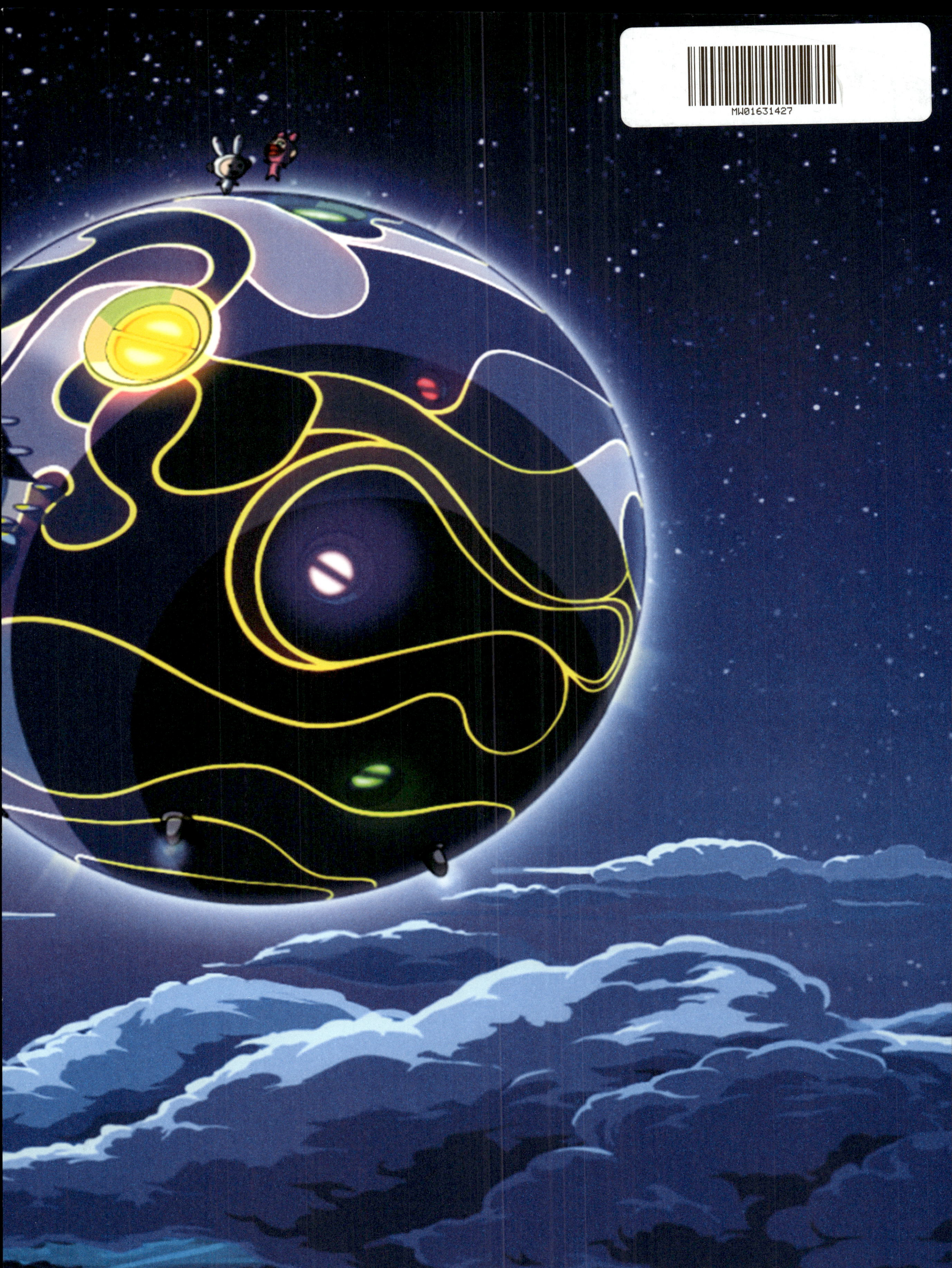

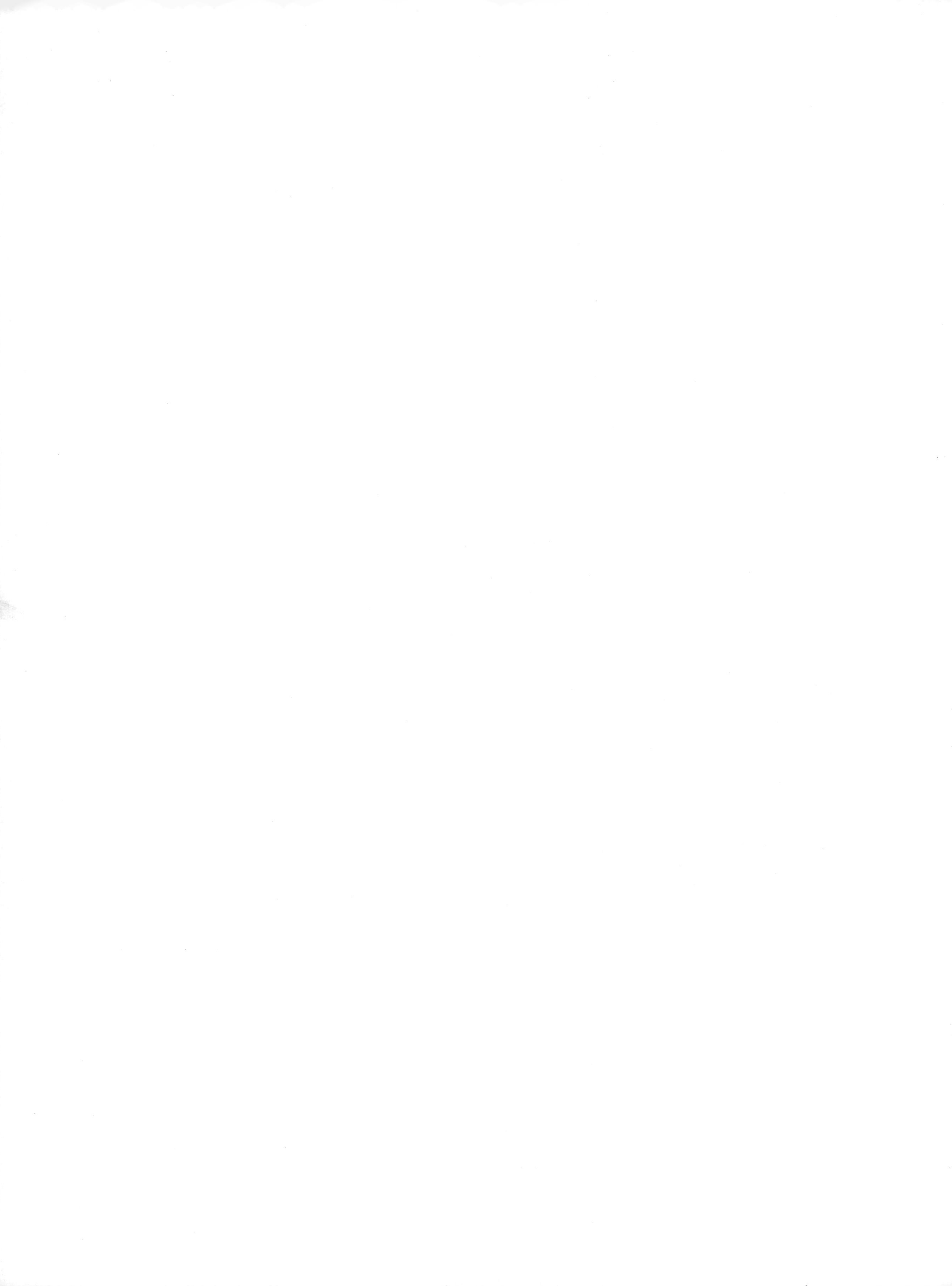

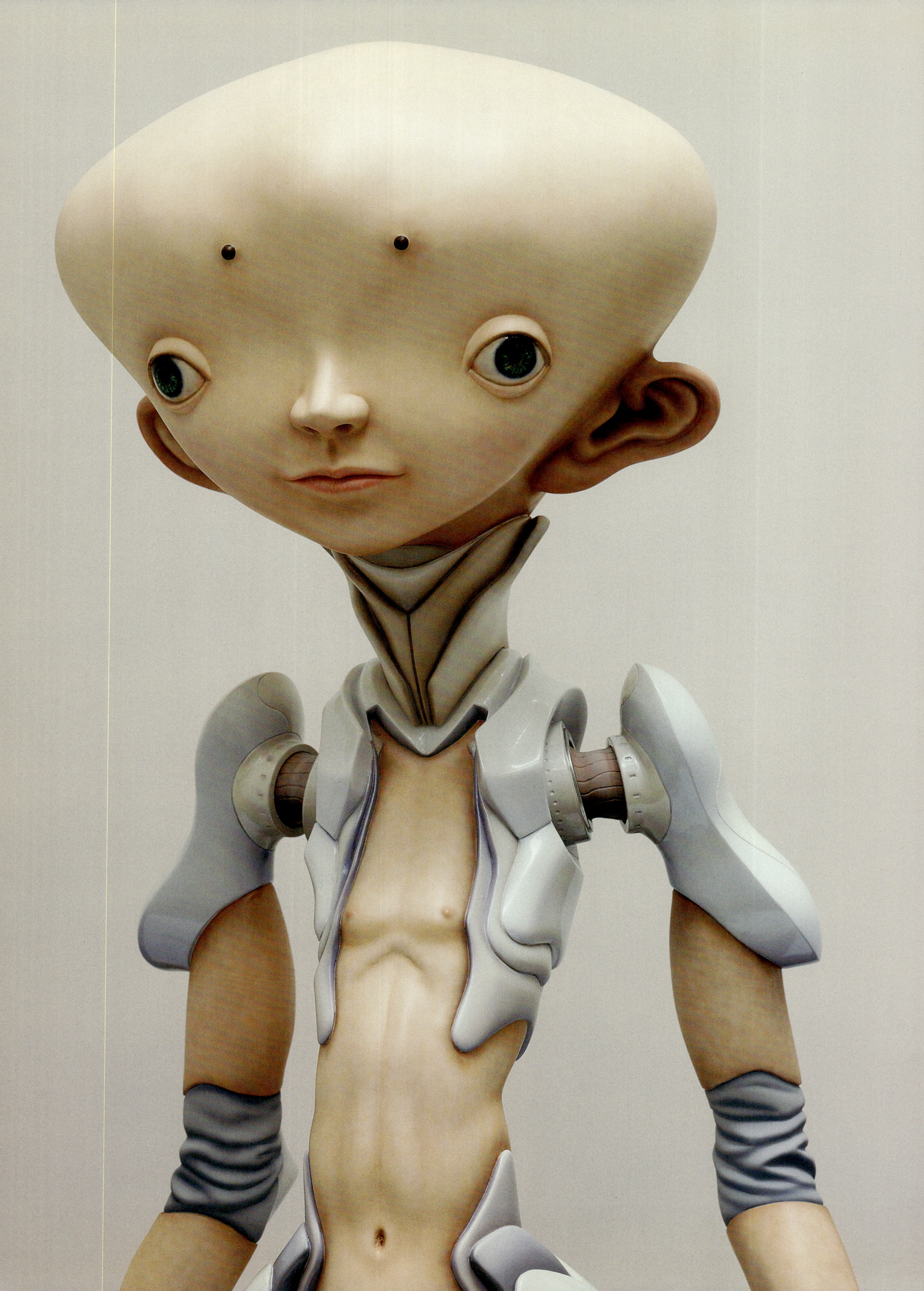

organized by
PAUL SCHIMMEL

essays by
DICK HEBDIGE, MIDORI MATSUI,
SCOTT ROTHKOPF,
PAUL SCHIMMEL, *and* MIKA YOSHITAKE

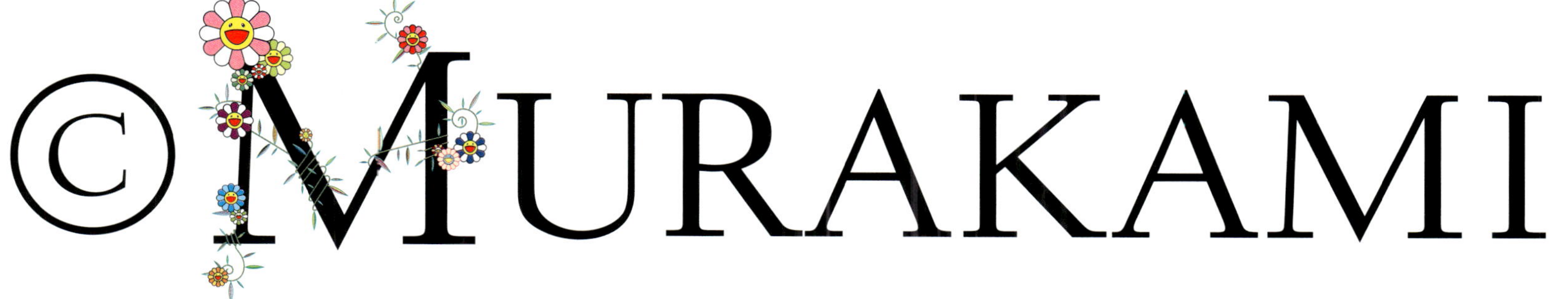

©MURAKAMI

THE MUSEUM OF CONTEMPORARY ART
Los Angeles

RIZZOLI INTERNATIONAL PUBLICATIONS
New York

KAIKAI KIKI CO., LTD./
KAIKAI KIKI NEW YORK, LLC
Tokyo/New York

This publication accompanies the exhision

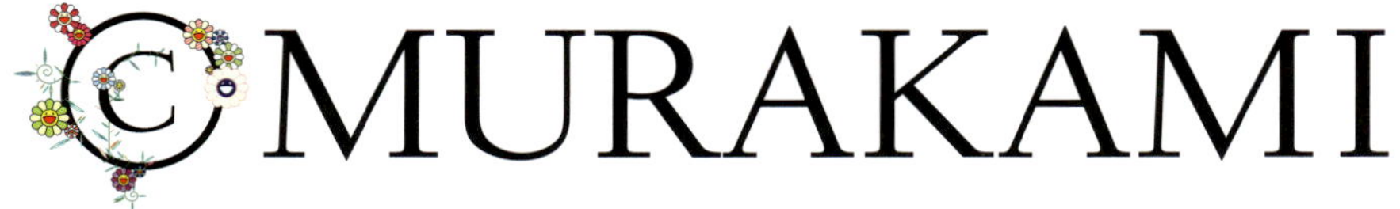

organized by Paul Schimmel
and presented at The Museum of Contemporary Art, Los Angeles,
MOCA at The Geffen Contemporary,
29 October 2007–11 February 2008.

Tour Itinerary
Brooklyn Museum of Art, Brooklyn, New York
4 April–13 July 2008

Museum für Moderne Kunst, Frankfurt, Germany
September–December 2008

Guggenheim Museum, Bilbao, Spain
February–May 2009

Note to the Reader
In this publication, Japanese names appear in Western order. Though the conventional order for listing names in Japanese is surname followed by given name, we have chosen to identify Takashi Murakami and his contemporaries as they are known internationally. Premodern names (pre-Meiji period, or before 1868), such as Kanō Sansetsu, remain in traditional order. Macrons are used throughout to indicate long vowels; exceptions are made for words and names standardized in the English language, such as Tokyo and Osaka.

Director's Foreword

JEREMY STRICK

The decisive influence of Japan upon the development of contemporary culture needs little recounting. Western artists, from Manet and Monet forward, have adapted design principles found in Japanese prints to create compositions of increasing flatness and abstraction. The philosophy of Zen Buddhism has influenced a range of practices in Western painting, music, and dance since the mid-twentieth century. In recent decades, Japanese consumer products—from electronics to automobiles—have profoundly affected societies worldwide, while the products of Japanese popular culture—*anime* and *manga* in particular—have found an international audience.

In his work and unique practice, Takashi Murakami seemingly picks out and reconfigures the disparate threads of Japanese influence that have been woven into the fabric of international culture over the last one hundred–plus years. If only for this reason, Murakami has swiftly risen to the position of one of the most influential and acclaimed artists to emerge from Asia in the postwar era. Murakami is now a distinct "brand"; his career is marked by extraordinary levels of ambition and achievement, and his work offers a brilliant and unique synthesis of the personal and the commercial.

Trained in the school of *nihonga*—traditional Japanese-style painting—Murakami has created works that bridge that tradition and the worlds of contemporary art, design, animation, fashion, and popular culture. Extending the trajectory of production by artists such as Andy Warhol and Jeff Koons, his oeuvre not only includes painting, sculpture, installation, and animation, but also a wide range of collectibles, multiples, and commercial products. Murakami expands the role of the artist well beyond its traditional boundaries—Western or Japanese. In conjunction with heading his international corporation Kaikai Kiki Co., Ltd., which has three locations in Japan and New York, he continues to incorporate a vast range of activities, taking on the responsibilities of curator, entrepreneur, publisher, lecturer, events coordinator, and manager.

The Museum of Contemporary Art, Los Angeles (MOCA), has been privileged to host Murakami on several previous occasions. In 2001, the influential "Superflat," a Murakami-organized exhibition of work by young Japanese artists, inaugurated MOCA's Pacific Design Center gallery. That same year, his work was featured in "Public Offerings," organized by Chief Curator Paul Schimmel. In 2004, Aya Takano, an artist managed by Murakami who also participated in "Superflat," launched *The world after 800,000,000 years* for MOCA's online digital gallery. Most recently, in 2005, Murakami's *DOB in the Strange Forest* and *Super Nova* (both 1999) were on display at The Geffen

Contemporary at MOCA as a part of "Ecstasy: In and About Altered States," also organized by Schimmel. MOCA's ongoing relationship with Murakami culminates in "© Murakami," the artist's largest survey exhibition to date, including over ninety works from his extensive oeuvre, a broad range of Kaikai Kiki merchandise, and a fully operational Louis Vuitton boutique featuring new designs by the artist as an integral element of the exhibition. "© Murakami" continues the museum's long-standing dedication to the organization and presentation of exhibitions by exceptional and challenging mid-career artists, including Douglas Gordon, Rodney Graham, Barbara Kruger, Gabriel Orozco, Charles Ray, and Christopher Wool.

This exhibition would not have been possible without the tremendous vision of Paul Schimmel, whose own passion and excitement for Murakami's work has fueled their ongoing relationship over the years. Schimmel, who gained Murakami's attention with his landmark 1992 show "Helter Skelter: L.A. Art in the 1990s" at MOCA, has been pivotal in creating a basis for understanding the artist's work in Los Angeles through exhibitions such as "Public Offerings" and "Ecstasy." Working closely with the artist with the assistance of Mika Yoshitake, project coordinator, and Yuko Sakata, executive director of Kaikai Kiki Co., Ltd., Schimmel has tailored an outstanding exhibition that will present Murakami's work in its full breadth to American and European audiences.

Exhibitions like "© Murakami," unusual for art museums in their scale, ambition, and complexity, rely upon the most devoted and visionary supporters for their realization. I wish to express my unending gratitude to MOCA's extraordinary Board of Trustees, led by Chair Clifford J. Einstein, President Dallas Price-Van Breda, and Vice Chair Michael Sandler, for their commitment, with special thanks to Audrey Irmas through the Sydney Irmas Exhibition Endowment, William and Maria Bell, Dallas Price-Van Breda, and Tom and Janet Unterman for their particular support. I am deeply grateful to exhibition sponsors Blum & Poe, Steven and Alexandra Cohen, Kathi and Gary Cypres, Gagosian Gallery, Galerie Emmanuel Perrotin, The Norton Family Foundation, Marianne Boesky, David Teiger, The MOCA Contemporaries, The Japan Foundation, and the E. Rhodes and Leona B. Carpenter Foundation.

My most profound gratitude goes to Takashi Murakami for his revelatory and transformative work, his commitment to MOCA, and his tireless dedication to this exhibition. His energy and the amazing efforts of Kaikai Kiki Co., Ltd., have brought this exhibition to the highest level.

Acknowledgments

PAUL SCHIMMEL

The organization of "© Murakami" has been profoundly inspiring. Even after thirty years of organizing exhibitions, I have been and continue to be surprised by an artist of such expansive vision, unrelenting ambition, and boundless generosity. Maybe because he runs multiple studios with over one hundred employees—or maybe in spite of it—Takashi Murakami has demonstrated tremendous empathy to the challenges presented by this exhibition and has lent his support to all facets of its organization. The staff of The Museum of Contemporary Art, Los Angeles (MOCA), developed the exhibition plan, catalogue, and installation in consultation with Murakami and members of his studio staff who, in turn, met each proposal with thoughtfulness, respect, and a demand for clarity and specificity that brought out the best in all of us.

Certainly one significant decision Murakami made during the process of organizing this exhibition was to approve and ultimately embrace its title, "© Murakami." A distillation of the complex apparatus through which the artist's output is conceived, produced, promoted, distributed, received, theorized, and historicized, the title is deceptively simple and reductive. In ways unlike Murakami's previous exhibitions, which often focused on aspects of his studio, his collaborations with other artists, or his broader curatorial and theoretical concerns, this exhibition first and foremost focuses on his work and how it functions in the world. The concept of copyright holds an exalted position within Murakami's practice for a multitude of reasons that are both personal and political; it represents something at the very foundation of his practice that is intimately felt yet representative of his work's public dimension—its status as a corporate, legal, and commercial entity. "© Murakami" reflects the complex relationship between the artist and his image and between the artwork and its identity.

MOCA has a relatively long and successful history of working with Murakami. Beginning in the mid-1990s, I became increasingly familiar with the artist through preparations for my exhibition "Public Offerings" (2001), which included the early work *Sea Breeze* (1992), a complex installation with a performative element. Murakami knew of MOCA not only for its commission of Arata Isozaki's first building outside Japan, but through the catalogue accompanying "Helter Skelter: L.A. Art in the 1990s" (1992), an exhibition focusing on the work of Los Angeles–based artists that he appreciated for the international resonance it gave to the work of local artists. For Murakami, MOCA was just the sort of institution with which he desired to collaborate. MOCA was also an American venue for the artist's group show "Superflat," which originated in Tokyo and was expanded and reorganized for touring in the United States under the supervision of former MOCA Associate Curator Michael Darling.

"© Murakami" is the most comprehensive retrospective of Murakami's work to date and focuses first and foremost on the artist's own oeuvre, bringing together his most significant paintings, sculptures, and installations, as well as his recent large-scale works. Hundreds of people have contributed to the success of this exhibition, whether by lending artworks; offering administrative, promotional, or financial support; providing scholarship and consultation; or simply extending their friendship. However, two people stand out as having made exceptional contributions on a day-to-day basis. MOCA Project Coordinator Mika Yoshitake—to whom I am unendingly grateful and without whom it would have been impossible to realize this project—began as a research assistant and became a full partner as the show developed. As a respected art historian and Ph.D. candidate at the University of California, Los Angeles, she contributed enormously both to the content of the exhibition and the catalogue. Mika has been an art historian, research assistant, translator, loan administrator, catalogue contributor, editorial assistant, and proofreader, and she has handled the various commercial, logistical, and financial aspects with assurance and grace. Her ability to communicate with great specificity, clarity, and elegance in both Japanese and English also made her indispensable in building a strong and productive relationship between the two very diverse teams at MOCA and Kaikai Kiki Co., Ltd. Her extraordinary intelligence, resourcefulness, commitment, and passion have made working with her a privilege. We were also very fortunate that in Yuko Sakata, executive director of Kaikai Kiki, New York, Murakami has an exceptionally informed, intelligent, dedicated, and accomplished collaborator. Yuko has been an extraordinarily professional and committed team leader, guiding and coordinating both logistical and financial aspects of the project on behalf of the artist. Mika and Yuko have been my partners in the realization of "© Murakami," and I am deeply grateful to both of them.

I also extend my gratitude to the dedicated staff of Kaikai Kiki. In the Tokyo office, I thank Chiaki Kasahara, project director, for the organization of the Tokyo press event and overall support of Murakami's career; Jun Tagawa and Takumi Kaseno of the sculpture department, for their incredible assistance with the floor-plan maquette, coordination of the large-scale sculptures, and shipping arrangements; Kazuhiro Mizuno and Masaya Irabe, for their design expertise; and finally, Kaikai Kiki's exceptional animation crew. In addition, I thank Hiroki Iijima of Lucky Wide and Kurotani Bijutsu, Ltd., for their incredible realization of *Oval Buddha* (2007). In the New York office, I thank Joshua Weeks for his assistance with the editorial process in translating catalogue essays and for coordinating aspects of the exhibition; Saori Tanaka, for compiling and coordinating merchandise; Kanako Yagi, for facilitating the image-license agreement; Kyoko Okano and Sawa Yamamoto, for catalogue image assistance; and Shunsuke Watanabe and Shino Takagi, for administrative assistance.

Few were more engaged and enthusiastic at the prospect of this retrospective than MOCA Director Jeremy Strick. He has taken up the cause of an immensely complex and challenging show with gusto, embracing the ways in which it questions the boundaries between public institution and private enterprise and making MOCA's relationship with this artist the very hallmark of his leadership throughout his eight-year tenure. As well, Emily Sudd, executive assistant to the chief curator, played a pivotal role, handling logistics, travel, scheduling, and communication between MOCA and Kaikai Kiki staff.

Before "© Murakami" was conceived, Tim Blum of Blum & Poe had been the most significant contact between MOCA and Murakami. His relationship with the artist, which dates back to the early 1990s, is the bedrock on which this exhibition has been built. I am very grateful to Blum, his partner Jeff Poe, and members of their staff, including Silke Taprogge and Renée Martin, for their significant role in both the instigation and support of this project. During the three years of its development, Marianne Boesky has been an exceptional supporter, and her gallery has made numerous loans available through the assistance of its director, Adrian Turner. Her particularly generous personal support of the exhibition is deeply appreciated. I am also grateful to Murakami's earliest supporters—Tomio Koyama of Tomio Koyama Gallery, Masami Shiraishi and his staff at SCAI The Bathhouse, and Tsutomu Ikeuchi of Röntgenwerke AG—for assistance with the loans of some of the important and lesser-known early works. In Blum & Poe, Galerie Emmanuel Perrotin, and Gagosian Gallery, the museum had three strong gallery partners who assisted in the project's development, lending significant administrative and financial support to the exhibition and to MOCA's extensive marketing campaign. I especially thank Emmanuel Perrotin, for his special assistance in the loan of some key European works, as well as staff members Etsuko Nakajima and Director Peggy Leboeuf. At Gagosian Gallery, I thank Larry Gagosian and his staff, Melissa Lazarov and Emily Florido.

Among the most significant aspects in the organization of "© Murakami" was the development of an international tour to the East Coast and to Europe. It has been a privilege to work with the Brooklyn Museum of Art, New York, especially Director Arnold Lehman, Deputy Director for Art Charles Desmarais, and Exhibitions Manager Megan Doyle Carmody. The Museum für Moderne Kunst, Frankfurt, committed wholeheartedly and with great enthusiasm as the first of two European venues, and I am very grateful for the support of Director Udo Kittelmann and longstanding curator Dr. Mario Kramer. I am very pleased that the Guggenheim Museum, Bilbao, committed to be the fourth and final venue thanks to the enthusiasm of Thomas Krens, director of the Guggenheim Foundation; Lisa Dennison, director of the Solomon R. Guggenheim Museum; and Alison Weaver, director of program and operations, affiliates. I am also grateful to Juan Ignacio Vidarte, director general of the Guggenheim Museum, Bilbao, for agreeing to participate in and round out the tour.

The catalogue accompanying "© Murakami" stands as the most comprehensive and substantial publication on the artist to date. A new model of partnership between artist and institution defined the production of the book; in fact, the title of the exhibition suggested itself during catalogue discussions regarding copyright. We are grateful to Charles Miers, Dung Ngo, Ellen Nidy, and Jessica Napp at Rizzoli International, our co-publisher, for their efforts and enthusiasm. Under Director of Publications Lisa Gabrielle Mark's exceptional leadership, MOCA's award-winning editorial team has produced a catalogue of exceptional quality, which benefited from the dedication and expertise of Senior Editor Jane Hyun, who managed countless details relating to editing and production; Editor Elizabeth Hamilton, who oversaw photography acquisition and assisted with editing; and Publications Assistant Dawson Weber, who tracked down hundreds of images and coordinated various administrative responsibilities. Editorial and proofreading assistance was provided by John Alan Farmer, Brooke Hodge, and Joshua Weeks, and photo acquisition in Japan was conducted by Maki Izumikawa, whose assistance was invaluable. This publication has been blessed with an incredibly high level of scholarship thanks to outstanding contributions by Dick Hebdige, Midori Matsui, Scott Rothkopf, and Mika Yoshitake. Its exquisite design is the result of the thoughtfulness, sensitivity, and rigor of Lorraine Wild and Victoria Lam at Green Dragon Office, who worked tirelessly to bring our collective vision to fruition.

Every member of MOCA's staff has in some way enhanced the organization of "© Murakami." Curatorial colleagues Ann Goldstein, Brooke Hodge, Philipp Kaiser, Rebecca Morse, Alma Ruiz, Bennett Simpson, and Librarian Lynda Bunting lent moral support. Director of Exhibition Management Susan Jenkins handled the significant contractual and administrative responsibilities for this project with her usual dedication and professionalism. The complex construction and installation requirements were ably overseen by Brian Gray, director of exhibitions; Sebastian Clough, exhibition designer and production coordinator; Jang Park, chief exhibition technician; and David Bradshaw, technical manager. I am especially grateful to Shin Kitahara for returning to MOCA at the artist's request to assist with installation; as a former MOCA employee, his successful history of working with Murakami made him an essential part of the team and has served as a reminder that the members of MOCA's exhibition crew are among the very best, their creativity and flexibility in working with artists legendary.

The registrarial staff, under the direction of Robert Hollister and day-to-day oversight of Melissa Altman, has done an exceptional job bringing together works of art from museums and private collections scattered throughout Australia, Asia, Europe, and the United States, coordinating the delivery of monumental sculptures along with numerous paintings and multiples. The transport of each object, no matter how large or small, has been handled with professionalism. Jennifer Arceneaux, director of development, and Laurie McGahey, deputy director of development, have done a terrific job in cultivating support among corporate and individual donors. I am grateful for their hard work, not only in funding the exhibition but also in organizing the gala under the direction of Development Special Events Director Vanessa Gonzalez and Support Programs Manager Michelle Bernardin. I also extend my appreciation to Grants

Officer Elizabeth Jordan and Development Writer/ Researcher Janet Lomax.

Both Director of Education Suzanne Isken and Education Programs Manager Aandrea Stang have brought years of experience to the development of programs that take advantage of Murakami's far-reaching impact. Bret Nicely has developed a special website as part of moca.org. Director of Communications Lyn Winter has brought great energy to the development of media and marketing plans, with the assistance of former Senior Designer David Rager, Marketing Coordinator Lauren Reilly, Production Coordinator Breanne Chappelle, Writer/Editor Cristin Donahue, and the consultation and coordination of public relations firm Rogers & Cowan. The work of former Public Relations Coordinator Rebecca Taylor in particular was fully realized under the supervision of Elizabeth Hinckley at Rogers & Cowan. John Melick and Lucy Toole of the public relations firm Blue Medium and Prap Japan worked with Kaikai Kiki to develop of press conferences in New York and Tokyo, respectively. I am especially grateful to Blum & Poe, Emmanuel Perrotin, and Gagosian Gallery for their special support of media initiatives surrounding "© Murakami." Finally, Assistant Director Ari Wiseman lent his assistance and legal expertise to the contractual agreements between MOCA and Louis Vuitton.

Murakami's collaborations with other artists and brands have been a distinguishing characteristic of his career. I thank Louis Vuitton—in particular, chairman and CEO of Moët Hennessy Louis Vuitton (LVMH) Bernard Arnault, CEO of Louis Vuitton Malletier Yves Carcelle, and Head of Architecture David McNulty—for their willingness to develop a fully operational Louis Vuitton shop incorporated into the body of the exhibition. This was an unprecedented initiative that involved the development of a new line of merchandise featuring new designs by Murakami working in collaboration with his good friend Marc Jacobs, artistic director of Louis Vuitton, who first brought Murakami to the company. Everyone at Louis Vuitton, including Store Network Director Eleanor De Boysson, Vice President for Store Planning and Development John Mulliken, and Procurement and Resource Project Manager of the Architectural Department Guillaume Galloy have proven their commitment to this extraordinary partnership, which both acknowledges and transcends the boundary between commercial and high art to reflect such conceptual leanings in Murakami's work. Special thanks to Johnston Marklee for their design of the Kaikai Kiki Merchandise Display Room.

This year's gala coincides with the opening of "© Murakami" and honors Murakami's long-time friend and collaborator Marc Jacobs. Although there is traditionally a separation between curators and gala organizers, given the complex interrelationship between Murakami's world and those of entertainment and marketing, it was inevitable that the gala accompanying this exhibition would involve a high level of communication between the planning committee and the curatorial staff. I am very grateful for the commitment, vision, and leadership that Gala Chair Maria Bell has provided for this event and also thank honorary chair Eileen Norton. We extend our immense gratitude to Kanye West and Don C for their extraordinary generosity and commitment in participating.

I want to thank a number of people for special assistance, including Patricia Marshall, a close and particularly important ally in this project, for initiating contact with the LVMH group. Philippe Segalot and Suzanne Pagé provided assistance with a number of significant European loans, and Sandy Heller and his assistant Kelly Culbertson facilitated significant loans in the United States. Finally, the early and very important support that I received from three of Murakami's most significant collectors, David Teiger and Kent and Vicki Logan, is especially appreciated.

Among the fifty-four lenders to the exhibition, I would like to single out Eileen Harris Norton and Peter Norton, assisted by Gwen Hill at the Norton Family Foundation; Marianne Boesky; Steven A. Cohen; David Teiger, assisted by Cabrina Potente; Vicki and Kent Logan; and Takashi Murakami/Kaikai Kiki Co., Ltd./ Kaikai Kiki New York, LLC. In addition, I thank the following lenders: Director Yuji Akimoto, former Director Yutaka Mino, Registrar Daisuke Murata, and Archivist Reiko Ishiguro at the 21st Century Museum of Contemporary Art, Kanazawa; Matt Aberle; Ruth and Jake Bloom, assisted by Amber Noland; Giancarlo Bonollo; Harry David; Martin and Rebecca Eisenberg; Margrit Brehm of Fluid Editions and Archives; Naomi Seike at the Fukuoka Jisho Co., Ltd.; Amalia Dayan and Adam Lindemann; Director Michael Govan at the Los Angeles

County Museum of Art; Rachel and Jean-Pierre Lehmann; Linda and Harry Macklowe; Martin Z. Marguiles; Halsey Minor; Javier and Monica Mora; Peter Morton; The Museum of Modern Art, New York; Thomas Olbricht of the Olbricht Collection; Douglas and Sherry Oliver; Emmanuel Perrotin; François Pinault; Suhanya Raffel, head of Asian, Pacific, and International art at Queensland Art Gallery; Alan and Darryl Reichbart; Rubell Family Collection, assisted by Mark Coetzee and Juan Valadez; Richard B. Sachs; San Francisco Museum of Modern Art; Ann and Mel Schaffer; Florence and Philippe Segalot; John A. Smith and Victoria Hughes; Ryutaro Takahashi; Walter Vanhaerents-Desanghere; and seventeen lenders who wish to remain anonymous. Without the willingness and commitment of its lenders, "© Murakami" would have been unthinkable.

I would also like to thank the following institutions, foundations, and individuals for their generosity: Audrey Irmas and the Sydney Irmas Exhibition Endowment; Maria and Bill Bell; Blum & Poe; Steven and Alexandra Cohen; Kathi and Gary Cypres; Gagosian Gallery; Galerie Emmanuel Perrotin; The Norton Family Foundation; Dallas Price-Van Breda; Janet and Tom Unterman; Marianne Boesky; David Teiger; The MOCA Contemporaries; The Japan Foundation; and the E. Rhodes and Leona B. Carpenter Foundation. From the outset, MOCA's Board of Trustees has shown tremendous enthusiasm for Murakami, and several of his most significant collectors have long been associated with the museum. I am particularly grateful to MOCA Chair Clifford J. Einstein, President Dallas Price-Van Breda, and Trustees William J. Bell, Ruth Bloom, Audrey Irmas, and Peter Morton for their steadfast support.

Finally and unequivocally, I thank Takashi Murakami, who essentially invited MOCA and me to become an extension of his vast and complex studio practice. He allowed me to experience both directly and vicariously the great traditions of the guilds, schools, and studio practices—a hallmark of Japanese artistic and corporate history—on which his own epic vision is based. This has been a great honor that I will never forget.

On behalf of the artist,
I wish to thank the entire team at Kaikai Kiki:

Catalogue Editing Assistance
Joshua Weeks
Masami Nakagawa
Miyako Hara
Nozomi Kobayashi
Mai Miyazaki

Catalogue Image Assistance
Kyoko Okano
Sawa Yamamoto

Painting Production
Data Production Director
Ira "Becky" bucho

Data Production
Chiho Aoshima
Chika Tamagawa
Yoshiyuki Mashimo
Kazuhiro Mizuno
Masako Izumi
Tsuyoshi Takasaki
Tsuyoshi Yamamoto

Painting Directors
Yoshikazu Hirata
Kentaro Eguchi
Tomoko Sugimoto

Painting Co-directors
Kaori Kawauchi
Keiko Tanaka
Rei Sato

Painting
Yoko Matsuno
Chihiro Shimizu
Yoko Akiyama
Tetsuko Nagano
Yuichi Ban
Chie Otake
Kouhei Ino
Takae Inoue
Motoko Akahori
Shinobu Takayanagi
Masami Inaba
Tomomi Kariya
Chika Ogura
Tomotake Yanagisawa
Misako Akiba
Kei Naitou
Miyako Okukawa
jagaichiro
Toshinobu Sakuma
Miho Yanagihara
Naoko Oda
Maki Momono
Koichiro Endo
Osamu Kuga
Yuji Yamada
Akihiro Ueda
Maiko Ito
Ran Kawano
Ako Takashima
Michiyoshi Sano
Izumi Fujiwara
Sawako Waha
Kisara Nigawara
Asami Tajima
Takayuko Nakano
Atsushi Takagi
Fish ! Matsumoto
Aiko Shinohara
Masahiro Murayama
Kentaro Eguchi
Mariko Suzuki
Rei Idehara
Tomomi Izuka
Pong★Fey
Mihoko Shimoji
Kyoko Watanabe
Yohei Kawakami
Takehiro Aso
Yuki Tanaka

Takuya "Men" Kato
Haruki Iwai
Norito Sakai
Era
Yasumi Tei
Ai Torii
Kenji Etoh
Rie Harimoto
Yoko Toshima
Saori Watanabe
Tetsuo Maruyama
Kiyofumi Oshima
Kaori Kimura
Rika Hirata
Naoto Moriwaki
Aso Men the Third Eye
Atsushi Saga (Over Drive)
Miho Ogai
Satoko Yoshikane
Emet Sosna
Kay Cho
Stacey Beach
Liam O'Brien
Cybele Pritchett
Ivanny Pagan
Suzy Kim
Marsha Pugachevsky
Jeff Vreeland
Mel Alvarez
Sarah Nawrocki

Interns
Risa Nakayama
Minah Kim
Nikolai Shveitser
Germaine Chang
Taehun Lee
Debra Zechowski
Miguel Jiron
Kevin Fey
Titania Inglis
Eunnam Hong

Sculpture Production
Shuichi Miyawaki (Kaiyōdō)
Hirohisa Yoshizawa (Lucky-Wide)
Hiroki Iijima (Lucky-Wide)

Model Production
Bome
Tetsuya Tamanoi
Yasuhiro Wakajima (Studio Cubics)
Masahiko Asano (Studio Cubics)

1:1 Figure Production
Tetsu Saegusa (Shadow Moon)
Fuyuki Shinada (Vi-shop)
Hisoka Miyauchi (Earth Work)
Tatsuo Kurotani (Kurotani Bijutsu)
Hajime Horii (majic BOX)
Takafumi Tanibuchi (incom arts)

Painting
Tomohiro "Shisho" Hoshino
Tsuneto Baba
Kouji Miki (cinq-art)

Installation
Jun Tagawa
Takumi Kaseno
Mitsuo Hosokawa

Animation Conception
Toshiaki Okuno (OLM. Inc + OLM Digital)
Chiaki Kasahara

Animation Production
Shukichi Kanda (OLM. Inc + OLM Digital)
Yuichiro Ichige
Takahiko Itakura
Tomiyuki Shiraki
Yasutaka Shinohara
Fujihiko Matsumoto
Gordon Wang
Shiho Oshita

Merchandise
Saori Tanaka
Mitsuru Oguma
Kazumi Muto
Yoshimi Yamagishi

Management
Noriko Hiraki
Chiaki Kasahara
Nobu Azuma
Kaoru Hayashi
Sho Sato
Shunsuke Watanabe
Shino Takagi

Press
Kyoko Nishimoto
Craig Barnes

Project Management
Yuko Sakata

Flat Boy vs. Skinny: Takashi Murakami and the Battle for "Japan"

DICK HEBDIGE

Umpire of Signs

"Orient and Occident cannot be taken here as 'realities' to be compared and contrasted historically, philosophically, culturally, politically. I am not lovingly gazing toward an Oriental essence... What can be addressed, in the consideration of the Orient, are not other symbols, another metaphysics, another wisdom...it is the possibility of difference, of a mutation, of a revolution in the propriety of symbolic systems. Someday we must write the history of our own obscurity—manifest the destiny of our narcissism."

ROLAND BARTHES[1]

In 1970, Roland Barthes published *L'empire des signes* (Empire of signs), his miscellany of essays on the "faraway" semiotic system which, he wrote (almost in parenthesis), "I shall call: Japan" as an ironic homage and a sincere riposte to nineteenth-century *Japonisme* and as the latest in his (calligraphic) brushes with the emptiness of Zen. The little book appeared at a time when the absolute demise of Japan's ultra-Left student movement; through-the-roof real-estate prices; exploded bubble economy; Godzilla-sized corporate tax evasion and money-laundering scams; and manipulation by Japanese players, linked directly to these scandals, of the French Impressionist art market all lay two decades off along with, on the larger stage, the collapse in November

1 Roland Barthes, *Empire of Signs*, trans. Richard Howard (New York: Hill & Wang, 1982), 3–4. The original French edition *L'empire des signes* (Geneva, Switzerland: A. Skira, 1970) appeared eight years before the English translation of what, prior to the anti-multicultural backlash following 9/11, must have seemed for some readers like Edward Said's *terminal* skewering of Orientalism (Said, *Orientalism* [Vintage: New York, 1978]). Rather than trying to skirt the issue of Orientalism in the present essay, I have attempted to follow Barthes's example, i.e., to stage a contest between "Oriental" and "Occidental" systems by consciously exaggerating/essentializing and then flattening the differences between them.

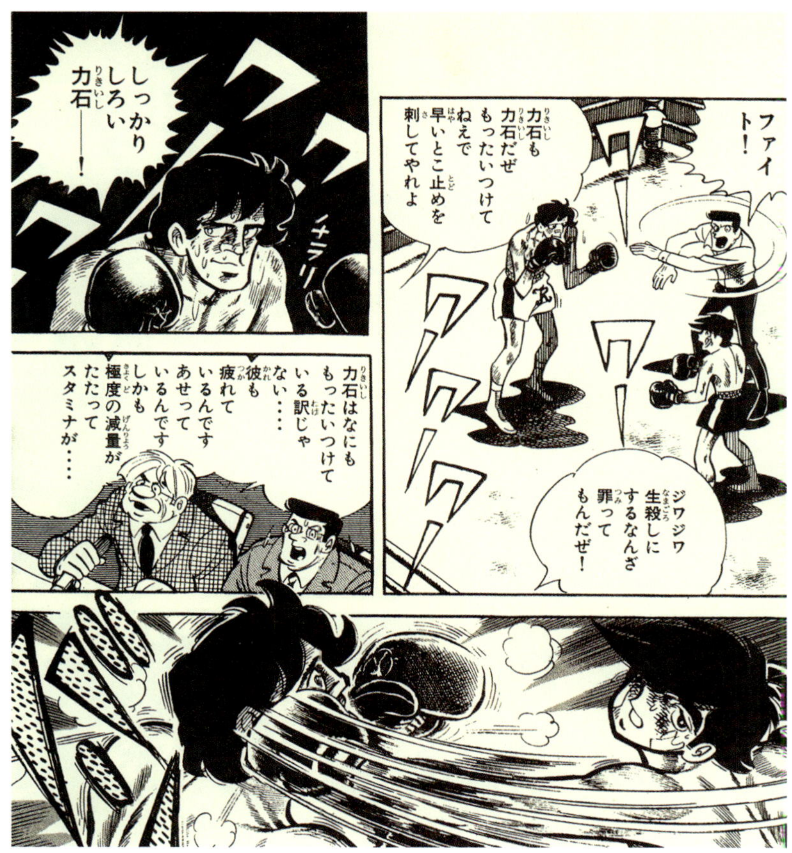

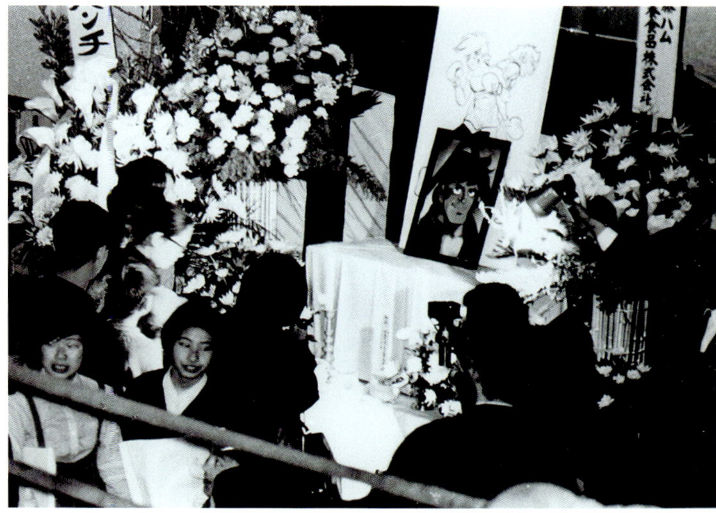

Panels from *Ashita no Joe* (Tomorrow's Joe), 1968–70, and view of funeral for Tōru Rikiishi, a character from the series, 1970

1989 of Soviet Communism and the simultaneous rise, linked to that collapse, of truly global markets and big-splash international art shows.[2]

Equally remote from Barthes's concerns when he set about collating his (im)personal impressions of "an unheard-of symbolic system…altogether detached from our own"[3] (he wrote, among other things, about chopsticks, bowing, *pachinko*, *kabuki*, *bunraku*, *haiku*, and the Japanese eyelid) was the thriving world of Japanese *manga* (comic books), today a five-billion-dollar industry. For, in addition to the 64.2 million people who poured into Osaka for Expo '70, Asia's first world trade fair, 1970 was also the year when more than seven hundred real-life *manga* fans attended a funeral service in Tokyo conducted by a Buddhist priest for Tōru Rikiishi, a comic-strip character who had succumbed after a boxing match with Joe Yabuki, the protagonist of the wildly popular series *Ashita no Joe* (Tomorrow's Joe) (1968–73) published by Kodansha.[4] According to Reiko Tomii, it was not

---

2 Ibid., 3. Julian Stallabrass gives a concise summary of the Japanese manipulation of the European Impressionist art market in *Contemporary Art: A Very Short Introduction* (Oxford, England: Oxford University Press, 2006), 75. The book also provides a systematic critical exploration of the structural links between the heavily advertised "freedom" of contemporary art as a fundamentally Western institution (freedom, for example, from moral or religious proscriptions, ethical constraints, political ideologies, use value, etc.) and the globalization of free markets after 1989. See also Peter Watson, *From Manet to Manhattan: The Rise of the Modern Art Market* (London: Hutchinson, 1992).

3 Barthes, *Empire of Signs*, 3.

4 See Paul Gravett, *Manga: Sixty Years of Japanese Comics* (London: Lawrence King Publishing Ltd., 2004). Gravett quoted Tomorrow's Joe creator Tetsuya Chiba's account of the funeral service for the fictional character, which was held in March 1970 in an actual boxing ring in Tokyo: "A famous poet in Japan, Shūji Terayama, had called for a funeral to be held…. The streets were packed, even though it was a weekday. People had taken time off work, businessmen, students. They were all dressed in black, they had black armbands and black ribbons on, many had brought flowers and incense" (52).

until 1983 that Japan's *manga-* and *anime-* (henceforth in this essay, *animanga-*) fixated stay-at-home geek subculture was publicly outed and named *otaku* (literally, "your household") by critic Akio Nakamori.[5]

It is this subculture with which Takashi Murakami remains historically affiliated and from which he has drawn the trademark themes, representational techniques, and visual and rhetorical figures that coalesce at the contemporary (as opposed to the art-historical) end of his epic Superflat thesis presented in a trilogy of exhibitions ("Superflat," 2000; "Coloriage," 2002; and "Little Boy: The Arts of Japan's Exploding Subculture," 2005). What Barthes probably could not have anticipated is that the agent most single-handedly responsible within the contemporary art world for affecting the kind of reversal Barthes was hoping for ("the mutation...the revolution in the propriety of symbolic systems") turns out to be not one of "Us" ("Someday *we* must write," etc.) but one of "Them."

Murakami-*san*—son not of the (European) *haute bourgeoisie* but of a Tokyo taxi-driver father and a homemaker mother, equipped with a Ph.D. in the Euro-Japanese *nihonga* style of painting from Tokyo's prestigious National University of Fine Arts and Music—could surely qualify as the de facto engineer of a version of Barthes's projected revolution in East-West sign relations. What Barthes would have made of Kaikai Kiki Co., Ltd., is anybody's guess, but one feature of the brand he would surely have appreciated is that in Murakami's monstrous East-West hybrids, the dominant gene is always Japanese. For in addition to his Dr. Moreau–type experimental monster-making *persona*, Murakami is also an archaeologist of the occluded Japanese "national character" (what Barthes might refer to as the Japanese "essence"). Despite his high-art training, Murakami is, for instance, able to find among his marginalized *hetare* (loser) *otaku* peers the living embodiment of the outcast *burakumin*. As Noi Sawaragi pointed out, the *burakumin*, Japan's disposable shadow people, were often entertainers or craftsmen and excelled in the arts in Japan's thousand-year-old feudal caste system,[6] a system that remained intact, thanks to the isolationism of the shogunate, until the archipelago's forced accommodation (via U.S. gunboat diplomacy) with capitalist modernity in 1868.

The excavation of forgotten or overlooked continuities like this one,

5 See Reiko Tomii's annotations for "Otaku Talk: Toshio Okada and Kaichirō Morikawa, Moderated by Takashi Murakami," in Murakami, *Little Boy: The Arts of Japan's Exploding Subculture*, exh. cat. (New York: Japan Society; and New Haven, Connecticut: Yale University Press, 2005), 182 n 1.

6 Noi Sawaragi, quoted in Murakami, "Superflat Trilogy: Greetings, You Are Alive," trans. Office Miyazaki Inc., in *Little Boy*, 158.

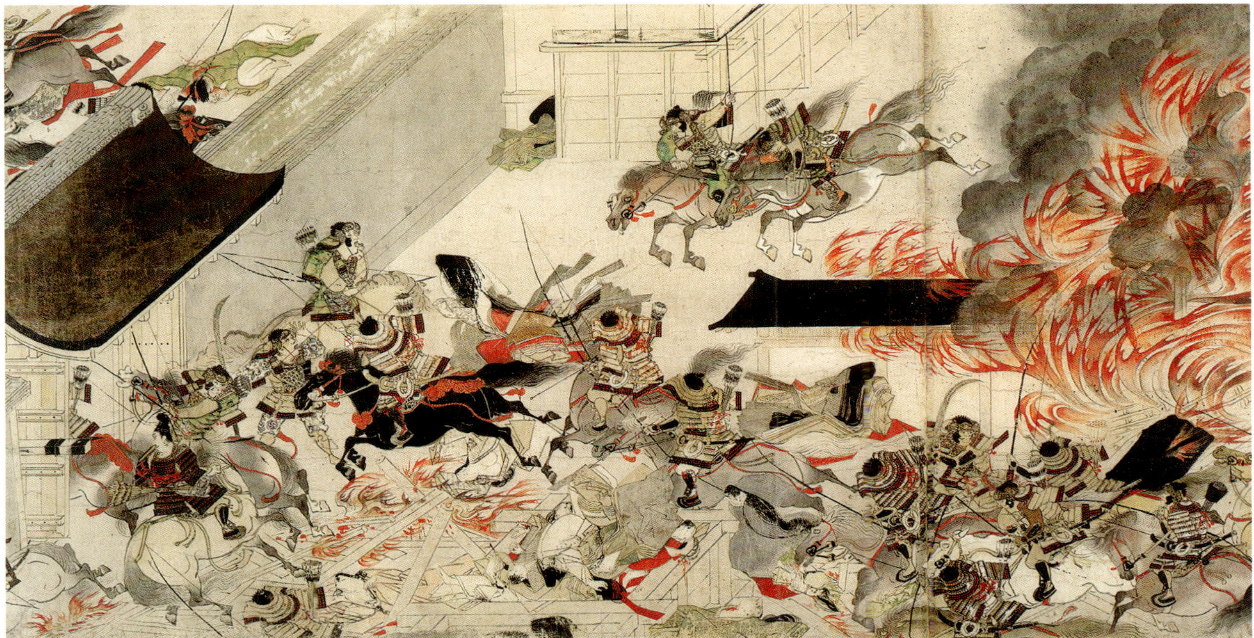

Night Attack on the Sanjō Palace, from the *Heiji monogatari emaki* (Illustrated scrolls of the events of the Heiji era), Japanese, Kamakura period, c. 13th century, detail
Handscroll: ink and color on paper
16 1/4 x 275 1/2 inches
Museum of Fine Arts, Boston, Fenollosa-Weld Collection

between *otaku* and earlier Japanese art traditions, forms an important part of Murakami's national-historical redemption project: his battle with the demons of Americanization. Murakami's goal in his catalogue for the "Superflat" exhibition, to establish an organic line of connection across the centuries in Japanese representational aesthetics, leads him beyond a simple listing of the obvious precedents for today's *animanga* (e.g., the twelfth- and thirteenth-century *Genji* and *Heiji monogatari* scrolls, the nineteenth-century caricatures of Hokusai Katsushika) to explore in detail continuities in the spatial and formal dynamics of the work of a contemporary animation master like Yoshinori Kanada and a group of Edo-era artists that includes Kanō Sansetsu, Itō Jakuchū, and Sōga Shōhaku.[7]

None of this, of course, is likely to matter one way or the other to most of the people who come to view the MOCA exhibition or who end up buying a Murakami-designed accessory at the Louis Vuitton store that formed part of its installation. No one needs a dictionary or a survey of Japanese art history to get what (or who) DOB is getting at or to be left gaping open-mouthed at the base of a seven-foot statue of the ko² super-babe morphing into an airplane. A credit card or cash is all it takes for anyone who wants to walk away with a Murakami bag or figurine.

7 Nobuo Tsuji, *Kisu no keifu* (The lineage of eccentricity) (Tokyo: Bijitsu Publishing, 1988), discussed in Murakami, "A Theory of Super Flat Japanese Art," in *Superflat*, exh. cat. (Tokyo: MADRA Publishing Co. Ltd., 2000), 9.

And who, after all, actually sits down and *reads* an art catalogue anyway? The discrepancy between the immediate eye-striking impact and accessibility of Murakami's artwork and the volume and interpretive "thickness" of the discursive support provided for it by the artist in his persuasive and densely data-rich essays, manifestos, and interviews is no doubt part of the deadpan serious joke that inheres within the project and is intrinsic to the paradoxical character of "Superflat" as a "Japanese" conceptualist conceit. ("Super flatness is an original concept of the Japanese, who have been completely Westernized."—Murakami[8])

For the duration of this essay I intend, nonetheless, to take Murakami's statements at face value and to move back and forth between his textual and visual works, giving equal weight to each while considering both in the light of Barthes's remarks about "Oriental" and "Occidental" symbolic systems. Following Barthes's lead in marking the distance separating his own construction of "Japan" from the three-dimensional island nation-state, I have put "Japan" (and "America") in quotation marks at those points in the argument where they act as surrogates for these larger systems or where the magical talismanic (or evil fetishistic) functions of the terms themselves are foregrounded.

My own conceit in the structuring and composition of what follows is to take the contention put forward by art critic Midori Matsui that there is a "fundamental affinity" between postmodern narrative poetics and Murakami's "conjuring of alternate dimensions of reality, unfettered by the mimetic demands of rational space or logic,"[9] and to run, or at least to jog, with it. According to Matsui, such a poetics is characterized by "metonymic chains of association and the schizophrenic juxtaposition of fragments that collapses time and draws one's attention to the materiality of signs."[10] The titling in my essay of the various sections and the neologisms, similes, and puns developed and explored within them form part of an emergent, incrementally elaborated schizo-system in which, for instance, "Flat Boy" functions in relation to the actually existing individual, Murakami, as Superman functions in relation to Clark Kent, or, to invoke a contemporaneous example from *manga*, as Ribon no Kishi (Princess Knight) functions in relation

8 Murakami, "Superflat Trilogy," 155.

9 Midori Matsui, "Toward a Definition of Tokyo Pop: The Classical Transgressions of Takashi Murakami," in Amada Cruz, Dana Friis-Hansen, and Matsui, *Takashi Murakami: The Meaning of the Nonsense of Meaning*, exh. cat. (Annandale-on-Hudson, New York: Center for Curatorial Studies Museum, Bard College, 1999), 27.

10 Ibid.

to Sapphire.[11] That system, in turn, represents my attempt to utilize the narrative conventions of *anime* and *manga* evolved within *otaku* subculture.

2
Flat Boy vs. The Silver Wig

> *"Business art is the step that comes after Art. I started as a commercial artist,*
> *and I want to finish as a business artist.*
> *After I did the thing called 'art' or whatever it's called, I went into business art.*
> *I wanted to be an Art Businessman or a Business Artist."*
>
> ANDY WARHOL[12]

IT IS MURAKAMI'S PREOCCUPATION with issues of Japanese national-cultural identity that distinguishes him from the practitioners of American Pop, though the debt to Andy Warhol tends to be the most serviceable trope available to critics faced with the task of introducing his work to an international audience. Given the scope and nature of Murakami's Kaikai Kiki operation, the broad appeal and affordability of his mass-marketed icons, and his unqualified commitment to "Business Art," the comparison is unavoidable and is acknowledged as such by Murakami himself. From a Western art-historical perspective, Warhol's shadow tends to loom so large over the younger artist that it threatens to obscure the radical specificity and originality of Murakami's project. That shadow is best confronted and to some degree deflected at the outset through a brief consideration of where the two converge and differ.

Both Warhol and Murakami gained attention in the art world by positioning themselves as outsider-*savants* not so much hostile as oblivious to the boundary-marking rituals and etiquettes that continue to protect institutionally sanctioned contemporary art from contamination by other forms of production and exchange. Both are seen as radical levelers: flatteners of the representational picture plane and of high/low, art/commodity, art-world/*fashionista* hierarchies. Both

11 Ribon no Kishi (literally, "Knight in Ribbons," translated into English as "Princess Knight") is the superhero(ine) alter ego of Sapphire in *manga* master Osamu Tezuka's first long-form story for girls serialized from 1953 in *Shōjo Club*. See Gravett, *Manga*: "A girl named Sapphire is born with both a girl's and a boy's soul, but to take her place as heir to the throne she has to disguise herself in public as a prince. She becomes known as Ribon no Kishi...By obliging her to conceal her feminine nature and her love for a dashing prince charming, Tezuka created an exquisite world of indecision... Princess Knight...was a prototype for the magical girls and the sexual ambiguities that would become central to *shōjo* (girls') manga" (76).

12 Andy Warhol, quoted in *Andy Warhol: A Retrospective* (New York: The Museum of Modern Art, 1989), 459.

appropriated business as an art form[13] and adopted corporate branding strategies. Both put those strategies in service of the global projection and promotion of exotic metropolitan taste formations: Manhattan's bohemian art-fashion-music scenes in Warhol's case, Tokyo's new media-savvy subcultures in Murakami's.

But the differences are in the end more telling. Whereas Warhol's Factory was as much a catwalk and a stage for social/art events as an actual production house, Murakami's Kaikai Kiki (formerly Hiropon Factory) is the real deal: a product-development and fabrication company with a regular salaried workforce operating much like any other flexibly organized software or digital-production business.[14] Warhol's Factory was a conceptualist joke directed at the idea of the lone artist-amateur sequestered in his/her studio, with Taylorism (the industrial rationalization of the labor process) and Constructivism (the socialist idealization of labor) thrown in as secondary targets. However, the gest, together with its baggage of historical associations, sinks somewhere in the passage across the Pacific.

Building on Noriaki Kitazawa's observation that the term "fine arts" (*bijutsu*) was only imported to Japan in 1873 as part of the Meiji government's modernization program, Murakami argues that art in Japan has still not secured the kind of autonomy from craft and commerce claimed for it since the beginning of the Industrial Revolution in the West. Hence the division of labor between master painters (*eshi*) and their artisan assistants, a system established in early twelfth-century *yamato-e* painting,[15] still predominates in Japan's *animanga* industries and at Kaikai Kiki, where Murakami's promotion of the art careers of his Kaikai Kiki–branded protégés—Chiho Aoshima, Chinatsu Ban, Akane Koide, Mahomi Kunikata, Mr., Rei Sato, and Aya Takano—seems, in its paternalist generosity, to operate on principles opposed to those governing Warhol's somewhat vampirish collaborations at the end of his life with Jean-Michel Basquiat.[16]

However, it is in the relation to expository language that the two artists part company most decisively. For where Warhol always spoke in character as "Andy" (a sort of Polish-Pittsburgh equivalent to Sasha Baron Cohen's "Kazakh" Borat), opting for blank aphorisms and Madison Avenue–style *koans* over earnest exegesis, Murakami is a public businessman-intellectual whose project involves

13 "Being good in business is the most fascinating kind of art. During the hippie era people put down the idea of business—they'd say 'Money is bad,' and 'Working is bad,' but making money is art and working is art and good business is the best art." Warhol, quoted in ibid.

14 For a full account of Kaikai Kiki's mode of operation, see Arthur Lubow, "The Murakami Method," *The New York Times*, 3 April 2005: "At 8:30 every weekday morning, unless he is not in Tokyo, Murakami leads the staff of his art studio...in a round of calisthenics. Then the employees go off to their various jobs... Murakami's 60 employees punch in with computerized timecards, and the company has training manuals for new hires. The hours are regular—and long. One daily ritual is the question-and-answer period, in which staff members book a slot of specified duration to ask the chief a question; when I attended, 14 had requested interviews, typically of 2 minutes each."

15 See Joan Stanley-Baker, *Japanese Art*, rev. ed. (London: Thames & Hudson, 2000), 79.

16 For master-apprentice relations and the division of labor in the Japanese *manga* industry, see Timothy R. Lehmann, *Manga: Masters of the Art* (New York: HarperCollins, 2005). Murakami promotes and curates the work of Kaikai Kiki artists internationally and takes a ten-percent commission from the gallery's share of the sales, not the artist's (see Lubow, "The Murakami Method"). For the late-career Warhol-Basquiat collaborations, by way of contrast, see Pat Hackett, ed., *The Warhol Diaries* (New York: Simon & Schuster, 1989). This volume tracks the alternating rhythms of opportunism, fear, and fascination that shaped Warhol's relationship with his young protégé in the last years of both artists' lives. Basquiat appears to be the only black person Warhol ever got in any way close to.

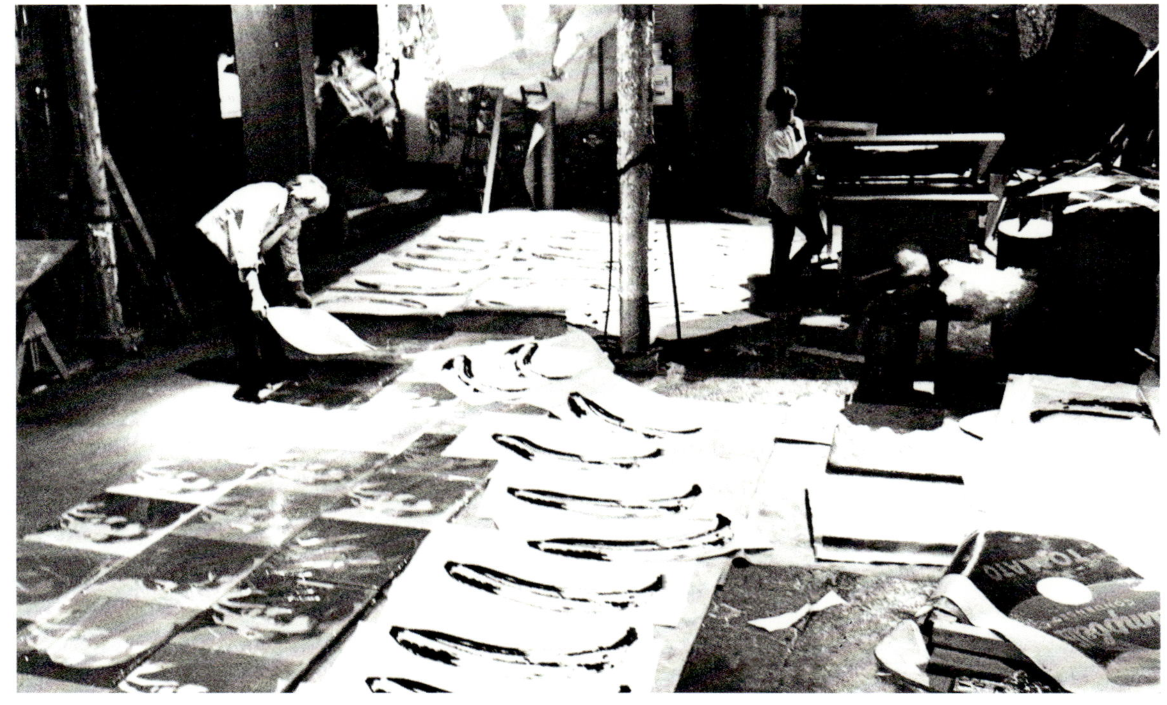

Andy Warhol making banana and self-portrait silkscreens at his Silver Factory, New York, 1967

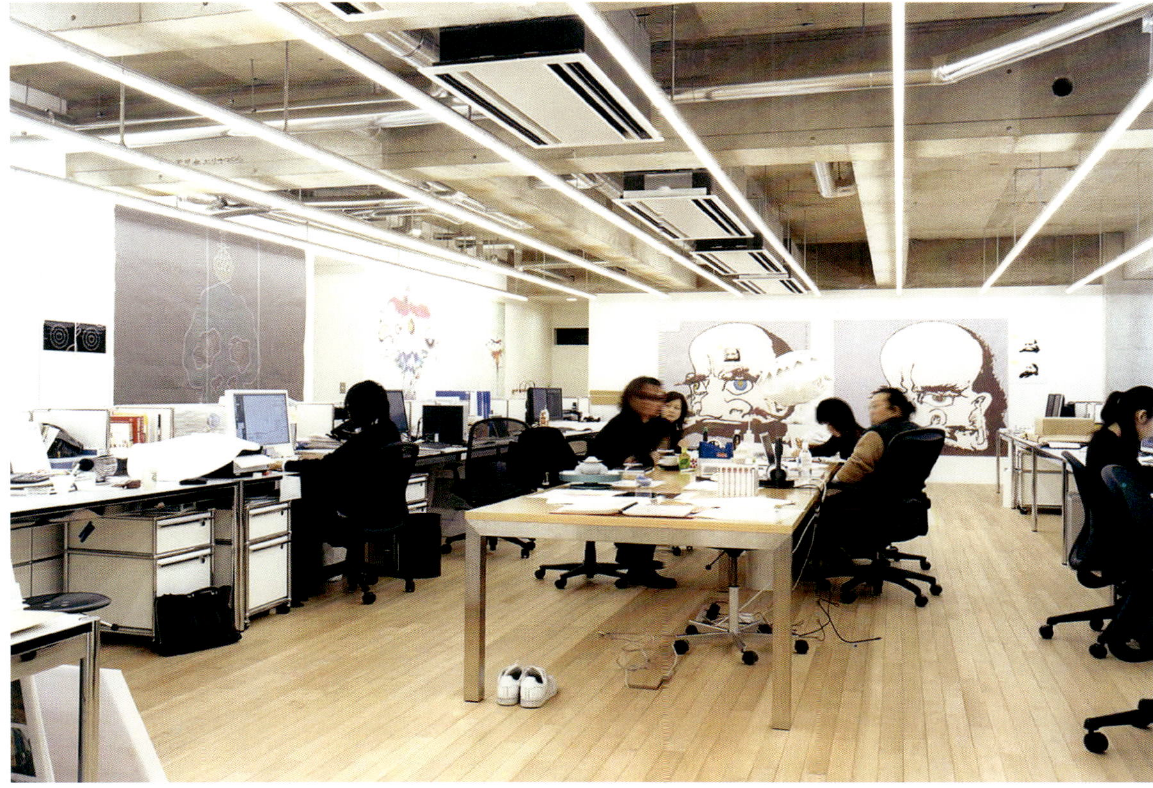

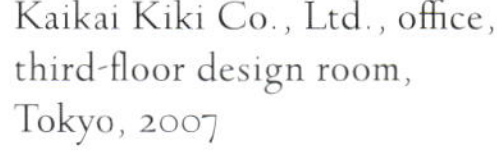

Kaikai Kiki Co., Ltd., office, third-floor design room, Tokyo, 2007

symbiotically connected visual and discursive propositions. ("The *Superflat* trilogy has been presented in two forms: publications and exhibitions."—Murakami[17]) Where Warhol initiates and leaves it at that, Murakami elaborates, then elaborates further. While Warholian blankness serves as both a dumb comment on the ultimate redundancy of any kind of language and as a mirror for the bluntness of American (business) English, Murakami's inclination towards art "that makes your mind go blank, that leaves you gaping"[18] finds its written correlative in a heightened sensitivity to wordplay and visual pun that is peculiarly Japanese.

Joan Stanley-Baker has traced back the Japanese penchant for punning to the coexistence at the inception in the sixth century of the Chinese-derived Japanese writing system, which offered two separate ideographic reading systems: *onyomi* and *kunyomi*,[19] a bifurcating fissure built into the very root of Japanese writing that effectively meant that several different (aural) syllables could be substituted for the same (visual) Chinese character. It is this potential for falling between two systems—*onyomi/kunyomi*; visual/verbal; visual art/ideographic; "Occidental"/ "Oriental"; "American"/"Japanese"—that pulls Murakami's publications for the trilogy onto the same radically superflat plane as the artworks exhibited under the Superflat rubric.

Warhol's verbal contribution to the theory of flat can be boiled down to one sentence: "If you want to know all about Andy Warhol, just look at the surface: of my paintings and films and me, and there I am. There's nothing behind it."[20] Murakami, by way of contrast, has devoted three exhibitions, two substantial catalogues, and numerous essays and interviews to the elaboration of the theory and practice of Superflat, a connotatively nomadic concept that he uses at different times to refer to any combination of the following: [i] traditional Japanese painting's anticipation of Occidental modernism's flatbed picture plane; [ii] the ocular kinetics and decentering decorative effects produced by art historian Nobuo Tsuji's "eccentric" line of seventeenth- and eighteenth-century Japanese painters (Murakami: "the freedom to enter into the reality of a scene through a gaze that can come from any angle"[21]); [iii] the horizontally organized nature of Japanese culture, in which Occidental art/craft, high/low distinctions do not apply;

17 Murakami, "Superflat Trilogy," 151.

18 Murakami, "Interview with Takashi Murakami by Hélène Kelmachter," in *Takashi Murakami: Kaikai Kiki*, exh. cat. (Paris: Fondation Cartier pour l'art contemporain; and London: Serpentine Gallery, 2002), 89.

19 Stanley-Baker, *Japanese Art*, 100. For an example of how this potential for phonetic complexity and "double talk" in Japanese written language functions in Murakami's work, see Murakami on the naming of his two "acolytes," Kaikai and Kiki, in his interview with Kelmachter: "As regards their names, in Japanese we have this adjective *kikikaikai*, which we use for strange things or phenomena, things that are frightening, disturbing or make us uneasy. But in this case, I was not referring directly to that expression but to another one, which, although based on the same sounds, is written with different Chinese ideograms, *kaikaikiki*. This term, that was used by an art critic in the late sixteenth century to define the works of the painter Eitoku Kanō, embraces several different notions: bravery and power, with all the seductiveness those traits may have and at the same time a keen sensitivity.... I thought that I too would like to create a form of art that was at once vigorous, sensitive and intelligent.... With these...characters... I wanted, I think, to create my own 'gods of art.'" "Interview with Takashi Murakami by Hélène Kelmachter," 87.

20 Warhol, quoted in *Andy Warhol*, 457.

21 Murakami, "Interview with Takashi Murakami by Hélène Kelmachter," 83.

[iv] the flat-screen world of digital imaging (Murakami: "the working environment of computer graphics, flat-panel monitors, or the forceful integration of data into an image"[22]); and [v] the ground-zero flattening of Hiroshima and Nagasaki in the nuclear strikes of 1945.

3
Mobile Superflat Redemption!

"Art is explosion!"

TARO OKAMOTO, ARCHITECT OF THE TWO-HUNDRED-AND-THIRTY-FOOT ARCHAIC-FUTURISTIC "TOWER OF THE SUN" FIGURE FOR EXPO '70, IN AN ADVERTISEMENT FOR HITACHI MAXELL VIDEOCASSETTES

FOR ANYONE WHO HAS READ MURAKAMI (at least for a reader, like this one, with very little prior knowledge of Japan), the experience can produce a shock as visceral and, in its own way, as uncanny as the jolt likely to be felt by an unsuspecting visitor to this exhibition who, turning a corner, suddenly comes across *My Lonesome Cowboy* (1998). To read a Murakami manifesto, interview, or essay is to be thrown immediately up against the depths of one's own ignorance and to be signed up on the spot for a crash course in Japanese art history (psychology, psychogeography, sociology, sexology, etc.). Any engagement with Murakami's catalogues more profound than a rapid skim is liable to leave the average Western art consumer (at least one old enough to be unaffected by the current Western youth fad for all things *otaku*) floundering in a sea of unfamiliar signifiers, feeling hooked, intrigued yet vaguely ill-at-ease, not unlike Bill Murray's character in Sofia Coppola's *Lost in Translation* (2003). The in-your-face hyperbolical nature of Murakami's fractally tripped-out paintings, psychedelic mushroom installations, hypersexual giant cartoon figures, and *kawaii* (cute) figurines is at once the bait, the snappy gesture that sets the hook, and the hand that reels us in—all of us, *otaku* initiates and novices alike.

22 Murakami, "Superflat Trilogy," 153.

Combining shock and awe in equal measure with a seduction/solicitation strategy aimed at winning over jaded hearts and minds, Superflat functions like the ancient Trojan horse to penetrate the art and fashion world's defenses and to neutralize whatever vestiges remain in the age of the corporate-sponsored art opening of the hermeneutics of suspicion. Or, to retrofit the simile, Superflat resembles a stealth bomber flying under the radar to perform its bombing mission that nonetheless, when viewed at rest as a stationary object (e.g., *Second Mission Project ko² (Jet Airplane Type)*, 1999), appears like an emissary from another world, as Barthes wrote of the Citroën DS (goddess),[23] as the vehicle for our deliverance: our manumission from what Murakami called the "apocalyptic tragic paradise"[24] of post-postwar "Japan."

Superflat is a tactical domination device operated by its designer as a means for taking over/making over what provincial insiders still insist on calling the "art world" (as if it were a medieval guild) at the moment when that "world" is being redimensionalized and reterritorialized by the über-IED known as globalization. Like the round-eyed hero—Flat Boy!—in some apocalyptic time-reversal *tokusatsu* (special effects) sci-fi *meka* (mechanical/robot story), Murakami is engaged in the leveling business of historical redemption. In his blanket bombardment strategy—the artworks, group shows, manifestos, bags, and *shokugan* (snack toy) figurines that fly out of Murakami's Kaikai Kiki factory (with bases in Tokyo; Saitama, Japan; and Long Island City, New York), he demonstrates his skill as the master adept of a meta-video game—Mobile Superflat Redemption!—the goal of which is to upend all regional enemy victories in accordance with a loser-wins logic applicable *inter alia* to the following series: "America" vs. "Japan"/art vs. *otaku*/subject vs. object/adult vs. child/human vs. monster/homogeneous vs. multi-planar.

---

23 Barthes, "The New Citroën," in *Mythologies* (Paris: Editions du Seuil, 1957; translated into English by Annette Lavers, New York: Hill & Wang, 1972), 88–91.

24 Murakami, in a discussion at the Japan Society, New York, 10 November 2004, quoted in Alexandra Munroe, "Introducing Little Boy," in *Little Boy*, 256. In the same discussion, Murakami described the basic nature of this "paradise": "A pervasive impotence defines the culture of postwar Japan where everything is peaceful, tranquil, lukewarm. Our general removal from world politics and distorted dependence on the U.S. leaves us in a circumscribed, closed-in system, inhabiting an Orwellian, science-fiction realm" (246–47).

"Thank you very much, American people, for 'Love me Tender.'"

FORMER JAPANESE PRIME MINISTER JUNICHIRO KOIZUMI ON A STATE VISIT TO GRACELAND IN JULY 2006 WHEN, ACCOMPANIED BY GEORGE AND LAURA BUSH AND PRISCILLA AND LISA MARIE PRESLEY, HE SANG "LOVE ME TENDER" AND "CAN'T HELP (FALLING IN LOVE)" FOR THE ASSEMBLED INTERNATIONAL NEWS MEDIA, PLAYED AIR GUITAR, DONNED A PAIR OF ELVIS PRESLEY'S ORIGINAL SUNGLASSES, AND SWIVELED HIS ARMS, MIMICKING A CLASSIC ELVIS STAGE MOVE.[25]

REDEMPTION IS HISTORICALLY AND SPIRITUALLY LINKED to ritual and survival practices involving a descent trajectory such as self-abjection, rag-picking, dumpster-diving, or recycling, a truism borne out in the work of Occidental artists as various as Hermann Nitsch, Antonin Artaud, Bob Flanagan, Robert Rauschenberg, Walter Benjamin, and Agnès Varda.[26] It is perhaps not *just* because homeless gleaners, those disheveled Christs of the urban sidewalk who collect empty drink cans for the miniscule deposit, are literally engaged in the business of "value redemption" that they sometimes get referred to as "redeemers." The submersion-into-flight motif appears to be a universal trope for spiritual or psychic stumbling and recovery—though, in the right historical or mythological circumstances, the trajectory may be reversed as in the familiar tale of Icarus or, come to that, the by now no less familiar though probably apocryphal story of Joseph Beuys, the Luftwaffe pilot shot down over the Crimea in 1944, badly burned at the point of impact then saved/transformed into an artist-shaman courtesy of his immersion in lard by the nomadic Tartars who, according to the Beuysian fable, found him and nursed him back to health.

Murakami's tracking of the fate over a fifty-year period of the battleship *Yamato*, presented in installments in the *Little Boy* catalogue,[27] loops up and down the vertical sea-to-air axis from the oceanic depths to outer space before plummeting back to the earth's surface and farther down into the Tokyo subway system for the apocalyptic *finale* as redemption turns to toxic doom in the form of sarin gas:

---

25 Peter Wallsten, "Japan's Koizumi Shakes Up Graceland," *Los Angeles Times*, 1 July 2006.

26 I am referring here to the work of Viennese *Aktionist* and body artist Hermann Nitsch; Antonin Artaud's "Theater of Cruelty" and his psychotic experiences and experiments with peyote; the super-masochistic performances of cystic fibrosis–sufferer Bob Flanagan; Robert Rauschenberg's use of found materials in his 1950s Combines; Walter Benjamin's mystical-modernist fascination with rag-picking-as-epistemology; and Agnès Varda's film *The Gleaners and I* (*Les glaneurs et la glaneuse* 2000). The inclusion in this list of Benjamin as an "artist" rather than a "writer" or "critic" is a Murakamian gesture that aims to suspend the distinction between writing and art in terms of their functioning with regard to the Superflat project.

27 Murakami builds this allegory across two sections of the introductory plates and entries of the *Little Boy* catalogue, the first on Shigeru Komatsuzaki, 66–69, the second on *Space Battleship Yamato*, 70–71, and on pages 12[illegible], 122, and 133 of "Earth in My Window," the first of the two Murakami essays in *Little Boy*. The sequence is also mentioned in passing on pages 176 and 184 and is fleshed out again in detail by Sawaragi on pages 190–97.

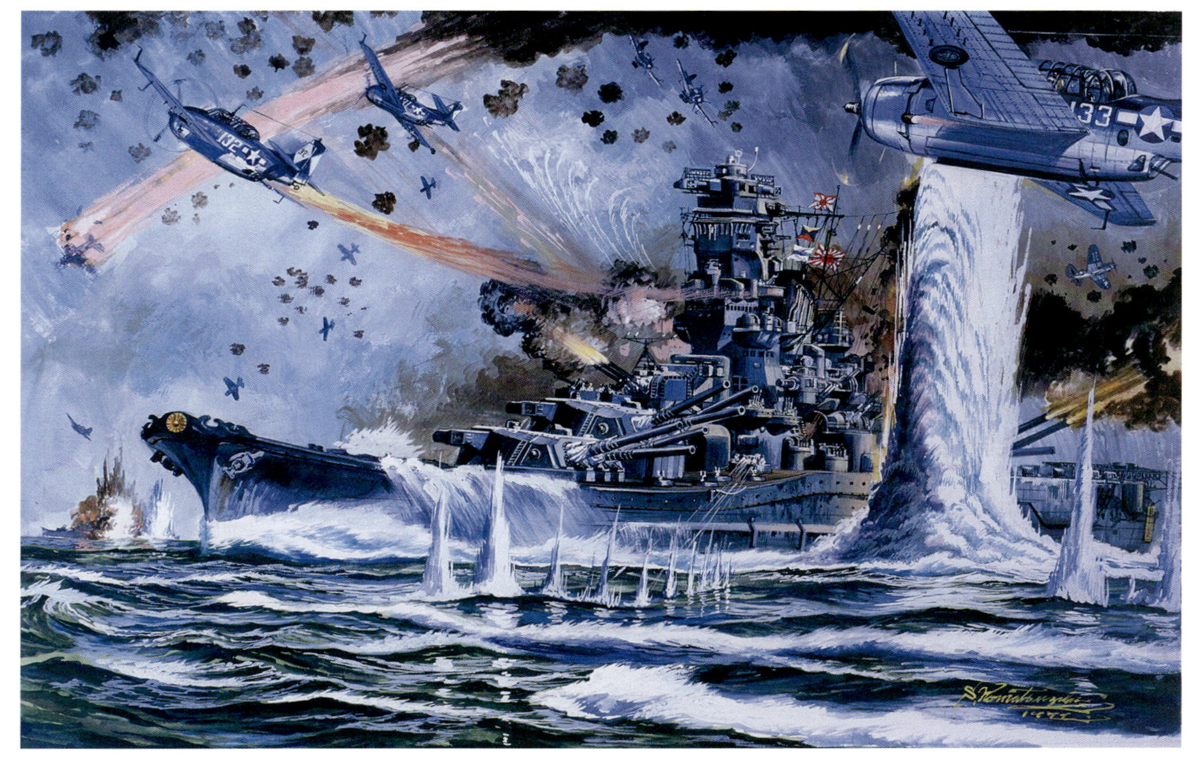

Shigeru Komatsuzaki
The End of Battleship Yamato, 1979
Watercolor, poster color, and gouache on paper
13 3/8 x 19 11/16 inches
Private collection
© Shigeru Komatsuzaki

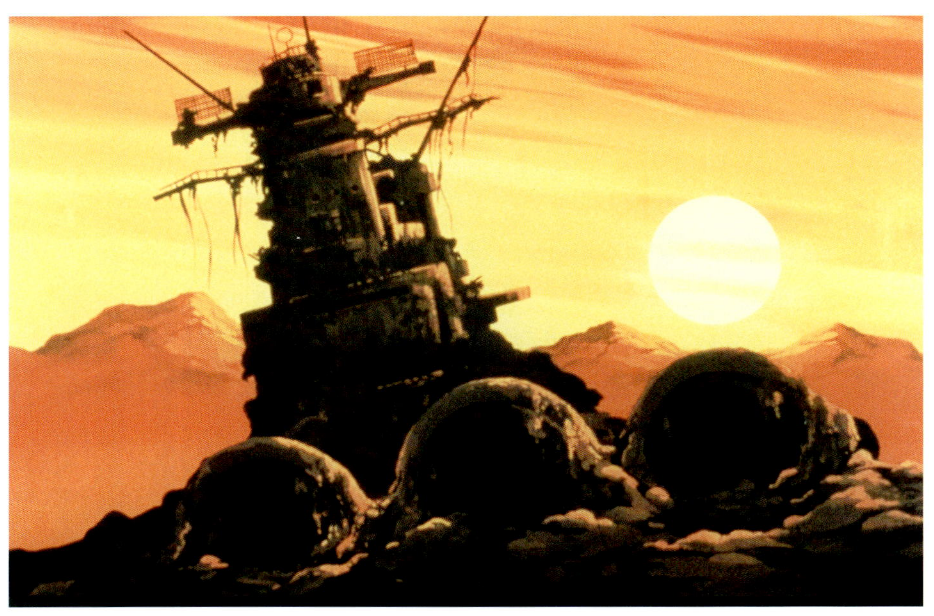

Still from
Space Battleship Yamato, 1974–75
Courtesy and © Tohokushinsha Film Corporation

EPISODE 1: The sinking of the *Yamato*, then the largest battleship ever built, on 7 April 1945 is typically presented in Japan as a tragic and unexpected reversal prefiguring defeat in the home team's heroic Pacific War narrative and is effectively depicted in those terms after the war by hyperrealist illustrator Shigeru Komatsuzaki on the box of the popular plastic-model kit of the ship that once had been the "pride of the Imperial War Fleet."

EPISODE 2: The *Yamato* shell is salvaged from the seabed and turned into a spaceship in 1974 for *Space Battleship Yamato*, a first-generation *otaku* TV *anime* series set in 2199, by a team of animators that includes Leiji Matsumoto, in his boyhood days a fervent Komatsuzaki fan. The redesigned *Yamato* is sent to retrieve the Cosmo Cleaner, a radiation neutralizer located on the planet Iscandar, to counter the toxic fallout from a nuclear attack launched from outer space by hostile aliens from the planet Gamilus.

EPISODE 3: Prior to its lethal 1995 Tokyo subway sarin gas attack, Aum Shinrikyo, the apocalyptic *otaku*-like religious cult, make a promotional *anime* video based on *Space Battleship Yamato* and market their air purifiers (for defense against predicted biological and chemical attacks) as "Cosmo Cleaners."

Redemption, in other words, as Murakami implies in this allegory, is a dirty tricky business. All bets are off when it comes to the apocalypse. All "conclusions" at this point remain contingent and reversible.

4
Little Boy, Dis-gnosis, and the Disney DOBblegänger

"Postwar Japan was given life and nurtured by America. We were shown that the true meaning of life is meaninglessness, and were taught to live without thought. Our society and hierarchies were dismantled. We were forced into a system that does not produce 'adults.' The collapse of the bubble economy was the predetermined outcome of a poker game only America could win."

MURAKAMI[28]

THE RAW FUEL THAT POWERS Murakami's Redemption War Machine is a mixture of the following:

[1] The trauma of and fallout from Hiroshima: the bombing of Hiroshima and Nagasaki is the foundational disaster on which Japan as a democratic state is posited. Hiroshima, the apocalyptic ending-as-beginning, is rerun and refigured in *animanga* sci-fi narratives like *Space Battleship Yamato*, *Akira*, *Mobile Suit Gundan*, *Neon Genesis Evangelion*, and *Time Bokan* (the 1970s TV series which furnishes the title and the distinctive death's head/mushroom cloud icon for Murakami's series of acrylic paintings).
[2] Article 9 of the United States–imposed 1946 constitution renouncing Japan's sovereign right to the threat or use of force in international relations. Prime Minister Shinzo Abe's pledge to abrogate Article 9 was probably the decisive factor in his 2006 electoral victory.
[3] Japan's postwar humiliation/infantilization under American occupation and in the ensuing dependency and post–Cold War "abandonment" phases.

Two epiphanous moments stand out in Murakami's national-humiliation narrative as triggers for the assembly and mobilization of his Redemption War Machine. The first is when, following his ouster in 1951 by Harry S. Truman, former Supreme Commander of the Allied Powers in Japan General Douglas MacArthur

28 Murakami, "Tokyo Pop" (1999), cited in "Superflat Trilogy," 152.

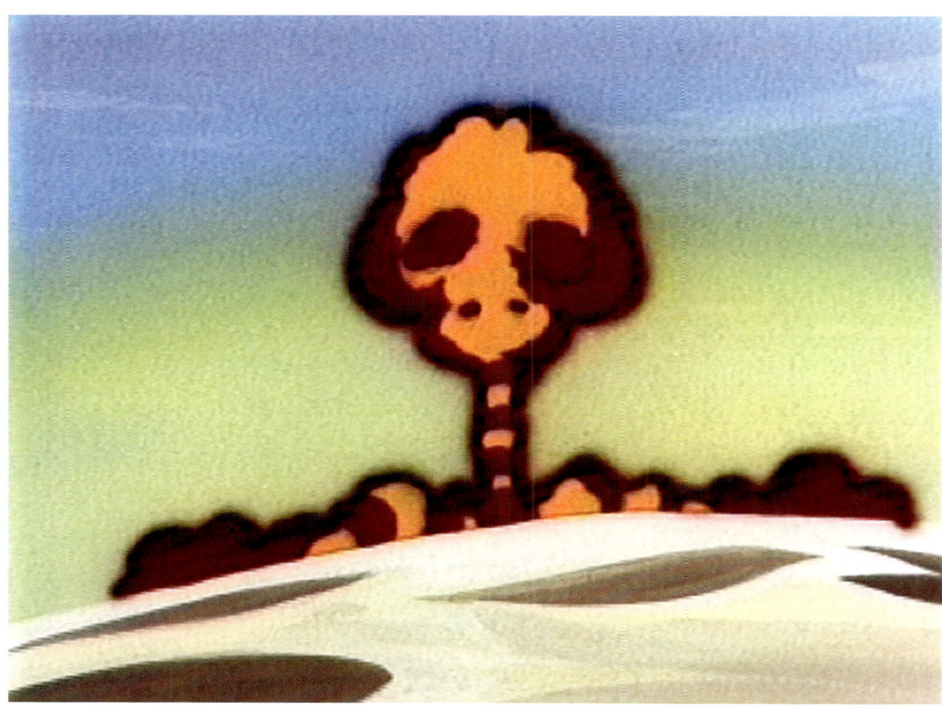

Still from *Time Bokan Series: Yatterman*, 1977–79

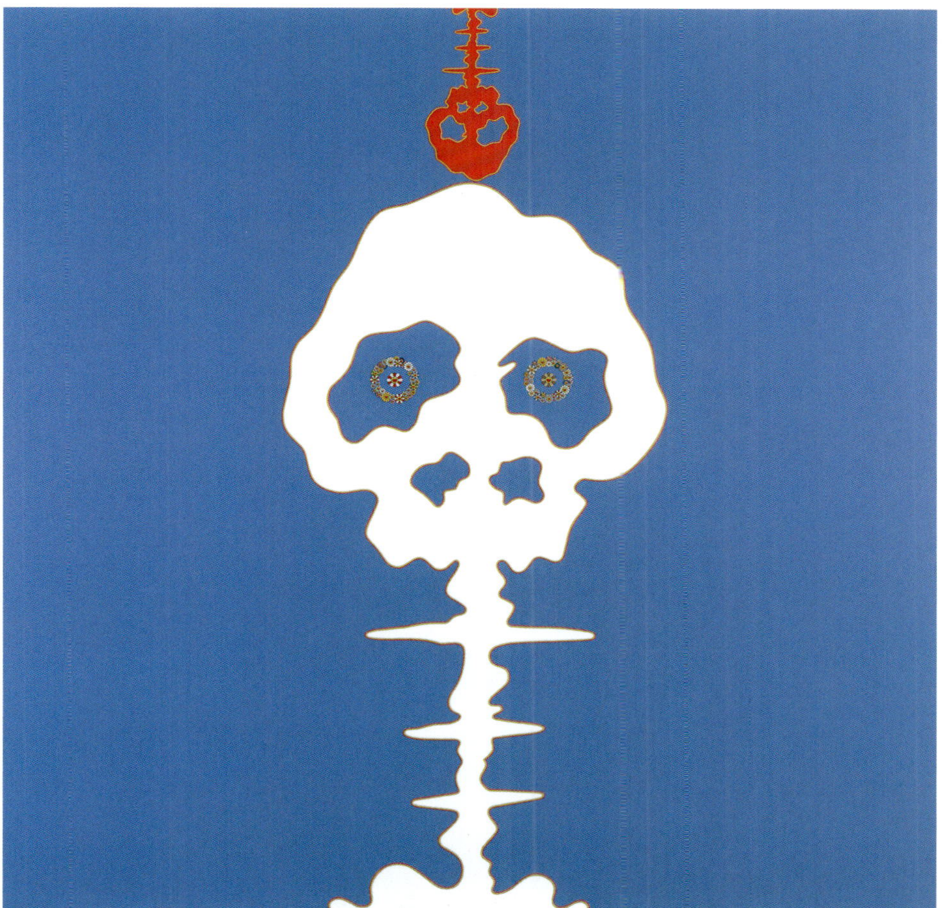

Takashi Murakami
Time Bokan—blue, 2001

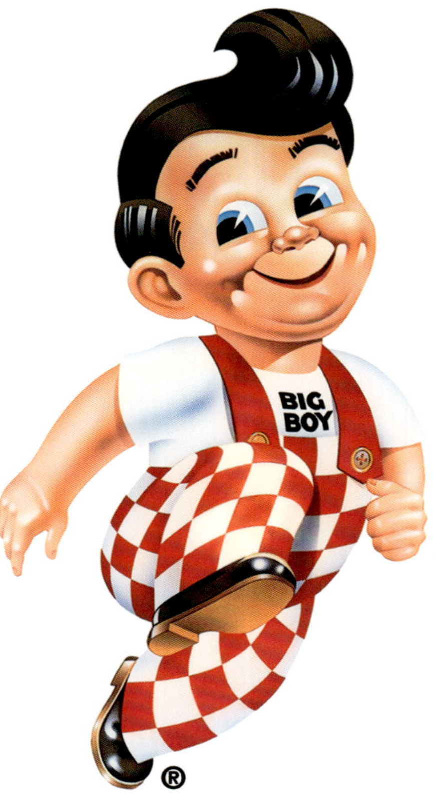

Bob's Big Boy restaurant logo
© Bob's Big Boy
Restaurants International

(nickname Skinny, a.k.a. American Caesar) stated in a speech to the United States Senate that "measured by the standards of modern civilization," the Japanese were "like a boy of twelve."[29] The second is when two of Murakami's Los Angeles gallerists, angling for a sales pitch while prowling in the artist's presence around his paintings, suddenly pounced: "How about this one? It's super flat, super high quality, and super clean!" According to the artist, the banality of this remark is what provoked him to develop his Superflat thesis. ("If Japanese culture could not transcend this flat surface, it would not achieve respectability as 'culture.'"[30])

Old Skinny's infamously patronizing comment about the "immaturity" of Japanese civilization triggered a similar psycho-semiotic response. In 2005, Murakami appropriated the U.S. Air Force's nickname for the weapon dropped on Hiroshima on 8 August 1945 for the title of his third and final exhibition in the Superflat trilogy: "Little Boy: The Arts of Japan's Exploding Subculture." Under the Little Boy rubric, he dispatches a small army of mutant figurines to New York City to take down a peg or two, David-vs.-Goliath–style, Little Boy's older sibling (Bob's) Big Boy, the oversized juvenile mascot for the once-ubiquitous burger chain founded in Glendale, California, in 1936 (with a branch still in Tokyo). Bob's Big Boy, the chubby all-American icon in checkered pants, appears to function in the Murakami system as (Little Boy's) "Big Brother," i.e., as an aggressively disarming metonym for the United States' aspiration, undisguised under the Bush administration, to achieve total global economic, military, and psycho-cultural dominance.

Prior to his invention of the Superflat system, Murakami's preoccupation with the matrix of humiliation as the key to postwar Japanese identity in particular and "Americanized" identity in general had found formal expression in a series

29 General Douglas MacArthur's remark, given during his three-day testimony to the United States Senate in 1951, is recycled at intervals throughout Murakami's published oeuvre and directly shapes Murakami's emphasis on the infantilization of Japanese culture that forms a dominant theme in the *Little Boy* catalogue. It is directly quoted in Lubow, "The Murakami Method," and in Gravett, *Manga*, 8.

30 Murakami, "Superflat Trilogy," 153.

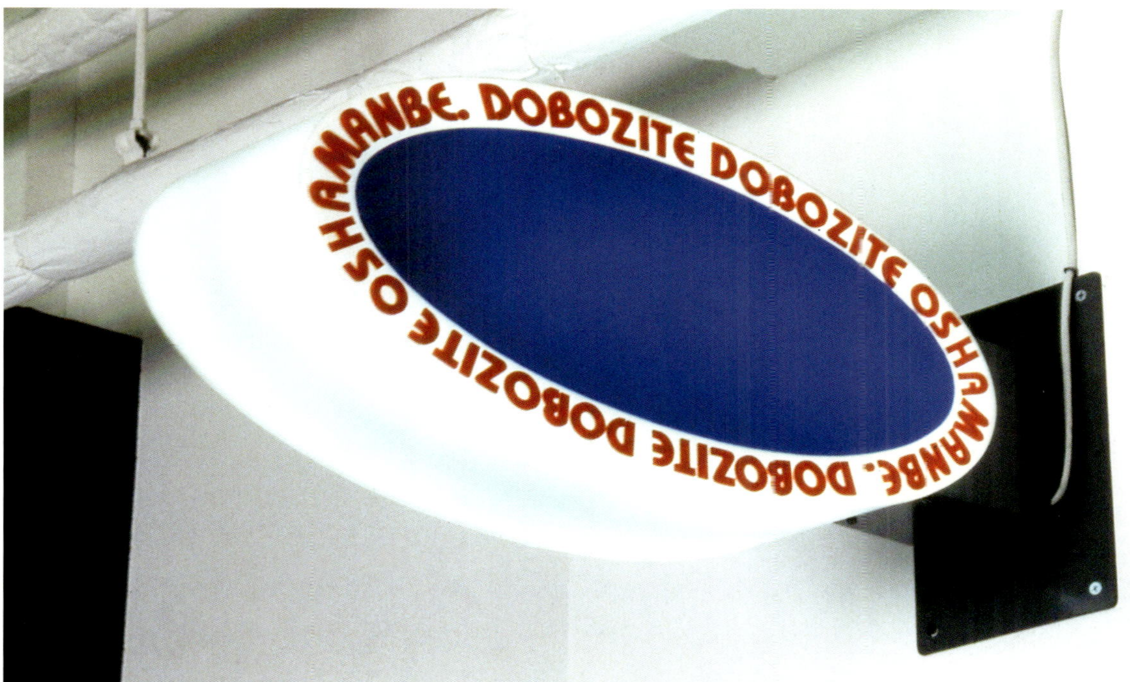

DOBOZITE DOBOZITE OSHAMANBE, 1993
Lightbox
10 7/16 x 29 15/16 x 7 7/8 inches
Courtesy Tomio Koyama Gallery, Tokyo

of heavily metaphorical works. *Randoseru Project*, produced for the 1991 exhibition "Sansei no hantai nanoda" (When I say yes, I mean no), consists of eight brightly colored school-children's backpacks (*randoseru*) hung on the gallery wall in a modular minimalist (or militaristic) formation. These decorative and innocent-seeming objects turn out on closer inspection/reflection to be: a) made from rare and exotic animal hides—hippopotamus, cobra, whale, etc. (this, at a time, coincidentally or not, when Japan was being ostracized for refusing to comply with the international ban on whaling); and b) direct descendants of the Japanese military backpacks modeled on Dutch army equipment and introduced as part of the Meiji-era Westernization program. In *Polyrhythm* (1991), Murakami plays back General MacArthur's "little boy" insult, sending it "home" to its source by exhibiting a seven-foot slab of pale yellow resin swarming with white American toy soldiers. The Superflat trilogy marked Murakami's maturation as an artist and as a major player in the art world as he moved beyond these reactive analogical responses to the infantilizing effects of foreign occupation to engage the infantilization-domination nexus digitally and critically at its root.

> DIS-GNOSIS 1. (neologism) combining dis- *prefix*, meaning opposite of, lack of (when placed before a noun), and gnosis, of or pertaining to knowledge. Hence, dis-gnosis means the opposite of knowledge, positively lacking in knowledge or a commitment to a state of denial. See also *dis-ingenuousness*, which refers to *simulated* candor, *calculated* frankness. Hence, dis-gnosis can also be used to connote *simulated* innocence.[31]

Having rejected as utterly unsuited to the Japanese context 1990s United States "message" art (Jenny Holzer, Barbara Kruger), Murakami first parodied the cult of the portentous slogan in his 1993 sign piece *DOBOZITE DOBOZITE OSHAMANBE*,[32] then sidestepped language and American conceptualism altogether in the abbreviated form of his first cartoon avatar, Mr. DOB. With the debut of DOB, Murakami-*san* morphs immediately into Flat Boy and takes the war with Skinny and his minions directly to the enemy, staking a claim to the previously uncontested subliminal terrain of the castrated Disney id, the sterile, soundless, de-libidinized artificial animation chamber situated, like the Wizard's miserable hidey hole concealed behind the curtain in Oz, at the (dead) center of America's postwar industrial-military-entertainment complex.

In *DOB in the Strange Forest* (1999), Mickey Mouse's Asiatic cousin stands, his white-gloved palms extended outwards like some nervous rookie traffic cop at a busy intersection, as an encircling gang of eye-encrusted mushrooms (psychedelic, phallic, or atomic?) appear ready to move in. By dragging the Mickey Mouse silhouette through a series of alternately ecstatic, carnivorous, lobotomized, vulnerable, and super-cute permutations, Flat Boy mangles the Disney corporation's copyright-protected rodent DNA and the presumption of eternal innocence encoded at its core, waiving its immunity to foreign infection, exposing it to the universally disfiguring fallout from the Little Boy and Fat Man detonations.

---

31 I coined the term "dis-gnosis" for an essay accompanying the exhibition "Never Never Land," curated by Omar Lopez-Chahoud at Florida Atlantic University in 2000. The exhibition included Disney-influenced works by twenty-five artists, including Murakami. An expanded version of the essay appears under the title "Dis-gnosis: Disney and the Re-tooling of Knowledge, Art, Culture, Life, Et Cetera," in *Rethinking Disney: Private Control, Public Dimensions*, ed. Mike Budd and Max H. Kirsch (Middletown, Connecticut: Wesleyan University Press, 2005). A further definition concocted for that essay is relevant to the concerns addressed here: DISNEY-FICATION (diz·ne·fik·a·shun) *n* 1. (neologism) combining Disney (surname of Walt, founder of Disney Studios, etc., etc.) and -fication (from Fr *fication*; Lat *ficatio*, from unstressed form of *facere*, to make, to do), a suffix meaning making, creating, as in calci-*fication*, morti-*fication*, mysti-*fication*. See also imagineering; theming (esp. of built environments); hyper-realism (also hyper-retailism, hyper-conformism); privatization (of public spaces, services); Californication (formerly "Americanization"); repression (esp. libidinal); mono-logism (also mono-theism, mono-gamyism; mono-railism); bowdlerization, a.k.a. sanitization (of history, myth, existence, etc.); homogenization (of cultures, differences); casualization (of labor).

32 The full text of the piece reads *Dobozite Dobozite Oshamanbe*, the latter word referencing "a place-name and double entendre used as a calling card by a Japanese comic" according to Katy Siegel in "In the Air," in *Little Boy*, 272, though Lubow also cited in "The Murakami Method" "a sexual innuendo, the indigenous Ainu people and who knows what else" as possible meanings. Murakami provided the following genealogy for DOB in his interview with Kelmachter: "I realized that by lining up totally unrelated words—to be specific, the phrase *dobojite, dobojite, oshamanbe*—you could make a 'Jenny Holzer–style' art.... I thought, if we are going to be ashamed, it might as well be with the kind of stupid jokes I was making...In the beginning, then, Mr. DOB did not arise as a character, but simply as a figure with two ears (the left one showing the letter D, the right one the letter B, and the face forming an O), DOB being the abbreviation of the joke I have just mentioned." "Interview with Takashi Murakami by Hélène Kelmachter," 75.

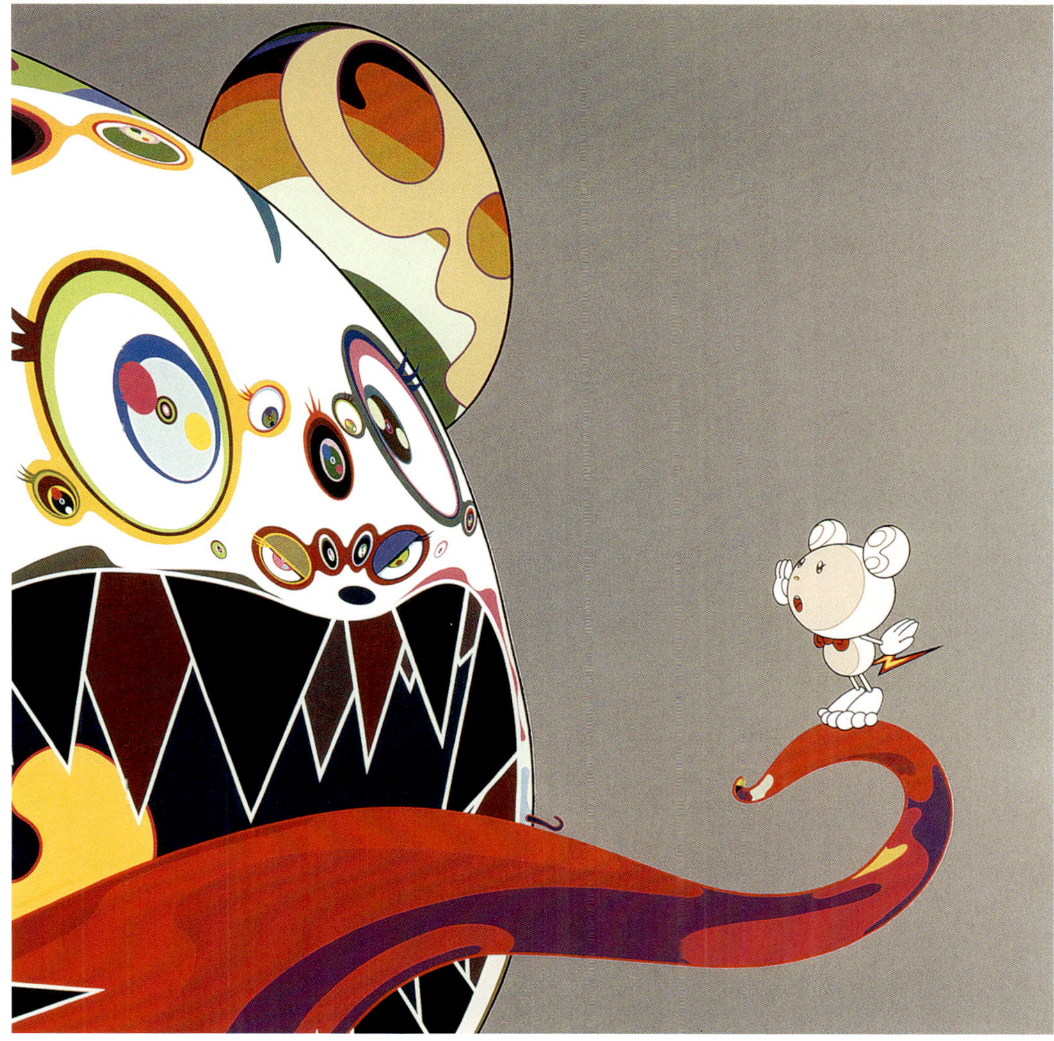

Takashi Murakami
Homage to Francis Bacon (Study of George Dyer), 2002, detail

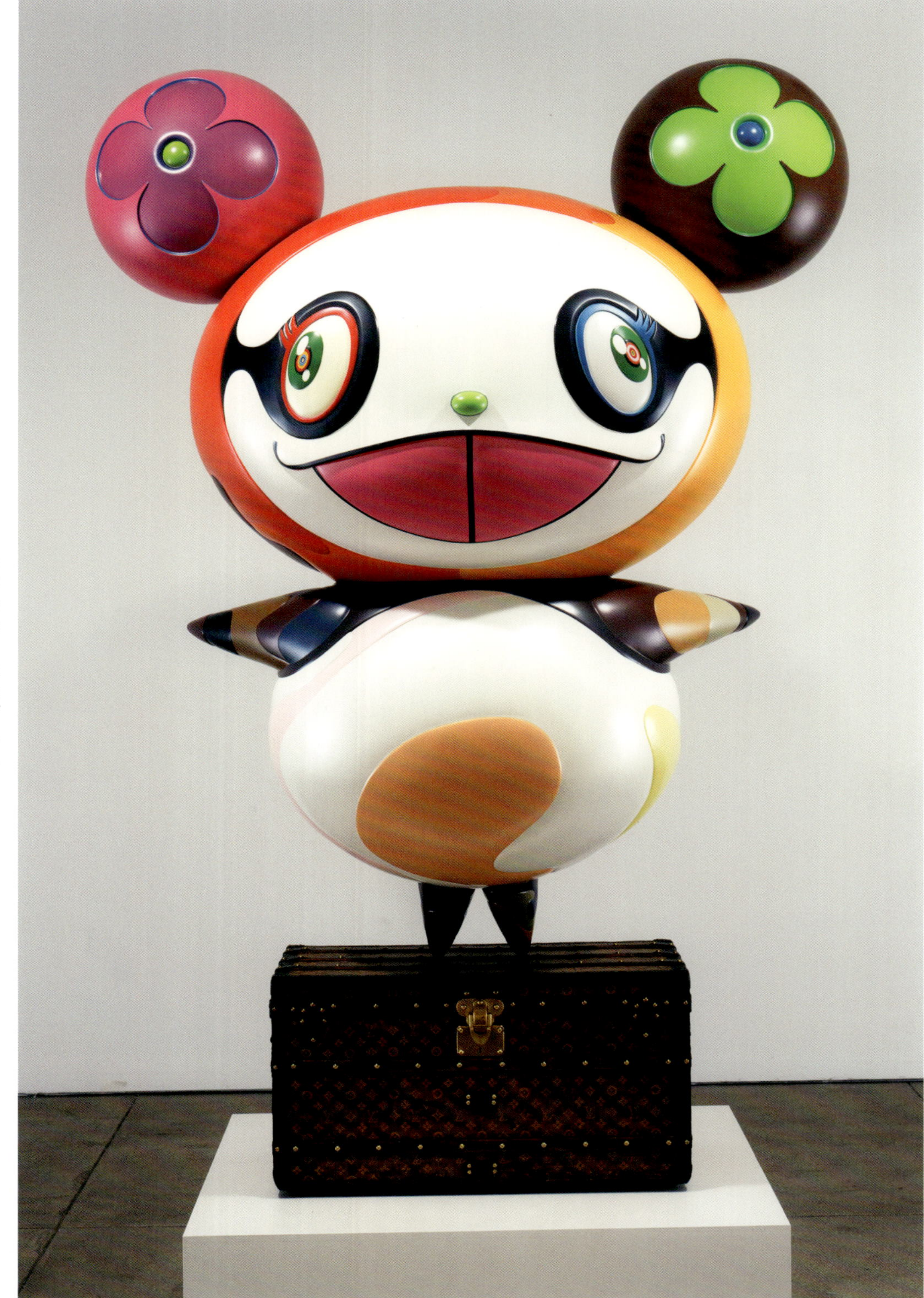

Takashi Murakami
Panda, 2003
Acrylic on fiberglass with antique Louis Vuitton trunk
100 3/8 x 64 15/16 x 42 15/16 inches
Courtesy Marianne Boesky Gallery, New York

In *Panda* (2003), the makeover is complete: "Mickey" (by this point the androgyny inherent in "his" moniker has been fully hyper-realized) perches *en pointe* (without his trademark boots, or even feet to put inside them) on an antique Louis Vuitton trunk. The ears are fiberglass balloons decorated with Murakami's signature floral motif, the body a Fabergé egg over-easy. As if in homage to his Master-Maker, the arms consist of a single stubby fiberglass pencil sharpened at both ends (the viewer's eye is drawn, as it were, to the [non-existent] hands). Panda-Mickey's eyes are elongated at the edges, the mouth pulled open in a grin to expose a single bisected front tooth—the classic cartoon Nipponese overbite—though in this case the foregrounded molars are a shocking pink, as if coated in lipstick (and indeed, when seen from a distance, the entire embouchure looks for all the world like a cosmetically enhanced, pumped-up pair of lips). Mickey, metaphorically outsourced to China (for which the panda is a synecdoche), no doubt for the sake of cost-cutting, has been hijacked for "Japan" (and Louis Vuitton).

In addition to cropping up again in two dimensions on Louis Vuitton's Murakami-designed tote bags and in the painting *The World of Sphere* (2003) along with the bipolar twins Kaikai and Kiki, both of whom appear solidly planted in flower *matangos*—*Panda* marks Murakami's move away from the sequestered seriousness of U.S.–centric political and conceptual art to a subliminal engagement with the *dis-gnostic* and infantilizing effects of an aggressively Americanized global corporate culture. That transition in turn entails a shift away from the Oedipal structures sanctioned in the art world that are typically organized in dyads around a contest of proper names (e.g., Murakami vs. MacArthur, Murakami vs. Warhol, Murakami vs. Disney, etc.) onto an anti-Oedipal track that is liable to spin off at any moment in any direction in pursuit of a constantly hybridizing set of minor differences, e.g., Orient vs. Occident vs. *otaku* vs. *orident* vs. *occirent* vs. *otakudent* vs. and so on, etc., *ad infinitum*.

5
Pornu(s)copia and the Immaculate Emission

PORNUCOPIA *n* 1. (neologism) overflowing with porn, c.f. *cornucopia* (myth) Lat, *cornu copiae* "horn of plenty," the horn of the goat Amalthaea placed in heaven, emblem of fruitfulness and abundance.

THE FAMOUS PERVERSITY OF *otaku* erotics, founded on the farside of the *ukiyo-e* (floating world) tradition and updated for the fully floating wireless generations, plays a major part in that differential splitting beyond the Oedipalizing binary effect. (Why, after all, as the queer theorists keep saying, do we always have to think in pairs [this and this] and couples [this/not this] rather than in threes or fours or solitary singulars or multiples or minus-ones or Hardt and Negri's "multitudes"?[33]) The ennui and epidemic wanderlust produced by psycho-socio-sexual binarism jamming up against the promiscuity of contact enabled by the web no doubt accounts for what, if internet economics add up in any way at all, amounts to nothing less than the *universally ineluctable pull of porn*.[34]

In his over-the-top *animanga* sculptures, Murakami explores this mutational dialectic together with the possibility contained within it that digital porn and its *cyborgian* derivative effects may be simultaneously convening and disseminating a new post-humanist set of universals, an idea which is at once postmodern and as old as Marx's prediction that capitalism's indifference to the sacred will eventually lead to the commodification of the body and the self. We could count along with the more immediately foreseeable of those derivative effects (e.g., further spikes in the rates of couples therapy, sexual performance anxiety, pathological narcissism, single-occupancy households, etc.) the following:

33 Michael Hardt and Antonio Negri, *Empire* (Cambridge, Massachusetts: Harvard University Press, 2000). Hardt and Negri argued that the rise of globalized/digitized markets in the post–Cold War era has weakened the sovereignty of the nation-state while metastasizing corporate capitalism into a new form of planetary empire that cannot be moderated or held to account by the forms of collective organization/representation developed in modernity. Instead, they advocate the formation of loosely structured autonomous sub- and supra-national resistance movements which they call "multitudes." In an alternative application, Murakami uses the word "multitudes" to invoke Shinto's polytheistic system of belief: "'multitude' is metaphorically referred to by the expression *yaoyorozu no kami*—literally, 'eight million gods'.... In this view, any natural element, any object, has its own life." "Interview with Takashi Murakami by Hélène Kelmachter," 103.

34 I am not arguing that porn is universally appealing (see, for instance, *inter alia*, American feminists Robin Morgan, Catherine MacKinnon, Andrea Dworkin, and their odd bedfellows on the American cultural and political right) though the number of free and pay-per-view porn and hook-up sex sites currently available online and the incessant proliferation of new, increasingly specialized/"far out" categories within them would seem to indicate a level of internet traffic around pornography/casual-impersonal sex unmatched in most other areas. My argument, itself hardly novel, is that porn is universally *attractive* (even when it generates repulsion), insofar as it draws attention to itself, most spectacularly in the moral panics that periodically boomerang around it, launched by those who attempt to publicly suppress it or to regulate its distribution.

> [1] the ascendancy of what might be termed "ex-timate" (public, impersonal) over intimate (private, personal) relations and affects;
> [2] material/exteriorized over immaterial/invisible criteria in self-and-other assessments;
> [3] a major stumble in the perpetual tug of war between (self-)idealization and (self-)abasement that registers seismically in the physical strata of the current booms across the genders in cosmetic surgery, health-club enrollments, and eating disorders; and in the meta-physical of mutations in individual and collective patterns of worship and devotion, e.g., the mainstreaming of "babe" worship/the *moe* (coming into bud) *bishōjo* (beautiful young girl)-adoration subculture and S&M/fetish/Goth lifestyle-fashions, the rise of evangelical mega-churches, the proliferation of syncretic New Age and neo-pagan cults, celebrity culture (versus "hero worship"), etc.

From the floating, rooted trig point of "Japan," in a spirit both sarcastic and sincere, Murakami takes the measure of these psycho-cultural sexual-spiritual effects as they move tsunami-like outwards and inwards across the internet and the Pacific. Some of the most profound and contradictory transformations of twenty-first-century global culture effected by the digital revolution are surely attributable in part to the sudden accessibility for the technologically literate masses, in formerly unimaginable variety and volume, of porn and its associated spin-offs. A comprehensive list of such transformations would include the exponentially connected rise of reactive religious fundamentalisms and the documentation and circulation on an unprecedented scale (if we bracket Jesus-on-the-cross) of sadistically eroticized humiliation rituals (e.g., reality TV shows, broadcast footage of bound and kneeling hostages videotaped by kidnapper-*jihadists*, the U.S. National Guard's Abu Ghraib jpeg picture gallery). When cosmopolitanism was feted by utopian postmodernists during the 1980s as an emergent value in a borderless world, it seems unlikely that what they had in mind was this steady *porn-etration* of the public sphere that so conspicuously marks post-millennial visual culture, from downloadable celebrity sex videos to the display, more or less

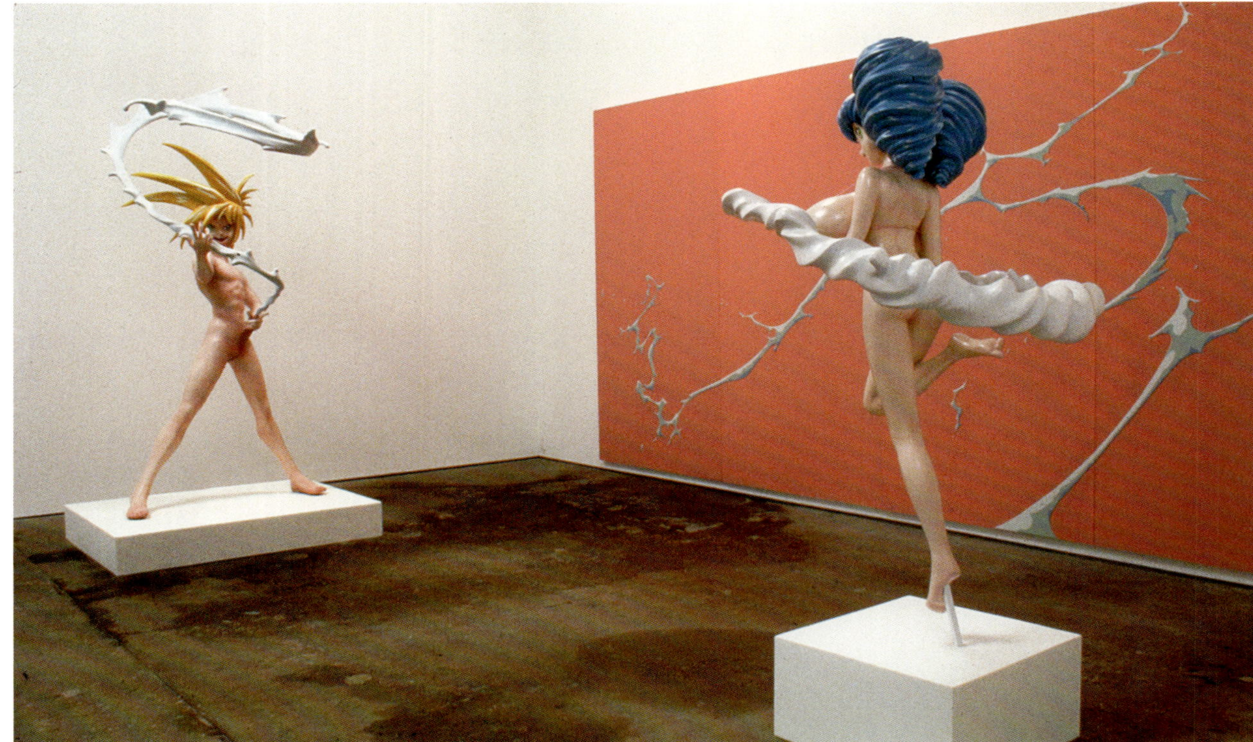

Takashi Murakami
My Lonesome Cowboy (left), 1998, and *Hiropon*, 1997, with *Milk*, 1998, in background
Installation at Blum & Poe, Santa Monica, California, 1998

ubiquitous throughout the Western world, of lower back tattoos and "I'm a Porn Star" T-shirt slogans.

It is the symbiosis between *pornu(s)copic* immersion (overexposure), emotional regression, and simulated innocence that forms the crux of Murakami's later work. His concern is to track—to analyze, accelerate, expose—the converging vectors of perversion and *dis-gnosis* as they play out across the meticulously crafted surfaces of *otaku*'s digital imaginary. Beginning with *Hiropon* in 1997, the artist has undertaken a systematic examination (part celebration, part critique) of the potentially globalizable *otaku* subculture as an aesthetic and a structure of feeling caught between insatiable sadistic voyeurism and a compensatory/weak redemptive pull toward exaggerated pathos.

By all accounts an object of loathing for the lacto/matro-phobic *otaku* community when it was first exhibited in Japan, *Hiropon* is now installed in museum settings opposite *My Lonesome Cowboy*, the priapic but androgynous figure that, since its debut in 1998, has proved somewhat more congenial to *otaku* tastes. Given the

35 Dave Hickey, "The Best of 1998," *Artforum* 37, no. 4 (December 1998): 94.

exaggerated symmetries linking the two figures (e.g., while built to scale, *Hiropon*'s plinth is slightly taller than *Cowboy*'s to accommodate an exact eye-line match), the nature of their relationship (are they strangers, siblings, rivals, partners, playmates, co-stars?) is not only *in* question, but becomes emphatically *the* question.

Though an ideal match on paper, the union of these two Dis-Disneyficated characters, each swathed in a ribbon of their own abundant discharge (a skipping rope for *Hiropon*, a lasso for the cowhand), remains eternally on hold. The union is suspended like the animation of the spatial composition in both pieces which, in its gravity-defying *brio*, its weightlessness, its coagulated mash-up of sexual and spiritual bliss, is comparable, as Dave Hickey has argued, to Bernini's *Ecstasy of St. Theresa* (1645–52).[35]

However, no actual contact or communication between the two figures is implied by Murakami in their pairing. On the contrary, each remains happily stranded on its own little plinth. Meanwhile, the colossal scale of their respective emissions (the breast milk and the sperm hanging in the air, unfettered absolutely from all reproductive functions) suggests a disciplined withholding on the part of the two principals that would surely tax the skill and will of the most controlling and mean-spirited of matrons, the most gifted (or pedantic) exponent of the mysteries of Tantric sex.

The very idea of an exchange of fluids between these two is anyway held in check by the nominal reference to homoeroticism and Warhol (e.g., *Lonesome Cowboys*, 1968) and by the ejaculated emphasis (!!) on onanism (the apodictic milking of the "cum shot"). The paintings *Cream* and *Milk* (both 1998) hung behind each figure rewind the arc of lateral spillage, though in these two-dimensional efforts the splashes appear flattened out like strands of DNA arrayed for our inspection across four panels in an abstract riff on Kanō Sansetsu's Edo-era screens *Pheasant on a Plum Tree* (1631) and *The Old Plum* (c. 1645), both cited by Murakami in his essay for the *Superflat* catalogue.

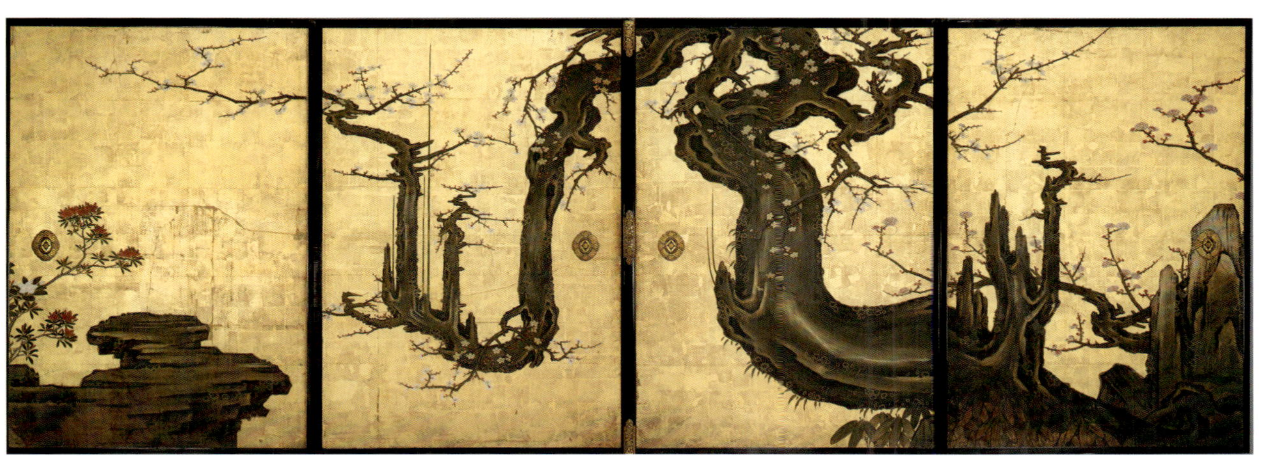

Kanō Sansetsu (attributed to)
The Old Plum, c. 1645
Four sliding door panels (*fusuma*)
Ink, color, and gold on gilded paper
68 3/4 x 45 11/16 inches each
The Metropolitan Museum of Art, New York

6
The Protocols of Sado-Cute

"Our...prescription for self-medicated denizens of a castrated nation-state may well be appropriated in the future world as an exemplary model of rehabilitation."

MURAKAMI[36]

IN THEIR IMMACULATE NARCISSISM, superhuman mastery of bodily functions, ecstatic porno exhibitionism, and vacuous *kawaii* facial expressions, *Hiropon* and *Cowboy* epitomize one hormonally supercharged variant of Sado-Cute, the psycho-sexual *habitus* where Murakami's Superflat formation feels most embodied and at home. Alternatively personified in a more literal and autistic iteration in the pairing of the rabbit-suited juvenile Kaikai and his rabid snag-toothed sibling Kiki, this Sado-Cute syndrome, though peculiarly "Japanese," is now an up-and-coming feature of youth-fixated sign-consumer cultures everywhere.

At the time of writing (November 2006), manifestations of Sado-Cute include *inter alia* the current sub-teen craze for time-travel (especially time-reversal); soft-porn, sci-fi, and sorcery *animanga* narratives and video games; pedophiliac *loli-com* (Lolita-complex) fashions, model kits, and signage; Sanrio's still phenomenally successful thirty-year-old Hello Kitty icon (today a billion-dollar-a-year business); the "dark" *kawaii* paintings of Yoshitomo Nara; and last but not least the international popularity of the Murakami brand, now franchised to include an expanding inventory of artworks and accessories produced by his Kaikai Kiki protégé-assistants. Sado-Cute's defining tactic is the tease, i.e., the taunt (e.g., "girls rule, guys drool") and the simultaneously calculated stimulation and baffling of desire which, as Adam Phillips has written with reference to flirtation, "eroticizes...by making ambivalence into a game."[37]

Linked structurally to long-term changes in the workplace—including the decline in the role and status of organized and manual labor in the West, the mass entry from the late 1960s on of women into the full-time workforce, and the rise of

36 Murakami, "Earth in My Window," trans. Linda Hoaglund, in *Little Boy*, 141.

37 Adam Phillips, *On Flirtation* (Cambridge, Massachusetts: Harvard University Press, 1994), xxiii. Phillips suggests that flirtation, "the saboteur of a cherished vocabulary of commitment," sets out to complicate the mundanely imagined ends and goals of social interaction by sexualizing them, then deferring or denying that such a move should necessarily have consequences. He suggests that flirtation manipulates perspective by setting at a distance the literal resolution of the amorous possibilities it provokes. Phillips pursues the widespread fear of flirtation "as sado-masochism with a light touch" to its root in a larger societal commitment to commitment (xvii).

the female corporate executive—Sado-Cute signals the apotheosis of "girl power" and the emergence of what Laura Kipnis has recently described as a new and more equitable "distribution of vulnerability"[38] (i.e., femininity) across the sexes. Prefiguratively identified thirty years ago in punk rock's rhetoric of male abjection, the feminization of the male psyche is registered culturally in trends like the invention and floating of the "metro-sexual" as a marketing category and in accelerating spikes in the incidence of male eating disorders and cosmetic surgery.

In Japan, the constitutional ban on militarized masculinity together with the collapse of the bubble economy and job-for-life *salarīman* positions has accentuated these patterns. The inversion of the traditional gender hierarchy is now so advanced there that, according to Japanese folklorist Eiji Ōtsuka, *shōjo* (adolescent girls) have displaced alternative figures (e.g., the farmer, the soldier, or the corporate male office worker) as the representative surrogate for the *jōmin* (the common people).[39] Where Hollywood's Imaginary and Symbolic systems in the twenty-first century are shaped around and pitched toward the fabled "fourteen-year-old boy from the San Fernando Valley," the Japanese media machine is stereoscopically fixated on the globally appealing dreams of *kawaii* school girls (in uniform) from the Tokyo 'burbs and the overheated voyeuristic fantasies of the older *otaku* and, increasingly, non-*otaku* males that trail along like Nabakov's Humbert in ecstasy and misery behind them.

As Arthur Lubow has pointed out, *anime* and *manga* qualify today as "global signifiers of cool"[40] despite the fact that most Western fans are likely to miss the more esoteric *otaku* references and subtexts. Nonetheless, there are enough similarities between the United States in particular and Japan (e.g., the prolongation in both countries of adolescence and its inherent structures of dependency for many young "adults" well into their twenties[41]) to guarantee affinities of interest and affect. As for the current craze for Murakami in America, it seems probable, as Lubow has argued, that "Americans feel they understand Murakami without conducting research because he is reacting to a hyperstimulated and decontextualized Japan that looks a lot like their own society."[42] By stressing the exportability and viral impact of *otaku* and *animanga*, together with the passive-aggressive, Sado-Cute

38 Laura Kipnis, *The Female Thing: Dirt, Sex, Envy, Vulnerability* (New York: Pantheon, 2006). "With status loss for men just around the next corner or the next downturn…it starts to seem like gender equality may not have to mean liberating women, it may just mean redistributing vulnerability more equally between the sexes. Between downsizing, vanishing retirement funds, corporations defaulting on pension obligations—say hello to the new male vulnerability…. Are men the new women?" (31–32). See also Susan Faludi, *Stiffed: The Betrayal of the American Man* (New York: Putnam, 1999).

39 Eiji Ōtsuka, *Shōjo minzoku-gaku: Seikimatsu no shinwa wo tsumugu "miko no matsuei"* (Folklore of young girls: "Shamans' descendants" who create the end-of-the-century mythology) (Tokyo: Kōbunsha, 1989), quoted in Matsui, "Beyond the Pleasure Room to a Chaotic Street: Transformations of Cute Subculture in the Art of the Japanese Nineties," in *Little Boy*, 212. Not being able to read Japanese, I have no idea whether Ōtsuka mentions farmers et cetera as possible former surrogates for the common people in his original research.

40 Lubow, "The Murakami Method."

41 A recent poll established that the majority of United States citizens now believe that a young American person does not achieve full adulthood until age twenty-eight.

42 Lubow, "The Murakami Method."

emotional formations that underpin and drive them, Murakami demonstrates that, contrary to what you might read in *The Economist*, we are today (in fact, all of us) going "Japanese"—all of us, that is, in the now fast-waning West (a zone that since the American occupation in 1945 includes, of course, Japan itself).

After seventeen years of stagnation, Japan, once dubbed "the Asian economic miracle," tends to be regarded in 2006 as dysfunctional and maladaptive, its faltering corporations overshadowed by the surging Chinese Dragon, its aging population afflicted by multiple pathologies, paralyzed by a general ambient unease. Whereas Japan's birthrate now ranks among the lowest in the world, it has the highest suicide rate among wealthy industrial nations, including a growing number of group suicides convened over the internet. It is also home to an estimated one million *hikikomori* (literally, "pulling away and retiring") domestic-space dropouts, the majority of them young(ish) men who subsist, sometimes for decades at a stretch, barricaded in their bedrooms in the parental apartment.[43]

Like those other little island Big League art-world players, the 1990s BritArt pack (Damien Hirst, Marcus Harvey, Tracey Emin, Sarah Lucas, Gary Hume, et al.), the Japanese proponents of Tokyo Neo-Pop, Superflat, and Sado-Cute (Murakami, of course, bridges all three) have turned the national tropes, common to both Britain and Japan, of imperial decline, cultural decadence, religious agnosticism/pluralism, poor-to-middling economic performance, and a sixty-year history of subordination to American power into a super-smart weapon launched against the status quo and the hegemony of New York's postwar art world. While in drawing up their respective invasion plans, the Brits could call upon indigenous traditions of cheeky visual/verbal wit, provocative advertising, and punkish insubordination, the Japanese had recourse to an equally productive legacy of canny appropriation, a formally strong but perverse and playful decorative crafts tradition, and a thousand-year immersion in *bushidō* and the martial arts.

In his elaboration of the Superflat thesis, Murakami has addressed at length the role of appropriation/reverse engineering in the creation of "Japan" and the subversive work of the rebus in classical Japanese decoration.[44] However, the strategic logics of Oriental combat—though not, perhaps for obvious reasons, explicitly

43 Michael Zielenziger, *Shutting Out the Sun: How Japan Created Its Own Lost Generation* (New York: Nan A. Talese, 2006), 9. This is Zielenziger's estimate based on his own research in the face of the silence and denials of Japanese officialdom and widespread *hikikomori*-family shame. In 2001, the Japanese Health Ministry finally acknowledged that at least six thousand families had visited public clinics seeking help and that a study team had been assembled. "A follow-up survey conducted in 2002 in rural Mie prefecture found that sixteen families out of 1,420—more than one out of every hundred surveyed—reported having a *hikikomori*. Projected across the entire national population of 126 million, the survey indicated that, at a conservative estimate, at least 410,000 families suffered from the syndrome" (47). The government-owned NHK TV and radio network now gives the higher number of between one million and 1.2 million *hikikomori* (60).

44 Murakami's devotion to art that stupefies, that, beggaring language, "leaves you gaping," draws him toward the recursive work of the rebus, where meaning is dispersed across and embedded in the "superflat" surface. When referring to *Hiropon* in an interview with Matsui for *Index* magazine in 1998, Murakami described the original image for the figure that he had appropriated from a comic book as a "rebus of the *otaku* sexuality." For more on the role of the rebus in classical Japanese art, see Matsui, "Toward a Definition of Tokyo Pop," 28.

mentioned—may be equally or more germane to an understanding of his project. For instance, "passive aggression" tends to be categorized in American English as symptomatic of "low self-esteem," a concept that East Asian scholar Michael Zeilenziger has argued has no equivalent in Japan.[45] Negatively evaluated, it tends to be regarded in the Anglophone world as a sign of weakness, strategically and morally inferior to either "aggressive aggression" or "passive passivity." But something like the idea of passive aggression is encoded etymologically at the very root of the Japanese words used to designate the major ancient Chinese-Japanese martial arts disciplines: *jūjitsu* and *jūdō*, i.e., *jū* (soft, yielding), *jitsu* (science), and *jūdō* (gentle way).

Murakami and his cohorts eschew the Big Boy "Army of One" *tokusatsu-meka* approach to engaging the enemy favored by the hyper-masculinist U.S. military in its current feud with Terror, just as they abstain from the abjection-fests and adolescent tantrum tactics that still pass in the U.S.–centric art world for "defiance" of a suspiciously abstract and now largely superannuated patriarchal order. What they opt for instead is the ocular *jūjitsu* of Sado-Cute: an insinuative, seductive, and ultimately neutering succession of moves designed to throw the viewer into what Barthes called "the very fissure of the symbolic...in which a certain disturbance of the person occurs...a shock of meaning lacerated...without the object's ever ceasing to be significant, desirable."[46]

Despite the erotic floral decor arranged around its rim, this fissure into which the viewer falls is an opening up to (our latent disavowed desire for) death or rather nonexistence, rather than to desire pure and simple (though when was desire ever pure or simple?). The regressions orchestrated in Sado-Cute do not return us to some familiar scene from childhood or adolescence rendered weird through irony (as in a Mike Kelley installation) or histrionics (as in a Paul McCarthy or Georgina Starr performance) but to the place of laceration itself, the sub- or super-human space, spooky rather than uncanny, sited in the wound within the wound of culture in the floating fetal time-space before sexes are assigned: the living undead space-time behind the trauma of the origin, set back before the trouble even starts.

45 Zielenziger, *Shutting Out the Sun*, 156: "The whole concept of self-esteem in which I, a Westerner, was immersed, was rooted in the Judeo-Christian tradition's teaching that each individual is infused with an ineffable spirit of the Creator, [Masahiro] Yamada [a sociologist] told me. 'But in Japan, we don't have self-esteem,' Yamada said flatly. 'We only have the identity of groups.'" Christianity was violently suppressed in Japan during the Tokugawa era (1603–1868), and the ban remained in place even during the Mejii Westernization program, ensuring the survival until 1945 of a feudal system based around the primacy of *ie* (clan) affiliation over individual or bloodline-based family identities. The remarks of an American theologian interviewed in this context by Zielenziger are worth quoting at length: "We find in the Japanese account no marked emphasis on any of the following: the individual (soul) as the primary unit of spiritual, moral, and political meaning; the notion of a set of universal principles applying to all humankind as the ideal of behavior; the idea of a legalistic, contractual relationship among persons or between a people and their God; the idea of a divine plan worked out in natural and human history to which we feel responsible; or the hierarchy of rationality as what sets off the human from other animals" (129).

46 Barthes, *Empire of Signs*, 4.

7
The War of Monster vs. Human

"It has become clear now, in light of the current global situation, that the notion of 'human' that informs high art and nationalism was invented in modern times to conceal the fact that humans themselves are a kind of 'monster' or 'cyborg'...Art is, at its root, made by these 'demons,' and is at odds with the everyday life we live. In this sense, art is fundamentally antagonistic to humanity.... I believe that the time has come to return art to the hands of the monsters, who were here before humans."

MURAKAMI[47]

THE OMINOUSLY MONSTROUS CAST of so much contemporary Japanese art and media culture stems from a broader, more accommodated sense of disenchantment with the human project than is (re)presentable in either the "pathological apocalypse"[48] scenarios of the *otaku* subculture or the metaphor, pursued across the interlocking surfaces of Superflat, of the postwar "crippling" of Japan. Far from being minor and subcultural, that mounting sense of mundane disenchantment is structured in for the declining Western subject, most acutely for the demi-Western subject in *faraway* "Japan," at the core of the current globalized conjuncture. Framed and animated by the twin delivery systems of the globalizing process—the flat screen and the Box,[49] by digital technologies and the shipping container—the sign-manipulating citizen-consumers of the affluent debtor nations appear these days not so much "de-centered" as outsourced: stoked in the short term on internet libido and cheap imported goods, yet aware at some level that the present setup cannot last. Anxiously resigned to some impending planetary eclipse yet at the same time in denial, we sit with one ear open, hunched inside the babble of our cell phones and our iPods, waiting for the other shoe to drop.

> MONSTER *n* misshapen creature; horribly cruel or savage person; huge object; from Lat *monstrum*, something marvelous or prodigious, orig. divine portent.

---

47 Murakami, "Superflat Trilogy," trans. Office Miyazaki Inc., 161–61.

48 Susan J. Napier, quoted in Munroe, "Introducing Little Boy," 255.

49 For a fascinating well-researched history of the shipping container and its revolutionary impact on distribution and international trade, see Marc Levinson, *The Box: How the Shipping Container Made the World Smaller and the World Economy Bigger* (Princeton, New Jersey: Princeton University Press, 2006). Digitization is often cited as the principal technological engine of economic globalization but, as Allan Sekula and others have long pointed out, the role of the shipping container in the transformation of maritime-terrestrial trade is at least as, if not more, important. An approximate audit of the trade deficit in the affluent-for-now West can be made by attempting to monitor the uncountable number of empty containers piling up on Western land masses and in the mounting number of experimental design/affordable–avant-garde housing projects centered round the shipping container currently initiated by Occidental nonprofit organizations, architectural practices, and art, design, and architecture schools. Communism may have lost the Cold War, but China may still sink the West, jujitsu-style not with bombs but with cold steel in the form of a rusting floor-to-floor continent-wide carpet of empty shipping containers.

In "Japan," this sense of closure and foreboding is concentrated in the recurring image of the monstrous infant. Mutilated or deformed, diabolically cute or unnaturally "advanced," sexualized or old or dead before its time, the depthless eyes of the sick or ruined child gaze and glower back at us from the pages of Katsuhiro Ōtomo's *Akira* (1982–90) and the paintings and sculptural installations of Izumi Katō, Aoshima, Nara, and the rest. Transposed onto DOB or surgically removed and turned into Jellyfish Eyes wallpaper, they stare back at us from the spotlit heart of Murakami's Mag(s)ick Kingdom.

> "A father complained about his twenty-nine-year-old [*hikikomori*] son, whose only communication over the past five years was through written notes left on the kitchen table with instructions such as, 'Get me a video game magazine,' or 'Do something about the dog that keeps barking.'… Attacking a parent has become one of the most common forms of domestic violence in Japan."[50]

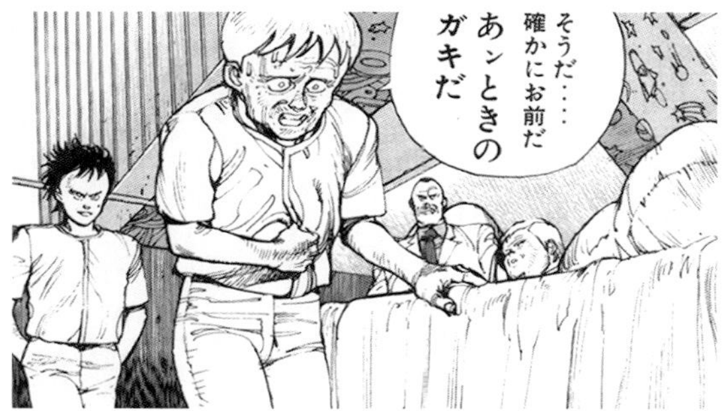

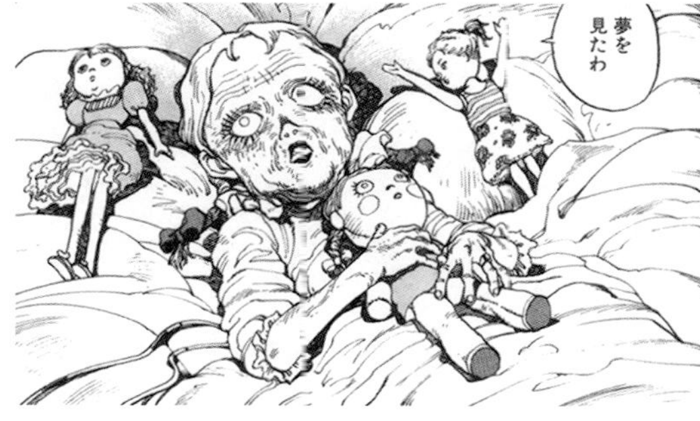

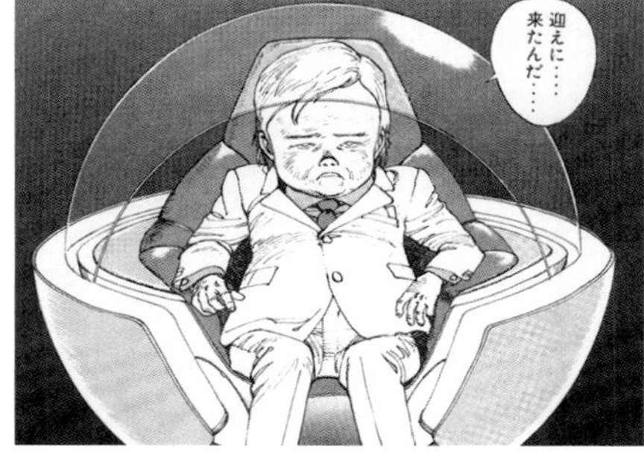

Katsuhiro Ōtomo
Panels from *Akira*, 1982–90
Courtesy and © Kodansha Ltd., Tokyo

As metonym for the end not just of an irradiated postwar lineage but of the myth of new beginnings, period, the inhuman gaze of the uncannily detached infant—like a cold reprise of Johnny Rotten's mad "No Future" glare, only infinitely creepier—signals a deepening crisis in (social) reproduction in the West. It suggests not just the repeal of the parenting "instinct" (some Japanese towns now offer cash incentives for couples willing to have children[51]) or a reluctance on the part of generations X and Y to "grow up" and follow their parents into rigidly

50 Zielenziger, *Shutting Out the Sun*, 48, 43.
51 Kipnis, *The Female Thing*, 76. She also noted that seventy percent of young Japanese women say they are not interested in marriage. She went on: "The United States isn't far behind, with its own Social Security drain, and its own graying population turning the national pension system into an impending Ponzi scheme and spawning a national debate over immigration amnesty—after all, someone has to pay in to forestall the whole thing collapsing" (76).

gendered *salarīman*-homemaker roles, insofar as those options still exist. It also suggests the lifting of the bar between fantasy and prohibition, the incursion into the Real of the eternally malleable, digitally generated model to such a degree that "the world of the living is no longer secure"[52] from the shadows of the monstrous, the unformed and the deformed, the dead and disavowed that silently surround it, stand over and sustain it.

At a time when the return of the murdered child as an angry or avenging ghost forms a persistent motif in contemporary Japanese films like *Tomie: Rebirth* (2001), *Jū-On* (2000), and *Jū-Rei* (2004), the parents of the reclusive *hikikomori*, the dysfunctional embodiment of *otaku*, subsist alongside their invisible offspring, haunted by the living ghosts, the poltergeists and demons they themselves have brought into the world: "In November 2004, a twenty-eight-year-old man, who had been a *hikikomori* for eight years, admitted killing his parents and older sister with a hammer and a kitchen knife. He had committed this crime after his father, a city worker, had demanded that he find a job. 'My father and my sister robbed me of my space to live in,' Masaru Iijima told the police...'I thought I'd kill them before they killed me.'"[53]

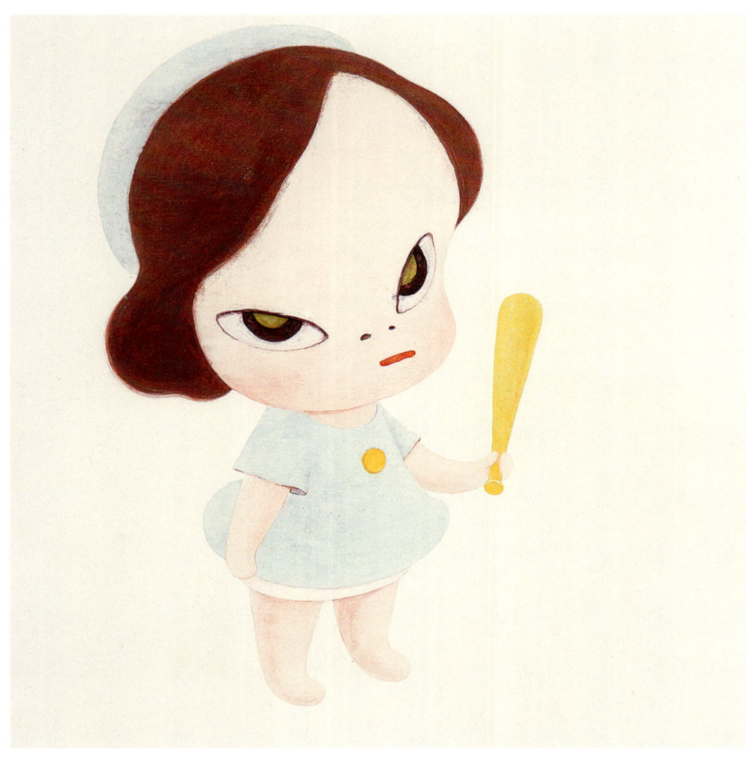

Yoshitomo Nara
Girl with Bat, 1996
Acrylic on canvas
47 1/4 x 43 3/8 inches
Courtesy Blum & Poe, Los Angeles
© Yoshitomo Nara

In the meantime, behind the closed door of Junior's bedroom where sleepless homicidal avatars cruise Nintendo-world, slaughtering anything that moves, and the robot kits pile up in the corner, the larger specters of the national past cast their shadows across Japanese school history books in the form of silences, omissions, euphemisms, and denials, sparking street riots in China and demands

52 Hiroki Azuma, "Super Flat Speculation," in *Superflat*, 151. Azuma used the phrase in the context of a subtle and sustained Lacanian argument concerning the gaze and how it is both orchestrated and signified in Murakami's work via "spectral eyes" that signal the simultaneous failure of linear perspective and the "mechanism of castration."

53 Zielenziger, *Shutting Out the Sun*. Zielenziger wrote: "Although there are no accurate data for it, the consensus among psychiatrists seems to be that at least half of all *hikikomori* treat their parents with some sort of violence. Beating them with an aluminum baseball bat is common; some children just use their fists.... So common is the violence that many counselors tend to associate the term 'domestic violence' not with wife-beating or child abuse by adult males as Americans do, but with abuse of parents by adolescent children" (43).

from Japan's neighbors for acknowledgment and compensation for atrocities committed by the Imperial Forces during the Pacific War. In May 1998, the surviving British remnant of the emaciated ghosts who, as prisoners of war in the midst of that conflict had built the Burma railroad, turned their arched-but-at-attention backs in protest on the motorcade conveying Japanese Emperor Akihito and U.K. Prime Minister Tony Blair down the Mall to meet the Queen while whistling "Colonel Bogey," the anthem of the defiant P.O.W.s in the 1957 movie *The Bridge on the River Kwai*. *The Daily Yomiuri* in Tokyo noted in response that "Britain was the largest colonial power before World War II, and although it was responsible for many barbarous acts, such as the 1840–42 Opium War, the country has hardly offered any apologies to its former colonies."[54] The empty stare of the post-mature late-arriving infant, emblem of amnesia, unattested guilt, and trauma-in-denial, makes no distinction between one claim or the next, implicating each with equal indifference as it scans in close-up from the *faraway* horizon one super-flattened object after another.

Conclusion

Second Mission Project ko² (Human Type): Free from Occupation

> *"The Western eye is subject to a whole mythology of the soul, central and secret, whose fire, sheltered in the orbital cavity, radiates toward a fleshy, sensuous, passional exterior; but the Japanese face is without moral hierarchy; it is entirely alive, even vivid (contrary to the legend of Oriental hieratism), because its morphology cannot be read 'in depth,' i.e., according to the axis of an inwardness; its model is not sculptural but scriptural: it is a flexible, fragile, close-woven stuff (silk, of course), simply and as though immediately calligraphed by two lines; 'life' is not in the light of the eyes, it is in the non-secret relation of a surface and its slits: in that gap, that difference, that syncope which are, it is said, the open form of pleasure."*
>
> BARTHES, *EMPIRE OF SIGNS*[55]

---

54 "The View from Japan," 27 May 1998, available at http://news.bbc.co.uk/1/hi/world/asia-pacific/100635.stm.

55 Barthes, *Empire of Signs*.

AS ONE WOULD EXPECT WITH WORK made in accordance with the protocols of Sado-Cute, the "monstrous" aspects of Murakami's oeuvre are mitigated and held in abeyance by his sustained and calculated teasing: by the hyperbolic motor-show style of presentation, the openly hilarious wit, and the luxuriously consummated surfaces: the visually stunning, "super-clean" finish of the works. No trace remains of the putatively "subversive" Bataillean mode of address, the Occidental meta-sexual-physics of dirt and desecration, that sense of Freud on acetate being played backwards complete with the "old-school" analog scratch-and-crackle that one gets with French surrealism.

Murakami's monstrous conjunctions—the lactating babe, the Mickey Mouse sublime—arrive uncontaminated by smudgy fingerprints or human grease, immaculately transmitted via that other plastic mouse that digitally directs all on/in-screen procedures from the "other (*cyborg*-monster) side" of the human-animal condition. In Murakami's work, the original Latin root of "monster"—*monstrum*: "something marvelous or prodigious"—decisively predominates, though the overall tone and effects are the opposite of what Occidental critics call "Wagnerian" (*animism*, after all, is at the "heart" of the Shinto religion; hence it might be said to function as the "essence" of Japanese spirituality).

Murakami's "tooning" of the Valkyrie in *Second Mission Project ko²* is at once a respectfully tongue-in-cheek translation of the heavy-duty Nordic prototype and the storming by litotes of Wagnerian *Sturm und Drang*: a bringing down to size and surface of Occidental "depth" and soulful gravitas. Like the substitution of Adam's demonic first wife, Lilith, for Christ as the crucified "savior" at the end of the world in *Neon Genesis Evangelion*[56]—like the Siniticization/sin-ification of Mickey Mouse, patron saint of globalized Californicated capitalism in Murakami's Panda icon for Louis Vuitton—the blown-up-beyond-life-size "reduction" of the Valkyrie is serious, almost reverential in its sacrilege.

Miss ko², bodacious secret-agent girl turning inter–aero-planar on her elevated plinth, is monstrous in the dictionary sense, i.e., "a huge object"; huge, one might add, though hardly grandiose: "divine," as in "absolutely fabulous," a "portent" of pure emptiness. Conceived originally in micro-scale through digital

56 Murakami dubs *Neon Genesis Evangelion* a "meta-*otaku* film." Made in the mid-1990s and set in 2015, it opens with a sudden attack on the new city of Tokyo 3 by airborne Angels, unidentified enemies including monsters and computer viruses that are countered by robotic weapons called Evangelions, manned (so to speak) by two fourteen-year-old girls, Rei and Asuka, and a fourteen-year-old boy, Shinji, who are working for NERV, a special UN agency. The story mashes Judeo-Christian mythology/Gnosticism up against speculative bio-science and New Age psychology with devices like the Spear of Longinus (derived from the legendary spear used by the eponymous centurion to pierce the crucified Jesus) and the AT (Absolute Terror) Field (a breachable barrier separating an individual's ego from the surrounding world). The film ends with the naked forms of Shinji and Rei lying on a beach about to merge with the crucified body of Lilith, then separating as Shinji wakes up to find himself strangling Asuka who caresses his cheek, inducing Shinji, weeping, to desist, though a tear falls on Asuka's cheek, causing her to snarl "That's disgusting," at which point the film abruptly ends. See Murakami, *Little Boy*, 127–31.

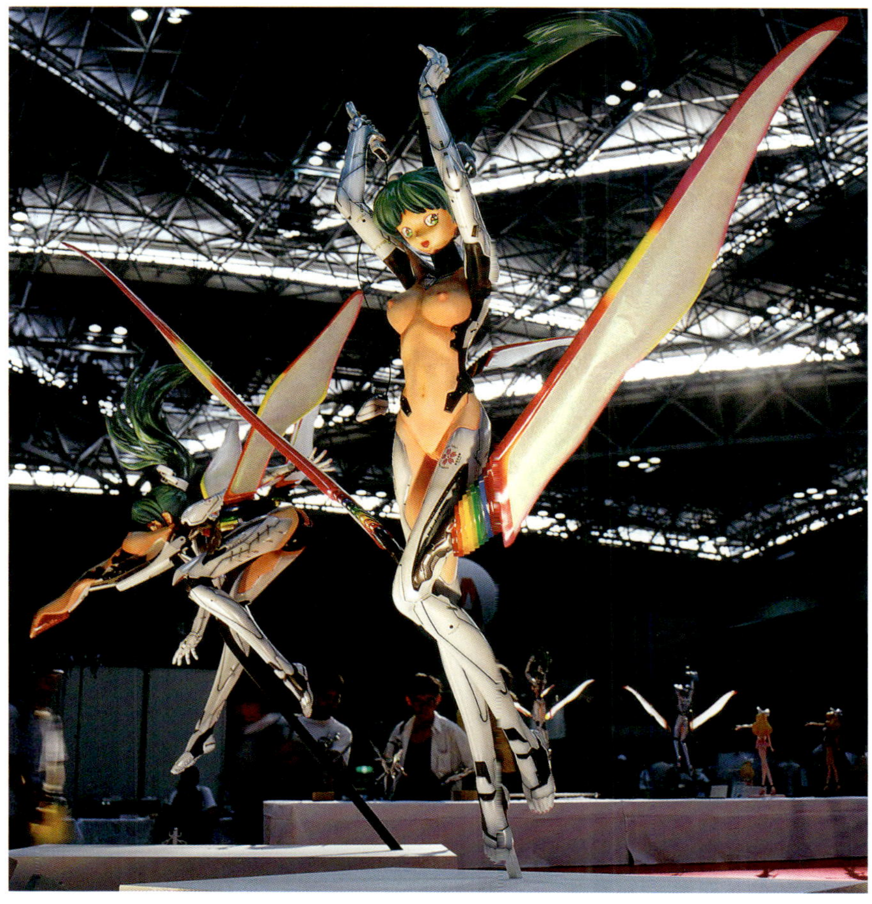

Takashi Murakami
Second Mission Project ko^2, 1998
Installation at "Wonder Festival 2000 Summer," Tokyo

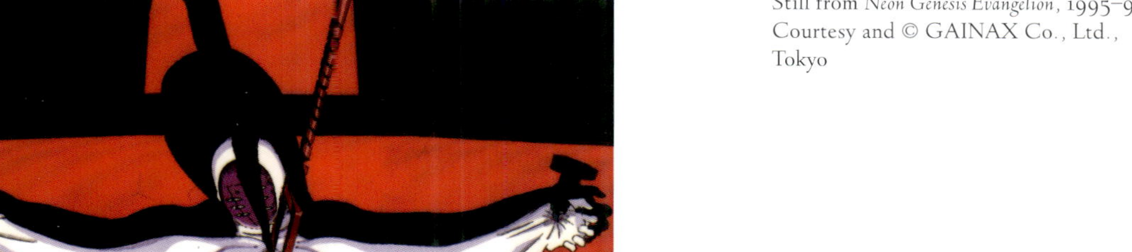

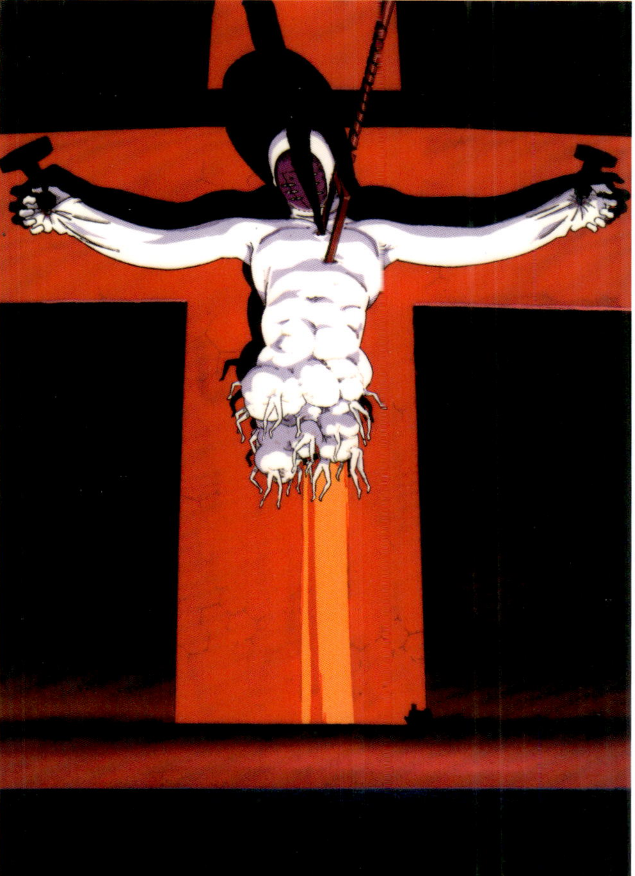

Still from *Neon Genesis Evangelion*, 1995–96
Courtesy and © GAINAX Co., Ltd., Tokyo

manipulation, subsequently rendered as a mass-produced miniature, then blown up to epic proportions (and in her glorious apotheosis, given wings), *Second Mission Project ko*² is a literal taking off of Leda and the swan. Beautiful but also "pretty" in the sense of "crafty, wily, clever, ingenious"; occupying space but also "vacant" in the sense of "devoid of contents; free from occupation," *ko*² is nothing less than "the history of our own obscurity"[57] inscribed in three dimensions. She represents, to borrow from the Barthes quote at the opening of this essay, the destiny of our narcissism made manifest: Flat Boy's triumph over Skinny.

"What do you think of Takashi Murakami?"
mu-ra-kam-mi ta-ka-shi o do o-moy-mas ka?
PHRASE THREE OF THE SEVEN PHRASES ON "ART"
INCLUDED IN YOSHI ABE, *LONELY PLANET JAPANESE PHRASEBOOK*,
IN THE FIVE-PAGE "CULTURAL DIFFERENCES" SECTION.[58]

Postscript

"Whoever is ignorant of the past remains forever a child."
CICERO

IN JUNE 2005, THE LONDON *Independent*[59] ran a story by Tokyo-based journalist David McNeill about the friendship developed against all odds between Takashi Nagase, a retired English teacher who more than sixty years ago worked as an interpreter for the Japanese military police during torture sessions in the prison camp made famous in *The Bridge on the River Kwai* (1957), and former P.O.W. and torture victim Eric Lomax, then a twenty-two-year-old Scottish Signal Corps engineer.

"I couldn't bear his pain," Nagase is reported as saying. "He was crying, 'mother! mother!' And I thought: what she would feel if she could see her son like this. I still dream about it...I wanted to help him in some way. I searched my brain for the right English expression, and as he was leaving the camp I said to him quietly, 'Keep your chin up.' I still remember his astonished face."

---

57 Barthes, *Empire of Signs*, 4.

58 Yoshi Abe, *Lonely Planet Japanese Phrasebook*, 4th ed. (Oakland, California: Lonely Planet Publications, 2004), 255.

59 David McNeill, "The Railway of Death: Bridge Over a Troubled Past," *Independent* (London), 20 September 2005.

The two men spent the intervening decades attempting to recover from the infernal context of their original encounter. Lomax, who almost died as a result of his injuries and spent the rest of the war in a brutal military prison, nursed his hatred for the "hateful little" interpreter with the flat inflectionless voice and for half a century said he "wished to drown him, cage him and beat him."

Nagase spent the same half century seeking to atone, building memorials across Thailand, including a Buddhist peace temple near the Tham Kham Bridge over the Kwai Noi River, the famous "Bridge on the River Kwai." Beginning in 1976, he organized a series of reunions between ex-P.O.W.s and Japanese soldiers on the same bridge, a crossing point for the 258-mile Thai-Burma Railroad that is estimated to have cost the lives of one hundred thousand slave laborers enlisted for its construction. McNeill reported that it was not until 1993 that the former interrogator finally met Lomax face to face on the banks of the Kwai.

"Although not yet ready to forgive, Lomax had been disarmed by an 'extraordinarily beautiful' letter from Nagase. He had gone to Thailand not knowing what to expect and ended up comforting a shaking, crying Nagase, who simply kept saying: 'I am so sorry, so very, very sorry.'"[60]

The two octogenarians still meet at regular intervals, and Nagase, who publicly criticized former Prime Minister Koizumi's politically expedient visits to Tokyo's Yasukuni Shrine, which contains the ashes of convicted World War II criminals, is also highly critical of current United States–United Kingdom foreign policy: "What the Americans are doing in Iraq is not good," he said. "In war people identify exclusively with their country. It makes people crazy. There has to be other ways of solving problems."

All "conclusions" after all are in the end reversible, all disasters, however great, with great difficulty, redeemable: after the humans, the monsters; after the monsters, the humans.

60 Ibid.

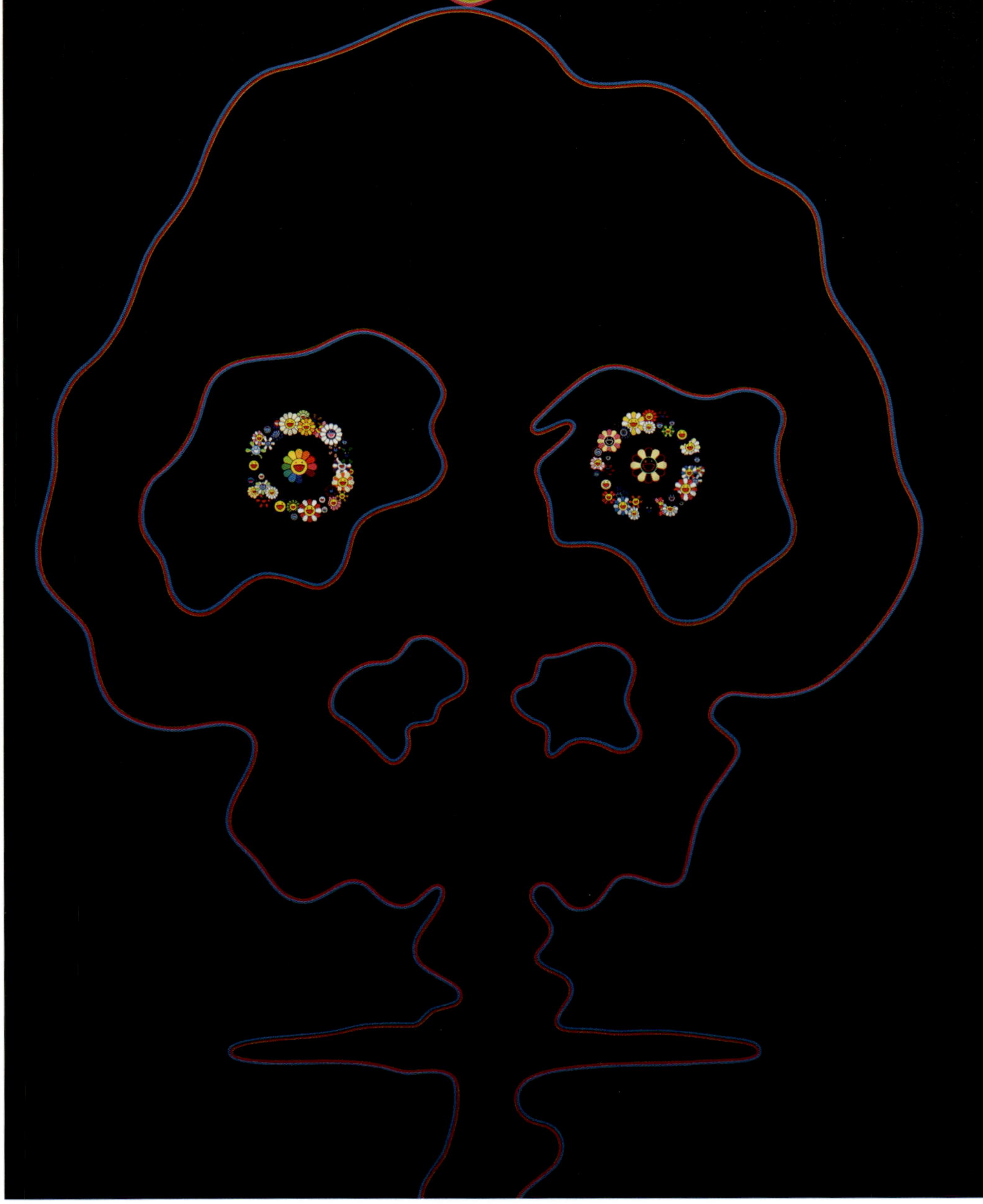

Takashi Murakami
Time Bokan—black + moss green
2006, detail
Acrylic on canvas
mounted on board
70 7/8 x 70 7/8 x 1 15/16 inches
Courtesy Blum & Poe,
Los Angeles

Making Murakami

PAUL SCHIMMEL

An atomic bomb, Fat Man, exploded over Nagasaki at 11:02 a.m. on 9 August 1945; it, and the bomb that exploded over Hiroshima three days earlier, ended the war between Japan and the Allied Powers. That morning the B-29 bomber Bockscar had abandoned its initial target, Kokura,[1] because of smoke cover caused by American bombing. Takashi Murakami's mother, who lived in that city, would say to him until he was ten years old (when he refused to listen any longer): "Takashi, you are very lucky. If Kokura had not been cloudy, you wouldn't be here today." From this perspective, it is understandable that mushroom clouds, which appear in many of Murakami's works, hold a special significance for the artist, especially as they allude to the complex relationship that has existed between Japan and the United States since the aftermath of World War II. More than a love/hate relationship, U.S.–Japan relations fostered a rich history that has shaped Murakami's reality since his childhood.

Japan's defeat in World War II began the transformation of an imperial culture in all of its dimensions, which in turn produced tremendous social upheaval for Murakami's parents' generation. After the war, his mother, Itsuko, studied needlepoint and designed textiles. His father, Fukujurō, born in Shimonoseki, did menial work on an aircraft carrier in Shimonoseki Bay in Yamaguchi-ken, near

All quotes and biographical information are from Takashi Murakami, in conversation with the author, 28 and 29 November 2006, unpublished transcript, unless otherwise specified.

1 Kokura is located in Kitakyūshū in the southern prefecture of Fukuoka, Japan

Kyushu. Afterwards, he gave up going to college because of his family's economic situation and, seeking employment, entered the Self-Defense Forces (SDF) that were formed immediately after the war. After training for several years to be a tank operator, he quit the SDF. Following Japanese tradition, Murakami's parents' marriage was arranged and, like many men and women of their generation, in the late 1950s they gravitated to Tokyo to find work and start a family.

Murakami, their first child, was born in Tokyo in 1962. For his generation, once removed from the survivors of the war, the necessity of reconciling traditional cultural practices with contemporary social conditions, including the growing influence of American culture, was an urgent reality. Murakami received a relatively traditional Japanese upbringing, but was also exposed to Western culture. In particular, his mother was interested in textiles and art. Murakami's childhood activities ranged from participating in Buddhist rituals to taking calligraphy classes to visiting museum exhibitions of Auguste Renoir and Francisco José de Goya y Lucientes. His parents sometimes had him write papers on exhibitions he had seen, on subjects such as Goya's representation of children. If he refused, a supper-less evening of punishment awaited him. In this competitive environment, he learned to think and write quickly.

Though Murakami developed an early appreciation of both traditional calligraphy and nineteenth-century European painting, Japanese animation had the most significant impact on him during his formative teenage years. One of his favorite animated television series was *Uchū senkan Yamato* (Space battleship Yamato, 1974–75). Its story, which betrays an obvious complex about Japan's defeat in the war, revolves around the greatest battleship in all of Japan's history—the Yamato. (Since it was named after an ancient Japanese province, one might surmise that the ship was named with national prestige in mind.) The Yamato sank right after its sortie in World War II, but in the television series it is resurrected and used as a spaceship to protect Earth when it is invaded by aliens. Another popular series at the time (though Murakami was not a hard-core fan) was *Time Bokan*, which was broadcast in Japan on Saturday evenings from 1975 to 1976. Each episode of the series ended with the demise of a villain, who would be brought back

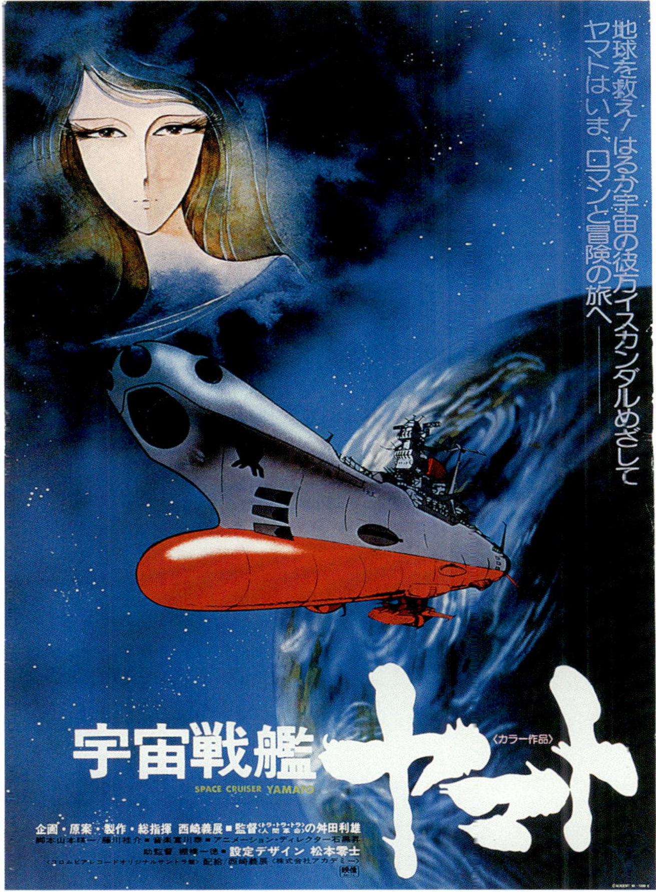

Poster for *Uchū senkan Yamato* (Space battleship Yamato), 1974–75
Courtesy and © Tōhokushinsha Film Corporation

in subsequent episodes with no explanation. The demise was often symbolized by a skull-shaped mushroom cloud.[2] Murakami also enjoyed *Galaxy Express* 999—a hugely popular comic and animation by Leiji Matsumoto (who also created *Uchū senkan Yamato*) consisting of an eighteen-volume *manga* and 113-episode animated television series that aired between 1975 and 76, followed by three animated films released between 1979 and 1981. The original model for this series was Kenji Miyazawa's *Ginga tetsudō no yoru* (Night on the galactic railroad). Murakami recalled Kyūshū-born Matsumoto stating that the origins for the creation of this piece lay in his personal experience coming to Tokyo on a night train and feeling like he was on a "galactic railroad." Murakami was particularly impressed by a thirty-second exploding meteor scene in one of the films, which he and his *anime*-viewing friends talked about:

2 "Time Bokan Series: Yatterman," in *Little Boy: The Arts of Japan's Exploding Subculture*, ed. Takashi Murakami, exh. cat. (New York: Japan Society; and New Haven, Connecticut: Yale University Press, 2005), 12.

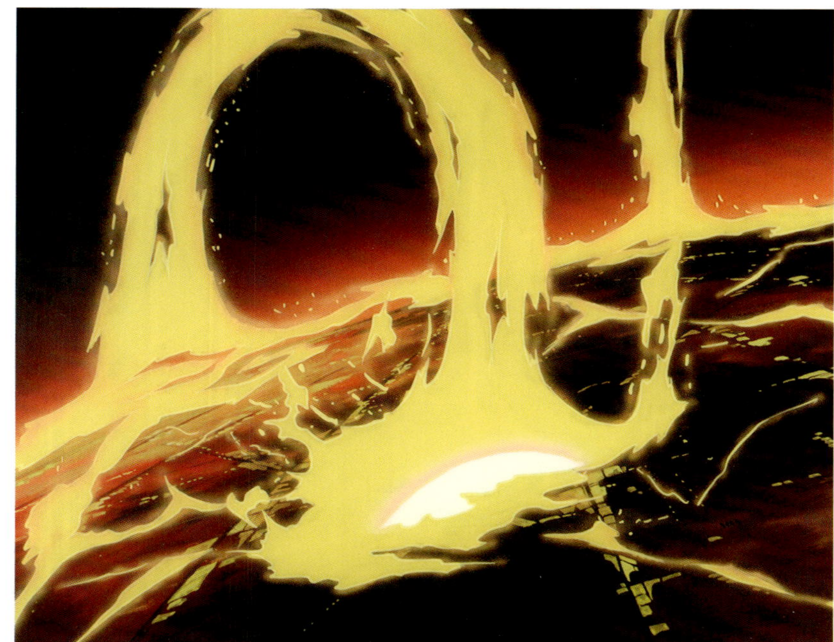

Still from
Galaxy Express 999, 1979–81
© 1979 Leiji Matsumoto,
Tōei Animation

> I was so impressed...when I realized that by putting together tens and hundreds of drawings...one could actually lead us to this grand, swelling movement.... I realized not only that monstrous effort, but also began to imagine the degree to which people could be moved by such an effort. I think you could call it a point where I opened my eyes to "image expression." The explosion was created by animator Yoshinori Kanada and was the major debut of the special techniques later dubbed "Kanada effects" that he had just begun to develop. ("Kanada effects" are becoming major again even now in Japan, twenty-five years later, as a basic form of animated expression.)[3]

He admired the complicated beauty of the explosion so much that he returned to the theater six or seven times just to see it again. He believes that the scene has been a persistent influence on his work to this day.

By the time that *Galaxy Express* 999 became a hit and "Kanada effect" Asian animation was being produced in mass quantities, Murakami knew that he wanted to become an animator. In 1980, he enrolled in the *nihonga* department

3 Murakami, email correspondence with the author, 27 June 2007.

of the prestigious Tokyo National University of Fine Arts and Music (GEIDAI). At the time, the entrance rate for the *nihonga* department at GEIDAI was one in forty-two, whereas the oil-painting department, known as an elite department, accepted only one in sixty. *Nihonga*, or "Japanese-style" painting, was developed during the Meiji period (1868–1912) to pose a resistance to the influence of Western art through the revitalization of the traditions of Japanese painting and their synthesis with aspects of Western art. After years of rigorous study, Murakami learned many of the techniques of *nihonga*, which continue to influence his work.

Though he did not specifically want to study *nihonga*, he had the idea to study background art for animation within the *nihonga* major. The animator who most influenced his desire to enter the field was Hayao Miyazaki, whose service-oriented ambition to entertain the audience, originating from highly critical self-references, was much appreciated by Murakami. Particularly impressive were Miyazaki's scene designs for Isao Takahata's animated television series *Anne of Green Gables* (1979), which he still speaks of to this day (especially a scene in the first episode featuring an abundance of blossoming apple trees that Murakami, moved by the beauty of the tree-lined street, thought he could somehow re-create).

In addition to diligently studying the techniques of *nihonga* at university, Murakami made eight-millimeter animation in classes outside of school. Although he recognized that the characters he was drawing were not good enough technically, he thought he might possess sufficient talent to become a background artist and to find more opportunities in the animation industry with a degree in an area of expertise. But after realizing the extent of the challenging technical demands and quick and precise drawing skills required, he decided otherwise. One valuable lesson from his foray into animation, however, was understanding

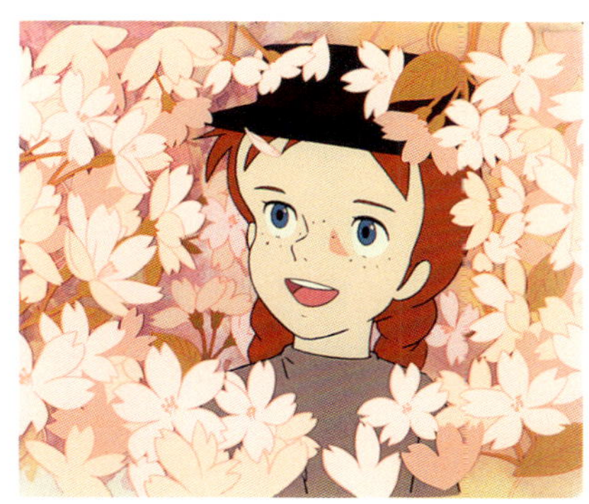
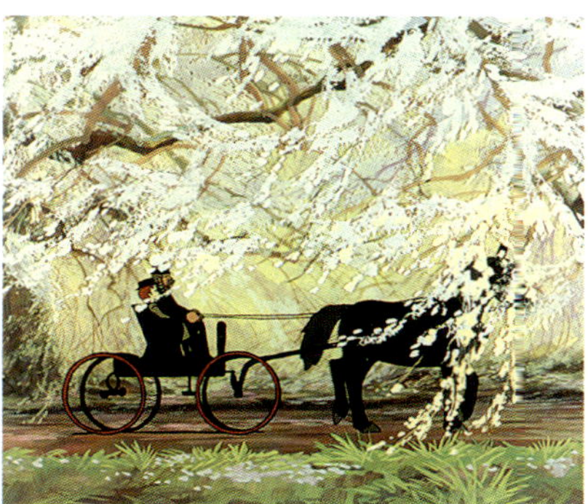
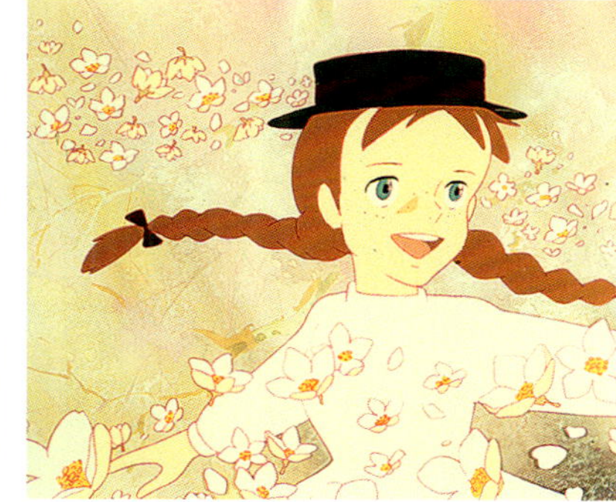

Stills from *Anne of Green Gables*, 1979
Courtesy and © 1979
Nippon Animation Co., Ltd.;
© EM Entertainment Gmbh

the necessity of hiring other artists with specific areas of expertise to aid in executing his artistic vision. (Nevertheless, thirty years after his first failed attempts, he has managed to establish his own animation production studio.)

Murakami reluctantly gave up studying animation in his fourth year, when he was thinking about graduate school and had to address time constraints. As a result, he developed his unique work schedule, painting with intense concentration for forty minutes and then sleeping for ten, seven days a week, from 6:00 a.m. until midnight. One work might take him roughly four months to complete. (Once, calculating how many paintings he would be able to make at this rate by the time he died, he regretted how low the number would be.)

During what would become an eleven-year odyssey as a *nihonga* student, which included four years of undergraduate, two years of graduate, and three years of doctoral coursework, as well as two years of dissertation writing, Murakami realized in his seventh year that his ambition was to become a contemporary artist. That said, both animation and *nihonga* have had a profound impact on his work, both in terms of technique and subject matter. From his study of animation, he learned about the complexities of creating characters, backgrounds, and dynamic compositions, and, particularly, how to work collaboratively. From his study of *nihonga*, he learned technical skills such as how to produce a particular hue of blue, as well as how to create *washi* (Japanese paper) and use it effectively in collage. From both, he developed the patience and concentration necessary to produce a work of art.

Murakami learned about contemporary art from a variety of sources, including important artists from abroad that he met through his school's visiting-artist program. In 1984, for example, Christo, Mario Merz, and Joseph Beuys gave lectures at the school. Merz's lecture, in which he spoke about production concepts relating to Fibonacci numbers and answered every question with double-talk and baffling tangents, left a deep impression; to Murakami, he seemed like a "magician of modern art." Beuys both inspired and infuriated Murakami. Very much a celebrity during that period of his life, Beuys came dressed in his usual uniform—jeans, a fisherman's vest, and a felt hat—that was part of his public persona. When one of the students asked about his vest, Beuys ignored the question. When another student asked why he used a blackboard, Beuys said, "Next" and "This question has no meaning. I would like a more meaningful question." This attitude upset Murakami, who felt that dismissing eager but uninformed Japanese painting students who had lined up the night before in anticipation of the lecture seemed too easy and too self-protective. (He was also angry with the sculpture professor who had organized the Beuys lecture because, while the students were enraptured, the professor was obviously trying to procure the blackboard that Beuys had drawn on.) Finally, Murakami was upset at the students who, despite their pretentiousness and aspirations to become fine artists, could not provide Beuys with a good question. This experience marked a turning point, as he realized that he needed to become more knowledgeable about contemporary art, while simultaneously recognizing the art-world elitism of GEIDAI and disdaining that elitism as the product of ignorant individuals with a group mentality.

Around this time, he visited exhibitions of contemporary art, seeing the works of Jannis Kounellis and Merz in shows that Fumio Nanjō brought to Japan; Julian Schnabel at Akira Ikeda Gallery; and Jean-Pierre Raynaud and Daniel Buren at the Hara Museum of Contemporary Art. In addition, the pages of *Bijutsu Techō* (Art notebook), the journal now known as *BT* that Noi Sawaragi often wrote for, proved a steady source of photos of the contemporary art world, including new directions in art as exemplified by Matthew Barney and Damien Hirst as well as Californians Paul McCarthy and Charles Ray.

Moving toward a more conceptually oriented practice, Murakami began using plastic World War II toy soldiers to explore his personal history—specifically, his connection to the complex relationship between Japan and the United States that emerged in the aftermath of World War II. *Polyrhythm* (1991) introduced some of the key features of the artist's subsequent oeuvre; its title was derived from a magazine interview with David Byrne, who embraced polyrhythm during the 1980s and discussed the music made by a particular African tribe during war time. An ensuing mental game led Murakami to use the word for his work's title: "It's certainly true that both in the movies and in reality heroic music is important for war, there is a tie between war and heroism...war is actually a tragedy, but if you change your mindset it's exotic. Our society's paradox is that we create plastic toy models that create a background for aggression and murder."

Prompted by friend and mentor Masato Nakamura, Murakami began to question many of the realities he had grown up with. As he later recalled, "I felt that I had to understand the relationship between Japan and the U.S. The reason being that growing up swimming in images of the Vietnam War and World War II on television, I felt confronted by the question: 'the contradictions in this world are a reality, but if we flip them around, perhaps they can become functional?' So I began using plastic World War II toy soldiers in my work." For *Polyrhythm*, he affixed scores of plastic 1/35 scale U.S. Infantry models (West European Theater) made by the popular Japanese toy company Tamiya to a tall slab made of synthetic resin that evokes a Minimalist object by Donald Judd. The theatricality of this object covered with an army of toy soldiers was also inspired by the fact that "we use horrible, non-recyclable material, which essentially becomes oversized garbage when you work with it to make our 'dream' discos, Disney Lands, and theme parks."

Murakami's next major work was *Randoseru Project* (1991), first exhibited at Tokyo's Hosomi Gallery, a space now buried under the Roppongi Hills development, and subsequently at Japan's first International Contemporary Art Fair and Aoi Gallery. *Randoseru Project* comprises eight backpacks (*randoseru*) that mimic the leather backpacks that many Japanese children wear, whose design is originally based on a military pack. Thus, in addition to evoking the omnipresent Prada bags that many Japanese consumers covet, these backpacks have a more bellicose connotation. Murakami exaggerated this quality by making the backpacks not of leather but of materials such as great blue shark, cobra, crocodile, two types of harpseal, hippopotamus, ostrich, and sei whale skins. He was of course aware that certain materials were controversial, if not illegal, for use in luxury goods; seeing a leaflet littered on the platform of Shinjuku station advertising panda and tiger skins, he knew the transgression—"a moment of darkness," as he described it—he would commit by calling the number. He began to look for companies that sold exotic

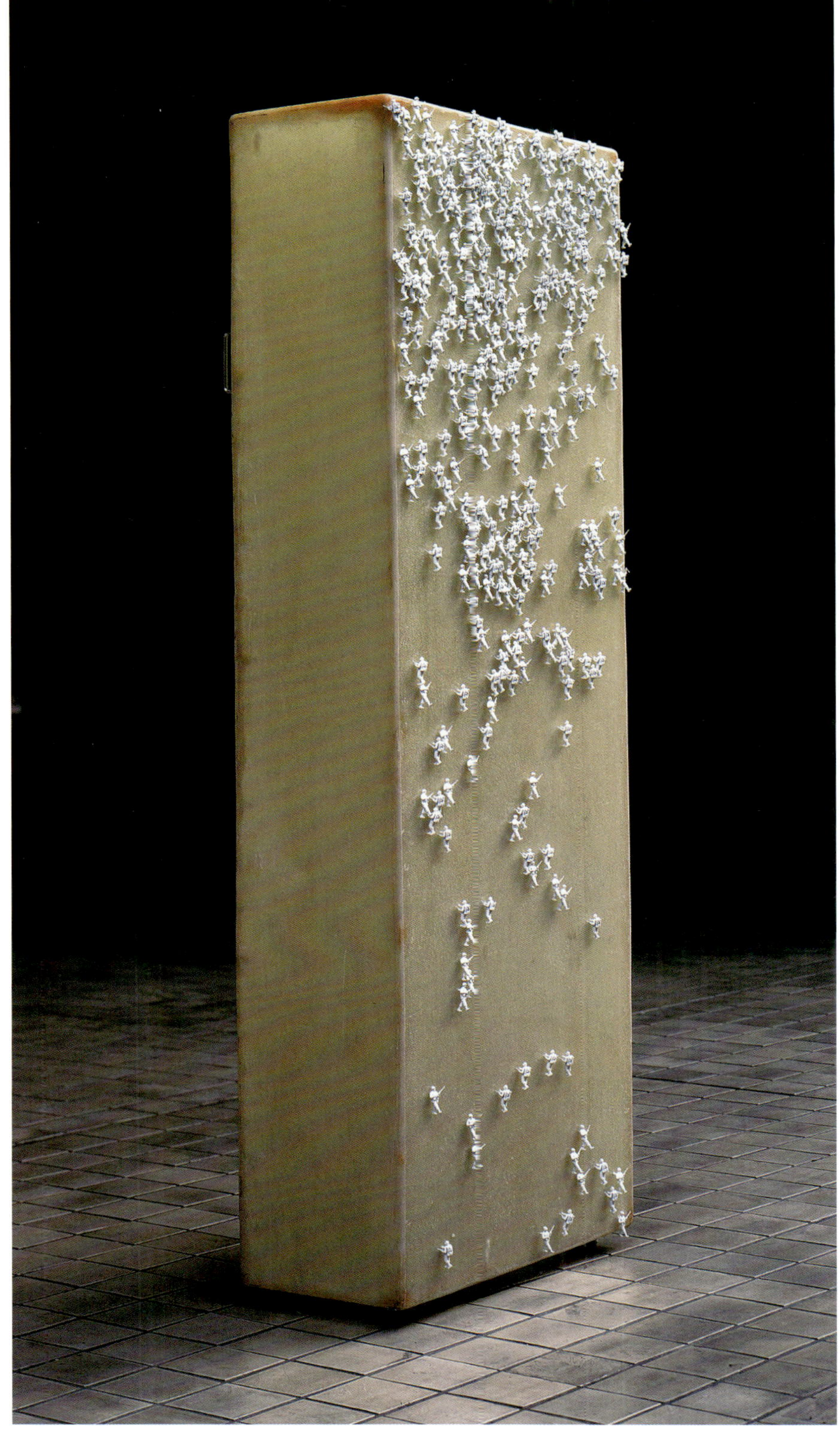

Takashi Murakami
Polyrhythm, 1991
Synthetic resin, iron, and plastic Tamiya 1/35 scale U.S. Infantry models (West European Theater)
92 1/8 x 14 3/16 x 4 15/16 inches

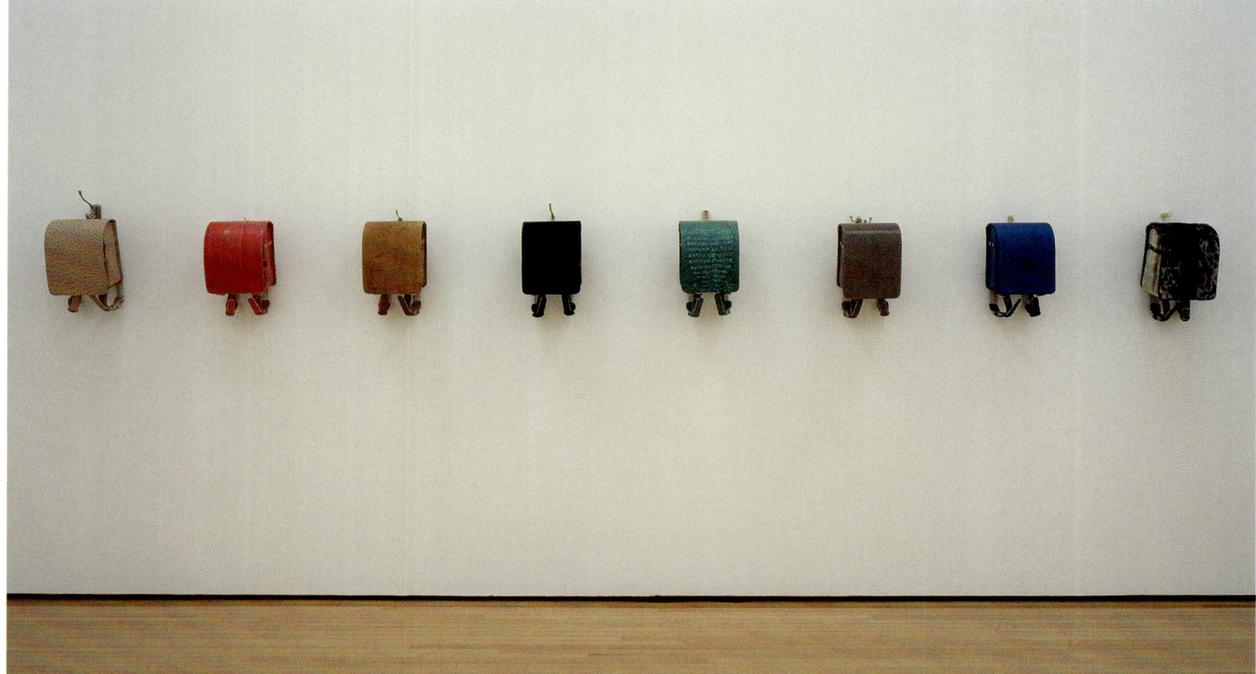

Takashi Murakami
Randoseru Project, 1991
Children's backpacks
in various animal skins
12 x 9 x 8 inches each
Toyota Municipal Museum of Art,
Aichi, Japan

animal hides and learned that while cobra and elephant skin could be sold legally, panda skin could not—and tiger and crocodile skins occupied a grey area. With *Randoseru Project*, Murakami intended to comment on the exploitative use of endangered species to produce luxury goods, but not to do so cynically. He was also exploring art's status as a luxury good, an issue he would mine further in collaborations with Marc Jacobs for Louis Vuitton. For the opening of the exhibition, he organized a combination performance-cabaret-Shinto ceremony in an attempt to highlight the conceptual underpinnings of the project. A Shinto priest prayed before the backpacks to honor the animals from which they were made.

Sea Breeze (1992) was made on the heels of *Polyrhythm* and *Randoseru Project* after Sawaragi invited Murakami to participate in a group exhibition at Röntgen Kunst Institut in Tokyo.[4] He saw this invitation as an opportunity to take on several of the leading artists of his generation, including Kenji Yanobe and Kōdai Nakahara, who he held in high regard. Ultimately, Murakami decided to produce what was initially intended as a reference to the ancient Japanese myth *Ama no iwato* (Gate of the celestial rock cave),[5] but in retrospect it could be read as

4 The performative aspects of *Sea Breeze* have become increasingly significant in its public presentations. Murakami hired a hula-hoop dancer to perform with the piece at the opening of "Anomaly" (1992) at Röntgen Kunst Institut, Tokyo; the artist himself dressed up as a pro wrestler for a talk show for the opening of "Ground Zero Japan" (1999), Mito Art Tower, Ibaraki, Japan; and he hired a male exotic dancer for the opening of "Public Offerings" (2001) at The Museum of Contemporary Art, Los Angeles.

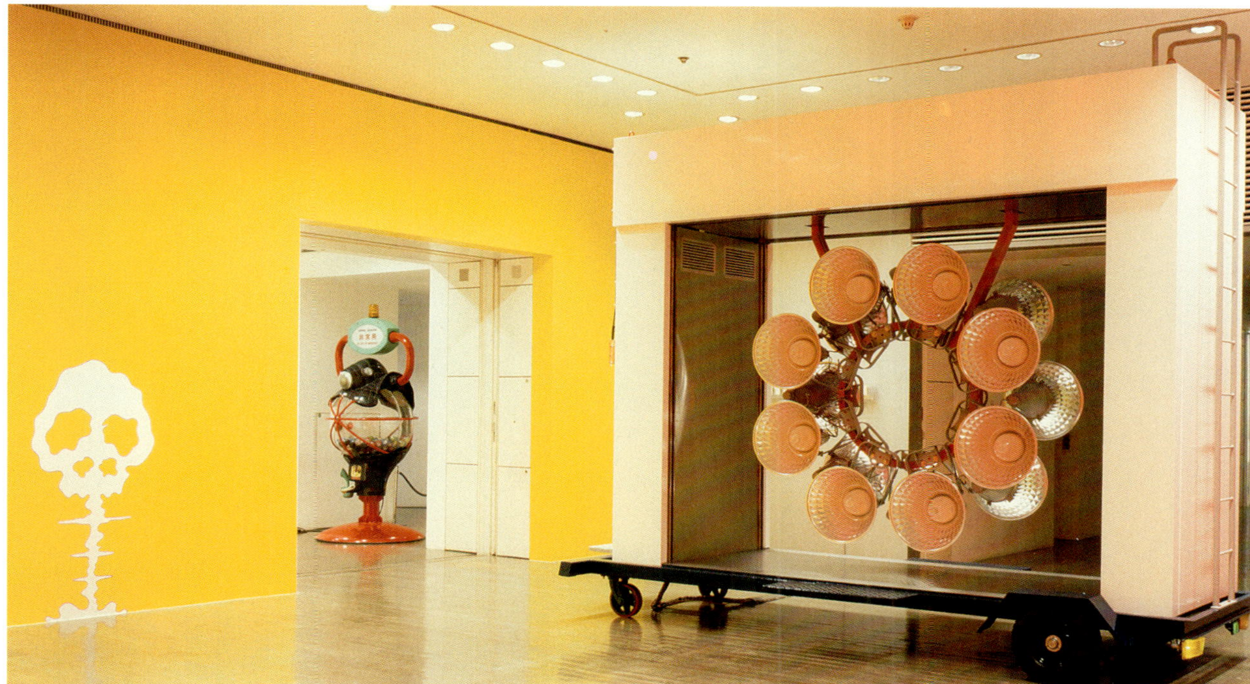

Sea Breeze, 1992
Iron, stainless steel, shutter, mercury lamp, caster, wheels, ventilator, and flashing lamps
137 13/16 x 189 x 98 7/16 inches
Installation in "Ground Zero Japan," Art Tower, Mito, Japan, 1999

his first reference to the atomic bomb: sixteen Klieg lights arranged back-to-back in a circle, encased in a square metal cabinet with roll-up doors. When the doors open, they expose the viewer to a blinding white light that suggests the flash before destruction; when closed, light seeps through and suggests a voyeuristic element, reminiscent of Duchamp's *Etant donnés, 1. La chute d'eau, 2. Le gaz d'éclairage* (1946–66). Murakami has also suggested that the bright lights are surrogates for the blasters of the American spaceships that inspired him in his youth, the halos encircling representations of the Buddha, or the sun goddess Amaterasu's emergence from the cave in *Ama no iwato*.

In 1994, Murakami traveled to New York on an Asian Cultural Council Fellowship to participate in P.S.1 Contemporary Art Center's International Studio Program. His friend, gallerist Tomio Koyama, had encouraged him to apply for the fellowship, which would give him the opportunity to develop and promote his art in New York. Knowing that both Tadashi Kawamata and Yukinori Yanagi, among the most internationally recognized Japanese artists of that generation, had also participated in the program, Murakami concluded that the

5 The myth is told as follows: terrified of the wrath of her brother, the storm god Susanoō, sun goddess Amaterasu went into hiding in a cave and the earth became dark. In order to lure Amaterasu out of the cave, the dawn goddess Ama-no-Uzume began an erotic dance near its entrance, a sight that made the other gods laugh. Amaterasu heard the laughter and looked outside to see what was happening. Catching her reflection in a mirror that Ama-no-Uzume had placed in a tree, she emerged from the cave. At that moment, the god Ame-no-Tajikarawo-no-mikoto blocked the entrance and prevented her from returning to the cave. The gods convinced her to rejoin them, and light was restored to the earth.

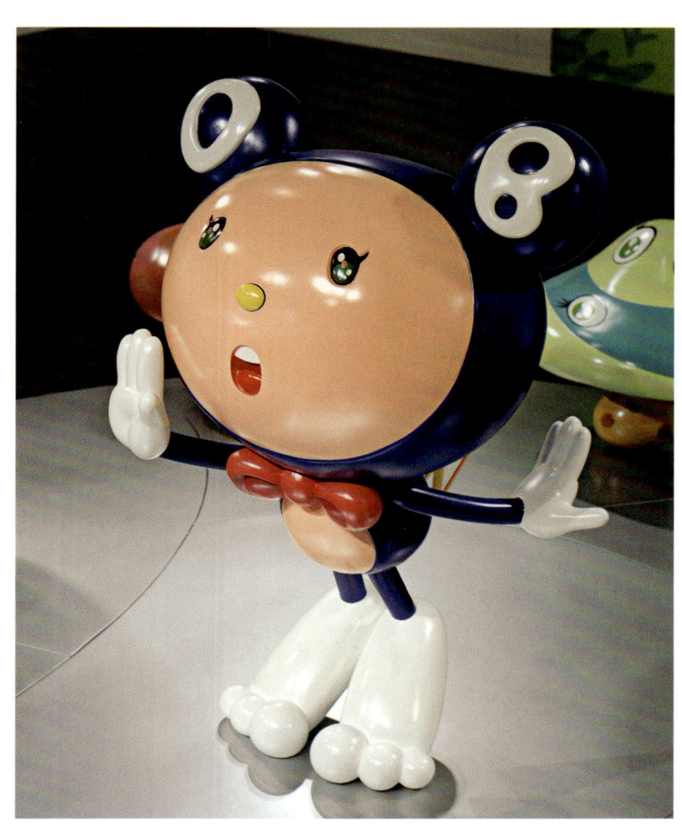

Takashi Murakami
DOB in the Strange Forest, 1999, detail

Doraemon
Courtesy and © Fujiko-pro

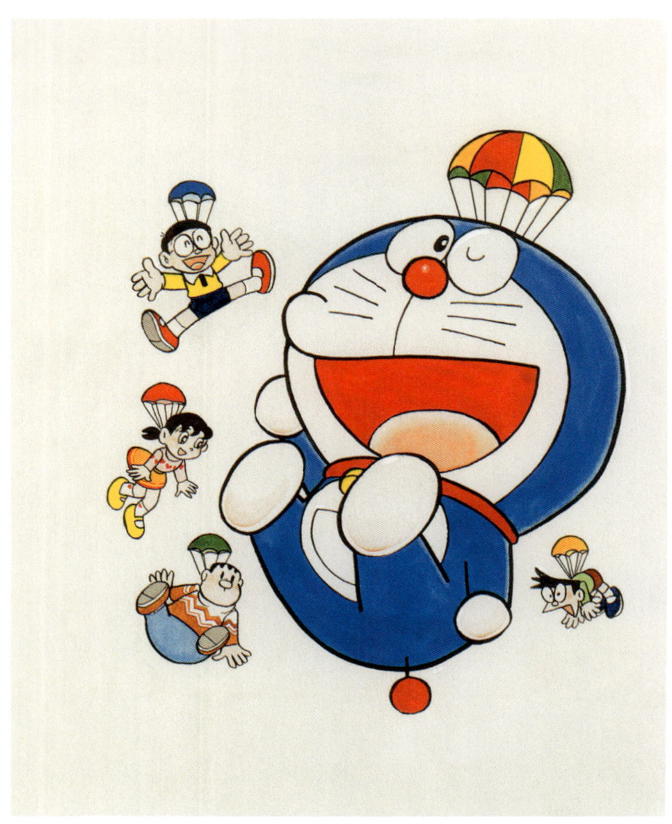

experience would be worthwhile. He lived at 14th Street and 7th Avenue, spending the first several months of the residency fixing up his studio and painting its walls white.

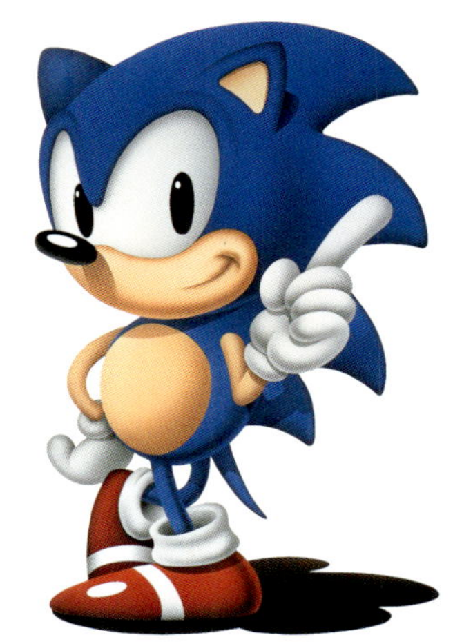

Sonic the Hedgehog
Courtesy and © SEGA

Prior to his departure for New York, Murakami had begun to develop a concept for an exhibition in 1993 that eventually led to his signature character, Mr. DOB. He has described how the character came out of a late-night word game using nonsense words: "For one or two hours, we said '*dobozite, dobozite*' [a phrase popularized by Noboru Kawasaki's 1970s *manga Inakappe taishō* (Country general), in which characters deliberately mispronounced "*dōshite*" (why) as "*dobozite dobozite*"].... A female friend said '*oshamanbe*,' which was a popular gag [associated with the comedian Tōru Yuri], maybe a sexual reference. I wanted to create a *dobozite, dobozite oshamanbe* show." He asked Manabu Koga, a young artist who had been assisting him with his work, to help him create a logo for the show. Looking at Koga's well-made logo, Murakami thought that the phrase "*Dobozite, dobozite oshamanbe*" was too long and that the acronym "DOB" was too simple, so Koga suggested that Murakami invent a character, which Murakami thought should be a combination of Doraemon (the cat-like robot character from *manga* and *anime* series) and Sonic the Hedgehog (the character in video games and *anime* that serves as the Sega mascot). This was the genesis of DOB, a two-eared character whose head spells its name ("D" appears on its right ear, "O" is its round face, the "B" on its left ear).

For his first exhibition in New York at the Angel Orensanz Foundation in 1995, Murakami showed a group of DOB-shaped inflatables. In contrast to his previous exhibitions in Japan, this show did not receive any significant critical attention. However, through a serendipitous encounter at the then-new Gramercy Art Fair, he reunited with gallerist Emmanuel Perrotin, who he had met some years earlier. For several hours that day, he helped Perrotin install a piece by Maurizio Cattelan and works by other artists. He then offered to exhibit in Perrotin's space some T-shirts he had designed and brought with him from Japan. The character printed on them was Hiropon, which he would later revisit in a 1997 sculpture. Hudson, director of the gallery Feature, saw the T-shirts, contacted Murakami through P.S.1, and arranged for a studio visit. In anticipation of that visit, Murakami created the first drawings for what would become *Second Mission Project ko²* (1999–2000).

Murakami knew of Hudson because his friend Tim Blum of the gallery Blum & Poe had introduced him to the works of Charles Ray, Hirst, Barney, and Jorge Pardo through catalogues. Murakami's eventual inclusion in a 1996 group exhibition at Feature demonstrated that he was becoming recognized as a member of a generation of international artists who were reviving interest in the figure in broad and diverse ways. His recognition of the achievements of these artists gave him permission to realize his own ambitions—a fusion of Japanese popular culture, international figurative tendencies, and the direction set off by that late-night word-game that led to the development of DOB.

After a period in New York—during which he was far from his family, friends, and professional success in Tokyo—he began Stew (1995), a series of five modestly scaled paintings. Among the first works he made in his New York studio, each painting features a figure, painted on a flat monochrome background, with a broadly smiling face (four with DOB ears, one without) and a body rendered in diffe rent states of liquidity, from fluid puddles to mere drips and splatters. This second, more developed incarnation of DOB gave Murakami his first inkling that it was a humanoid character who could eventually take on a life of its own. While DOB's first incarnation had begun as a simple phrase, a joke, a visual pun, it was to have a lasting impact on his iconography and identity. Ultimately, it would become a stand-in for the artist—a type of self-portrait that reflects the persona of its creator. While Murakami attributes its formation to his collaboration with Koga (and the designer Gento Matsumoto, who had developed its rough outline), DOB also has similarities to Mickey Mouse, from whom Murakami struggled to distinguish it, and a monkey-like collectible from Hong Kong based on a Russian character called Chebrashka. However, the inclusion of letters on each of DOB's ears is distinct.

DOB has become the single most represented subject in Murakami's oeuvre. From its early manifestations as signage, it has become the subject of numerous paintings, sculptures, inflatables, and collectibles. But in contrast to Walt Disney, for whom the character Mickey Mouse became the brand identity with which he built his corporation, Murakami has created a constantly evolving character that embodies all the complexities and nuances of his ever-changing personal and corporate identity. How DOB came into existence and what it symbolizes are two different things; what began as a flat, humorous, benign character morphed into one who can be alternately monstrous, irrefutably dark, and frighteningly aggressive, while simultaneously evoking cuteness. *DOB Genesis* (1993) features DOB's simple iconic head isolated in the center of a field of blue. *ZuZaZaZaZaZa* (1994) presents a more fully realized DOB without the liquid gestural drip; inspired by the work of Kanada, it is repressented as a minute figure on a red ground with an explosive form. By 1995, DOB had become more menacing but also more personal. In another important painting of this period—*And Then, And Then And Then And Then And Then (Blue)* (1996), begun in 1994—the subject is again DOB, but Murakami focused dramatically on the character's head, which fills the entire canvas of sanded-down layers of paint, creating a richly textured surface that almost resembles skin.

Around this time Murakami had been thinking about making a freestanding work inspired by the figurines that the artist Bome made for Kaiyōdō, a Japanese manufacturer of collectibles inspired by *anime* and other sources, that would play off the dichotomy between the marketplace and the insular, almost cult-like world of *otaku*. As Murakami observed in his essay "Impotence Culture—*Anime*" (2001), *otaku* originally derives from a word for another person's family or home that is used as an honorific second-person pronoun. In his historic series of articles "Otaku no kenkyū" (An investigation of *otaku*), published in the magazine *Manga Burikko* in 1983, Akio Nakamori drew attention to its contemporary usage as a word that geeks used to address one another.[6] Specifically, the word refers to obsessive fans of *anime*, *manga*, or video games who spend most of their time at home pursuing their hobbies. For many Japanese people, the term conjures up

6 Akio Nakamori, "Otaku no kenkyū" (An investigation of *otaku*), *Manga Burikko* (June–August 1983).

certain negative stereotypes of socially dysfunctional, sexually frustrated, perverted, and occasionally psychotic young men who live in fantasy worlds. This perception, however, has begun to change, and some *otaku* have attempted to reclaim the term as a positive one.

During this period of his life, *otaku* became an obsession for Murakami, who was both inside and outside of it. But in spite of the fact that he has not been fully accepted into *otaku* culture, it is important to note the distinction between the relationship that Murakami has to his sources in *otaku* and the relationship that Pop artists such as Roy Lichtenstein and Andy Warhol had to theirs. Although the latter artists borrowed liberally from popular media such as comics, they did not presume to elevate the status of the comic artists whose work they appropriated. By contrast, Murakami does. One of his ambitions is to change Japanese culture so profoundly that the Westernized distinctions between high and low are no longer part of the critical dialogue. As Midori Matsui has observed, his commitment to elevating the "debased" products of *otaku* culture through his art has influenced both his work as an artist and a curator.[7] In exhibitions he has curated, such as "Ero Pop Tokyo" (1998), "Hiropon Show" (1999), and "Tokyo Girls Bravo" (1999), he has mixed his own work with that of his studio assistants and professional *otaku* artists in a nonhierarchical manner that at once illuminates the similarities that unite them and the differences that divide them.

After returning to Japan in 1995, Murakami worked on producing a series of major sculptures inspired by *otaku* culture at a production facility he christened Hiropon Factory. A synthesis of a traditional Japanese art workshop and a contemporary Japanese corporation, Hiropon Factory integrated aspects of a school, workshop, studio, and corporation. Its Eastern precedents can be found in the Japanese guilds, such as those producing woodblock prints, where each phase of production was compartmentalized. Its Western precedents include Peter Paul Rubens—who dealt with his success as the "most harassed man in the world" by establishing a well-organized studio enterprise for which he hired talented assistants trained in various areas of expertise to execute under his supervision large-scale projects for prestigious clients—and Warhol, who by the 1970s

7 Midori Matsui, "Toward a Definition of Tokyo Pop: The Classical Transgressions of Takashi Murakami," in *Takashi Murakami: The Meaning of the Nonsense of Meaning* (New York: Harry N. Abrams, 2000), 27.

had transformed his studio into a production facility that generated paintings, films, television programs, and a magazine. In 2001, Murakami renamed Hiropon Factory as Kaikai Kiki Co., Ltd., which has evolved into a highly organized corporation employing about fifty people at its headquarters in Tokyo; forty at a satellite facility in Long Island City, New York; and ten others in a Tokyo animation studio, who work in precisely defined divisions ranging from creative to administrative, financial, and legal. With Murakami at its helm, Kaikai Kiki produces and promotes art; manages artists; operates the GEISAI art fair; organizes collaborative projects with individuals and companies in fashion, music, and entertainment; and develops animation works.

Murakami initially conceived his first *otaku*-influenced sculpture while confronting his isolation as a foreigner living in New York. Though modeled indirectly on the *otaku* fantasy of a 1950s-style American roller-skating waitress, *Miss*

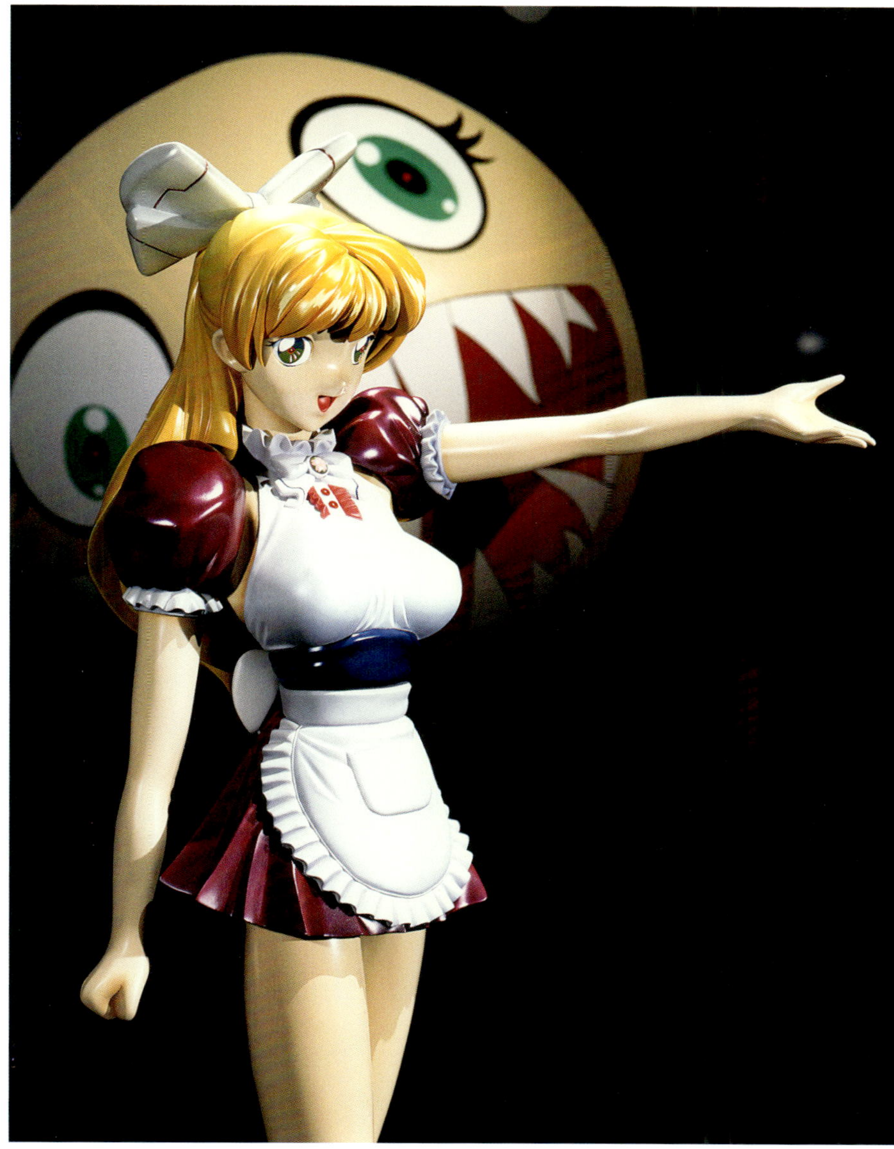

Takashi Murakami
Miss ko^2, 1997, detail, with *Mr. DOB*, 1995, in background
"Konnichiwa, Mr. DOB," installation at Kirin Art Plaza, Osaka, Japan, 1996

ko² (1997), like its prototype painting (1996), was based more directly on the iconic waitresses of the Hawaiian/Japanese chain restaurant Anna Miller's. Their uniform—a white blouse, a short orange or pink jumper-style dress starting just below the breasts, an apron, and a heart-shaped name tag—is instantly recognizable to the Japanese. Particularly popular among *otaku*, characters representing these waitresses appear in video games such as Variable Geo, in which they battle one other.

Kaiyōdō Company fabricated the first 1/5 scale model of *Miss ko²*, which recalls the simple figures used to advertise *pachinko* parlors. Murakami showed the first version at Feature in 1996; however, like his previous New York exhibitions, it received no significant critical reaction. He showed a second version in the exhibition "Konnichiwa, Mr. DOB" at Kirin Art Plaza in Osaka, also in 1996. For this version, he commissioned the specialist Toru Saegusa, who started out as an unknown sculptor but went on to create props for the hardcore *otaku* live-action film convention DAICON, to work on it. Yet another version, *Second Mission Project ko²* (1998), was shown at the 1999/2000 Carnegie International. The installation comprised a three-part sculptural work in which the figure transforms into an airplane; it was accompanied by a do-it-yourself model kit. Underscoring the erotic dimension of the work, Murakami observed that its prototype "originally started as a project, by expressing a girl valkyrically transforming into an airplane to somehow define a kind of current Japanese sexual complex, which equals a girl, which equals an airplane."[8]

Murakami's next major sculpture was *Hiropon* (1997). "Hiropon" is a Japanese slang term for crystal methamphetamine, a highly addictive stimulant widely used in Japan after World War II until it was banned in 1952. To Murakami, it signifies the dark void that existed in Japan after the war; in adopting the term, he was not seeking to make a literal connection between his art and drug culture, but wished to evoke the popular association between *otaku* culture and illicit forms of entertainment. *Hiropon* was inspired by several illustrations of large-breasted characters in a *dōjinshi* (self-published works) by a person who called himself Floppy Disc. The images showed females with sausage-like nipples

8 Murakami, quoted in the press release for "Takashi Murakami: Second Mission Project ko²" (2000), P.S. 1 Contemporary Art Center, Long Island City, New York, available at http://www.ps1.org/cut/press/murakami.html.

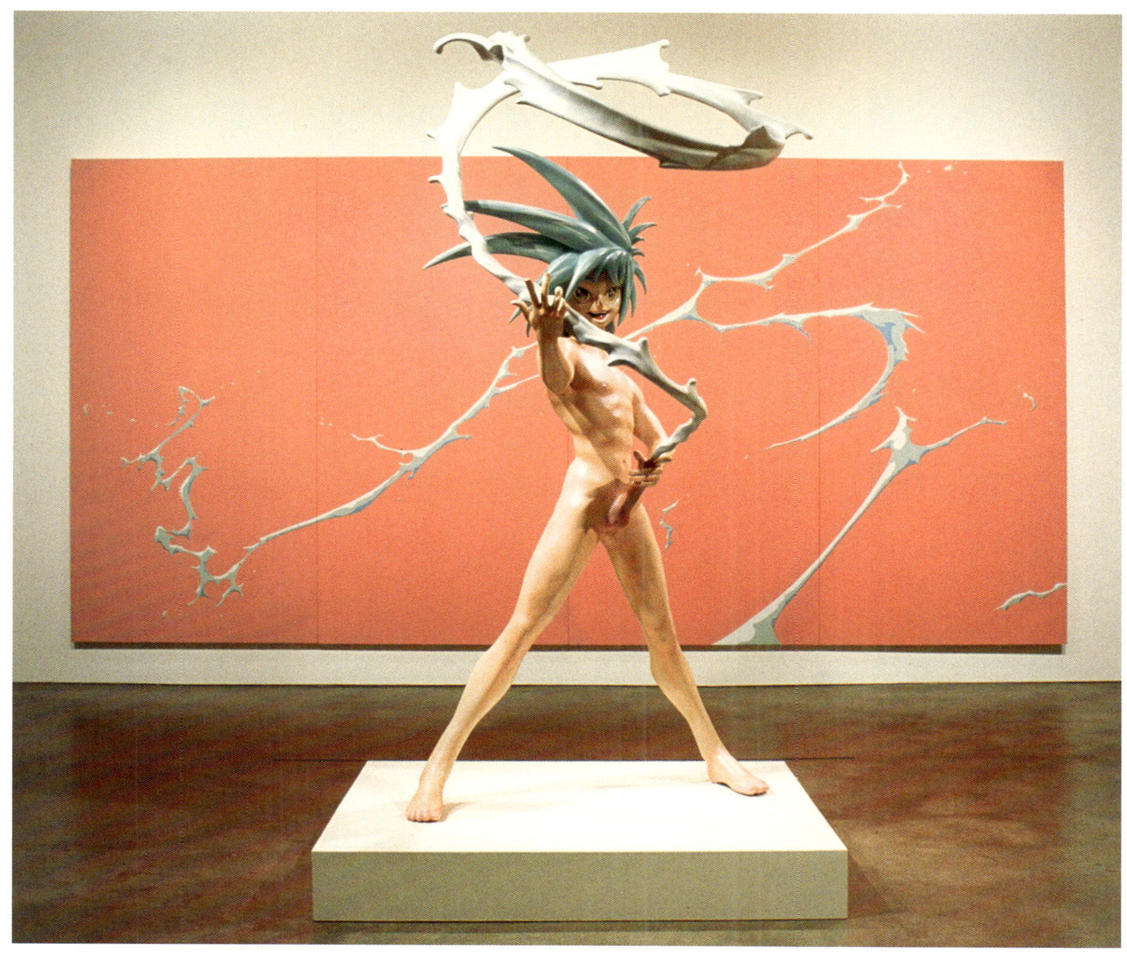

Takashi Murakami
My Lonesome Cowboy, 1998,
with *Milk*, 1998, in background

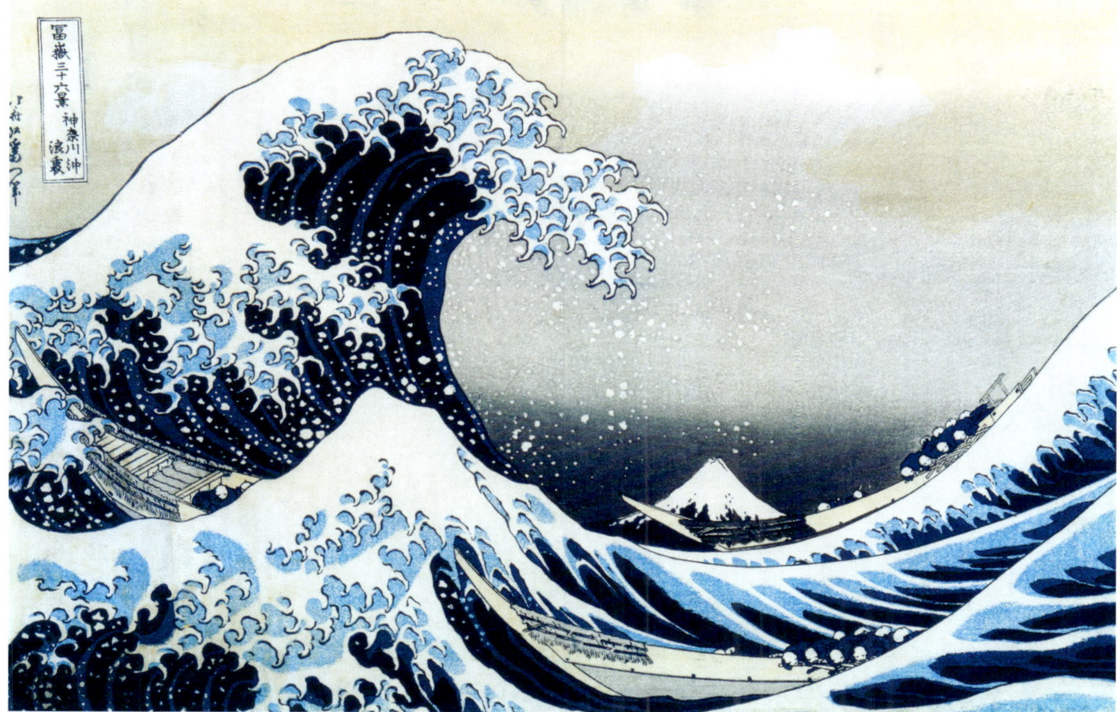

Hokusai Katsushika
The Great Wave of Kanagawa
from *Thirty-Six Views of Fuji*,
c. 1830–32
Color woodblock print
10 1/8 x 14 15/16 inches
Private collection

from which milk spurts expressively like ejaculating penises. He contacted the illustrator, who refused even to respond. But he was able to convince Kaiyōdō to fabricate the sculpture, which presented enormous technical challenges. If *Miss ko²* is provocative, *Hiropon* is even more so—combining sweetness and perversion in a sculptural tour de force. At first glance, this over-the-top three-dimensional realization of an *otaku*'s fantasy woman, with her adorable cartoonish face and baroque tornado hairstyle, is awesome, though it ultimately manages to draw more attention to its cultural references than its technical aspects.

For his next sculpture, *My Lonesome Cowboy* (1998), Murakami created a space-age, spiky blue-haired naked youth ejaculating a stream of semen that transforms into an encircling lasso—again, a difficult figure to fabricate in three dimensions. The carving was executed by Fuyuki Shinada at a workshop that makes costumes for film, and the painting was done by Murakami himself. A counterpart to *Hiropon*, this sculpture was created at the suggestion of Toshio Okada,[9] perhaps the foremost authority on *otaku*, having written several books on the subject. While he credits Okada with conceiving the idea for *My Lonesome Cowboy*, Murakami remarked that both *My Lonesome Cowboy* and *Hiropon* were fundamentally inspired by Kanada. In addition, the title bears a coincidental resemblance to Warhol's film *Lonesome Cowboys* (1968), which parodically explored the ongoing homoerotic fascination with the cowboy, an icon of American masculinity. Despite the connection to Warhol's film, its real source is the novelist Yoshio Kataoka's story *Rōnsamu kauboi* (Lonesome cowboy, 1975) about a truck driver who travels across the United States. The swirling stream of semen in *My Lonesome Cowboy* and the milk in *Hiropon* also recall the renowned nineteenth-century print artist Hokusai Katsushika, perhaps the best-known Japanese artist in the United States, whose depictions of frothy ocean waves have become emblematic of Japanese art.

Murakami also produced a series of major paintings during this time. The title of 727 (1996) was inspired by a Japanese cosmetics company of the same name, one that struck the artist as odd, given the association with the American airline industry. The surface of the painting—created by applying and then sanding away layer upon layer of paint to produce a rich patina—reveals the

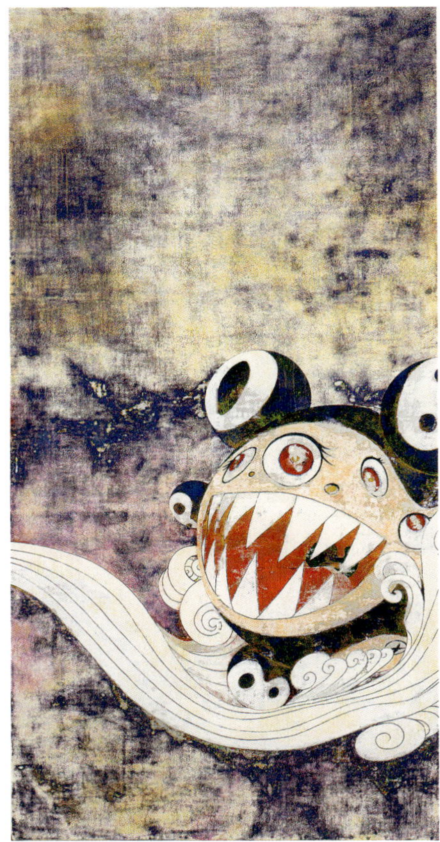

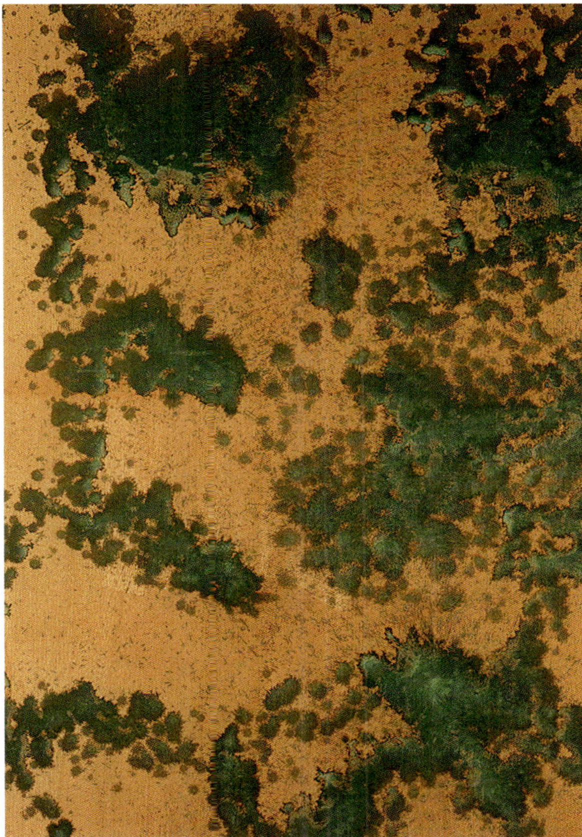

Takashi Murakami
727, 1996, detail

Andy Warhol
Oxidation Painting, 1978
Urine and metallic pigment
in acrylic medium on canvas
76 x 52 inches
The Andy Warhol Foundation
for the Visual Arts
© The Andy Warhol Foundation
for the Visual Arts/ARS, New York

painstaking process by which the work was created, yet it also evokes *nihonga* and lacquerware techniques and the surfaces of Shinro Ohtake's abstract canvases, as well as Warhol's Oxidation Paintings (1978). *727* owes another debt to American art in that its core is an image of DOB as a mutant, post-apocalyptic Mickey Mouse. Vicious, grotesque, and fierce, flashing a toothy grin and peering with multiple eyes that see everything yet care for nothing, this DOB is the antithesis of Disney's sentimental characters.

The two-dimensional abstract paintings *Cream* and *Milk* (both 1998), like *Hiropon* and *My Lonesome Cowboy*, reference bodily fluids and exaggerated sexuality, this time in a pared down, minimal style. Their gestural lines also evoke explosions depicted in animated films such as Kanada's *Goodbye to Galaxy Express 999* (1981); in fact, the fluids might resemble what Jackson Pollock drips would look like if done by Kanada, but for Murakami, they suggest improvised

9 Murakami, in conversation with Amada Cruz, 24 June 1999, cited in "DOB in the Land of Otaku," in *Takashi Murakami*, 18.

gestures such as those found in Abstract Expressionism, without seeking to imitate them.

Similarly, *Cosmos* (1998) responds to the traditions of Edo-period painting in its flattened representation of nature in hyper-detail. On a silver background sits a tangle of branches sprouting flowers with smiling faces, a recurring motif in his art that is in some respects a counterpart to DOB. Flowers are a classic motif in traditional Japanese painting, and Murakami drew them for two years as he was preparing for his university entrance examinations. After graduation, when he was teaching at a preparatory school, he also showed his students how to draw them. In *Cosmos*, he created a non-space that achieves a landscape quality in which flowers seem to float on the flat surface, achieving a certain intimacy with the viewer.

In 1999, Murakami began *Super Nova*, one of his most complex works. Spread over seven panels are dozens of different cartoon-ish mushrooms, from abstract to humanoid, elegant to deformed, sweet to scary, political to animistic. At the center is a giant mushroom with fractured shard-like teeth beneath its monstrously beautiful, eyeball-covered cap; an army of smaller mushrooms is arranged in a neat horizontal band that spans the length of the composition. *Super Nova* began as a highly detailed schematic drawing by Murakami, which he developed and refined. He mapped out the work on a computer, enabling multiple individuals to produce the composition at the same time without sacrificing consistency or coherence.

Super Nova serves as a compendium of Murakami's various mushroom motifs and might be interpreted as a joking reference to himself as a rising star in the art world. The title refers to a song by the British band Oasis called "Champagne Supernova" (1995) and stems from the artist's interest in how drug culture moves into the mainstream via popular music, such as with the Beatles' *Sgt. Pepper's Lonely Hearts Club Band* (1967). Hallucinogenic drugs like "magic mushrooms" are often associated with spiritual awakenings, a poetic sentiment expressed in the song. Exquisitely crafted and frighteningly horrific, *Super Nova* is inspired by Itō Jakuchū's *Compendium of Vegetables and Insects* (1790), which focuses on mushrooms, long revered in Japanese culture for their gastronomic qualities, diversity, and

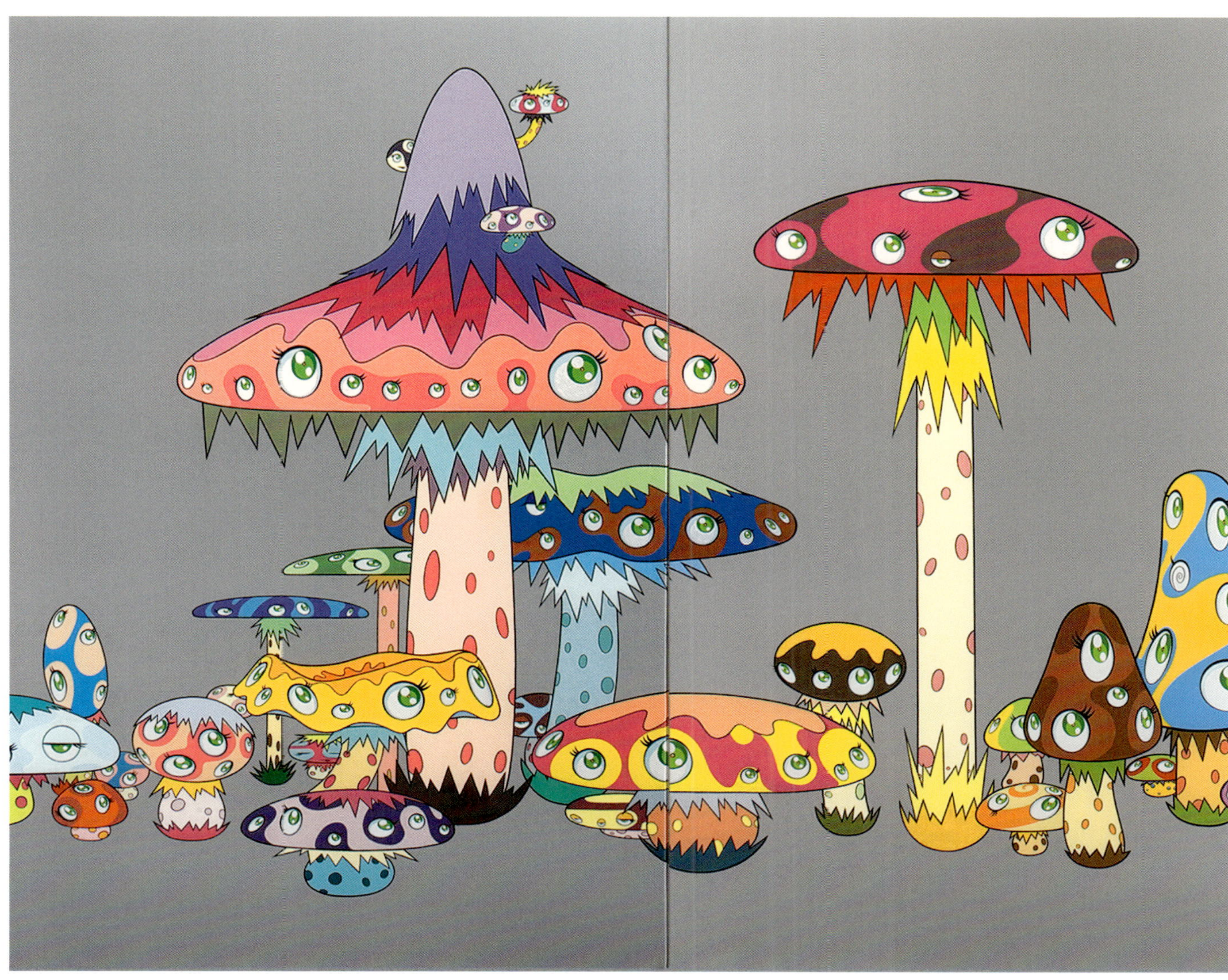

Takashi Murakami
Super Nova, 1999,
detail

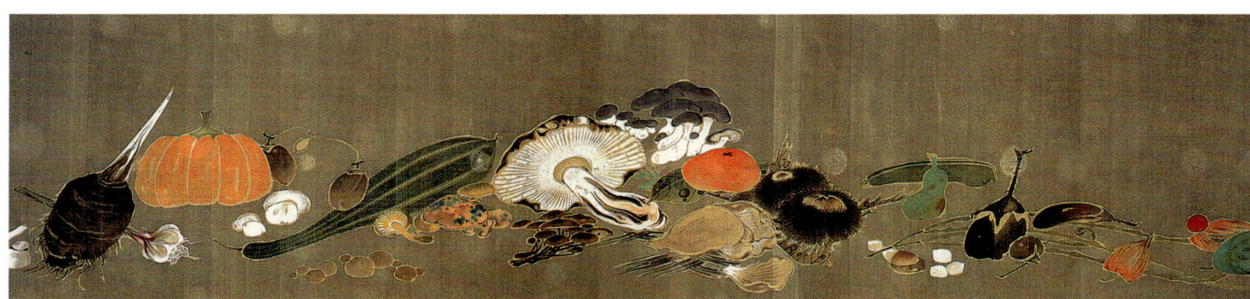

Itō Jakūchū
Compendium of Vegetables and Insects, 1790, detail
Handscroll
Approximately 40 feet
Yoshizawa Memorial Museum of Art, Sano, Japan

evocation of ephemerality. Murakami also acknowledged as a precedent the work of artisan Yumeji Takehisa, who created scarves and collectibles decorated with mushroom designs "which were very cute, but they were poisonous mushrooms."

While there are distinct autobiographical references throughout Murakami's work of the 1990s, it was not until *Tan Tan Bo Puking—a.k.a. Gero Tan* (2002) that he made a work that he himself regarded as expressive of his physical and mental states. Towering above the foreground is an enormous Jabba the Hutt–like figure who vomits forth everything that he has consumed in his orgy of gluttony. His large head features a compendium of the artist's most iconic images: it hosts a plethora of figures represented from multiple perspectives and in discontinuous spaces, including dozens of mutating DOBs and hands derived from Steven Spielberg's film *E.T.* (1982). It is a disturbing image that also draws on his memories of having nightmares after seeing horror films like *The Thing* (1982), in which people transform into monsters after their bodies are infected by invading foreign entities. Finally, like a contemporary version of Oscar Wilde's *The Picture of Dorian Gray* (1890), the monster in this painting is a dark, grotesque, putrid, and perverted image of the artist purging his demons—Murakami stated plainly that it "is very much a self-portrait."

Entirely different in tone is *Kawaii! Vacances d'été* (2002), a heroically scaled six-panel painting that is in some ways a counterpart to *Super Nova*. *Kawaii* is the Japanese word for "cute." As is well known, cuteness has become a lucrative commodity in Japan, as exemplified most famously by the Hello Kitty phenomenon. Murakami has analyzed cuteness with the rigor of a professional trend-spotter to produce a multitude of works that embody its aesthetic. If *Super Nova* presents a post-apocalyptic vision with a menacing mushroom at its center, the focal point of *Kawaii!* is a band of flowers that runs across the entire length of the work against a blue sky. This painting fully realizes the joyous reverie that Murakami hinted at in the landscape of *Tan Tan Bo Puking*. He described the world represented here as his "heaven": "I really love Japanese summer. It's a summer image—blue sky. It's kind of a Buddhist offering during the summer equinox."

In 2003, Murakami began his Moët Hennessey Louis Vuitton (LVMH) series at the invitation of designer Marc Jacobs. In a series of handbags called Eye Love Monogram, Murakami combined Louis Vuitton's signature monogram in ninety-seven different colors with his own signature eyes repeated on black or white backgrounds. A second series, Cerises, featured the iconic brown Vuitton monogram overprinted with Murakami's cartoon cherries. While he was already adept at using systems of commercial distribution to disseminate his own "brand" (he had been producing merchandise for a mass market since the days of the Hiropon Factory), this project gave him the opportunity to produce a brand-name luxury item with a high degree of visibility through advertising. Rather than lose his identity in the LVMH brand during their collaboration, he catalyzed a process of cross-pollination in which he was able to tweak the brand to incorporate his own identifiable aesthetic. Murakami also produced a series of acrylic-on-canvas paintings (2003–04) that feature the colorful monogram and the eyes on black or white backgrounds.

Murakami's sculpture series Inochi (2004) is rooted in postwar Japan's fascination with robots. Deprived of a place at the forefront of world events, the Japanese focused inward, often making smaller versions of themselves in the form of robots (which appeared in toys, films, animation, etc.). Part human child, part cyborg, Inochi has delicately refined head, hands, and feet, and yet is grotesque. One of the artist's most exquisitely crafted figures, the work is based on traditional Japanese figurative sculpture. The artist produced four variations, each featuring distinctive coloration (albino, pink, olive, and black); each is dressed in a modified schoolboy uniform complete with a backpack, which references *Randoseru Project*. Murakami was more closely involved in its fabrication than was

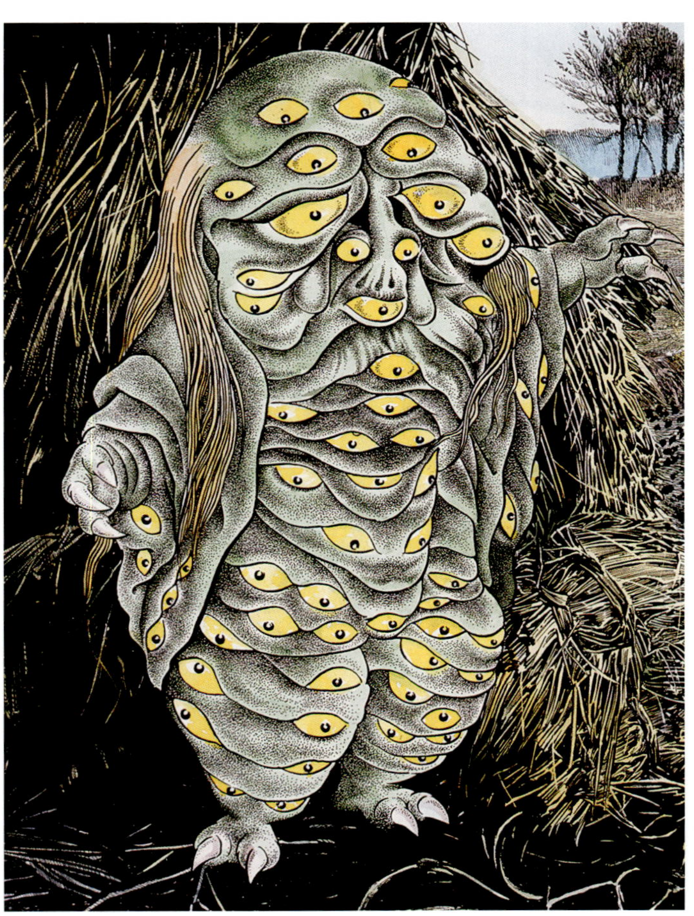

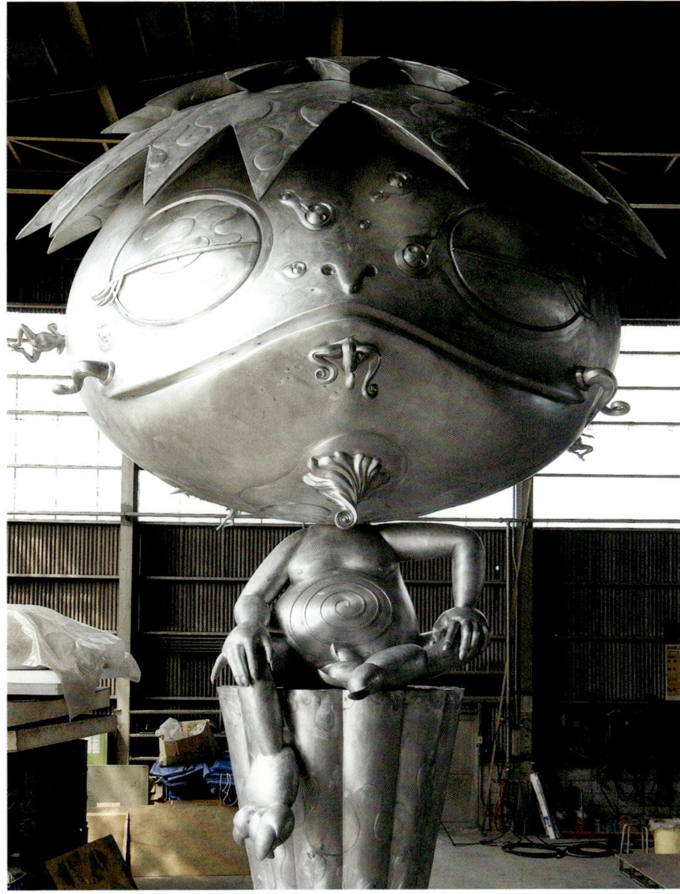

Hyakume
Courtesy and © Mizuki-Pro, Tokyo

Takashi Murakami
Oval Buddha, 2007, detail

typical at the time. A self-portrait of sorts, *Inochi* can be seen as an avatar of the artist adopting various cultural identities. He also created a series of commercials based on a made-up narrative in which Inochi, a junior-high-school boy, discovers his sexuality through an encounter with a female classmate.

In contrast to Inochi, whose intimate scale and lifelike delicacy invites a relationship with the viewer, *Oval Buddha* (2007) resembles a public monument, drawing from both Buddhist art and Western sculpture traditions. Murakami invented the character in response to Naoki Takizawa, a designer for Issey Miyake, who challenged him to create a character based on Humpty Dumpty. In response, he combined Humpty Dumpty with Hyakume (Hundred Eyes) to create a round figure covered with Murakami's signature eyes. Like many of his characters, Oval has gone through many incarnations in a range of media, including paintings, sculptures, inflatables, and collectibles. The figure, resembling a mutant emperor who by his sheer size awes his subjects, evokes the most private dreams and nightmares.

Throughout his career, Murakami has mined his personal and artistic heritage, a conflicted amalgamation of Japanese, American, and European traditions. He has combined these to develop a unique aesthetic that has generated a proliferation of distinct images and icons. Murakami is an artist with the ability to plumb art history, popular culture, and corporate entities ranging from Disney to Louis Vuitton and an entrepreneur with the skill to promote his artistic and cultural vision to a global audience that spans a range of nationalities, social classes, and ethnicities.

Murakami Matrix: Takashi Murakami's Instrumentalization of Japanese Postmodern Culture

MIDORI MATSUI

1
The Murakami Machine: Instrumentation of Postmodern Imagination

Takashi Murakami is now recognized as an innovator of contemporary Japanese art, creating an entirely new genre, changing the perception of art within his own country, and influencing the reception of contemporary Japanese art as an original development in response to the conditions and sensibilities of the current postmodern and global age. His most conspicuous strategy is the incorporation of imagery and production methods associated with Japanese *manga* and *anime* into his own artistic creations, curatorial projects, and diverse public activities. *Otaku* culture, the subculture of science-fiction animation and *manga* aficionados, was central to the evolution of Murakami's artistic development. Not only did the eccentric but original expressions of *anime* and science-fiction television and film inspire him to pursue a new style of representation, but Murakami's idea of an effective and stimulating art practice was influenced by the rigorous craftsmanship of *otaku*, along with its internal but highly developed system of critical evaluation. From the earliest stages of his artistic career, Murakami made his purposes explicit: [1] to break open the closure of contemporary Japanese art; [2] to present a new artistic style and perspective; and [3] to make that new brand of artistic production and presentation internationally recognized and influential. For Murakami, *otaku* creations provided a model both in terms of formal style and production methods.

In one of his earliest interviews, Murakami stated that he finds the expressions of *anime* and science-fiction films significant because their creators possess the operative "structure" of public presentation, through which "they take the audience seriously and try to win their interest and support," subsequently nurturing an enthusiastic and experienced audience.[1] He explained that contemporary Japanese art, in contrast, does not yet have an audience with its own criteria for judgment because artists and critics play by the predetermined rules and speak the language of international contemporary art, exchanging prescribed professional interpretations within a closed circuit of insiders. He argued that artists should leave the "sacred zone" of contemporary artistic expression and strive to attain the power and influence with which they might contend with the commercial market and systems of distribution, the actual social forces run by the power of money. He then proposed a fundamental upheaval of the Japanese art system via "explosive" art that takes advantage of the chaotic social situation brought about by the bust of the "bubble economy":

> I think the market of contemporary art should be more visible. I don't understand why artists pretend as if the market did not exist. The 1980s, in which art went commercial, is now over, and we are in the period in which the economy is bad after a big boom. And that gives us a ground on which we can create something as explosive as the art of Andy Warhol. Ours is the time in which the true quality of contemporary art must be discussed.[2]

He also argued that Japanese society, in which everything has been leveled to flat equality and therefore lacks class conflicts, remains a weak ground for nurturing strong artists:

> Japanese society has no real class system. There's no sense of absolute defeat about climbing social ladders, nor a visible evidence of class difference. We

1 Takashi Murakami, "Seiiki kara hanareta kyōjin na āto e" (Towards a strong art that departs from a sacred zone), *Atelier* (Tokyo) (March 1992): 96–97.

2 Ibid., 97.

> don't have the condition in which the enormously rich class or aristocrats buy big art with big money. But I feel that art fundamentally emerges from the friction of a class or society. For that reason, art should be exposed to a general audience, entering in an open competition for their approval or purchase.[3]

This interview, from 1992, contains all the fundamental concepts of Murakami's art. First, it reveals his deep interest in the revolutionary potential of original expressions made by marginalized groups, especially *otaku*, frequently associated with childishness. Second, it underlines his conviction that a revolutionary art practice must be supported by power and influence operative in the real world. And third, it outlines his ambition to create an open art market that encourages artists to be conscious of their purposes and positions.

Murakami's ideas about revolutionary art deeply reflect his relationship to Japan's postmodern condition. By "postmodern," I mean the period between the 1960s and the present; narrowly defined, the word specifically points to the overblown consumer culture and commodification of knowledge and information during the 1980s. This was the period during which Murakami came of age as a member of the first postwar generation to enjoy the abundance of commodities and growth of indigenous popular cultures like *manga* and *anime*, while suffering from the absence of a totalizing theory ("grand narrative"), whether humanism or Marxism. His was a generation named by the media in the early 1980s as *shinjinrui* (new human race) for their deviations from traditional Japanese tastes and behaviors.

Otaku—which emerged during the late 1970s among enthusiastic fans of science fiction, *anime*, and *manga*, becoming a minor industry by the late 80s—is the central cultural backbone of Murakami's generation. He grew up exposed to a vision of the future presented by science-fiction comics, *anime*, and films with robots, rockets, and other technological wonders constituting the collective fantasy of his generation. Later, with the success of the *anime* production company GAINAX, *otaku* turned professional, presenting to Murakami the possibility of putting the childlike hobby in the service of cutting-edge expression to make a strong impact on the popular imagination.

3 Ibid.

Murakami's condemnation of an apparently egalitarian Japanese society for dampening artists' opposition to preexisting systems reflects a popular conception of Japanese society as "predominantly middle class" during the 1980s. In addition, the "childishness" of Japanese consumer society was frequently debated. For instance, Akira Asada, a political philosopher who had a charismatic influence on youth throughout the 1980s, characterized Japanese society as overrun by "infantile capitalism":

> [I]n Japan, there are neither tradition-oriented old people adhering to transcendental values, nor inner-oriented adults who have internalized their values; instead, the nearly purely relative (or relativistic) competition exhibited by other-oriented children provides the powerful driving force for capitalism. Let's call this infantile capitalism.[4]

Asada argued that in the context of such infantile capitalism, the fundamental purpose or value of individual work is obscured or undefined, and childlike passion and the spirit of play are exploited for the development of a new technique or fashion to enhance the economy: "Engineers are cleverly maneuvered into displaying a childlike passion whereby they are easily obsessed with machines," while in advertisements, "people become carried away by word play, parody, and all the other childlike games of differentiation."[5] He pointed out that this cycle of play enhancing the economy was only possible under the protection of some political power. He found this "power" not enforced by a "hard" ruling structure that is "vertically centralized," but reinforced through a "soft" seduction "by a seemingly horizontal, centerless 'place.'"[6]

Asada's view anticipated a number of cultural studies that have established an analogy between Japanese imperialism and consumer culture, which would go on to influence the theoretical strategy of Japanese Neo Pop art in the early 1990s. More importantly, the ambivalent point of Asada's statement that Japanese society, without a spiritual center, remains "infantile" in relation to a society supported by traditional or modern spiritual principles—but produces various

4 Akira Asada, "Infantile Capitalism and Japan's Postmodernism: A Fairy Tale" (1987), reprinted in *South Atlantic Quarterly* 87, no. 3 (summer 1988): 631.

5 Ibid.

6 Ibid.

technical skills precisely because of childishness—reappeared in Murakami's own statement "Tokyo Pop Manifesto" in 1999. In fact, the points Asada made and those of Murakami's early interview constitute the central paradoxes that sustain the artist's conceptual operation. Murakami's uniqueness lay in his dialectical thinking, which inspired him to turn negative conditions of postmodern Japanese society into new methods of creating and interpreting a uniquely Japanese art.

This essay examines how Murakami utilized these negative conditions—childishness and flat social structure—as vehicles to develop a unique aesthetic, a method of cultural interpretation, and rules of artistic operation to bring about a revolutionary change in the structure of Japanese contemporary art. I maintain that Murakami held this revolutionary purpose from the beginning, and his diverse projects are consistent with his claims. These include his invention of the idea of Superflat and exhibitions illustrating the idea, his foundation of the studio and company Hiropon Factory (later transformed into Kaikai Kiki Co., Ltd.), his collaboration with Louis Vuitton, and his direction and sponsorship of GEISAI, the combination open art forum and flea market where anyone can display his or her own art, for a small entry fee, to art-world professionals.

I propose to reconstruct the evolution of Murakami's strategies for revolutionizing Japanese art in three steps. The first is an examination of his early style of appropriation—considering its relevance as a Japanese equivalent of American Neo Geo, a typical response of contemporary art to the postmodern condition—by comparing Murakami's method to two definitions of allegory, the interpretation of cultural signs, posited by Craig Owens and Walter Benjamin. The second is a reevaluation of Murakami's redefinition of Pop as Tokyo Pop, especially focusing on the idea of Po+Ku, the amalgam of Pop and *otaku*, in which childishness and an awareness of malevolence become the resources of a new aesthetic. The third is a survey of Murakami's organization of GEISAI and an analysis of its effects, including the emergence of Mahomi Kunikata as an artist embodying the spirit of GEISAI. As inheritors of artistic methods and attitudes explored by Murakami, the works of video artist K.K. and cartoonist Daisuke Nishijima will also be discussed.

2
Monuments to Emptiness, Vehicles of Transcendence: Neo Pop as a Mirror of Japanese Postmodern Unconscious

THE TERM "NEO POP" FIRST APPEARED in the March 1992 issue of the art magazine *Bijutsu Techō*, coined by editor Kiyoshi Kusumi and critic Noi Sawaragi. The category represented artists whose work evidenced the influence of *otaku* taste, including Murakami, Kodai Nakahara, and Kenji Yanobe. The special feature, titled "Pop/Neo Pop," was a strategic attempt to promote the Neo Pop generation as a Japanese counterpart to American Neo Geo.

Sawaragi's essay "Lollipop: That Smallest Form of Life" functioned as the central apparatus of defining Japanese Neo Pop as a species of postmodern appropriation ("simulationism") with the ability to deconstruct the invisible structures of social power. Presenting American Neo Geo's disruption of the authority of the social system of representation through the appropriation of pop culture fragments and their "cute" alterations, Sawaragi also viewed Japanese Neo Pop's simulation of "cute" details of domestic consumer products and cultural icons as a deconstruction of Japanese imperial power.[7] Sawaragi's argument was simultaneously influenced by Owens's theory of appropriation and the critique of Japanese imperialism as a structure of "soft" seduction made by Asada in a 1989 article, and Eiji Ōtsuka's comparison of this "soft" imperialism with the functioning of Japanese consumer culture in his books *Shōjo minzoku gaku* (The ethnology of young girls, 1989) and *Shōjotachi no kawaii tennō* (The cute emperor of young girls, 1991).

Appropriation was the dominant method of postmodern art defined by Owens, who described it as an "allegorical" operation that "does not invent images but confiscates them," laying "claim to the culturally significant, pos[ing] as its interpreter," adding a new meaning to the original that "supplants the antecedent one."[8] In other words, by mimicking an image in contemporary culture, whether part of an advertisement, film, or photography, appropriation makes a small ironic change to reveal a concealed message. This strategy is a method of

7 Noi Sawaragi, "Roripoppu—sono saishōgen no seimei" (Lollipop: That smallest form of life), *Bijutsu Techō* 44, no. 651 (March 1992): 90–94.

8 Craig Owens, "The Allegorical Impulse: Toward a Theory of Postmodernism" (1980), reprinted in *Beyond Recognition: Representation, Power, and Culture* (Berkeley: University of California Press, 1990), 54.

interpreting a cultural sign through the application of semiotic cultural analysis to contemporary art. Making this function of "simulation" a central characteristic of Japanese Neo Geo, Sawaragi attempted to shape Japanese Neo Pop as a vehicle of ideology critique.

Sawaragi's formulation of Neo Geo as a branch of cultural critique was also a response from the field of contemporary art to the provocation of New Academicism, an academic trend extremely influential among college students in the early 1980s. An independently developed Japanese equivalent to cultural studies or cultural materialism, New Academicism was represented by scholars of linguistics, anthropology, sociology, and film studies who applied semiotic analysis in their own fields while encouraging the interdisciplinary application of their methods to contemporary cultural phenomena.[9] In the milieu of such a radical intellectual upheaval, Asada held an exceptional position. His book *Kōzō to chikara* (Structure and power, 1983), which summarized theoretical points of poststructuralist studies, especially those of Michel Foucault and Gilles Deleuze and Félix Guattari, became an instant bestseller, even a social phenomenon. The most influential section was the preface, however, in which Asada invited young college students to use theory instead of obeying it, applying poststructuralist methods of analysis to the "turgid world" of postmodernism.[10]

In his first solo exhibition at a commercial gallery in December 1991, Murakami presented an installation that invited an association with the critique of the complicitous relationship between Japanese popular culture and imperialism. At Hosomi Gallery, Tokyo, he showed a row of *randoseru* (school backpacks for children whose shapes have a military origin) that had been manufactured in various skins of mammals and reptiles and installed in a single row on the gallery wall in a cool Minimalist arrangement. The installation was accompanied by drawings appropriated from the Japanese comic *Tensai Bakabon* (Genius and stupid kid), popular for its destructively nonsensical humor, redrawn on the surface of boxes of the same kind as those in which imperial gifts are delivered. The installation opened itself up to political interpretation while remaining fundamentally ambiguous.

---

9 Scholars representing New Academicism were Keiichirō Maruyama (linguistics), Yoshihiko Hasumi (film studies), and Shin-ichi Nakazawa (cultural anthropology), among others.

10 Akira Asada, *Kōzō to chikara* (Structure and power) (Tokyo: Keiso Shobo, 1983), 3–6.

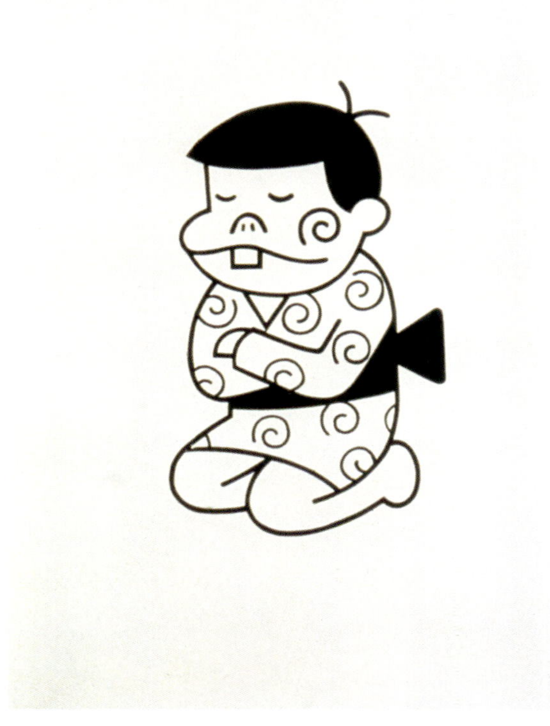

Takashi Murakami
Bakabon Project, 1991, detail
Oil on board
Five panels:
19 5/16 x 15 2/8 inches each

Illustration: Akemi Suetsugu
Cooperation: Fujio Production

Murakami himself was not entirely committed to the condemnation of postmodern Japanese culture by decoding its signs. Instead, the cultural icons in his work served a more loosely allegorical and thought-provoking end. Initially interested in the technical innovation of *otaku*, he wanted to incorporate its unorthodox imagination into the practice of contemporary art. In the round-table talk "Post-Hobby Art in Japan," also included in *Bijutsu Techō*'s Pop/Neo Pop issue, Murakami emphasized the importance of "paying attention to marginalized production, things looked down upon for being meaningless," because he wanted to "turn the present system of contemporary Japanese art upside down."[11] He also found it commendable that *otaku* were dedicated to "the invention of a new technique, especially through the use of overlooked elements, finding an 'empty space' between existing methods of production or criteria for judging works." He maintained that art must find the same "empty space" to revolutionize itself.[12]

Murakami's appropriation of an *otaku* image in his 1992 sculpture *Sea Breeze* exemplifies his productive application of an "insignificant" fragment of popular

11 Murakami, Kenji Yanobe, and Kōdai Nakahara, "Posuto hobbī āto in Japan" (Post-hobby art in Japan), *Bijutsu Techō* 44, no. 651 (March 1992): 69, 78.

12 Ibid., 74.

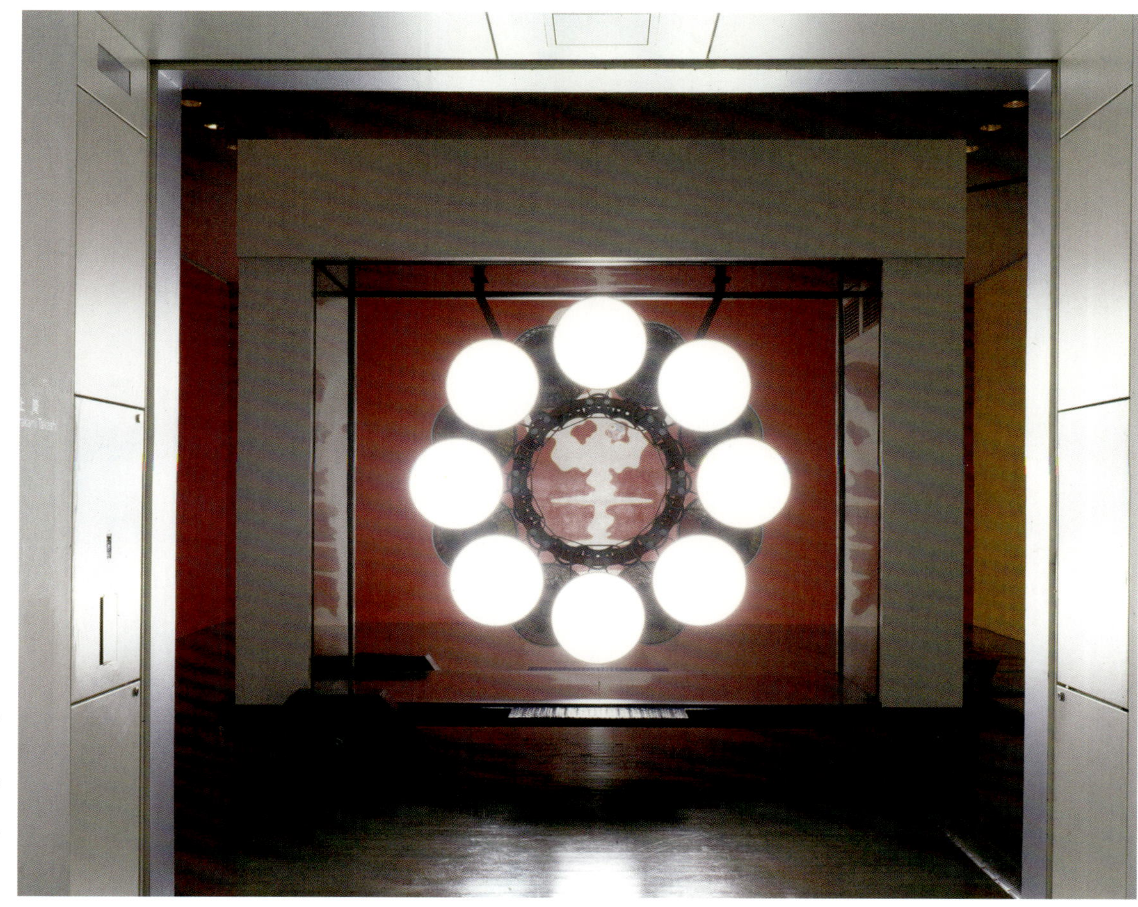

Takashi Murakami
Sea Breeze, 1992
Iron, stainless steel, shutter, mercury lamp, caster, wheels, ventilator, and flashing lamps
137 13/16 x 189 x 98 7/16 inches
Installation in "Ground Zero Japan," Art Tower, Mito, Japan, 1999

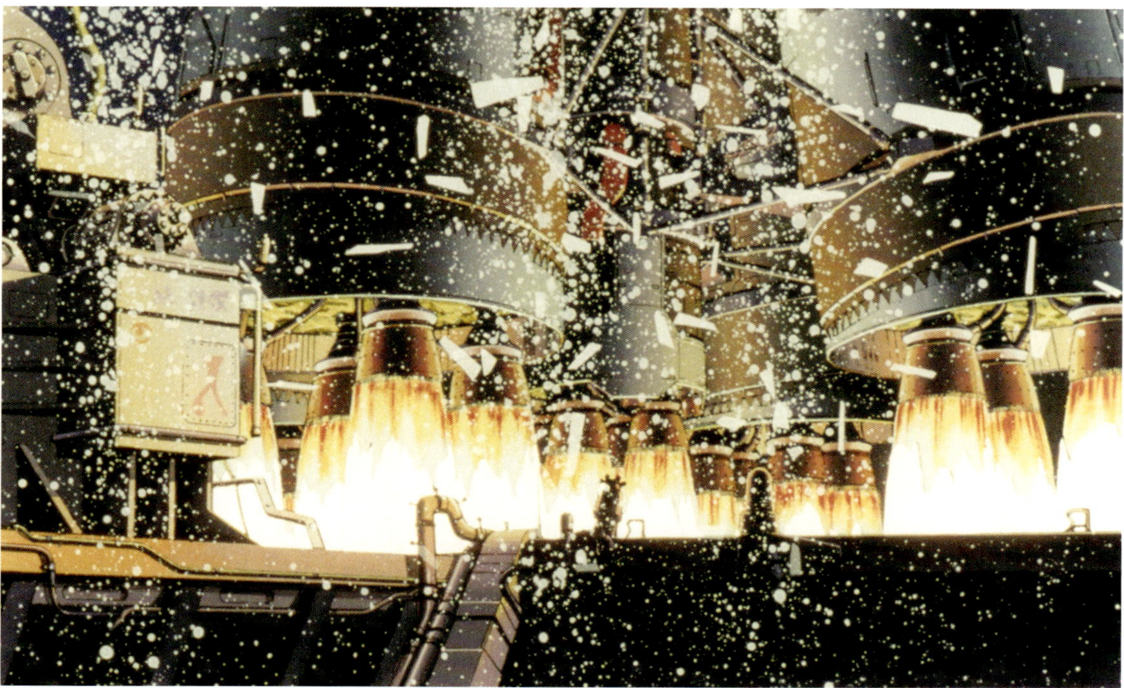

Still from *Royal Space Force: Wings of Honneamise*, 1987

culture. The sculpture features two back-to-back rings of eight gigantic stadium lights contained in a square box on wheels. The arrangement of lights resembles the view of a rocket seen from below; when switched on, the intense heat and dazzling flash of the lights evoke the moment of its launch. The work references a scene from *Royal Space Force: Wings of Honneamise*, the first feature-length *anime* movie produced by GAINAX in 1987. Although the reference is almost cryptic, it is salient to *anime* lovers, as GAINAX, founded and operated by a group of former *otakus*—including Toshio Okada, Hideaki Annō, and Hiroyuki Yamaga—possessed vanguard status. Producing high-quality animation that appeals to a large audience using the aesthetic and technical expertise of *otaku* but still subject to the prejudice against *otaku*, GAINAX represented, for Murakami, a model of marginalized yet cutting-edge cultural production. Referring to their film was Murakami's homage to GAINAX's independent spirit. At the same time, the fact that the burning wheel was contained inside a box signified passion confined within a conventional frame, evoking the failure of *Honneamise* to present a uniquely Japanese expression as it remained under the influence of Western science-fiction films.[13]

Stylistically, *Sea Breeze* recalled Jeff Koons's classic Neo Geo sculpture *Two Ball 50/50 Tank (Spaulding Dr. J Silver Series, Spaulding Dr. J 241 Series)* (1985), in which two basketballs are suspended in a tank. Like *Two Ball*, *Sea Breeze* featured a vernacular image associated with a particular subculture within a geometric frame. However, the Murakami has a stronger emotional content than the Koons. By taking a scene fragment from an *anime* movie, enlarging it, and making it aggressively physical, *Sea Breeze* simultaneously evokes a heroic narrative from science fiction, the aspiration of *otaku* creators to make something brilliantly new, and their failure to depart from circumscribed limitations. (Incidentally, the rocket launch in the *anime* also was unsuccessful.) In its intense heat and sudden flash, the work also suggested an atomic explosion, seen in the

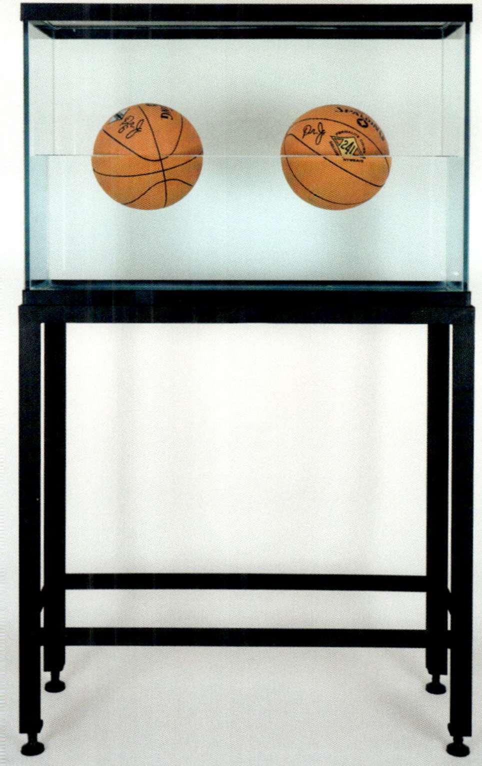

Jeff Koons
Two Ball 50/50 Tank (Spalding Dr. J Silver Series, Spalding Dr. J 241 Series), 1985
Glass, steel, distilled water, and two basketballs
62 3/4 x 36 3/4 x 13 1/4 inches
Courtesy and © Jeff Koons

13 Ibid., 78.

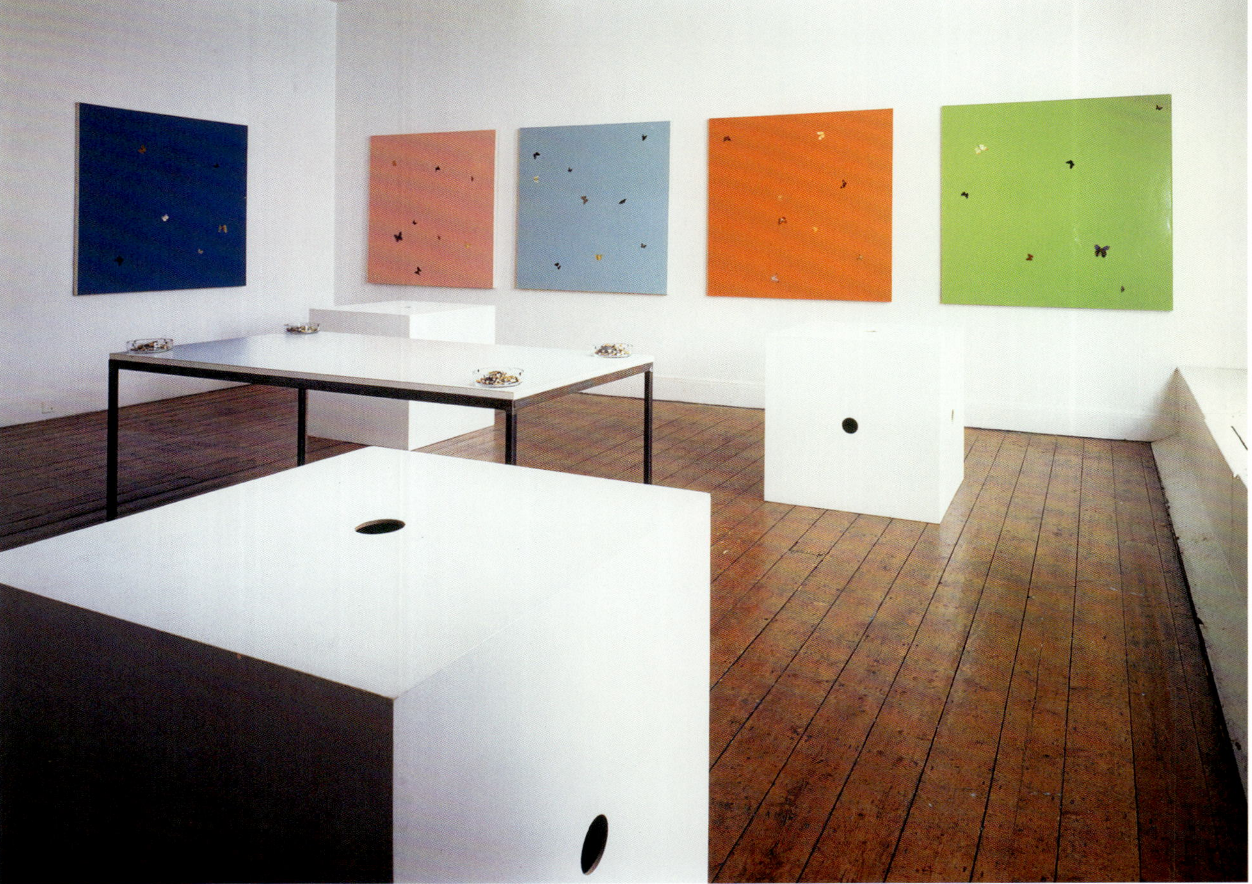

Damien Hirst
In & Out of Love, 1991
Household paint on canvas, boxes, table, and four glass ashtrays with cigarettes
Eight paintings: 60 x 60 inches each; four boxes: 36 x 36 x 36 inches each; table: 84 x 42 x 36 inches
Collection Yale Center for British Art, Paul Mellon Fund
© Damien Hirst

apocalyptic images of both 1970s classical *anime* and 80s cyberpunk *anime*. The metaphor of explosion was frequently applied by Murakami to describe the total change of the Japanese art system. *Sea Breeze* thus became an emblem of the specific cultural milieu of the early 1990s, in which science fiction and *otaku* expressions carried the promise of a brilliant new art.

In communicating emotion through an image appropriated from vernacular culture then presented in a Minimalist format, *Sea Breeze* bears more affinity with Damien Hirst's *In & Out of Love* (1991), an installation displaying the cycle of birth and death in butterflies alongside spent ashtrays. Both are allegories conveying themes pertaining to collective lives. Exaggerating the symbolic features of national stereotypes—the *anime*-crazed Japanese and the British obsession with the monumentalization of death (as in Madame Tussauds Wax Museum)—

both works nevertheless indicate the passionate desire to break free of confining structures, whether belonging to the art world or society at large. They bring a touch of cheekiness or crudeness into the neutralized academic presentation of art, using geometric forms as inverted signs of an iconoclastic act and the alibi of being "a work of art." Both works are allegorical in that they communicate a discursive message—with subversive content—through fragmentary images that suggest a larger socio-cultural context.

Still, Murakami's use of a cultural fragment to evoke an emotion shared by a specific social group belonging to a specific historical period indicates a more complex use of allegory than Owens's. It recalls Walter Benjamin's analysis of cultural products as reservoirs of the collective vision of utopia. Benjamin emphasized the importance of discerning ("remembering") the patterns of "dreaming," the ways in which the nineteenth-century bourgeoisie perceived their organic relation with their society and time through their relations to popular images and products:

> But the modern—*la modernité*—is always citing primary history. Here, this occurs through the ambiguity peculiar to social relations and products of this epoch. Ambiguity is manifest of dialectic, the law of dialectic at a standstill. This standstill is utopia and the dialectic image, therefore, dream image. Such an image is afforded by commodity per se: as fetish.[14]

Benjamin also believed that a study of the "primary history" of the present culture, the origin of the many material conditions characterizing the present time, would give interpreters not only the political knowledge of the past but an awareness of the specific problems characterizing their own time. In his "Exposé of 1935," a prototypical blueprint for *The Arcades Project*, he stated:

> The Copernican revolution in historical perception is as follows. Formerly it was thought that a fixed point had been found in "what has been," and one saw the present engaged in tentatively concentrating the forces of knowledge on this ground. Now this relation is to be overturned, and what

14 Walter Benjamin, *The Arcades Project*, trans. Howard Eiland and Kevin McLaughlin (Cambridge, Massachusetts: The Belknap Press, Harvard University Press, 1999), 10.

> has been is to become the dialectical reversal—the flash of awakened consciousness. Politics attains primacy over history. The facts become something that just now first happened to us, first struck us; to establish them is the affair of memory.[15]

According to Benjamin, while a true utopia cannot be attained without a drastic social change, the present society compromises the revolutionary desire of the people by producing commodities that present images of "Utopia," which, after the fashion passes, will be revealed as nothing but kitsch—hence the ambiguity underlying the collective fantasy of utopia. Nevertheless, by studying kitsch, those analyzing cultural signs after the fact can comprehend the specific ways in which a given people imagined the ideal world to come. Kitsch is thus an archaeological token of the imaginary lives of people during a specific period. Murakami applies the same method of analysis to products of *otaku*. The glaring image of lights in *Sea Breeze*, evoking the scene of a rocket launch, captures the subconscious desire of Japanese youth to break out of the materialistic and fragmented life of postmodern Japan as well as the artist's own ambition to go beyond the ineffective "institutions" of the Japanese art world, along with the frustration and anger at the difficulty of escaping.

An analysis of popular images as matrices of collective dreaming and trauma is recapitulated by Murakami in a more mature and comprehensive form later in his thematic organization of the 2005 exhibition "Little Boy: The Arts of Japan's Exploding Culture," a survey of Japanese *anime* and pop culture and its influence on the contemporary artistic production of younger Japanese artists. The show revealed the sustained fear of the atomic bomb felt by Japanese people after World War II, in contrast to the "euphoria" associated with the economic prosperity enjoyed under the protection of the United States. The "limited freedom" of postwar Japanese democracy produced a childish culture lacking a mature capacity for self-reflection, creating instead an endless flow of cultural signs. For "Little Boy," Murakami applied allegorical interpretation in the manner of Benjamin to

15 Ibid., 388–89.

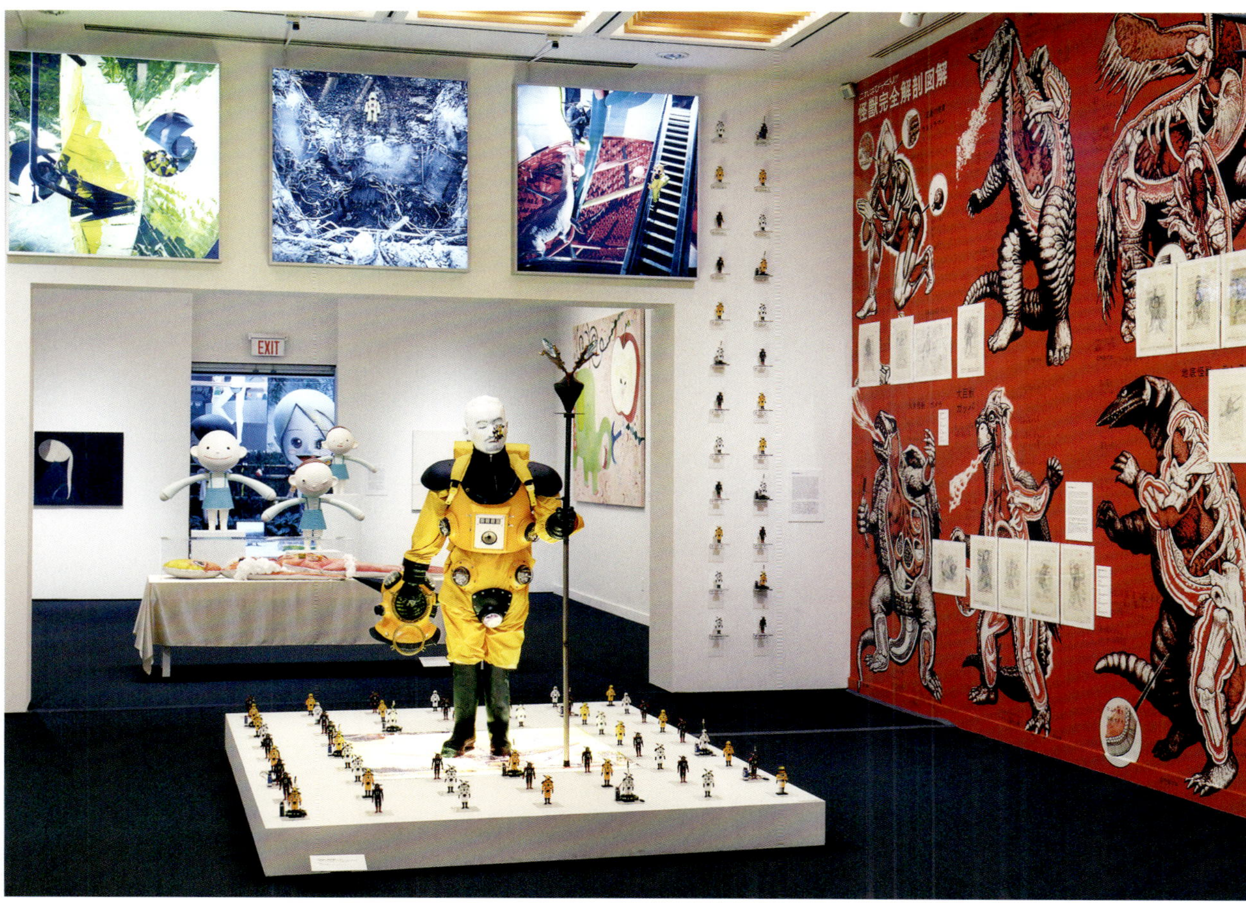

"Little Boy: The Arts of Japan's Exploding Subculture," installation at The Japan Society, New York, 2005

reveal the political meaning of a historical period—in which lay the origins of the present culture—through the analysis of popular products.

Murakami learned this allegorical method from a group of Neo Geo critics and artists associated with the Tokyo gallery Röntgen Kunst Institut. They tended to attribute the origin of *otaku* imagination to the *anime* and science-fiction culture of the 1960s. In a 1992 issue of *Radium Egg*, a magazine issued by Röntgen, popular-culture historian Kentarō Takekuma introduced the work of editor Shōji Ōtomo, whose book *Kaijū zukan* (Monsters encyclopedia) and futuristic articles about robots, three-dimensional theater, and others greatly influenced the construction of a utopian vision for Japanese children during the late 1960s.[16] Murakami included Ōtomo's *Kaijū zukan* in "Little Boy," deploying the fruits of a cultural historiography of the early 1990s.

16 Kentaro Takekuma, interviewed by Sawaragi, "Tōtaru sukōpu shiatā—anomarī to Ōtomo Shōji" (Total scope theater: Shōji Ōtomo and anomaly), *Radium Egg*, no. 3 (Tokyo: Röntgen Kunst Institut, 1992): 4–11.

3
Redefinition of Tokyo Pop: The Paradox of Childishness and Impoverished Culture as Conditions of New Creation

"HELLO, YOU ARE ALIVE: TOKYO POP MANIFESTO," published in the magazine *Kōkoku hihyō* (Advertisement criticism) in 1999, was Murakami's first attempt at a public declaration of his ideas about a uniquely Japanese approach to contemporary art. The two-page manifesto enumerated the disadvantages of Japanese contemporary society and presented strategies for producing an entirely new artistic expression, reiterating his comments from 1992. Murakami posited an infantile mind incapable of constructing a solid structure of meaning (system of legitimation), an absence of a class society that produces ultra-rich citizens, and a tendency toward amateurism as conditions contributing to the apparent "poverty" of contemporary Japanese culture.[17] He ascribed the absence of a value-determining structure to postwar Japan's having been placed in the political custody of the United States, thereby unable to define its political identity. Murakami saw Japan as a society of children driven by the insatiable desire for the production of, and interest in, details without a centralized purpose—the most typical manifestation of which is *otaku*. He suggested that the lack of a teleological conception of time progressing linearly toward some goal may not be so "negative" from a Japanese standpoint. In fact, for an *otaku*, who only believes in the consistency of his inner universe fortified with individually significant details, time does not run linearly.

Murakami praised *Love & Pop*, a 1998 film by Hideaki Annō, the director of the extremely popular *anime* television series *Neon Genesis Evangelion* (1995–96). *Love & Pop* depicts, with live actors and actresses, the urban odyssey of a high-school girl confronting the squalor of Tokyo and the absence of true love while accepting to live in this world. Its impressive last scene shows four girls marching in a dirty shallow river, their faces lifted and looking straight ahead. The film was a bold adaptation of the 1997 novel of the same title by Ryū Murakami, who attempted

---

17 Murakami, "Haikei kimi wa ikite iru, Tokyo poppu sengen" (Hello, you are alive: Tokyo pop manifesto), *Kōkoku hihyō* (Advertisement criticism), no. 226 (April 1999): 58–59.

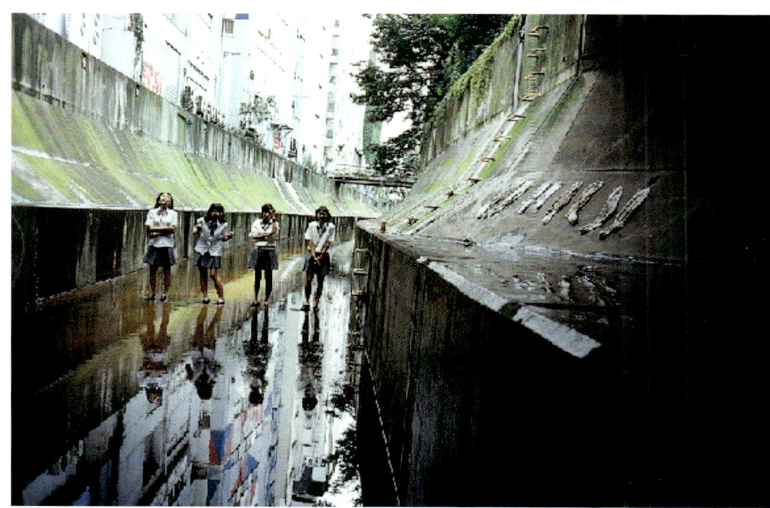

Hideaki Annō
Still from *Love & Pop*, 1998
© 1998 Love & Pop Production Organization

to present the contemporary chaos of Tokyo as a Japanese version of Pop. For Takashi Murakami, Annō's film transformed the book's central message by revealing the absence of epiphany in contemporary Tokyo, thus capturing the city's reality. Murakami pointed out that Annō's existential acceptance to live in the emptiness of a Tokyo life and his formulation of this awareness into an aesthetic expression provided him with a new creative position, enabling him to transcend the closed *otaku* sensibility. The new position nevertheless differed from the bold embracing of the surface championed by American Pop. Being an "externalization of an introverted *otaku* aesthetic," the new creative position of Tokyo Pop was to be called "Po+Ku," an abbreviation of Pop and *otaku* combined, denoting a "post-*otaku*" sensibility.

With Murakami's new reading, the idea of Pop was transformed. No longer a cool appropriation of cultural icons or their aesthetic monumentalization in a hard-edged design, "Pop" now signifies a standpoint and principle of the production of marginalized individuals empowered by a reflexive analysis of their situation and creative impetus. Murakami asserted that this new creative position can form a unique artistic genre, "Made in Japan," in response to Tokyo's chaos and emptiness.

What Murakami percieves to be Japan's political dependency on the United States, which caused a confusion of national identity, resembles a postcolonial situation. He thought that it could be transcended by dialectically transforming its negative conditions into a creative resource. The absence of an ontological core, a progressive view of history, and professional expertise—signs of Japan's "childish" postmodernity—become advantages for a postmodern art that supersedes the humanism and teleology that dominate modern cultural institutions.

Murakami's definition of Tokyo Pop corresponds with widely accepted definitions of postcolonial and postmodern cultural production. The use of a decentered imagination that produces details without a guiding principle or hierarchy as a driving force of a much freer cultural production recalls the "schizophrenic" production of the postmodern anti-subject posited by Deleuze and Guattari in *Anti-Oedipus: Capitalism and Schizophrenia* (1972). They posited that capitalism produces "through its process of production...an awesome schizophrenic accumulation of energy or charge, against which it brings all its vast powers of repression to bear, but which nonetheless continues to act as capitalism's limit."[18] To Deleuze and Guattari, "schizophrenic" is not a pathological category, but a metaphor for the individual acting in response to the driving force of an advanced capitalism of the postmodern age that does not obey the definitions of a centered integrated subject of modernity, but "wanders about," carried away by the flow of his desire, "scrambl[ing] all codes," discovering his reality at the disintegration of a conventional integrity of a social body.

Taking the American category of Pop and inverting its meaning with resources from his own culture, Murakami transformed Pop, making it a vehicle for a postcolonial redefinition of Japanese cultural identity and turning the tables against modern Western cultural authority. This method of critical reinterpretation and transformation is precisely the application of postcolonial "articulation" proposed by Stuart Hall as an effective means of political transformation, in which the colonized subject uses a prominent theoretical category of the dominant culture to shape a new language of cultural operation, endowing them with a new identity and enabling them to "speak in a new language."[19]

In its primary stage, Tokyo Pop then was a term for Tokyo's cutting-edge youth culture and art, which had a vivid reality by 1998, produced by those who

18 Gilles Deleuze and Félix Guattari, *Anti-Oedipus: Capitalism and Schizophrenia* (1972), trans. Robert Hurley, Mark Seem, and Helen R. Lane (Minneapolis: University of Minnesota Press, 1983), 34. They continued: "He plunges further and further into the realm of deterritorialization, reaching the furthest limits of the decomposition of the socius on the surface of his own body without organs" (35).

19 Stuart Hall, "On Postmodernism and Articulation: An Interview with Stuart Hall," ed. Lawrence Grossberg, in *Stuart Hall: Critical Dialogues in Critical Studies*, eds. David Morley and Kuan-Hsing Chen (London: Routledge, 1996), 143: "In the case of the Rastafarians in Jamaica...the Bible—that did not belong to them; they had to turn the text upside down, to get a meaning which fit their experience. But in turning the text upside down they remade themselves; they positioned themselves differently as new political subjects; they reconstructed themselves as blacks in the new world: they became what they are. And, positioning themselves in that way, they learned to speak a new language" (143).

creatively deployed their childlike, amateur, and border-crossing sensibilities. Murakami's selection of ten Tokyo Pop creators—including Yoshitomo Nara (artist), Annō (animation and film director), Cornelius (techno-pop musician and producer), Hiromix (photographer), and Bome (sculptor of dolls based on *anime* characters)—typically excluded his own work. Instead, he acted as a critic and curator who defined and evaluated the still "invisible" production of Tokyo Pop, playing the role of a conscious "adult" in relation to the "child" creators.

The "Superflat" exhibition, which showed at Parco Gallery in Tokyo and Nagoya in 2000 before touring internationally, was reshaped as a glamorous "adult" exhibition. Although it preserved aspects of Tokyo Pop through the inclusion of Nara and photographers who employ a snapshot aesthetic, like Hiromix and Masafumi Sanai, the show's central thesis was shifted to the inheritance of the uniquely nonrepresentational, playfully distorting expressions of eighteenth-century Edo Mannerist paintings by contemporary cartoonists and *anime* directors, positing a new aesthetic that consciously integrated characteristics of both

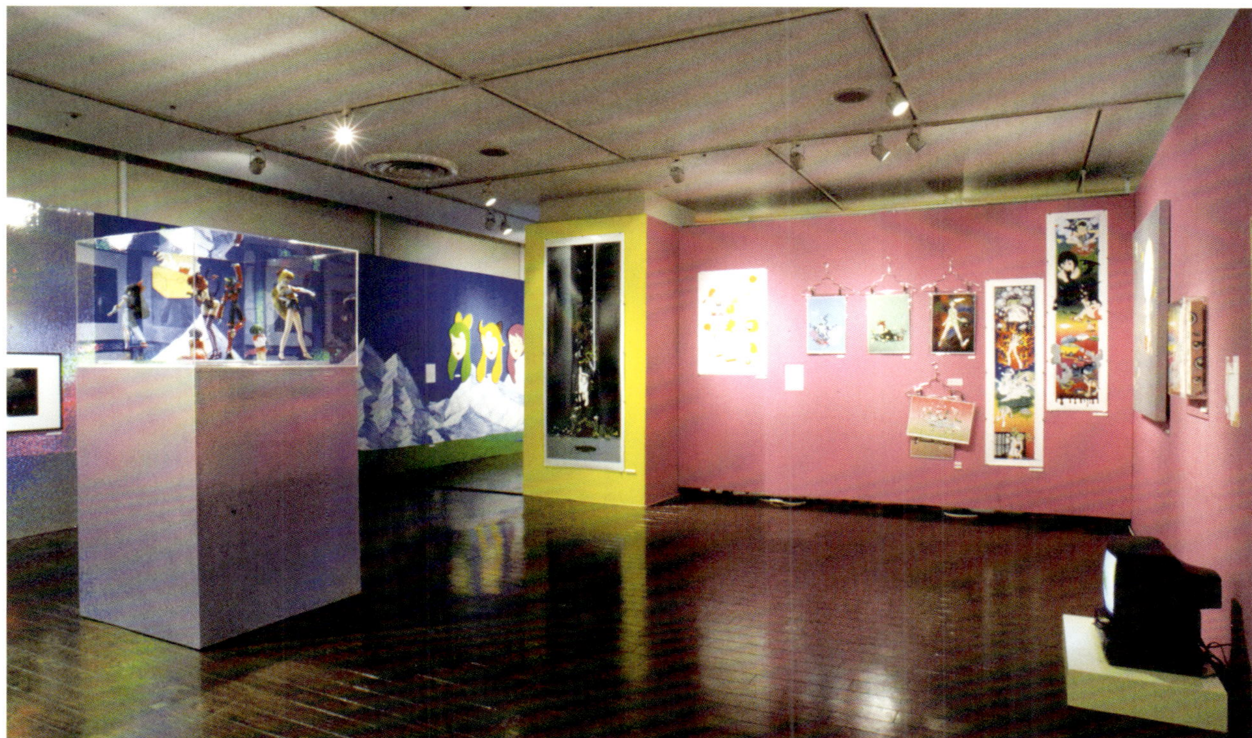

"Superflat," installation at Parco Gallery, Nagoya, Japan, 2000

premodern and postmodern art. The combination of analogically related premodern and postmodern styles was asserted as a vehicle for transcending the subservience of modern Japanese art to Western artistic models, clearly showing a postcolonial inclination.

The initial assertion of Tokyo Pop as an "externalization of an introverted *otaku* aesthetic" was thus presented in an enlarged definition. The coexistence of two different species of Superflat art—one professional, glamorous, and strategically conscious, the other amateurish, youthful, and spontaneous—resulted in the enrichment of the presentation while somewhat suppressing the originality of marginal production. Nevertheless, the sublimation of Tokyo Pop into Superflat as an aesthetic of a postmodern age was successful, as the "Superflat" exhibition had an enthusiastic reception throughout its American tour in 2001, leading to second and third exhibitions—"Coloriage" in 2002 at the Fondation Cartier pour l'art contemporain in Paris and "Little Boy" in 2005 at the Japan Society in New York.

3
Building an Arena of Free Competition: GEISAI as a Vehicle of Transforming Japanese Art Presentation

GEISAI WAS A LOGICAL DEVELOPMENT of Murakami's earlier assertion that the art market should be made an integral part of contemporary art practice in Japan. It was also an application of the idea of Superflat to the structure of art evaluation and dealing, breaking down the boundaries between professionals and amateurs. GEISAI started in March 2002 as an art competition and flea market, open to anyone who purchased a one-square-meter booth for ¥15,000, with prominent artists and art critics acting as judges and professional gallerists, magazine editors, and directors of design offices and *anime* production studios going about the booths as "scouts." Professional galleries were also invited to participate as business competitors. Held for one day twice a year, GEISAI completed its tenth launch on 17

September 2006. Starting with 270 entries and 3,531 visitors at the first launch, GEISAI has grown into a large art festival with more than eight hundred booths and nine thousand visitors at its latest incarnation, counting 791 artists, sixteen gallery/shop participants, and 9,809 visitors altogether.

Although its practical format was borrowed from the Design Festival and Comic Market, the market where *otakus* sell personally created *manga* works, the conceptual model of GEISAI was also inspired by PRIDE, a tournament of mixed wrestling that allows fighting between those practicing different genres of martial arts. Started in 1997 and restructured in 2000 as a fighting ground for everyone regardless of weight or genre, PRIDE permits former Olympic medalists to battle first-rate martial-arts professionals twice a year and has become top entertainment, in competition with Ultimate Fighting Championship and K-1 Fight Club, under the powerful leadership of Naoto Morishita, president of Dream Stage Entertainment.

In the round-table talk "The Superflat Relation Between Professional Wrestling and Art" published in *Kōkoku hihyō* in March 2000, Murakami pointed out the affinity of PRIDE with the idea of Superflat. He considered professional wrestling as another example of marginalized people making interesting social performances. PRIDE was a new form of professional wrestling that superseded the convention of presenting fighters as stereotypical parodies of their classes. Annihilating the sense of borders, PRIDE presented a model of a new performing platform:

> Professional wrestling was an entertainment that showed fighting among marginalized people, who were given characters exaggerating the stereotypes of their classes. I found that very sympathetic to the position I am taking in the field of contemporary art. But the condition of professional wrestling can be applied to the reflection on the ambiguous stratification of class in Japan. This is like the idea of Superflat. Japanese "class system" is not a three-dimensional pyramid. It has layers of difference, but everything is flattened out, overlapping or becoming contiguous with each other. This

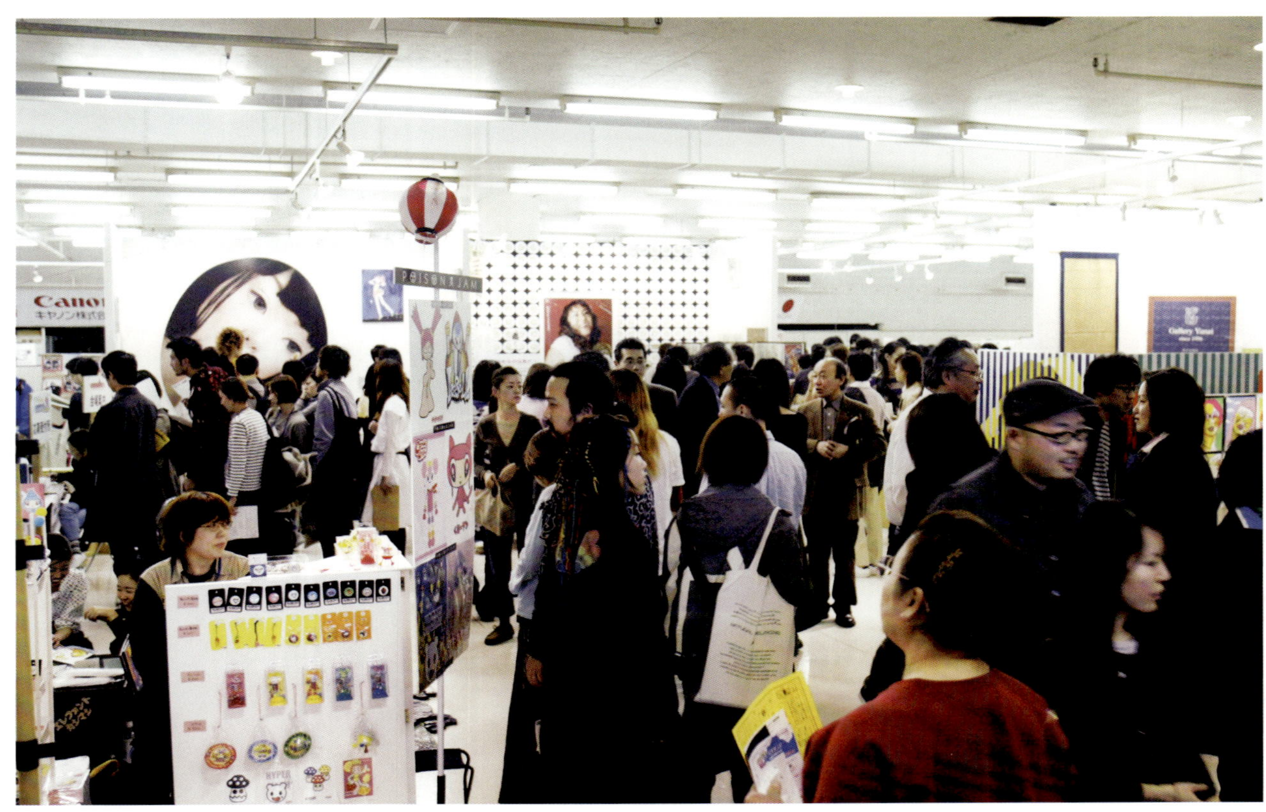

View of first GEISAI festival, Tokyo, 2002

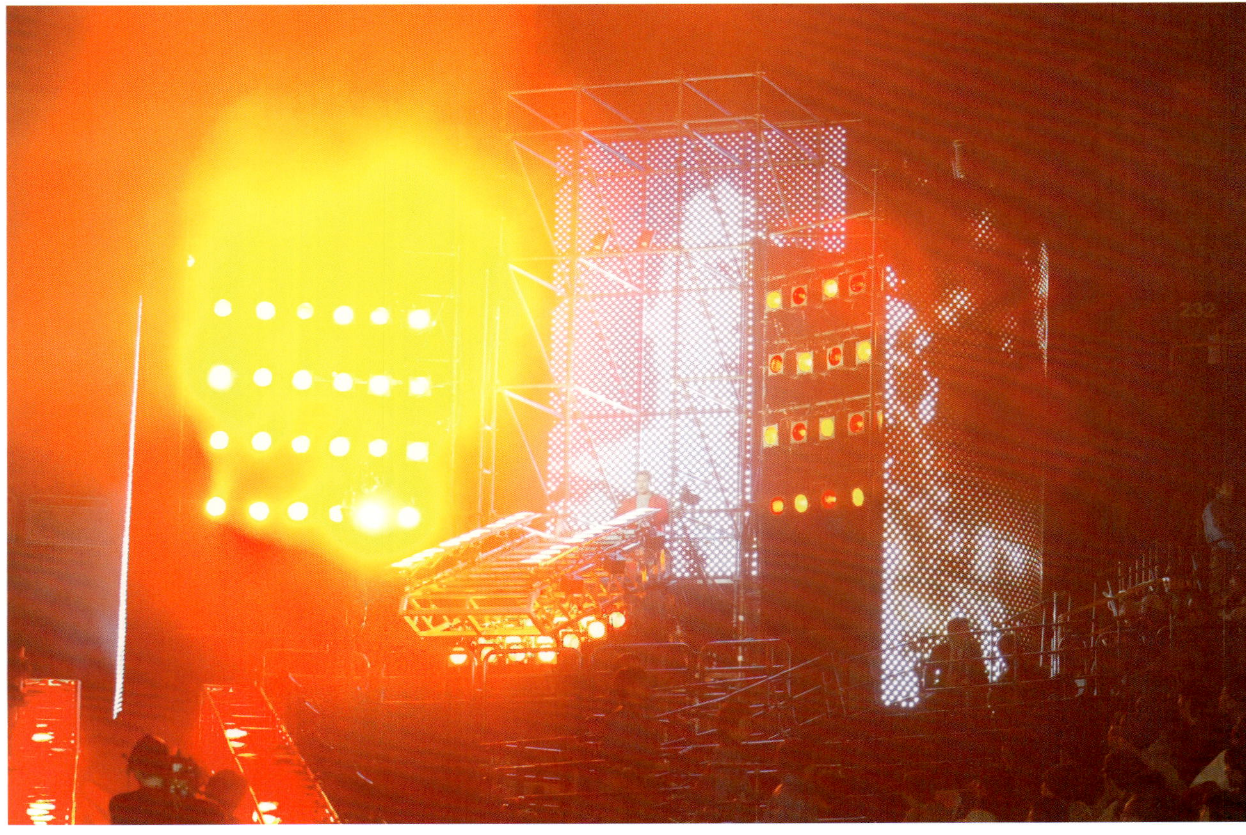

View of PRIDE 29 "Fists of Fire" tournament, Tokyo, 2005

> structure influences all the unique expressions of Japanese culture. I want to interpret that.[20]

As discussed in "Tokyo Pop Manifesto," the ambiguous stratification of class in Japanese society is one of the negative elements of Japan's postmodernity. However, Murakami proposed to use this flat juxtaposition of class difference as a model for a functioning system in Japan. He stated that Morishita was creating "a new language of professional wrestling with PRIDE" by using the unintelligibility of the Japanese class system to define genre-free fighting. He even stated that PRIDE can propose a "common world language" of wrestling originating in Japan. In the same way, by combining the models of the Comic Market and PRIDE, he constructed a new arena in which "an art created in Japan can become a global currency." GEISAI is regarded as another system by which those belonging to the lowest strata of society, here represented by *otaku*, can "disrupt the hierarchical structure of evaluation in the West."[21]

GEISAI has earned a place in the art world, positively affecting the careers of its participants. Its breaking down of the distinctions between professionals and amateurs has been commended by art magazines and newspapers for challenging the conventional system of the art market and art competition, where one must be selected to present one's work.[22] It has also trained young artists to develop their communication skills. The invitation of prominent judges from Japan and overseas, including Tom Eccles of Public Art Fund; Douglas Fogle, curator of contemporary art at the Carnegie Museum of Art; and François Pinault, president of the multinational holding company PPR and an art collector, among others, has given artists the opportunity to receive a critique and evaluation from international perspectives, and sometimes even chances to show their work abroad.

One of the aims of GEISAI is the discovery of young artistic talent. Kunikata, the third-prize winner of GEISAI #2, has an especially important symbolic relation with the fundamental attitude of GEISAI. Kunikata initially presented an almost unmediated transcription of her adolescent abjection: a cartoon narrative, scribbled in several notebooks, depicting an adolescent female body dismembered,

---

20 Murakami, Sawaragi, and Kenji Motohashi, "Puroresu to āto no sūpā furattoteki kankei" (The superflat relation between professional wrestling and art), *Kōkoku hihyō* (Advertisement criticism), no. 236 (March 2000): 115.

21 Ibid., 117–18.

22 Hisako Hara, "Ātokai kōzō kaikaku e no fāsuto raundo" (The first round in the battle for reforming the structure of the art world), *Bijutsu Techō* (May 2002): 128–32; and Kyōji Maeda, "Nihon āto hasshin naruka—Murakami Takashi shi no Geisai" (Could this be a chance to export Japanese art?: Takashi Murakami's GEISAI), *Yomiuri shinbun* (Tokyo), 28 March 2006, 4.

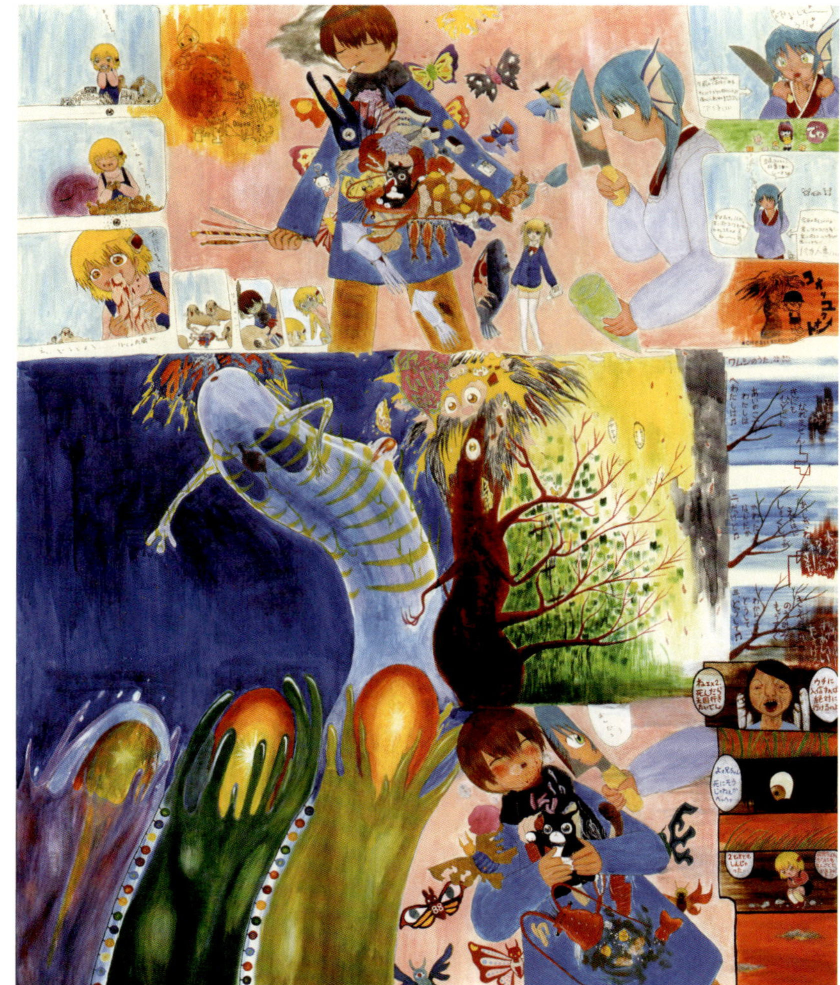

Mahomi Kunikata
Sound of Body and Mind Freezing: The Story of Gyūi No. 5, 2005
Acrylic on canvas
63 3/4 x 51 3/16 inches
Courtesy Reflex Gallery, Amsterdam

devoured by a monster, steeped in blood and vomit, or encountering the death of her brother. There is an intense negation of self, accompanied by the desire to be integrated into the body and mind of the loved other through the pain and ecstasy of disintegration. Kunikata's paintings amalgamate all the narrative threads of her drawings into oneiric tableaux in which scenes of beheading, stabbing, and fragments of human bodies merging with alien or non-human bodies are juxtaposed with images of small animals, toys, flowers, and butterflies, constituting an erotic but innocent rebus of adolescent longing.

Kunikata's work embodies the power of "alien" imagination sublimated into an aesthetic style, recalling Murakami's statement that Tokyo Pop is sustained by "the externalization of the introverted *otaku* aesthetic." Now an artist with Kaikai Kiki, Kunikata participated in the group shows "Little Boy" and "J'en rêve" at the Fondation Cartier pour l'art contemporain in 2005 while making a strong impression and selling out her works at large overseas art fairs and gallery shows. Her work embodies the intense originality of marginalized art production genuinely growing out of the dark soil of Japanese *otaku* culture.

Her relation to Murakami as a protégé embodies the relation of marginal and childlike production of young Japanese artists to the "adult" clarity of his critical judgment. The relation also reflects the contradiction of GEISAI, which is a platform for younger artists and is partially funded by the profit gained by the sales of Murakami's own work. Kunikata's evolution into a promising professional artist is an exceptional case for GEISAI participants. The gap between Murakami's intent to nurture original Japanese talents and participants' general dependency on the given platform of GEISAI indicates the challenge of dialectically shaping the "childishness" and "flatness" of Japanese postmodern sensibility into a positive medium to transform the system of art.

4
Empowerment of Marginal Production: K.K. and Daisuke Nishijima

MURAKAMI CULTIVATED TWO SIGNIFICANT METHODS OF ARTISTIC PRODUCTION for younger artists. One is the critical reflection on Japanese postmodern cultural representations through the appropriation of images in popular media. The other is the dialectic transformation of "closed" *otaku* aesthetic into an artistic expression open to critical judgment. The artist K.K. and the cartoonist Daisuke Nishijima respectively extend these methods.

K.K's. video *WARATTEIITOMO_* (You can laugh, 2002) appropriates footage from the enormously popular TV variety show of the same title, framing it in a metanarrative in which the artist himself watches the show in his living room. Broadcast since 1982 weekdays from noon to 1 p.m., the show of light talk and games was hosted by the popular comedian Kazuyoshi Morita, alias Tamori. The secret of the show's long popularity lies in Tamori's skillful control of the audience in the open studio. When he occasionally addresses them with light questions, they answer in unison, creating an atmosphere of total inclusiveness.

K.K.'s editing of the show focuses on the moments of laughter, which, sped up or doubled, fragmented and interpolated between other episodes, grow convulsive, increasingly taking on an aspect of mass hysteria. The video's "chapters," parodying the show's daily changing theme, include Tamori's biography told through documentary footage that reveals the process by which he became a media icon, a sort of mock father of the Japanese nation, supplanting General MacArthur. Introducing an episode about Morita's loss of sight in his left eye, K.K. highlights the irony of his wearing dark glasses to hide a personal handicap and in doing so ultimately enhancing his charismatic appeal. Revealing the relentless public ritual of devouring Morita's identity, K.K. exposed the spiritual dependency that nurtures the structure of "soft" power in postmodern Japanese society, indicating its origin in the spiritual vacuum created by the loss of a strong father figure. Parallel to his scapegoating of this media icon, K.K. presents his own vulnerability by leaving his living room to visit Studio Alta, the show's venue. The picture of himself buried in the wave of people, reduced to a tiny dot on the screen, demonstrates his powerless anonymity, in contrast to the omniscience and autonomy experienced in front of the TV. The double perspective showing the reversal of the viewer's and media icon's roles indicates their dependency on the euphoria provided by television, as well as their entrapment.

Nishijima published his narrative comic *Ōson sensō* (O Village wars, released as *The Universal* in English) in 2004. The book was published by Hayakawa Shoten, prominent publisher of Japanese and overseas science fiction (not specializing in the publication of comics); as of its ninth printing, it had sold twenty-thousand copies. From the perspective of a junior-high-school boy, it relates the consequences of a Martian attack on a small village surrounded by mountains, where no airwaves can reach. Confronted by the crisis, the village does nothing, as everyone is satisfied with a closed happy life. The name of the village, Ō, meaning "concave" in Japanese, suggests both its homogeneity and the sense of existential entrapment felt by someone awakening to an awareness of the outside world. The story recounts the desperate but comic effort of the boy to warn everyone about the attack and eventually to depart for Tokyo. The last scene finds him standing on top of a damaged building in Tokyo, looking for the high school where he will take his entrance examination.

Ōson sensō has been acclaimed as a post-*otaku* work, inheriting the type of meta-narrative inspired by Annō's *anime Neon Genesis Evangelion*, which accumulates references to classical and new-wave science-fiction novels, modern philosophy, psychoanalysis, and Biblical themes, but treats the genres critically. After *Evangelion*, numerous *anime* and *manga* works were made that present a world on the verge of destruction from the perspective of an individual absorbed in his personal relationship with a Romantic other. Called *Sekai-kei* (World maniacs), the genre's

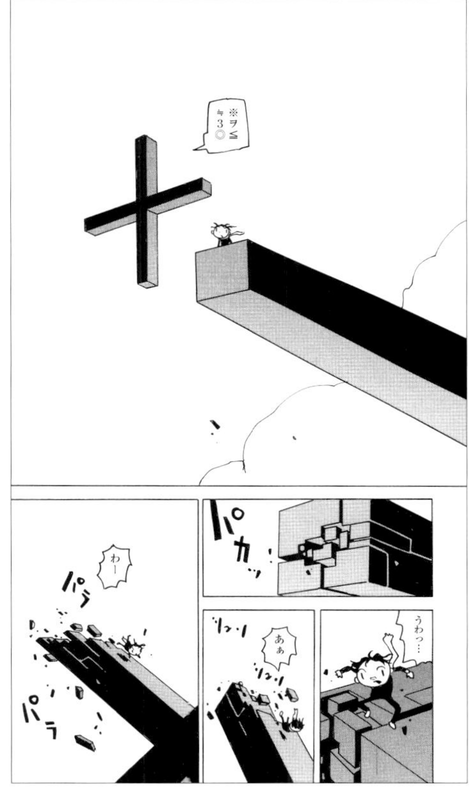

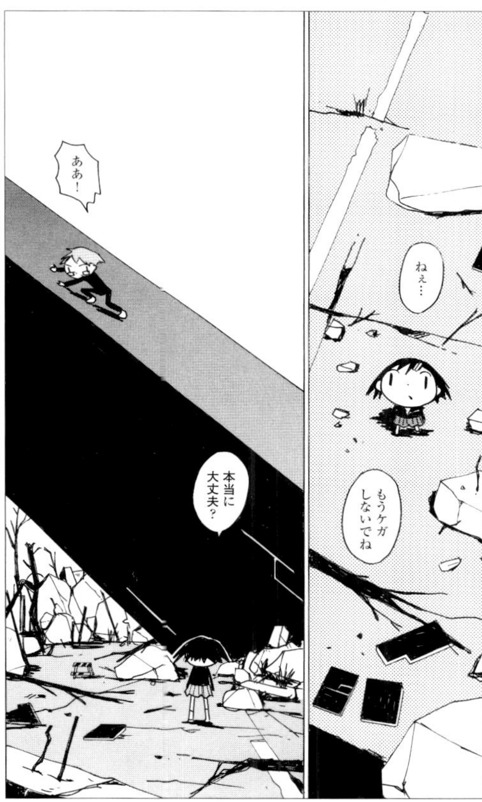

Panels from *Ōson Sensō* (Ō Village wars; published in English as *The Universal*), 2004
Courtesy and © 2004 Daisuke Nishijima/Hayakawa Publishing, Inc.

name ironically refers to the seamless conjunction of an apocalyptic theme with a character's absorption in an inner world.

Nishijima's comic narrative presents a self-reflexive critique of *Sekai-kei* fiction. Piecing together numerous references to classical science-fiction novels and popular films while reflecting contemporary youth's perception of living in a hopeless flatness of the everyday, Nishijima still emphasized his protagonist's will to break through to a fractured but open world outside.[23]

Both K.K. and Nishijima present "the externalization of an introverted *otaku* aesthetic" in innovative artistic ways. At the same time, the existential orientation of their works indicates their post-*otaku* standing, reminiscent of Annō's film *Love & Pop*. The emotional weight of their work evokes Murakami's statement in 2003 about the *otaku* generation born in 1970s. Describing them as second-generation *otaku* who mostly consume the creations of the first generation, he pointed to the dichotomy of their fetishizing of details on the one hand and almost aggressive pursuit of personal emotion on the other.[24] He suggested that the "maniacal pursuit" of the details that constitute their private universe might create a new Japanese expression that could be a dark counterpart to the American Pop of the 1960s. Where American Pop reflected the dissolution of the weight of culture in high consumer society, Japanese *otaku* art expresses the "weight" of yearning for the reality of life. Murakami suggested that young *otaku* people, "attaining the intensity of their life" through involvement in the apparently meaningless ("nonsensical") activities of "critically commenting on *otaku* culture, or pursuing their personally dictated taste," could create a genuinely post-*otaku* art, resisting the lightness of American Pop, although both are responses to the emptiness of life caused by postmodern capitalism.[25]

---

23 Haruki Kazano, "SF Book Scope Japan," *SF Magazine* (Tokyo) 45, no. 6 (June 2004): 122; Ryō Okikata, "Daisuke Nishijima's Ōson Wars," *SF Magazine* 45, no. 11 (November 2004): 46–47.

24 "Beat" Takeshi Kitano and Murakami, *Tsū āto* (Two art) (Tokyo: Pia Corporation, 2003), 158.

25 Ibid., 159.

5
Doing "Business": Everything for Creating New Rules of Art

IF CONCEPTUAL ART LOOKS FOR NEW RULES for thinking about art rather than merely presenting a new aesthetic style, Murakami is a conceptual artist. He has created a unique genre that integrates neglected local practices, finding a potentially new language in the communicative processes of people largely unrelated to the world of high art. In the formation of this conceptually vernacular artistic consciousness, Murakami resembles Mike Kelley, who found in the exchange of handmade gifts or drawings of high-school students a semiotic process, building a new kind of conceptual art on his interpretation. In fact, Murakami's dialectical integration of kitsch materials and methods of production to create a new genre of art and a new critical perspective opened up an entirely new category for the Japanese art world while proposing an example of an internationally relevant art emerging as a critical response to the conditions of a postmodern age, turning the deficiencies of a culturally postcolonial condition to its advantage.

In his appropriation of cultural signs, Murakami even recapitulates the original impetus of American Pop art. Just as Andy Warhol deliberately used icons of American popular culture, including advertising, cartoons, and images of celebrities that reflect a subconscious collective longing for wealth, glamour, and happiness in spite of high art's scorn for the popular and the vernacular, Murakami focused on the denigrated arts of *otaku* and professional entertainment as cultural symbols of people's relationship to contemporary society.[26] In so doing, Murakami invented a new brand of Japanese contemporary art that had outgrown Japan's cultural dependency on the West, which is analogous to the then-new visual language created by Warhol in resistance to the overwhelming cultural authority of modern European art.

In *Two Art* (2003), a book co-authored with film director and comedian "Beat" Takeshi Kitano, Murakami expressed his intention to "set new rules for playing the game of art."[27] While he had been providing new frames for thinking about

26 Ibid., 123–24.

27 G. R. Swenson, "The New American 'Sign Painters'" (1962), reprinted in *Pop Art: A Critical History*, ed. Steven Henry Madoff (Berkeley, California: University of California Press, 1997), 34.

Japanese art, he now wanted to establish a system of "supporting young artists showing and selling works of art, and cultivating a new audience" with rules proposed by those who make art "from the rock bottom of society."[28] Although he has played by the rules of the West, becoming a conceptual artist of a kind, Murakami now wants to play his own game, applying vernacular resources to their best advantage without depending on any pre-existing Western model.[29]

In his 2006 book *Geijutsu kigyōron* (The theory of art entrepreneurship), Murakami drew a parallel between artists and founders of new businesses. Underlying this provocative message is the urge to take the initiative in changing the ways art operates in Japan and to present art that is a unique product of post-modern Japan to a Western audience. Murakami proposed that Japan's postwar mentality, its "worldview without the essential ground," could attain sympathy and influence all over the world in a global age.[30]

With this new "entrepreneurial" phase, Murakami is taking great risks as an artist. First, his art-business analogy, coupled with his assertion of Japanese postmodern culture as a potential paradigm for the art of the global age, ironically allies him with cultural expansionism in spite of post-colonialist strategies. Second, the contradiction between the fundamentally private character of the "marginal" production that he draws from and his own aggressive pursuit of public influence remains unresolved. But the importance of his work is precisely owing to the visibility and scale of his ambition, as well as his ability to see possibility in obscure and despised corners of cultural production. His critical acuity, formed in response to the negativity of the postwar Japanese condition, takes him beyond its limits.

28 Ibid., 124–25.

29 Ibid., 150–51.

30 Murakami, *Geijutsu kigyōron* (The theory of art entrepreneurship) (Tokyo: Gentosha, 2006), 177–78.

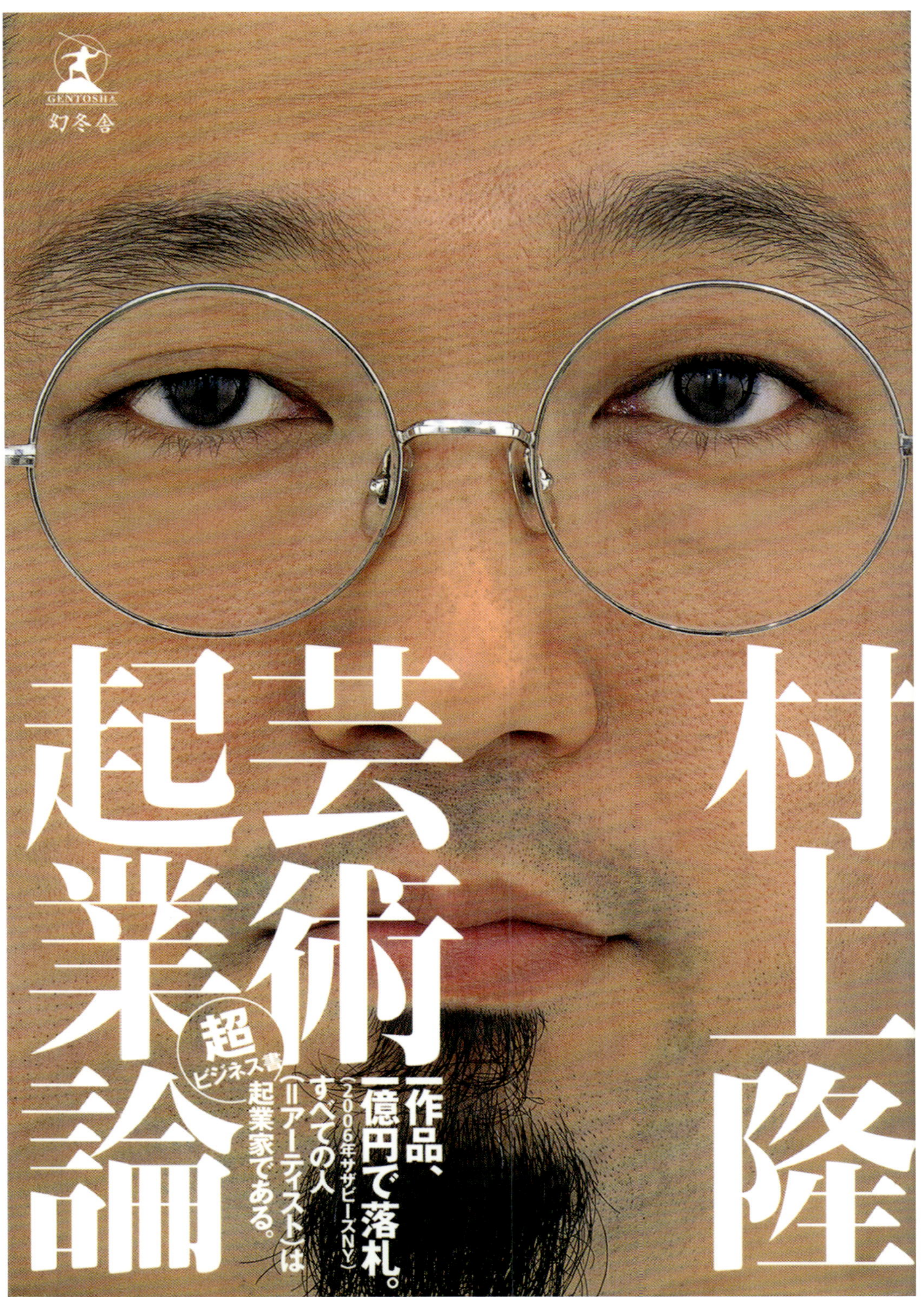

Cover of Takashi Murakami, *Geijutsu kigyōron* (The theory of art entrepreneurship) (Tokyo: Gentosha, 2006)

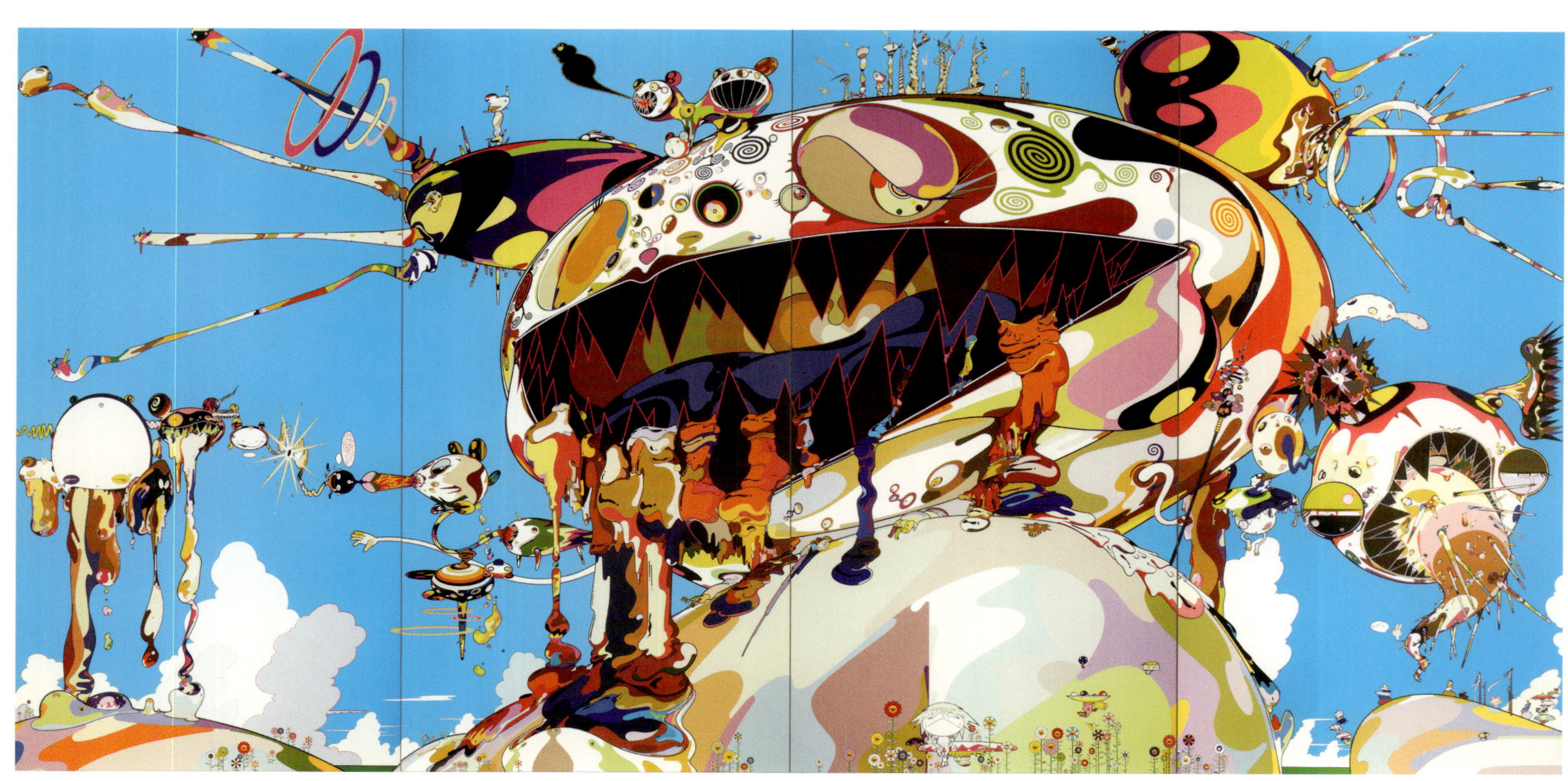

Takashi Murakami
Tan Tan Bo Puking—a.k.a. Gero Tan,
2002

The Meaning of the Nonsense of Excess

MIKA YOSHITAKE

"Vomiting uncontrollably, together with the stench of my breath, my phlegm curdles. As my tongue flays to pieces, my headache intensifies, and my eyes have become blind. As shit and piss flow, an excruciating pain runs through my entire body and I sense death is near. As I cry for help, I regret my cowardly behavior, preventing others from loving me until now; as I feel the futility of my escape, my nausea continues endlessly."

INSCRIPTION ON *TAN TAN BO PUKING*
—*A.K.A. GERO TAN* (2002)

An apocalyptic prefiguring of death, this scatological entry lies buried inside a miniscule thought bubble in Takashi Murakami's panoramic painting stretching over twenty-three feet wide, *Tan Tan Bo Puking—a.k.a. Gero Tan.*[1] Against a bright cerulean-blue sky, the enormous Gero Tan (literally, "vomiting phlegm boy") radiates the atmosphere like a violently exploding sun stretching light in painful slow motion. Like a viral DNA string, Murakami's mascot Mr. DOB transfigures into a nightmarish head with gaping carnivorous black teeth, while salamanders consume the liquid waste below. DOB's ears have transformed into Venus flytraps, while tentacles spurt from the pores of its meaty tongue. Unlike the slickly rendered DOBs of previous work, Gero Tan represents its ebullition: a figure on the verge of explosion, decimated by consumption and waste.

1 The figure was adapted from Tan Tan Bō (Phlegm Boy), a character from Shigeru Mizuki's serial manga *Ge Ge Ge no Kitarō* (1966–70) about modern-day Japanese demons.

Tan Tan Bo Puking made an unprecedented appearance in Murakami's oeuvre, offering flat singular portraits toward a grand-narrative landscape representing the birth and death of his characters. On Gero Tan's massive head, decorated with legions of eyes and spirals, is a web of three DOBs, each derived from different stages of their mythological evolution. The earliest DOB bears two monstrous multi-eyed twins, one of which emits an ominous black cloud from its mouth. To the right and left of Gero Tan, a multitude of DOBs formlessly shifting between eyes, phalluses, and embryos are linked by external organs that extend beyond the frame of the image as if to wrap around and consume the viewer's body.

Apart from the web of DOBs, tripartite guardians—Oval, Kaikai, and Kiki—diminutively make their stage appearance. Oval, the round all-knowing arbitrator, sits humbly, hand on knee, at bottom center on a wide-eyed mushroom in a candy-cane field of smiling flowers. To the right, the tiny rabbit-eared Kaikai leans out on the tips of his toes from a prickly tentacle of a DOB's contorted tongue, crying out "Daijōbu kayō?" (Are you alright?) to Gero Tan. Finally, to the far right, Kiki rests in a shrine on a plateau marked by four Shinto staffs dangling with sacred paper strips (*gohei*), signaling that the figure has transcended into a spirit (*kami*) about to cross into an ethereal afterlife. The shrine represents an offering (a manifestation of the *o-higan*, a Buddhist observance centered on the equinox during which prayers are read at an ancestral grave). Gero Tan holds a long staff clad with a tangle of skulls signaling his impending death.

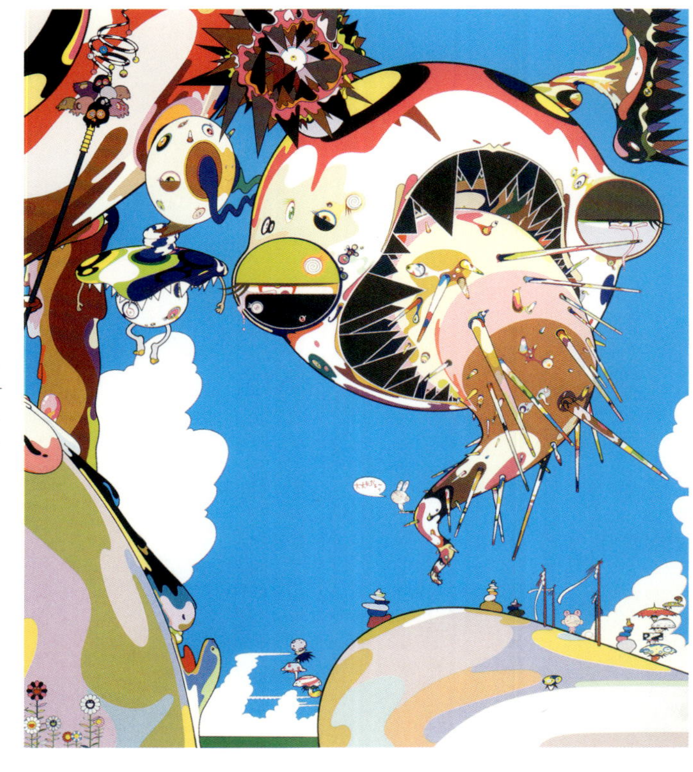

Takashi Murakami
Tan Tan Bo Puking—a.k.a. Gero Tan, 2002, detail

At the heart of Murakami's spectacular narrative is an allegory for society's unending desire for consumption, in which Gero Tan embodies this desire in a powerful image of sacrificial death. This idea of consumption is a correlative to Georges

Bataille's vision of expenditure in his theory of the general economy. In *La part maudite* (The accursed share, 1949), Bataille noted that every culture produces excess that must be expended and annihilated in order to sustain its own development. Bataille's vision is based on cultural surplus and society's need for an unproductive form of expenditure (exemplified in the rituals of the potlatch in archaic societies) rather than economic scarcity. If one extends Bataille's vision, surplus in contemporary capitalism becomes replaced by capital through the process of investment as a source of constantly multiplying surplus value (a reserve of excess). This vision of excess is key to understanding the evolution and life cycle of DOB in *Tan Tan Bo Puking*, where Murakami literally takes up the accumulation of capital to the point of self-destruction. One can think of Murakami's images as placed in a cyclical reserve (capital) that is dependent on their very loss.

It is my intention to examine the symbolic operations in Murakami's work, specifically the understanding of consumption as a destructive tendency, beginning with his early experiments with parody and spectacle; the evolution of his branding of DOB; and finally, *Tan Tan Bo Puking*. Murakami's visual language in the work can be positioned within a larger trajectory of destructive aesthetics in postwar Japanese countercultural art, and thus I situate his practice in an alternative narrative from the Pop art context within which he is predominantly associated. By examining Murakami's visual language, I will describe an operation rooted in tensions between consumption and excess on the one hand, and loss and intimacy on the other.

Consumption, Parody, and the Aesthetic of "Nonsense"

DURING THE EARLY 1990S, Murakami's work emerged from the discursive terrain of a new generation of Japan's "Neo Pop" simulationists (a term first coined by Japanese art critic Noi Sawaragi in 1992 to describe artists such as Kōdai Nakahara, Tarō Chiezō, Yukinori Yanagi, and Kenji Yanobe)[2] who, like the appropriation

2 See Noi Sawaragi, "Roripoppu—sono saishōgen no seimei" (Lollipop: That smallest form of life), *Bijutsu Techō* 44, no. 651 (March 1992): 90–94.

Takashi Murakami
Signboard TAMIYA, 1991

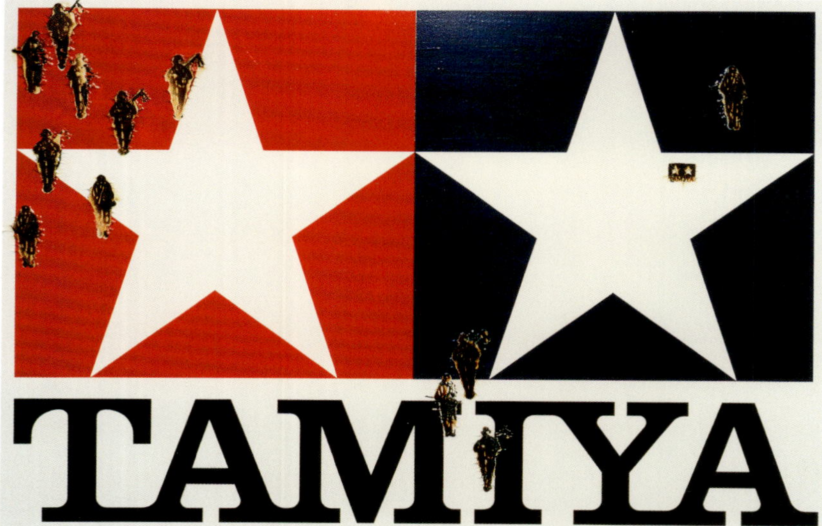

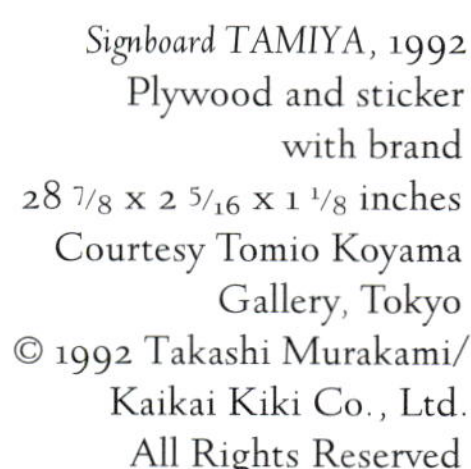
Signboard TAMIYA, 1992
Plywood and sticker
with brand
28 7/8 x 2 5/16 x 1 1/8 inches
Courtesy Tomio Koyama
Gallery, Tokyo

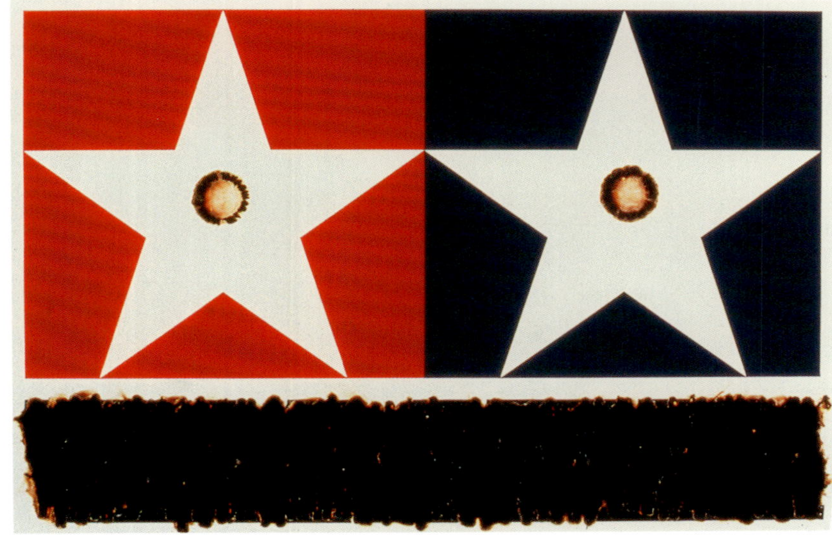

Signboard TAKASHI, 1992

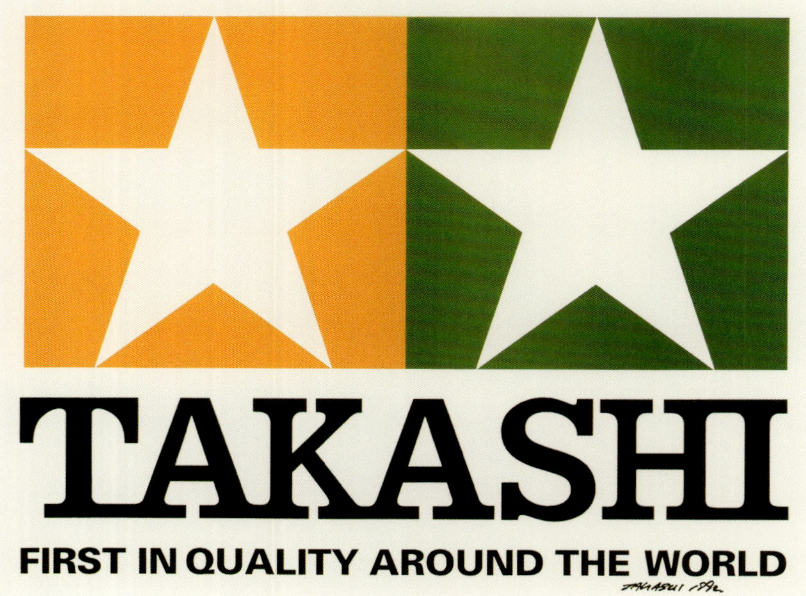

artists in the United States, deployed commodities and consumer products in their practice to "demythologize their charm through a sarcastic modification."[3] According to critic Midori Matsui, works by these artists "featured pop icons and consumer products to show the complicity between the lack of critical reflection (represented by 'cute' consumer products) and the tendency to absorb individual difference into 'the eternal embrace' that underlies Japanese fascism."[4] The absorption of "individual difference" within the context of Neo Pop's mode of simulation is a key reference to understanding how their work addresses problems of cultural reification, which distinguishes them from 1980s appropriation art in the United States.

Already in circulation are clichéd perceptions by French poststructuralist critics who have constructed Japan as a signifier for the purposes of their own semiotic advancement.[5] Citing Japan's "bohemic" sensibility of nature and quick assimilation of technology as emblematic features, Matsui explained in her essay "Beyond Signs: Hybridity in Japanese Art" (1995) how these scholars posit a "Japanese subject (that) cancels its active agency and paradoxically fulfills its spiritual potency."[6] Not only does this type of Orientalist interpretation lead Japan to be perceived as an "exotic Other" or as a "spectacle," which discredits the production of a rational subject, but the Other becomes "internalized by the Japanese themselves and exploited as a strategy in the sale of Japanese 'culture' to the West."[7] It is Homi Bhabha's term "hybridity" to which Matsui turns to define the Neo Pop artists and their ability to retain difference and resist the temptation to fetishize form. Neo Pop thus critiques the condition of Japan's own internalization of foreign perceptions of Japanese subjectivity.

In his Tamiya series (1989–91), Murakami assembled hundreds of plastic 1/35 scale U.S. Infantry models (West European Theater) manufactured by Tamiya (a Japanese toy company specializing in model kits) and placed them on boats and minimalist boxes made out of synthetic resin. Through this series, he began revealing the duplicitous structure of consumption: that is, the marketing of difference (Tamiya) in the structure of the same (toy companies) by exposing the sign-value of the commodity, the Tamiya brand. As Hal Foster noted, "We consume more than the object as such; it is the brand name that triggers our desire, the

3 Midori Matsui, "Murakami Takashi: Nihilist Agonistes," in *Takashi Murakami: "Which Is Tomorrow?—Fall in Love"* (Tokyo: SCAI The Bathhouse, 1994), 35.

4 Matsui's characterization is based on Sawaragi's conversation with curator Fumio Nanjō, published in "Dangerously Cute," *Flash Art* 25, no. 163 (March–April 1992): 77. See also Matsui, "Beyond Signs: Hybridity in Japanese Art," in *The Age of Anxiety*, exh. cat. (Toronto: The Power Plant, 1995), 65.

5 The most famous of which is Roland Barthes's *Empire of Signs* (1970), trans. Richard Howard (New York: Hill and Wang, 1982).

6 Matsui, "Beyond Signs," 64.

7 Ibid.

commodity-as-sign that becomes our fetish."[8] In *Signboard TAKASHI* (1992), he took the radical step of appropriating the Tamiya motto "first in quality around the world," substituting his name for Tamiya's in the same lettering and font along with the brand's double-star logo, thereby replacing the fetish of the commodity-sign with the aura of the artist himself. Surprisingly, however, we do not learn anything about the artist, whose qualities are purposely obscured and made irrelevant. Rather, the work highlights the universalizing power of the Tamiya brand as a sign of "qualitative difference," though a simulated one, not unlike the perceptions of French semioticians who particularized aspects of Japanese culture to universalize their own agenda. Here are the beginnings of how Murakami's work is born from sign play through the structures of marketing and cultural reception: the consumption of "difference" as a simulacrum of Japan's identity, a fake form of particularity that has no origin or purpose but to serve the market or empower the desiring (universal) subject. As with his Neo Pop peers, Murakami critiqued the condition of Japan's own internalization of foreign perceptions of Japanese subjectivity by appropriating this simulacral identity and selling it as the epitome of the postmodern subject.

One might understand Neo Pop's particular strategy against the historical backdrop of Japan's own relational pairing with the West. Japan's drive for international and intellectual equivalence with the West in the modern era can be understood through the relation between particularity and universality as theorized by literary scholar Naoki Sakai. Sakai demonstrated how the country's mimetic desire to possess equal faculties of thought (such as philosophy) with the West has resulted in a hierarchy between Japan and the West that is driven by a constant sense of self-lack. Paradoxically, this mimetic desire has been the underlying impetus for Japan's intellectual progress and national strength. This relationship encompasses a reinforcement of "modernity" in Japan, which is articulated by Sakai as a relational historico-geopolitical pairing between premodern Japan (particular) and modern West (universal). In the process of modernization, Japan has affirmed itself through and against the West, as the West has been the assumed condition of possibility for the universal validity of knowledge. Sakai wrote:

8 Hal Foster, "1986," in *Art Since 1900* (New York: Thames and Hudson, 2004), 600.

9 Naoki Sakai, "The Problem of 'Japanese Thought': The Formation of 'Japan' and the Schema of Configuration," in *Translation and Subjectivity: On "Japan" and Cultural Nationalism* (Minneapolis: University of Minnesota Press, 1997), 172.

10 Jirō Yoshihara, quoted in Ming Tiampo, "Gutai & Informel: Post-War Art in Japan and France, 1945–1965," Ph.D. dissertation, Northwestern University, 2003, 61.

> Japan's uniqueness and identity are provided insofar as Japan stands out as a particular object in the universal field of the West. Only when it is integrated into Western universalism does it gain its own identity as a particularity...Japan becomes endowed with and aware of its "self" only when it is recognized by the West. [The] positing of Japan's identity in Western terms...in return establishes the centrality of the West. Universalism and particularism reinforce each other.[9]

In this relational logic, the interdependence between the two (particular and universal) necessitates a critique of not only the dominant West but of Japan itself.

In Murakami's early performances, he confronted this relational logic between Japan and the West by humorously exposing Japan's own aim toward particularity within its local context. This began with his 1992 reenactments of postwar Japanese avant-garde performances by Gutai and Hi Red Center. In his first performance, Murakami parodied Gutai's imperative for the "new," derived from its leader Jirō Yoshihara's famous dictum "Do something that no one before you has done...Do something new."[10] Crashing through a row of large paper screens with his entire body in *Kami yaburi—Murakami Sabotarō Saemon Ryūnosuke* (Paper-ripping—Murakami Sabotarō Saemon Ryūnosuke, 1992), Murakami restaged in fully absurdist mode Saburō Murakami's "heroic" action-based work

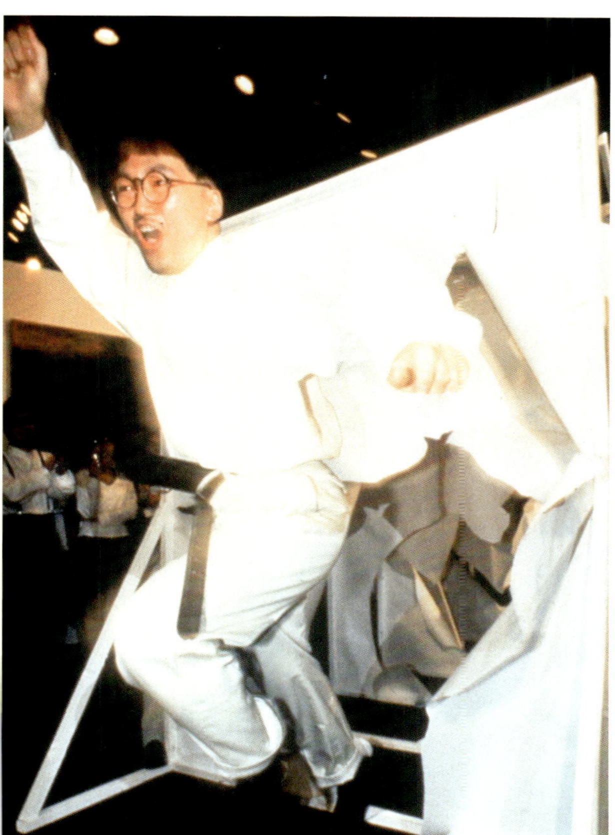

Takashi Murakami
Performance of *Kami yaburi—Murakami Sabotarō Saemon Ryūnosuke* (Paper-ripping—Murakami Sabotarō Saemon Ryūnosuke), Tokyo, 1992

from the 1950s. The piece was a perfect target for Murakami, who possesses the same last name as the elder Gutai artist and mimicked his look (helmet-shaped hair, white clothes, and black-framed glasses) for the performance. In the original context of the elder Murakami's performance—as well as of Kazuo Shiraga's *Challenging Mud* (1955), for which the artist wrestled against the earth with his bare hands and feet—the performer's body was a renewed site of liberatory action embodying the visceral effects of war's destruction. In its decontextualized restaging forty years later, instead of Gutai's sentiment for cultural renewal, Murakami's parody embodied gaps in the global historical reception of the group, whose particularity, born from an imperative for the new, was simply read as "nonsensical" in the Japanese mainstream art context.[11]

On the other hand, Gutai's experimental aesthetic was morphologically similar to the French Art Informel, and it was precisely this similarity that attracted Michel Tapié, Informel's ideologue, who "discovered" the group within his local agenda of existential materialism.[12] Murakami's restaging thus intervenes in this gap by hyper-accentuating the "exotically Japanese"[13] sentiment of the West and collapsing it with the local perception of "nonsense" by Japanese contemporaries. By integrating these two perceptions, Murakami in fact took up a different notion of "nonsense," which is not an "antithesis to sense"[14] but a nihilistic form of ambiguity between two disparate contexts. Murakami's satirical restaging was as much a humorous attempt to expose the gaps of cultural perception as it was a serious engagement with the potentiality of "nonsense" to serve as a productive site of meaning.

In another example, Murakami restaged 1960s Japanese avant-garde group Hi Red Center's street happening *Movement to Promote the Cleanup of the Metropolitan Area (Be Clean!)* (1964). In the original performance, the members of Hi Red Center—Genpei Akasegawa, Natsuyuki Nakanishi, and Jirō Takamatsu—wore face masks and lab coats and meticulously "sanitized" the streets of Tokyo with brooms, rags, toothbrushes, and magnifying glasses as a humorous gesture mocking the city's beautification project for the Tokyo Summer Olympics. For *Osaka Mixer Project* (1992), Murakami restaged the happening with fellow artists Tsuyoshi Ozawa

11 The group was never critically received within Japan until the 1970s. See Shigeo Chiba, *Gendai bijutsu itsudatsu-shi 1945–1985* (A history of deviations in contemporary art 1945–1985) (Tokyo: Shōbun-sha, 1986), 25.

12 For more on the problems of cultural translation between Gutai and Informel, see Tiampo, "Gutai & Informel."

13 Here I refer to the structure of exoticism "by which one language appropriates elements from a foreign or ancient language to recognize and rationalize its own contemporary atavisms." See Benjamin H. D. Buchloh, "Parody and Appropriation in Francis Picabia, Pop, and Sigmar Polke" (1982), in *Neo-Avantgarde and Culture Industry: Essays on European and American Art from 1955 to 1975* (Cambridge, Massachusetts: The MIT Press, 2000), 354.

14 Matsui, "Murakami Takashi," 37.

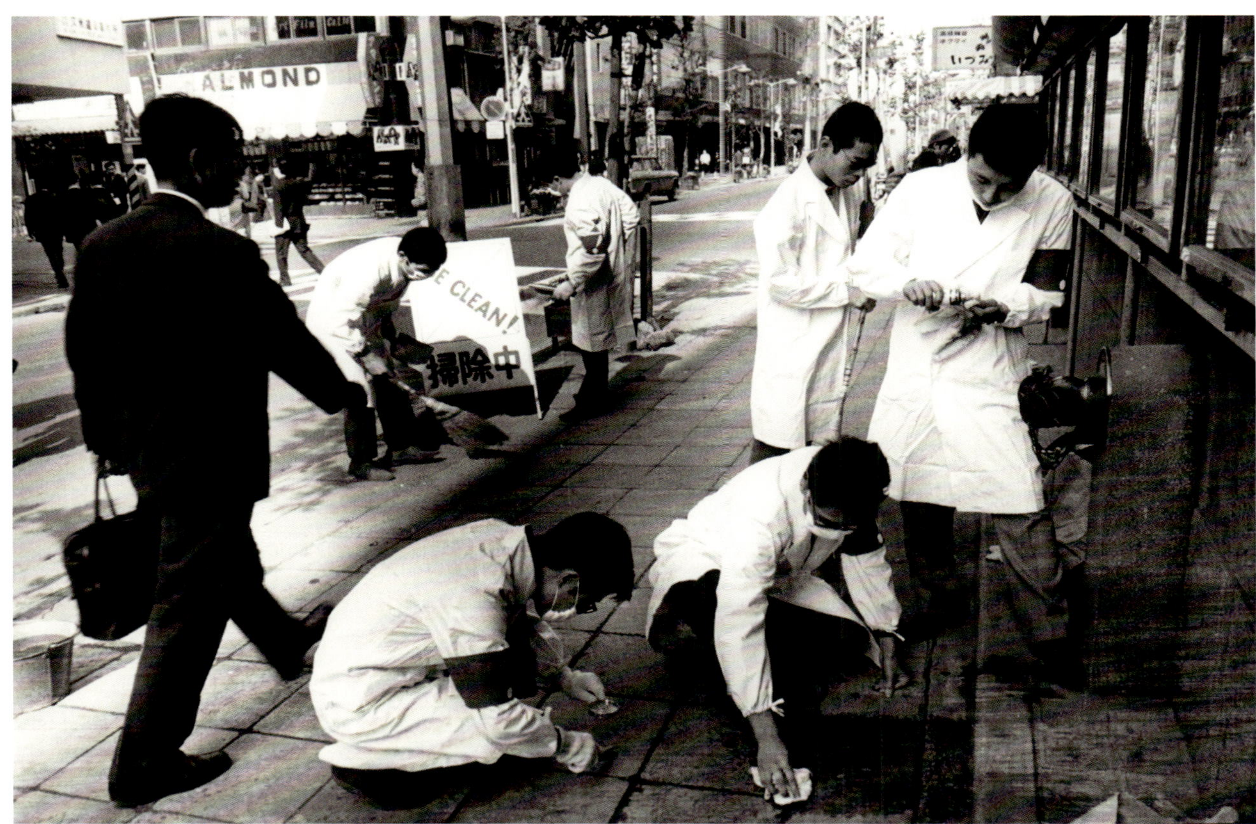

Hi Red Center
Movement to Promote the Cleanup of the Metropolitan Area (Be Clean!), 1964
Performance in Tokyo

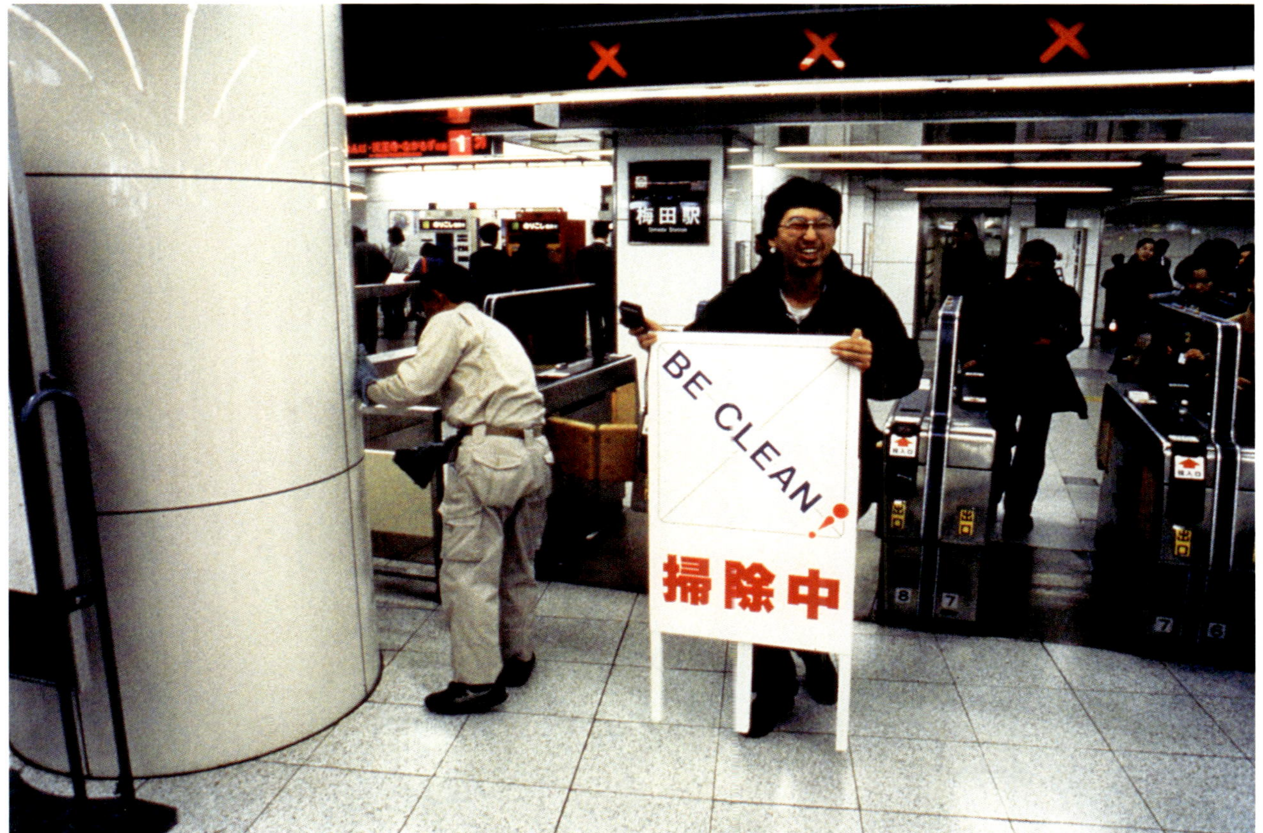

Small Village Center
(Takashi Murakami, Masato Nakamura, and Tsuyoshi Ozawa)
Osaka Mixer Project, 1992
Performance in underground shopping center, Osaka, Japan

and Masato Nakamura in and around the streets of central Osaka's Umeda station. Like Hi Red Center (whose group name was an acronym derived from the English translation of the first character of each artist's surname), they called themselves "Small Village Center" (Small from Ozawa, Village from *Mura*kami, and Center from *Naka*mura). Furthermore, they wore armbands with Hi Red Center's trademark logo (a red exclamation point) with an additional dot and carried the same exclamatory sign, "Be Clean! Sōjichū (Cleaning in process)," while police officers reprimanded them for public disturbance.

For Japanese avant-garde artists involved in the open-juried Yomiuri Indépendant exhibitions of the early 1960s,[15] the body was a site of both spectacle and self-degradation. Their works incorporate a vast storehouse of industrial and junk materials recalling Japan's historical avant-garde group Mavo (1923–25) and their anarchic assemblages of rifles, bottle caps, shoeboxes, and human-mechanized vending machines. Not surprisingly, some of the Yomiuri artists formed a collective called Neo Dada Organizers (or Neo Dada), marking a "return" to avant-garde strategies. Employing the material stuff of everyday life, Neo Dada artists infamously wrapped newspaper around their bodies and walked city streets advertising their shows or used boxing gloves dipped in black paint to punch across packing material. Their works were often discarded or set on fire after an exhibition, a comment on society's new imperative for consumption and waste as subjects of Occupation culture, as well as the decaying historical memory of the city.

Parodying Hi Red Center's happening, Murakami revealed his engagement with Neo-Dadaist strategies of humor combined with the locally specific trajectory of the insistence on the useless, the ephemeral, and the spectacular. His performances, reenacting and decontextualizing the original actions nearly three decades later, embrace the absurdity of the acts while simultaneously forcing the re-experience of a destructive aesthetics that could no longer contain a viable form of urgency in early 1990s Japanese culture.

Furthermore, by attaching his name to the history of Japanese avant-garde practices as well as to consumer culture vis-à-vis *Signboard TAKASHI*, he linked

15 The Yomiuri newspaper company launched the Yomiuri Indépendant exhibitions (1949–63), held annually at the Tokyo Metropolitan Museum of Art, one of the first venues that allowed artists to freely exhibit their work without a presiding jury.

himself to the proper pedigree of both arenas (the geographic specificity of the avant-garde and globally recognizable trademarks of pop culture). In doing so, the artist bridged these two contexts by addressing the ambiguity between the particular and the universal. That is, these local avant-garde practices were driven by critics (most prominently Ichirō Haryū) who were addressing the need for international contemporaneity (competitiveness)[16] with art practices in the West, while an overt form of national pride underlies the Tamiya brand motto "first in quality around the world."

"Nonsense" and Spectacle

THROUGH THE APPROPRIATION AND PARODY of Japanese avant-garde performances, what distinguished Murakami from his Neo Pop peers was his humorous engagement with fleeting acts of the absurd or, perhaps more specifically, spectacles intentionally stripped of meaning. He called this "the meaning of the nonsense of meaning" (derived from the title of his 1993 Ph.D. dissertation "Considering 'the Meaning of the Nonsense of Meaning' in Art"). Murakami's phrase encompasses a loose association of ideas that primarily affirm negation and the presence of meaninglessness in everyday life. Ideas range from the radical potential of "nonsense" (*nansensu*), a term popularized in early 1970s student demonstrations with references to *manga* of the period,[17] the elevation of useless objects to extraordinary status in Akasegawa's Tomason series (1972),[18] and the grand scale and mythic pastiche of Neo-Expressionist painters Julian Schnabel and Anselm Kiefer.[19] This last reference is peculiar as it is precisely Murakami's creation of a grand narrative in *Tan Tan Bo Puking* that aligns him with 1980s Neo-Expressionist painting. However, the work's reference to self-destruction and lack of synthetic pastiche distinguish it from the heroic subjectivity present in the Euro-American context.

Murakami brought forth the most elaborate form of spectacle in his most theatrical installation, *Sea Breeze* (1992). This piece comprises sixteen stadium Klieg lights displayed in two back-to-back rings and placed inside a stainless-steel box

16 See Reiko Tomii, "Historicizing 'Contemporary Art': Some Discursive Practices in *Gendai Bijutsu* in Japan," *Positions: East Asia Cultures Critique* 12, no. 3 (winter 2004).

17 Murakami interestingly appropriated Fujio Akatsuka's popular comic *Tensai Bakabon* (translated loosely as "genius and stupid kid") in *Bakabon Project* (1991). Akatsuka was often criticized for being status quo, which undoubtedly attracted Murakami even more.

18 Genpei Akasegawa, *Chōgeijutsu Tomason* (Ultra-art Tomason) (Tokyo: Byakuya shobō, 1985); pocketbook edition (Tokyo: Chikuma bunko, 1987). As Reiko Tomii described, "A compilation of *haiku*-like visual puns, the series consists of nameless works of art hidden in the everyday, such as *A Record of the Wind*, concentric traces left by wind-blown tree branches on a concrete wall that the artist and his followers uncovered and photographed." See Tomii, "State v. (Anti-)Art: *Model 1,000-Yen Note Incident* by Akasegawa Genpei and Company," *Positions: East Asia Cultures Critique* 10, no. 1 (spring 2002): 161.

19 See Murakami, "Bijutsu ni okeru 'imi no muimi no imi' o megutte" (Considering "the meaning of the nonsense of meaning" in art), Ph.D. dissertation, Tokyo National University of Fine Arts and Music, 1993.

on wheels. In its first installment at "Anomaly" (1992), an exhibition curated by Sawaragi at the Röntgen Kunst Institut in Tokyo, the sculpture was placed in the center of a room, its lights hidden behind stainless-steel shutters. On either side were walls painted lemon yellow and pink respectively, each marked with two vertical slits of the opposing color and spotlit between the slits. According to the artist, the slits had connections to philosopher Akira Asada's writings on "Klein's Pot,"[20] a mathematical theory derived from fusing two Möbius strips to form an intersecting bottle, where one is unable to distinguish between "inside" and "outside" surfaces. During the opening, a nude male performer danced on a tower spinning hula hoops, while the shutters slowly opened to reveal the canopy of flashing lights. Faced with the blinding halos and burning heat, as well as the circling hula hoops, viewers seemed to succumb to the work's heightened sublime, which resonated with a hyper-religious or carnal experience in an endless spiraling rhythm of light and heat. In an act of phenomenological violence upon the viewer, the artistic labor here seemed to be charged on the consumption of the audience's very presence.

What is at stake in *Sea Breeze* is the representational crisis in Japan at the height of consumer society: an allegorical failure between production and consumption, image and referent, self and body, in an era where heightened consumerism had fallen and one's nationhood challenged. In Asada's words, "What is 'excessive' is realized through capitalism's unending everyday forward progress, which itself *tries* to produce 'abundance' or 'surplus'... Everyday life itself has become a continuous, profane 'potlatch.'"[21] In this context, the 1990s Neo Pop artists can be seen as forming part of a wider response to this symbolic crisis: the phenomena of a nihilistic and ironic positioning of simulated identities emerging from subculture such as *kogyaru* (literally "young girl," referring to the cultural and stylistic fetish of teenage schoolgirls) and *otaku* (geek subculture) and a neo-nationalist attempt to recover an authentic identity through an existential imaginary.[22] On the heels of this crisis, we might read Murakami's work as situated between these two phenomena: simulated identities as well as a neo-nationalist imaginary predicated on consumption and excess.

---

20 "Klein's Pot" is the Japanese translation of nineteenth-century German mathematician Felix Klein's "Klein bottle." Murakami knew Akira Asada's famous book, *Kōzō to chikara* (Structure and power, 1983), which had many illustrations of Klein's Pot throughout. This idea would later be tied to Murakami's three amorphous DOB paintings *Klein's Pot A, B, and C* (1994–97). Murakami, interview with author, 28 November 2006.

21 Marilyn Ivy, quoting Asada's *Kōzō to chikara*, in "Critical Texts, Mass Artifacts: The Consumption of Knowledge in Postmodern Japan," in *Postmodernism and Japan*, ed. Masao Miyoshi and H. D. Harootunian, 5th ed. (Durham, North Carolina: Duke University Press, 2003), 44 n 6.

22 See Yumiko Iida, "Between the Technique of Living an Endless Routine and the Madness of Absolute Degree Zero: Japanese Identity and the Crisis of Modernity in the 1990s," *Positions: East Asia Cultures Critique* 8, no. 2 (fall 2000): 423–64.

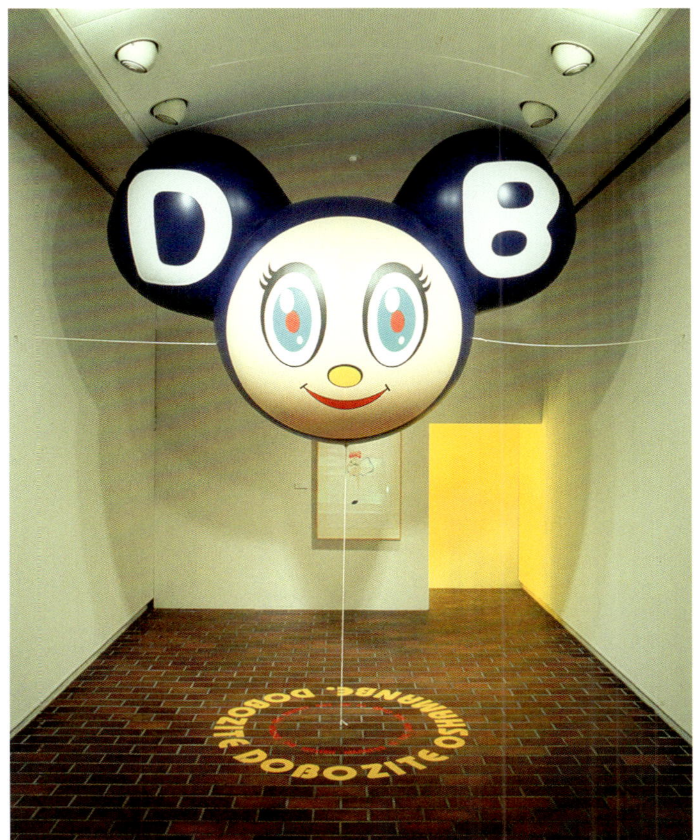

Takashi Murakami
Mr. DOB, 1994
Vinyl chloride, helium gas, and cutting sheet
92 1/2 x 120 1/16 x 70 7/8 inches
Courtesy Galerie Emmanuel Perrotin, Paris and Miami, and Tomio Koyama Gallery, Tokyo
Installation at Louisiana Museum of Modern Art, Humlebaek, Denmark, 1995

DOB™

SINCE THE BEGINNING, DOB has been a unique alibi for Murakami and his talent for branding. The dada-like phrase "dobozite dobozite oshamanbe," from silly gags found in early 1970s Japanese *manga* combined with the famous gag by comedian Tōru Yuri,[23] was conceived as a signboard and then condensed into the three-letter DOB to form a trademark pop character. With a large round O-shaped face and ears bearing the letters D or B, DOB straddles two sources of inspiration—the Sega mascot Sonic the Hedgehog and Doraemon, the intelligent and endearing Japanese cat-like robot from the future—yet its identity remains as evasive as the nonsensical phrase from which it was conceived. While DOB's origins as a product of language rather than commodity imagery has been a site of investigation more recently,[24] what is also at stake is how DOB symbolically operates as an agent

23 The phrase "dobozite dobozite" (why, why) is derived from Noboru Kawasaki s 1970s *manga Inakappe taishō* (Country general), in which characters deliberately mispronounced 'dōshite" (why) as "dobozite dobozite" when scolded or depressed in order to incite self-pity. The phrase was combined with Tōru Yuri's gag "oshamanbe," a pun on the name of a town in Hokkaido incorporating the syllable *man* as the slang term for female genitalia. See Murakami, "Life as a Creator," in *Takashi Murakami: Summon Monsters? Open the Door? Heal? Or Die?*, exh. cat. (Tokyo: Museum of Contemporary Art, 2001), 130–47.

24 See Sianne Ngai, "The Cuteness of the Avant-Garde," *Critical Inquiry* 31, no. 4 (summer 2005): 811–47.

of consumption in Murakami's visual lexicon: [1] an anonymous and malleable icon produced as a marketable brand, and [2] an abstract and fleeting morphing life-form representative of our endless desire to consume.

One of the first versions of DOB featured his tiny face in otutline floating atop a large square pool of deep blue in *DOB Genesis* (1993). During this period, Murakami was experimenting with monochromes and primary colors through a comparative analysis between *gunjō*, the most valued color of ultramarine blue unique to the field of *nihonga*,[25] and the blue most closely related to the one associated with Yves Klein. Murakami paid homage not so much to the formal reduction of the monochrome as to the qualitative value of Klein's patented color, International Klein Blue (IKB). For Klein, the immaterial presence of the pictorial field was vital from the beginning. His choice of blue came in 1957 with his "Proposte monochrome, epoca blù" (Proposition of the blue epoch) exhibition in Milan, for which he hung identically sized canvases of blue on a system of brackets so that they projected away from the wall. He found that spaces were saturated with invisible blue and proposed that the authentic quality of painting was found beyond the visible, which was the pictorial sensibility in a raw material state. The emphasis was not on painting as production in its display of seriality and repetition, but the spectacle of painting itself.[26] The fact that he sold them for different prices proved that, first, "the pictorial quality of each painting was perceptible by means of something else besides the material appearance," and second, "those who chose recognized this state of things which I call pictorial sensibility."[27]

In Murakami's case, the monochrome acts as a mere support for DOB. Reflecting back on the aims of his curatorial endeavor "Coloriage" (2002), in which the artist parodically commented on Japanese art's historic tendency to "outline" (mimic) the precedents of modern art in Euro-America,[28] here Murakami places his figure atop the blue planar field in a gesture that reverses the historical imperative toward modernist abstraction. Whereas Klein's is patented monochrome IKB as a symbol to legitimize the authenticity of his "pictorial sensibility" (a unique attribute of artistic identification), Murakami's icon remains anonymous, never completely interchangeable with an expressive artistic sensibility à la

25 *Nihonga* is the school of Japanese-style painting in which Murakami trained at Tokyo National University of Fine Arts and Music. *Nihonga* was created in 1890 during the Meiji period as a reaction against the importation of Western-style techniques (*yōga*) in Japan. Both are stylistic developments unique to Japan, but what makes *nihonga* distinct is the use of an opaque and non–water-soluble pigment that adheres to the surface with a type of glue called *nikawa*. One of the most characteristic colors in *nihonga* is the rich deep blue hue of *gunjō*.

26 Buchloh, "Plenty or Nothing: From Yves Klein's *Le Vide* to Arman's *Le Plein*" (1998), in *Neo-Avantgarde and Culture Industry*, 264.

27 Yves Klein, quoted in Thierry de Duve, "Yves Klein, or The Dead Dealer," *October*, no. 49 (summer 1989): 78.

28 Murakami, "Interview with Hélène Kelmachter," in *Takashi Murakami: Kaikai Kiki*, revised version (London: Serpentine Gallery; and Paris: Fondation Cartier pour l'art contemporain, 2002), 11.

Signboard TAKASHI. As the artist himself stated, "This is an inquiry into the 'secret of market survival,' or the 'universality' of characters like Mickey Mouse, Sonic the Hedgehog, Doraemon, Miffy, Hello Kitty, even the Hong Kong–made rip-offs."[29] Born from a simulation of language and cartoon imagery, Murakami's production of DOB comes from an engagement with how an icon emerges as an object of mass consumption and circulates as a distinctive registered trademark to be used, reused, bought, and sold. Like gold, it is a privileged and exclusive product of exchange, inherently useless, but an object of pure surplus and excess.[30]

DOB further takes on an anthropomorphic development through a fleeting form of desire and reification. Like the nonsensical phrase from which it was derived, DOB is directed by sound, speed, fluidity, and diffusion as super-sensuous attributes of the commodity fetish. In *ZuZaZaZaZaZa* (1994), which is derived from the onomatopoetia used in *manga* to express the sound of a baseball player sliding into home plate, DOB playfully leaps above a lightning splash of milky white fluid. Similarly, in *Pschiiit (red)* (1995), the name of a French soda stemming from the sound made when twisting a cap open and an obvious pun on the English word "shit," DOB's face emerges from a vapor of red bubbles. Further, Murakami charted DOB's initial evolution from a simple earless character (yellow) to a one-eared one (red), then to a fully formed DOB (blue) in the series Stew (1995), each generated from the same stylized liquid swirl. DOB's beginnings are thus imbued with its own disappearance, melting into a stream of waves or evaporating into thin air. (Like laughter, these fleeting moments are embedded with humor rather than as a tangible object.) The images alert us to the superfluous value of signs, the endless chain of reification stemming from the displacement of one's desires through consuming one object to the next.

29 Murakami, "Life as a Creator," 33.

30 See Jean-Joseph Goux, *Symbolic Economies: After Marx and Freud*, trans. Jennifer Curtiss Gage (Ithaca, New York: Cornell University Press, 1990).

Takashi Murakami
Pschiiit (red), 1995
Acrylic on canvas mounted on board
18 1/8 x 18 1/8 inches
Courtesy Galerie Emmanuel Perrotin, Paris and Miami

Murakami's DOB is not a character so much as an erratic manifestation of one's desire to consume and the ceaseless regeneration of this impulse.

In *The Castle of Tin Tin* (1998), with links perhaps to the famous Belgian comic *The Adventures of Tintin* (1929–86) by Hergé, Murakami featured multiple DOBs stacked atop one another in a swirling spiral indicating the speed of accumulation (the spiraling image is especially akin to the cover of Hergé's *The Seven Crystal Balls* [1948]); by contrast, in the amorphous figures of the Chaos series (1998–99), DOB disperses into a web of forms signaling desire's unstable diffusion, like a mood thermometer measuring varying degrees of satisfaction that never reaches fulfillment. As philosopher-sociologist Zygmunt Bauman recently pointed out, "consumerism is assumed to mean greed for acquisition; the wish to accumulate things, to have more and more...It now seems that it is the rapidity, the promptness of disposing of things, which is the secret of contemporary consumerism: not accumulation, not acquisition, but change."[31] Murakami's branding of DOB is thus an exercise in not only deconstructing the sign value of the art commodity, but in charting the effects of the hedonism, degeneration, and dispersion of desire in the process of consumption.

Excess

MURAKAMI'S PRACTICE HAS ENGAGED in a symbolic play of consumption through strategies of branding, historical parody, spectacular forms of excess, anonymity, and the futility of desire. These strategies stem back to Murakami's critical (albeit anarchic) affirmation of negation in his aim early on to define the "meaning of the nonsense of meaning." In *Tan Tan Bo Puking*, these terms are combined together to take on a destructive shift that one might describe as a turn toward intimacy.

In *Tan Tan Bo Puking*, one perceives the features of a history painting reflective of an uncensored release of primal need, lust, violence, suffering, and rebirth, all of which take place in the avarice of consumption. Here Gero Tan performs a heightened multiplication of waste, generating a chain of DOBs who take part

31 Zygmunt Bauman, "Liquid Arts," *Theory, Culture & Society* 24, no. 1 (January 2007): 123.

in this ritual act. On the left side of the painting, this chain is most graphically illustrated with a gout-like protrusion from the side of Gero Tan, morphing into a DOB that spews a large phallus, a black eye, and an open hand. Hanging from the cheek of a white DOB with an enlarged forehead is the whiskered Nezumi Otoko (Ratman), the filthy three-hundred-year-old rat ghost from Shigeru Mizuki's comic (the same comic from which Gero Tan was derived), full of ulcers and skin disease and whose breath and discharge are so toxic that they render unconscious those in its path.

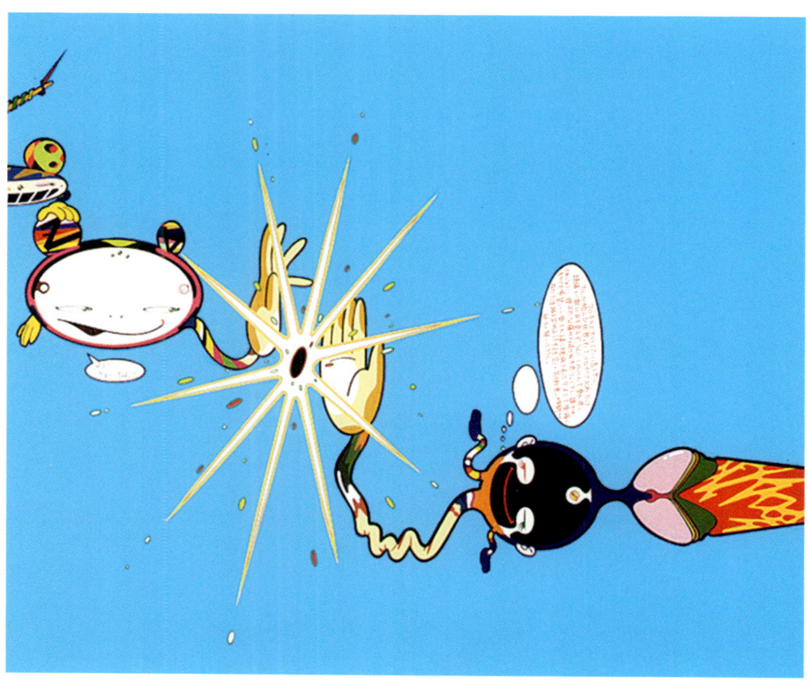

Takashi Murakami
Tan Tan Bo Puking—a.k.a. Gero Tan, 2002, detail

While the noxious nature of the painting overpowers any benevolent read, the hidden climax lies in the spark of light that flashes between two elongated hands as a synapse between the two chains; this is symbolic of an impulse for intersubjective communication that may be attributed to the famous heartfelt silhouette of E.T. touching the finger of a child.[32] This is also the point where the dramatic thought bubble (from which this essay began) appears. Cast in a different light, the artist's investment in the language of parody, spectacle, nonsense, and branding all testify to strategies of excess that have depended on the achievement of critical distance. However, these strategies seem to gain a different sort of meaning in this climactic space, wherein one witnesses an unprecedented shift toward the candor of intimacy. This painting is thus indicative of Murakami's imperative toward a communicative element of excess, albeit through a precariously destructive form, that manifests in the artist's practice as a necessary and regenerative source of life.

32 Murakami, interview with the author, 28 November 2006.

Takashi Murakami: Company Man

SCOTT ROTHKOPF

"Of everything Andy produced, the Factory...was one of his most important works of art. The Factory created a model for art to survive in a world dominated by the corporation, although so far it seems nobody has picked up on it."

GLENN O'BRIEN[1]

Walking west down 46th Road in Long Island City, New York, you get a picture-postcard view of the back of the old Pepsi-Cola sign and the United Nations' tower gleaming across the river. Get it while you can, though, because at the street's end, a luxury high-rise is under construction, and the view will soon be gone. As I made my way along the block on a gray fall day, this vista struck me as the perfect preamble for a visit to the New York outpost of Takashi Murakami's growing multinational corporate empire. Here was a symbol of a powerful American brand—the kind the Pop artists loved in their heyday—inverted, fading, and soon to be occluded by a speculative real-estate venture. And just before the end of the street, in the last building on the right, a low-slung old factory was humming not with the sound of light machinery, or even of silkscreens brushing canvas, but of whirring computer hard drives and shuffling slippered feet.

---

1 Glenn O'Brien, "A Portrait of the Portrait Artist," preface to *Unseen Warhol*, ed. John O'Connor and Benjamin Liu (New York: Rizzoli, 1996), 11.

Welcome to Kaikai Kiki Co., Ltd. Upstairs, an immaculate white office space houses rows of desks at which trendy kids, mostly of Japanese descent, work silently behind computer terminals.[2] They are attending to contracts and licensing agreements and merchandise orders related to Murakami's work or to that of the seven other artists represented under Kaikai Kiki's corporate umbrella. At one end of the space, a milky screen slides aside to reveal three more employees in the accounting department, where a sign taped to the wall provides current exchange rates in dollars, euros, yen, and pounds. In an adjacent office, I am shown the twin-size pine bed on which Murakami sleeps when he's in town. (Ordinarily, he prefers a sleeping bag on the floor, but the heat in the new space isn't working yet, so somebody borrowed an old mattress from somebody over in Brooklyn.) Downstairs is the studio, where a Japanese assistant in a blue camo parka is completing painting orders for the American market, with the strains of Barry White's "Can't Get Enough of Your Love, Babe" filling the air. When asked how this satellite studio works, I'm told that an exact template of each painting is transmitted electronically from the design office at the Tokyo headquarters, and that none of the finished canvases are released before the visiting master has given them his final seal of approval.[3] With this description in mind, the outpost atelier can seem something of a corporate redundancy, but it apparently saves on shipping and import/export taxes, and, perhaps most important, it serves as a kind of demo Santa's workshop to edify and impress Western curators, dealers, and critics like me.

---

2 The details of Takashi Murakami's studio described in this and the following paragraph are based on visits made there on 7 and 14 November 2006, which were led by Executive Director Yuko Sakata. I am extremely grateful to Sakata for her patient and insightful assistance in answering my questions during the research and writing of this essay, as I am to Tim Blum and, especially, Murakami himself. My gratitude is also due to Yve-Alain Bois, Carroll Dunham, Jordan Kantor, Julian Lethbridge, Don McMahon, and, as always, Matt Saunders, for providing thoughtful feedback and suggestions on earlier drafts and excerpts of this text. Finally, I owe special thanks to Anne H. Bass for generously providing the physical—and mental—space in which this essay, as well as with many before it, was written.

3 Although the detailed parameters of Murakami's painting practice lie beyond the scope of this essay, they merit brief description here. Generally speaking, each painting is based on a handmade sketch by Murakami, which is then developed into a schematic digital rendering with the help of technical assistants in his Japanese studio. Once the overall image is finalized, it is broken down into several diagrams, which provide the configuration of all of the contours to be rendered (similar to a "paint-by-numbers" picture), as well as detailed views of individual passages, which specify exact color choices for each of the myriad shapes on the canvas. The paintings are then executed (in Japan or the United States) by highly trained studio assistants, who deviate as little as possible from the original concept rendering. Finally, Murakami inspects each painting to make sure that it meets his artistic standards (however ineffably defined), and substandard works are corrected or repainted entirely. This process is directly analogous to the one now pursued by Jeff Koons, whose paintings are begun as handmade collages, then "designed" on the computer and finally executed by the hands of numerous assistants. Both artists' systems are marked by a clear division between the work's full-blown "conception" and its "execution," which can be traced back to academic studio practices of preceding centuries or, more immediately, to similar bifurcations in the planning and realization of much Minimal and Conceptual art of the 1960s. For an extraordinarily detailed account of Murakami's studio practice, see the exhibition catalogue for his retrospective at the Museum of Contemporary Art, Tokyo, *Takashi Murakami: Summon Monsters? Open the Door? Heal? Or Die?* (Asaka, Japan: Kaikai Kiki Co., Ltd.; and Tokyo: Museum of Contemporary Art, 2001).

Here it should be noted that the rejection or correction of individual works has come to play an important part in the mythology of Murakami's practice: Whether or not an outsider would be able to grasp a work's deficiencies, the pretense of final quality control functions as a kind of guarantee of the painting's "authenticity" as an expression of the master's vision, if not his hand. (Koons, who produces paintings at a far slower rate, is an even greater perfectionist in this regard.) This practice mimics the standards advertised by the makers of high-end luxury goods (a particularly germane point in the context of this essay), who often boast of rejecting raw materials or finished products that are insufficient in quality to bear the brand's name.

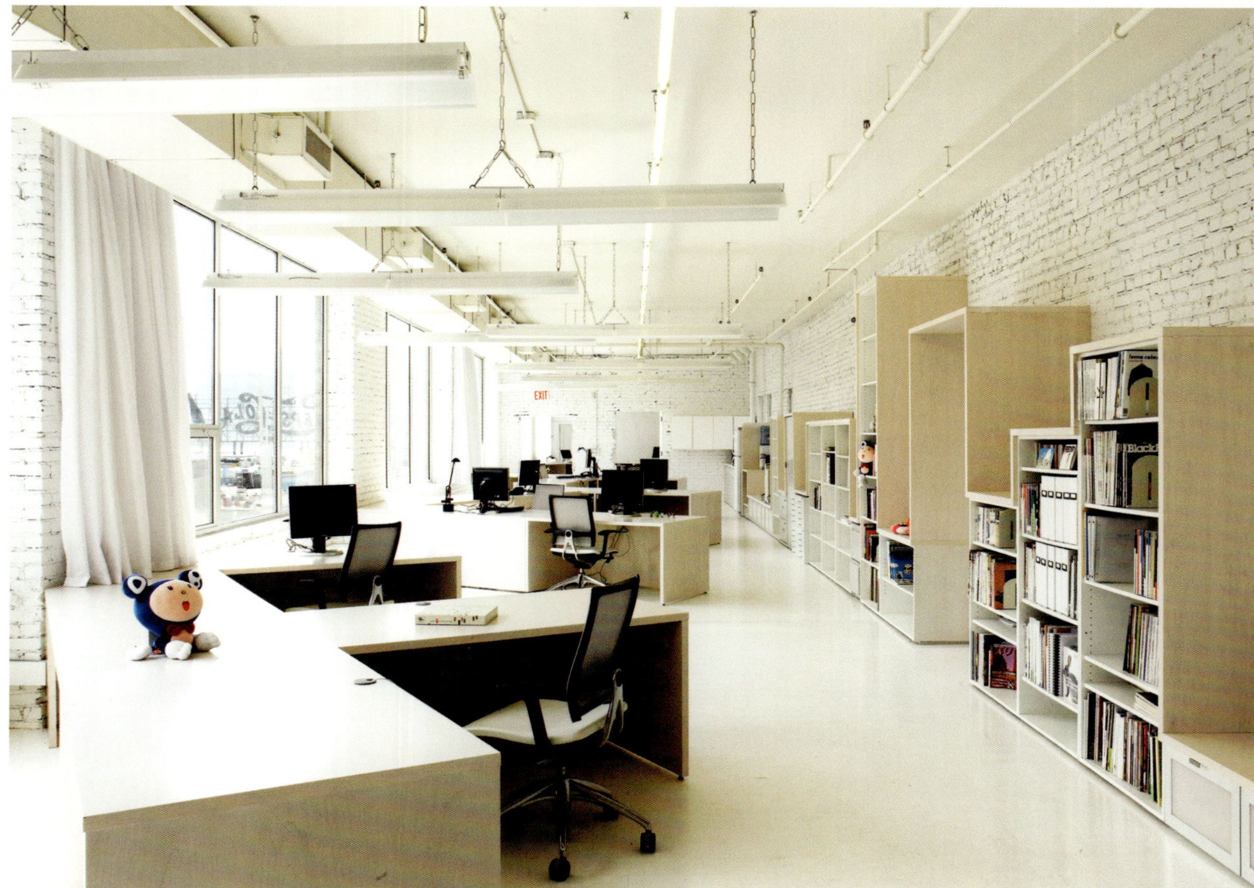

Kaikai Kiki New York LLC office, Long Island City, New York, 2007

Taking a closer look at the paintings nearing completion, I'm surprised to discover that they sport Murakami's candy-colored riff on Louis Vuitton's iconic monogram—surprised, that is, not because it seems an inappropriate subject, but because he notoriously exhibited similar canvases more than three years ago, when his collaboration with the venerable luxury house created something of an international *succès de scandale*.[4] The story is by now well known. In 2002, Marc Jacobs, the brand's art-savvy American mastermind, invited Murakami to offer his take on the classic LV monogram. The resulting handbags—which bore brightly hued logos as well as the artist's own signature "jellyfish eyes" and smiling cherry blossoms and fruit—wound up creating an overnight media sensation, appearing everywhere from the luxury glossies to O, *The Oprah Magazine* and *People* and grossing more than three-hundred million dollars in their first full year of production alone.[5] At

4 When Murakami's Louis Vuitton juggernaut hit, one would not have imagined that his LV paintings, like the bags still rolling out of Vuitton's workshop, would remain in production several years later. Indeed, the laws of fashion trends would ordinarily dictate that the multicolor accessories last only a season, but they have now escaped the style cycle to become as "timeless" as one expects good art to be. Conversely, one generally imagines that artworks are produced according to the inner "necessity" of a particular body of work, rather than as a way of satisfying pent-up consumer demand, which appears not to be the rationale behind the most recent paintings, destined as they are not for exhibition but for individual buyers.

5 Carol Matlack, "The Vuitton Money Machine," *Business Week* (22 March 2004), available at http://www.businessweek.com/magazine/content/04_12/b3875002.htm.

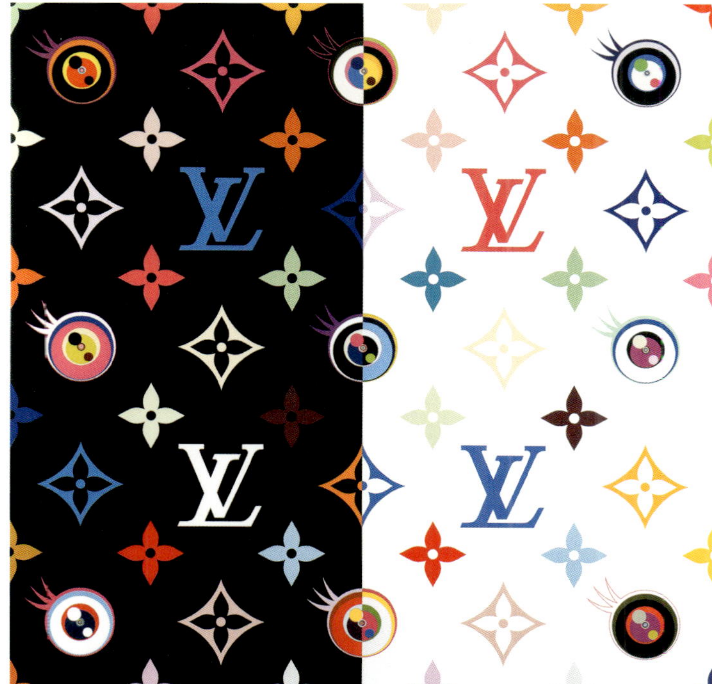

Takashi Murakami
Eye Love SUPERFLAT, 2006
Acrylic on canvas mounted on board
47 1/4 x 47 1/4 x 1 15/16 inches

the height of the feeding frenzy, while on assignment to review the 2003 Venice Biennale for *Artforum*, I was struck that the ubiquity of the bags—real and fake, on arms and street corners—allowed Murakami to handily steal the show's spotlight. Comparing his unintentional ambush to those official entries that posed accepted if futile challenges to the dominion of global capital, I wrote: "If Murakami's satchels seemed at all subversive in Venice, it was certainly not because they demonstrated the obviously critical—or, at the very least, ironic—relationship to the global culture industry that was de rigeur at the Biennale...This was clearly not a case of market infiltration, but rather *penetration*, which...was perfectly suited to an omnivorous oeuvre that engages questions of copyright and consumption with ruthless glee."[6] Little could I conceive, however, just how ruthless, gleeful, and, finally, penetrating his broader practice would turn out to be.

Indeed, during my visit to Kaikai Kiki's New York branch office—with its accountants and copyright and merchandising specialists—it became clear that Murakami's LV collaboration was only the most conspicuous (and, no doubt, lucrative) point in a constellation of activities that dwarfs his gallery-bound paintings

6 See my "In the Bag," *Artforum* 42, no. 1 (September 2003): 176.

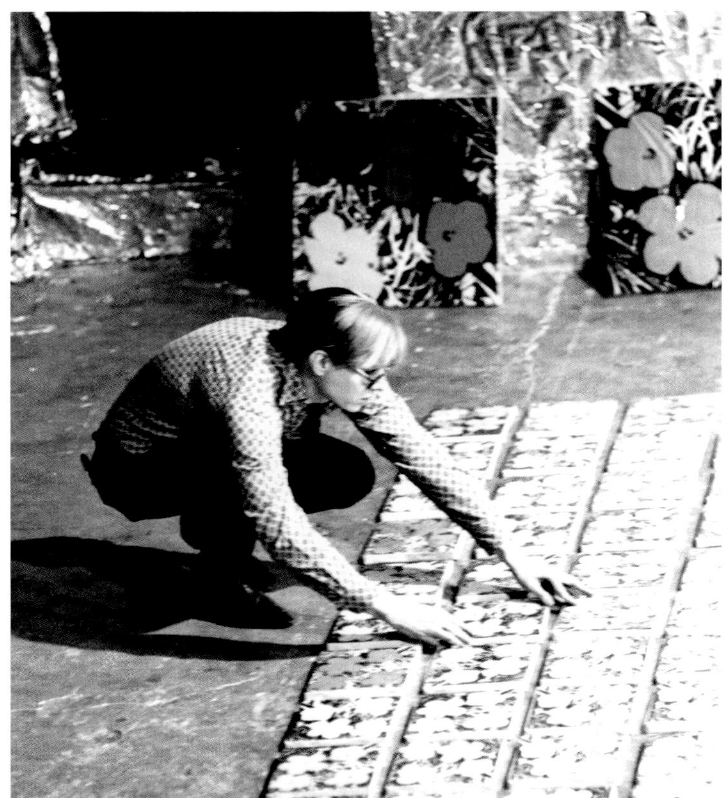

Andy Warhol arranging flower canvases on the floor of his Silver Factory, New York, 1966
© Billy Name/OvoWorks, Inc.

and sculpture in administrative scope and market reach. In addition to churning out finely crafted artworks, he is busy producing related merchandise; running an art fair; managing the careers of seven young Japanese artists; planning exhibitions and their accompanying catalogues; hosting a radio show and penning a newspaper column; pursuing commercial "collaborations" in the form of product tie-ins, advertising commissions, and corporate branding projects; and establishing an independent animation studio with an eye toward the eventual release of a feature-length film—all under the auspices of Kaikai Kiki, a business venture that may well constitute a kind of *Gesamtkunstwerk* for the new millennium. If Andy Warhol provided the model, Murakami has broken the mold.

All of these activities, of course, could seem a bit peripheral to the core of Murakami's *work*, but my aim in this essay is to question the locus of that term in relation to his larger practice, one which like Warhol's—but to an even greater degree—pushes that word closer to the common end of its connotative spectrum.

While it is by now a standard critical refrain to mention the reciprocities between Murakami's "art" and his gift-shop "merchandise," the stupefying intricacies of that relationship have remained largely unexamined, as have the details of the much broader corporate system in which they unfold. This is not without good reason. On the one hand, the neologism "Superflat," which Murakami coined to describe both the formal characteristics of a centuries-old strain of Japanese visual production and that culture's traditional lack of differentiation between the Western categories of "high" and "low," would seem to render moot any extended discussion of his complication of those terms.[7] (However, as we shall see, this level playing field is not without its wrinkles.) And, on the other hand, Western avant-garde art has long been premised, at least to some degree, on its fundamental antagonism to mass culture and on its ongoing critical reappraisal of its own conventions—twin aims that Murakami's corporate project cannot easily be claimed to fulfill. For perhaps even more antithetical to the cause of art than mass culture's endless stream of trinkets and divertissements are the multinational corporations that produce them. And here Murakami has turned the tables—if not the knife—by co-opting their structures as seamlessly as they have been accused of co-opting art's. This is a risky gambit when it comes to his critical (if not his financial) fortunes, and it is the character of this wager with which we are here concerned.

Catalogue Copies

ALMOST IMMEDIATELY AFTER MURAKAMI made a self-conscious decision in the early 1990s to forsake his training in traditional *nihonga* painting and pursue a career in what he endearingly calls "contemporary art," his work began to absorb the style and even the literal stuff of Japan's pop-cultural universe, and it was not long thereafter that he started spitting products of his own right back into the commercial muddle.[8] It is thus by now a critical commonplace to say that he "blurs the line" between "art" and "mass culture" by establishing a bidirectional network between

7 The fullest elaboration of Murakami's Superflat theory is to be found in several essays that he wrote for the catalogue of the traveling group exhibition he organized under that name. See Murakami, *Superflat*, exh. cat. (Tokyo: MADRA Publishing Co., Ltd., 2000). The concept has been further analyzed by Michael Darling in "Plumbing the Depths of Superflatness," *Art Journal* 60, no. 3 (fall 2001): 76–89.

8 Murakami has discussed this transition in his work in numerous interviews, though perhaps most clearly in his conversation with Hélène Kelmachter in *Takashi Murakami, Kaikai Kiki*, exh. cat. (Paris: Fondation Cartier pour l'art contemporain; and London: Serpentine Gallery, 2002), 75–78. For an insightful analysis of the Japanese critical and artistic context within which Murakami forged his early work, see Midori Matsui, "Conversation Days: New Japanese Art Between 1991 and 1995," in Paul Schimmel, ed., *Public Offerings*, exh. cat. (Los Angeles: The Museum of Contemporary Art; and New York: Thames and Hudson, 2001), 230–47.

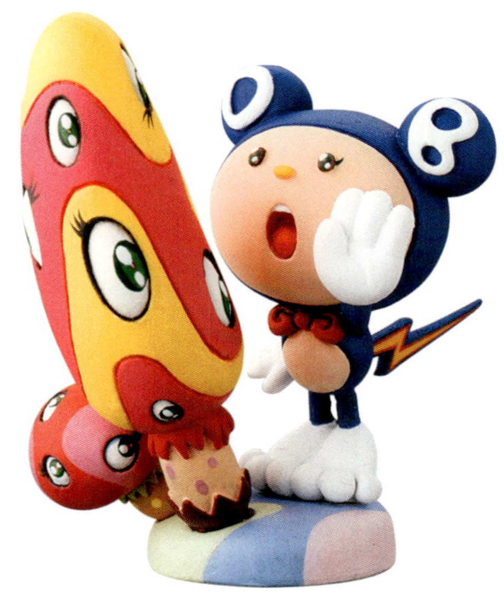

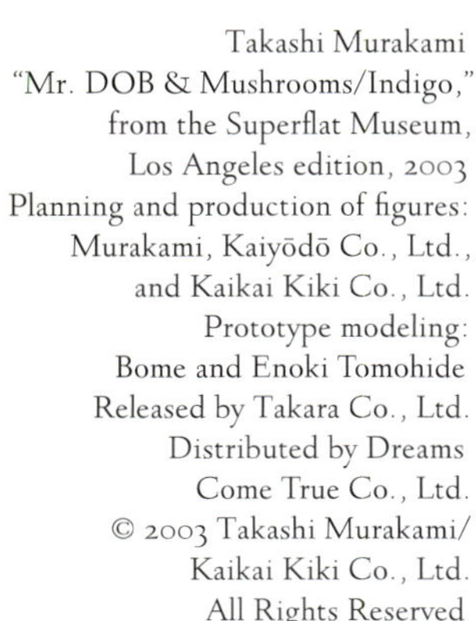

Takashi Murakami
"Mr. DOB & Mushrooms/Indigo,"
from the Superflat Museum,
Los Angeles edition, 2003
Planning and production of figures:
Murakami, Kaiyōdō Co., Ltd.,
and Kaikai Kiki Co., Ltd.
Prototype modeling:
Bome and Enoki Tomohide
Released by Takara Co., Ltd.
Distributed by Dreams
Come True Co., Ltd.
© 2003 Takashi Murakami/
Kaikai Kiki Co., Ltd.
All Rights Reserved

them. To begin, he has performed an acute reading of Japanese *otaku* culture (characterized by its obsession with the worlds of *manga* and *anime*), arriving at a potent distillate of their forms and subtexts, which then provides the basic design DNA for his work. This process has spawned motifs and characters such as the Mickey Mouse–like Mr. DOB and the leggy Miss ko², along with bands of mysterious mushrooms and rictus-faced daisies, all rendered in dazzling costume-jewel–tone colors. These beguiling creations serve as the basic subjects of Murakami's paintings and sculpture, while at the same time appearing on a range of merchandise, including key chains, plush dolls, stickers, mugs, file folders, cell-phone straps, buttons, and T-shirts that return them to the world of mass-market bibelots from whence their inspiration came. It is a brilliant strategy—one that borrows from Western Pop art's groundbreaking mass-cultural appropriations, but differs significantly in that Murakami gets to play both Walt Disney *and* Roy Lichtenstein, creating his own Mickey Muse that crosses the wires between boutiques and galleries far and wide.[9] It is also a strategy far more complicated than its now-standard two-way modeling suggests, particularly as evidenced in the *chef d'oeuvre* of his mass-market wares, the Superflat Museum.

Indeed, of all of Murakami's prodigious forays into the world of merchandising, none better exemplifies his Möbius-like marriage of high and low than the aptly named "museum," a kind of *boîte en valise* for the Cracker Jack set. Here he adopts the form and distribution mechanisms of popular Japanese *shokugan* (literally, "snack toy") figures, which are ordinarily found "free" inside packages of kid-friendly snacks and sweets. Each museum consists of a colorful cardboard box emblazoned with the artist's signature "jellyfish eyes" containing a minutely painted figurine, no more than a few inches tall, of one of his well-known artistic

9 Alexandra Munroe, for example, has incisively written that "Murakami does not merely appropriate the *manga*- and *anime*-based worlds of *otaku* subculture; he operates within them. His lushly bright, mutant characters, all of which have names, are coveted by convenience-store consumers as much as they are sought after by the international art community." Munroe, "Introducing Little Boy," in Murakami, ed., *Little Boy: The Arts of Japan's Exploding Subculture*, exh. cat. (New York: Japan Society; and New Haven, Connecticut: Yale University Press, 2005), 243.

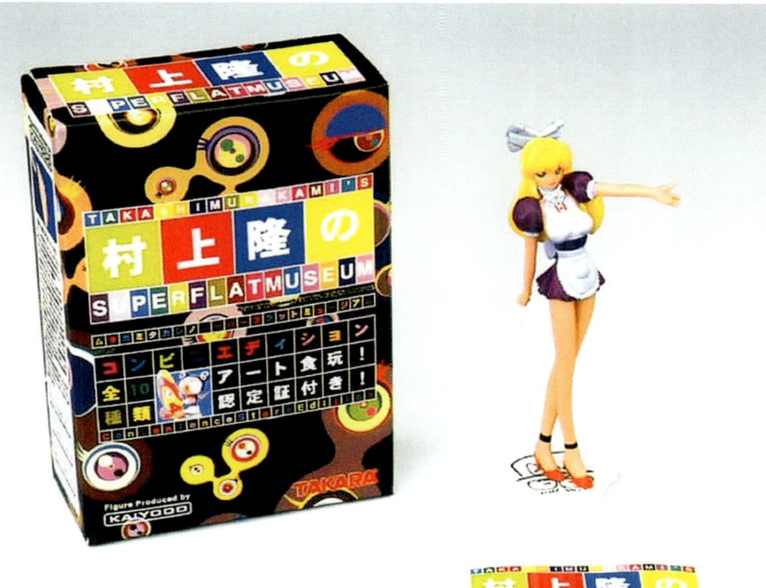

Superflat Museum, 2003
Plastic figures and figure-assembly kits packaged with gum, brochures, and certificates
Box: 5 1/8 x 3 9/16 x 1 9/16 inches
Planning and production of figures: Murakami, Kaiyōdō Co., Ltd., and Kaikai Kiki Co., Ltd.
Prototype modeling: Bome and Enoki Tomohide
Released by Takara Co., Ltd.
Distributed by Dreams Come True Co., Ltd.

Brochures from the Superflat Museum, 2003
Released by Takara Co., Ltd.
Distributed by Dreams Come True Co., Ltd.

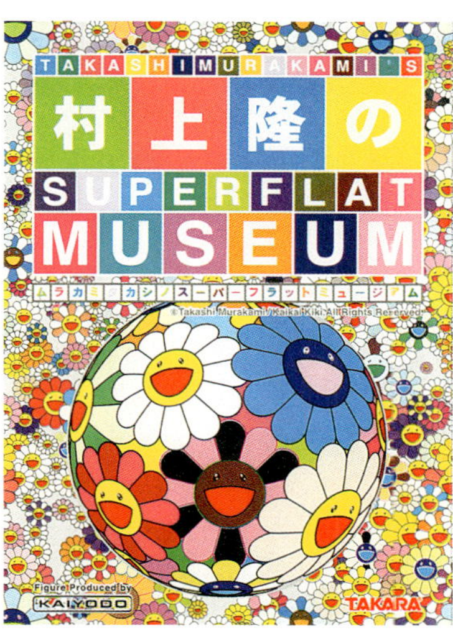

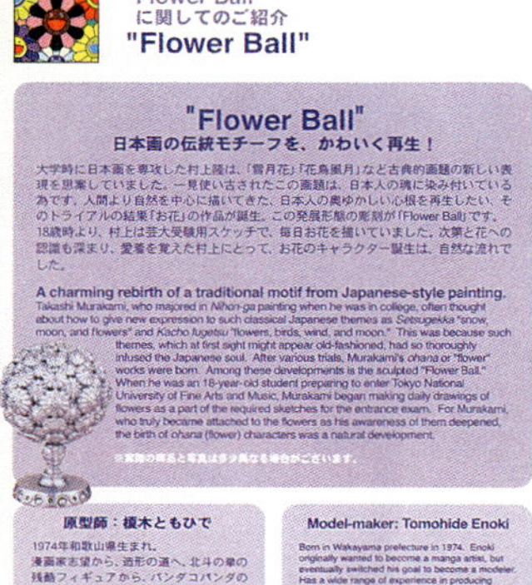

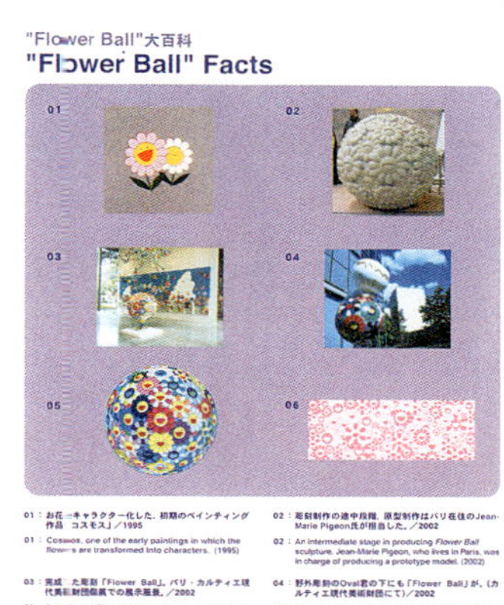

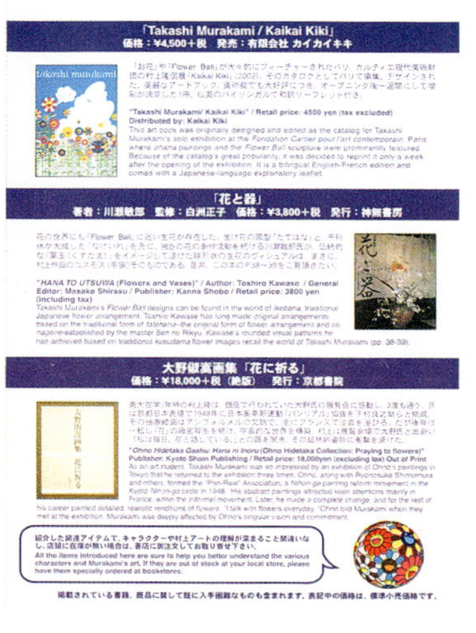

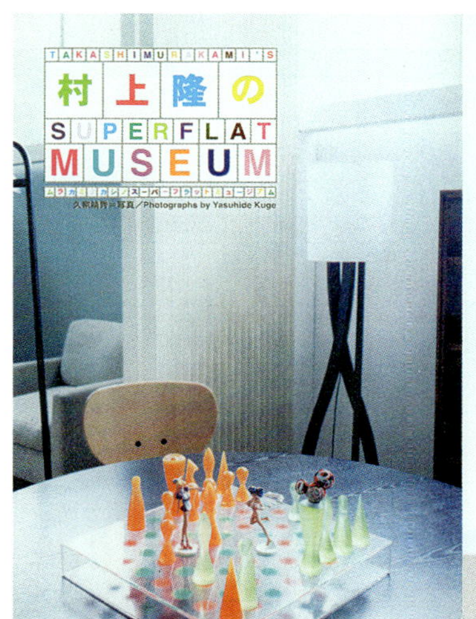

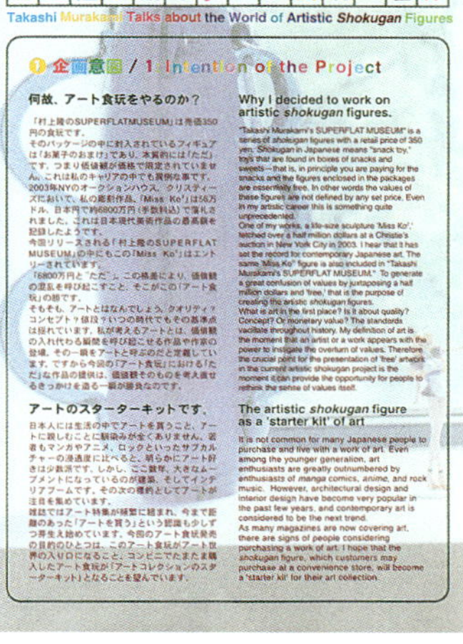

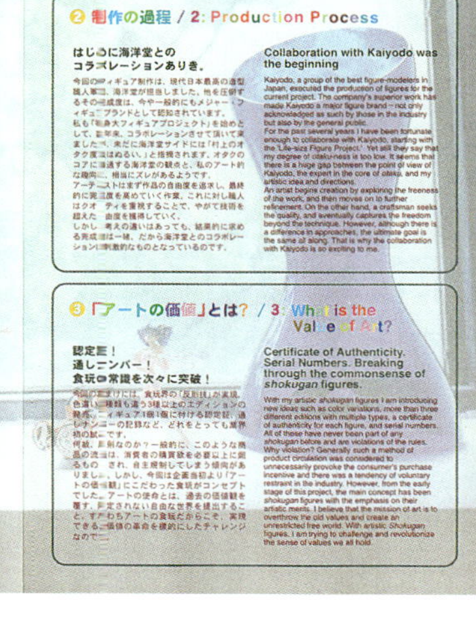

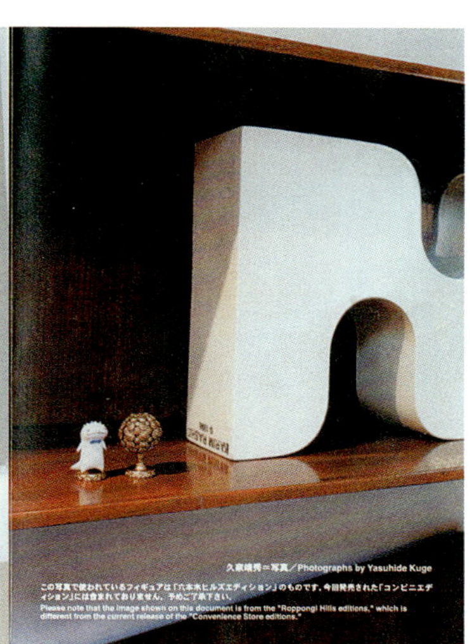

creations—DOB, Miss ko², or Flower Ball, for example—along with two pink pellets of fruit-flavored chewing gum. Released in late 2003 and early 2004, many of these could be purchased at Japanese 7-Eleven and Lawson convenience stores, among other retail outlets, for the price of only ¥350 (about $3.50), though amassing the complete collection hardly came cheap. That's because Murakami created five separate series (in limited editions of up to thirty thousand, as indicated on the accompanying serial-numbered "certificates of authenticity"), each comprising as many as ten different figures whose identities remained sealed in every box. According to the enclosed promotional literature, this blind marketing scheme was a "violation" of the usual *shokugan* "rules," since it "was considered to unnecessarily provoke the consumer's purchase incentive and there was a tendency of voluntary restraint in the industry."[10] One wonders what could possibly be meant by "unnecessarily" spurring sales in the case of a marketing gimmick intended to do precisely that, but perhaps the "collect-'em-all" advertising tactics of Happy Meals and chocolate Kinder Eggs have yet to colonize certain non-Western markets as efficiently as one might otherwise have thought. In any case, the fact that Murakami would co-opt (and then claim to outstrip) one of the food industry's most exploitative marketing tools is but one of the most glaring signs that he is flouting the rules of art's doctrinaire critical game.

Like any respectable museum, Murakami's comes with informational brochures elucidating the collection. Each tells in detail (in Japanese and English) the story of the figure it accompanies, explaining both who the character is (a narrative supplement common in the marketing of collectible dolls and figurines) and, more atypically, the history of its artistic genesis. We find in the DOB leaflet, for example, an early "rough sketch" from 1993; a biography of the model-maker, Tomohide Enoki, with whom Murakami collaborated on this and other figures; an image of the first plush DOB doll ("no longer available"); an image of DOB stickers priced at ¥300 (presumably still available); even a note offering that DOB was "created with an analysis of the 'survival secret' and 'universality' of various popular figures as its theme"—hardly the type of meta-disclosure that the culture industry's mythmakers would append to the very figures in question. In other

10 This quotation appears in the leaflet accompanying the Shachō figure that Murakami designed for the Roppongi Hills real-estate development, a topic to which we shall return. It is worth nothing that while the recto of each trifold leaflet varies depending on the character being discussed, the verso remains almost identical across the various series, except for a few minor modifications to the text, some of which omit the passage quoted (perhaps because its potentially exploitative claims proved even too incendiary for Murakami).

brochures, art-historical terms like *tondo* and a view of Murakami's Flower Ball in a prestigious museum jostle with images of Kaikai Kiki hand towels sporting the same motif. This catch-all compendium grows ever more mind-boggling when we turn to the adjacent suggestions for further reading (prices conveniently provided in yen, "tax excluded"), where a serious catalogue on the artist gets a plug alongside a comic book whose protagonist's signature phrase, "dobozite dobozite" (why, why?), lent DOB his name. It's as if these little brochures were instruction manuals for how to view Murakami's Superflat project as a whole: While we're not likely to encounter a DOB painting and keychain in the same physical space (the wall between a museum's gift shop and galleries still being stubbornly opaque), here we can observe Murakami's slippery alter ego trafficking among his various incarnations—mass and scarce, prior and post, cheap and dear.

For the artist, this delirium is precisely the point. While Bazooka Joe gave you a comic to ponder while chewing your sugary cud, Murakami bets the kids today are hungrier for an art-market primer. On the back of each leaflet, beneath the heading "Intention of the Project," he notes that the life-size version of Miss ko² (whose diminutive likeness you may have just acquired "free" with the purchase of two gumballs) was sold at Christie's in New York in 2003 for half a million dollars. He opines, "When comparing a half million dollars to 'free,' there's an overwhelmingly different sense of values, almost a confusion of values. This confusion is the purpose of creating the *shokugan* figures." But what really is the nature of this confusion, and is it of a different order than the relationship between a painting of DOB and all those key chains, and mouse pads, and plush dolls plastered with his shit-eating grin? The answer would seem to be yes, given that those products, no matter how ubiquitous or cheap, refuse the status of "replicas," that crassest of equivalences between an art object and its collectible copy. While we're now well familiar with images of contemporary artworks appearing *on* a postcard, T-shirt, or tote bag, the reproduction of the thing itself is usually reserved for the plastic Venus de Milos and facsimile Rembrandts on canvas that only the most vulgar—or dead—artist would condone. Here, fresh from the success of his Louis Vuitton project, Murakami beats so many licensing-happy foundations and heirs to the museum shop's posthumous punch. But in order to ensure his merchandise's "artistic merits" (his phrase, not mine), he boasts of collaborating on his figurines with Kaiyōdō, the very same, highly esteemed *otaku* modeling company that produced his "original" life-size sculptures. So, while the *shokugan* may differ in scale, finish, and edition size from their gallery-dwelling counterparts, they share with them not only the same basic forms and amorphous context (as elaborated in the leaflets), but also analogous design processes and quality standards. The (unintended) ironies here are rich, since Murakami is essentially invoking the name of a major commercial modeling concern to confer "fine art" status on "free" trinkets that would ordinarily be beneath even that corporation's lowly market purview.

With the artistic merits of his figurines intact, Murakami would have them pave the way for his next generation of collectors in Japan, where, his brochures contend, "it is not common to purchase and live with a work of art." "I hope," the artist writes, "that the *shokugan* figure, which customers may purchase at a convenience store, will become a 'starter kit' for an art collection." To that end, he helpfully provides three large photographs showing his mini minions arrayed in modish Design Within Reach–style interiors, where they nestle among the translucent rooks and pawns of a Plexiglas chess set or stand beside a white ceramic objet d'art stamped upside down with Karim Rashid's copyright insignia. A "starter kit" for art-collecting, then, but one strangely indistinguishable from the other accoutrements of the well-designed life.[11]

The purposeful confusions, clearly, are many. If, as Murakami has stated time and again, the Japanese aesthetic tradition makes little distinction between high art and mass culture, why claim for the *shokugan* artistic merits to separate them from the garden variety figurines they ape? And, if such a distinction is to be made, why picture the "starter kit" of this artistic insurrection amidst so many hackneyed markers of no-brow good taste? Internal contradictions abound (and Murakami readily acknowledges them, pointing to Warhol's interviews as his model), but to hold him to the letter of the law would be to betray the vestiges of a worldview ill-equipped to deal with his unencumbered—and, more frighteningly, unironic—cultural gymnastics.[12] What we are talking about here

11 The elision of the boundary between "art" and "design" is hardly a new one, although, as Hal Foster recently argued, we are living at a time when the "inflation of design" has reached an unprecedented level of cultural and economic power. Foster, "Design and Crime," in *Design and Crime, and Other Diatribes* (New York: Verso, 2002), 13–26.

12 When I asked Murakami about some of these contradictions, by way of explanation he immediately pointed to the many confusing statements within Andy Warhol's interviews (Murakami, conversation with the author, Long Island City, New York, 14 November 2006). The question of irony is an important one, because it would generally signal some knowing critical distance, a cover for Murakami's direct involvement with the commercial structures that advanced art is usually assumed to critique. Irony, for example, is often invoked as a way of sparing Warhol from the charges that he uncritically replicated the visual idioms of commerce and spectacle (though this is an extremely debatable point). Some writers on Murakami have tried to impute an ironic or critical edge to his commercial dealings, but for the most part this line of argument strikes me as a disingenuous (if often well-meaning) attempt to win space for his practices within a critical framework to which they are not particularly suited.

is a little plastic artwork in the guise of a tchotchke in the guise of an artwork in the guise of a tchotchke. Warhol may have accomplished that transmutation to the first degree, and Keith Haring to the second, but Murakami pulls off a kind of death-defying triple lutz.[13] His true aim, it seems, is not to have it both ways but to have it *every* way—to confound the categories of high and low to such an extent that we are no longer mired between them but launched into some outer headspace from which we look with amazement on his freewheeling play of signifiers.

We could also look on with well-justified disdain—which would really just be an intellectualized cover for that more visceral sensation, disgust. (If art critic Peter Schjeldahl once wrote "Jeff Koons makes me sick,"[14] one imagines Murakami might make him hurl.) Indeed, to follow the *shokugan* down the garden path requires the definitive suspension of modernism's, and even postmodernism's, foundational belief that some distinction can and must be made between capitalism's mass-cultural effects and art's quasi-autonomous ones—no matter how knowingly blurred, or ironically crossed, or dialectically reckoned we now accept these wobbly spheres to be.[15] Such qualifications, if tortured, are necessary, as they signal both our theoretical savvy and jaded realism. But when push comes to shove, they prove rather weak emotional armor. For no matter how many times we acknowledge the market's insatiable and omnivorous maw or concede that no critical space truly exists outside it, deep within our hearts we may still hope this is not the case—that the spheres are not entirely congruent—and so we develop ever more elaborate and audacious ways to find within this or that co-opted practice a subversive edge or critical aside. Yet Murakami's system lays bare our secret embarrassment. It portends a loss of faith we should know better than to have to endure once more—one we believe previous generations repeatedly experienced for us, whether in the time of Jean-Antoine Watteau or Edouard Manet, the Dadas or Warhol—and it is both a thrilling and potentially revolting affront to our sophisticated sensibilities that we might suffer this loss of innocence all over again.

---

13 Warhol, for example, made artworks, such as the Brillo Boxes, that took the form of mass-market commodities, while Keith Haring, to whom we will return, made products such as T-shirts and pins that shared imagery with his paintings, which themselves displayed visual affinities with vernacular sources. However, Haring, unlike Murakami, did not invest those mass-market products with either the physical qualities or discursive apparatus that might encourage them to be viewed as "artworks" in and of themselves (nor, conversely, did they as closely approximate preexisting products in the commercial marketplace).

14 Peter Schjeldahl, "Looney Koons," *7 Days* (14 December 1988): 66. Schjeldahl went on to opine that "Koons symbolizes the apotheosis of corporate culture," but as we will see, his work, in comparison with Murakami's, remains highly circumscribed within art's commercial and institutional confines.

15 In following this line of reasoning, I am gesturing to the many sophisticated arguments made over the last three decades (often drawing on and responding to the work of Theodor Adorno and Walter Benjamin) that have complicated the relationship between the arenas of fine art and mass culture (or high and low) to such an extent that these labels are rendered nearly useless. Yet, my point here is that no matter how nuanced such thinking has become (as, for example, in the brilliant and pioneering work of scholar and critic Thomas Crow), the residue of some distinction between these categories nevertheless remains a fundamental, if often tacit, critical premise—at least in the field of art history, as opposed to, say, cultural studies.

Yen and Cents

IT IS TEMPTING—COMFORTING, EVEN—for an art critic or historian to discuss Murakami's high/low trafficking in terms of his symbolic manipulations alone. We have already seen how fluently his branded personae slip from sculptures to figurines, paintings to handbags, galleries to convenience stores—all within a wildly permissive intellectual framework of the artist's own device. This would surely be enough to earn him a place near the head of Warhol's table, but it must be noted that such semiotic brinksmanship unfolds within a complicated economic system, braiding together a number of key precedents. Money, of course, has been a subject in art for centuries, and throughout the postwar period, figures as diverse as Yves Klein, Michael Asher, and Santiago Sierra have at times made financial transactions the raw materials of their art. Few, however, have openly adopted capitalist business models themselves as the very core and structure of their practice, and none has done so more vociferously than Murakami. This, after all, is an artist who unabashedly advertises his auction records in his own promotional literature ("a half million dollars"!) and who endlessly talks about artistic and financial success as if they were one and the same.

A lone forerunner in this department, one must concede, is Mark Kostabi, who has had the gall—or just bad taste—to advertise his sales figures for decades, trumpeting his trumped-up statistics not to gum-chewing teens but to an art-world audience dubious of his work's intrinsic merits. His (mostly losing) strategy has been to try and force the cultural higher-ups to accept the validity of his practice by virtue of its supposed popularity among certain market segments. Yet nobody at New York's Museum of Modern Art seems to be listening, and Kostabi, for his part, pretends not to care, today subsisting in a kind of alternate art universe with few points of tangency to the one at which he scoffs.[16] Murakami, by contrast, reverses the flow of information, conveying his record prices at Christie's—an arena where Kostabi's paintings are unlikely to change hands—to a broad (and, importantly, young) audience of brand-conscious consumers who may be duly impressed. On a more subtle level, increasing numbers of artists have made public

16 It bears mentioning here that many analogies exist between Mark Kostabi's practice and Murakami's. Following Warhol's example, Kostabi established his own "factory" in 1988 under the name Kostabi World. At the height of its output, the enterprise employed dozens of assistants who generated ideas for paintings and executed them while also minting products, including a Swatch watch, neckties, and scarves, as well as book- and album-cover art. Perhaps even more apposite, Kostabi carefully cultivated a high-profile public persona, which during the late 1980s and early 90s had a market reach as wide as Murakami's today. Through self-interviews and an advice column published in Artnet.com's online magazine, Kostabi has outlined the keys to artistic success in a brutally calculated manner that suggests "market research" is at the heart of his artistic project, a strategy that Murakami has also advertised in his many comments analyzing the Japanese and Western art systems. Yet if both artists approach their respective practices with a self-professed desire to attain broad sales, the reception of their paintings proper has differed greatly, with Murakami gaining far more serious institutional and critical traction (for one measure of his greater success in this regard, just compare his passel of major museum catalogues with Kostabi's equal number of self-published coffee-table tomes). This discrepancy may be due to the fact that Kostabi's paintings can feel more like props in a larger conceptual project, whereas Murakami's art has sustained a level of interest independent of the system in which it is generated and from which it is ultimately launched.

their financial attainments in photo pictorials of lavish studios and townhouses. This bid to claim socioeconomic parity with their patrons may also serve to reflect an understated halo of success back on their work. Yet if Julian Schnabel famously spends his days in Sulka silk pajamas, Murakami professes to spending his nights in a cheap sleeping bag. This may be a matter of personal taste, but it's also a mode of self-presentation perfectly in sync with a changing global corporate culture, one whose new-economy titans the artist would no doubt like to impress. So, while Henry Kravis may look rich in a bespoke suit, Murakami knows his hero Bill Gates looks even richer in a pair of Dockers. Such sartorial analogies are hardly beside the point, for if we are to take seriously the full gamut of Murakami's professional engagements, we should no doubt be concerned with the up-to-the-minute image of the company president he projects.

So too, of course, should we be concerned with the bottom line. While Murakami's merchandise is only the tip of an ever-expanding corporate iceberg, the economic implications of his *shokugan* might serve as an instructive point of entry, a node on his practice where his "confusion of values" takes on a decidedly pecuniary inflection. He claims (again in his leaflets) that the close kinship of his figurines and sculpture proper is a "dangerous gamble," one "with the potential to decrease the monetary value of my artworks." Here, Murakami gets points for bravado, but his protests can come off as a bit coy. After all, he better than anyone understands that while critics and theorists may be "confused" by his wild juggling of signs, the market certainly has no trouble distinguishing between a plastic figurine in an edition of thirty thousand and its big buxom sister in an edition of three—a power of discrimination to which the artist's ever-rising retail and resale prices attest. But this discrepancy does not undermine or annul his high/low manipulations so much as it confirms the masterful orchestration of his system as a whole.

Indeed, I would argue that no artist before him has been able to generate as great a price differential between such ostensibly similar stuff—all while maintaining audience credibility at equally far ends of the viewing spectrum (here, think the kids at 7-Eleven and the curators clamoring for his work). Koons, with whom Murakami is often compared, has succeeded in winning over an equally broad audience with icons such as his topiary puppies and glistening balloon dogs. Yet although he shares with Murakami a love of publicity, analogous modes of studio fabrication, and, above all, a magpie infatuation with the culture industry's effluence, Koons has shown almost no interest in moving beyond (or below) the production of objects that circulate in the most rarified market climes. For all the talk of how he and contemporaries like Haim Steinbach in the 1980s "played on the collapse of the dialectic of art and commodity, but in the form of the art-commodity,"[17] as Hal Foster succinctly put it, there's never any mistaking that art is the privileged term in this hyphenated equation. Even Warhol, for all his extra–art-world dabblings, never moved as much merch; the licensing of his images of images on everything

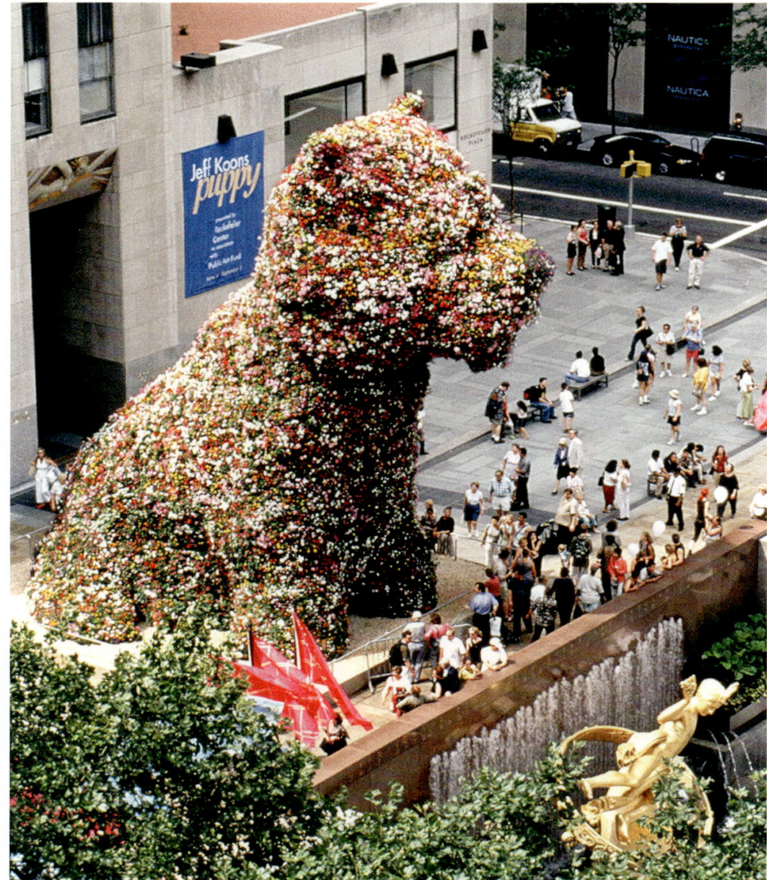

Jeff Koons
Puppy, 1992
Stainless steel, soil, geo-textile fabric, internal irrigation system, and live flowering plants
486 x 486 x 256 feet
Courtesy of the artist
Installation at Rockefeller Center, New York, 2000
© Jeff Koons

17 Foster, "The Art of Cynical Reason," in *The Return of the Real* (Cambridge, Massachusetts: The MIT Press, 1996), 116.

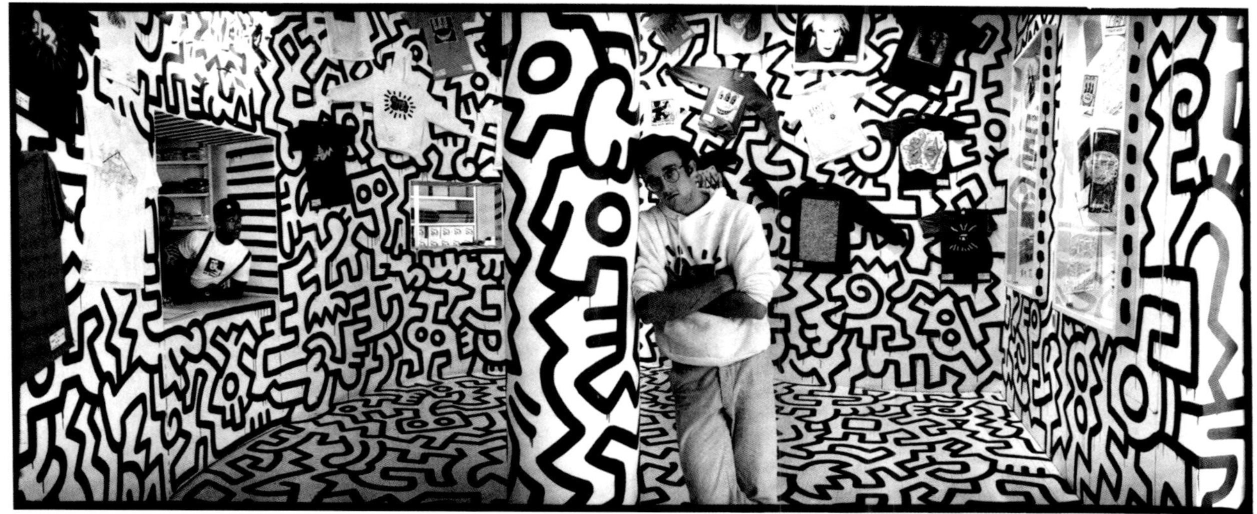

Keith Haring in his Pop Shop, New York, 1986
© Keith Haring Foundation

from, well, handbags to last year's Barney's Christmas catalogue ("Happy Andy Warhol-idays!") came only after his death. Nevertheless, Murakami would have a hard-to-beat edge on this front: The brilliance of his brand is that his characters, like Disney's, are entirely and unmistakably his own, yet their vernacular essence makes them supple surrogates in a world of pre-existing product lines.[18]

The most apposite precedent here would have to be Haring, whose Pop Shop Murakami visited on his first trip to New York in 1989, just three years after it opened with Warhol's fabled blessing.[19] Like Murakami, Haring had a stable of signature characters—the barking dog and radiant baby, to cite only the most iconic examples—that moved fluidly between his high-end paintings and sculptures and the T-shirts and magnets that filled Pop Shop's shelves. Also like Murakami, Haring's signature graphic style derived from vernacular sources and was instantly recognizable, lending itself to cross-branded collaborations, such as his series of Swatch watches, and occasional advertising commissions like those he undertook for Absolut Vodka and Lucky Strike. So aware was he of his brand's growing cachet that he permanently appended a hand-drawn copyright symbol to his signature as both an acknowledgment of its talismanic power and a mock

18 In a particularly compelling case study of Mr. DOB, Marc Steinberg contrasted Warhol's use of seriality (based on variations within particular painted motifs, such as soup cans, car crashes, etc.) with the serial transformations of Murakami's signature character, who changes color and form among different paintings but also metamorphoses across various product lines. While Steinberg saw Warhol's project as typifying Jean Baudrillard's canonical discussion of capitalist modes of seriality in *The System of Objects* (1968), he argued that Mr. DOB's multifarious guises speak to a "new seriality" exemplary of our current era. He wrote: "Where for Baudrillard the relation between objects—along with the variation in colour or shape which differentiated them—played out within an object type (a toaster), in other words *within* the series, what is important now is rather the connections *between series*. It is the creation of relations between the vacuum cleaner series and the car series, the pencil series and the toaster series, that defines the shift in relations under information-capitalism. In short, it is the age of branding and convergence. An object is no longer characterized by its secondary variation within a uniform series, but by its belonging to a greater series within which it is connected with a potentially unlimited variety of other objects...the brand grouping subsumes a number of disparate and previously unrelated lineages into a larger series governed by the brand image or label." Steinberg, "Characterizing a New Seriality: Murakami Takashi's DOB Project," *Parachute* 110 (April–June 2003): 90–109.

19 Murakami, conversation with the author, Long Island City, New York, 14 November 2006. On several occasions, Haring went on record to note Warhol's approval of his project: "I discussed the Pop Shop many times with Andy Warhol, and he was totally supportive of my taking the plunge, and not caring what people thought, because as long as I knew *why* I was doing it, then that was what was most important." Haring, cited in John Gruen, *Keith Haring: The Authorized Biography* (New York: Prentice Hall, 1991), 129. Of course, Haring obviously *did* care "what people thought" (indeed, perhaps too much), or he would not have taken such pains to justify his actions.

threat to would-be forgers. I say "mock," because Haring claimed that in keeping with the populist spirit of his work, he chose not to pursue litigation against those who used his imagery without consent—a decidedly different course of legal action than that taken by Murakami, who has sued the purveyors of look-alike DOB children's apparel and has never released a product too small or too cheap to bear a real copyright credit line.[20]

Indeed, Haring's merchandising mania, in contrast to Murakami's, was enveloped in a spirit of folksy populism left over from his tagging days, an aura of giving art to the people when he was selling it to them all the same. His interviews are filled with sanctimonious tales of refusal concerning lucrative corporate projects, and he openly worried about the "tightrope walk," as he called it, between the demands of art and the dangers of "crass" commercialism.[21] There's a certain pathos to Haring's crisis of conscience; his angsty reservations are those of a prophet who envisioned a future for art that he was unable to wholly embrace. It's hard to imagine Warhol or Murakami suffering similar qualms, petty commercialism being no crasser than the bourgeois pretense that art can be innocent of such charges. What seems in retrospect slightly embarrassing and problematic about Haring's cottage industry is the tortured contradiction between his humanist values (aptly embodied in the unremitting presence of his hand) and their dissemination in the form of so many mass-market commodities. Murakami obviates this dilemma formally by replacing Haring's muscular expressive line with a razor-sharp mechanical contour and ethically by giving up any pretense that his project is driven by anything other than the relentless pursuit of *success*—financial, critical, popular, or otherwise.

It is this aggressively unrepentant posture that makes Murakami the consummate figure for our artistic present, one whose "compromised" status, particularly in relation to today's hypertrophied market, seems less like a compromise than a supremely canny form of realism in an age of rapidly multiplying art fairs and "special art issues" published by the likes of *W* and *Vanity Fair*.[22] Murakami's claim to experiencing a certain "embarrassment" for James Turrell on encountering the elder artist's installation-*cum*-décor in Louis Vuitton's new Champs Elysées boutique is

20 Gruen, *Keith Haring*, 127–28. For details on Murakami's court case against and eventual settlement with Narumiya International Co., Ltd., see the report on Kaikai Kiki's official website: http://kaikaikiki.co.jp/regarding_the_amicable_settlement/.

21 Revealing a certain amount of inner conflict, Haring elaborated this tension as follows: "If I had accepted all the licensing offers that I had from big firms, like those that licensed Snoopy and Garfield, I could have made just pots and pots of money immediately. Really, there were endless proposals from television and manufacturers which *had* to be turned down, because there was a specific vision for the work which *had* to be followed. The fact is, I wanted to keep the work on an artistic level while still allowing it to communicate on a popular level." Ibid., 128–29. For more on Haring's rationale behind the Pop Shop and critical reactions against it, see Jade Dellinger, "Keith Haring: Art and Commerce," available on the Keith Haring Foundation online archive, http://www.haring.com/cgi-bin/essays.cgi?essay_id=15.

22 In a remarkable coincidence that speaks to contemporary art's rising prominence in the broader cultural imagination (and its power as a magnet for affluent brand-savvy consumers), *W* and *Vanity Fair* released back-to-back special issues devoted to contemporary art in November and December 2006, respectively.

an unexpected yet apt intuition on the part of the Japanese handbag maven: We may have known for ages that "advanced" art can be co-opted as nothing more than good design, but it's still hard to reconcile ourselves to the thought that an artist like Turrell might willingly deploy his supposedly sublime visual vacuums in the midst of so much commercial clutter.[23] (Where, one wonders, is the Dia Foundation when you need it?) Olafur Eliasson's 2006 holiday window designs for the same luxury house betrayed a similarly conflicted idealism. Although Eliasson stipulated that no products be shown alongside his freestanding sculptural lamps in order to preserve their integrity as "a serious work of art,"[24] for all their formal and conceptual interest, the gesture ended up looking less like a radical refusal than another tactic from the annals of cutting-edge advertising, which has long experimented with substituting an aura of chic mystery for the product being pushed. The point is not to blame Turrell, Eliasson, or countless others for wanting to share in commerce's attention-grabbing spotlight (while simultaneously wanting to preserve the appearance of standing just outside it), but rather to suggest that Murakami is far more unself-conscious—and thus, ironically, far more conscious—about his role in this system. His work anticipates and directly responds to the burgeoning market within which all art (no matter its price tag) is now to a greater or lesser extent necessarily implicated, and he goes one step further by directly demonstrating how that commercial network itself participates in much larger economic structures. We could call this stance complicit or collusive, or we could simply call it honest. Indeed, if anything is more morally suspect than "selling-out" (a term which itself seems almost hopelessly quaint today), it's the false hope that appearing not to have done so might serve as some form of expiation. Murakami clearly knows better, and his project helps us to as well.

The surprise in all this is that just when we think Murakami has reconciled himself more unequivocally and seamlessly than any of his predecessors to the flows of mass production and consumption, strange chinks open up in his business model. Returning to the *shokugan*, for example, we realize that at the moment it appears he has leveraged his brand to the fullest—the snack toys, remember, are

23 Murakami, conversation with the author, Long Island City, New York, 14 November 2006.

24 Olafur Eliasson, cited in Rachel Wolff, "How Much Is That Eye in the Window?," *New York Magazine: Daily Intelligencer* (9 November 2006), available at http://nymag.com/daily/intel/2006/11/how_much_is_that_eye_in_the_wi.html. Countless examples of the advertising industry's withholding of the product being promoted abound, though one of the most famous in the United States remains the launch of Infiniti cars in 1989, which was preceded with months of print and television advertising that never showed the vehicles nor, for that matter, even explained that Infiniti was the name of an automaker. This strategy has only grown increasingly common in the marketing of everything from prescription drugs to high-end fashions, as companies attempt to capture a viewer's attention and imagination or try to build cachet around a brand independent of its specific product lines.

According to a posting on the Moët Hennessey Louis Vuitton (LVMH) website (http://www.lvmh.com), Eliasson donated his fee for the Vuitton project, along with the proceeds from the sale of a related limited-edition lamp, to an organization he and his wife established for the benefit of Ethiopian children. While this philanthropic stance is extremely commendable, its public proclamation suggests that the artist may have experienced some concerns about collaborating with the luxury maker and felt the need to make clear that his motives for doing so did not involve his own financial enrichment. One can scarcely picture Murakami making a similar pronouncement, which is not to suggest that he values avarice over charity, but only to indicate that he is less conflicted about "colluding" with industry than some of his artist peers may be.

selling on the strength of his name, not Swatch's or Louis Vuitton's—Murakami may actually be pushing something of a high-volume loss leader. For even if he claims to have adopted a sales strategy more manipulative than Japanese big business allows itself, this is likely something of a hollow boast. After all, the profit margin on a few hundred thousand units—no matter how inexpensively hand-painted in China—would scarcely amount to the artist's take on the sale of a single large painting. (And this is not even to account for the tremendous in- and out-of-house staff hours and design fees invariably associated with such a complicated project.) The point, however, is not to hold up slim margins as a sign of anti-capitalist valor (à la Haring), the secret sacrifice that commutes "business art," to borrow Warhol's sobriquet, back into plain old art. Rather, it is to suggest that Murakami's "confusion of values" plays itself out on both symbolic and real economic registers, and that the most glaring signs of the artist's submission to the interests of mass culture may ironically point the way to his greatest conceptual gambit.

Model Business

WITH THE STAKES EVER-RISING, MURAKAMI's real gamble may be the ongoing growth and maintenance of his own multinational corporation, Kaikai Kiki Co., Ltd., whose multiple suffixes he brandishes with the same pride that others might flaunt "Esq." or "Ph.D." The venture started humbly enough as the Hiropon Factory, which Murakami established outside Tokyo in 1996 and named in obvious homage to Warhol. There, he assembled a motley band of assistants who helped produce his paintings and sculpture while also attending to related efforts like T-shirt design and the publication of *Hiropon*, a house organ in the form of a free newspaper. These products had a techno-DIY vibe, which is perhaps more than can be said of the first Factory itself. One former assistant (now an artist in his own right, known simply by the moniker "Mr.") remembered "Studio No. 1" as a prefab structure containing not much more than "a plank set on some wooden legs" and

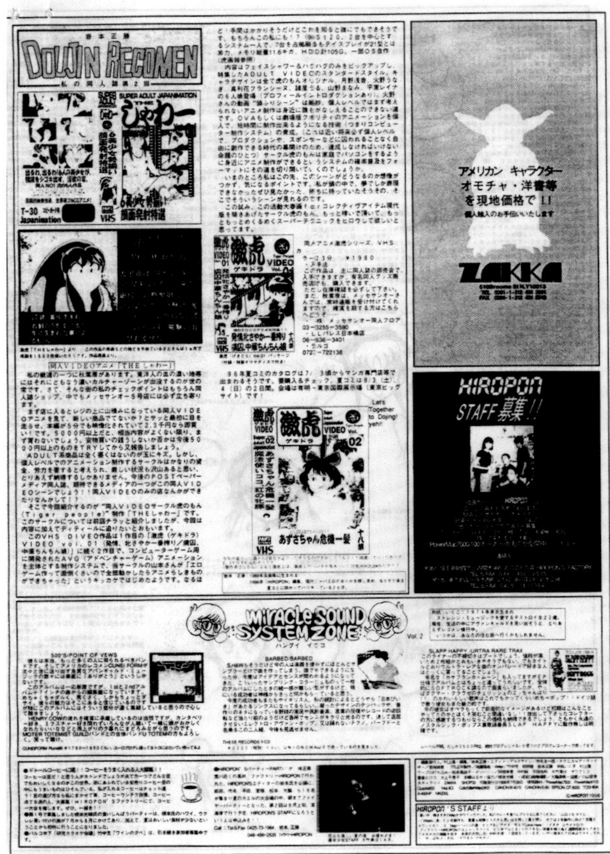
DOUJIN RECOMEN

アメリカン キャラクター
オモチャ・洋書等
を現地価格で!!

ZAKKA

HIROPON
STAFF募集!!

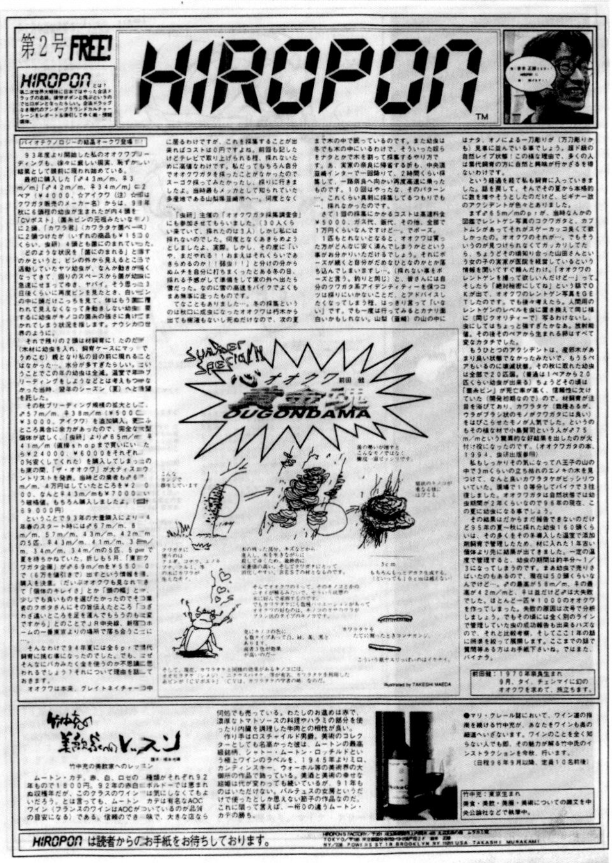
第2号 FREE!
HIROPON

OUGONDAMA

HIROPON は読者からのお手紙をお待ちしております。

Spread from *Hiropon*, no. 2 (1996)

furniture scrounged from the trash. There was no computer, no air conditioning, no shower, and during the summer "everybody was drenched with sweat." The Dickensian tale of these devoted acolytes—working without pay and racking up huge cell-phone bills and train fares commuting from school—reaches a kind of parodic fever pitch in Mr.'s recollection of feeding the merry tribe: "We really had no money back then," he recalled, "so sometimes we eat [*sic*] convenience store meals that had gotten too old to sell, or even boiled wild horsetails that I picked."[25] Factory life is grueling, exploitative even, and this one seems less suited to documentation by Billy Name than Lewis Hine. But Murakami's hard-scrabble beginnings do efficient double-duty as a calculated marketing ploy; for even more shocking than the appalling working conditions and menu is the fact that they were recounted not in a former employee's vengeful tell-all but in the

25 Mr., "Early Days of the Hiropon Factory," in *Takashi Murakami: Summon Monsters?*, 121.

catalogue of Murakami's 2001 survey exhibition at Tokyo's prestigious Museum of Contemporary Art. Here, we understand the extent to which Murakami has mastered the self-mythologizing drive of predecessors such as Salvador Dalí and Warhol, Damien Hirst and Martin Kippenberger, the latter being the proprietor of the all-purpose office-*cum*-studio Büro Kippenberger in Cologne (and, it should be said, Murakami is far more a Warholian celebrity in his native Japan than is generally understood in the West).[26] But in place of hard (or weird) living, we find simply hard *working*, an up-by-the-bootstraps success story less typical of bohemian chronicles than of the biographies than of America's self-made tycoons.

Palmier days, of course, lay ahead. In 1998, Murakami opened the tiny New York outpost that served as a necessary toehold in the capital of the international art market, and in 2001, he reincorporated the Hiropon Factory as Kaikai Kiki Co., Ltd. This move recalls Warhol's own eventual re-christening of the Factory as Andy Warhol Enterprises, and, more important, it mimics recent shifts among affluent nations from goods- to service-based economies. For although Murakami still attends to the production of an ever-expanding universe of "artworks" and "merchandise" (a distinction maintained in his corporate structure if not in his Superflat ideology), he has increasingly focused his energies on consulting and managerial projects. With roughly one hundred employees stationed between three branch offices in Tokyo and New York, the company pursues, according to its official website, some eighteen interrelated business functions, which merit enumeration in full:

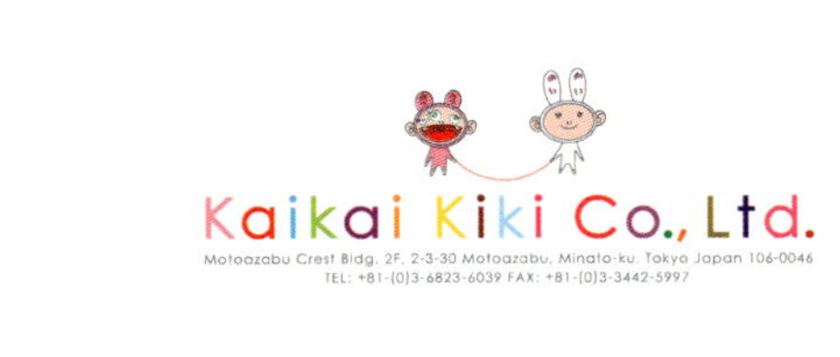

Kaikai Kiki Co., Ltd., stationery, 2007

26 Despite his tremendous media coverage in the West, it remains difficult here to understand the staggering cult of personality surrounding Murakami in Japan, where he is known not simply for his artworks, related merchandise, and Louis Vuitton bags, but also through numerous popular TV appearances, articles he has written for mainstream publications, and a radio program addressing a range of non-art topics, from film to professional wrestling. As Jim Frederick wrote, "In Japan, Murakami is now magazine-cover, mobbed-in-public, rock-star famous—something that a million gallery shows could never have made him." Frederick, "Move Over, Andy Warhol," *Time Asia*, 19 May 2003, available at http://www.time.com/time/magazine/article/0,9171,452870,00.html.

The drive to understand Warhol's persona not simply as a biographical supplement to his practice but as an integral component of it has been one of the main thrusts of much recent writing on the artist, including that of Kelly M. Cresap, Bruce Hainley, and Wayne Koestenbaum. Such readings have provided a basis for similar explorations of younger artists like Koons and Kippenberger. For an instructive study of the latter figure along these lines, see Alison M. Gingeras, "Performing the Self," *Artforum* 43, no. 2 (October 2004): 253–55, 304–05.

[1] Exhibitions in Japan and overseas, event coordination, contemporary art course-planning, and production
[2] Artworks: planning, production, sales, and imports/exports
[3] Books: planning, cover and binding design, editing, publishing, sales, and imports/exports
[4] Art textbooks: planning, production, sales, and imports/exports
[5] Clothing: planning, design, production, sales, and imports/exports
[6] Consumer goods: planning, design, production, sales, and imports/exports
[7] Packaging: product design, production, sales, and imports/exports
[8] Advertising: planning and production
[9] Websites: planning and production
[10] Antique sales
[11] Copyright and translation: rights, management, and trading
[12] Artists' and celebrities' performance, illustration, and manuscript management
[13] Characters planning, development, and design sales
[14] Film and video: planning, production, sales, and loans for promoting sales of broadcast programs and character products
[15] Art lecturer dispatch and introduction
[16] Animation planning, production, sales, and imports/exports
[17] Animal- and plant-handling and sales
[18] All tasks accompanying all of the above[27]

The list is dizzying. Purposefully so, one imagines, with its slight hint of Enron-style puffery. (When asked about the "animal- and plant-handling and sales," Kaikai Kiki's executive director explained that Murakami has occasionally sold killiefish at GEISAI, the semi-annual Tokyo-based art fair the artist founded five years ago and continues to oversee under Kaikai Kiki's auspices.[28]) Although it would be impossible in a short essay to describe comprehensively the full scope of his various ventures, a few bear elaborating here. For example, Murakami's involvement with advertising (item number eight) draws on a long, if seamy, undercurrent

27 Kaikai Kiki Co., Ltd., "About Kaikai Kiki: Business Description," http://english.kaikaikiki.co.jp/company/summary/.

28 Sakata, conversation with the author, Long Island City, New York, 7 November 2006.

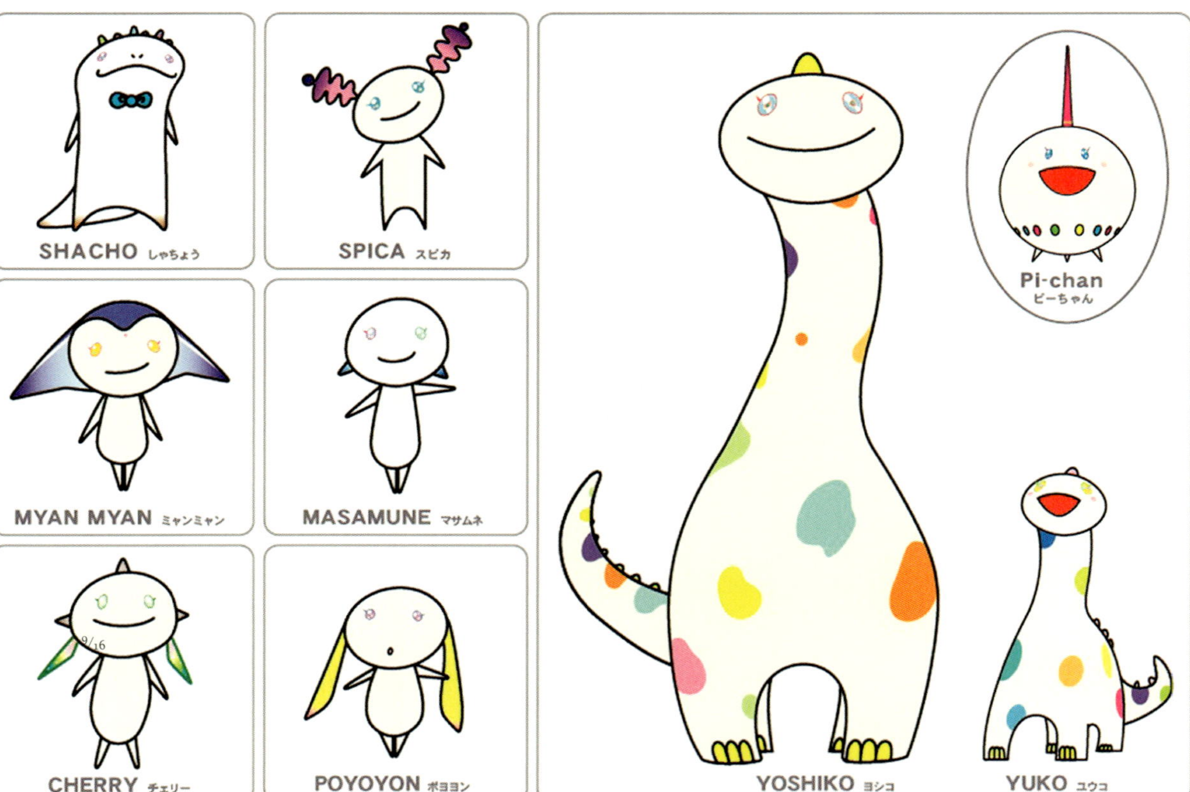

Takashi Murakami
Creatures of Planet 66, 2003
Courtesy Roppongi Hills

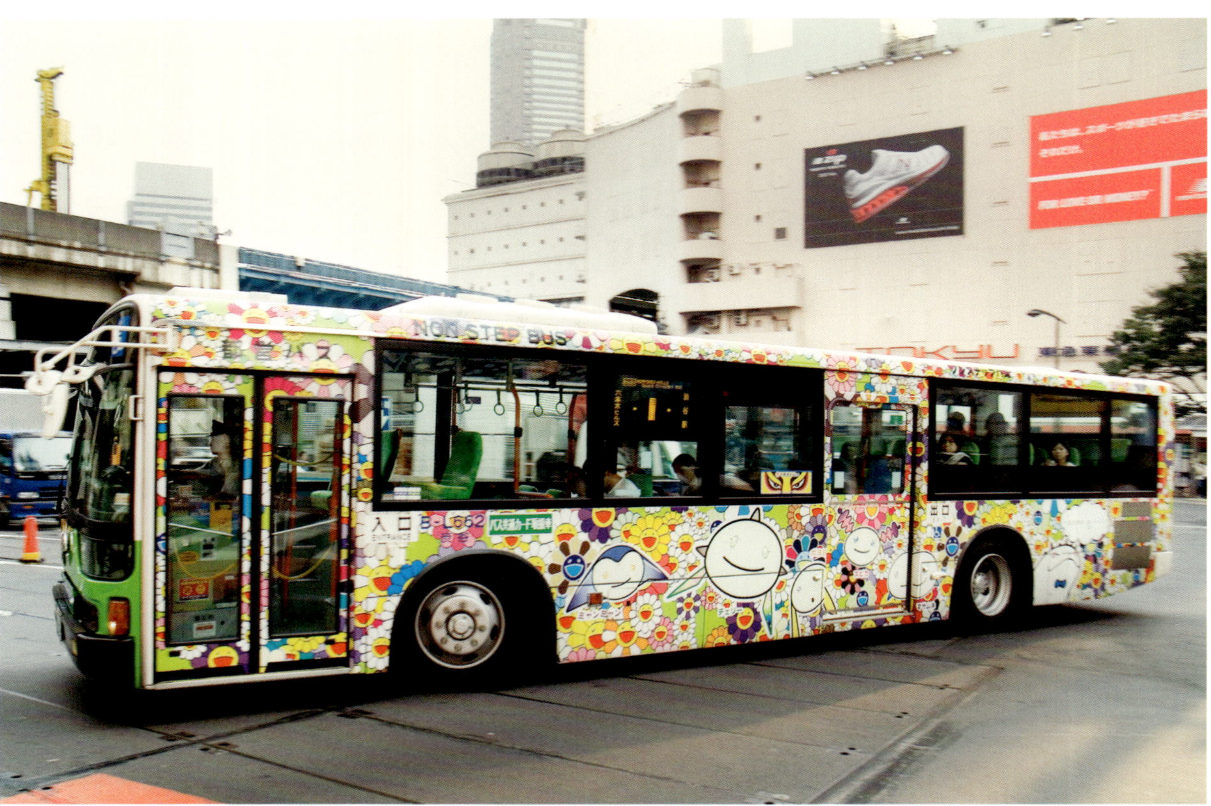

"Roku-Roku Go,"
Tōei shuttle bus linking Roppongi
Hills and Shibuya station, Tokyo,
in service since October 2003

of twentieth-century art. Dalí, to take only the most problematic case, infamously licensed images of his art and himself to almost anyone with the cash to pay for them, and he also produced new commercial work in the form of print ads for Bryans hosiery, posters for the French national railroad, packaging designs for Coup de Feu perfume and Osborne brandy, and even an unsuccessful television spot for Alka Seltzer, which showed the septuagenarian artist painting on a female model to simulate the medicine's salubrious effects.[29] Late in life Warhol, too, returned to the world of advertising that he had left behind to become a "real" artist, though his most notable command performances in the field took the form of celebrity endorsements—for Diet Coke, Braniff airlines (in a campaign also starring Dalí), and the investment banking firm Drexel Burnham—rather than design work for hire.

Taking permission from these debased precedents, Murakami has significantly upped the ante by acting as a full-service brand consultant for a Japanese television station and for billionaire Minoru Mori's mammoth Tokyo real-estate development Roppongi Hills. Mori, Japan's largest commercial landlord, called on Murakami to replace a major Japanese ad agency just four months before his center's 2003 opening, and the artist devised a family of smiley creatures from "Planet 66" to serve as mascots for the complex. Presided over by a not-so-veiled portrait of Mori himself in the form of a cuddly salamander whose name, Shachō, means "president" in Japanese, the characters were turned into sculptures to adorn Roppongi Hills' main entrance and appear in the center's promotional literature and signage, in addition to starring in animated television advertisements and decorating a line of briskly selling souvenirs. Importantly, they share a design vocabulary indistinguishable from Murakami's proprietary creations like DOB, and he has retained permission to use them in his painting and sculpture as he wishes. The fact that Shachō and a few of his friends from Planet 66 wound up in the Superflat Museum collection, along with miniatures of Murakami's most iconic sculptures, only indicates the utter futility of attempting to clearly differentiate between his art and commercial work—a border that in the case of Warhol or Dalí has been far easier to police.[30]

29 These projects, among others, are described most fully in the catalogue of Félix Fanés's exhibition "Dalí: Mass Culture" (organized by Fundación "la Caixa," Barcelona, Spain, and the Museo Nacional Centro de Arte Reina Sofía, 2004).

30 In what remains one of the most trenchant discussions of Warhol's art, Benjamin H. D. Buchloh has argued that Warhol's practice from the start "'embodied' the paradox of modernist art: to be suspended between high art's isolation, transcendence, and critical negativity and the pervasive debris of corporate-dominated mass culture." Buchloh, "Andy Warhol's One-Dimensional Art: 1956–1966," in Kynaston McShine, ed., *Andy Warhol: A Retrospective*, exh. cat. (New York: The Museum of Modern Art, 1989), 39. For Buchloh, it was Warhol's understanding of traditional artistic precepts that ensured his early success in the commercial field, just as his experience in that arena would later enable his greatest innovations in painting. Nevertheless, Buchloh, along with the majority of Warhol's most serious interpreters, had no trouble isolating the Pop master's "art" from his commercial work for hire, which did not entirely cease in the early 1960s but persisted in different forms intermittently until his death. It is only lately that serious scholars and critics have come to value Warhol's later commercial exploits as integrated within—rather than ancillary to—his oeuvre as a whole. See, for example, David E. James, "The Unsecret Life: A Warhol Advertisement," *October*, no. 56 (spring 1991): 21–41.

If Murakami's advertising projects take to new extremes the relatively modest practices of these predecessors, it is more difficult to find touchstones for many of Kaikai Kiki's other business activities. For example, several of those delineated in the list above pertain to the production and marketing (and licensing and shipping, etc.) of not only Murakami's art but that of several Japanese artists promoted under Kaikai Kiki's umbrella. Many of these artists—Chiho Aoshima, Chinatsu Ban, Akane Koide, Mahomi Kunikata, Mr., Rei Sato, and Aya Takano—began their careers as studio assistants of Murakami's or under the employ of Kaikai Kiki and have lately begun to garner attention in their own right. Rather than entrusting their professional development to far-flung Western galleries that may not have a full grasp of the specifics of their work or a single-minded interest in their advancement, these artists allow Kaikai Kiki to manage their careers in exchange, of course, for a cut of their sales. To this end, Murakami advises them on the direction of their studio practices, on where to show their work (brokering deals with overseas galleries, some of which may represent him as well), and on potential marketing tie-ins, collaborations, and merchandising opportunities. Kaikai Kiki then provides crucial administrative support by assisting with complicated tax and billing details, translation services, press contacts, and all of the other myriad issues that attend the nurturing of a career in what remains—despite the Western art world's self-congratulatory affirmation of its recent "globalization"—a somewhat alien cultural and commercial arena.

The most valuable service, however, may be the most intangible: the creation of a self-sustaining critical apparatus in which the work of these young artists can flourish. Here, I refer to the first business function outlined in the list above, the planning of major exhibitions both in Japan and overseas. Indeed, Murakami's phenomenal success in the West may depend as much on the strength of his individual artworks as on the cogent critical and curatorial framework that he has constructed around them, most famously in his Superflat trilogy of exhibitions, which began in 2000 with the show that lent the series its name and continued with "Coloriage" in 2002 and "Little Boy" in 2005.[31] This is not the place to provide a full account of Murakami's multilayered curatorial arguments, which merit

31 "Superflat" debuted at the Parco Gallery in Tokyo before traveling to The Museum of Contemporary Art, Los Angeles; the Walker Art Center, Minneapolis; and the Henry Art Gallery, Seattle. "Coloriage" appeared at Paris's Fondation Cartier pour l'art contemporain, and "Little Boy" was installed at the Japan Society in New York.

a detailed consideration all their own. Suffice it to say that few curators have ever proven themselves as persuasive a cultural critic as has Murakami in his examination of the relationship between a certain strain of contemporary Japanese art and key aspects of that country's mass- and subcultural production (such as *manga* and *anime*), all within the larger context of a postwar collective unconscious that he characterizes as severely conflicted and, ultimately, infantilized.[32]

Murakami is certainly not the first artist to argue on behalf of a like-minded group of practitioners. The prewar avant-gardes were full of such garrulous self-analysis (think of the Futurists, the Surrealists, and the Constructivists, to name a few), and the postwar period saw the rise of artist/critics, such as Donald Judd and Mel Bochner, who wrote survey articles or curated group exhibitions of their contemporaries. Two key differences, however, remain: the first being that these Western examples were primarily addressed to audiences within their own cultural milieu, and the second being that the success of their critical positions was not likely to directly enrich their respective spokesmen. By raising this latter point, I do not mean to cast in doubt either the validity of Murakami's extremely compelling theses or his motives, but make no mistake about it: his activities as a curator and critic function as a shrewd marketing device. By framing and advancing a new "movement" of sorts, he has gained for his cohorts significant traction in both foreign intellectual and commercial markets, all the while co-opting the imprimatur of serious institutions, such as the Walker Art Center; the Japan Society; the Museum of Contemporary Art, Los Angeles; and even Yale University Press, which co-published the *Little Boy* catalogue. The fact that all three of his major curated shows to date have included not only his own work but that of younger artists represented by Kaikai Kiki means that he has a direct financial stake in their success, in terms of both the firm's revenues and his status as an artistic paterfamilias.

32 This thesis is explored at length in Murakami's writings in the *Little Boy* catalogue. For an excellent overview of the exhibition's underlying premise and Murakami's art in general, see Arthur Lubow, "The Murakami Method," *New York Times Magazine*, 3 April 2005, 48–57, 64, 76–79.

The World's a Stage

SUCH DISCLOSURES—ESPECIALLY WHERE the entanglement of institutional credibility and profit potential is concerned—will likely provoke some serious hand-wringing. We might cringe at the image of museums handing art dealers the keys to the kingdom, but to a certain extent, of course, they already have. My goal, however, is not to launch a full investigation into the nagging issue of art-world conflicts of interest, but to show that Murakami is working the system with amazing dexterity in perfectly plain sight. Here we might turn to Jack Bankowsky's compelling recent discussions of artists such as Maurizio Cattelan and Richard Prince who, he claims, "perform" the art system by reframing within their practices some of its least reputable, if most fundamental, functions—whether mercantile, as in the case of Cattelan's the Wrong Gallery, a five-square-foot storefront parody of New York's mammoth commercial emporiums, or publicity oriented, as in the example of Prince's recent Spiritual America redux (2005), a semi-secret restaging of both the execution and exhibition of his notorious Brooke Shields photograph. For Bankowsky, these artists learned from Warhol that the secret to success depends on a two-pronged approach, based on a "reciprocity...between the broad proliferation of extra-art activities and the museum-ready icons that provide the freewheeling brand a graphic and institutional identity."[33] Murakami's core business strategy is much the same, except that his activities outside the white cube are a far more crucial part of the equation and, as we have seen, are less a burlesque of commercial and curatorial conventions than a deadly serious co-optation and embodiment of them. Indeed, if the Wrong Gallery's tiny storefront was recently moved from the streets of Chelsea to London's august Tate Modern, it's much harder to imagine a comparable transposition of Murakami's expansive business operations to such secure institutional confines. Similarly, while the Wrong Gallery and artists such as Tino Sehgal or Anthony Burdin have lately graced international art fairs with special projects that parody or attempt to disrupt the shows' seamless mercantile machinations, Kaikai Kiki has now begun renting stalls and promoting and selling young Japanese artists just as any other dealer might.[34]

---

33 Jack Bankowsky, "Tent Community," *Artforum* 44, no. 2 (October 2005): 231. See also related discussions in Bankowsky, "Openings: Anthony Burdin," *Artforum* 43, no. 7 (March 2005): 226–27; and Bankowsky, "Ciao Rensselaerville: The Other Richard Prince," forthcoming in Nancy Spector, *Richard Prince: Spiritual America*, exh.cat. (New York: Guggenheim Museum, 2007).

34 These projects by Tino Sehgal and Anthony Burdin are discussed in Bankowsky, "Tent Community," 230–31.

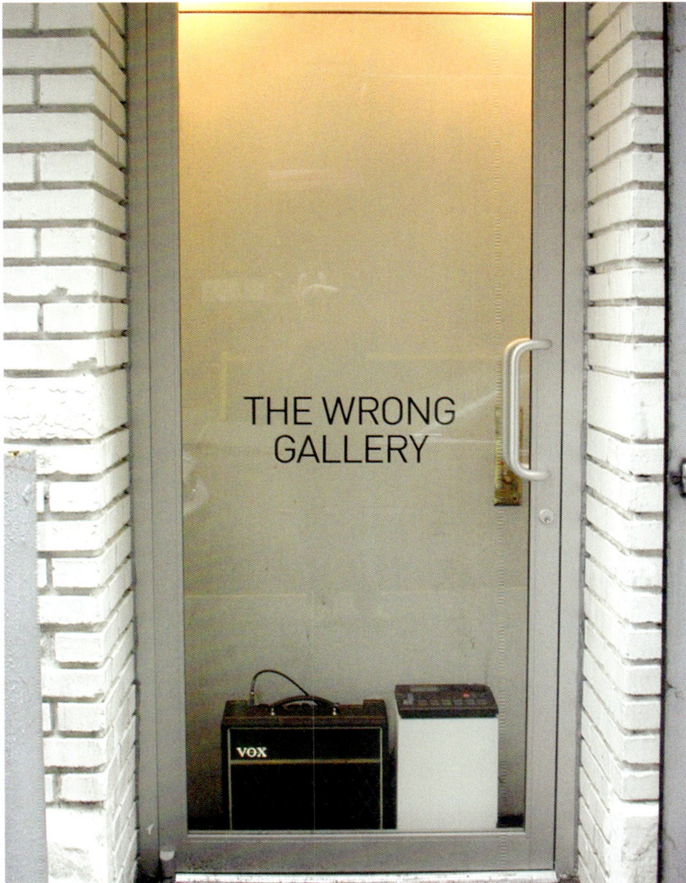

Martin Creed
Work No. 122: All the Sounds on a Drum Machine, 1995–2000
Drum machine, amplifier, and plinth
Dimensions variable
Courtesy of the artist and
Gavin Brown's enterprise, New York
Installation at The Wrong Gallery,
New York, 2002
© Martin Creed

Comparisons like these show that Murakami's practice, by its very nature, has a way of making most others look stagey and almost hopelessly bound within art's institutional parameters. This was certainly the case when his Louis Vuitton bags and their copies spread like pathogens in Venice, where United States representative Fred Wilson hired an African immigrant to hawk arty versions of fake designer purses outside the American pavilion as part of an extended meditation on the historical role of blacks in Venetian society.[35] The same could also be said of Pierre Huyghe and Philippe Parreno's Annlee Project, which revolved around their purchase in 1999 of the copyright to a gamine *manga* character that they then gave to colleagues for use in their artworks and eventually "set free" through legal procedures barring Annlee's further commercial (or artistic) use. Their project was an ingenious comment on the nature of intellectual property and its role in the

35 This contrast between Murakami's and Wilson's handbags galvanized my understanding of the former's Vuitton project in Venice. See my "In the Bag," 240.

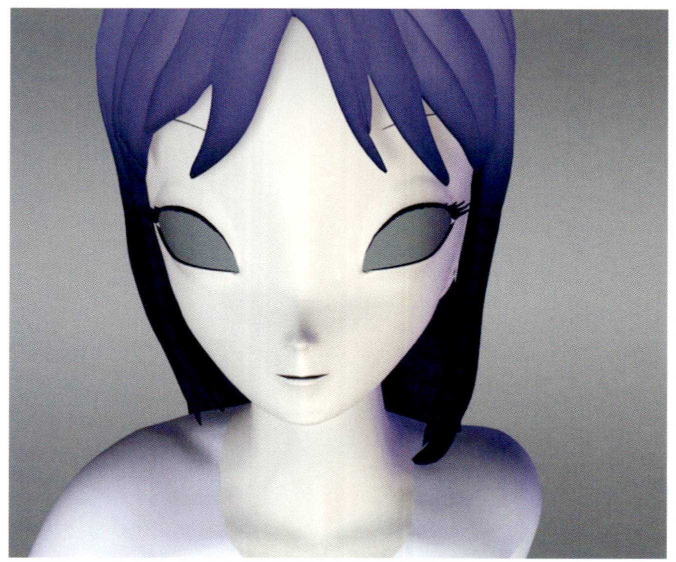

Philippe Parreno
Still from
Anywhere Out of the World, 2000
Video with sound
4 minutes
Courtesy Marian Goodman Gallery, New York
© Philippe Parreno

M/M, Paris
Annlee: No Ghost Just a Shell, 2000
Four-color silkscreen
69 5/16 x 47 1/4 inches
© M/M

creation and consumption of identity, yet for all its involvement of real commercial and legal precepts it was a *comment on them* all the same, which is far more difficult to say with certainty of Murakami's pesky DOB.[36]

Of course, we could hardly fault Annlee for her distance from the workaday world of mass-cultural commodities, since it is precisely this remove (the difference between being "reflective of" and simply *of*) that guarantees her ultimate status as art, by which we can only mean, at least since Marcel Duchamp, something—anything, really—bound within art's discursive matrix. This is the invisible frame or pedestal that makes possible the superhuman perceptual feat of seeing that imperceptible difference between a table and a sculpture (in the case of Jorge Pardo, or Isamu Noguchi before him) or a dinner party and an artwork by Rirkrit Tiravanija. If such a meal is more easily understood as art than is a sheet of stickers covered with beaming flowers, this is probably because it falls on the right side of the art/commerce divide, ostensibly partaking of a gift economy more readily than a capitalist one (though the fact that art has by now been rather well

36 For an in-depth discussion of the Annlee project, see Pierre Huyghe and Philippe Parreno, *No Ghost Just a Shell* (Cologne, Germany: Verlag der Buchhandlung Walther König, 2003); and Philip Nobel, "Annlee: Sign of the Times," *Artforum* 41, no. 5 (January 2003): 104–09. Gingeras contrasted Murakami's project with the critical aims of Huyghe and Parreno in "Pop After Pop: A Roundtable," *Artforum* 43, no. 2 (October 2004): 172–73.

absorbed into the latter system makes it increasingly difficult to argue its ontology on purely moral grounds). Regardless of where one stands on this ethical spectrum, it is nevertheless astonishing to recognize that, at this late date in Duchamp's reception, Murakami has managed to develop a practice that cannot be comfortably accommodated within art's otherwise infinitely elastic frame. This is no small achievement. We may smile with retrospective bemusement at the debates between Pop's early detractors and defenders over whether a painted soup can could count as art, but forty years later it's rather more astounding—and humbling—to find our enlightened certainties tested in the face of an animated lizard.

Warhol would be proud—or maybe jealous. After all, it is he—the first master of the diversified portfolio—who casts his long pale shadow over Kaikai Kiki's corporate sprawl. And it is with him that we must end. By the time he died, Warhol's brand had at one point or another included a magazine, a television studio (producing videos for the Cars and a show of his own for MTV), a rock band, books (an arena which Murakami has also lately entered), and a passel of films destined for release not in art houses but in honest-to-goodness movie theaters.[37] "Business art is the step that comes after Art," he famously wrote, "Being good in business is the most fascinating kind of art...making money is art and working is art and good business is the best art."[38] The remark has an aphoristic ring, but in retrospect, Andy Warhol Enterprises may actually look less like a proper commercial endeavor than a glamorous house of cards buttressed by the sale of its figurehead's paintings (the designation seems an apt one for Warhol here, given that the majority of his ventures, unlike Murakami's, were not overseen by him but by acolyte-entrepreneurs such as Paul Morrissey, Vincent Fremont, and Bob Colacello).[39] *Interview* magazine did, eventually, turn a profit, but everything else appears to have been rather less lucrative, except where generating the aura of hype was concerned. Murakami, however, holds Warhol to his word—chasing after higher-profile collaborations, a broader range of services, a larger market share, a bigger piece of the pie. When I asked him somewhat incredulously how he came to purvey Kaikai Kiki Chocolate Crunch, which is sold in blue or pink tins covered with his signature flowers, he replied in all seriousness that his Roppongi

37 These activities are described in greater detail in O'Connor and Liu, *Unseen Warhol*. Following Warhol's lead, Murakami recently published his own book elaborating the secrets of his success and analyzing Japan's lagging art market. As of this writing, it is only available in Japanese. See Murakami, *Geijutsu kigyōron* (The theory of art entrepreneurship) (Tokyo: Gentōsha, Inc., 2005). For an English-language discussion of this book, see Kay Itoi, "Murakami's Guide to Success," Artnet.com's magazine, 4 October 2006, http://www.artnet.com/magazineus/books/itoi/itoi10-4-06.asp.

38 Warhol, *The Philosophy of Andy Warhol (From A to B and Back Again)* (New York: Harcourt, Inc., 1975), 92.

39 Paul Morrissey, for example, directed many of Warhol's more "mainstream" films; Vincent Fremont served, among other capacities, as the studio manager and vice-president of Andy Warhol Enterprises and the producer of *Andy Warhol's TV* and *Andy Warhol's Fifteen Minutes*; and Bob Colacello was a longtime editor of *Interview*, in addition to participating in other projects.

Hills royalty checks revealed Mori's house-brand candy to be a big seller, and, quite simply, he wanted in on the action.[40]

If Murakami keeps a sharper eye on new market "opportunities" than did Pop's elder statesman, he thinks harder about the future, too. Warhol may have managed to hatch a brood of "Superstars," but none of them could sustain their status outside the Factory's make-believe hothouse, their celebrity always stuck like gaudy barnacles on the cult of his. Murakami, by contrast, is intent on establishing independent careers for his chosen sevensome, and he may have been wise to put the name Kaikai Kiki on the door rather than his own. After all, Andy Warhol Enterprises died with its namesake, but Murakami—perhaps taking a page out of Christian Dior's or Martha Stewart's playbooks—knows that a truly successful brand today must be able to survive its founder, and he claims that he may one day step down as president to become just another artist in Kaikai Kiki's fold.[41] It's hard to believe the famous micromanager on this score, but whatever the case, he has succeeded in masterminding a kind of self-sustaining organism totally unlike any before it. There are the artworks and the related merchandise, as well as the exotic hybrids between them; the corporate commissions and tie-ins that are as much Murakami's own as they are Vuitton's or Mori's; the budding disciples, along with the art fairs and marketing campaigns that promote them; and the curatorial and critical discourse that envelops the whole project in a vibrant intellectual firmament. And yet the beauty of this strange biosphere is not its independence from the external artistic, commercial, and critical structures that it replicates, but its imbrication within them. It is a world of Murakami's own device, and whether its effects are to be found in a gallery, comic shop, TV commercial, or fashion boutique, it is a world inextricably overlaid and intertwined with our own.

This, admittedly, is a potentially frightening future for art, but it's too late to turn back now. We could not be blamed for wanting to, though, as even Murakami himself flinched in the glare of the Vuitton-induced spotlight. "I need to rebuild the wall between the commercial art and the fine art I do," he said in the midst of the frenzy three years ago.[42] When I later asked him about this comment, he admitted to having experienced a moment of trepidation—like Dr.

40 Murakami, conversation with the author, Long Island City, New York, 14 November 2006.

41 Ibid. The example of Martha Stewart is instructive here, because during her much-publicized legal imbroglio, lasting from 2002 until 2005, executives at her company explored ways to maintain her brand's vitality and market position while minimizing to a certain degree the presence of her likeness and name on her products. Such a strategy may prefigure steps that will necessarily be taken as she ages, if the corporation is to continue after her death. Murakami, similarly, may also wish to avoid hinging the future success of Kaikai Kiki entirely to his star.

42 Murakami, quoted in Frederick, "Move Over, Andy Warhol."

Frankenstein facing his monster—when confronted with the orgiastic consummation of his system's implied promise. But it lasted just a moment, for he knew better than to try and stop the inexorable tide he had unleashed.[43] The wall, indeed, is broken beyond repair, and with it comes the loss of quotation marks and brackets that—unlike the invention of photography—may deal the true deathblow to art's still-resilient aura. But in place of this cosseting nimbus comes a new frisson, one derived from the tense intermingling of an artist's work with that of anyone else. This is the buzz one gets when spotting a colorful fake Louis Vuitton belt on the subway, or a DOB doll amidst so many mundane others, or a tiny photograph of a museum inside a box of gum. Both toxic and intoxicating, it is the buzz of injecting dye into a system like drugs into a vein. Warhol knew it well: "I didn't expect the movies we were doing to be commercial," he remarked of his more "mainstream" pictures. "It was enough that the art had gone into the stream of commerce, out into the real world. It was very heady to be able to look and see our movie out there in the real world on a marquee instead of in there in the art world."[44]

The headiness that Warhol described can be felt not only by the one who places the sign in the "real world" but by the one who finds it there, though that glimmer of perception is by no means universal. It derives from a tiny bit of information we carry inside of us—and here Murakami's work may surprisingly share a fundamental premise of Conceptual art and even of institutional critique—that allows us to spot within the commercial welter one of his advertisements or Warhol's name on a marquee, just as we might recognize, say, a patch of Daniel Buren's stripes in the street.[45] The ambition to be in the real world has haunted art at least since modernism declared its autonomy from it, whether in the revolutionary dreams of the Constructivists or in the financially motivated aspirations of Dalí. If fully realized, it is a dream that will lead to art's vanishing. But for now, at least, the sign still glows true.

---

43 With hindsight, Murakami has chosen not to retreat from the Vuitton project but to pursue other similarly high-profile ventures. When questioned about the lessons of this collaboration, he claimed that he now believes that the fashion industry's semi-annual product launches are a far more effective means of maintaining the public's attention than the traditional schedule of an artist presenting a solo show every two years in a particular city. Pressed further as to whether this logic would imply that he might seek multiple gallery shows within a year in the same city, he cited the activities of a rap impresario like Kanye West as a more suitable model, since West might release a new album every other year, but during the intervening months might produce tracks for like-minded artists, make guest appearances on their recordings, or find other outlets for maintaining a continuous public presence.

44 Warhol, *The Philosophy of Andy Warhol*, 92.

45 Perhaps the most incisive articulation of this condition is to be found in Andrea Fraser's writing on the legacy of institutional critique: "[Michael] Asher took Duchamp one step further. Art is not art because it is signed by an artist or shown i and consume it as art, whether as object, gesture, representation, or only idea.... What Asher thus demonstrated is that the institution of art is not only 'institutionalized' in organizations like museums and objectified in art objects. It is also internalized and embodied in people. It is internalized in the competencies, conceptual models, and modes of perception that allow us to produce, write about, and understand art, or simply to recognize art as art, whether as artists, critics, curators, art historians, dealers, collectors, or museum visitors." Fraser, "From the Critique of Institutions to an Institution of Critique," *Artforum* 44, no. 1 (September 2005): 281.

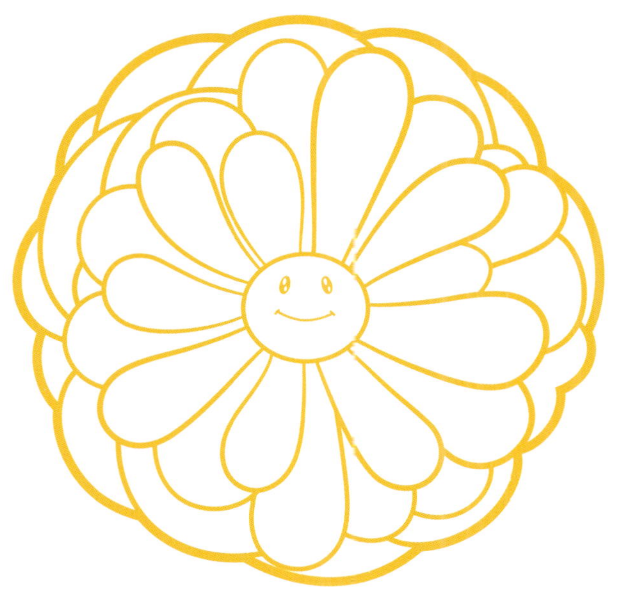

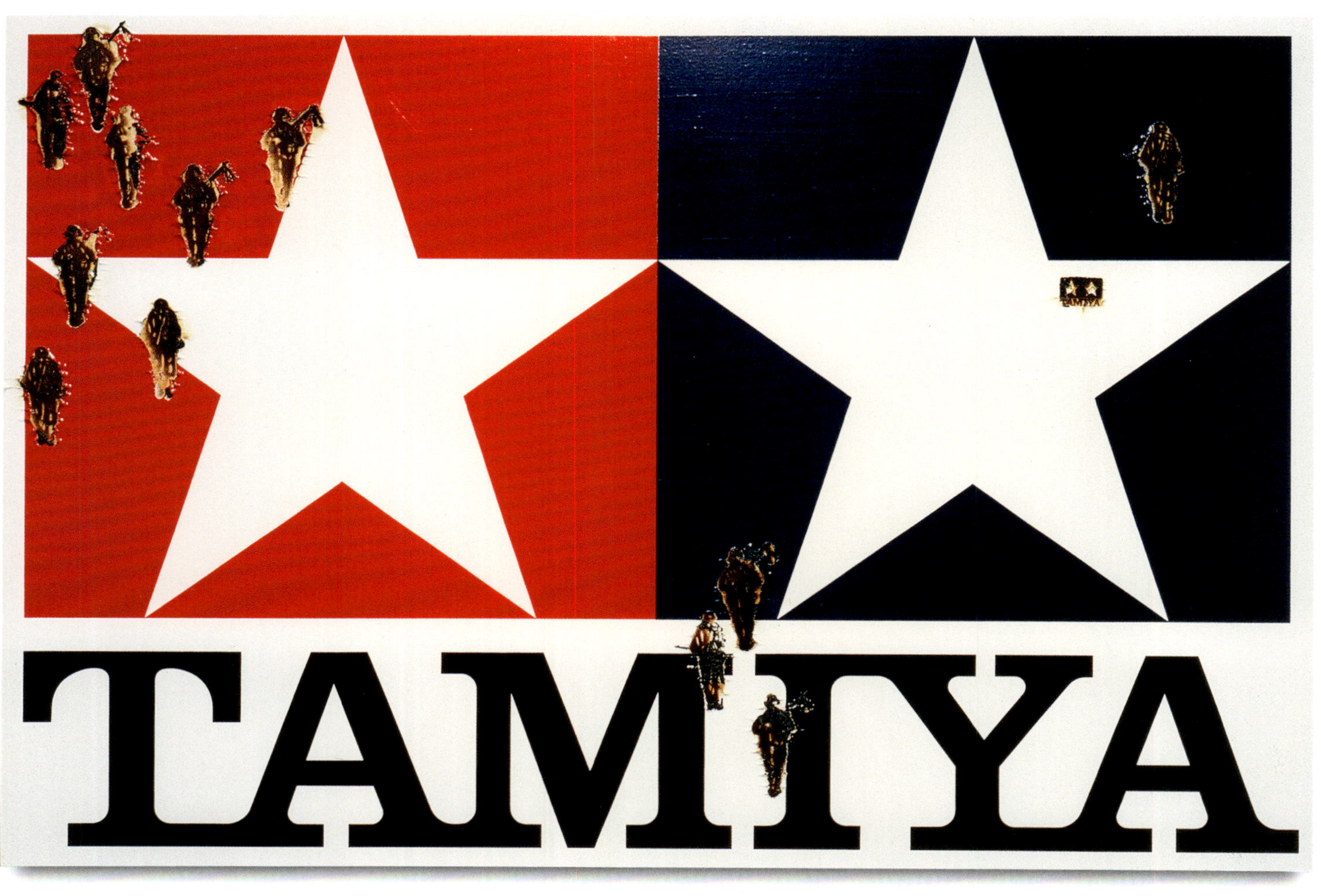

Signboard TAMIYA, 1991

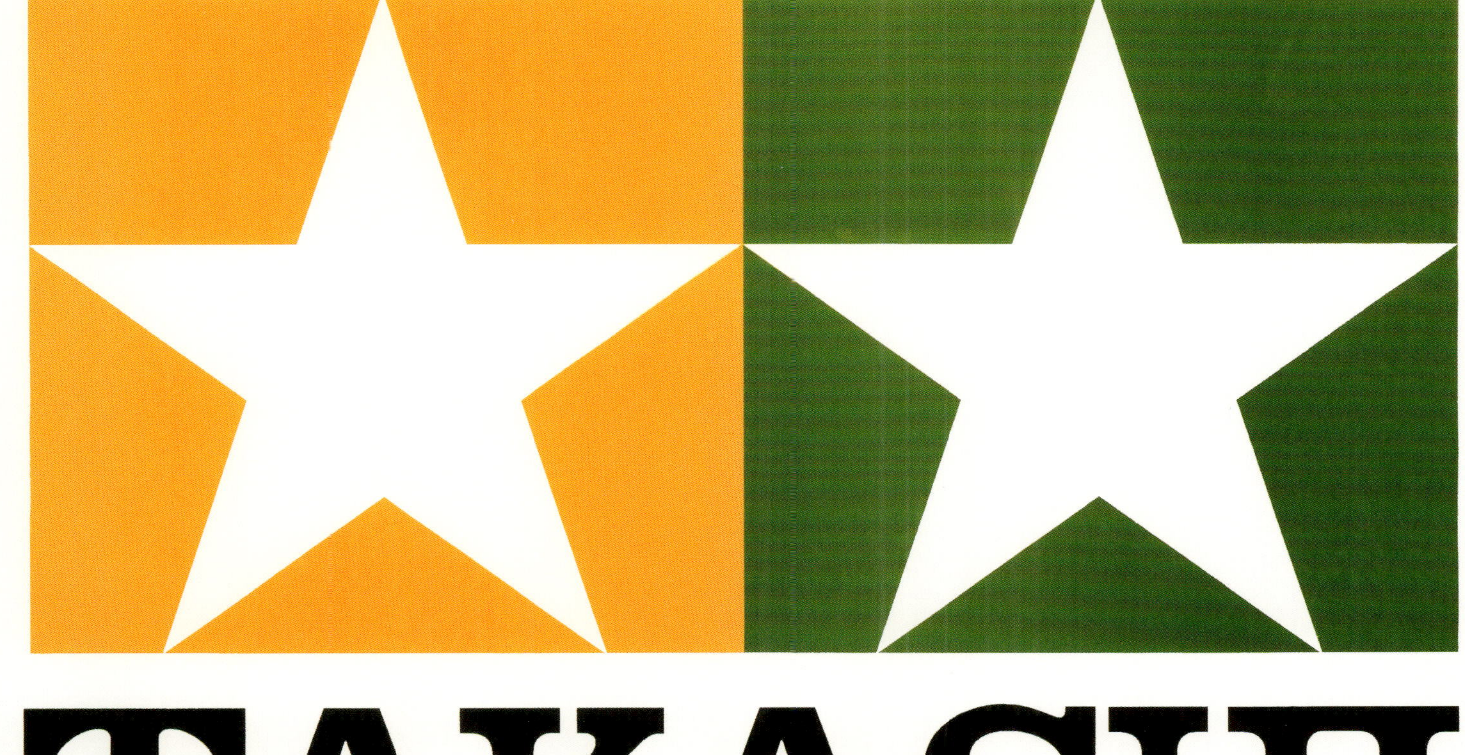

Signboard TAKASHI, 1992

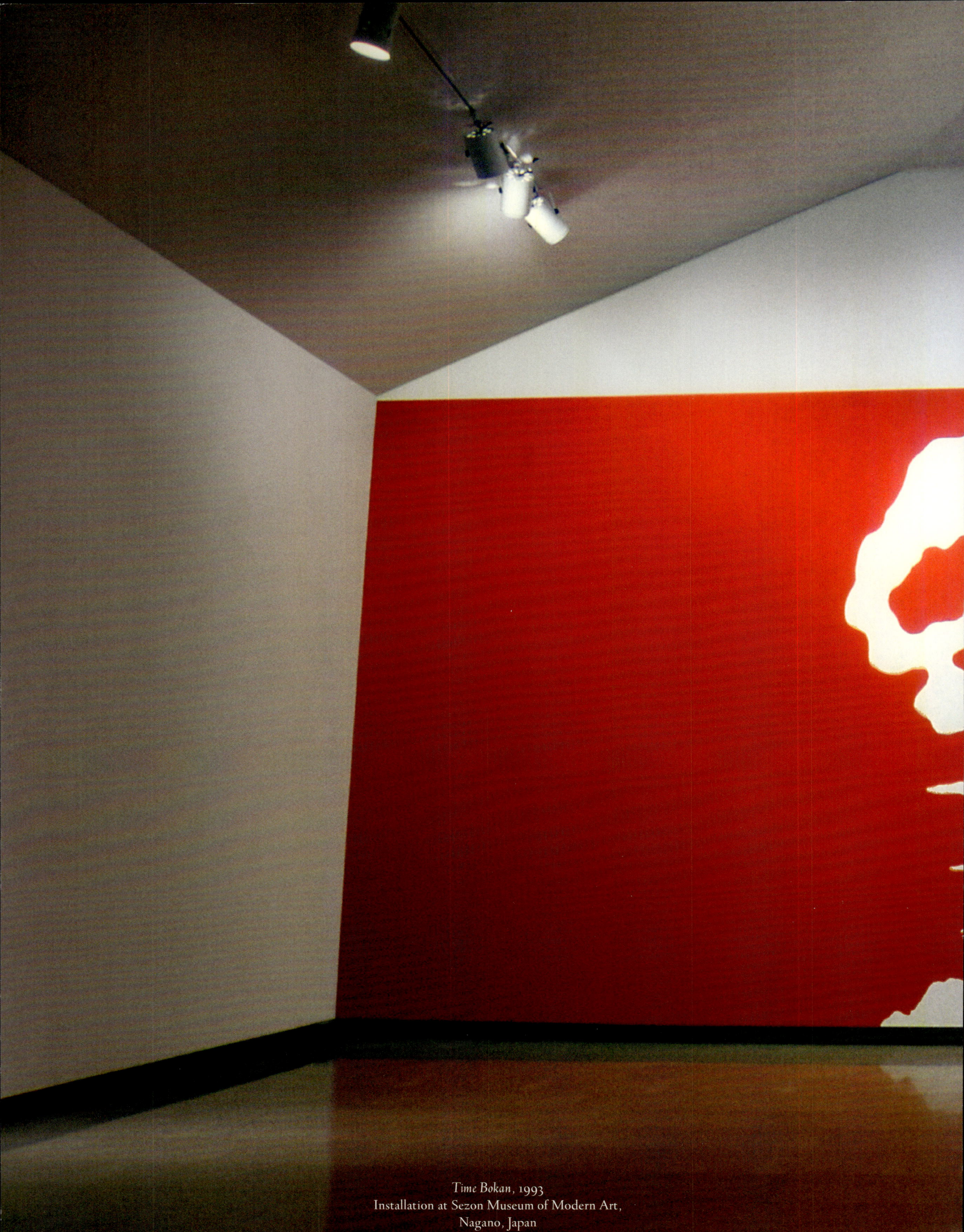

Time Bokan, 1993
Installation at Sezon Museum of Modern Art,
Nagano, Japan

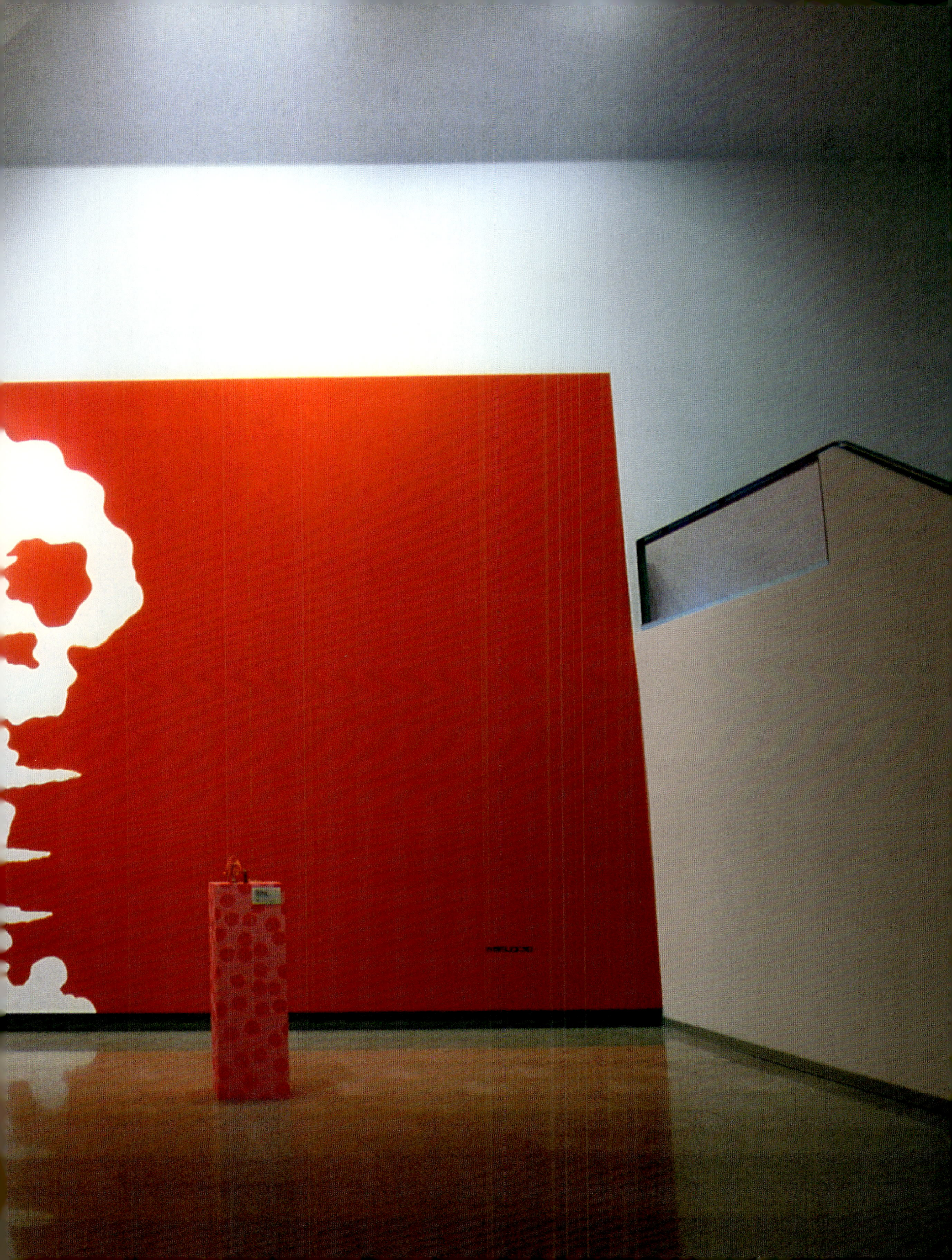

DOB *Genesis*, 1993

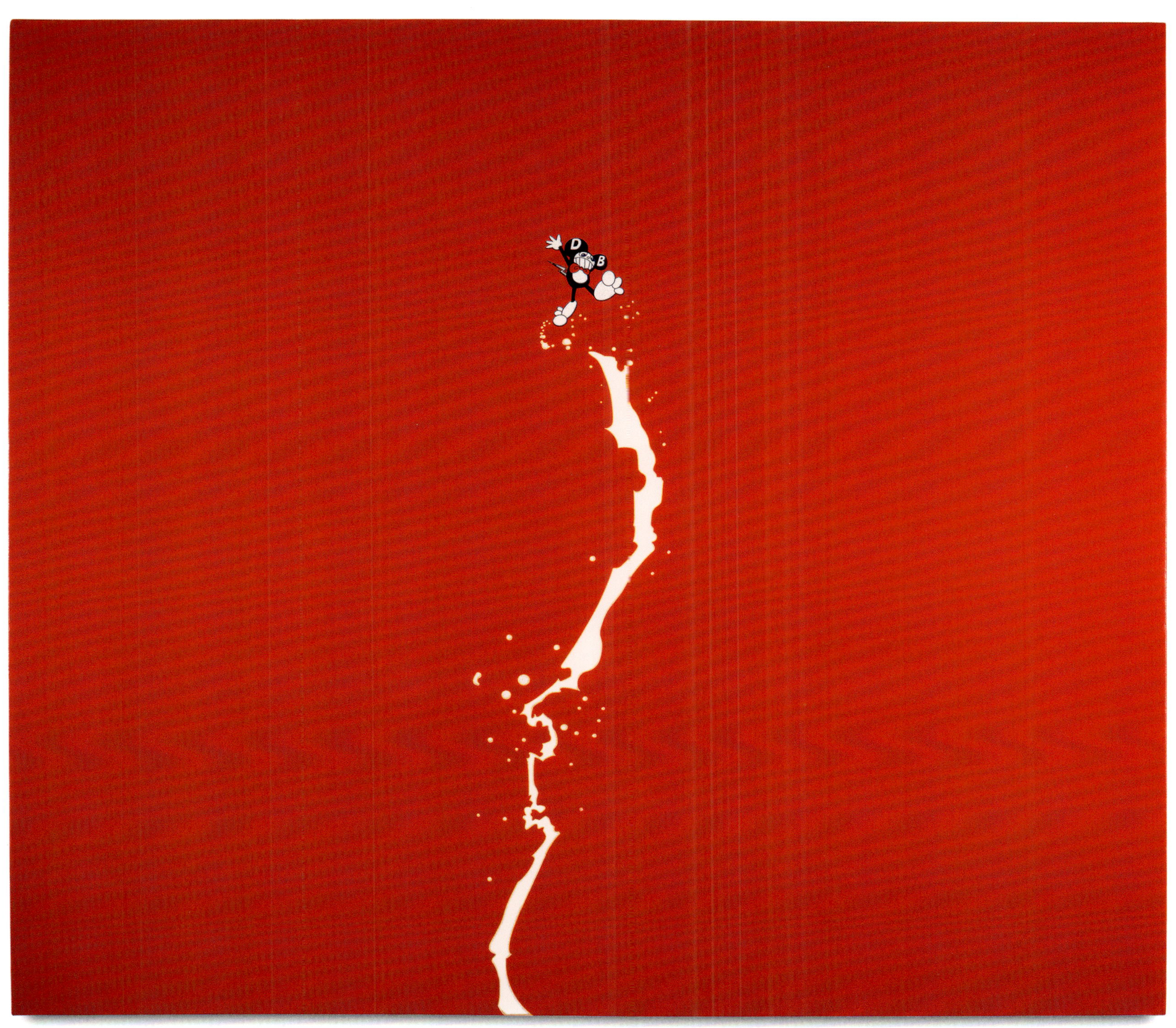

ZuZaZaZaZaZa, 1994

following page
top: *Stew (blue)*, 1995
bottom: *Stew (red)*, 1995

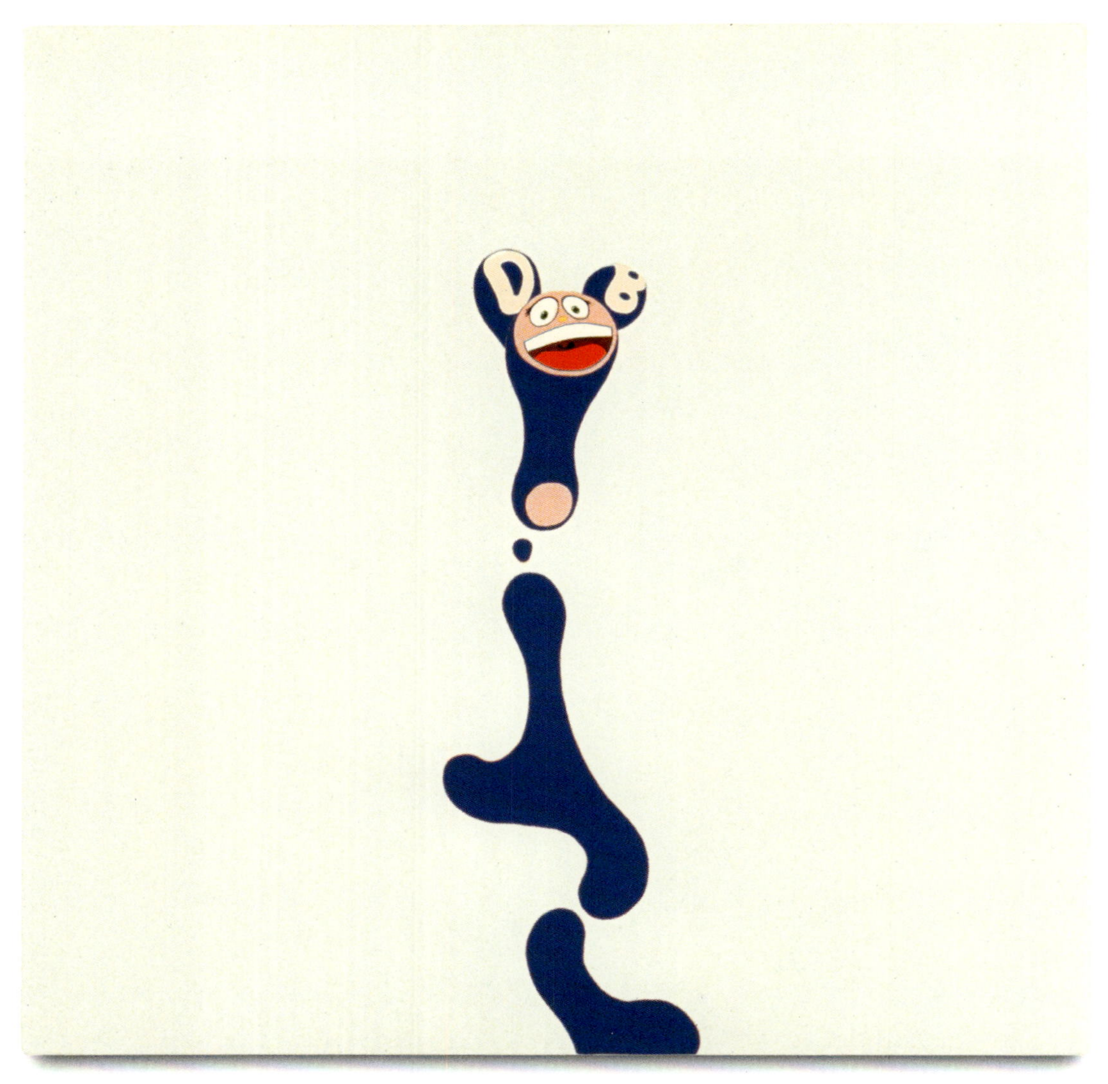
D
B

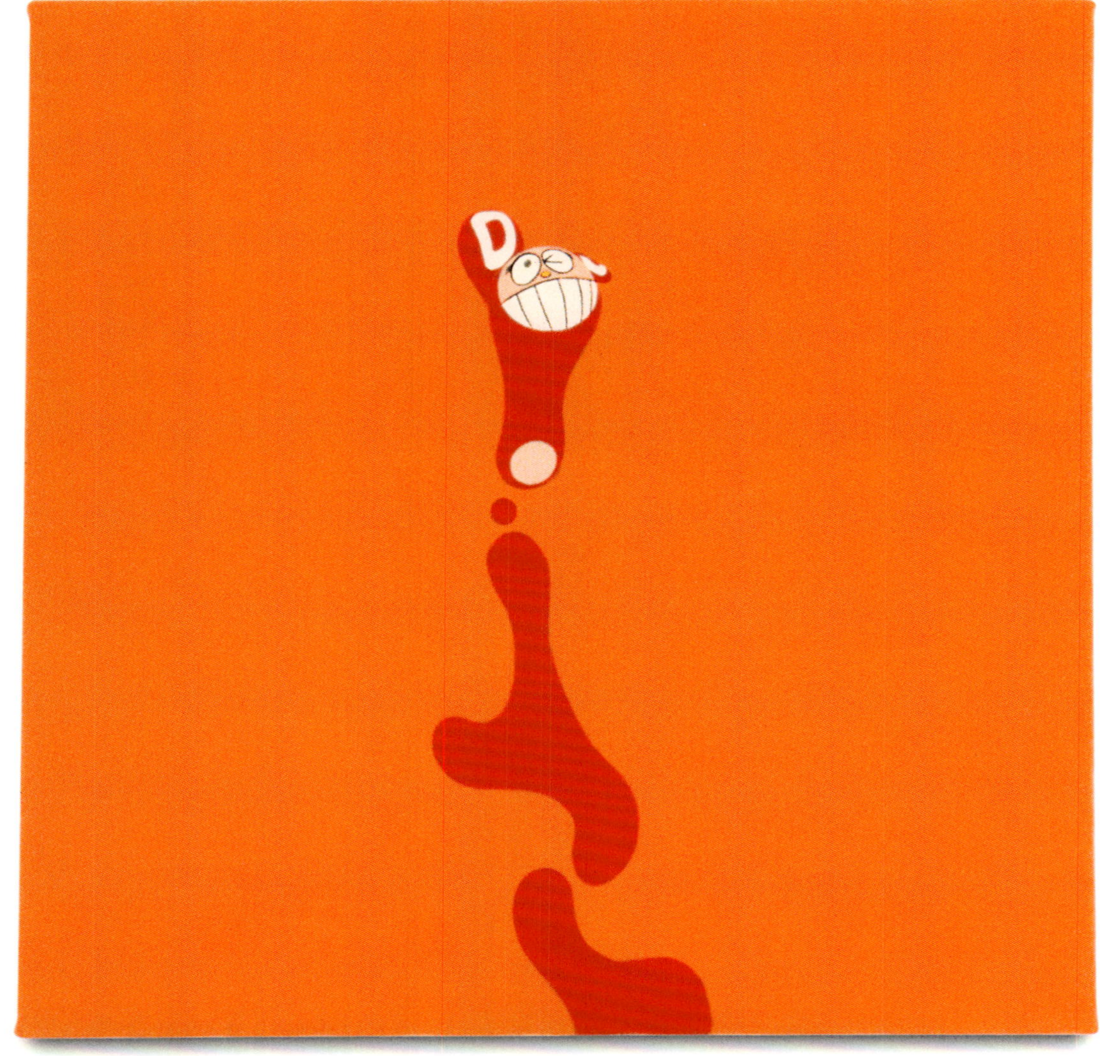
D

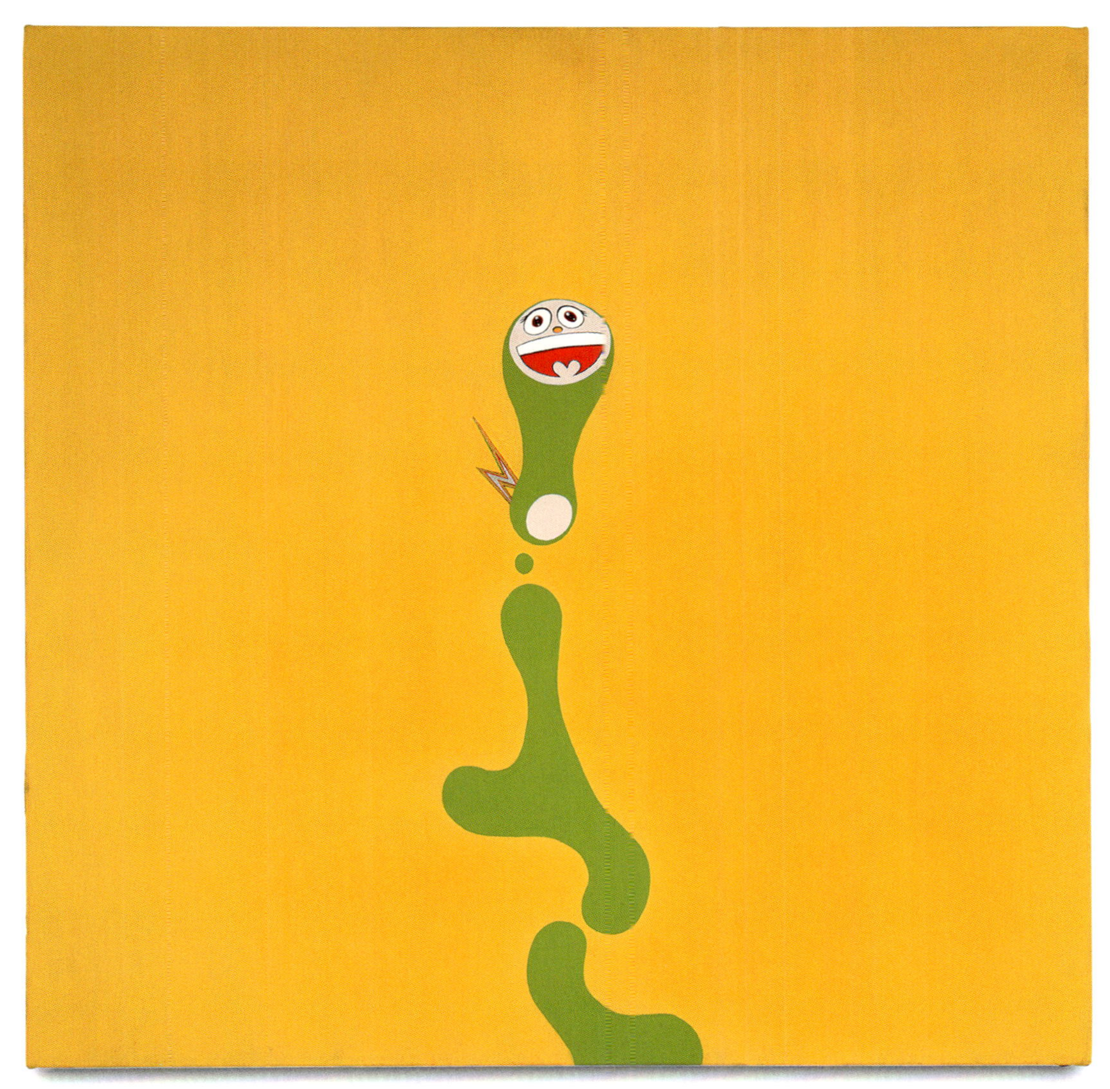

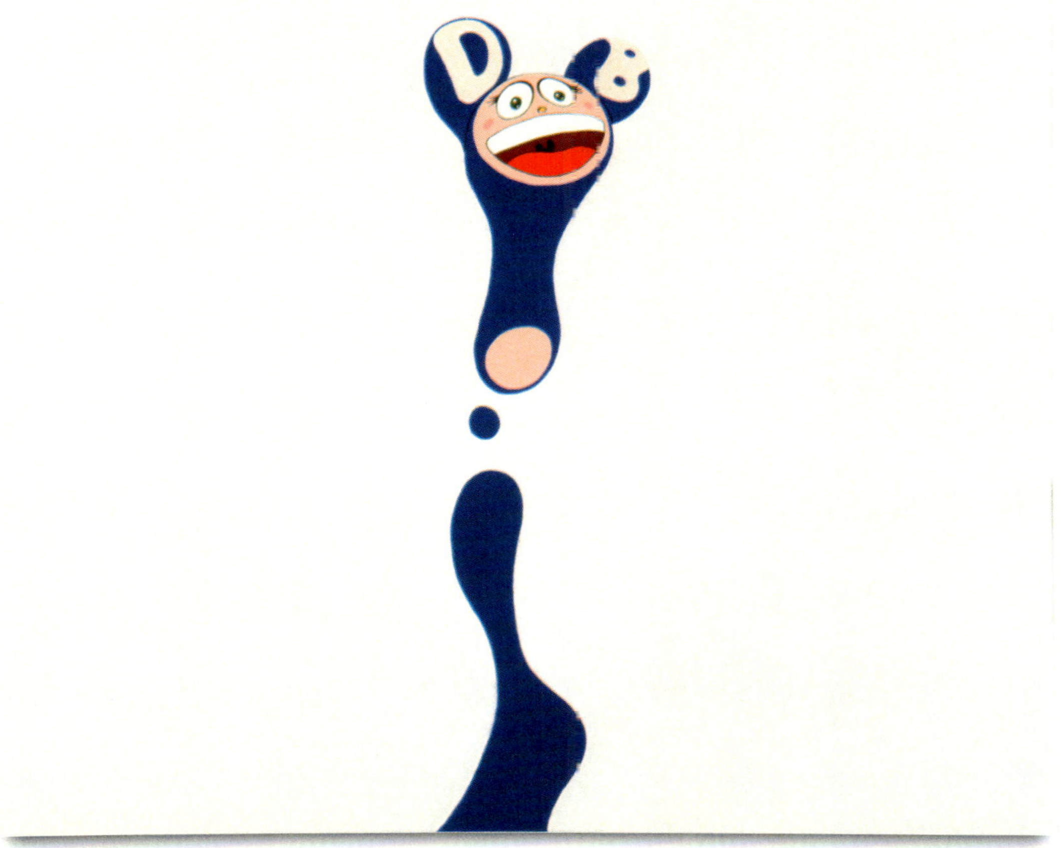

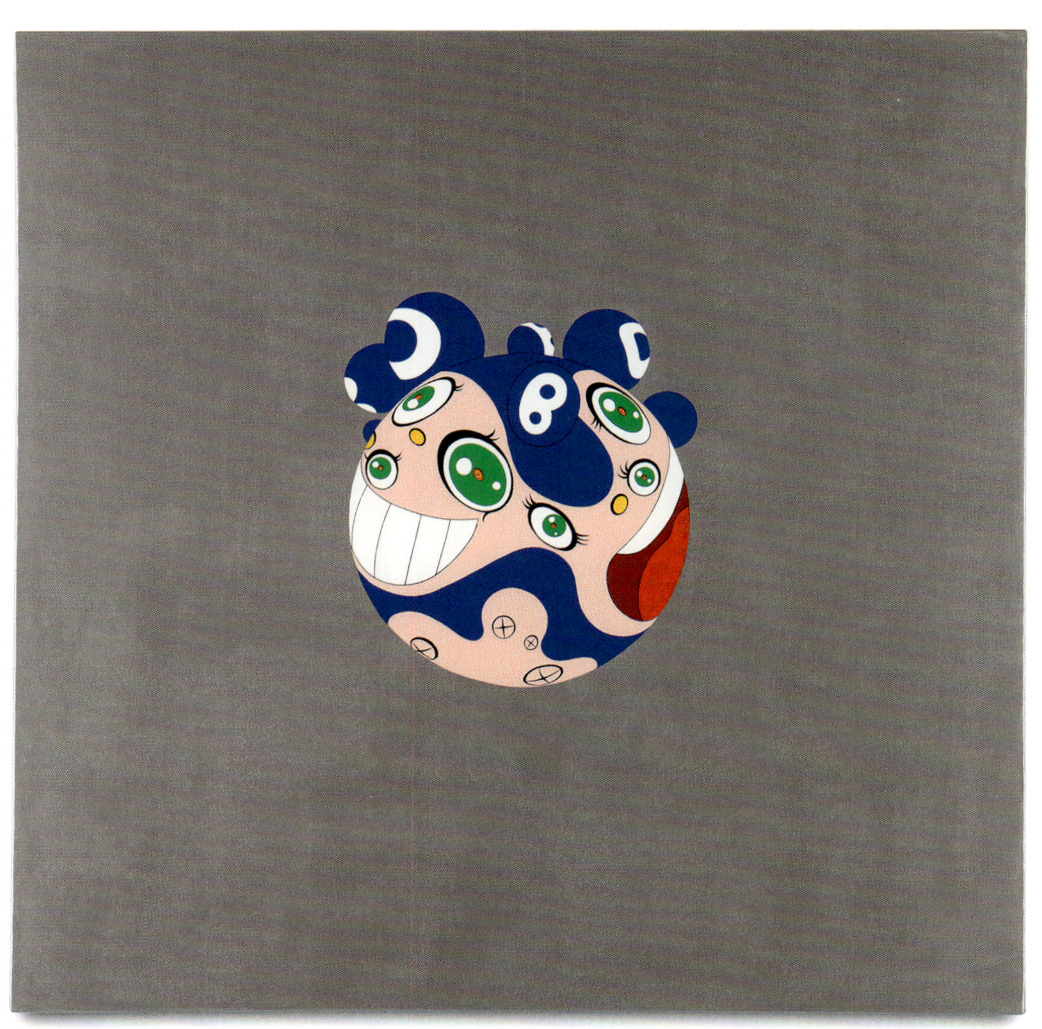

previous page
top: *Stew (yellow)*, 1995
bottom: *Pschitt (blue)*, 1995

Forest of DOB, 1995

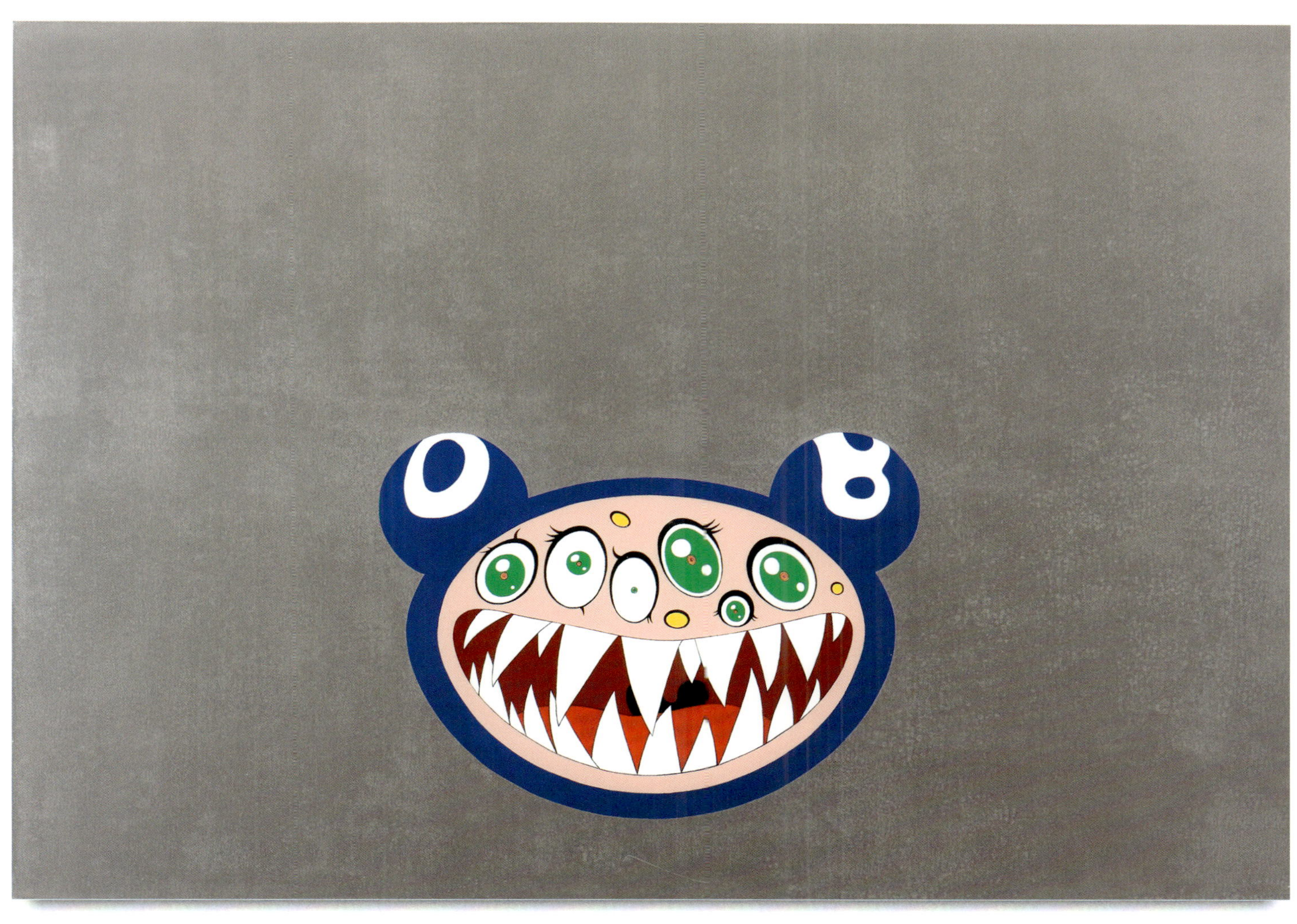

DOB's March, 1995

DOB's March (above) and *Forest of DOB*, both 1995
Installation at SCAI The Bathhouse,
Tokyo

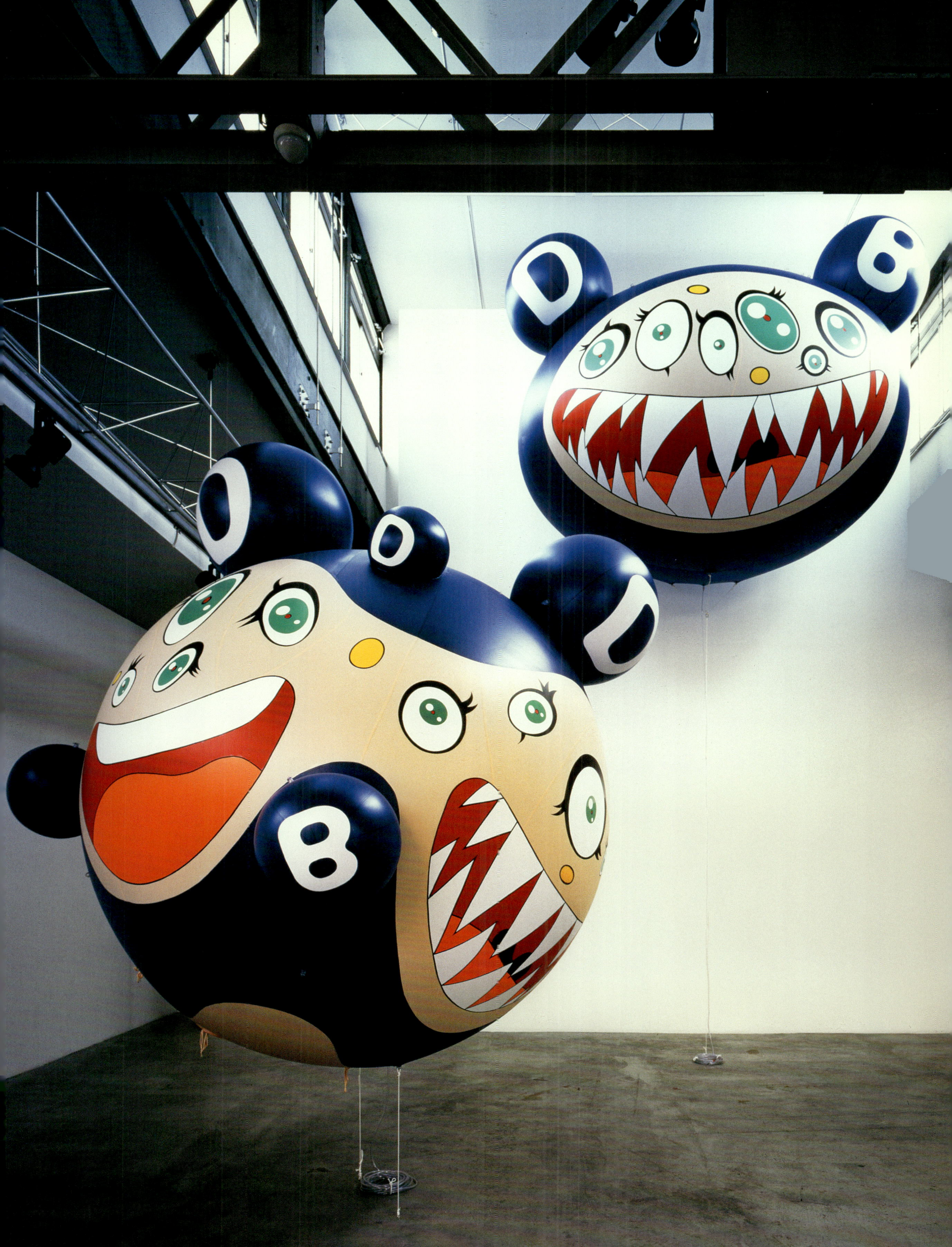

Chaos, 1996
Installation at Canal City Hakata,
Fukuoka, Japan

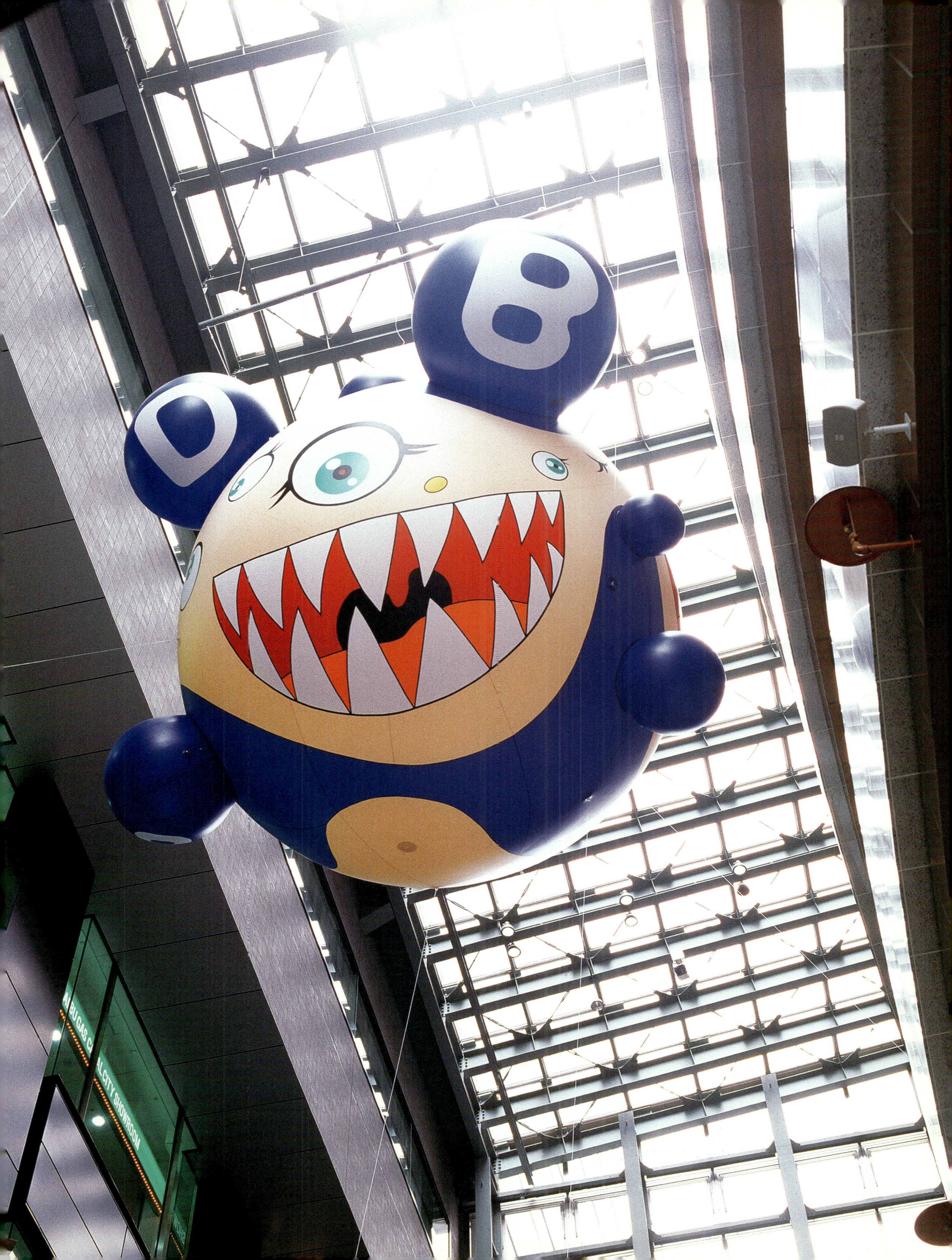
D
B
BU GAS
CITY SHOWROOM

Mr. DOB, 1995
Installation at Staatliche Kunsthalle
Baden-Baden, Germany, 2000

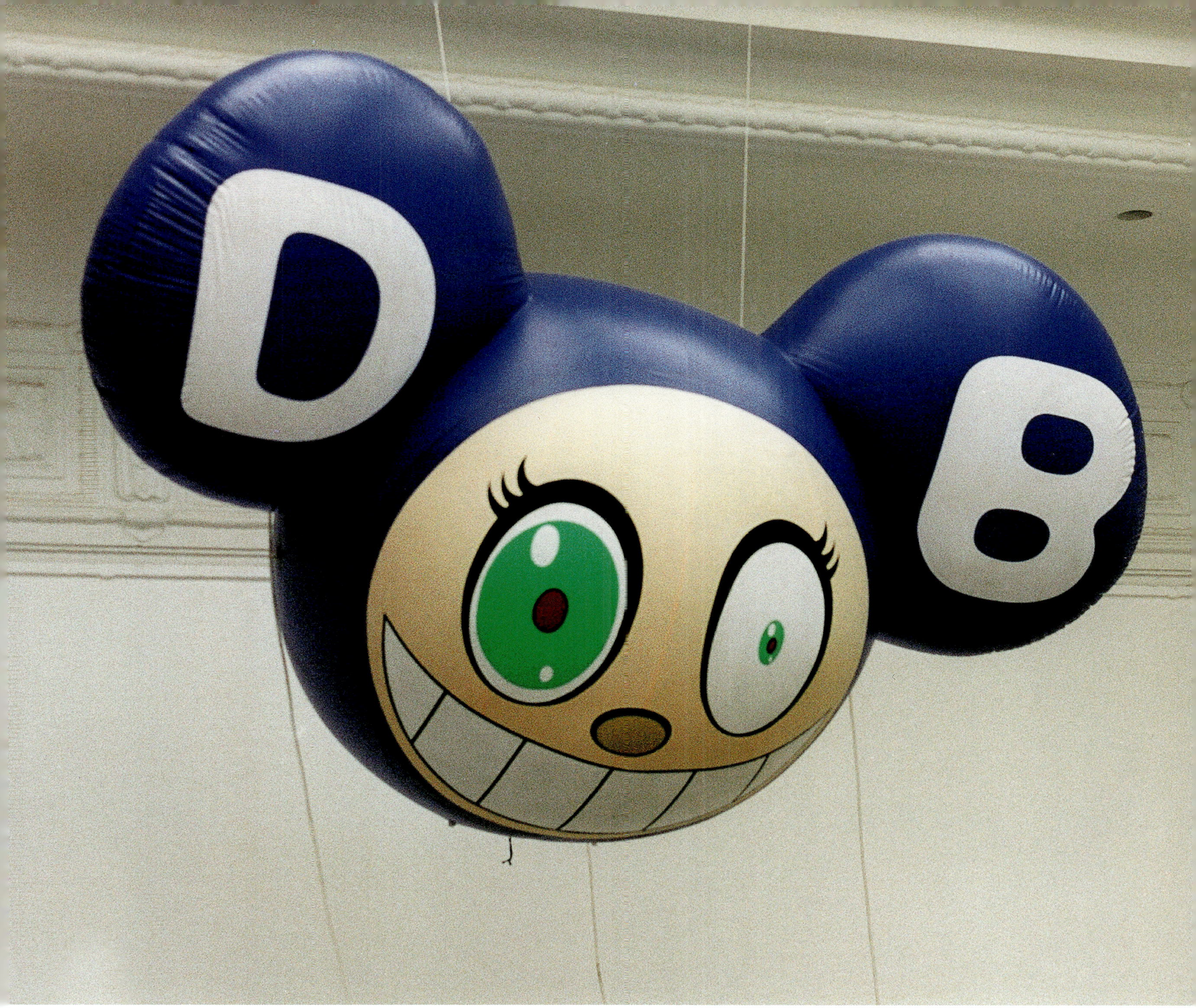
D
B

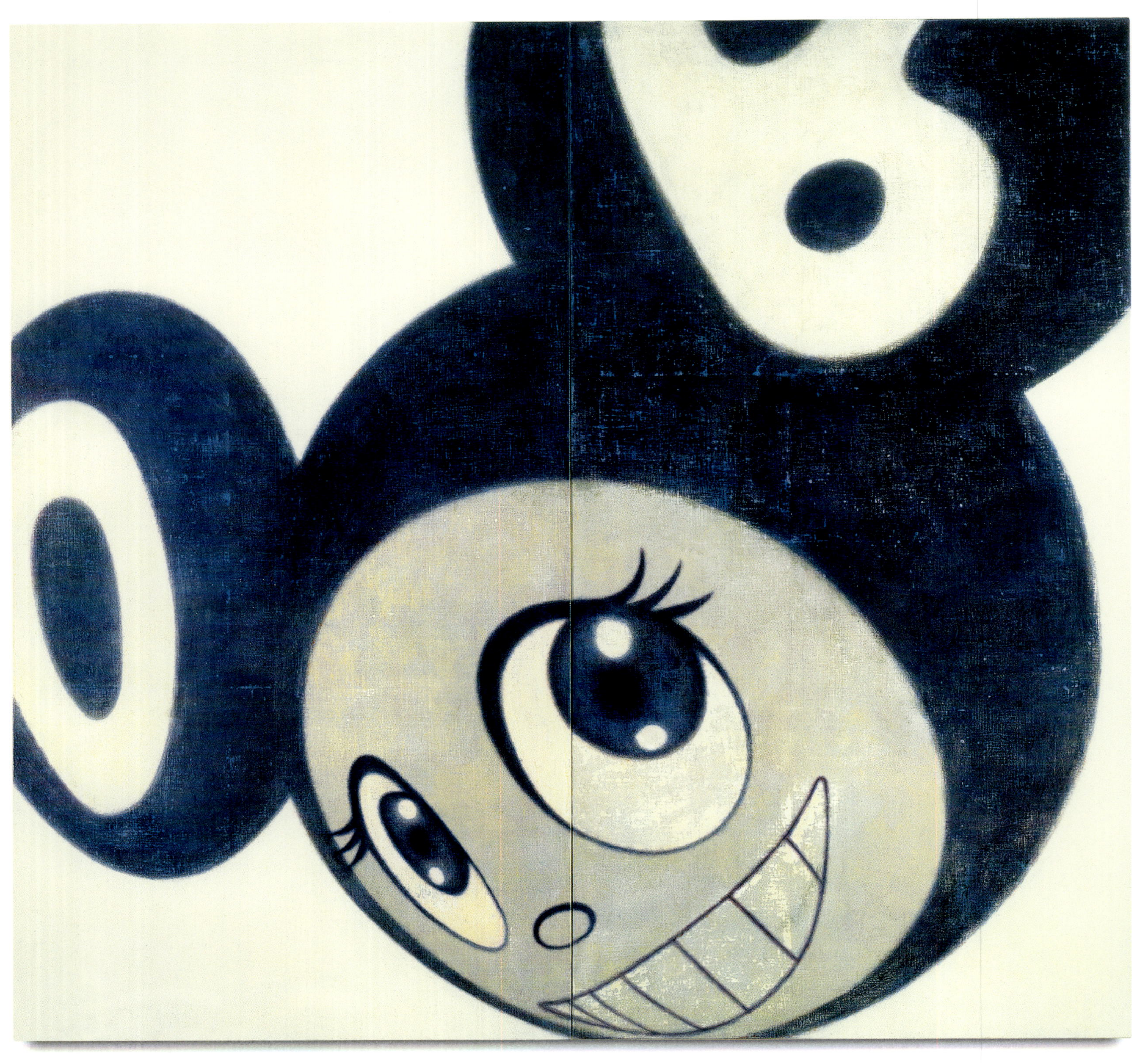

And Then, And Then And Then And Then And Then (Blue), 1996

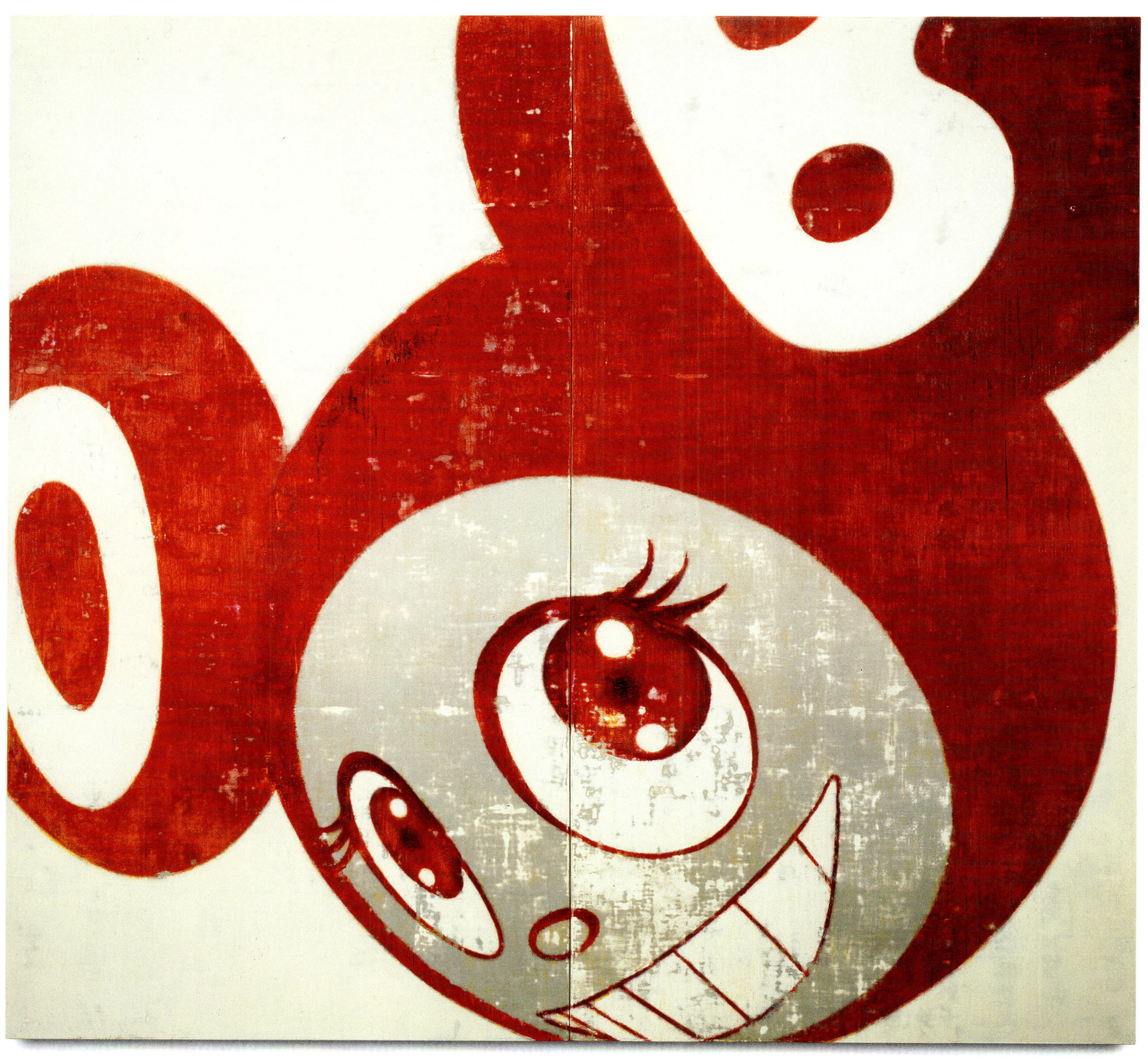

And Then, And Then And Then And Then And Then (Red), 1996

following spread
727, 1996

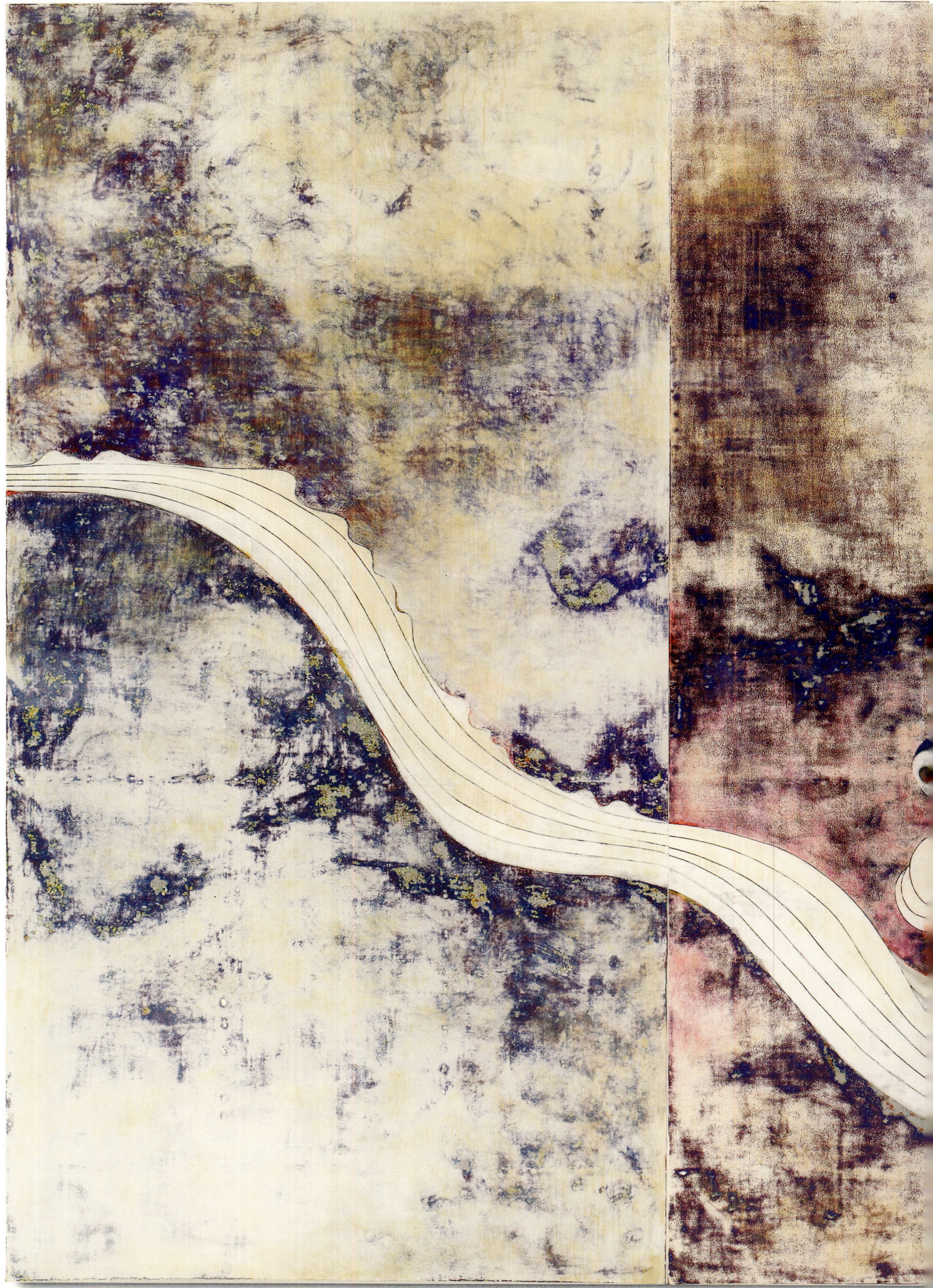

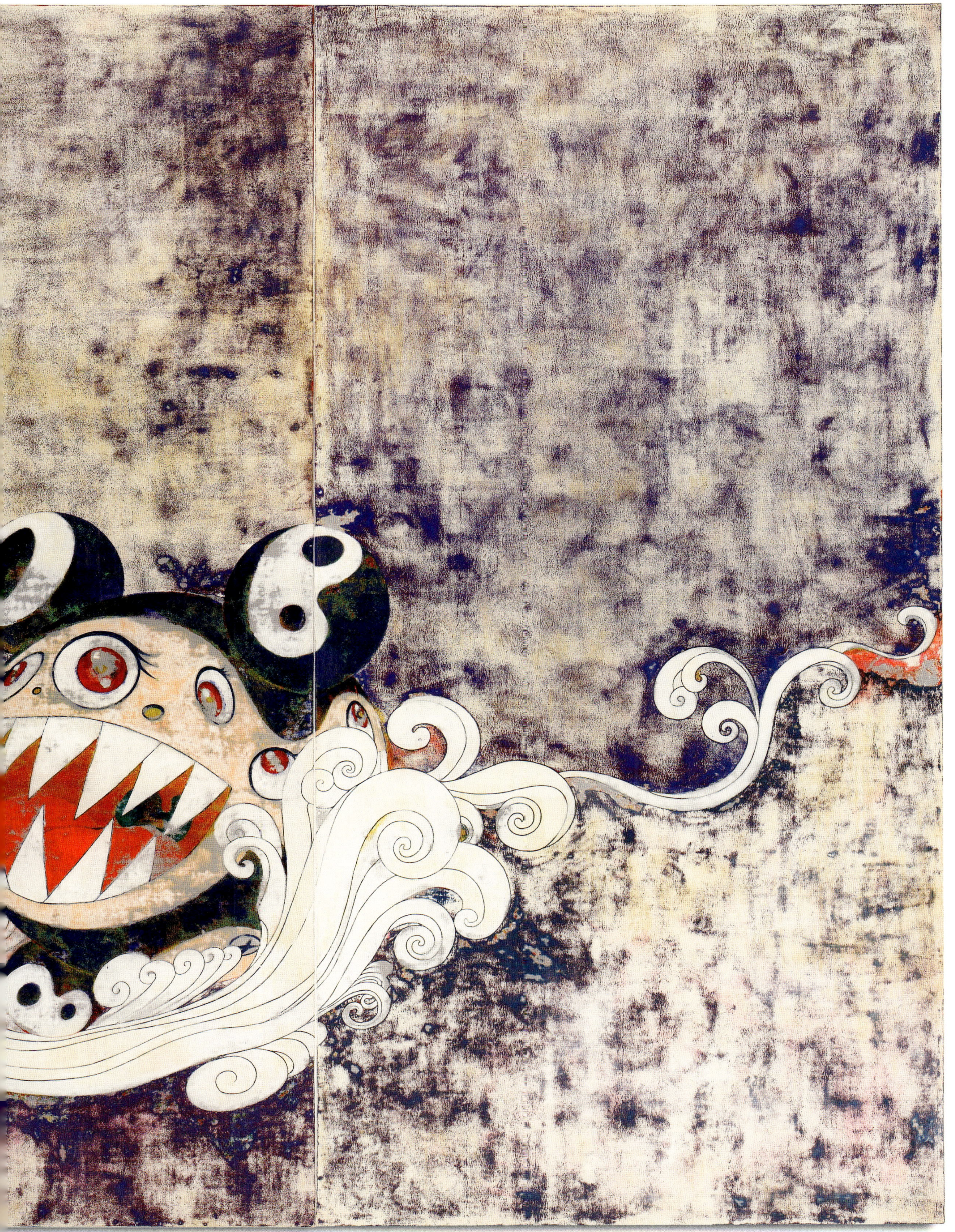

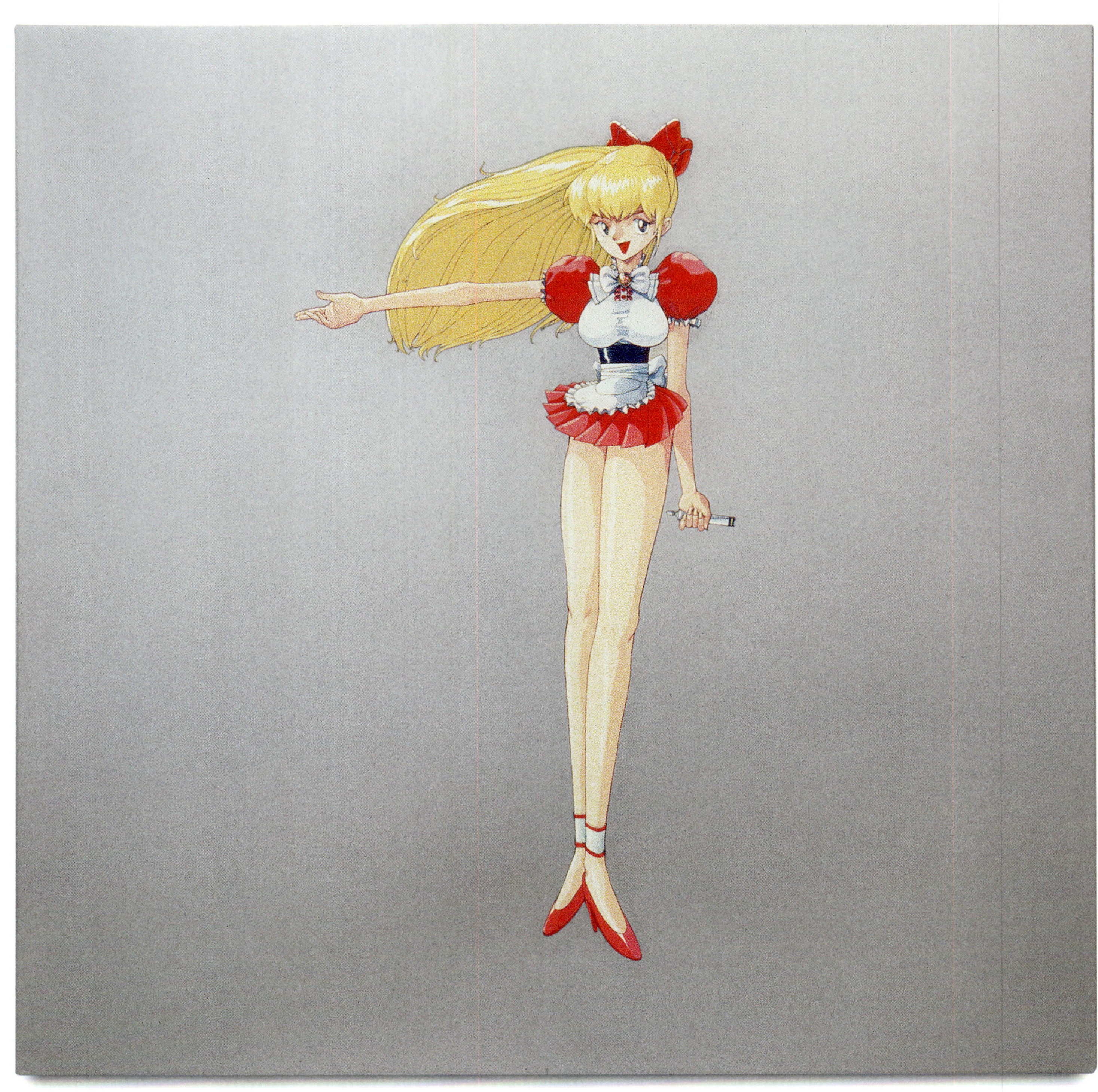

*Miss ko*², 1996

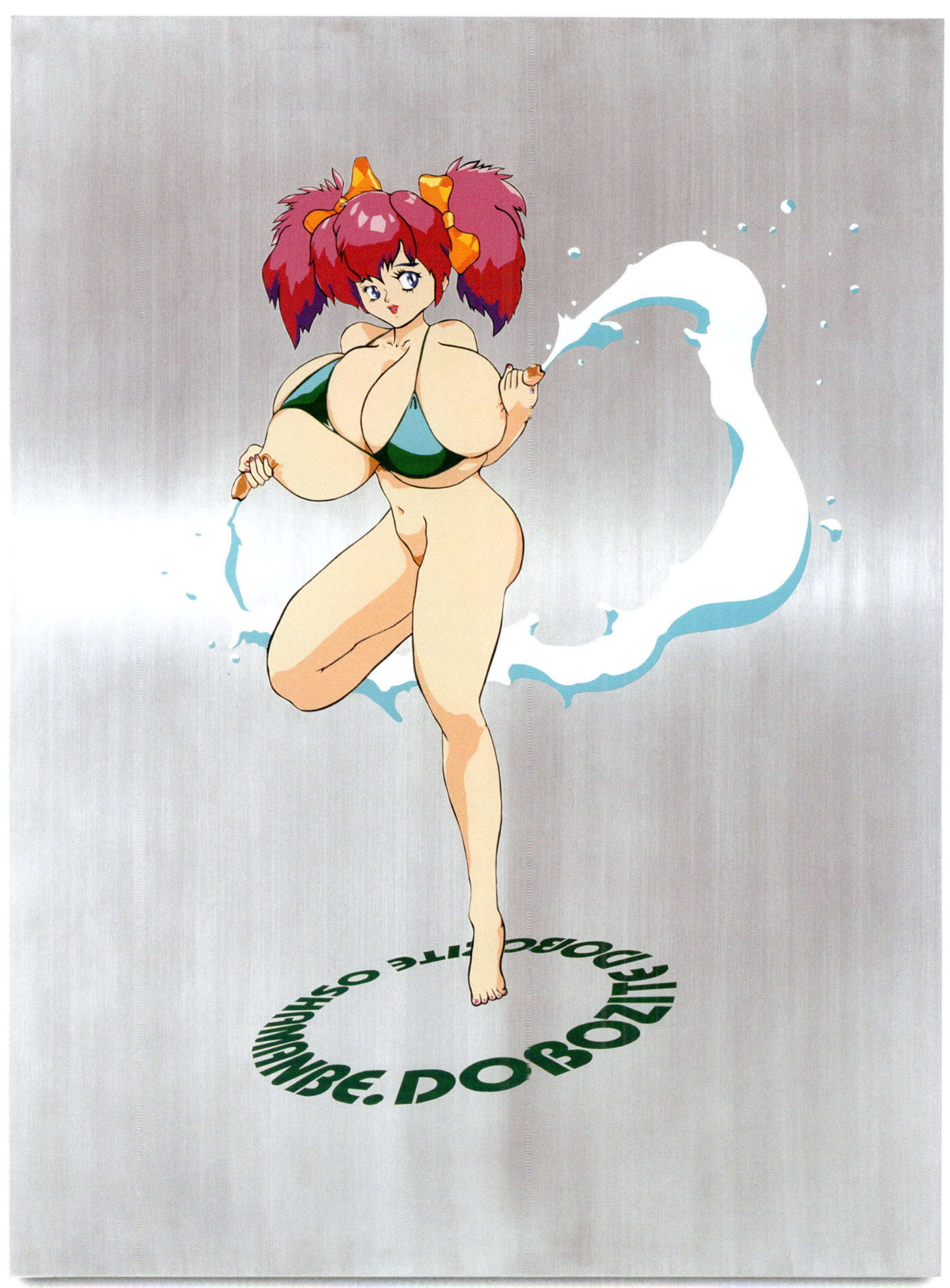

Hiropon, 1997

*Project ko*², 1997
Installation at "Wonder Festival 2000 Summer,"
Tokyo

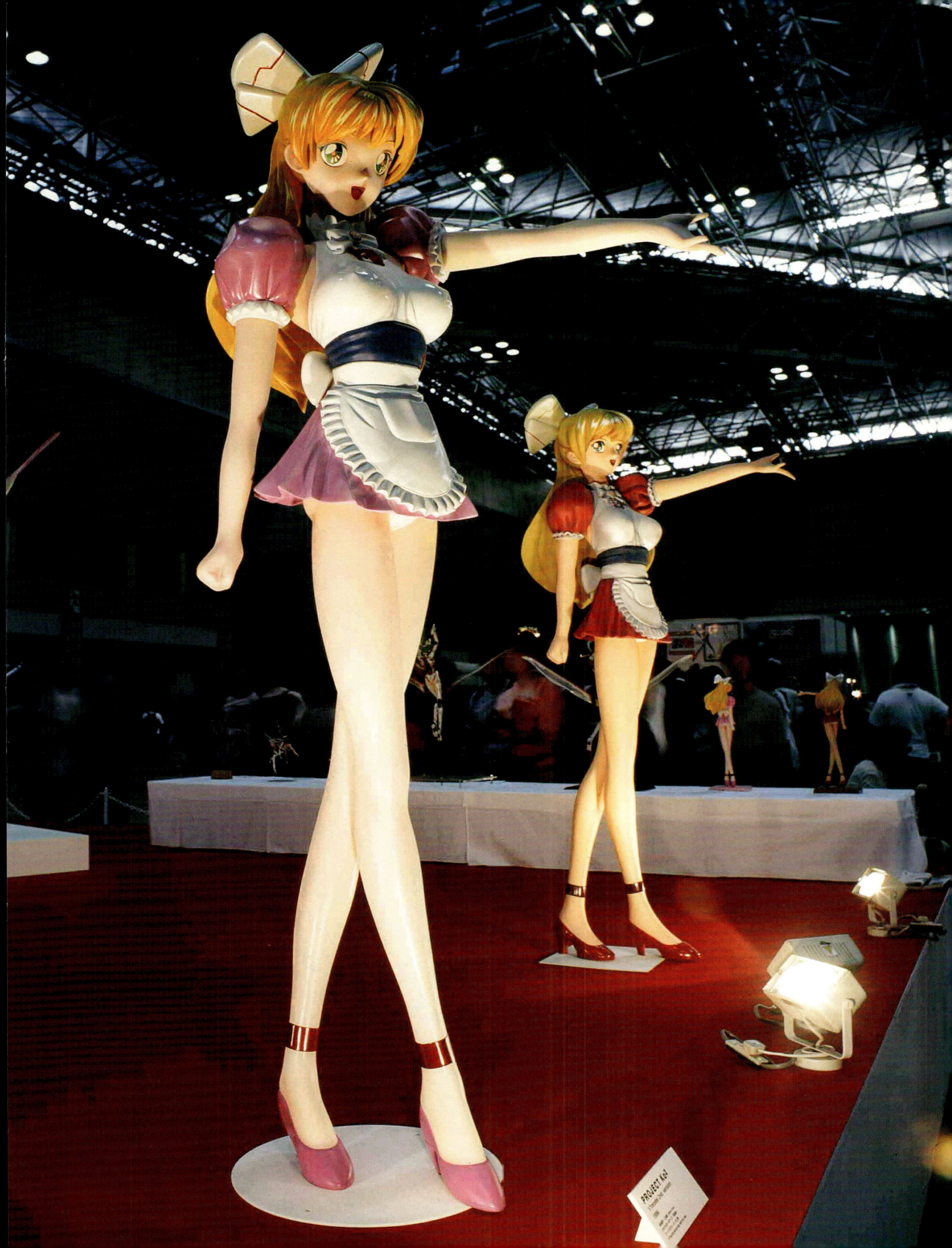
PROJECT Ko2

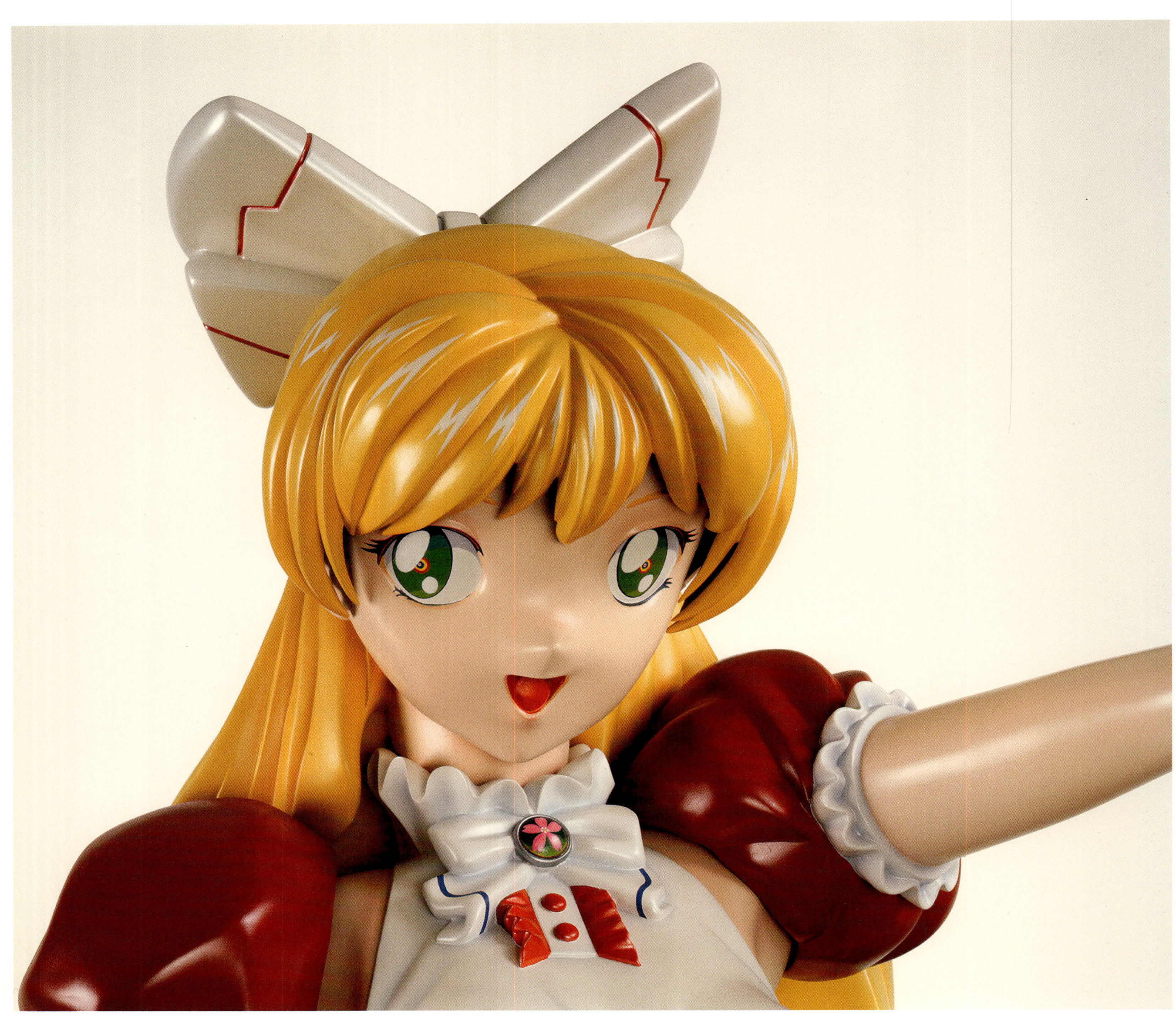

*Miss ko*², 1997, and detail

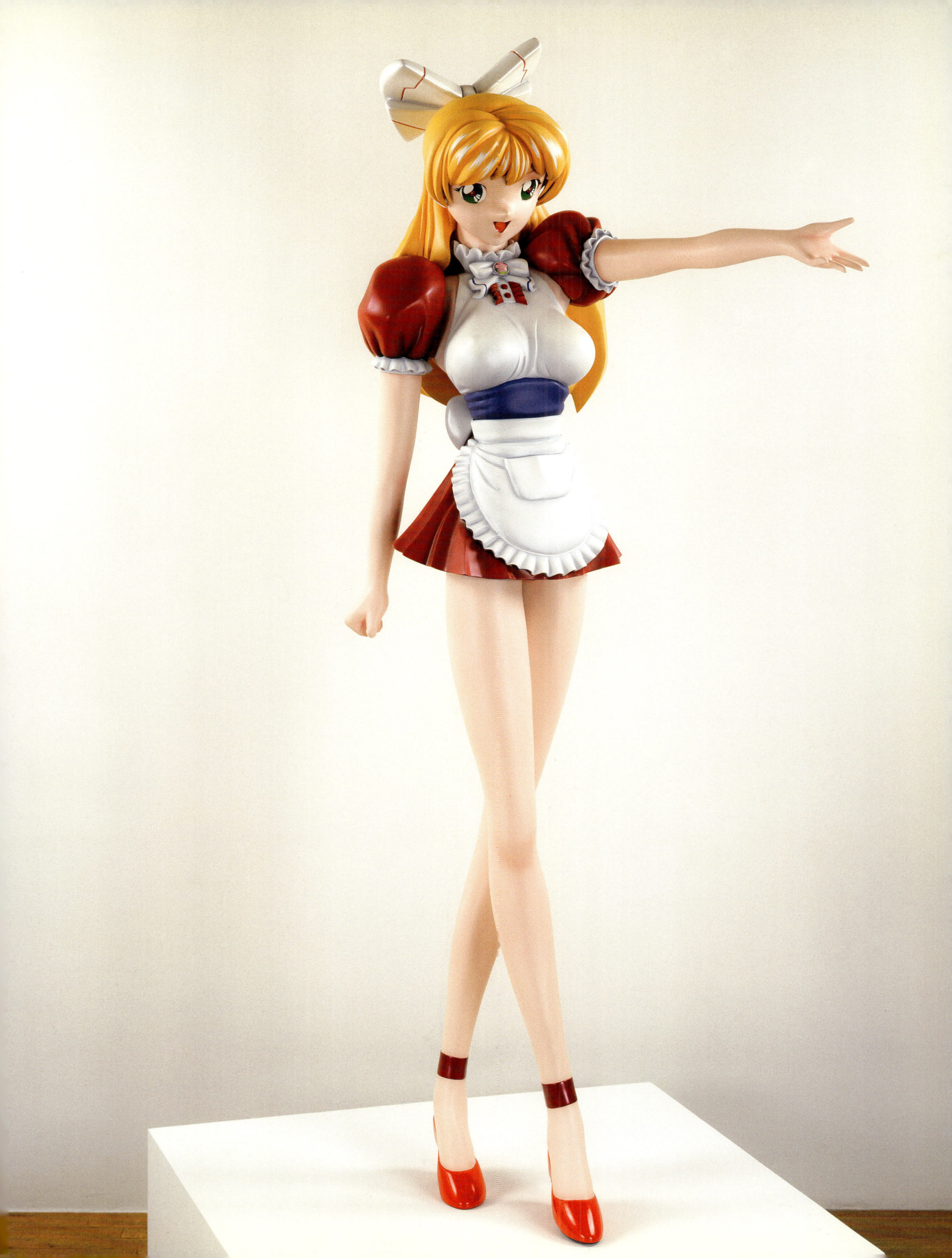

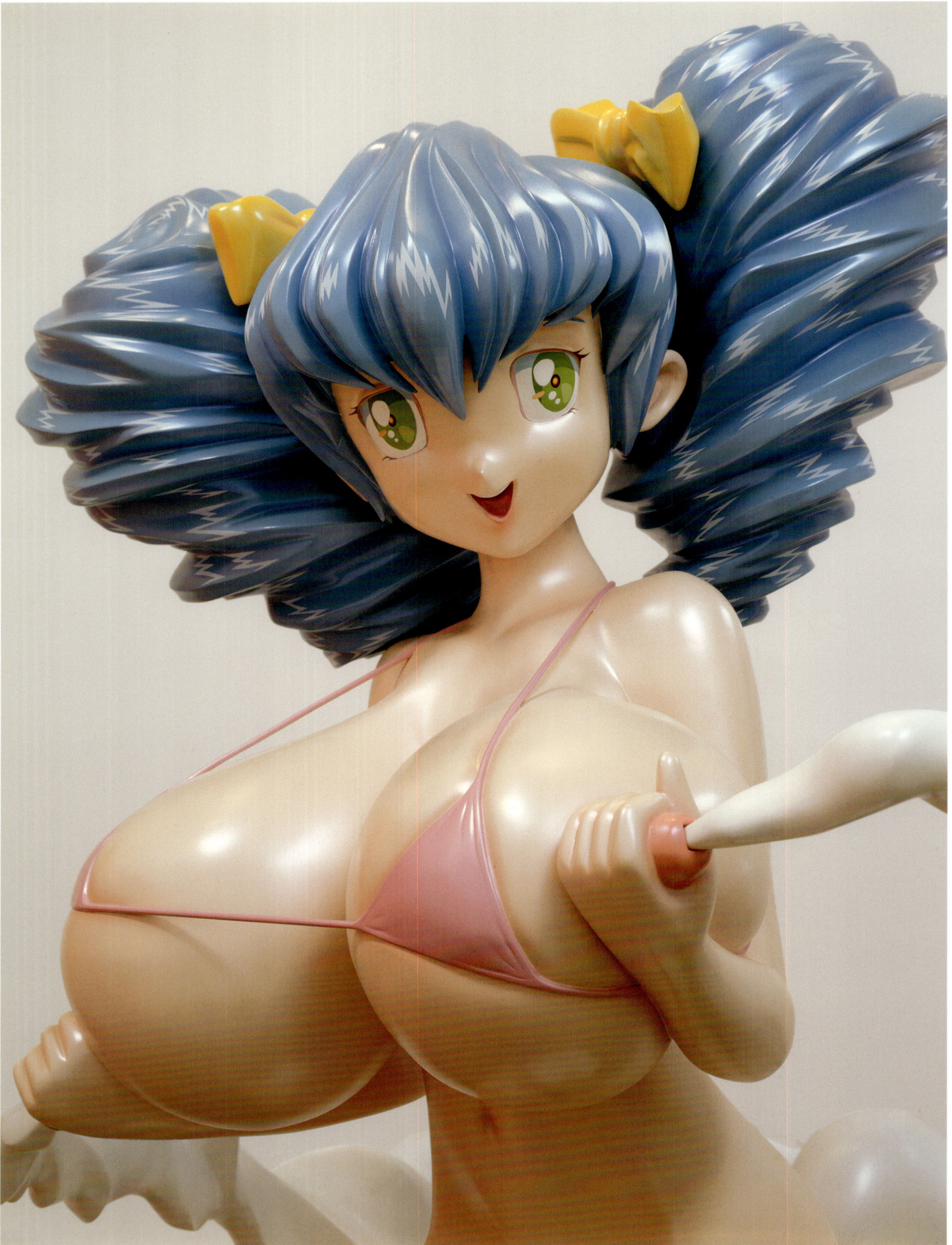

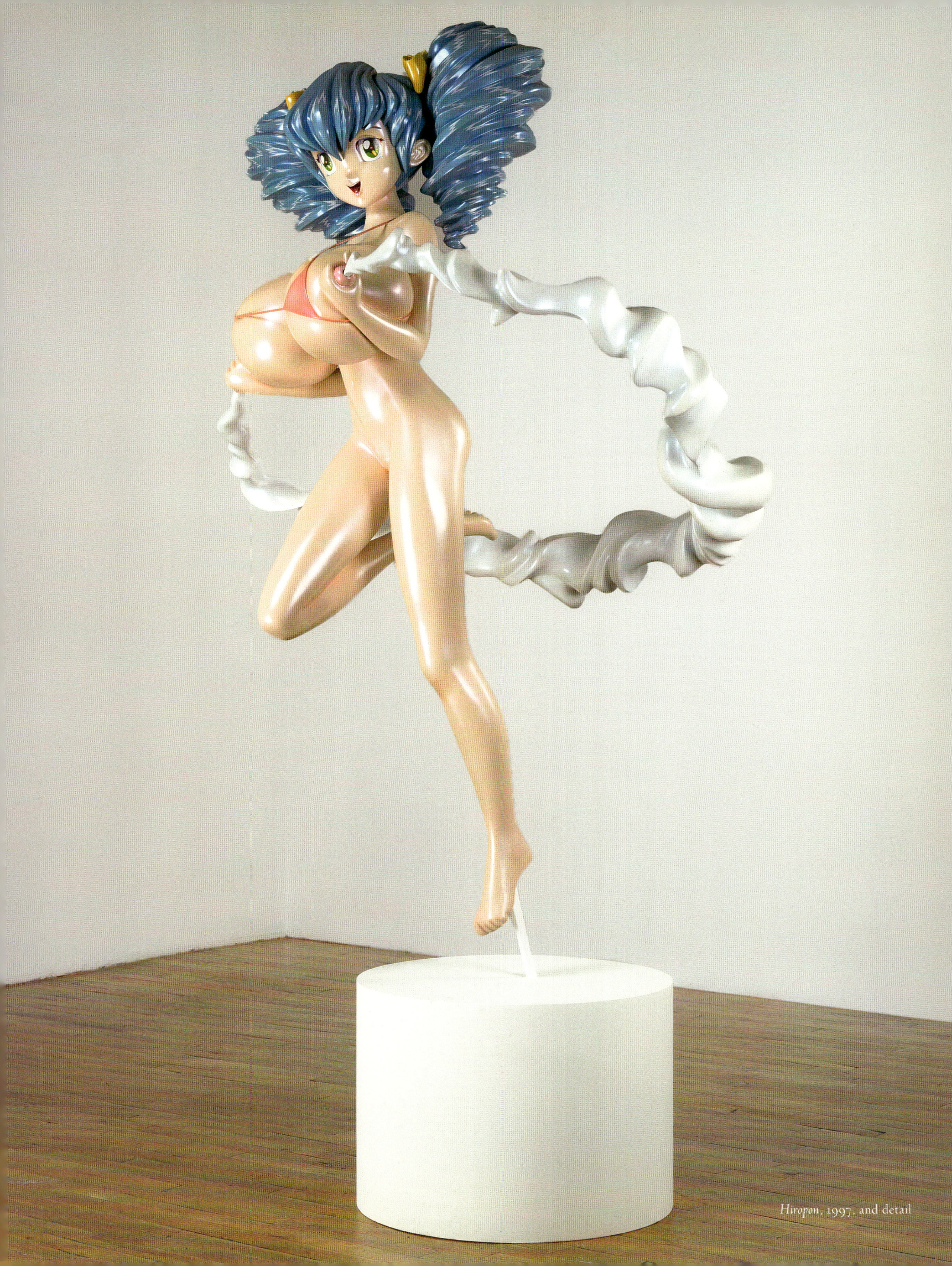

Hiropon, 1997, and detail

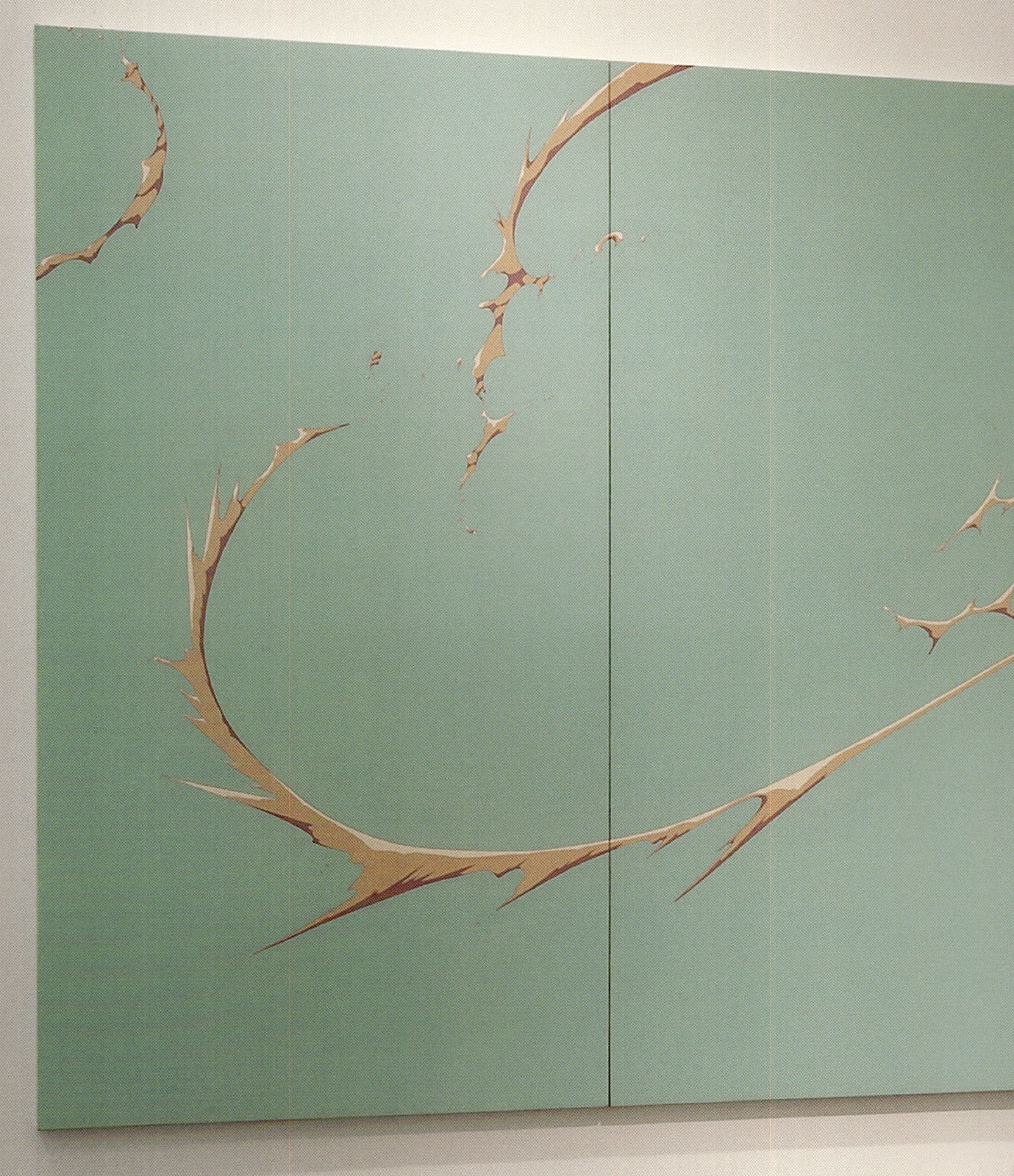

Hiropon, 1997,
with *Cream*, 1998, in background

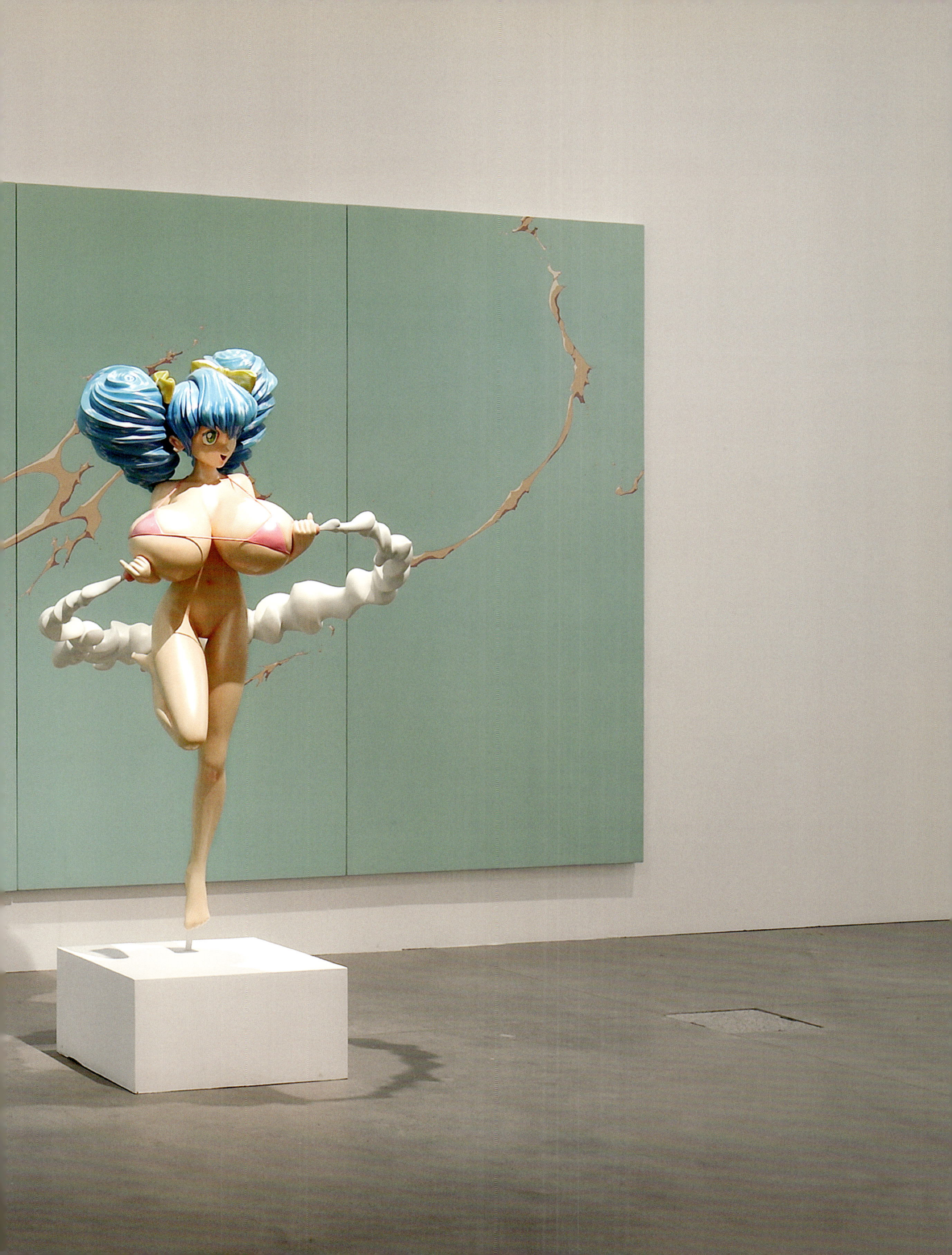

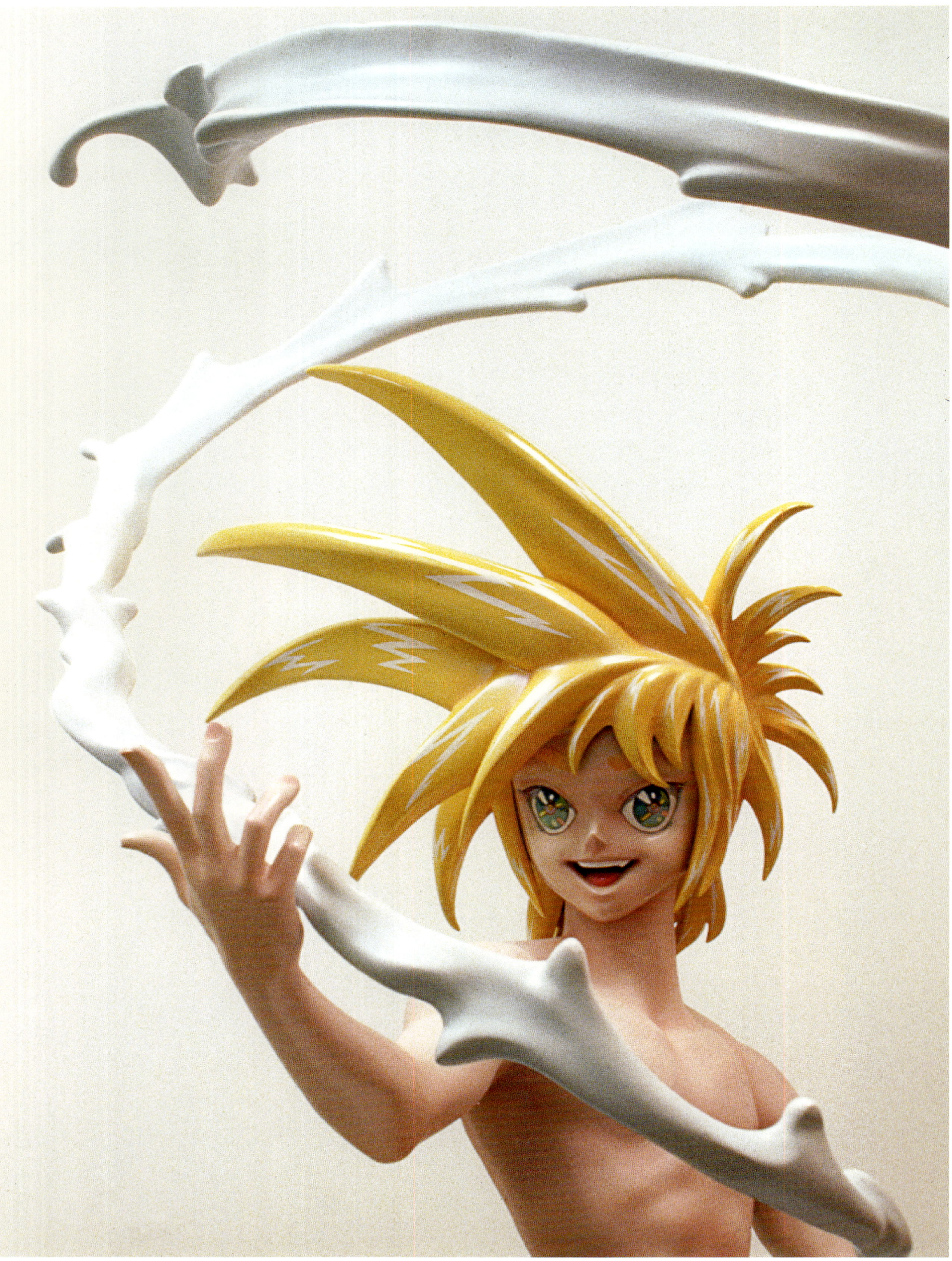

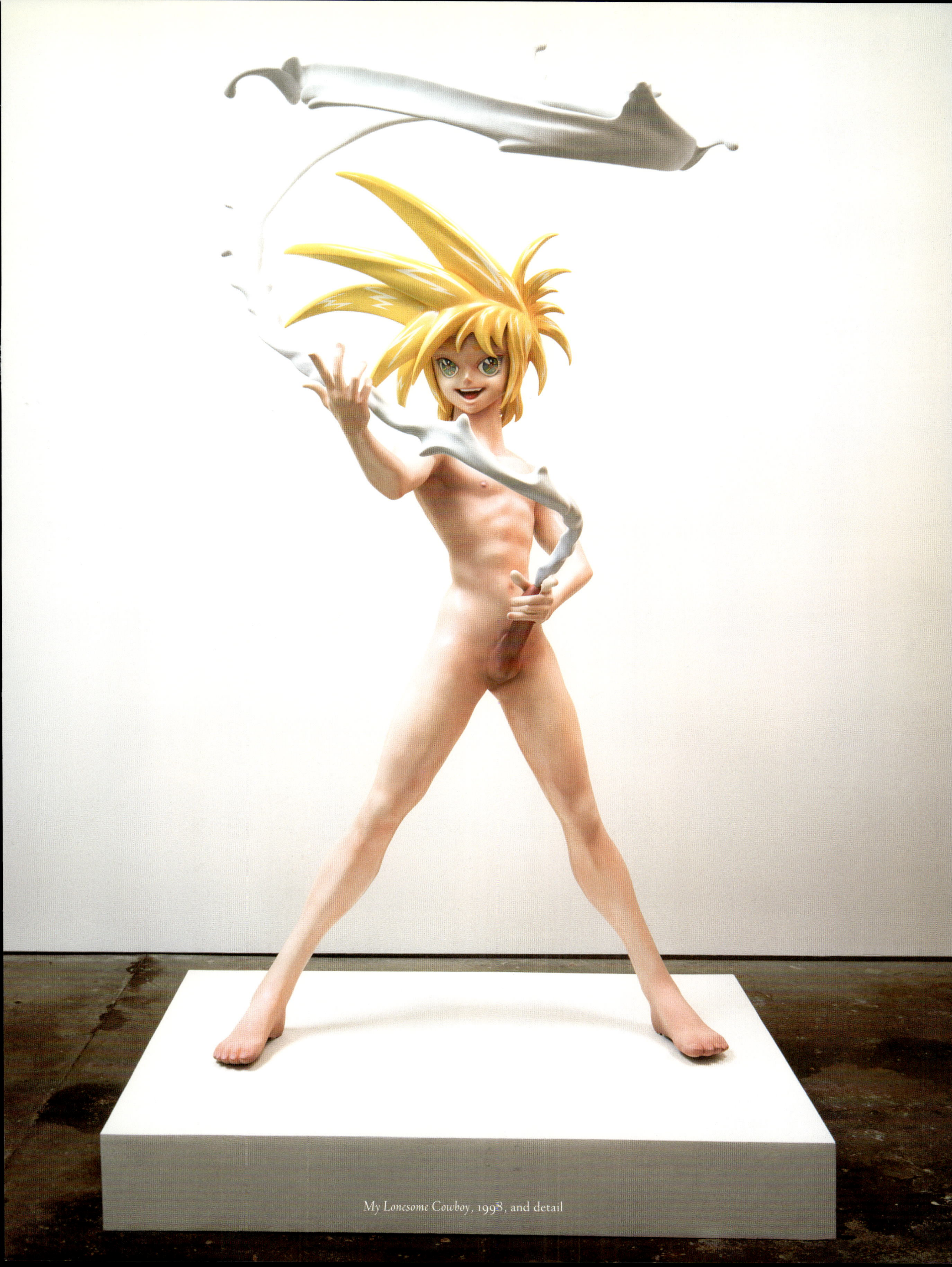

My Lonesome Cowboy, 1998, and detail

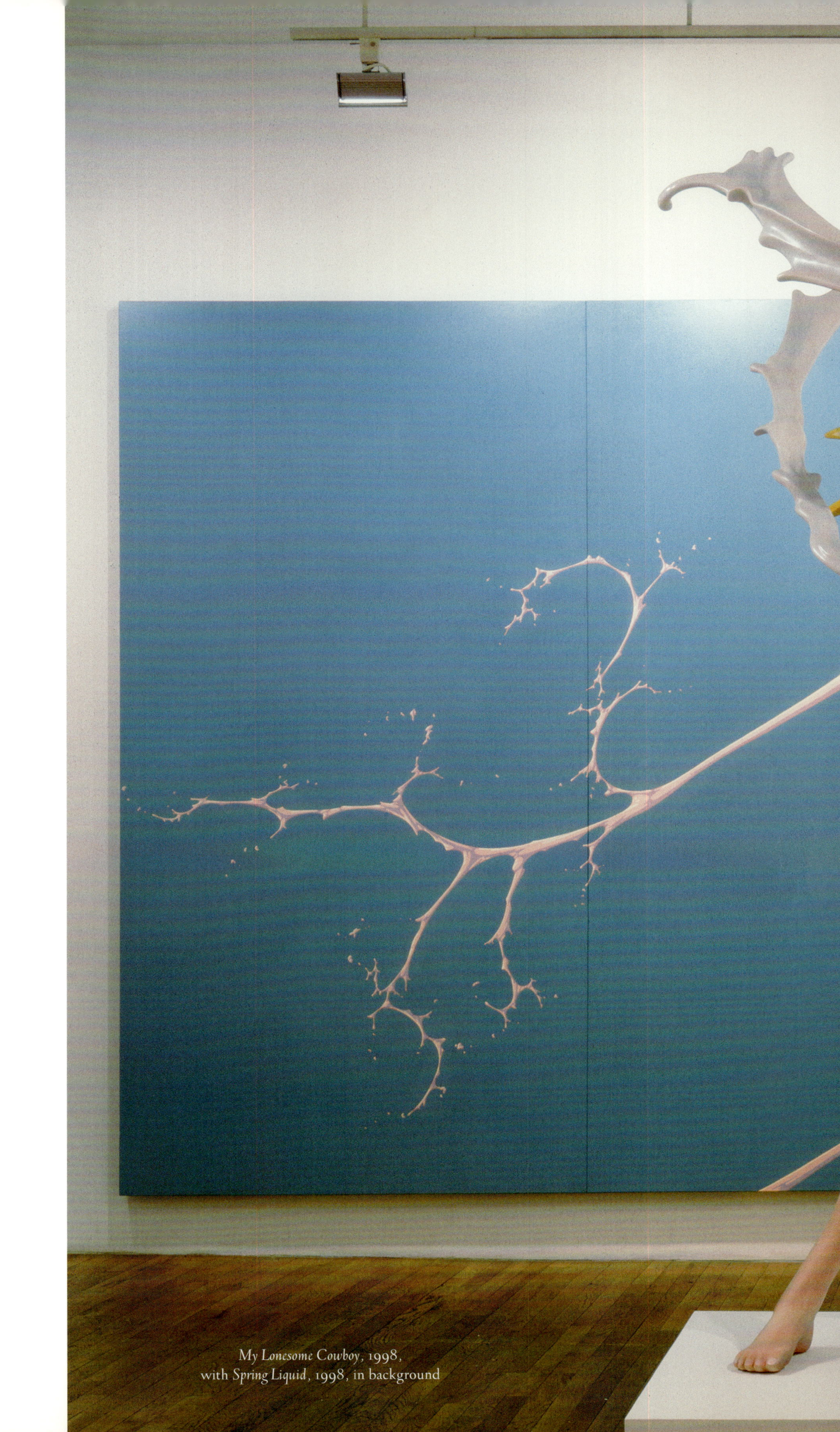

My Lonesome Cowboy, 1998,
with *Spring Liquid*, 1998, in background

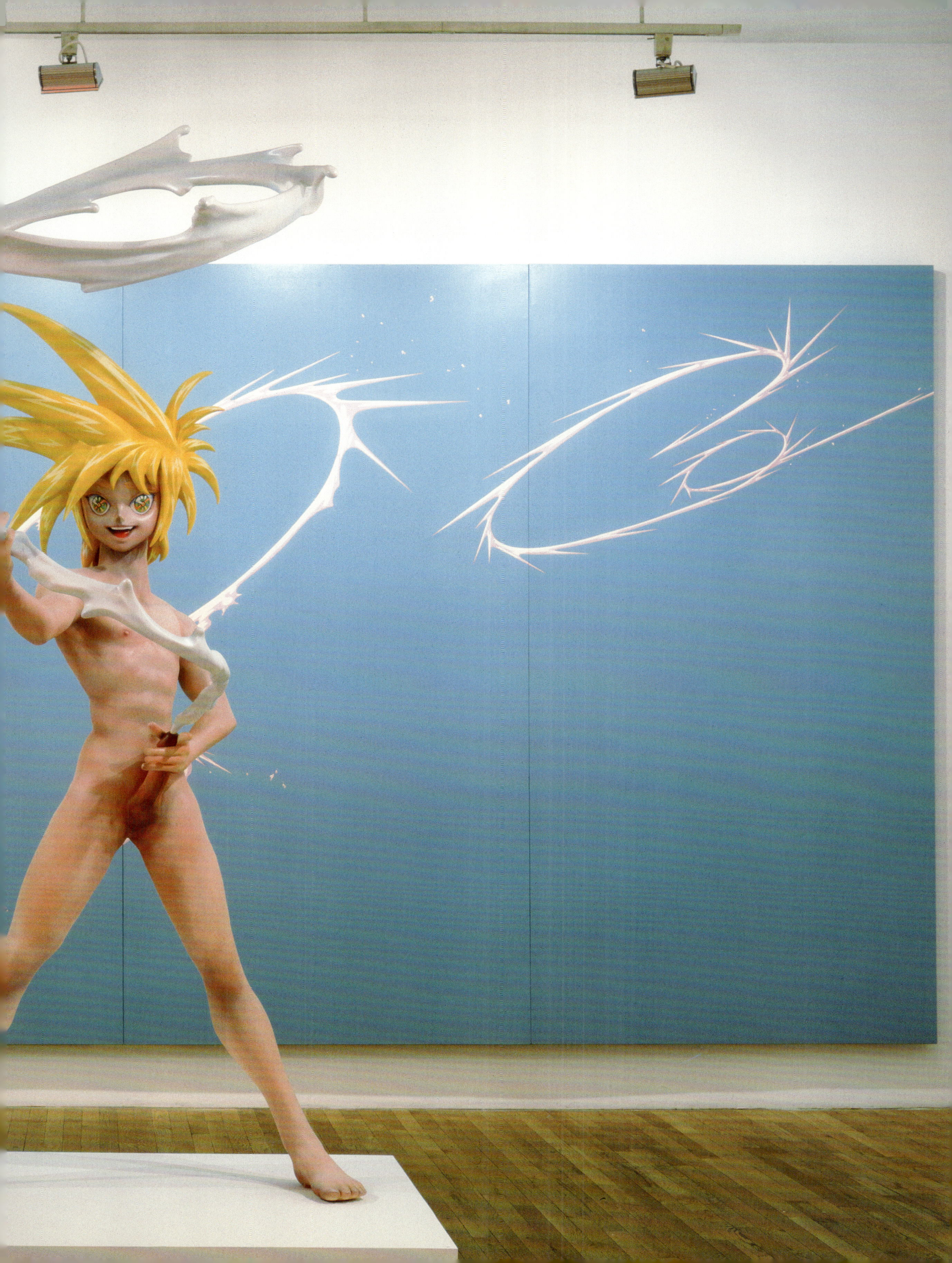

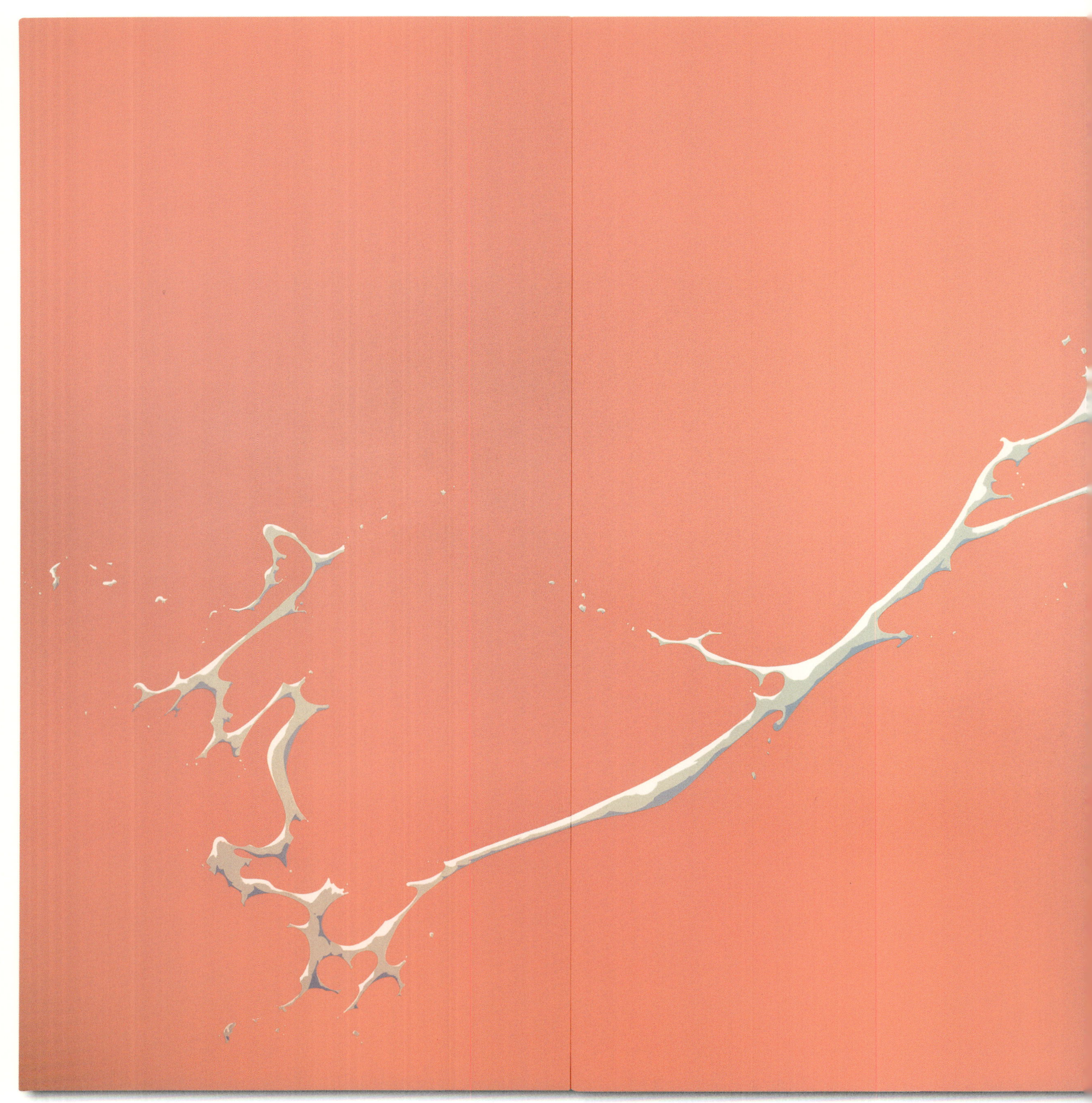

Milk, 1998

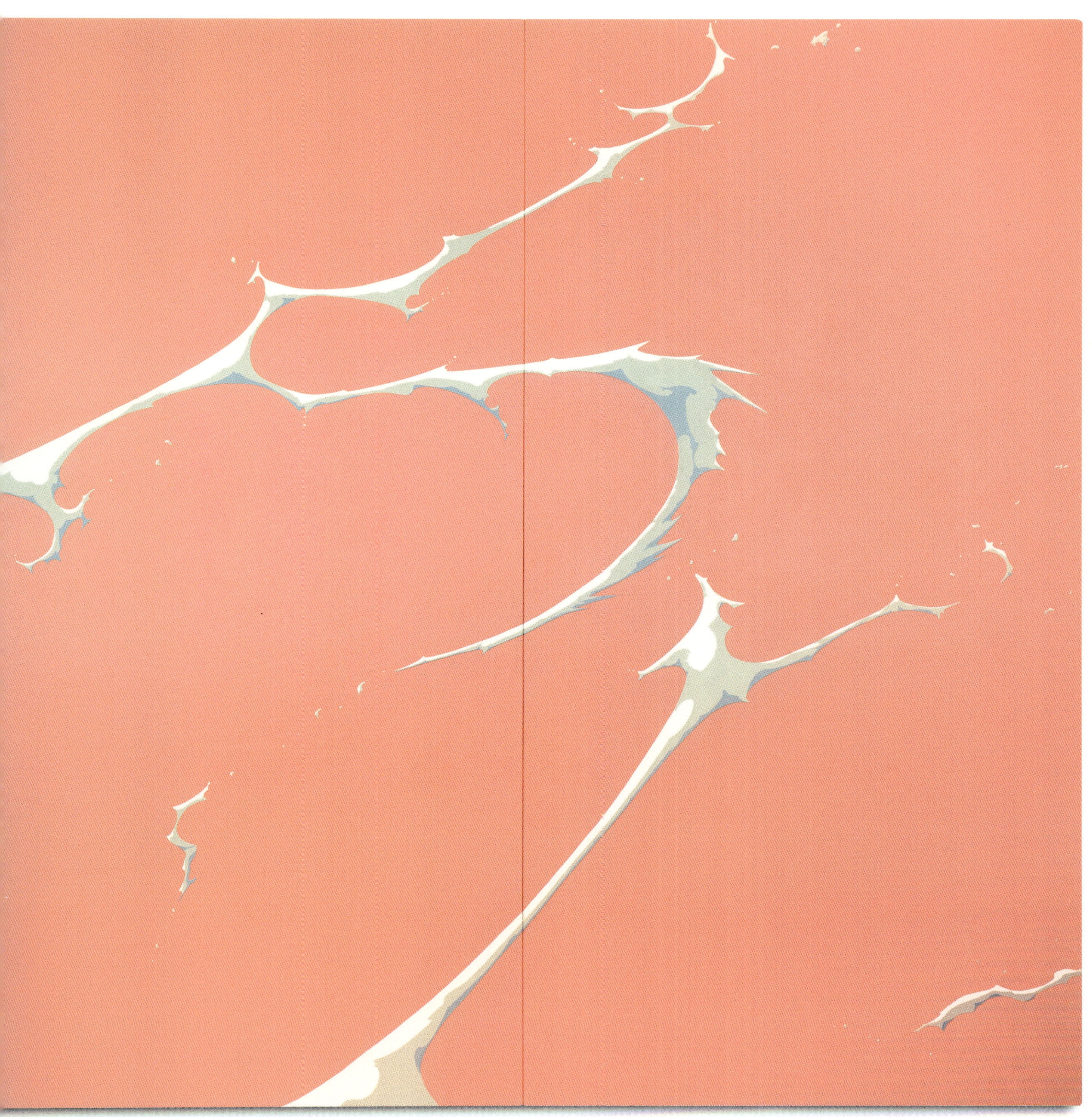

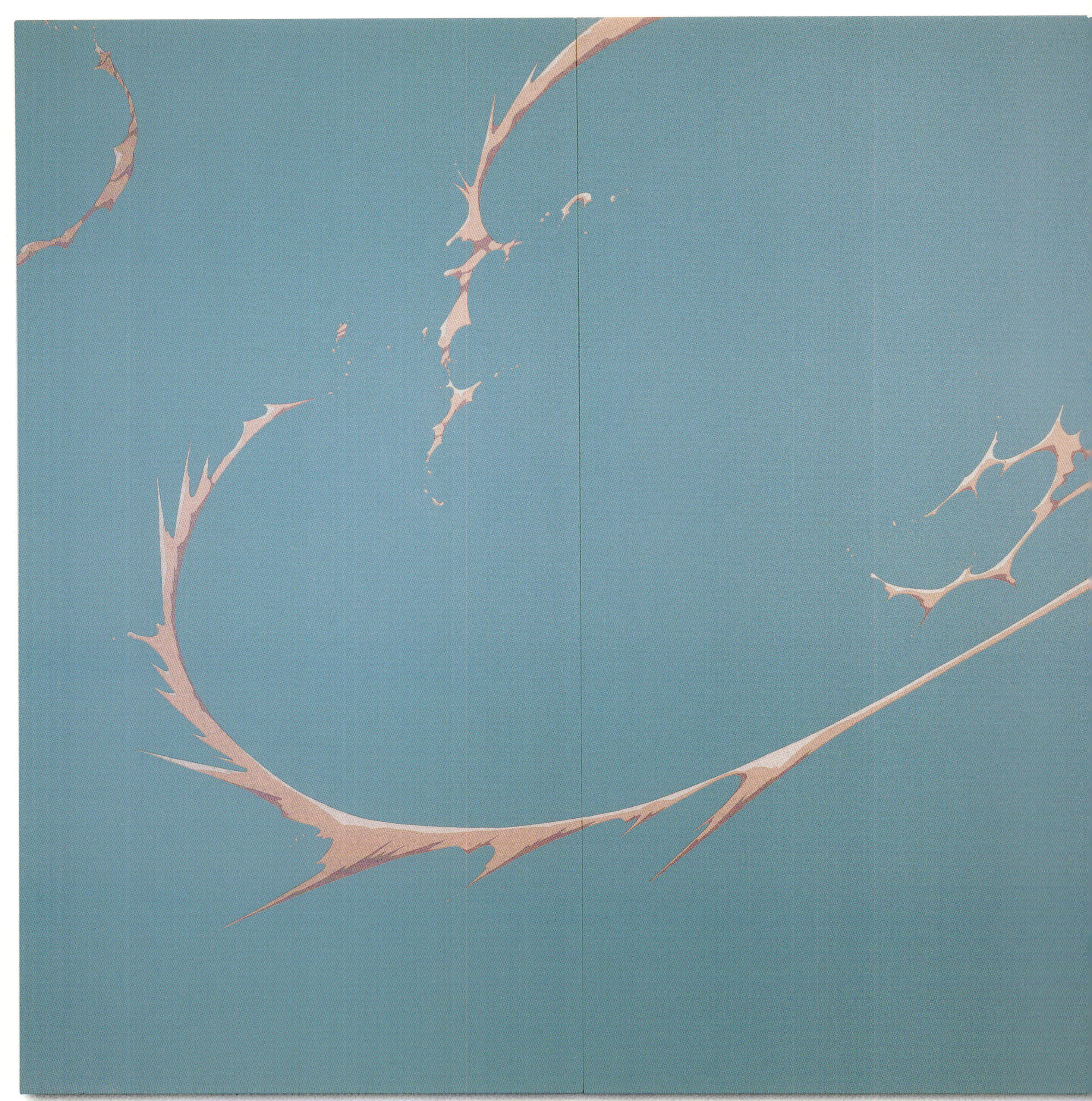

Cream, 1998

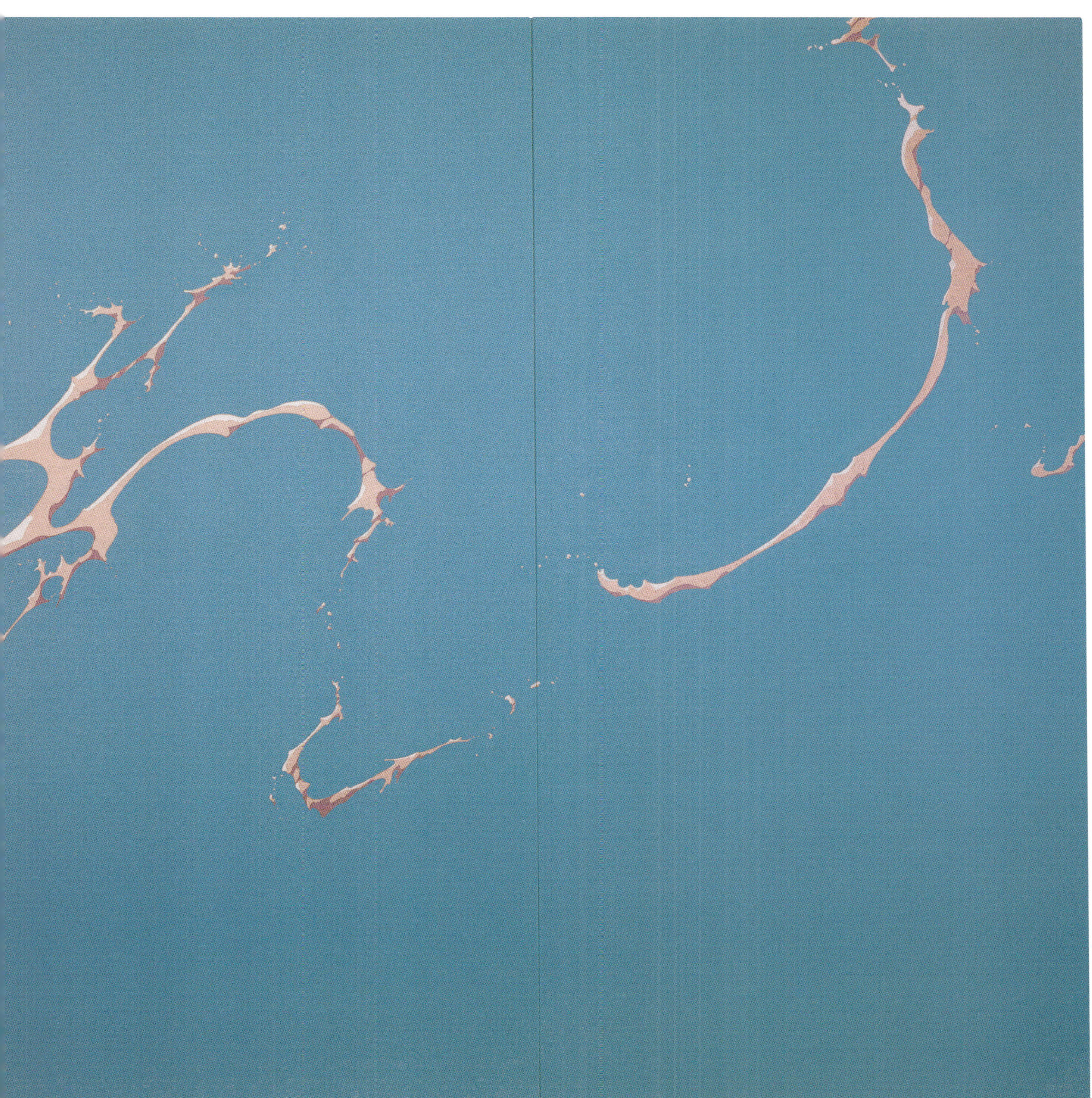

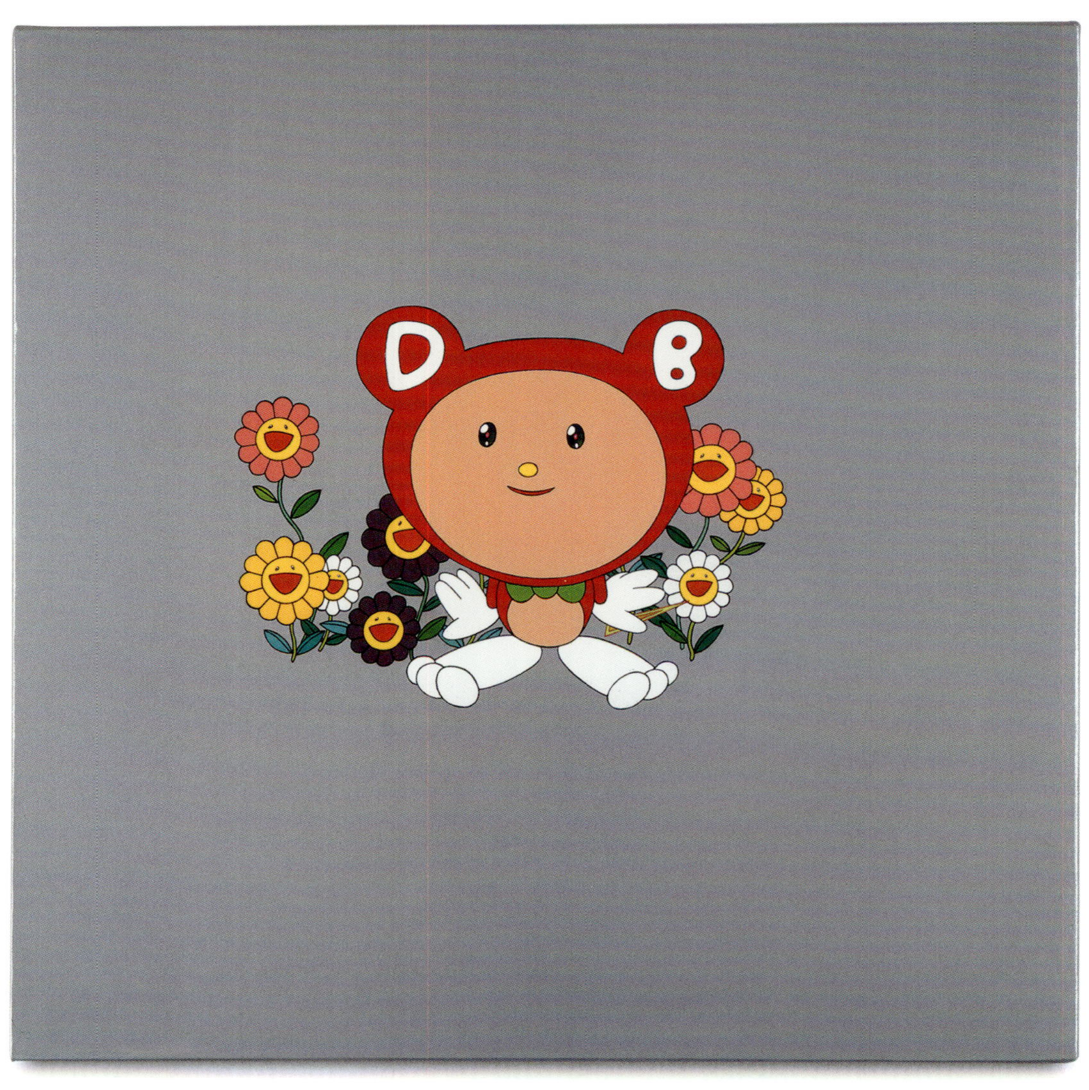

DOB with Flowers, 1996–98

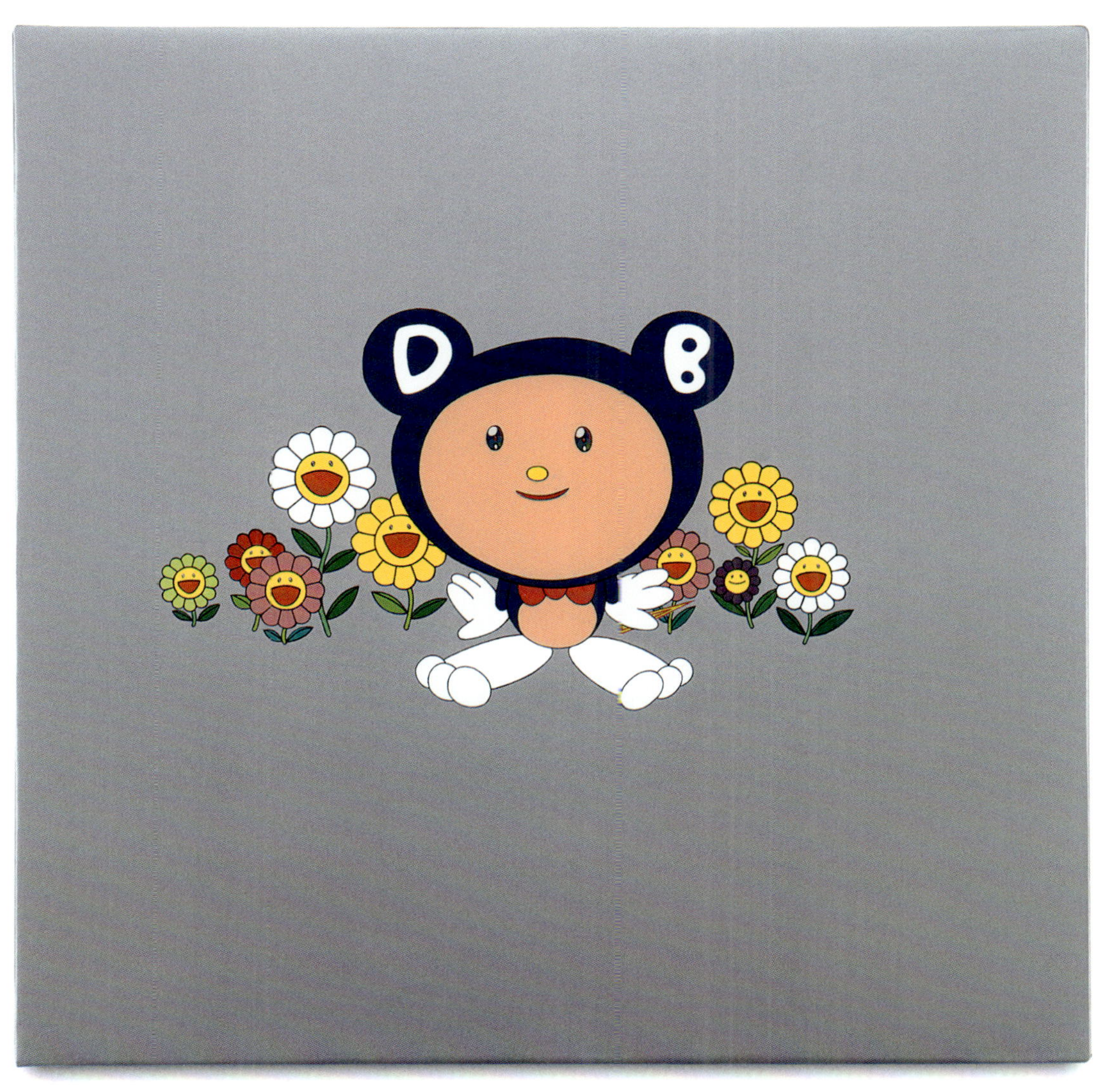

Mean of Blue, 1998

The Castle of Tin Tin, 1998

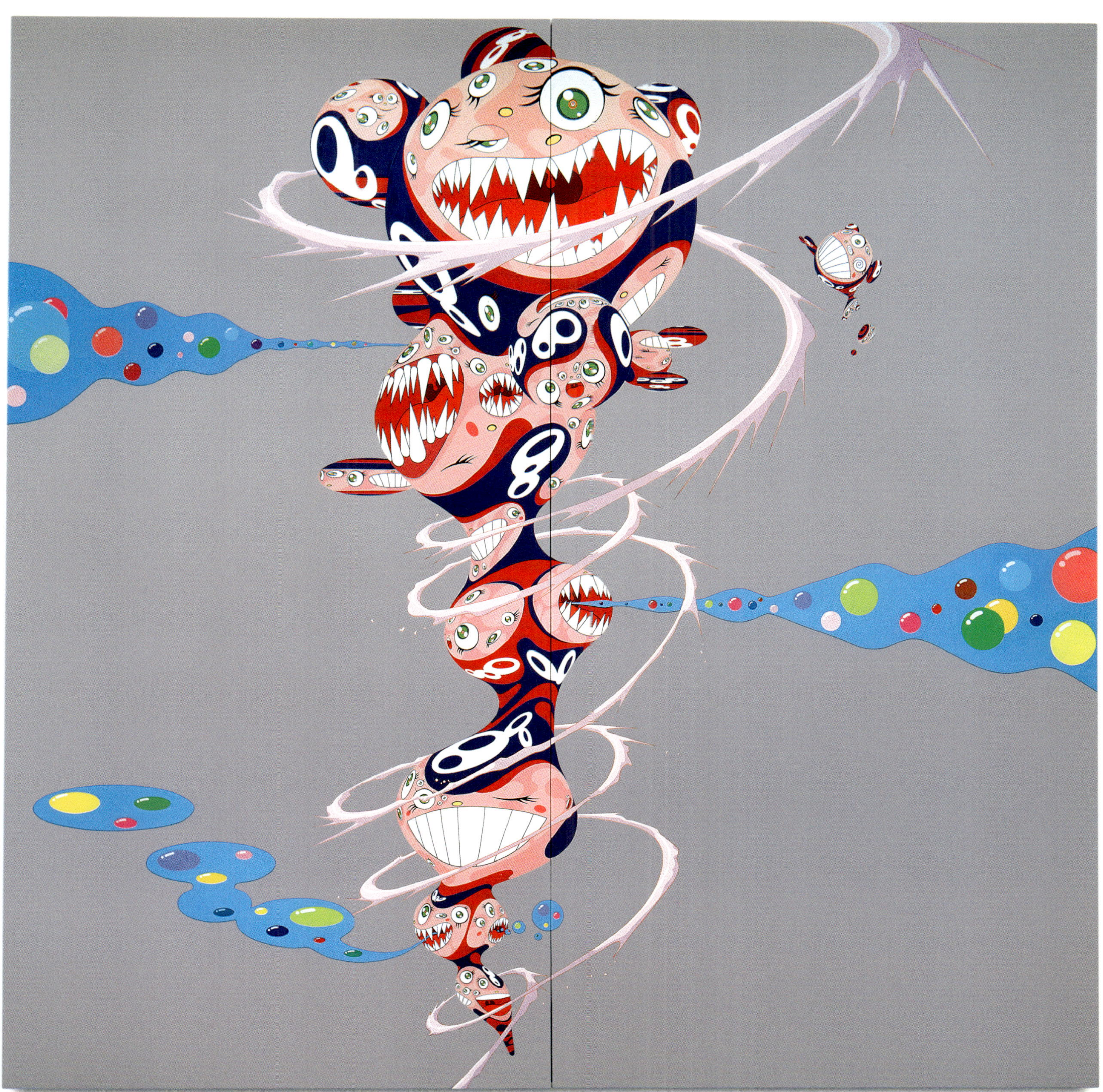

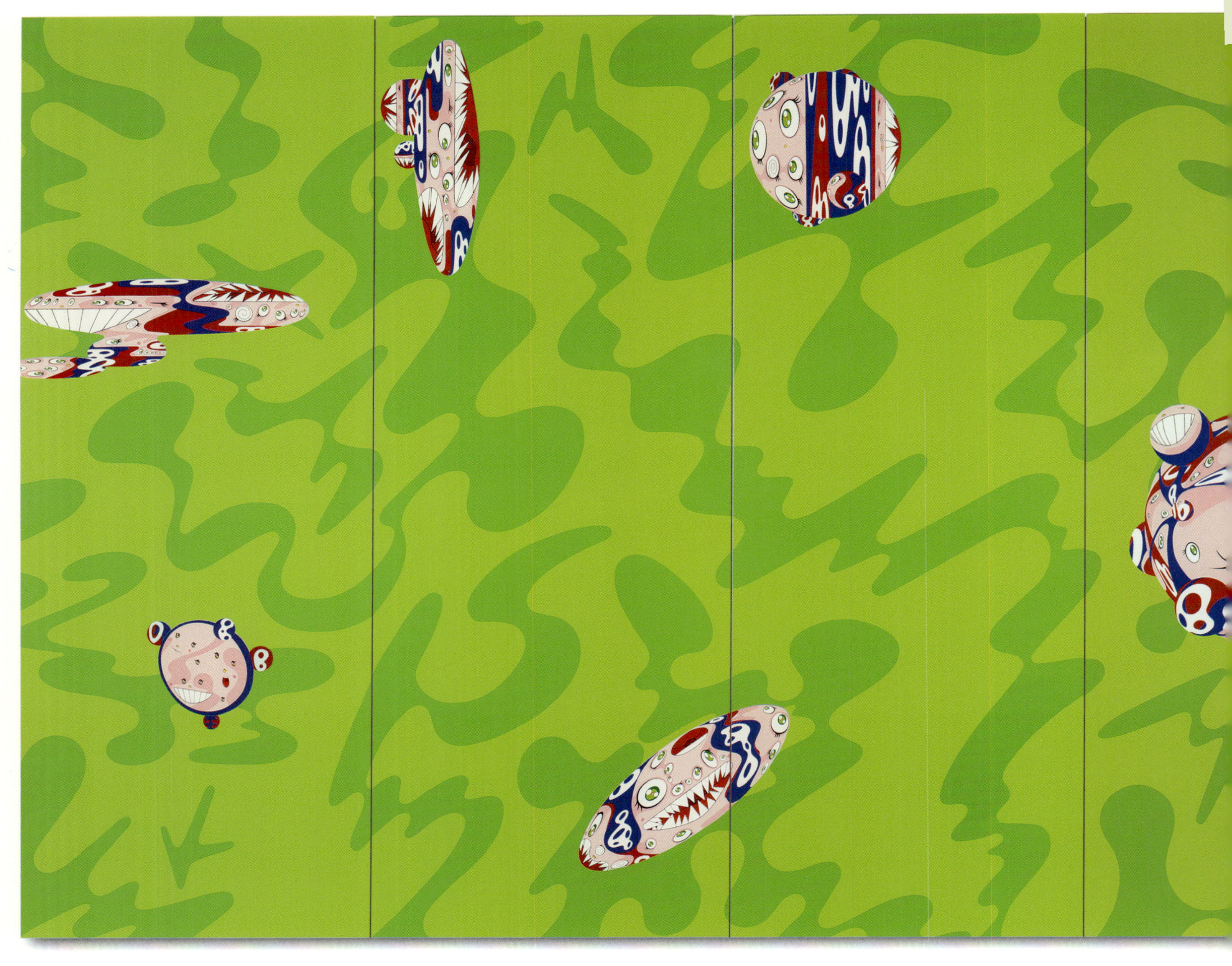

Magic Ball, 1999

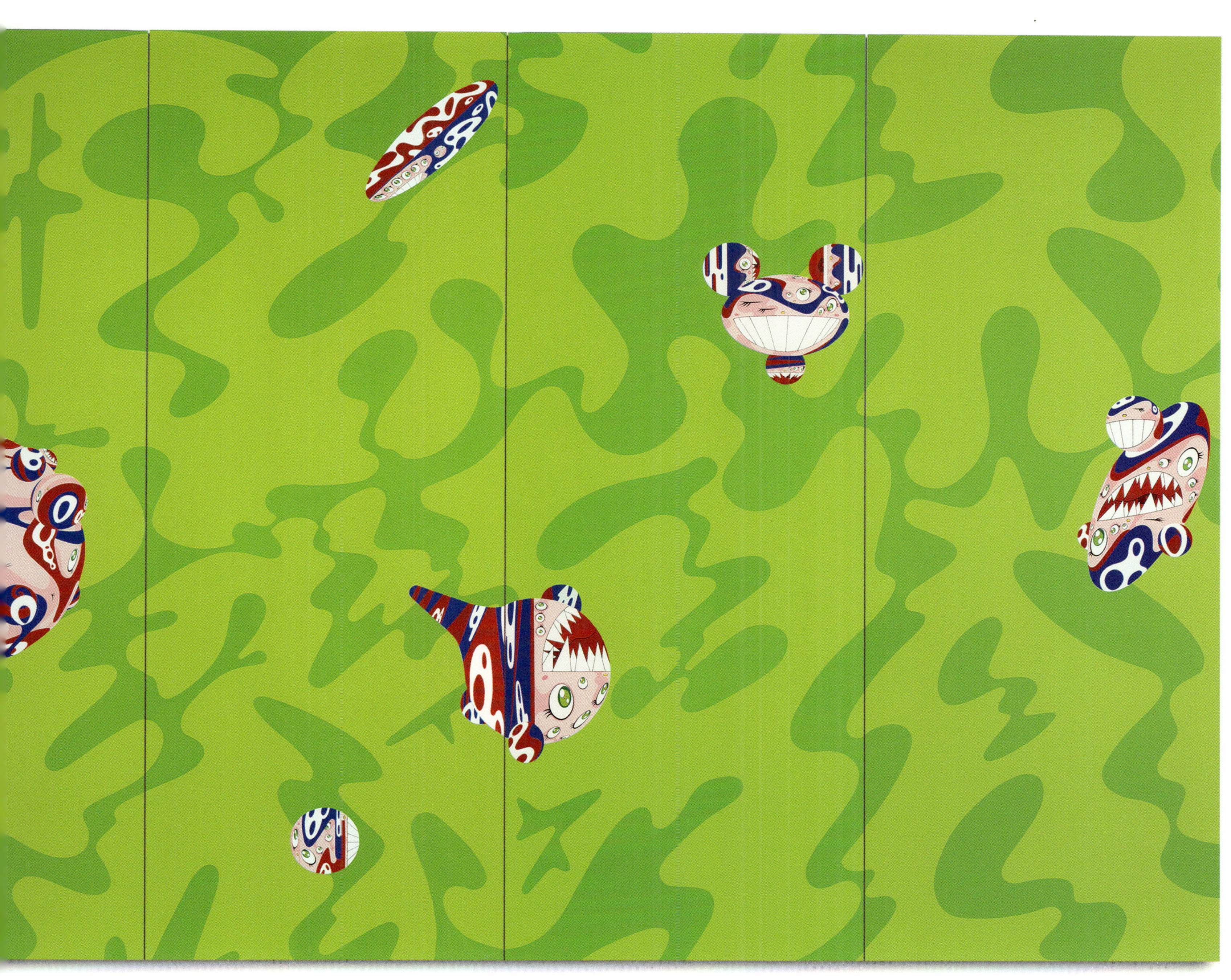

following spread
Cosmos, 1998

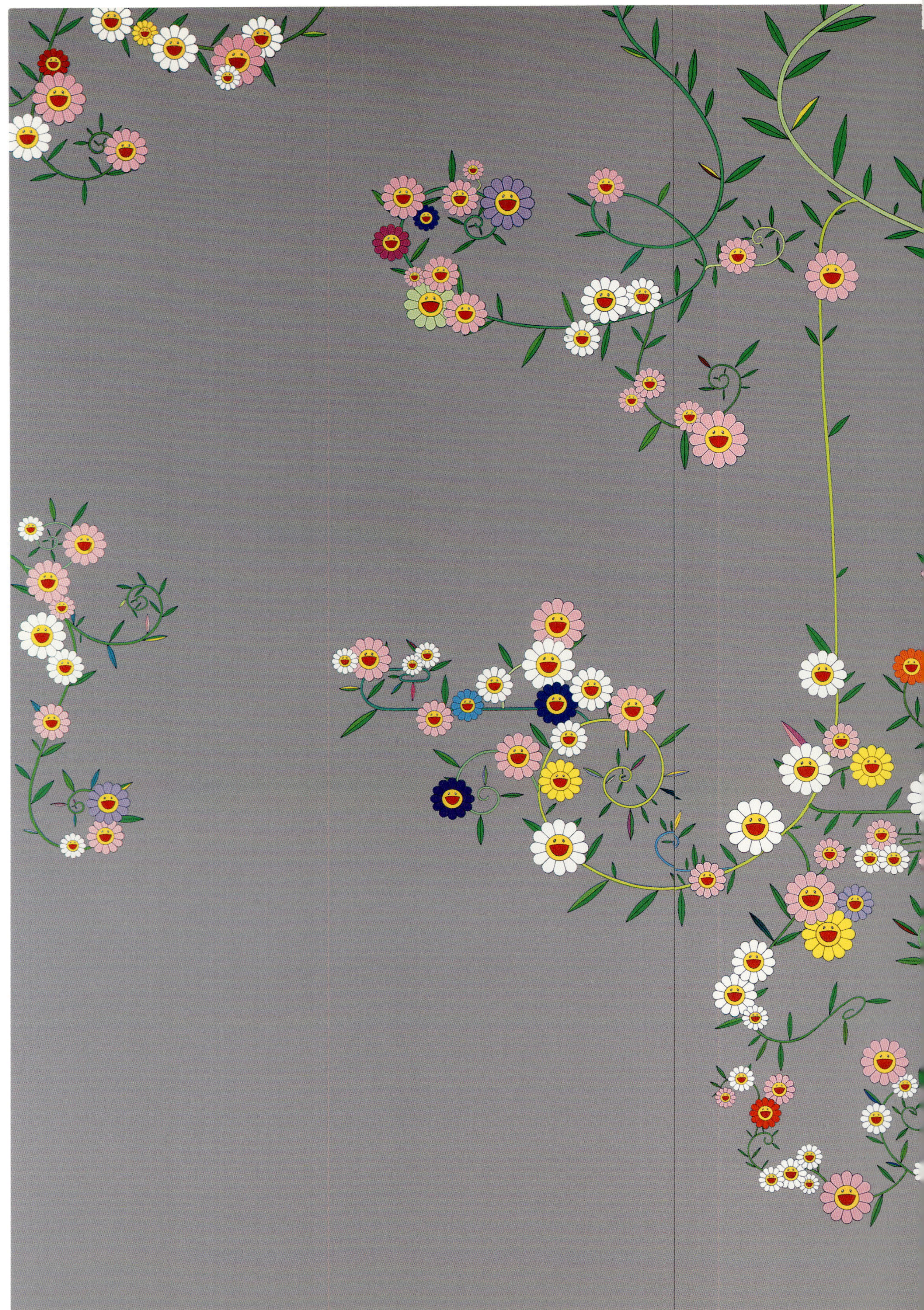

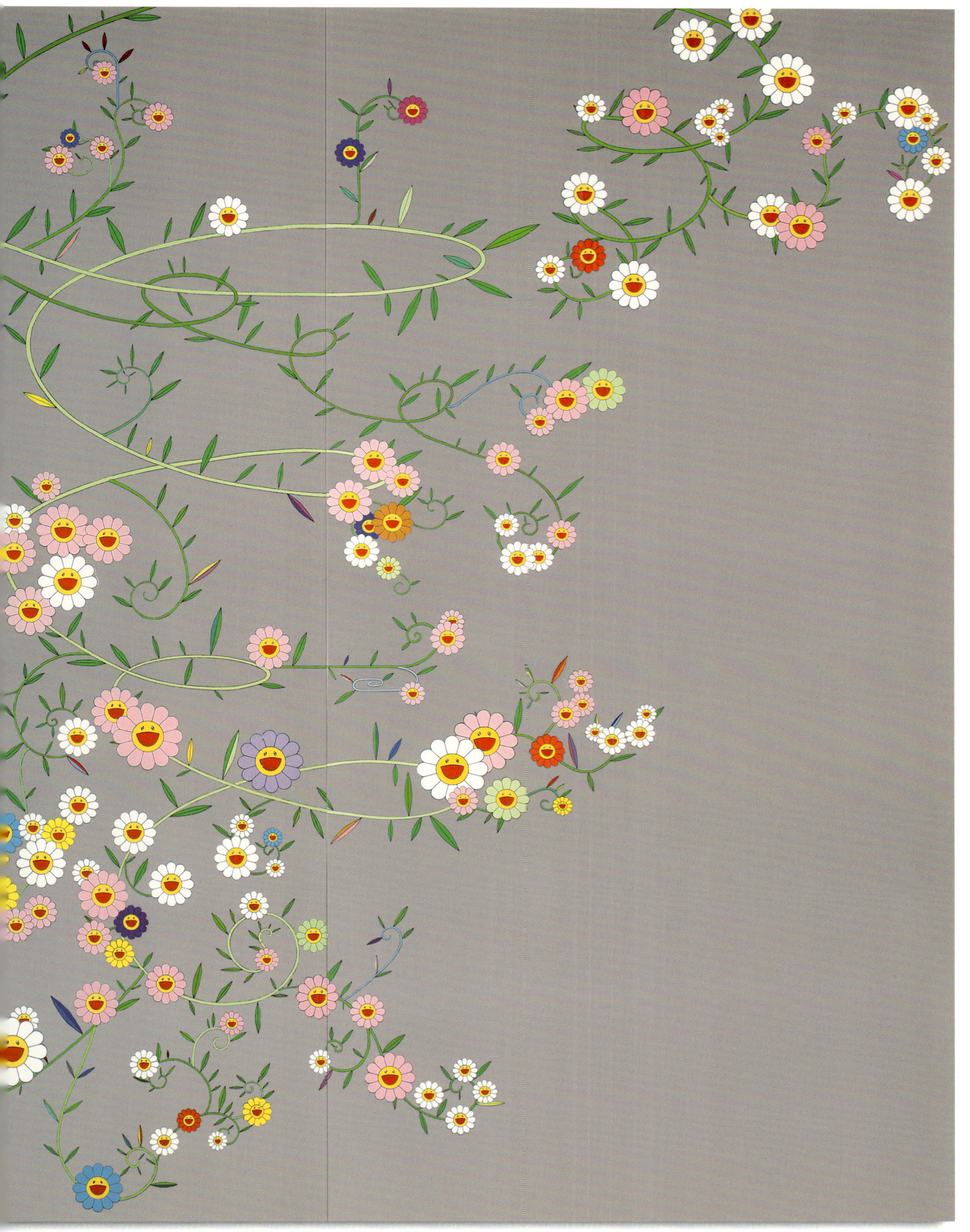

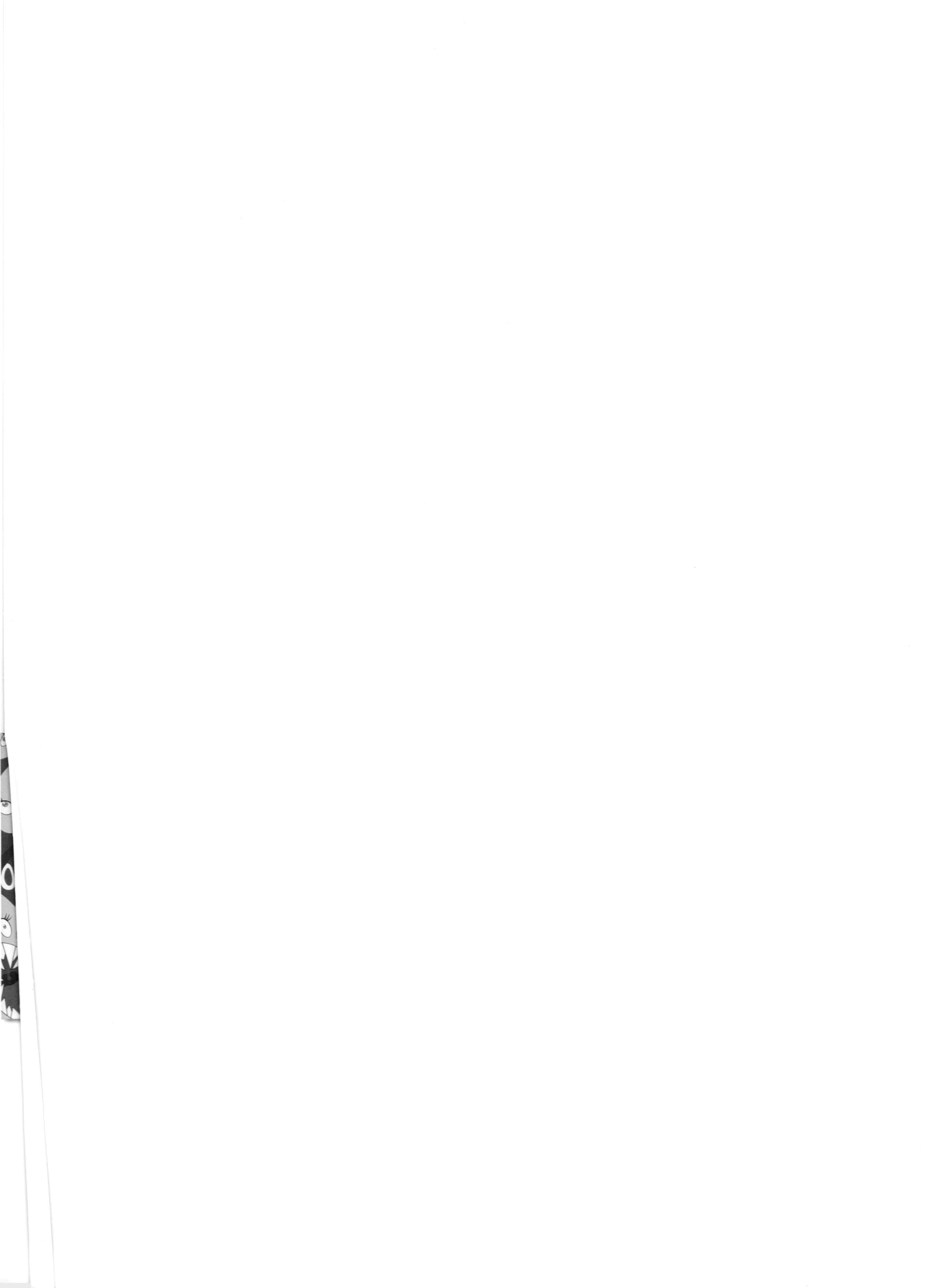

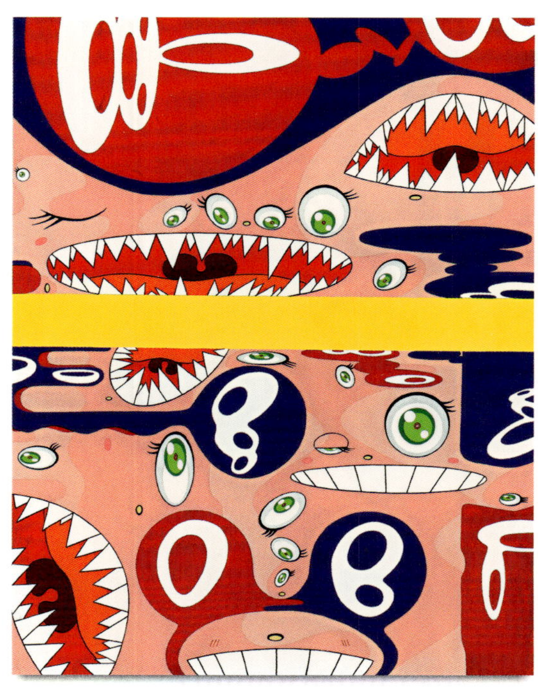

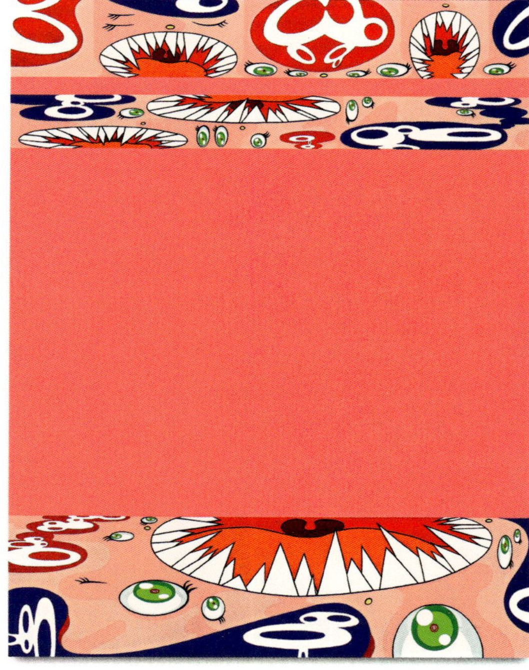

PO+KU *Surrealism Mr. DOB—Yellow, Pink, Blue, Purple, Green*, 1998

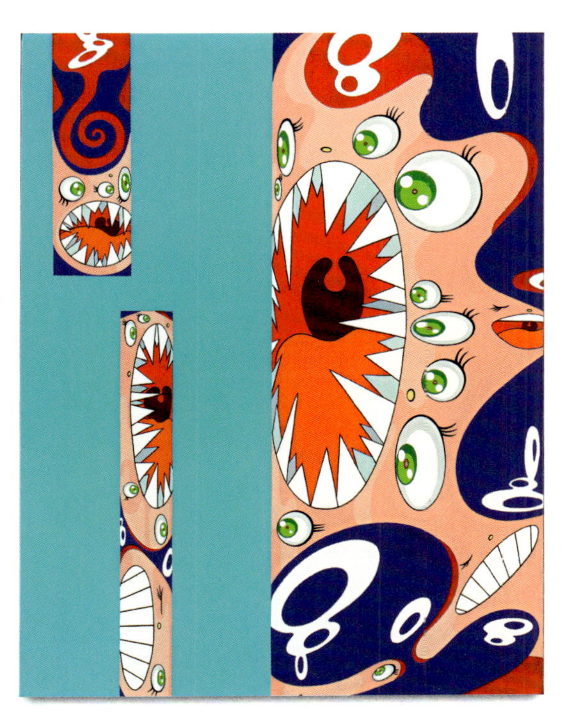
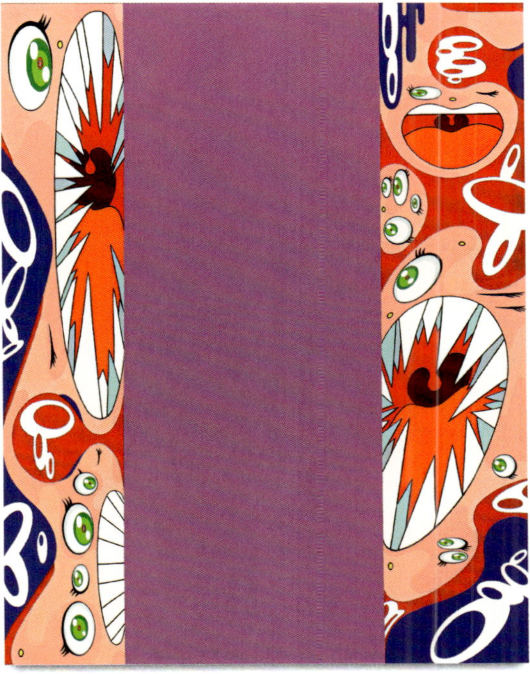
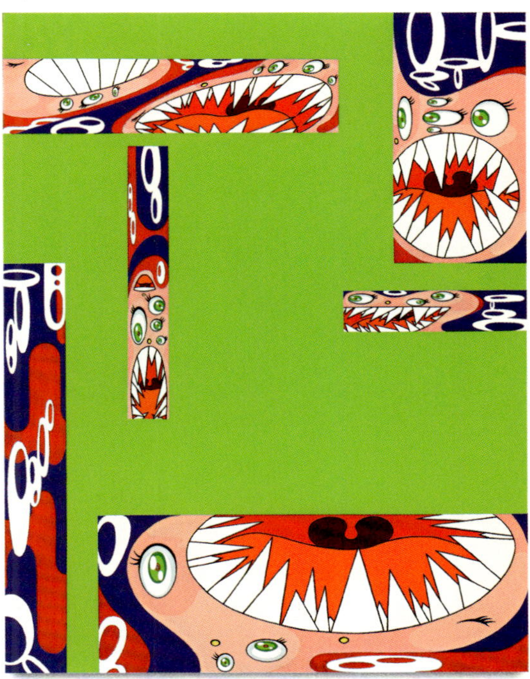

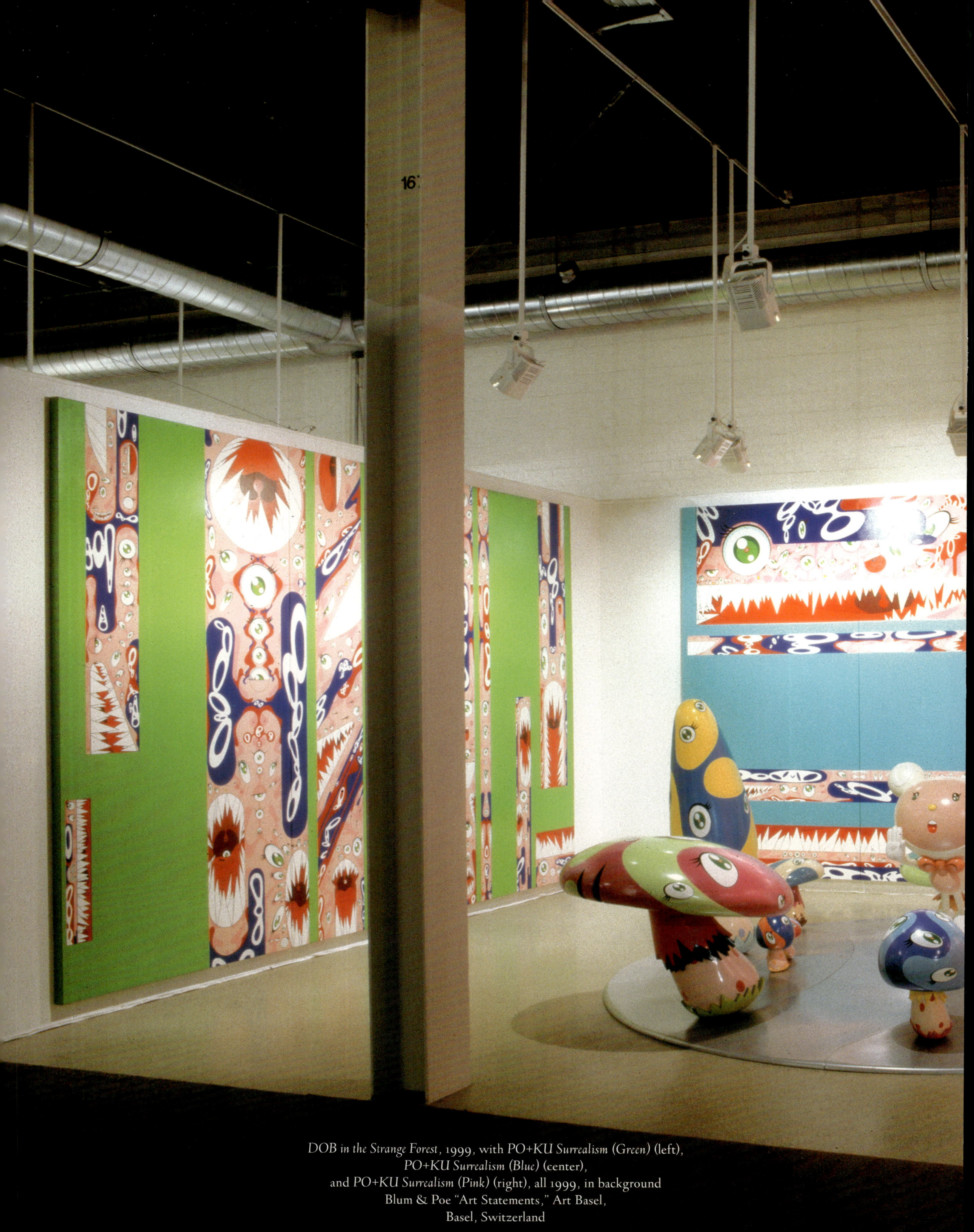

DOB in the Strange Forest, 1999, with PO+KU *Surrealism (Green)* (left),
PO+KU *Surrealism (Blue)* (center),
and PO+KU *Surrealism (Pink)* (right), all 1999, in background
Blum & Poe "Art Statements," Art Basel,
Basel, Switzerland

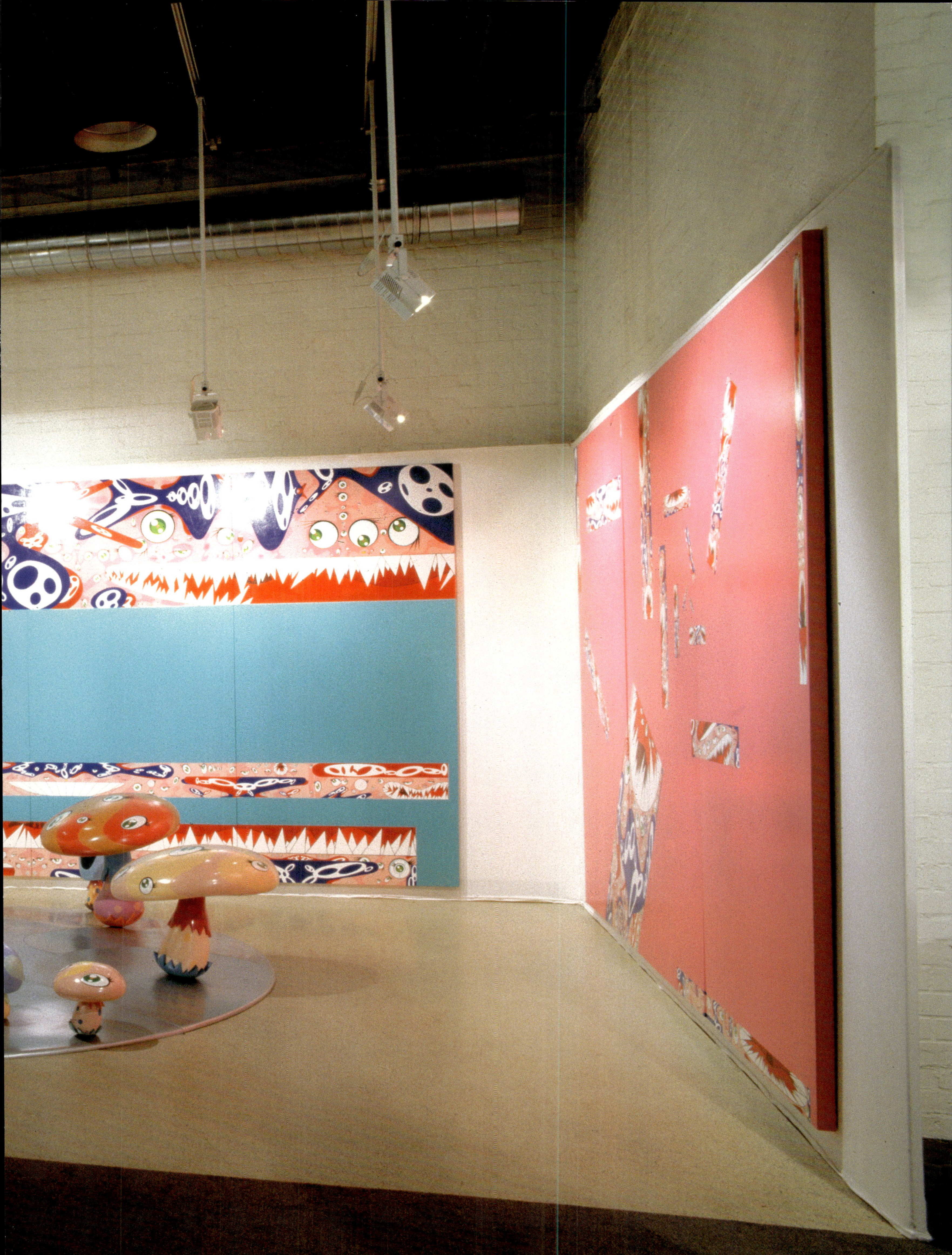

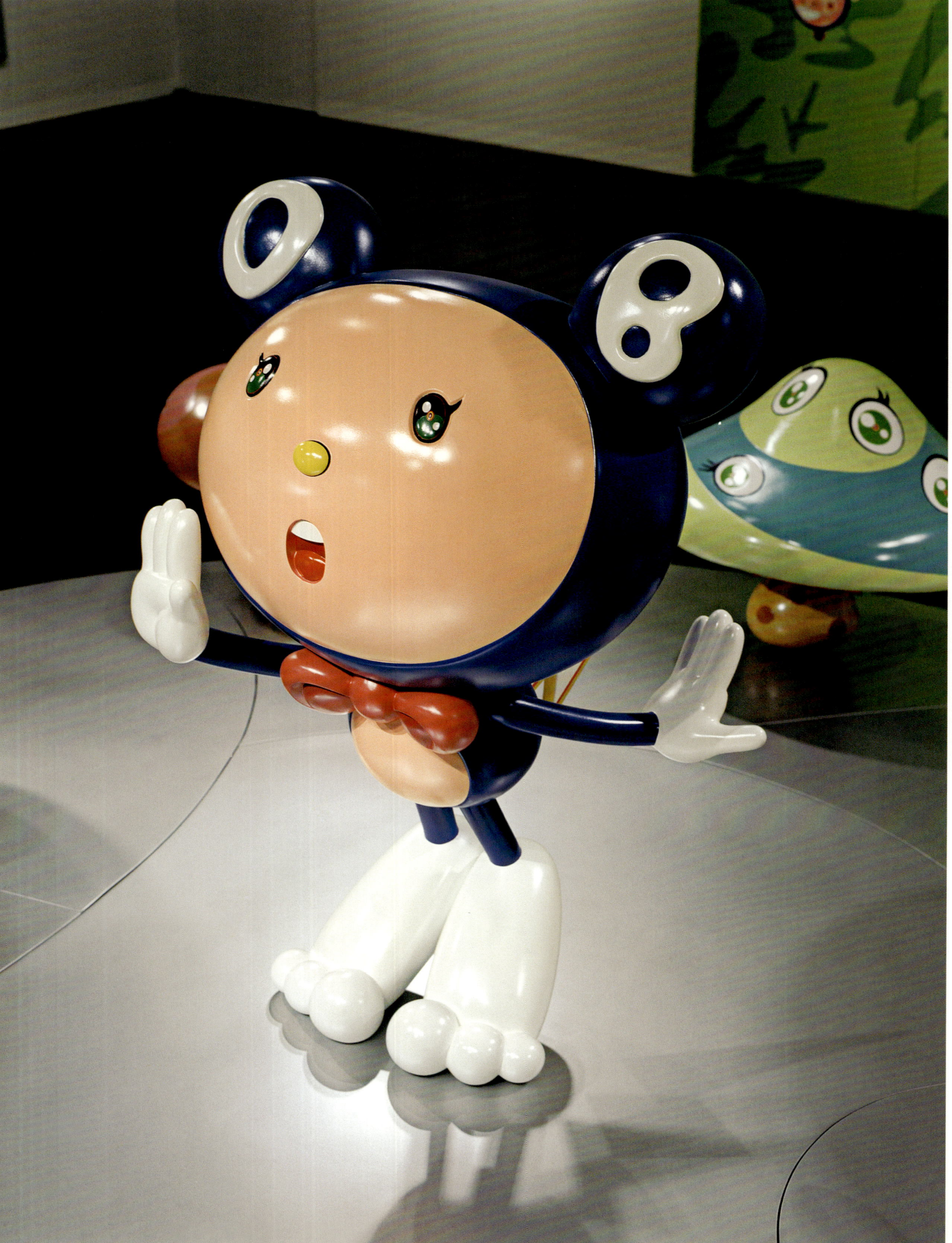

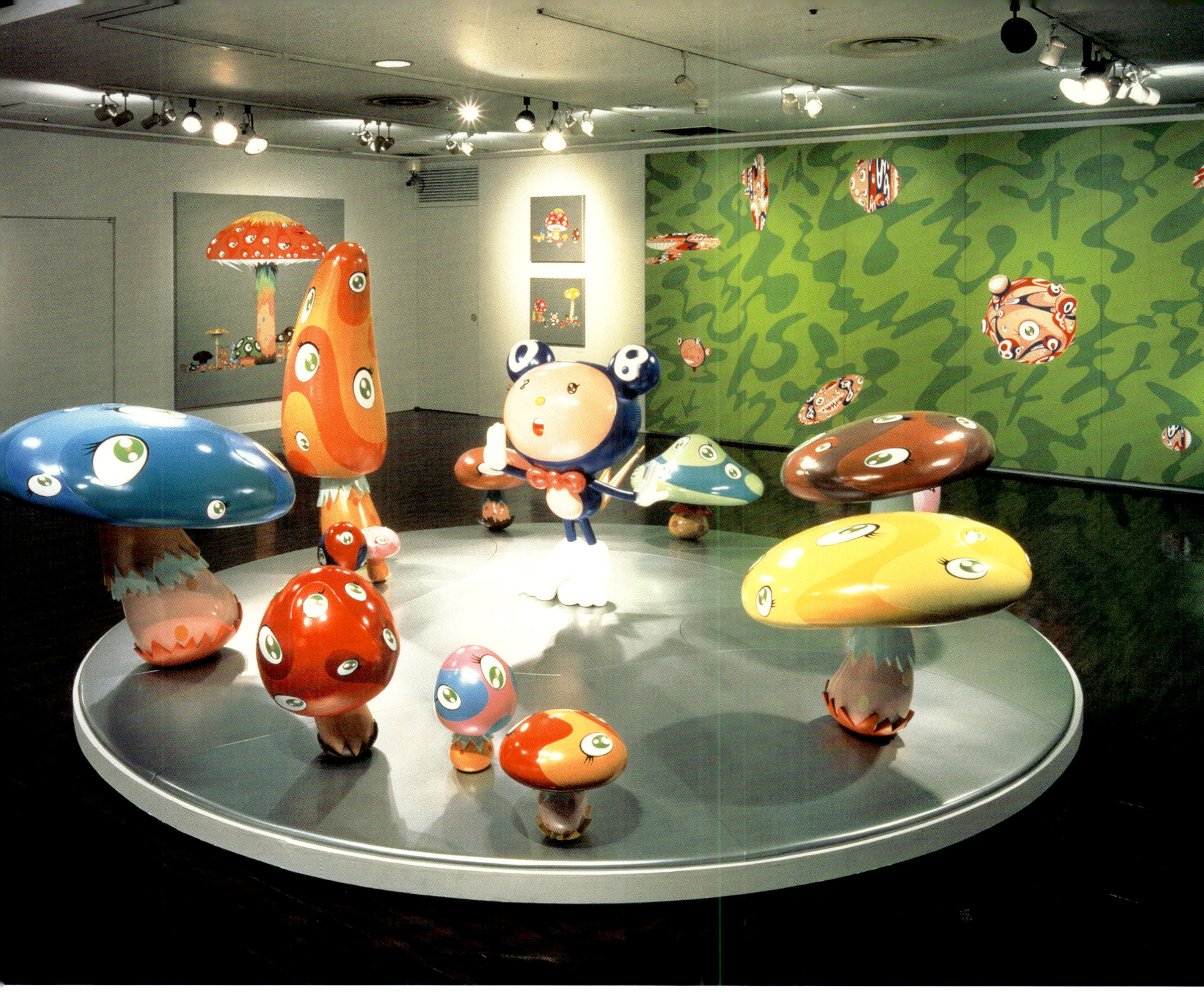

DOB in the Strange Forest, 1999, and detail
Installation at Parco Gallery,
Tokyo

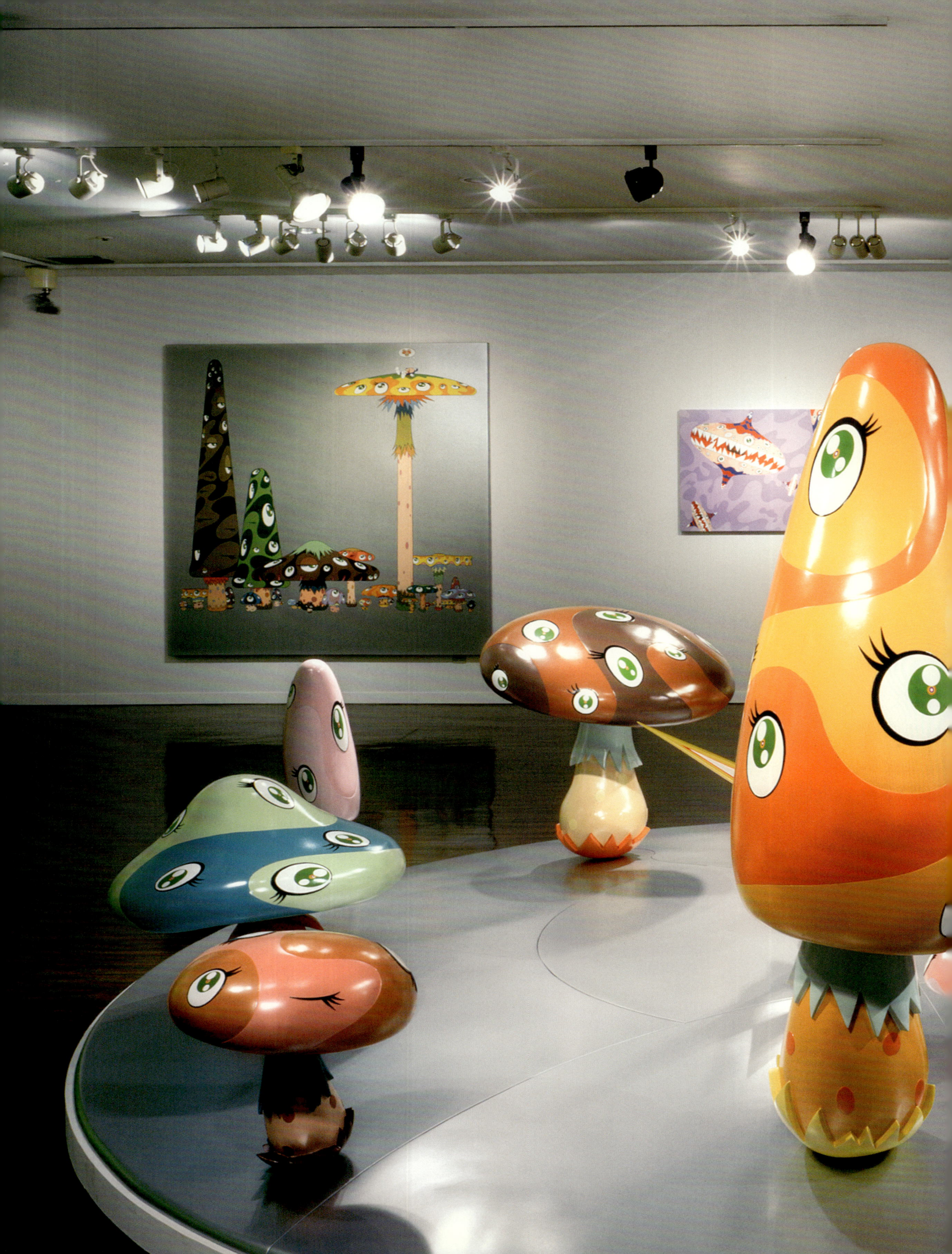

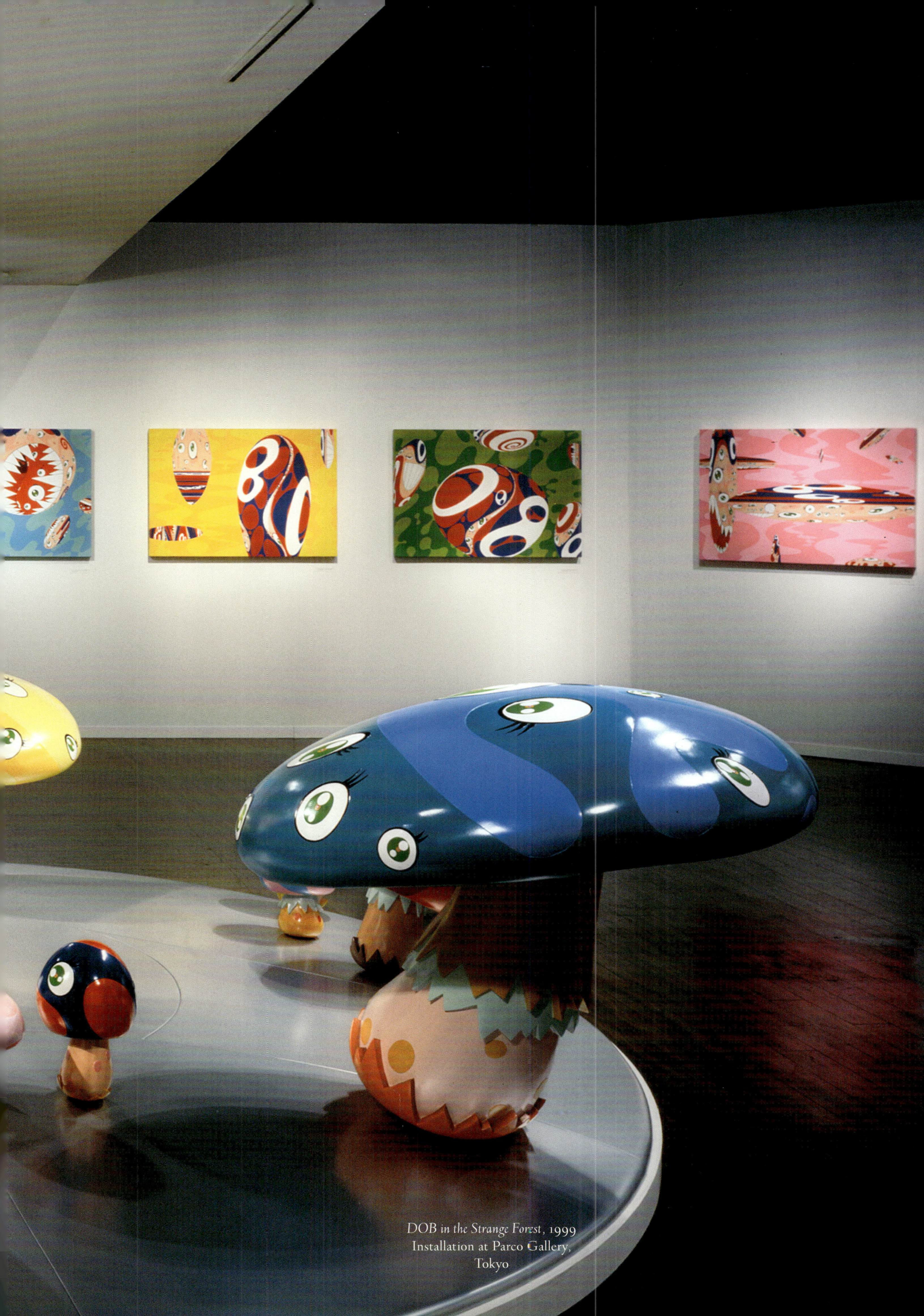

DOB in the Strange Forest, 1999
Installation at Parco Gallery,
Tokyo

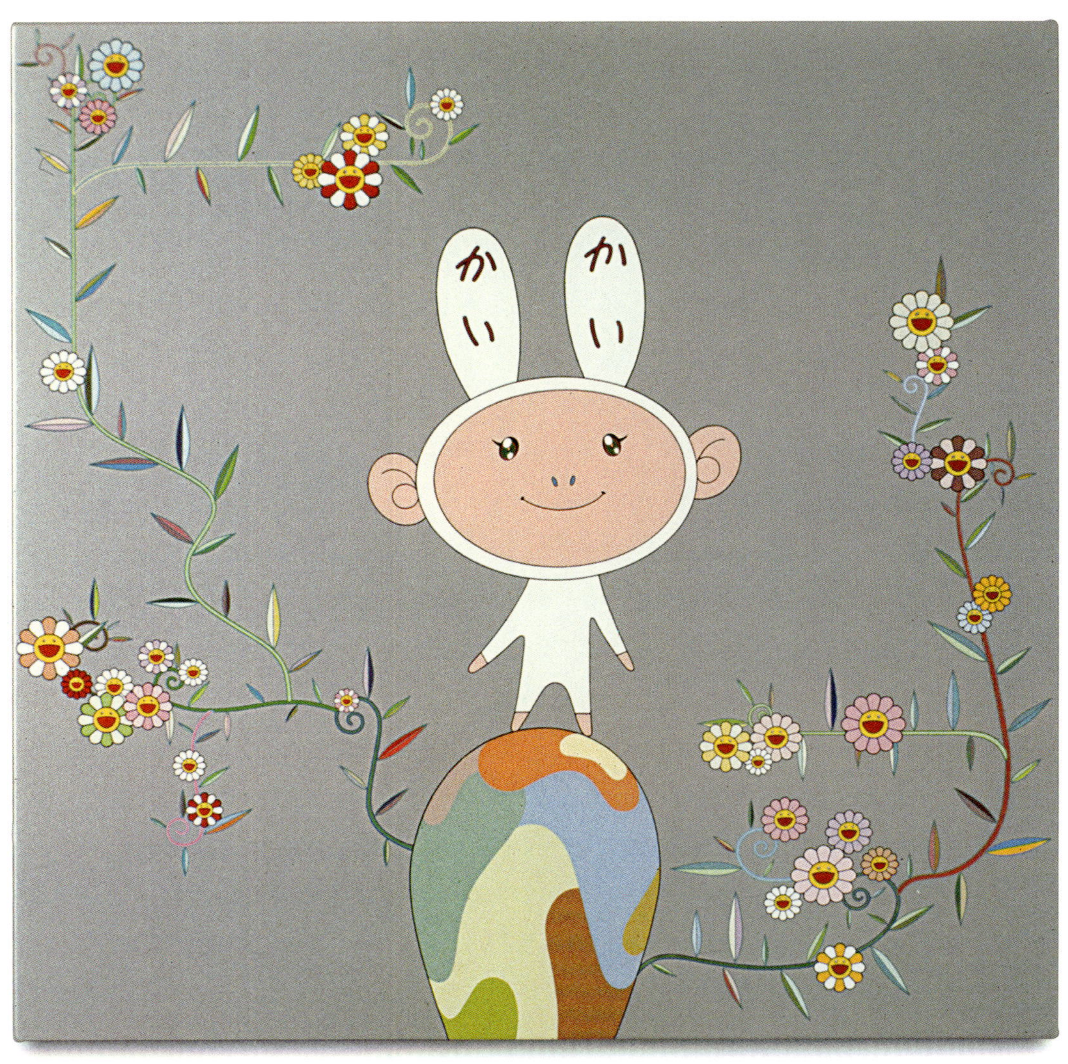

Kaikai with Moss, 2000

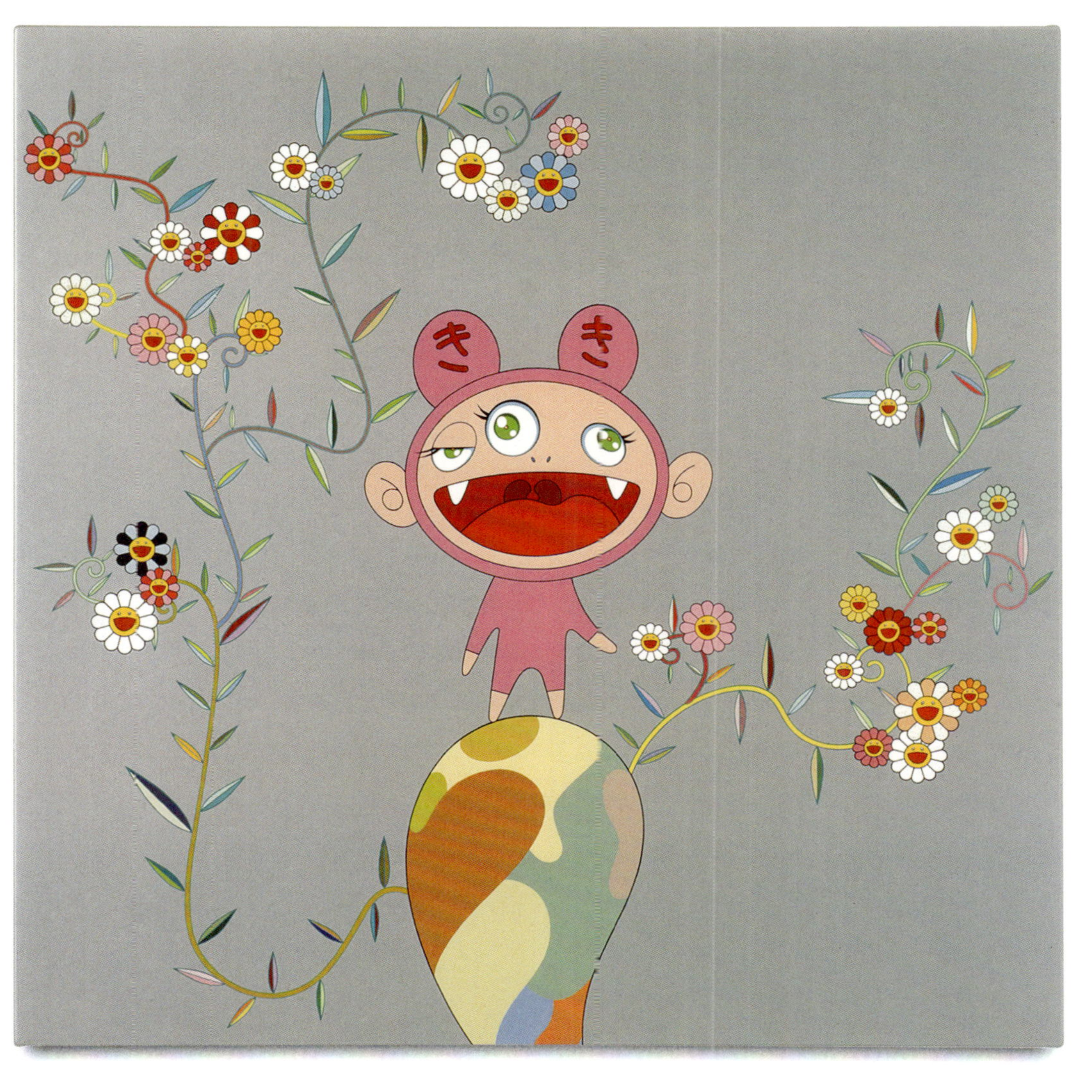

Kiki with Moss, 2000

Kaikai (left) and *Kiki* (right), both 2000,
with *Time Bokan—pink* on *Jellyfish Eyes* wallpaper, both 2001, in background
Installation at the Museum of Contemporary Art,
Tokyo, 2001

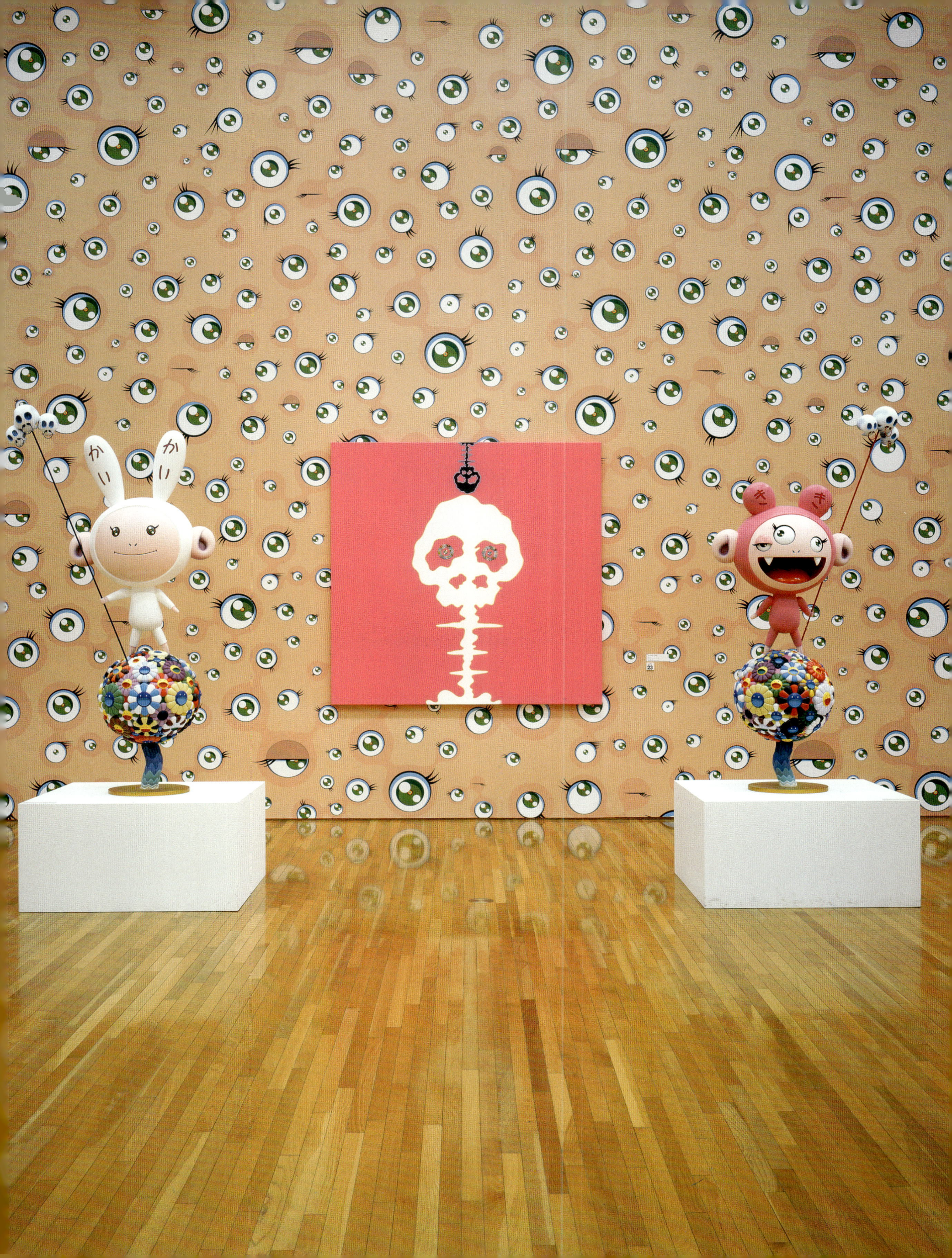
かい
かい
き
き

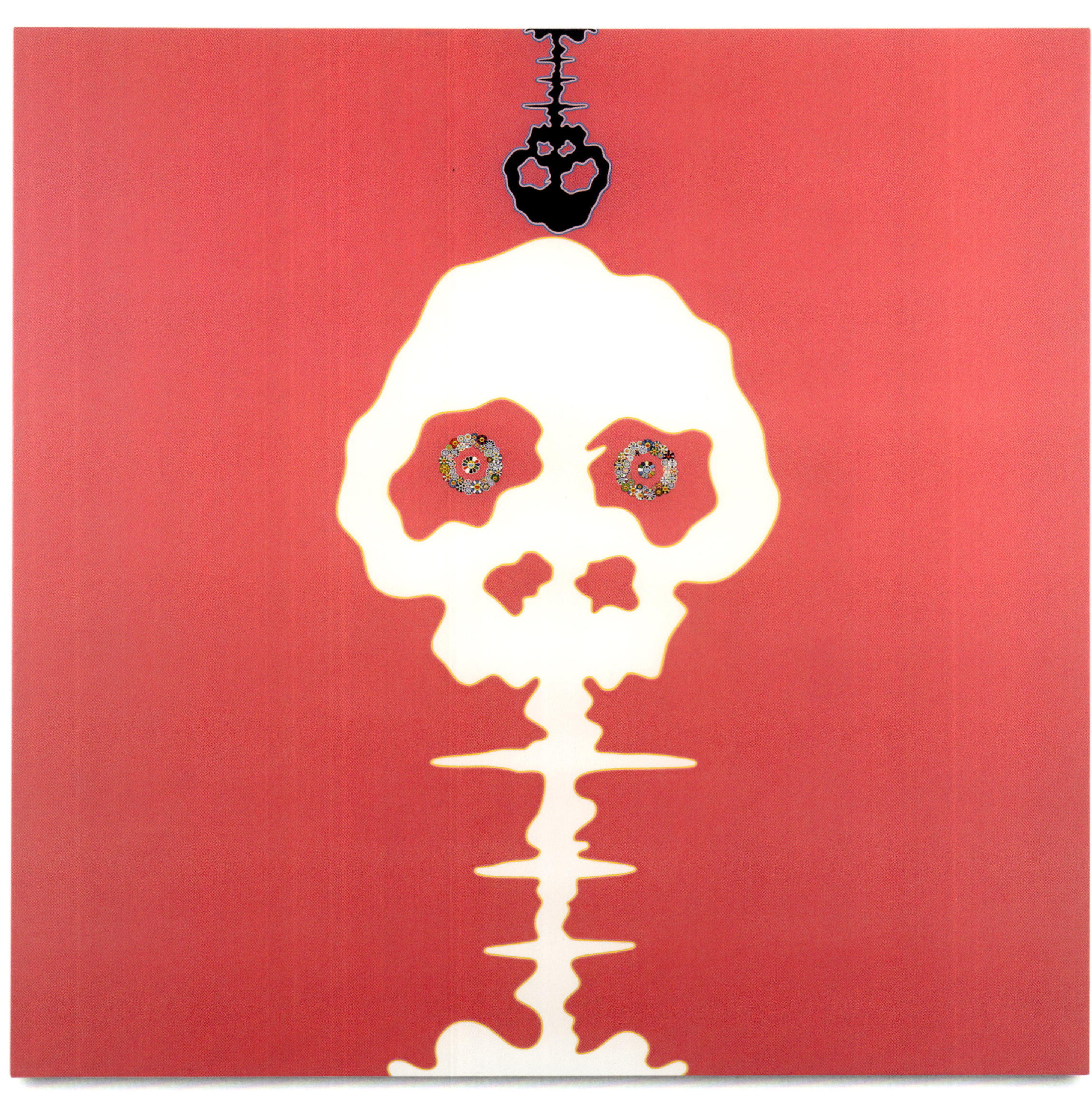

Time Bokan—pink, 2001

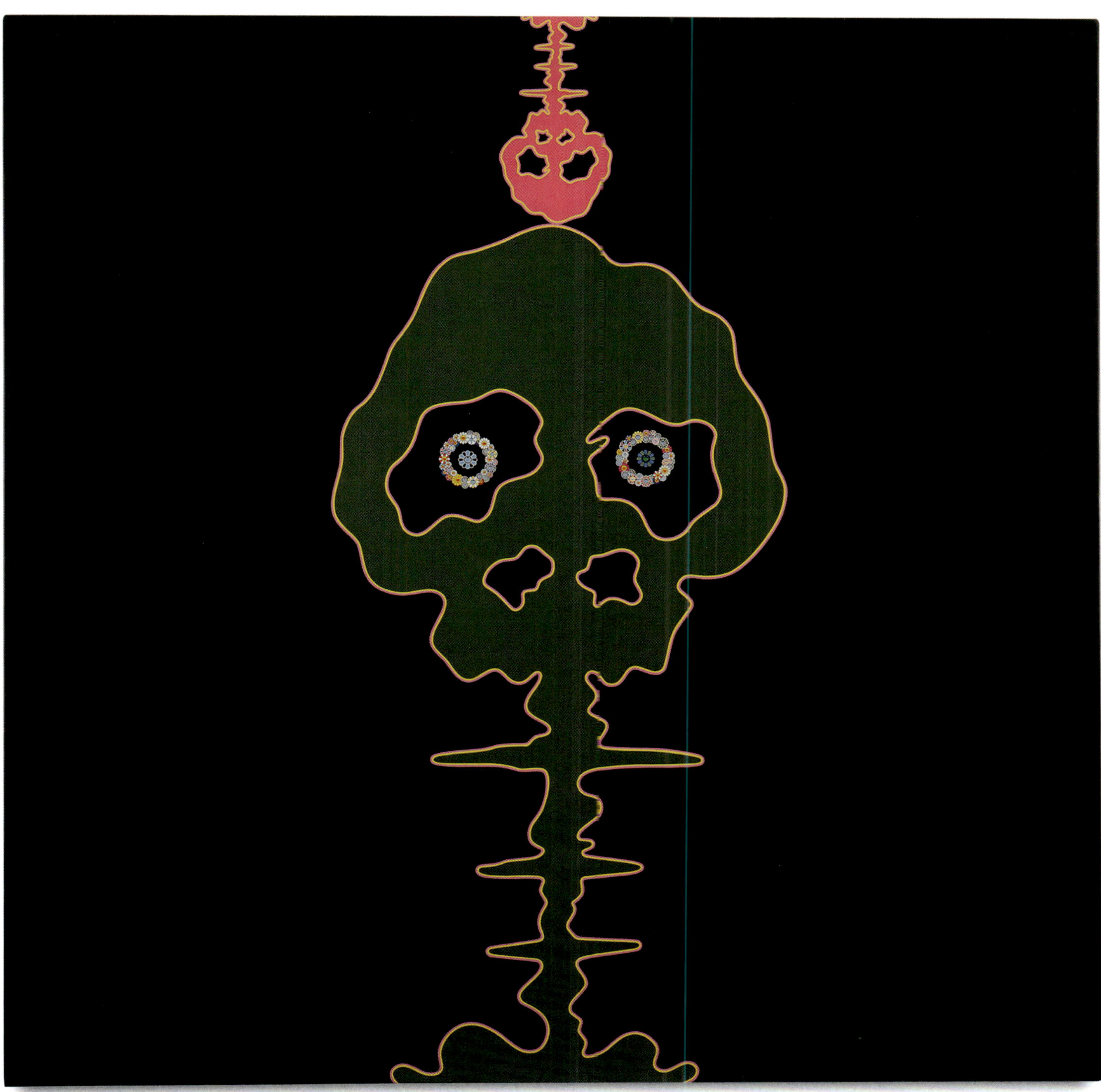

Time Bokan—black, 2001

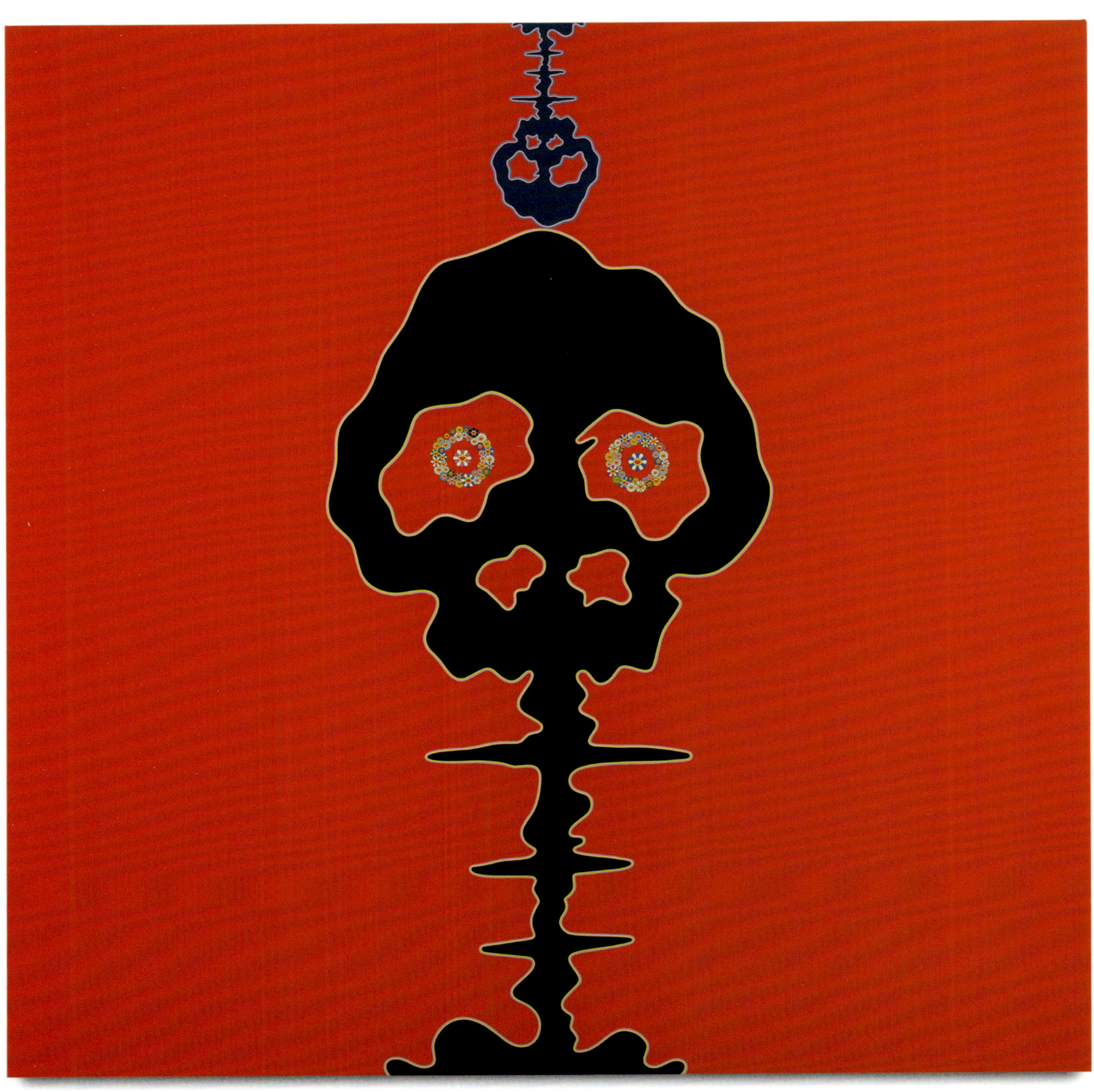

Time Bokan—red, 2001

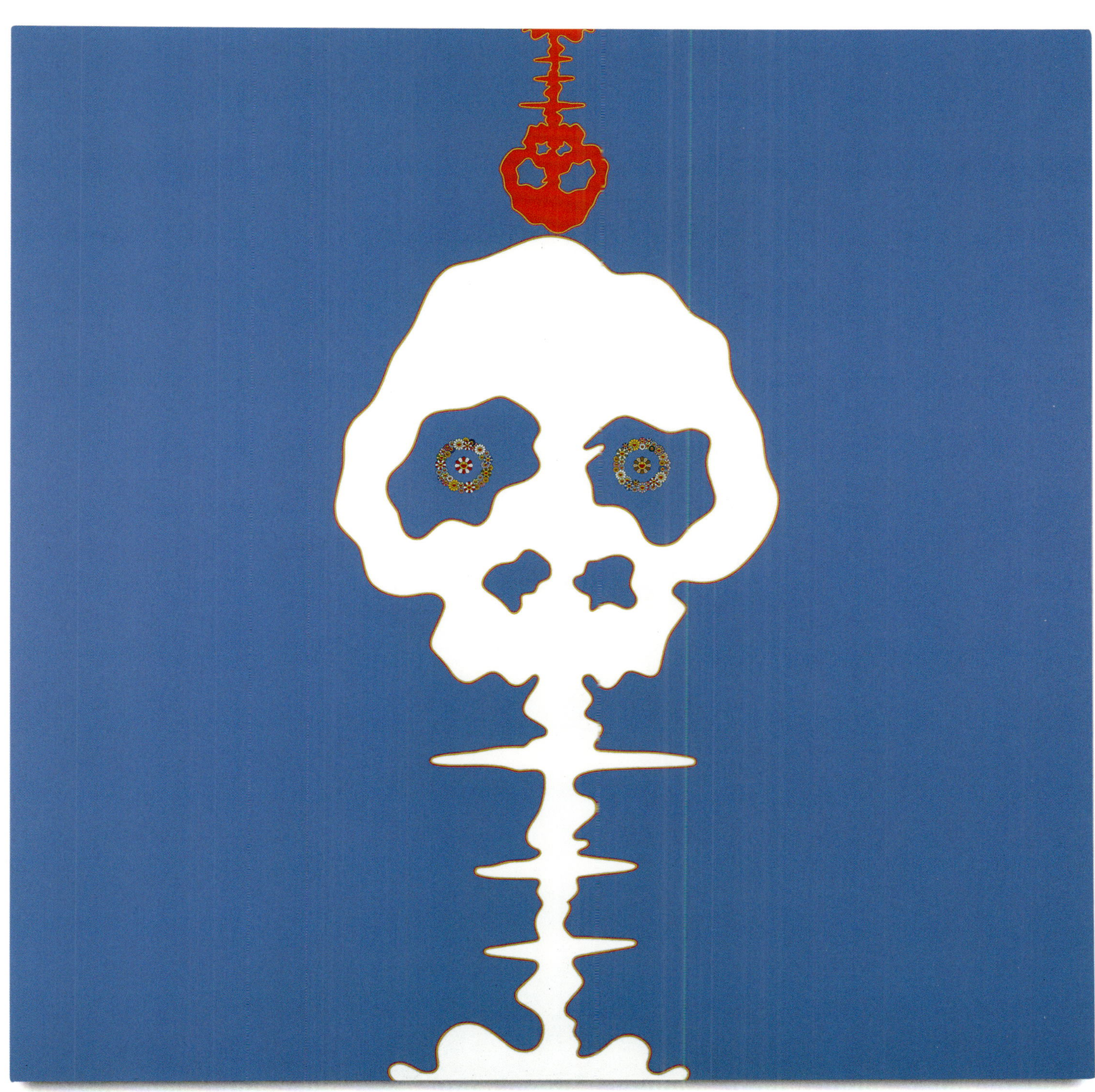

Time Bokan—blue 2001

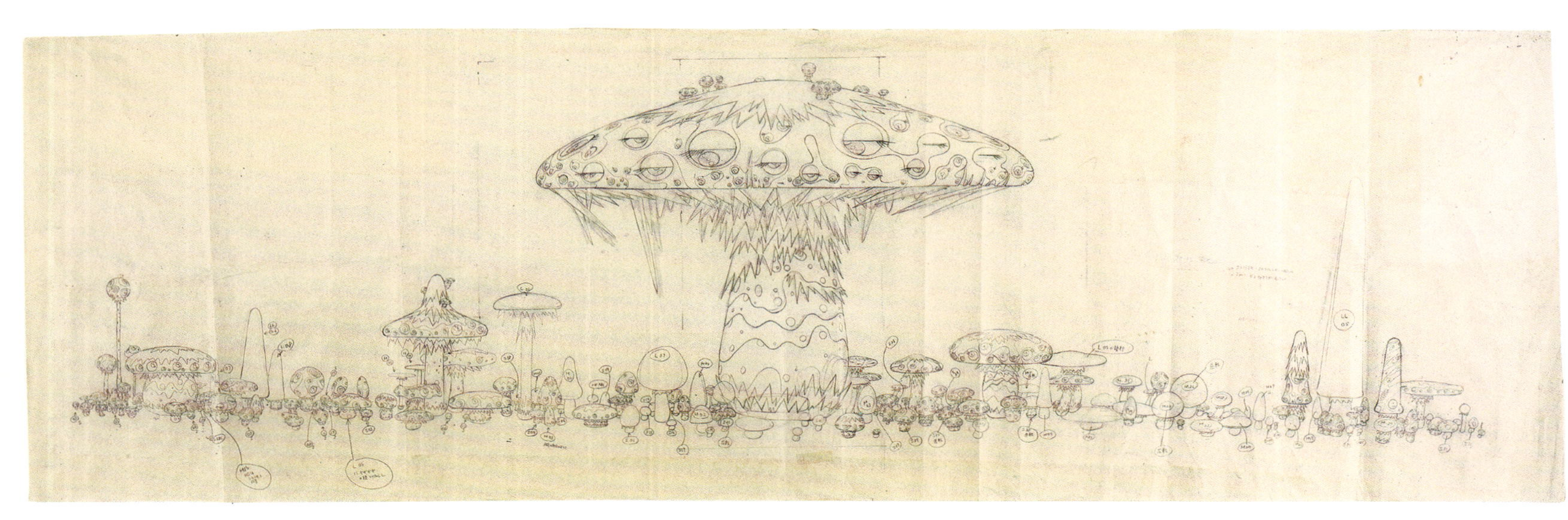

Mushroom Painting Drawing, 1999

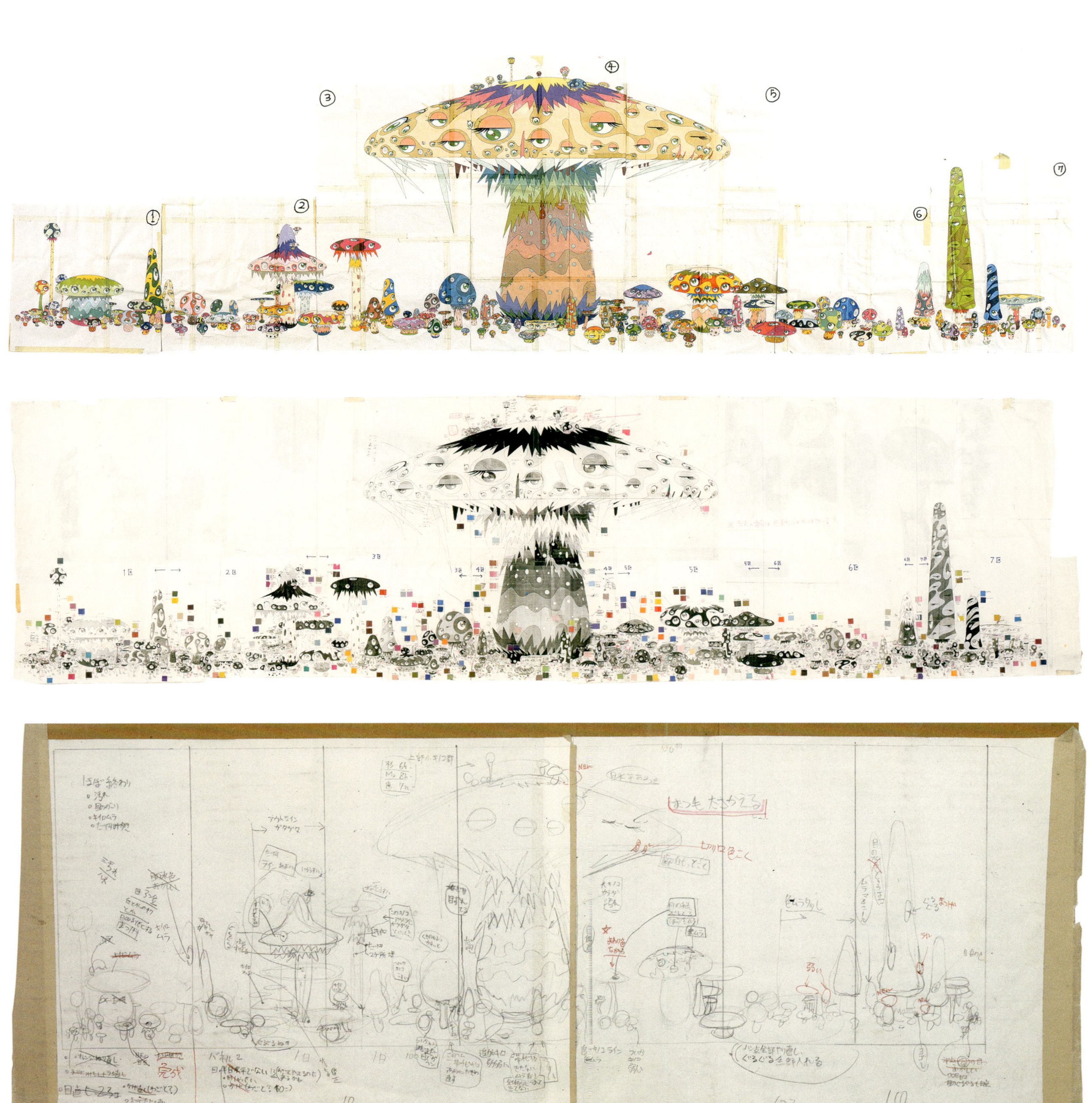

Untitled (Study for Super Nova), 1999
Study for Super Nova 1999
Study for Mushroom Painting, 1999

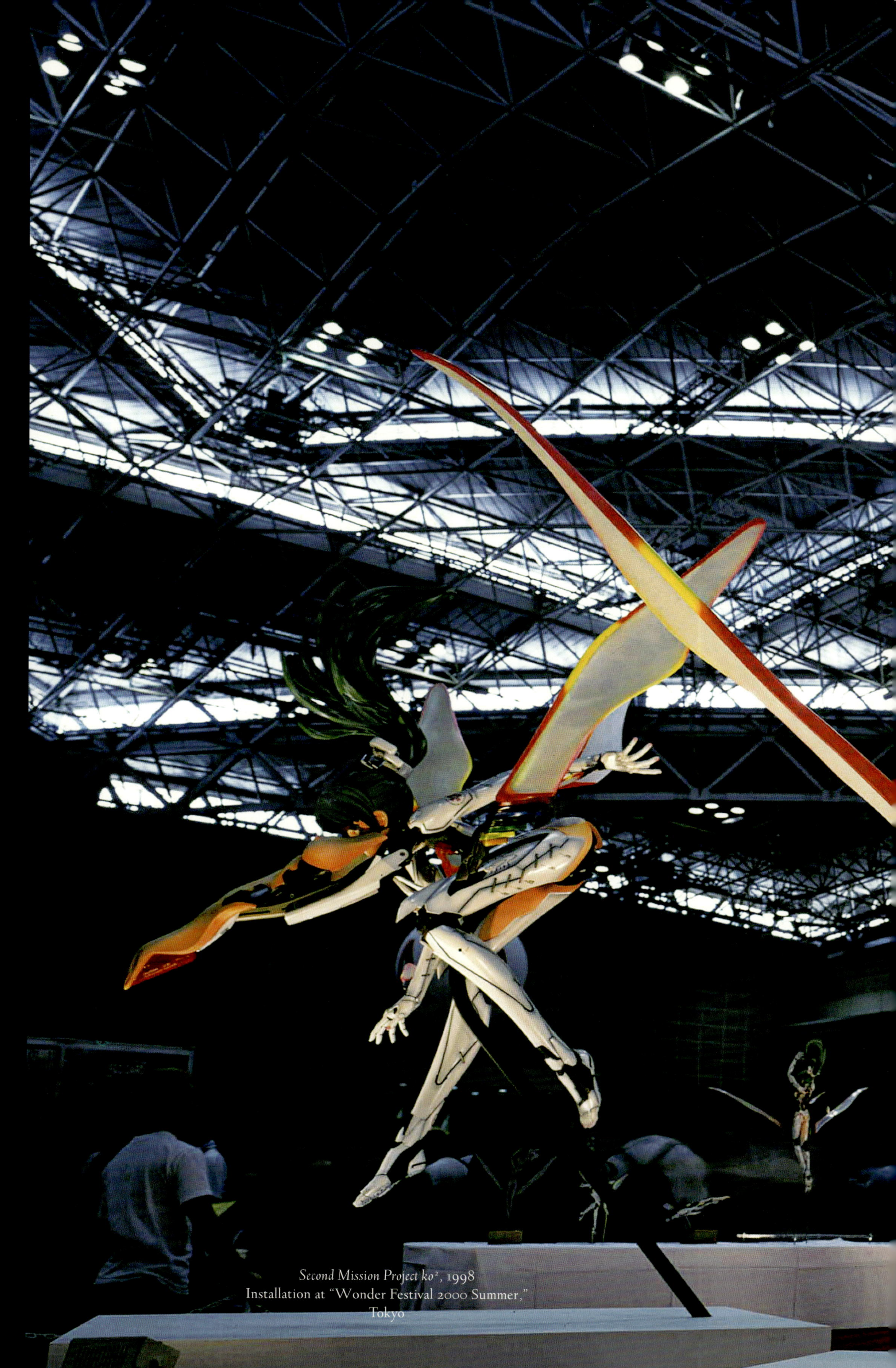

Second Mission Project ko², 1998
Installation at "Wonder Festival 2000 Summer,"
Tokyo

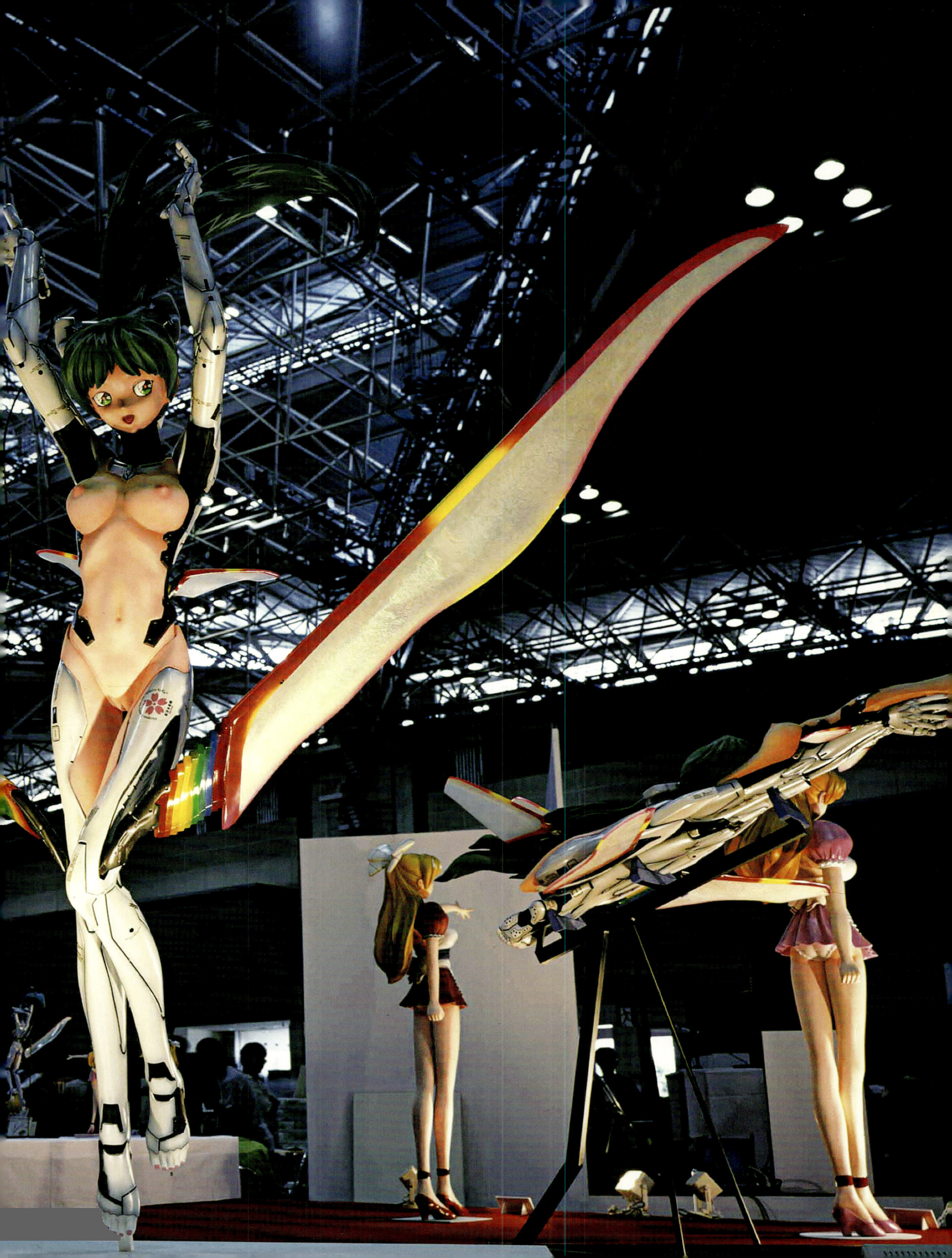

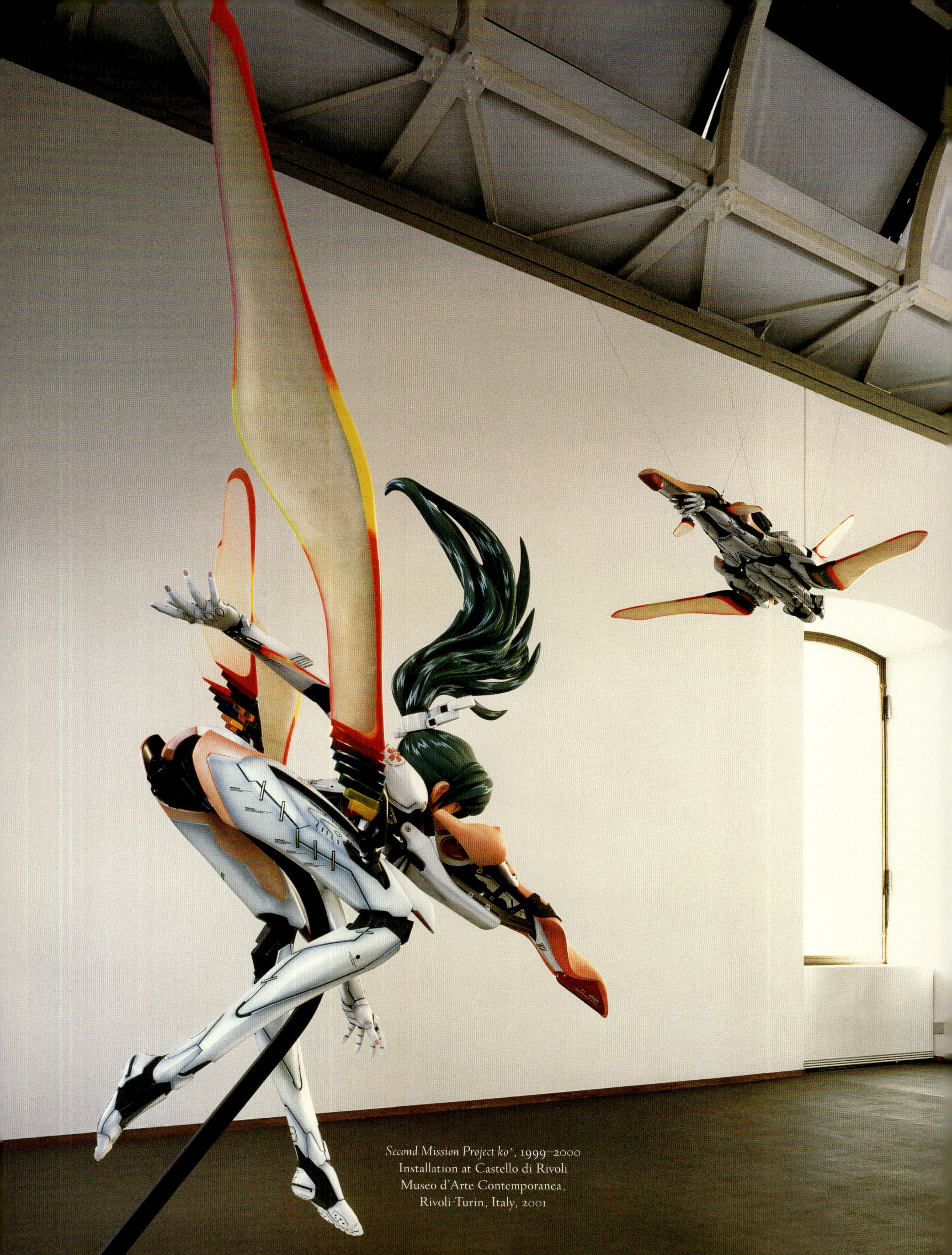

Second Mission Project ko², 1999–2000
Installation at Castello di Rivoli
Museo d'Arte Contemporanea,
Rivoli-Turin, Italy, 2001

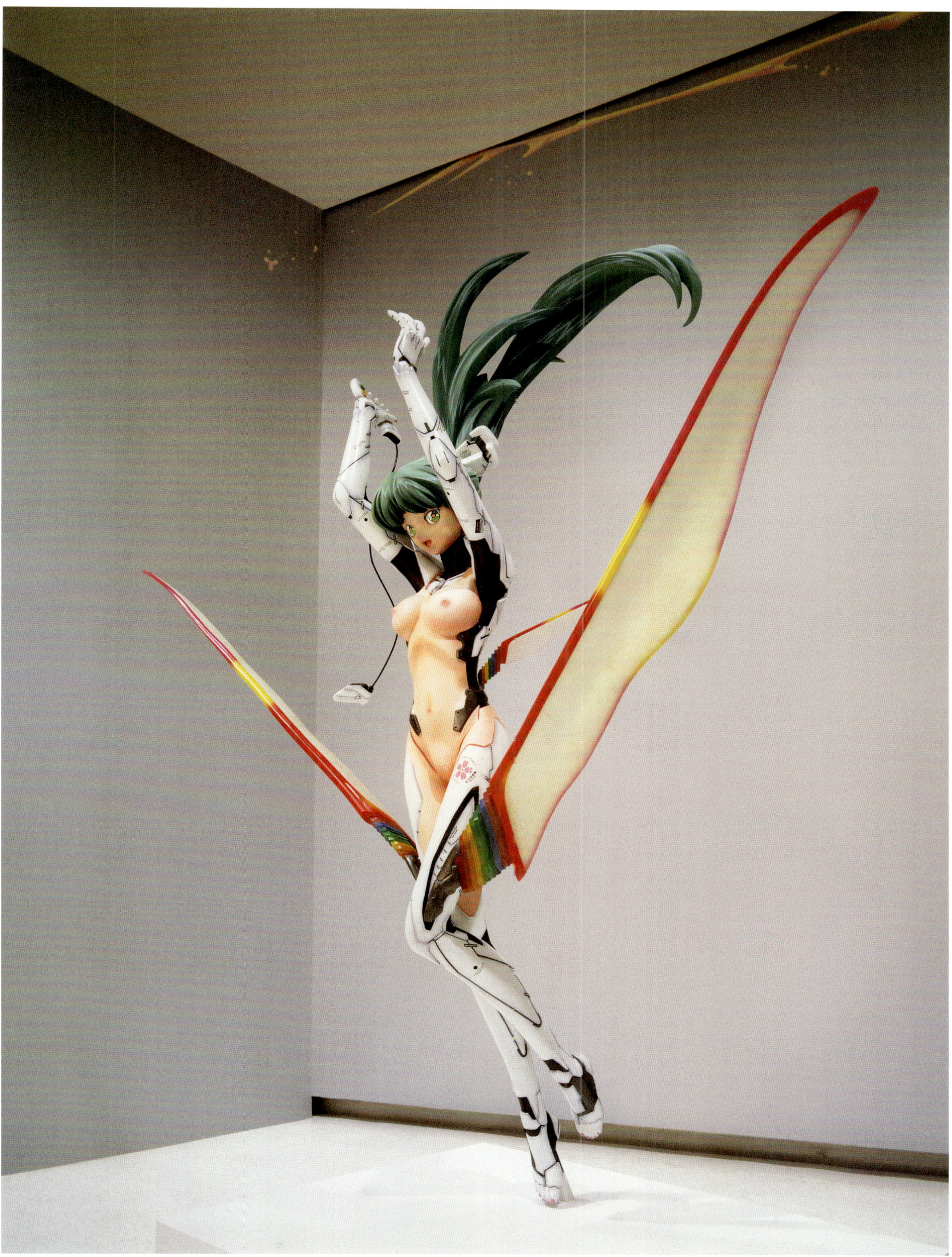

previous page
Second Mission Project ko[2]
(Human Type), 1998
Installation in Carnegie International 1999,
Carnegie Museum of Art, Pittsburgh

Melting DOB D, 2001

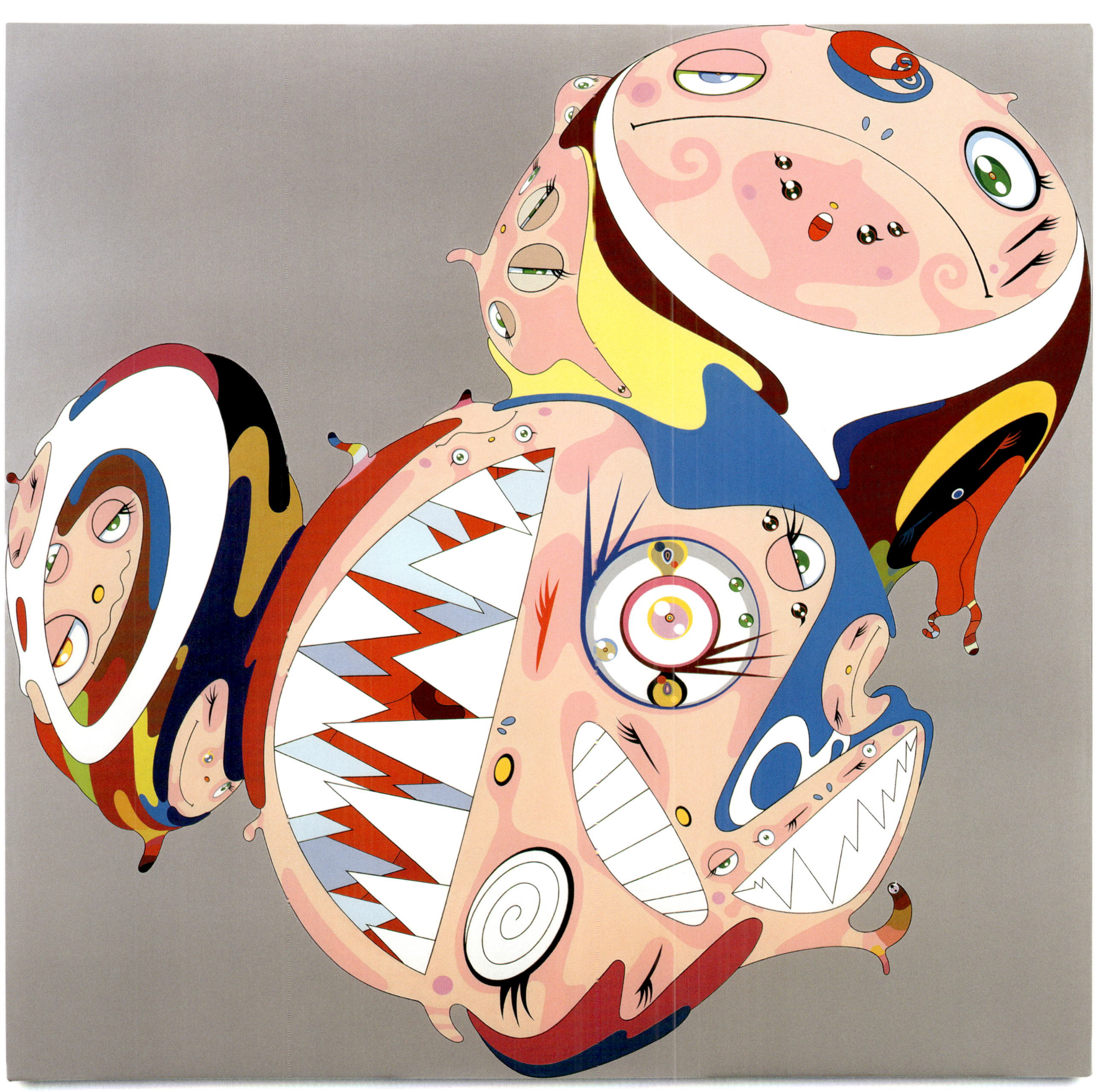

The Double Helix, Reversal, 2001

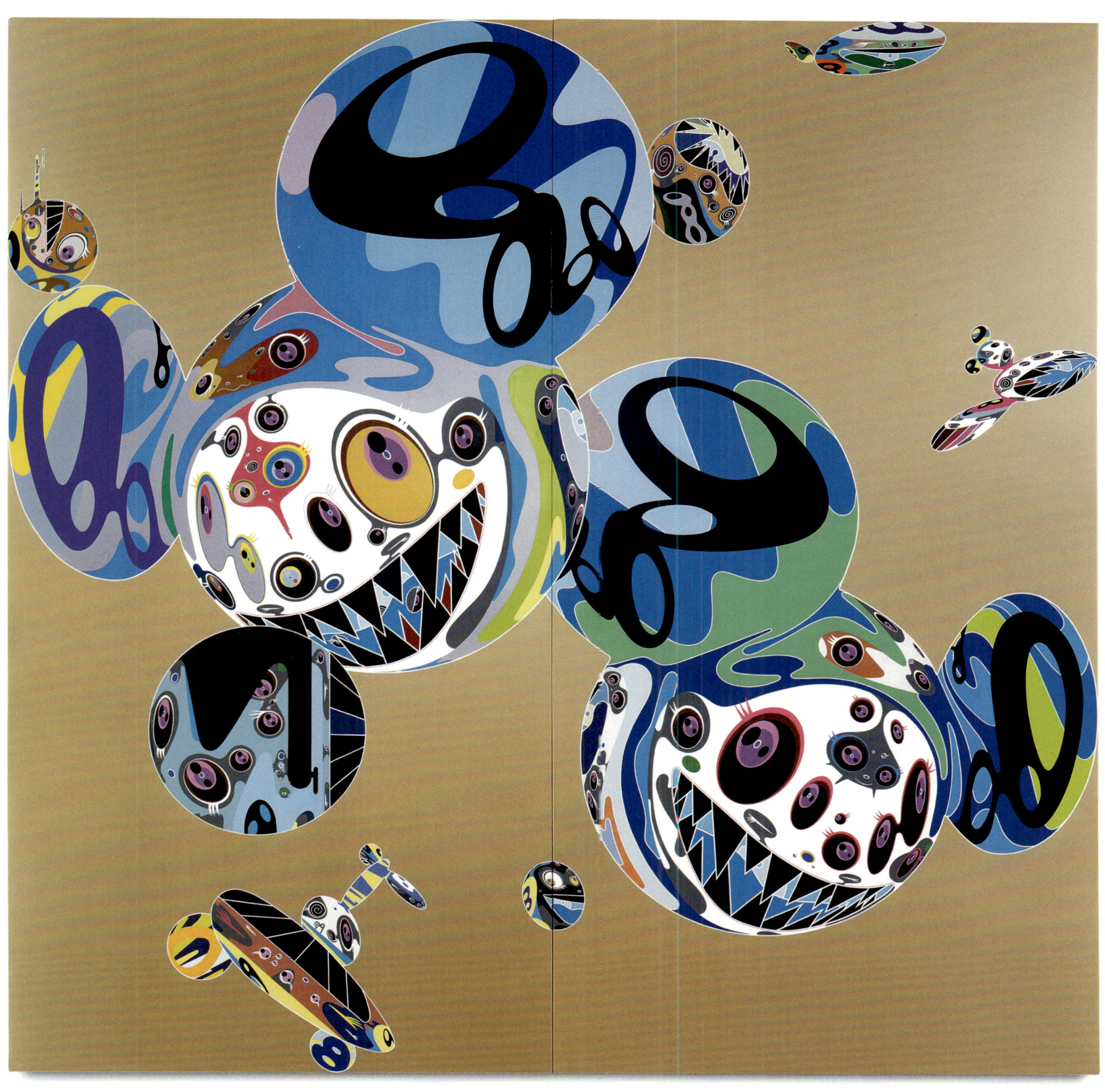

following spread
Tan Tan Bo, 2001

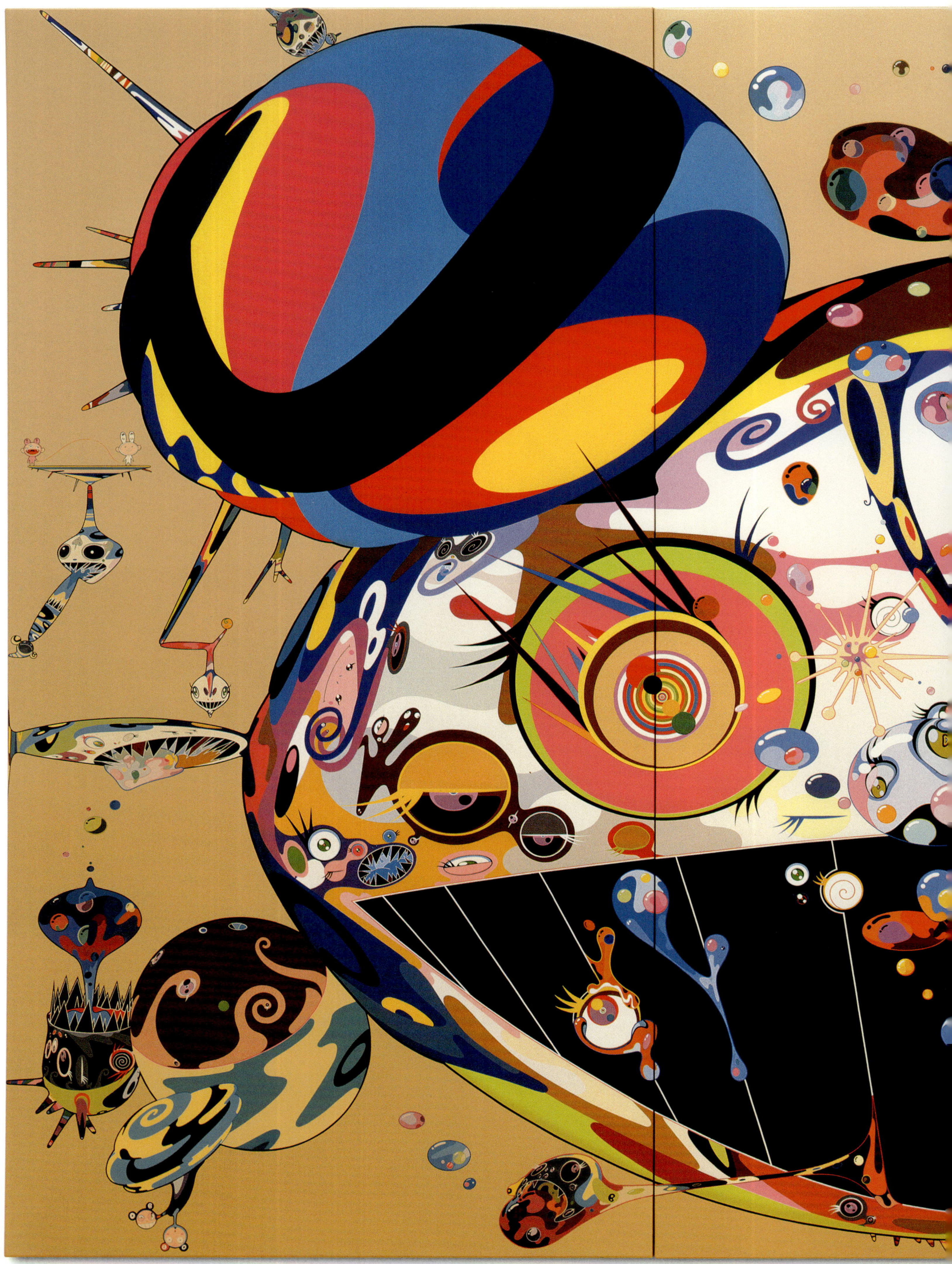

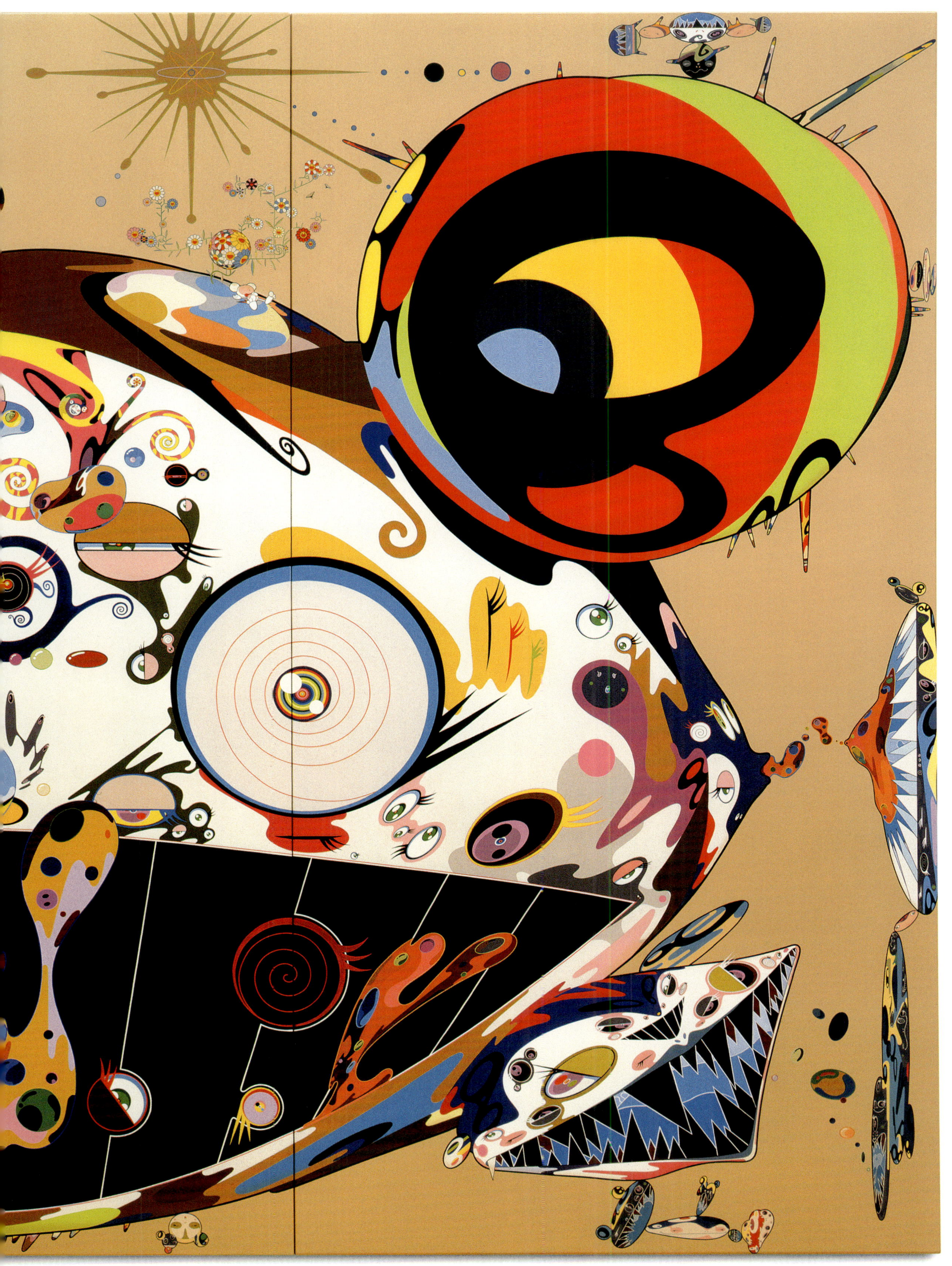

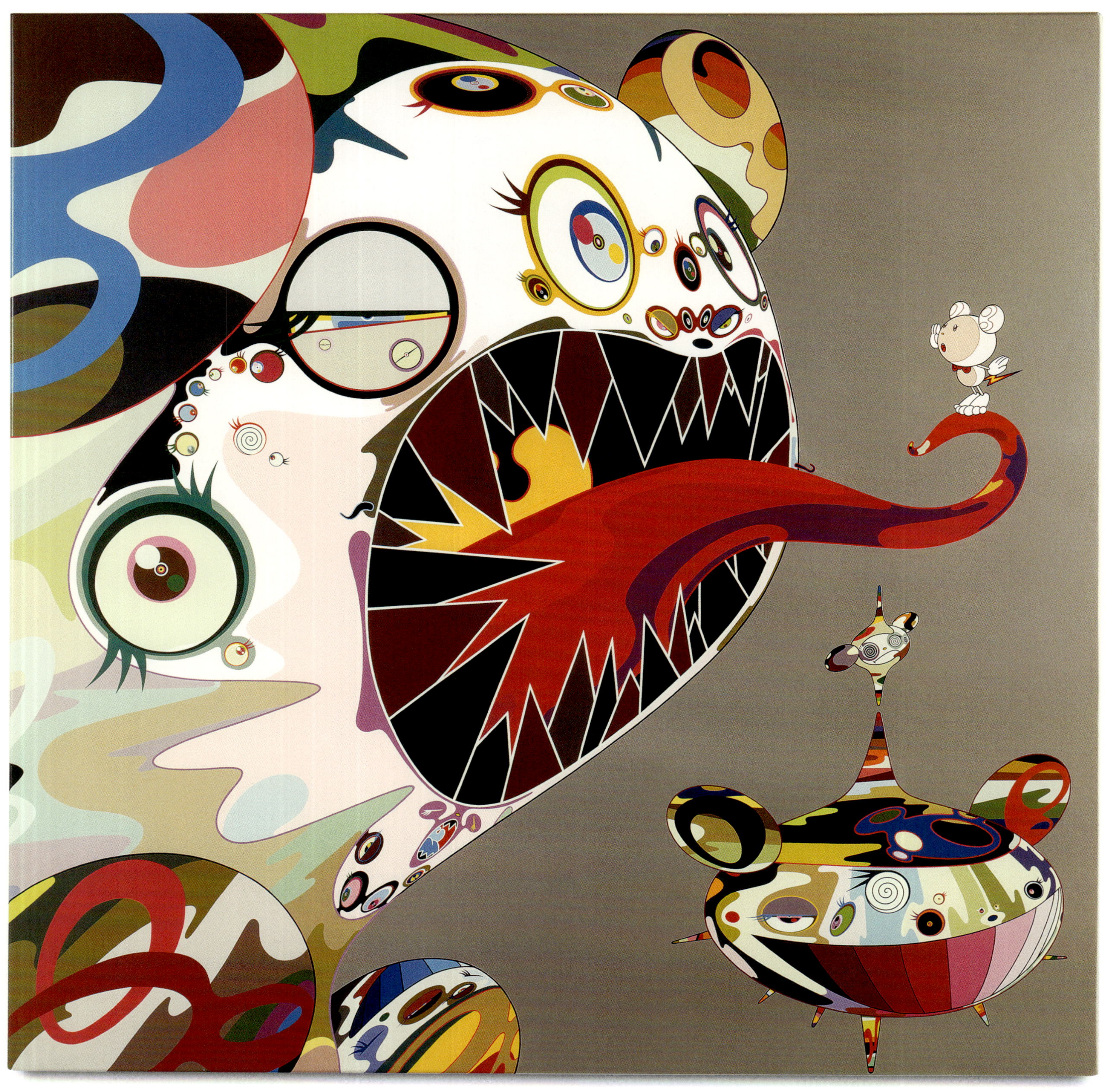

Homage to Francis Bacon (Study of George Dyer), 2002

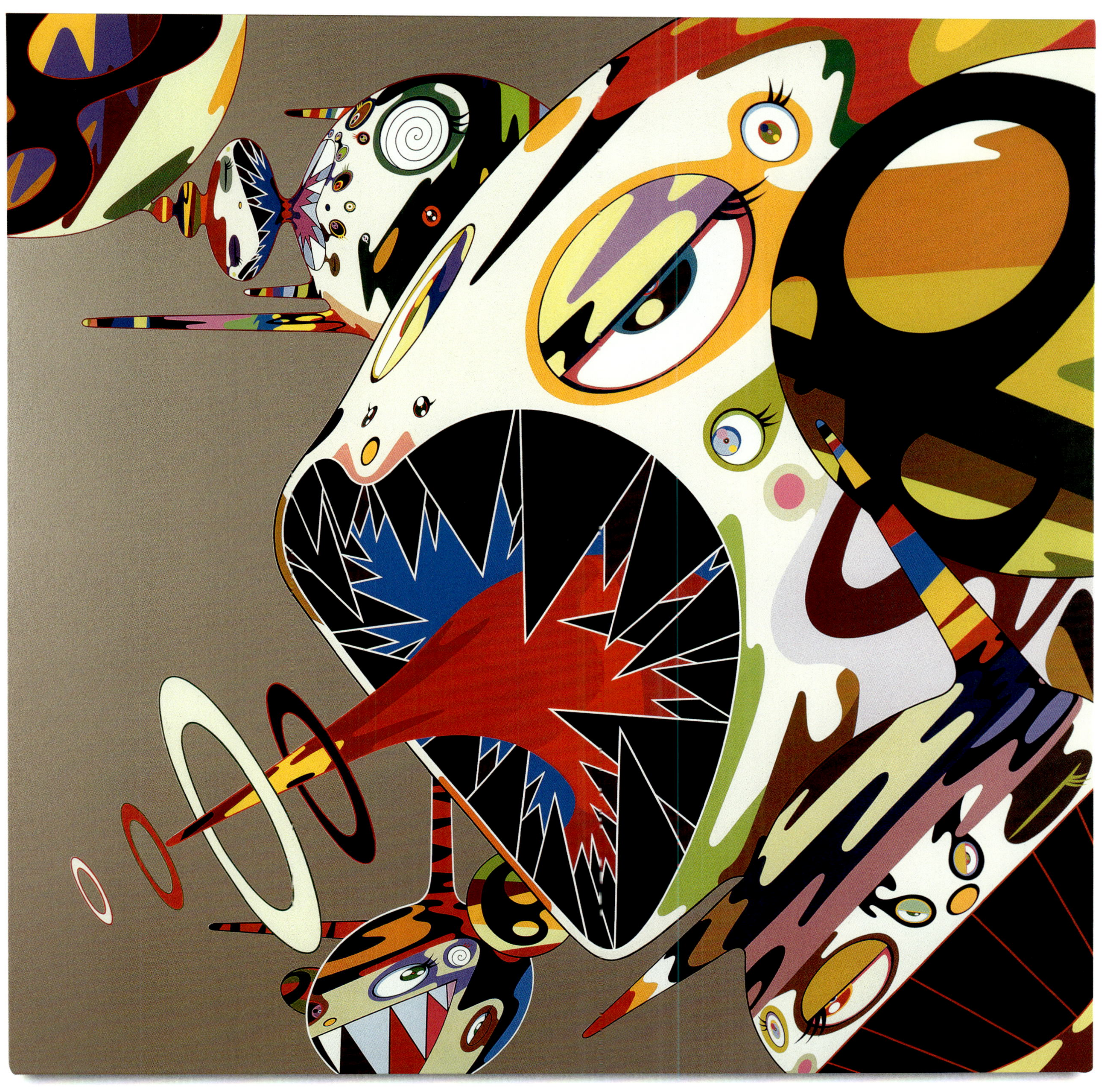

Homage to Francis Bacon (Study of Isabel Rawsthorne), 2002

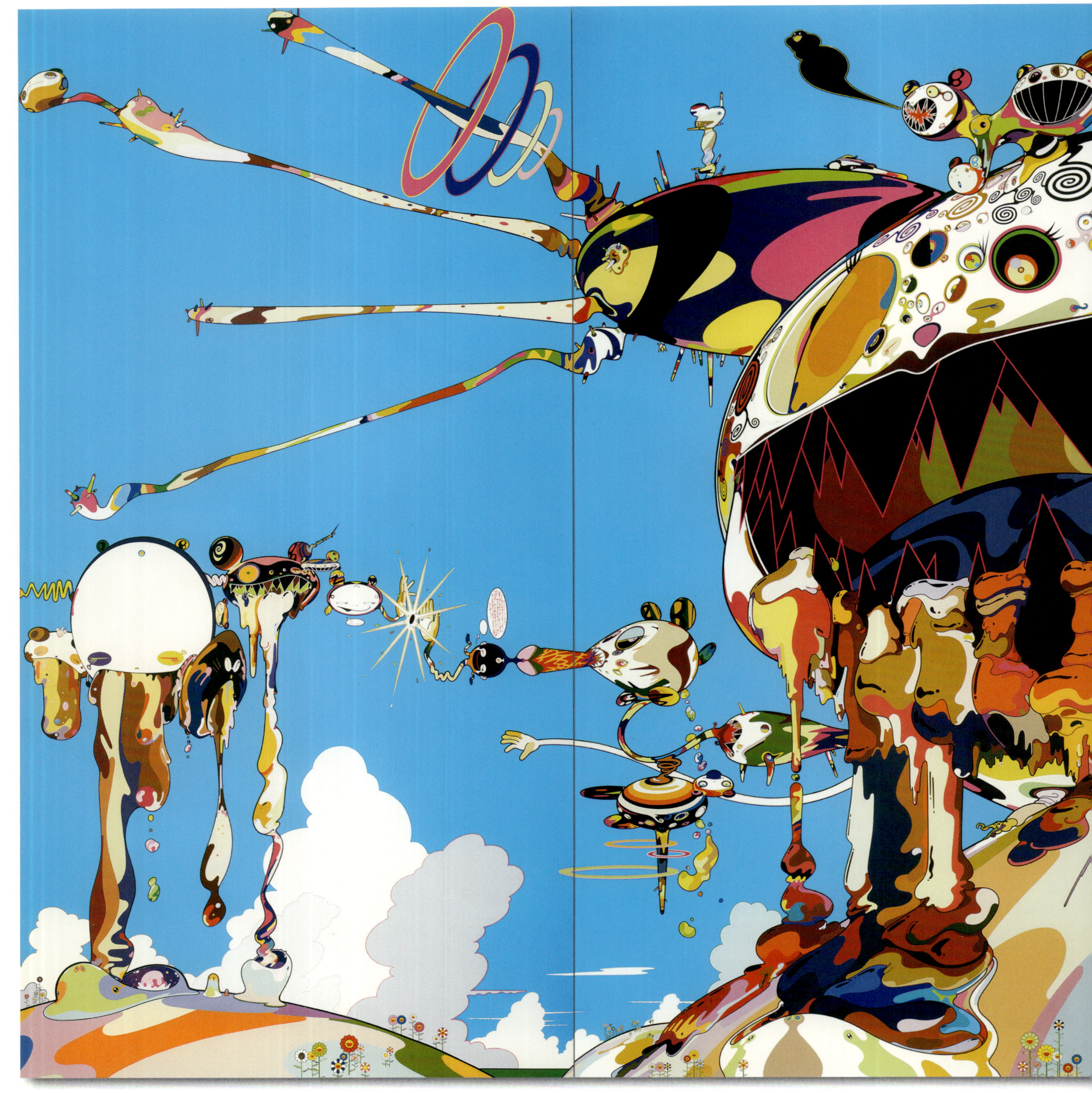

Tan Tan Bo Puking—a.k.a. Gero Tan, 2002

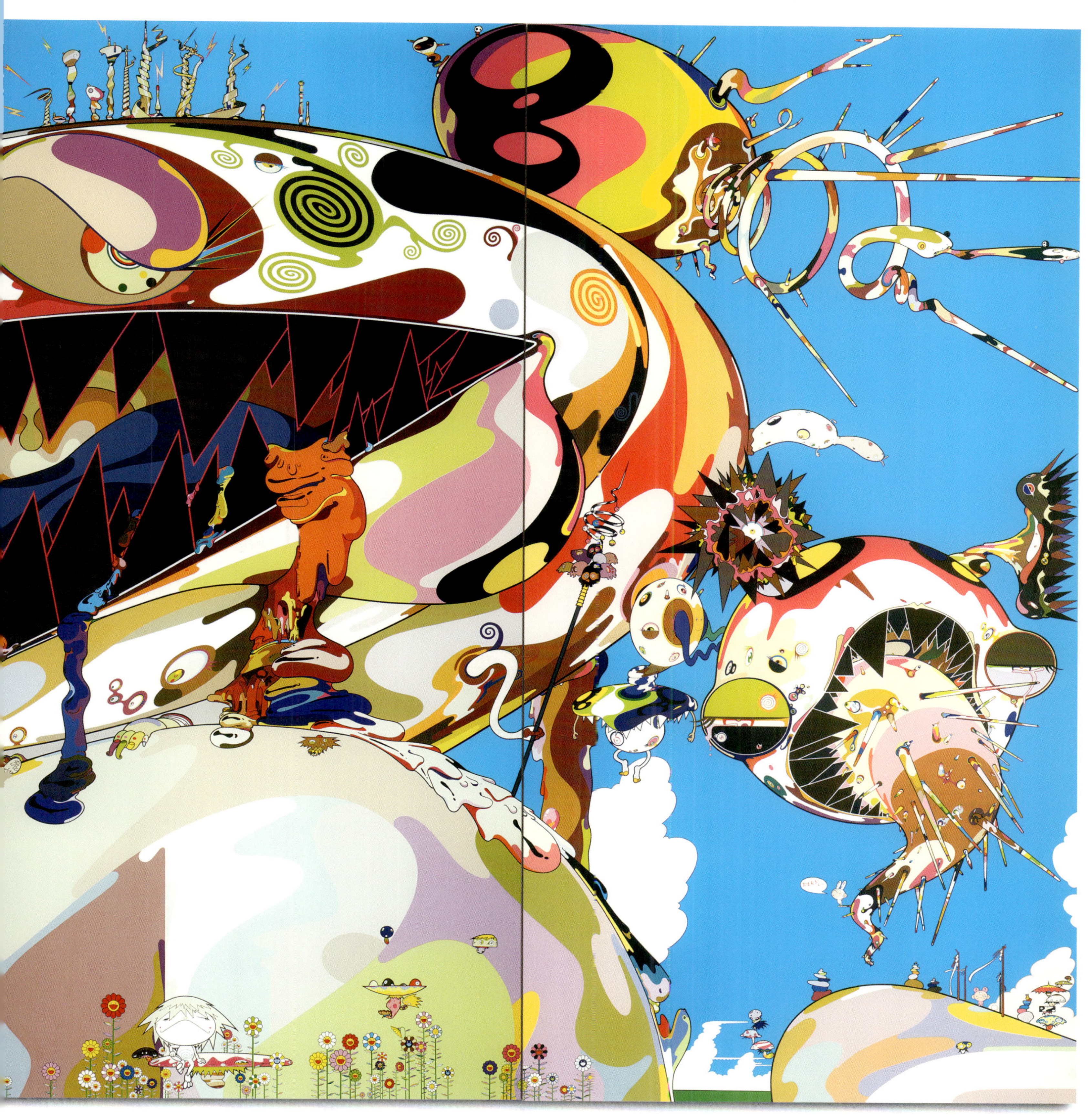

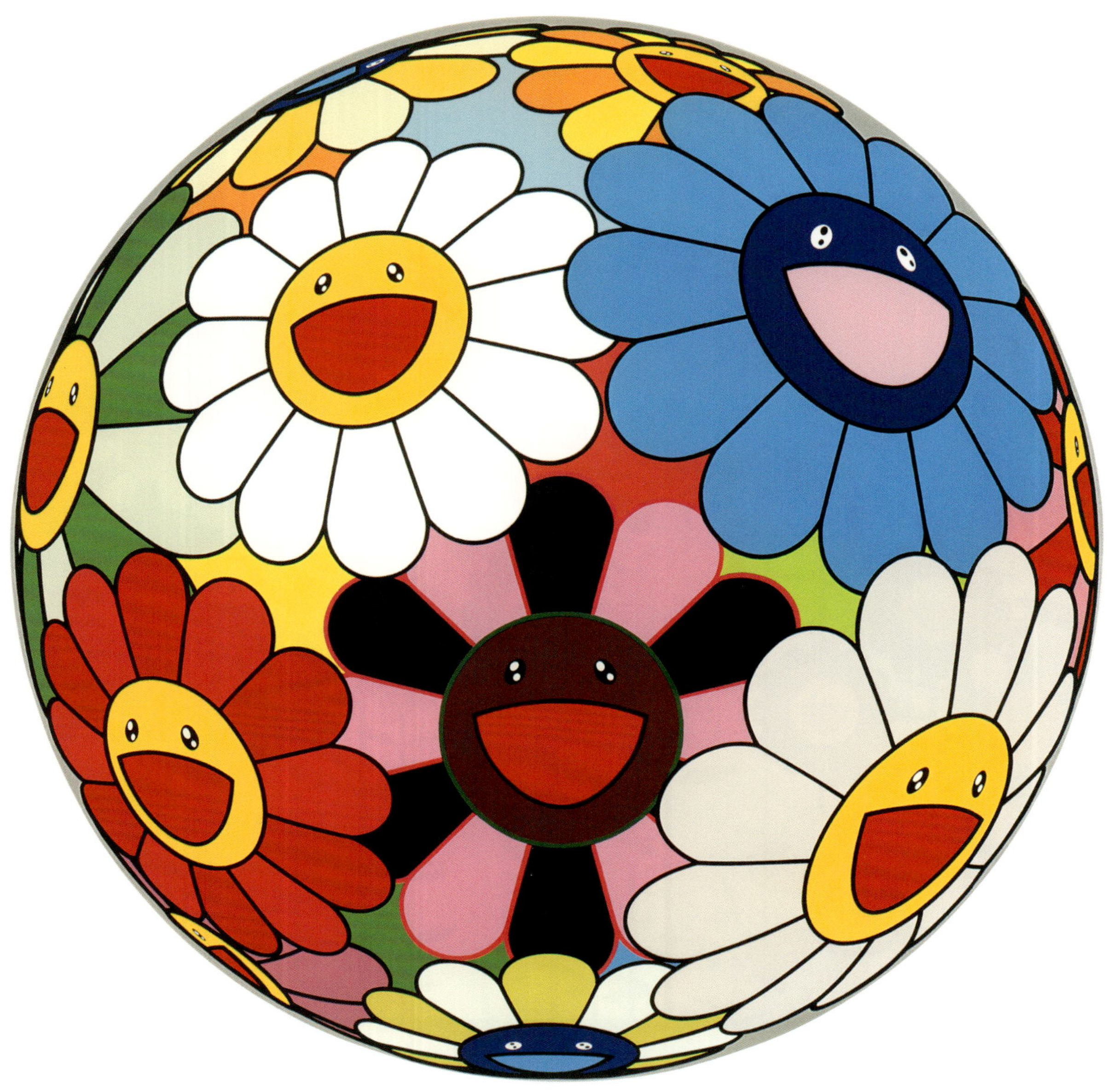

Flower Ball (Algae Ball), 2002

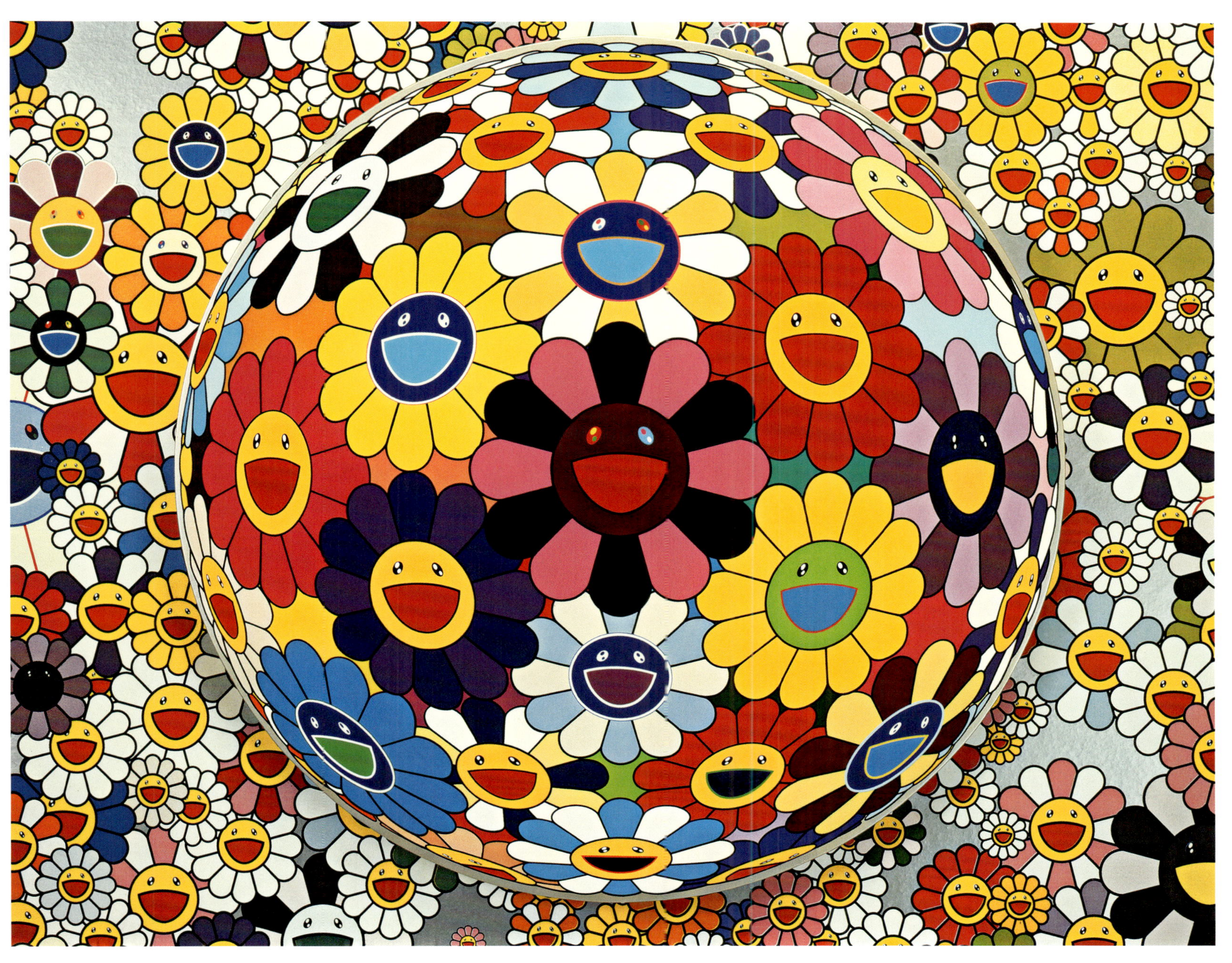

Flower Ball (Kindergarten Days), 2002

Flower Ball (3-D), 2002

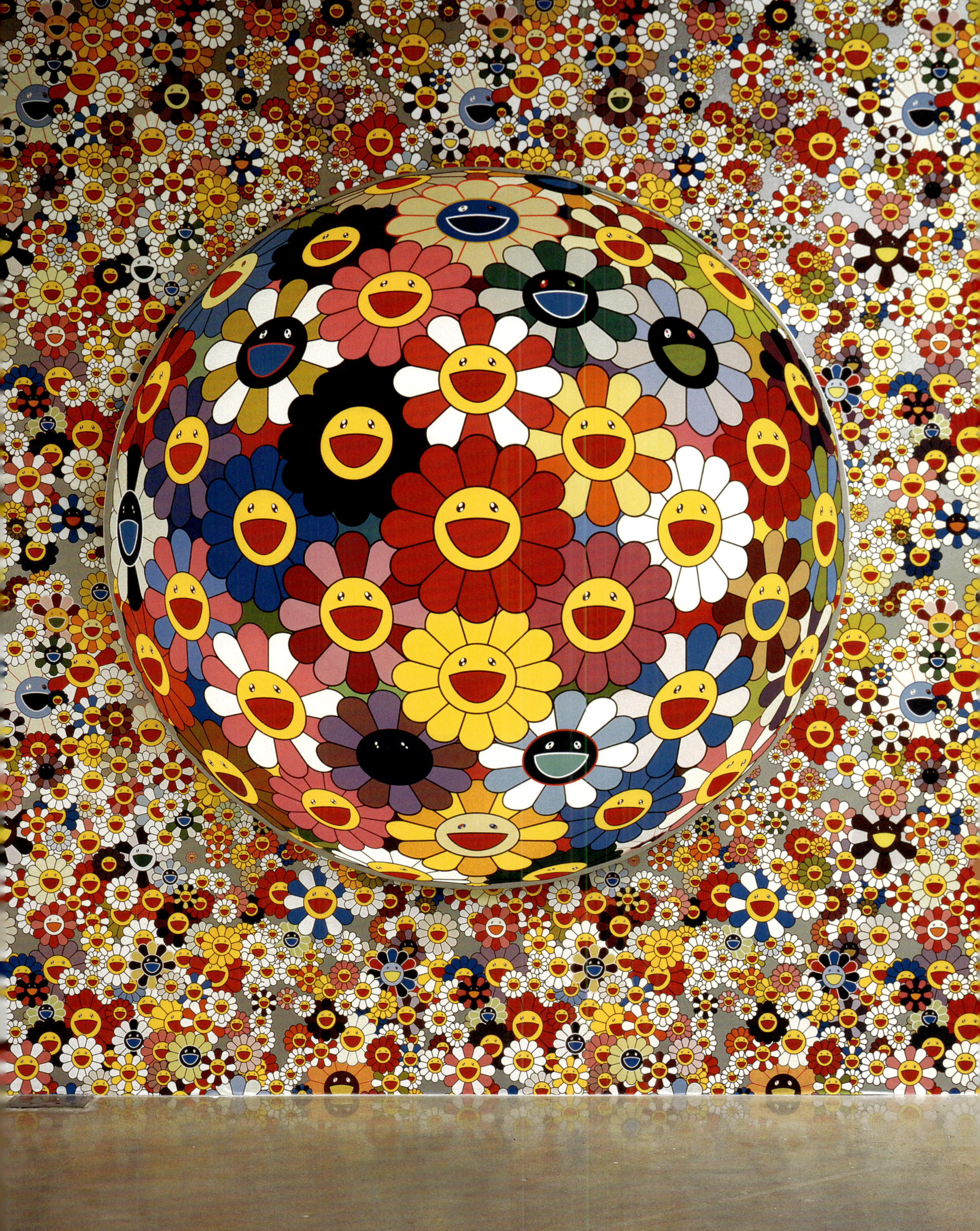

Kaikai Kiki News, 2002

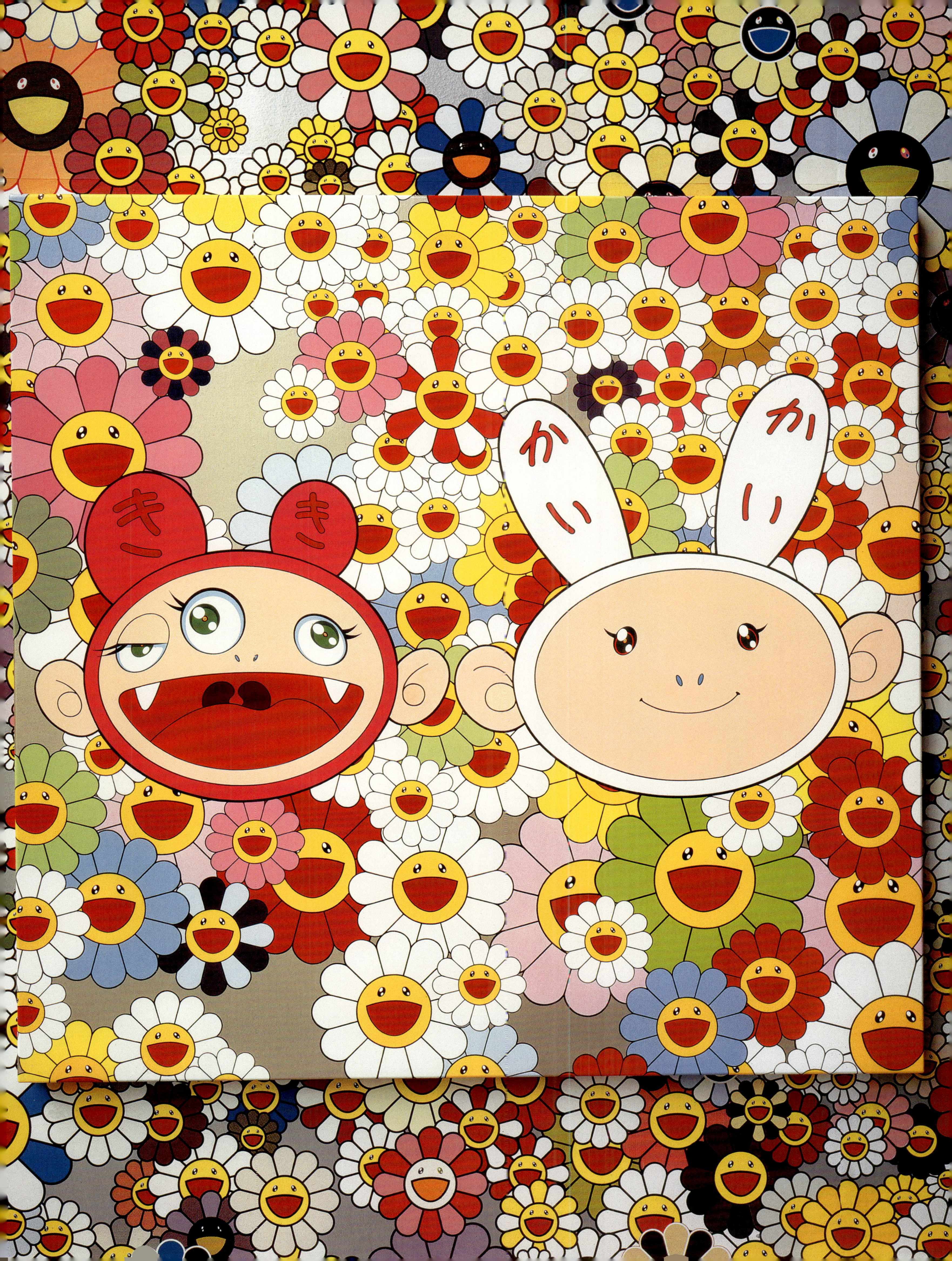
き
き
かい
かい

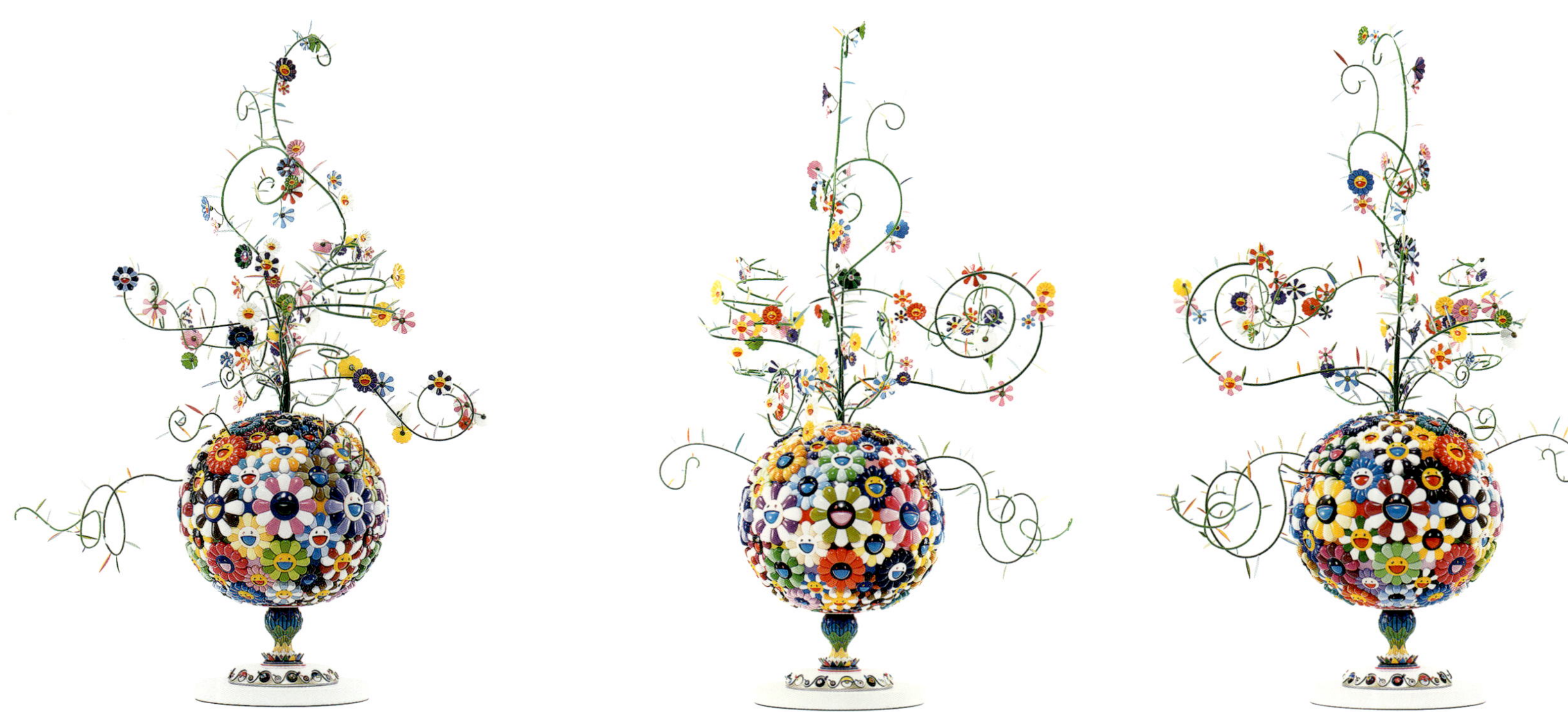

Views of *Flower Matango (b)*, 2001–06

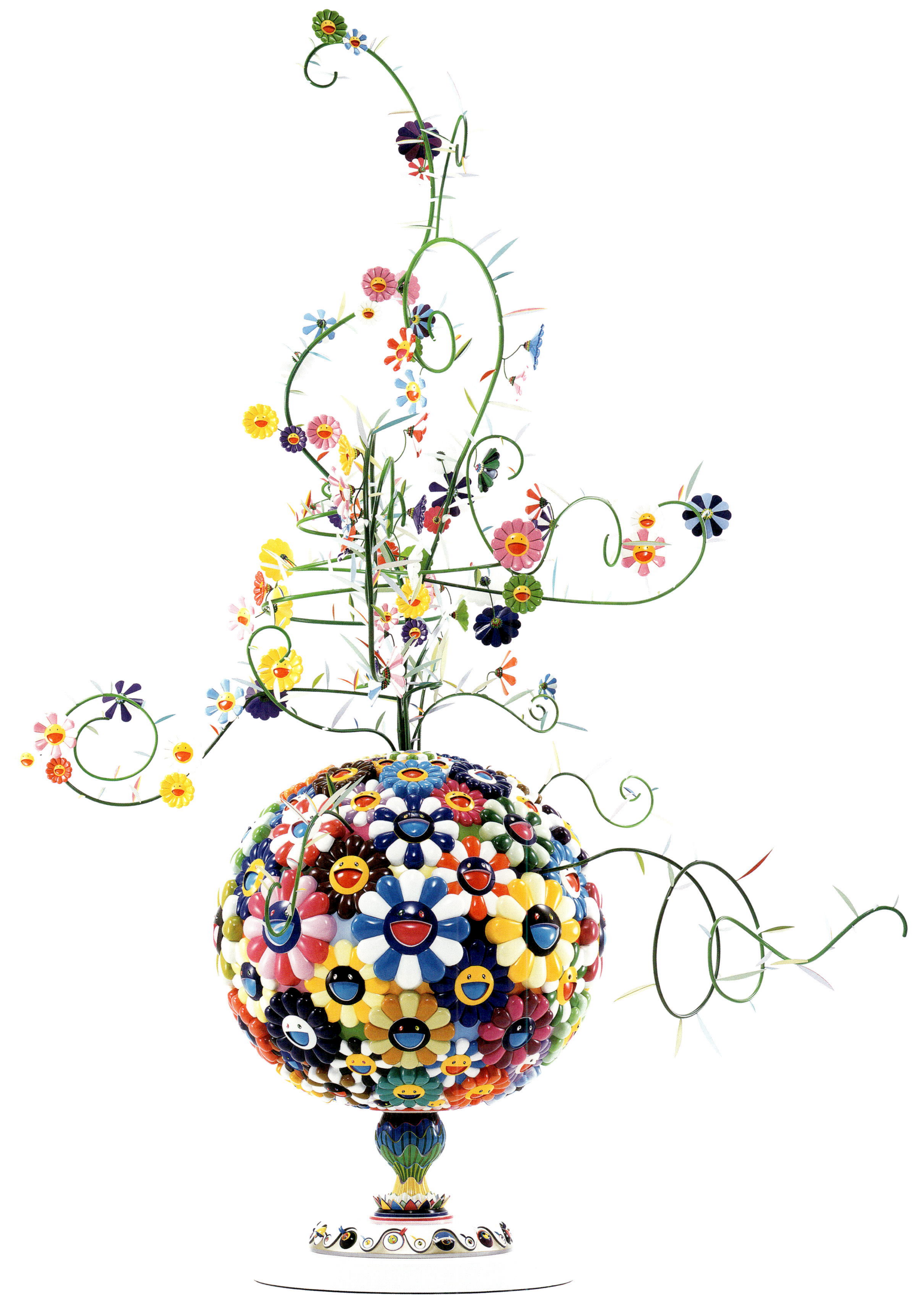

Flower Matango, 2001
Installation at Fondation Cartier pour l'art contemporain,
Paris, 2002

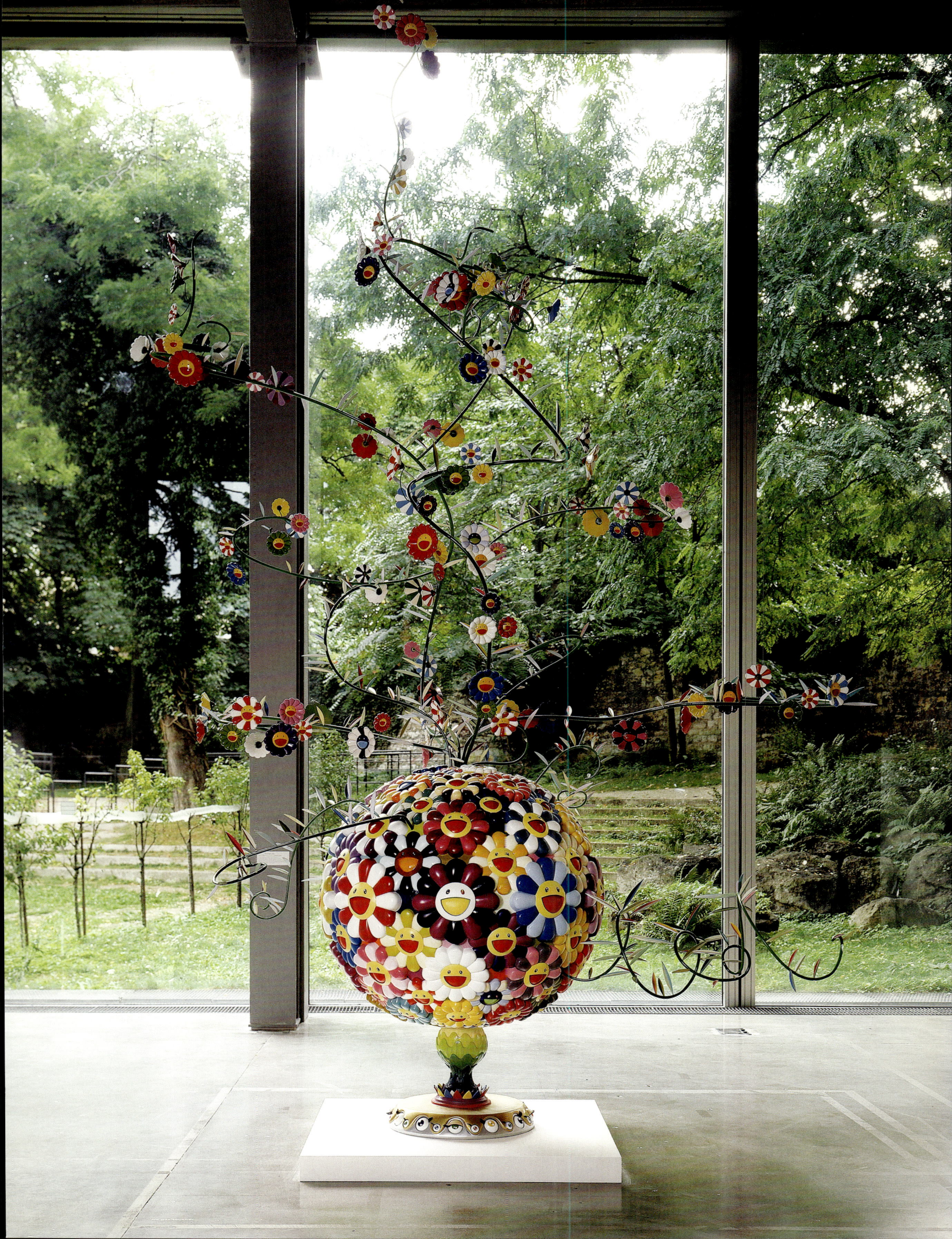

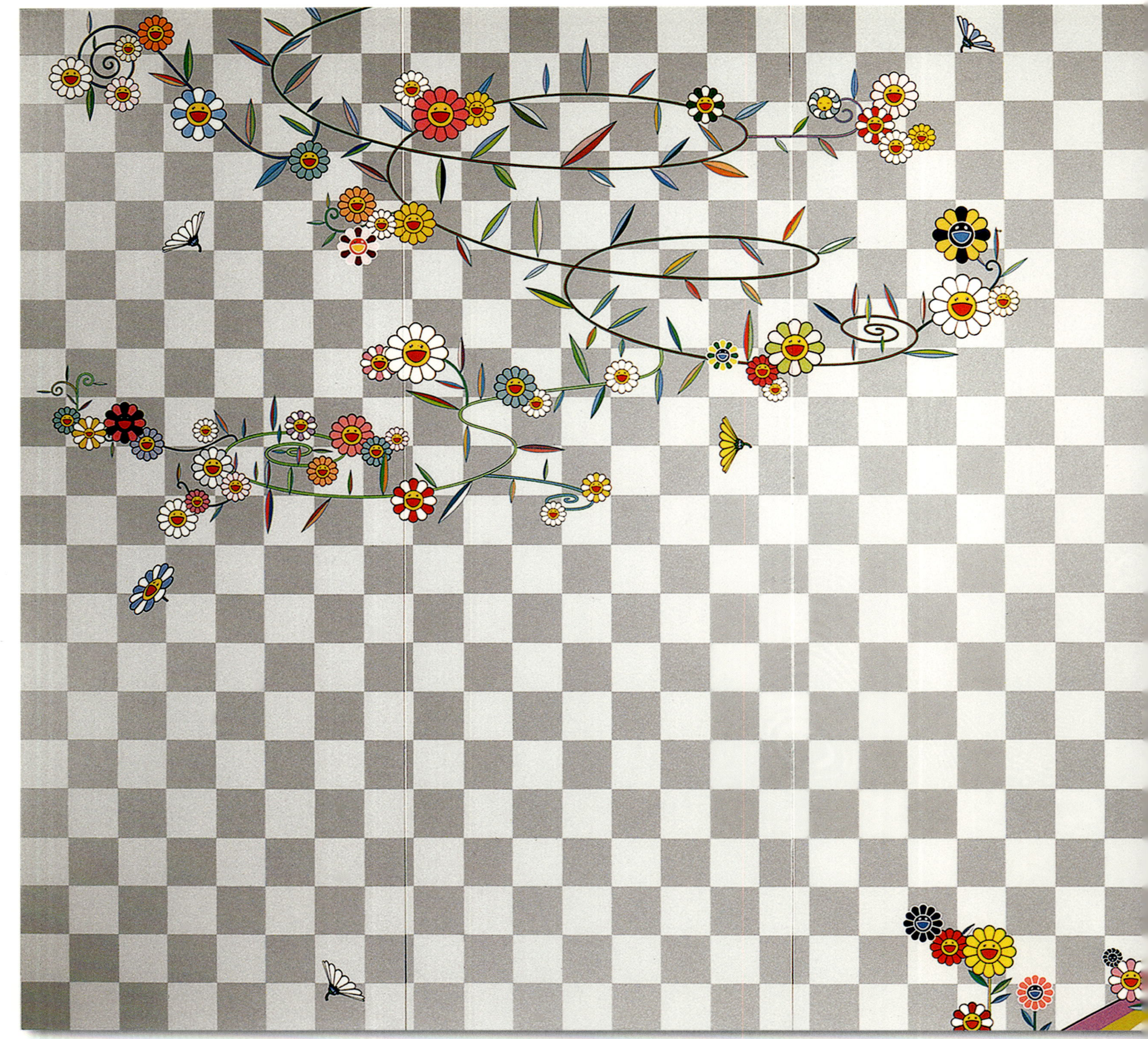

Kaikai Kiki in Peach Paradise, 2002

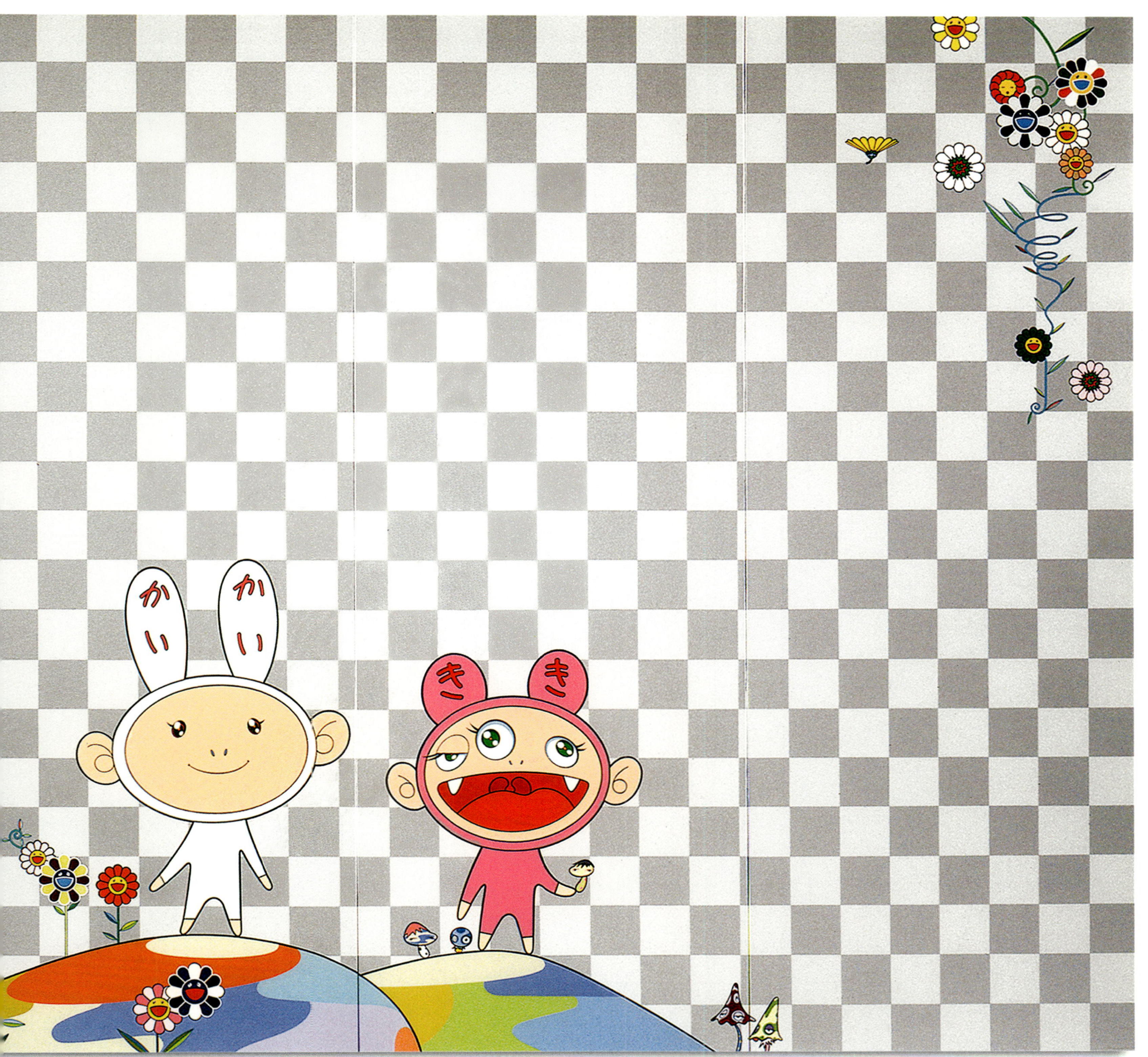
かい
かい
き
き

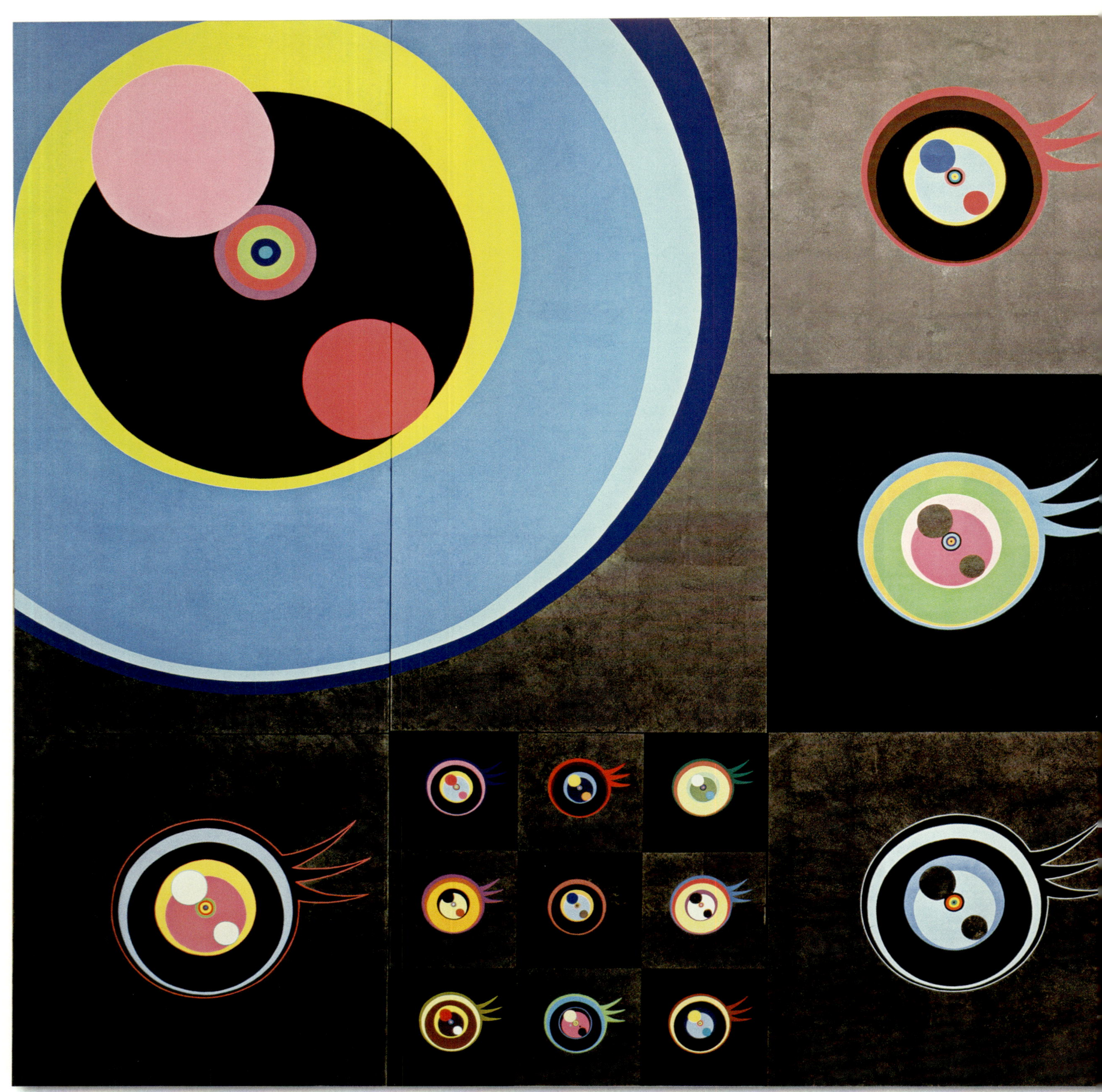

Superflat Jellyfish Eyes 1, 2003

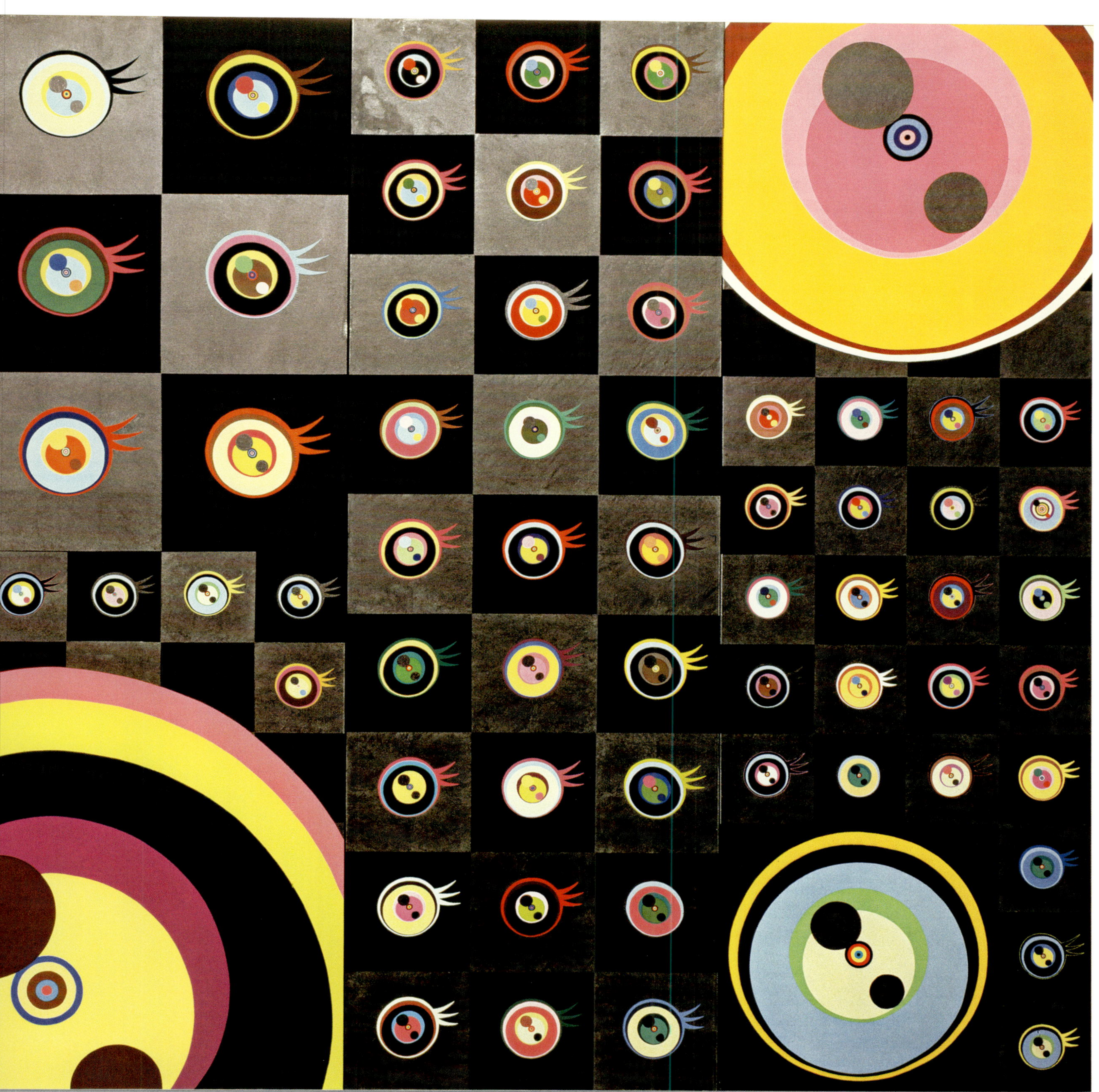

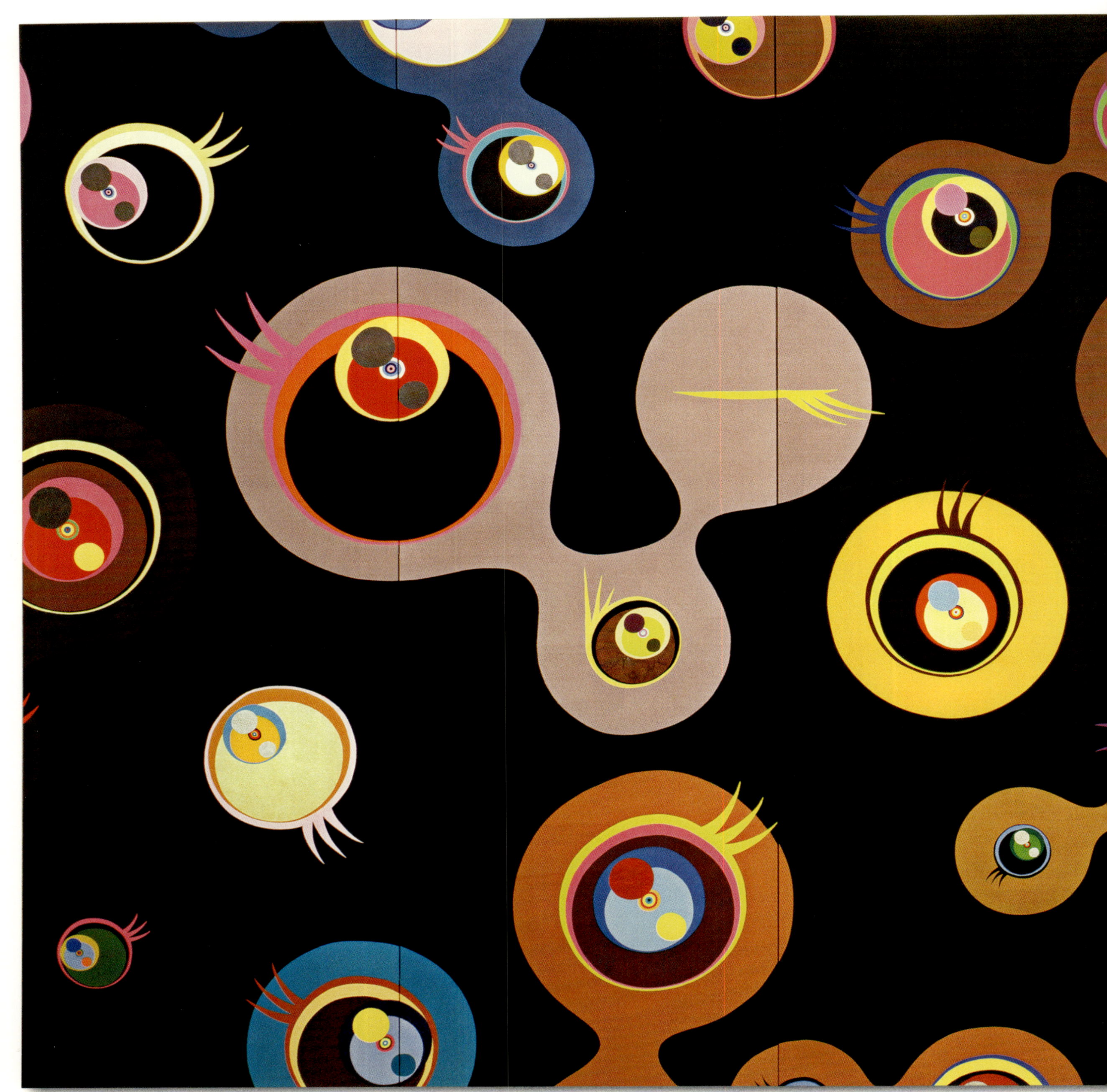

Superflat Jellyfish Eyes 2, 2003

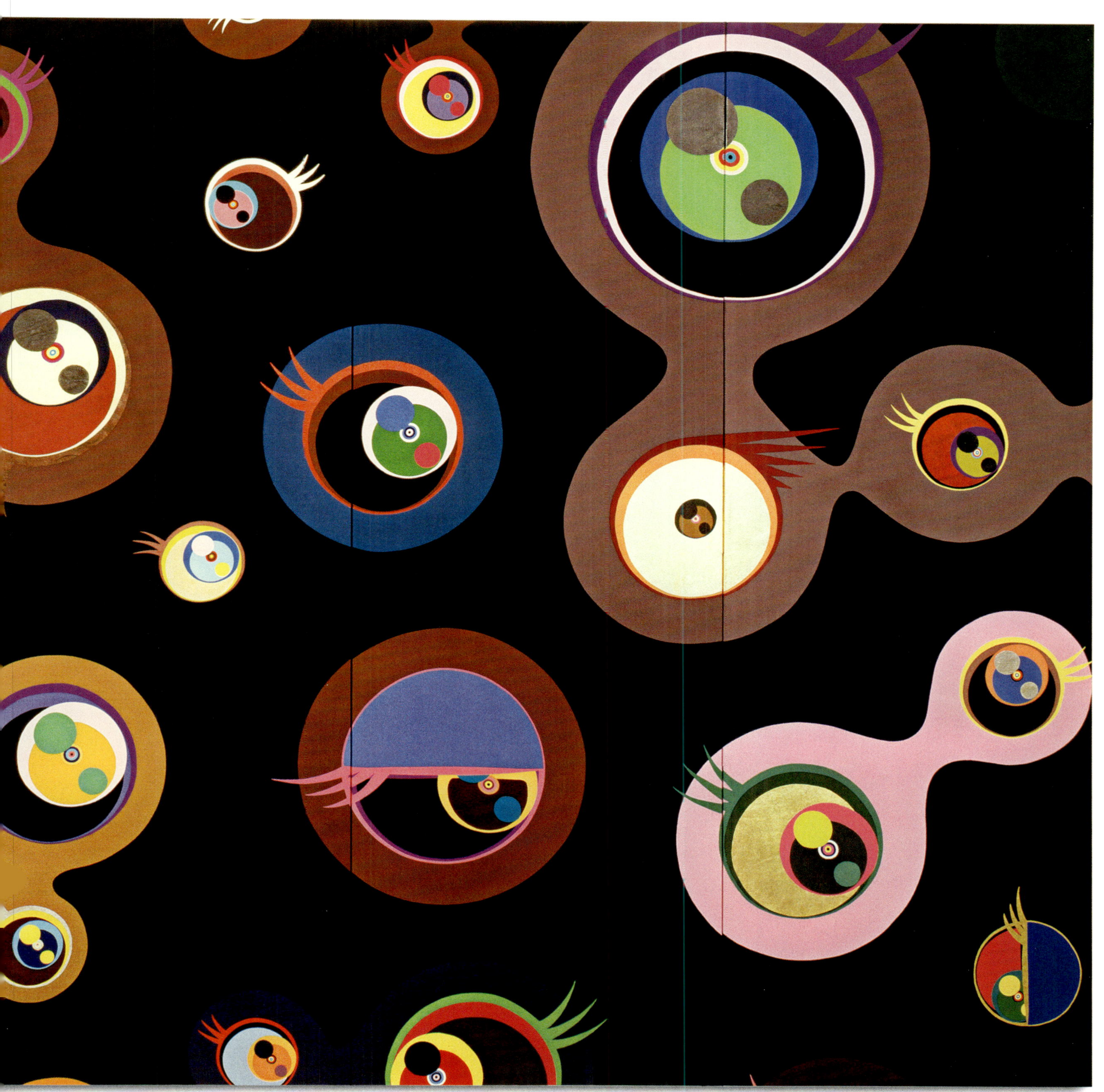

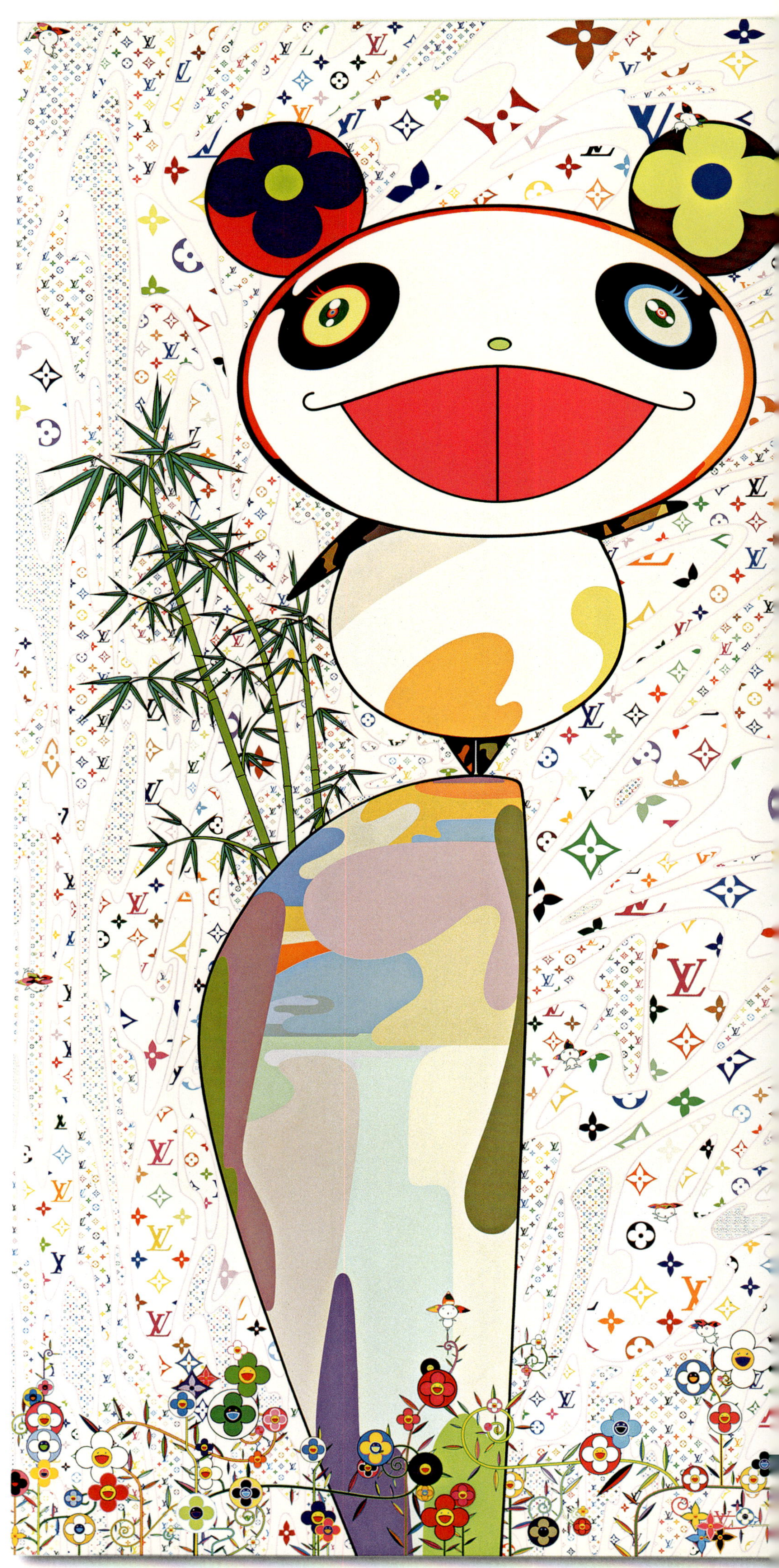

The World of Sphere, 2003

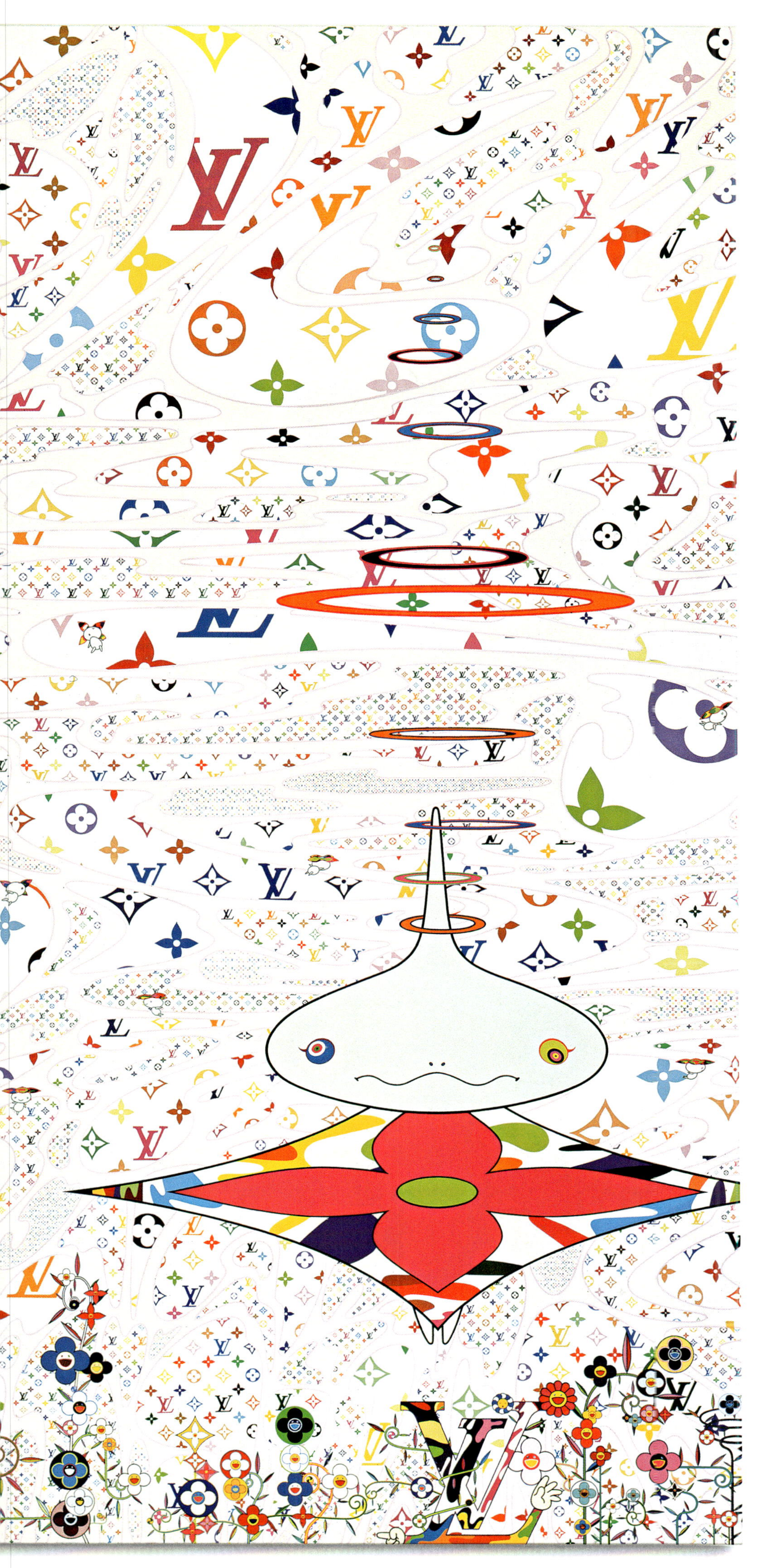

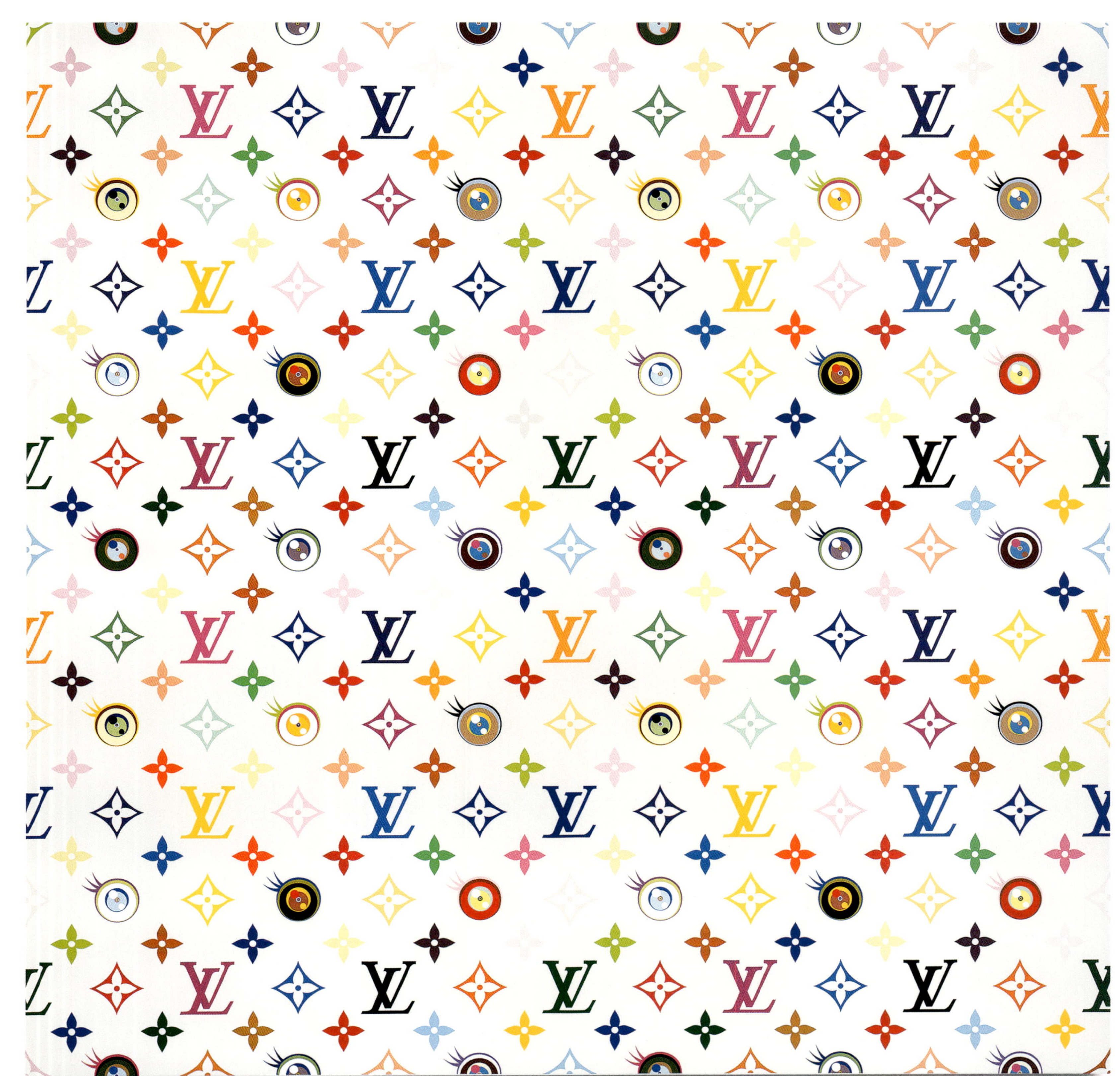

Eye Love SUPERFLAT, 2003

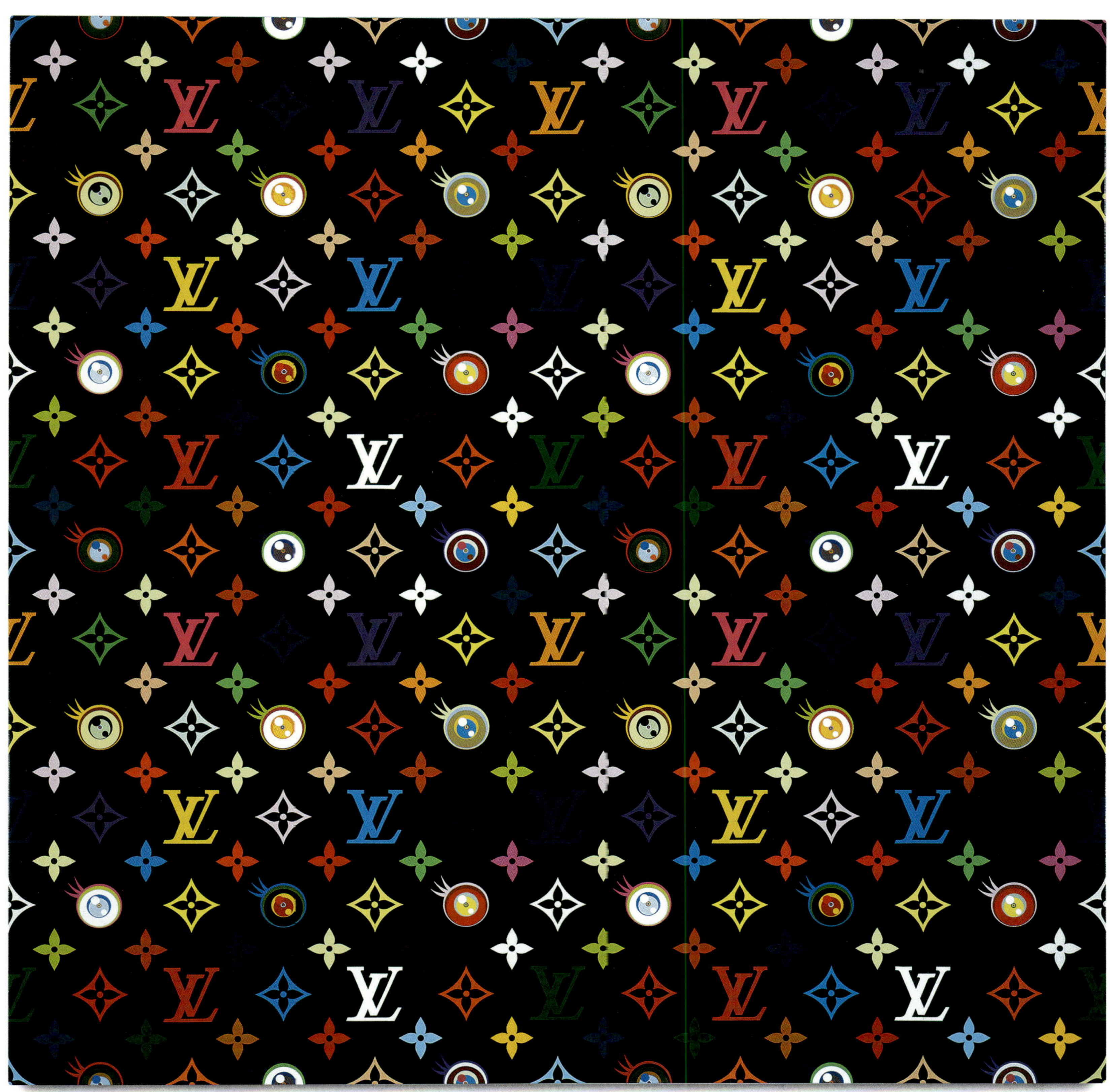

Eye Love SUPERFLAT 2004

Inochi, 2004, detail

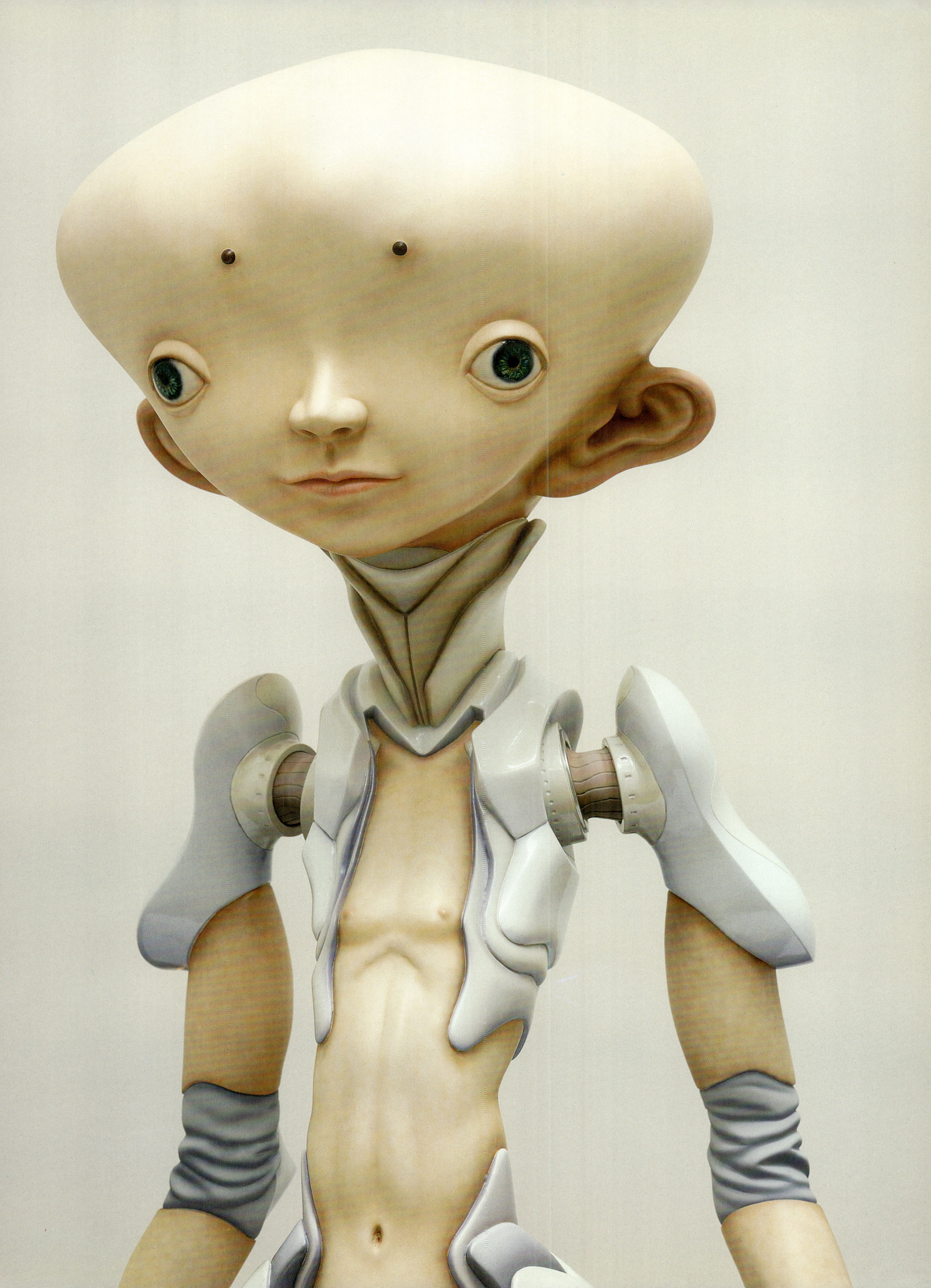

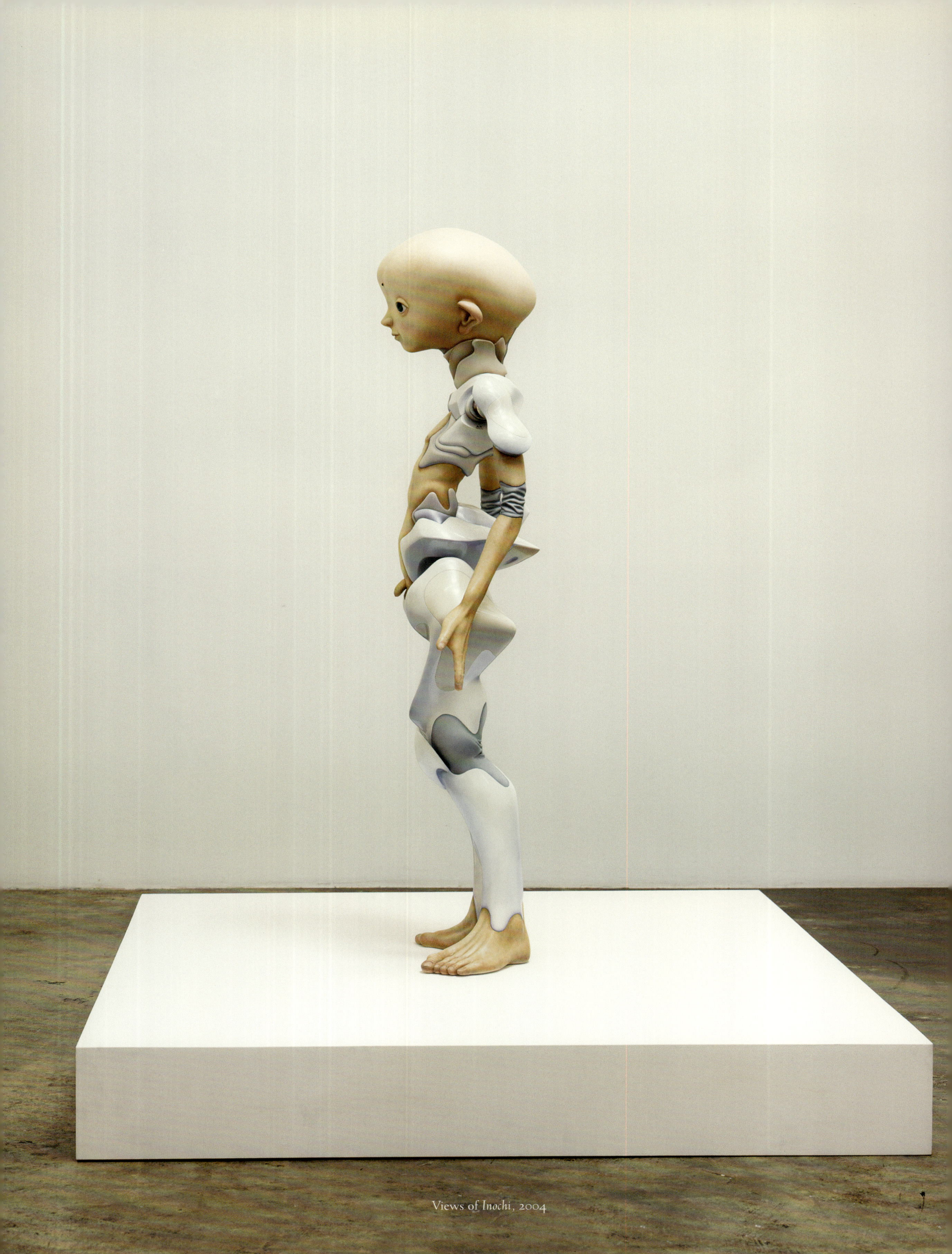

Views of *Inochi*, 2004

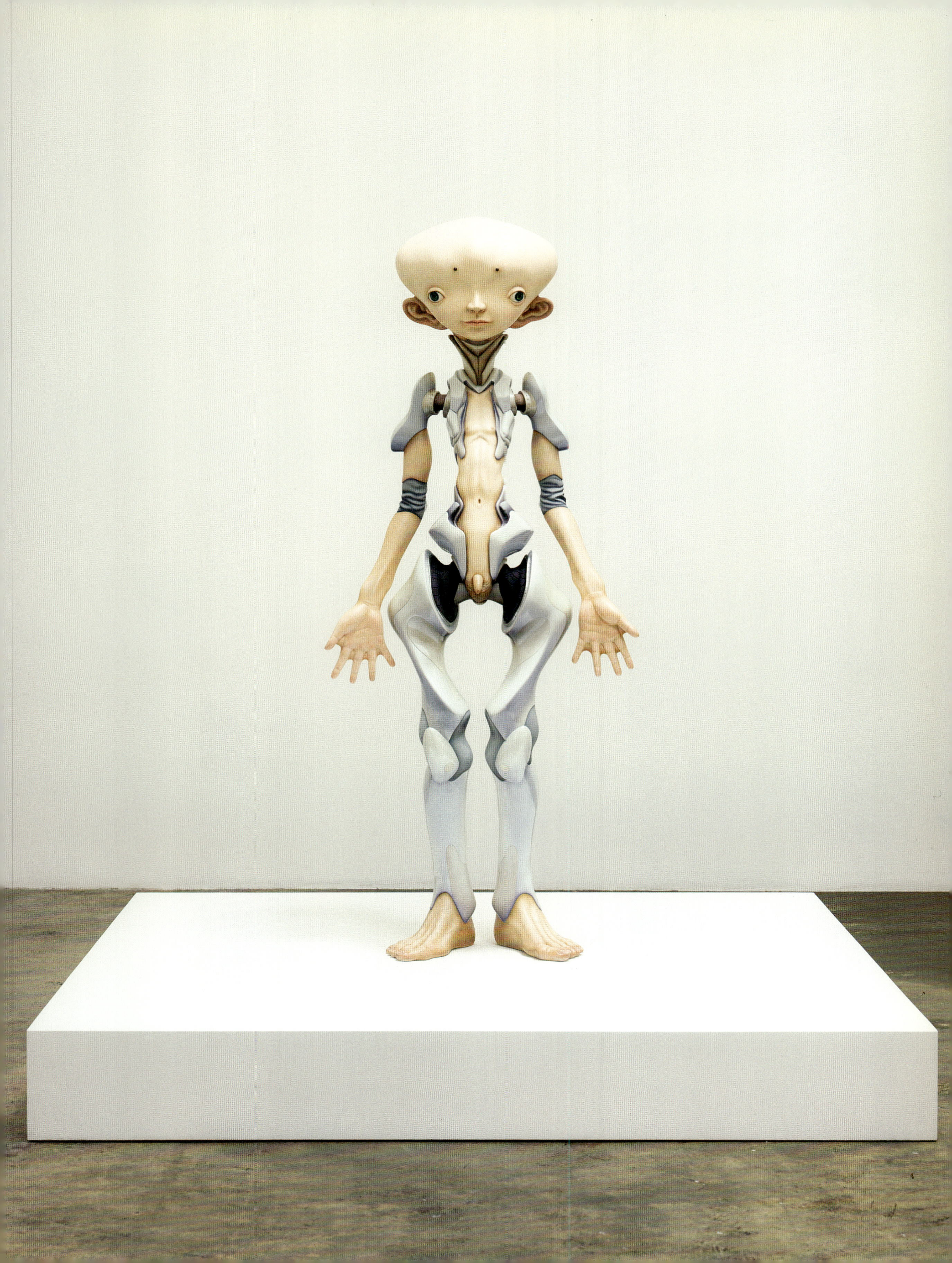

Inochi, 2004, detail

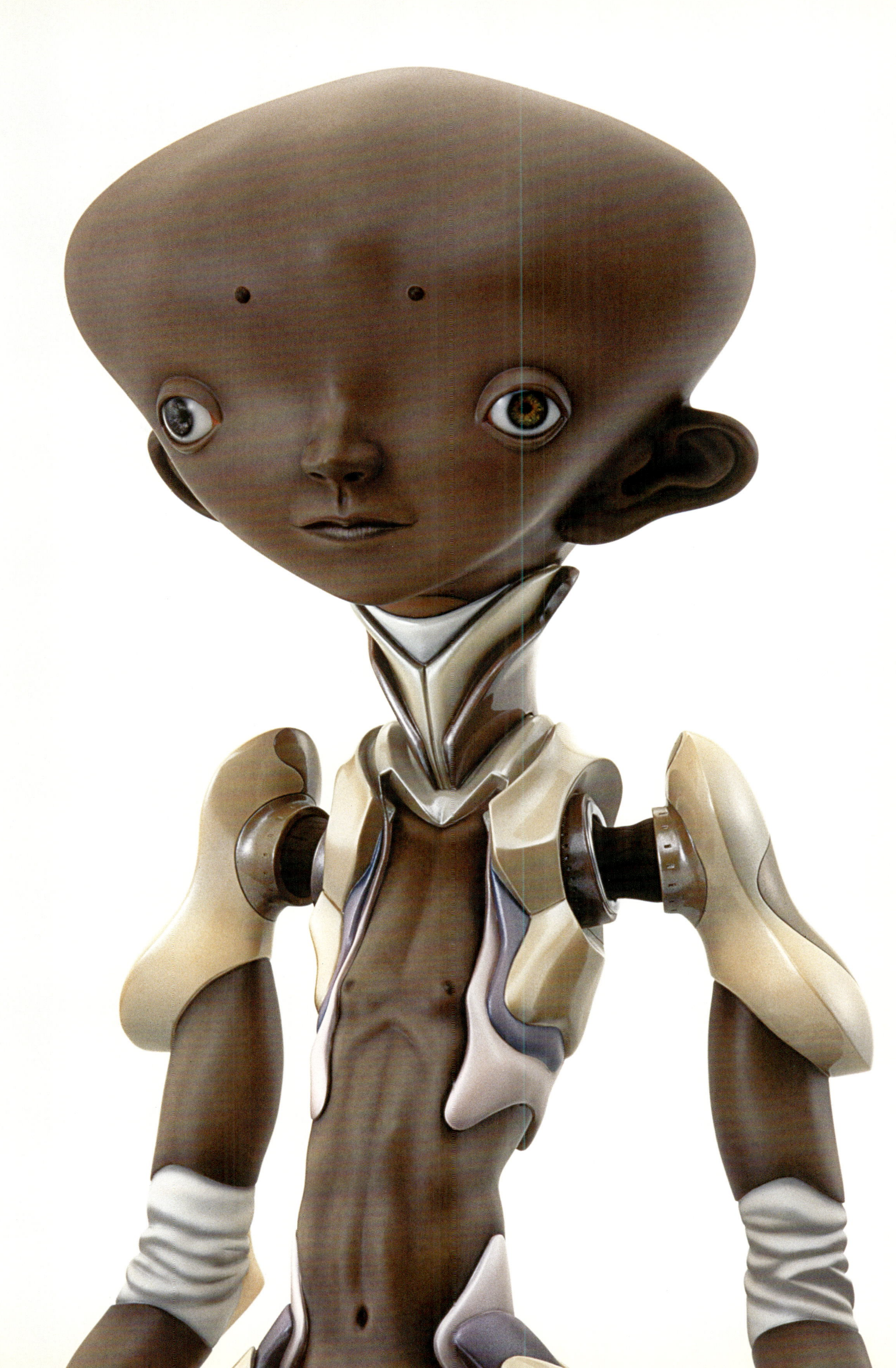

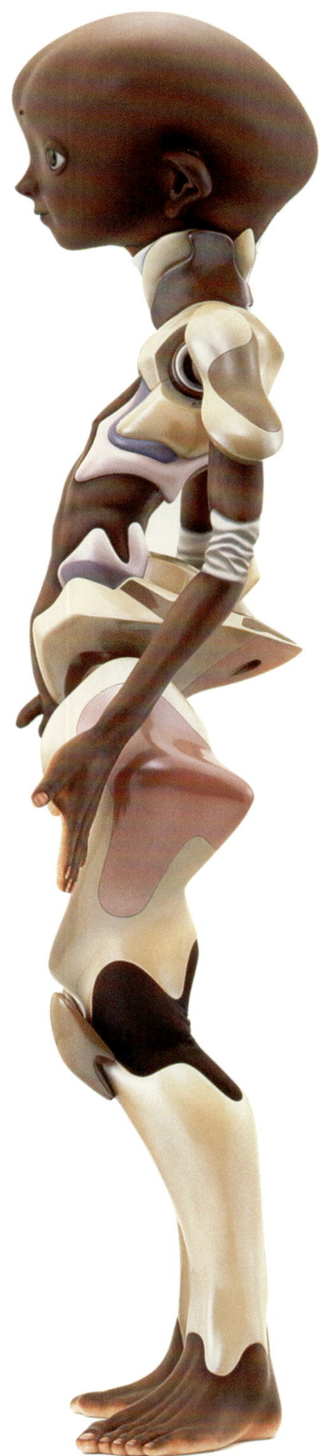

Views of *Inochi*, 2004

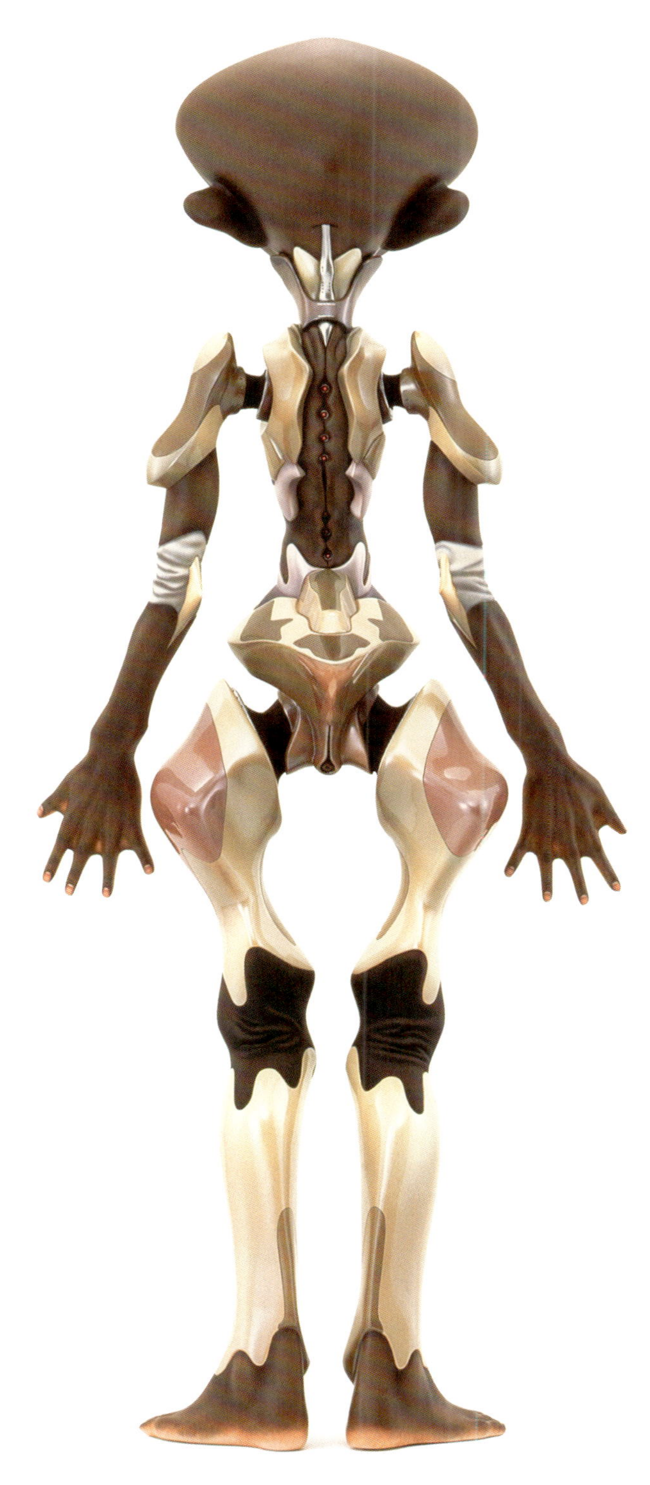

"Reversed Double Helix," 2003
Tongari-kun (center) with *Zoucho-kun*, *Koumokkun*, *Jikokkun*, and *Tamon-kun*
Installation at Rockefeller Center, New York

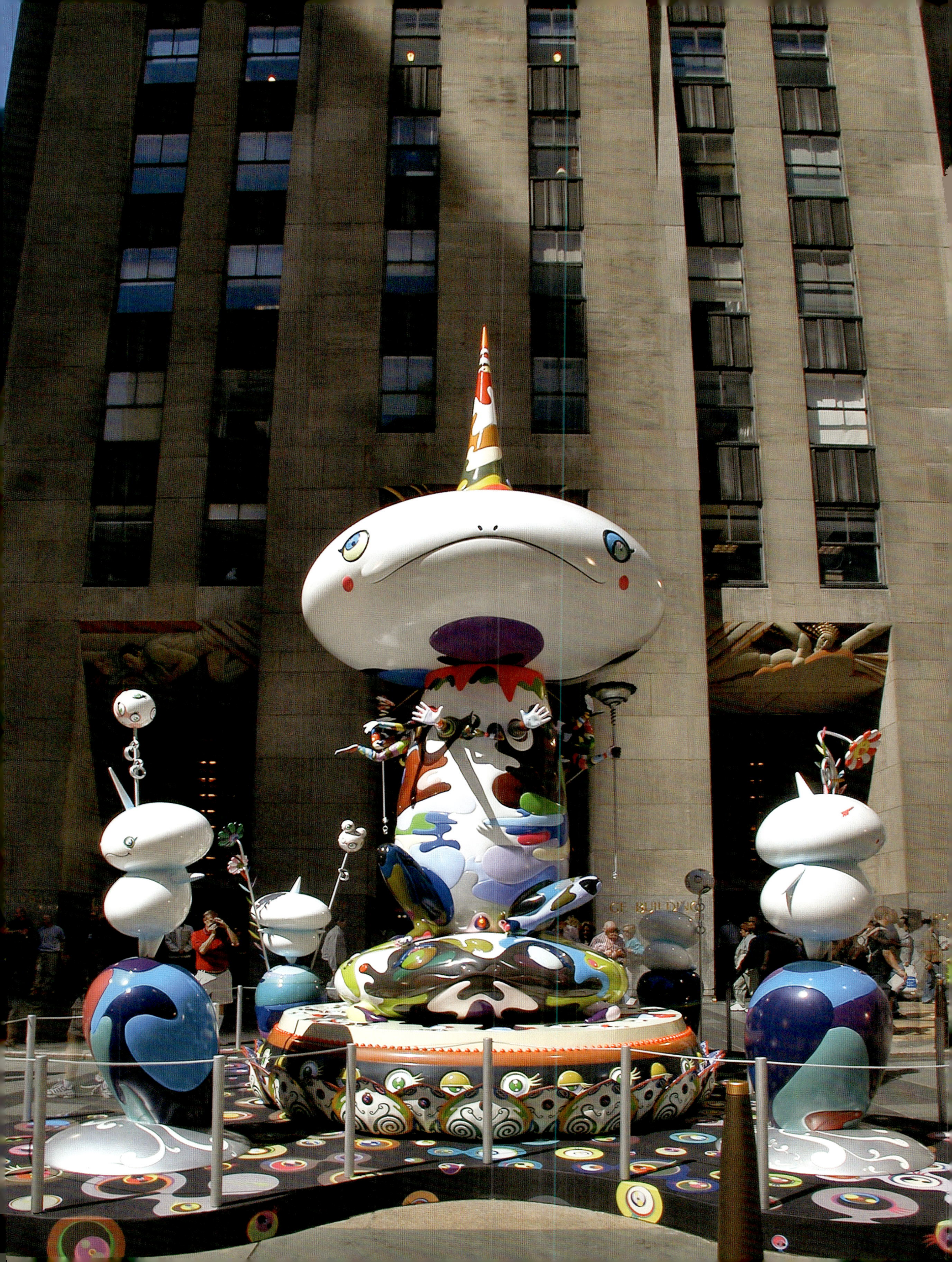
GE BUILDING

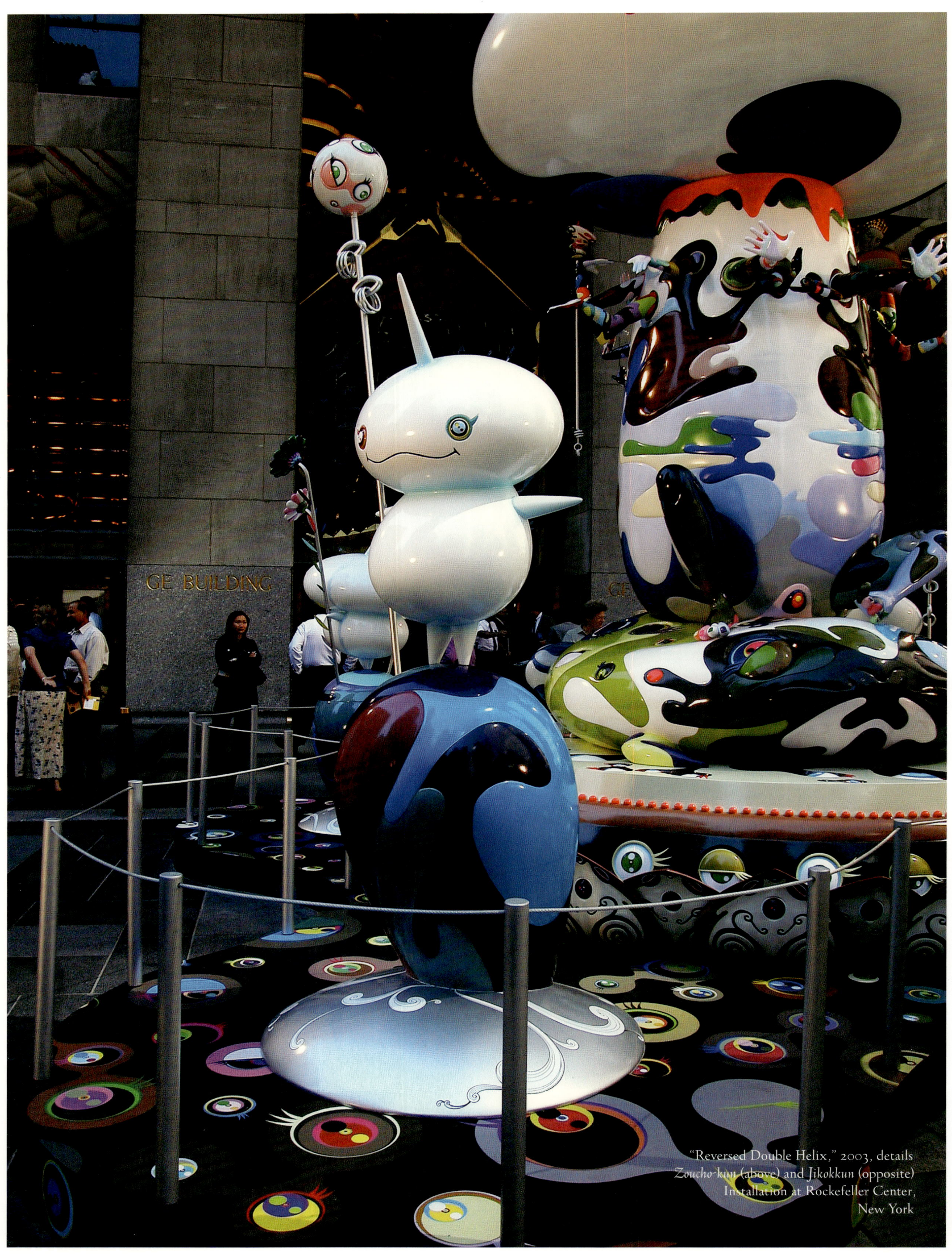

"Reversed Double Helix," 2003, details
Zoucho-kun (above) and *Jikokkun* (opposite)
Installation at Rockefeller Center,
New York

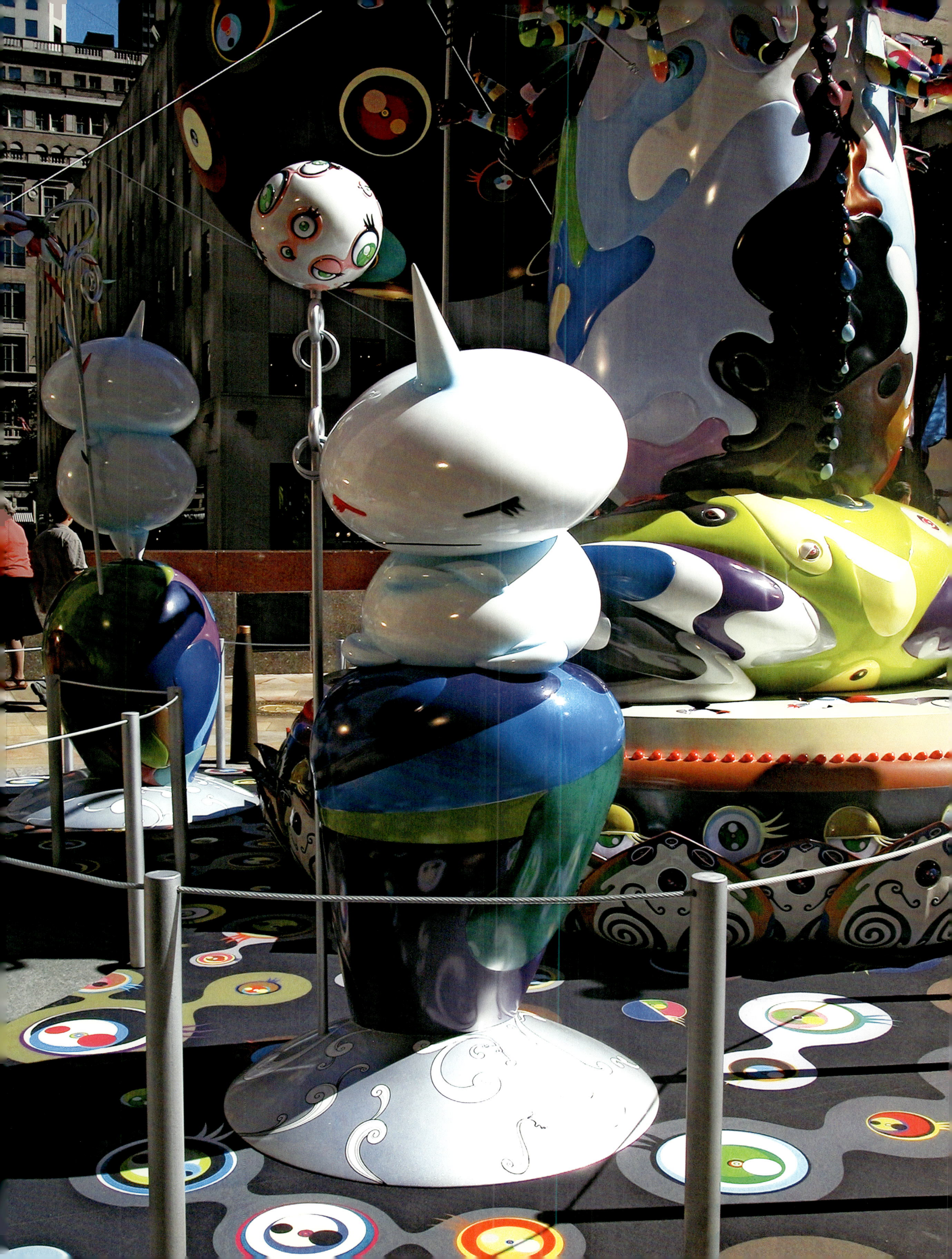

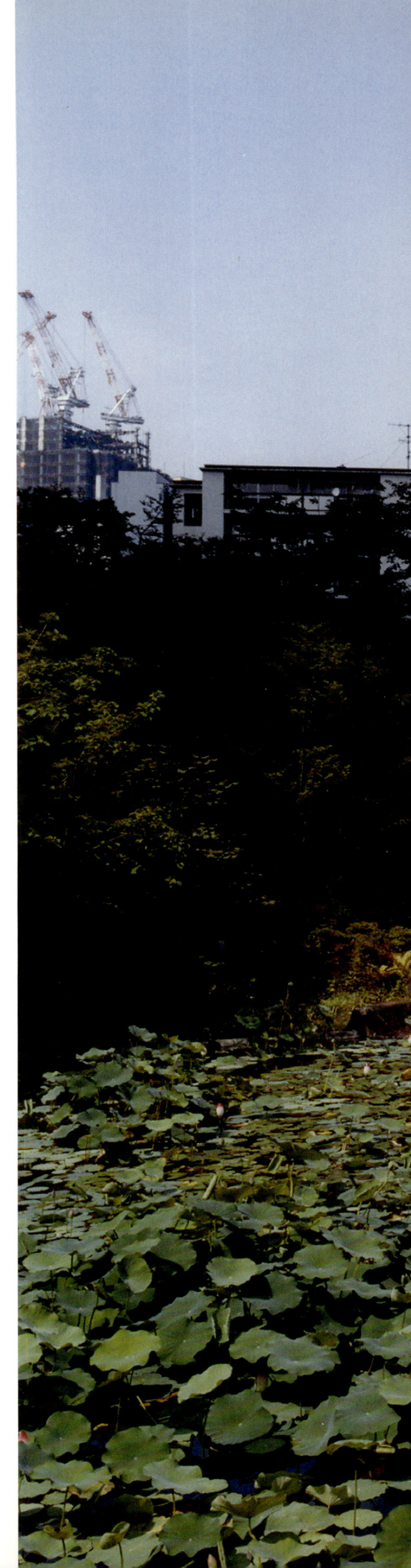

Tongari-kun (center) with *Zoucho-kun*, *Koumokkun*, *Jikokkun*, and *Tamon-kun*, all 2005
Installation at
Roppongi Hills, Tokyo

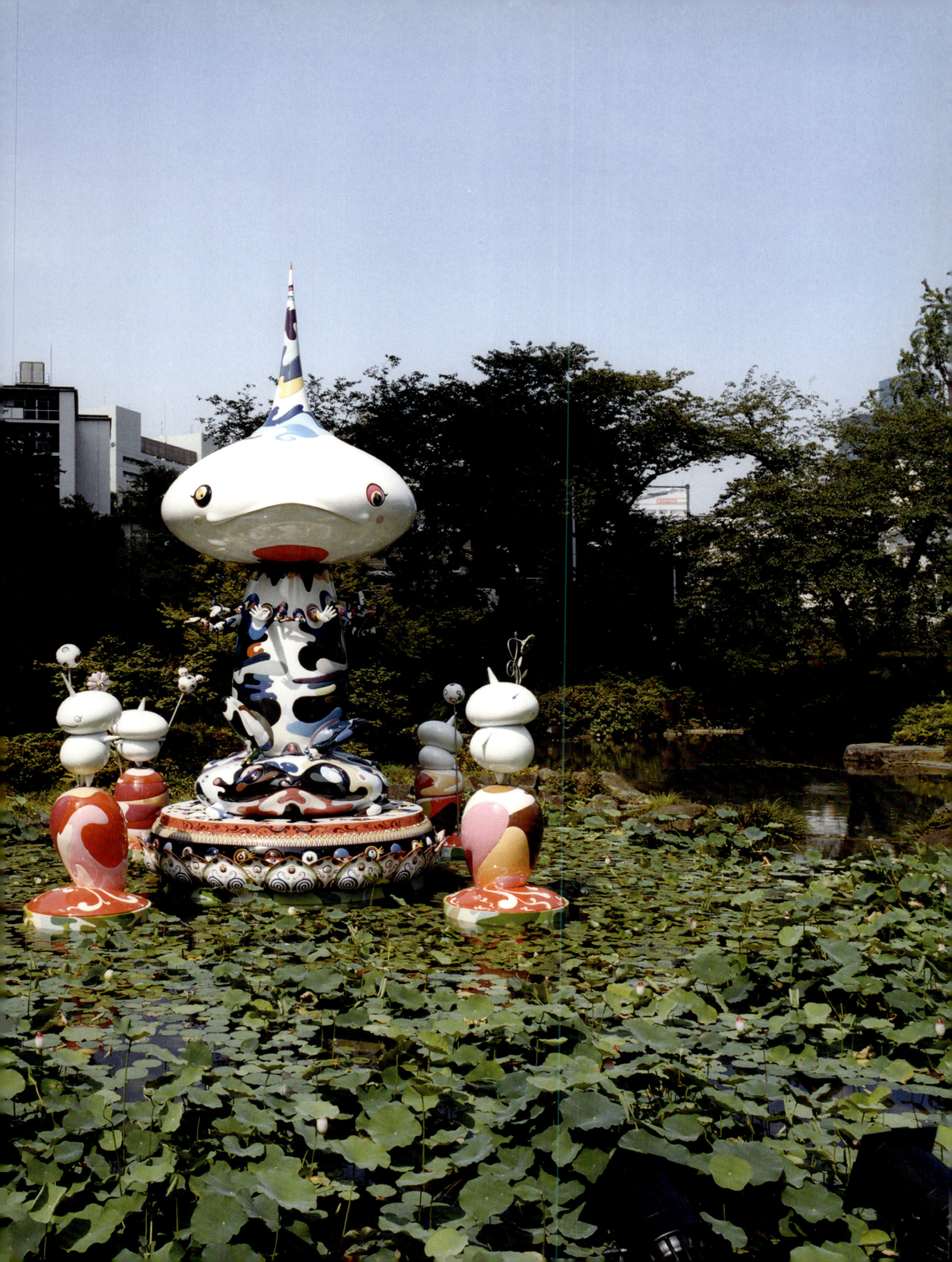

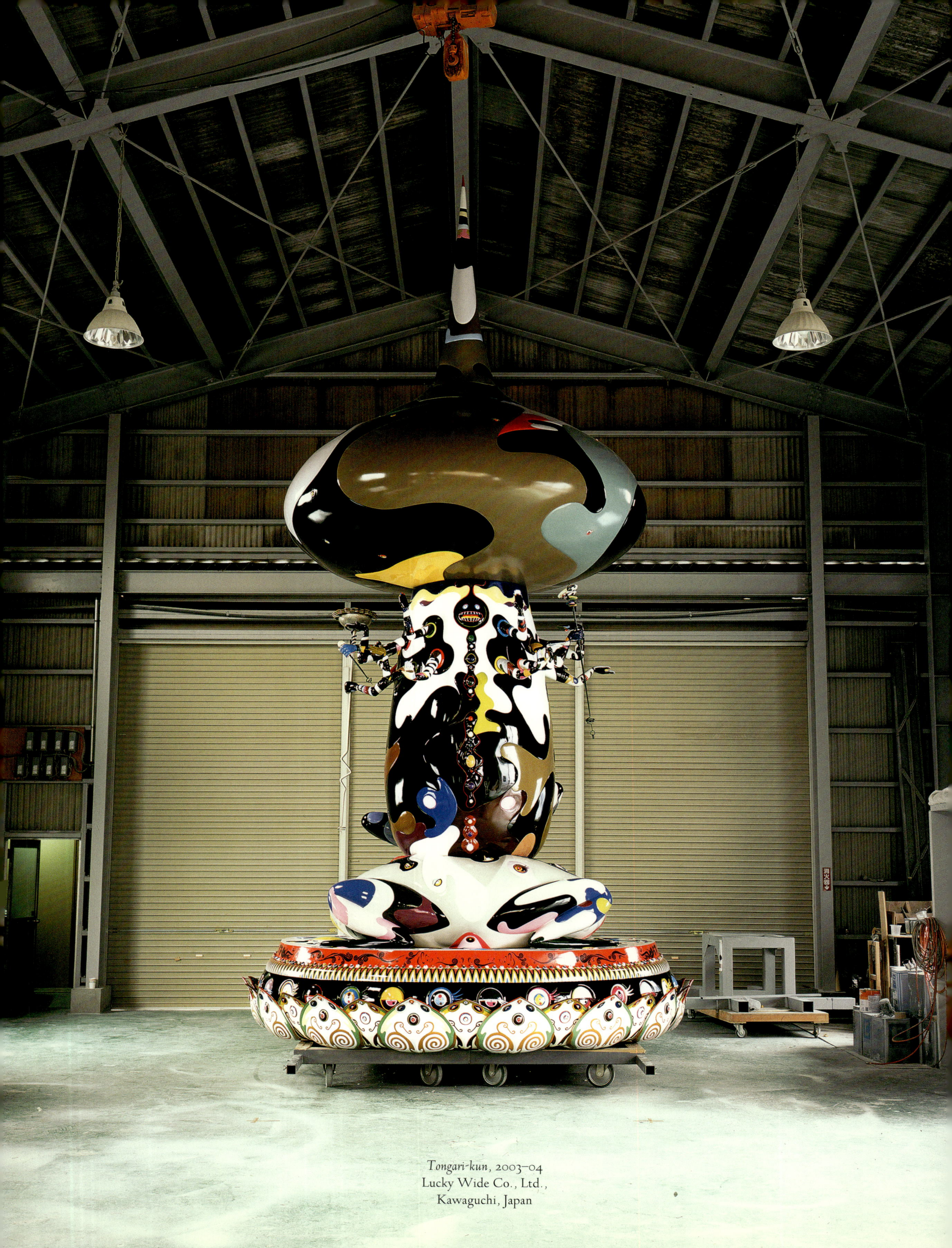

Tongari-kun, 2003–04
Lucky Wide Co., Ltd.,
Kawaguchi, Japan

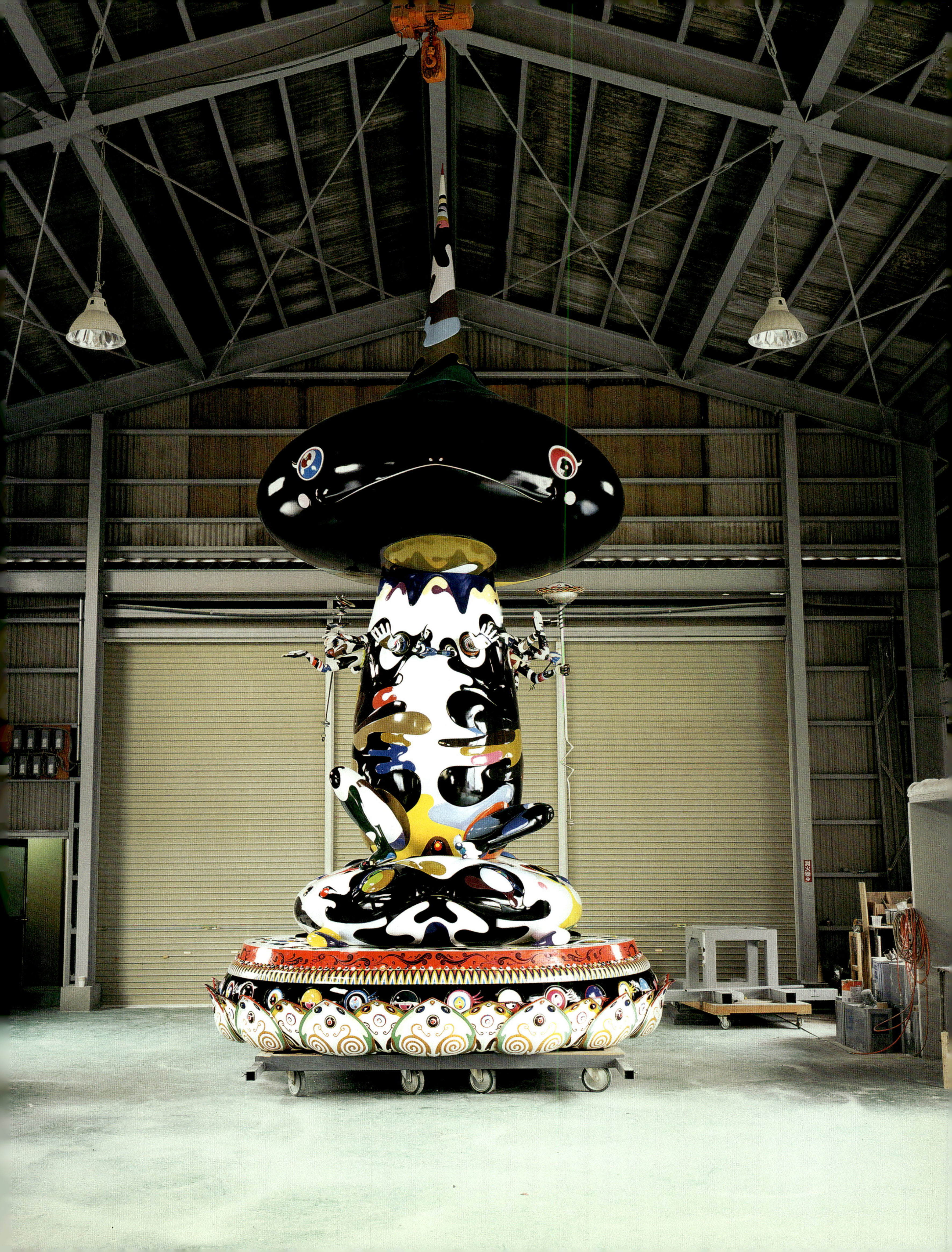

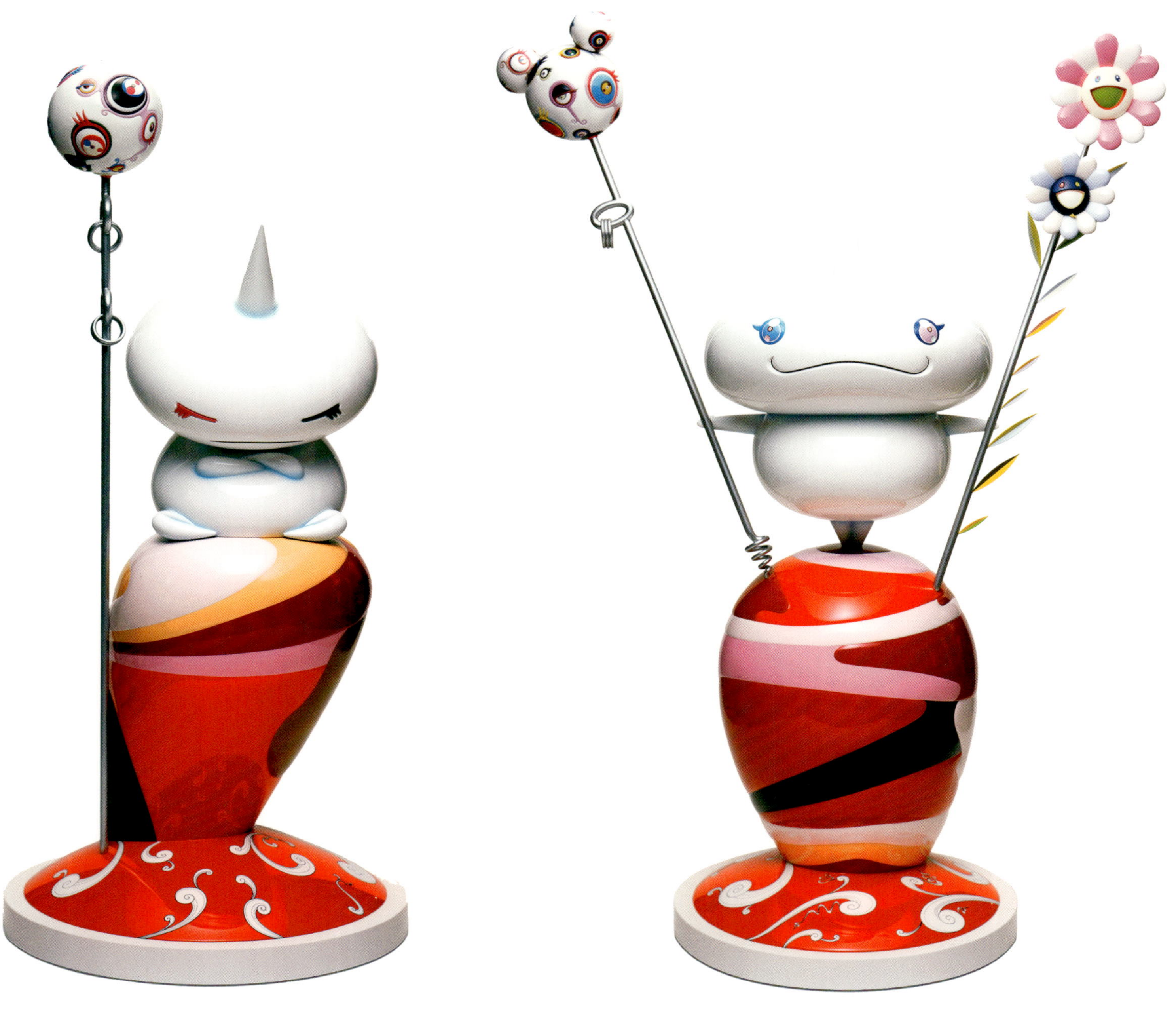

Jikokkun (left) and *Koumokkun*, both 2003–05

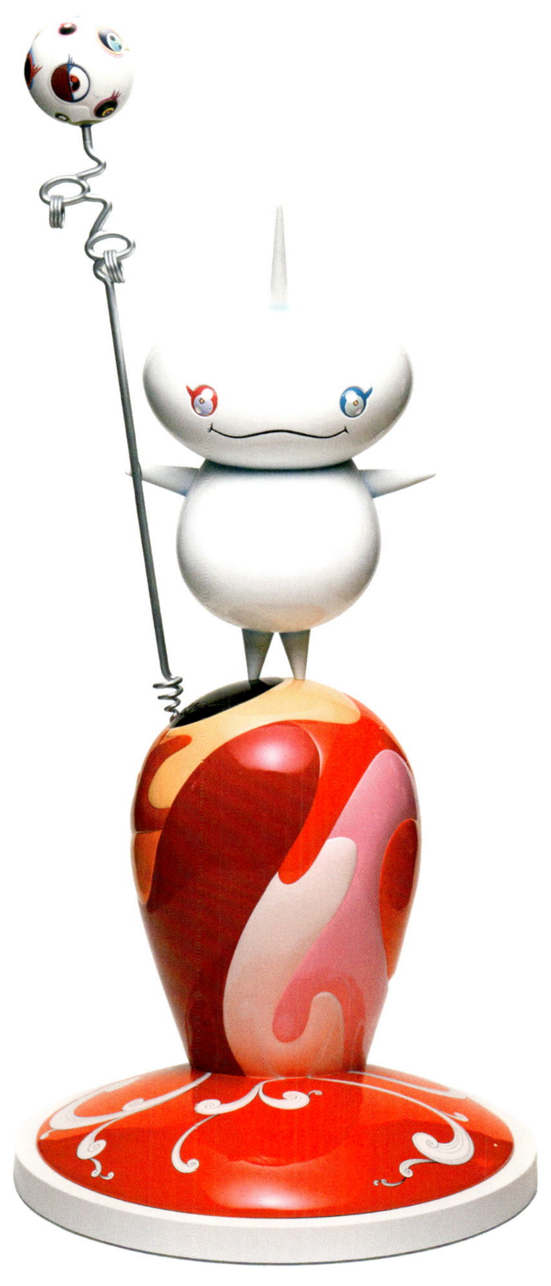

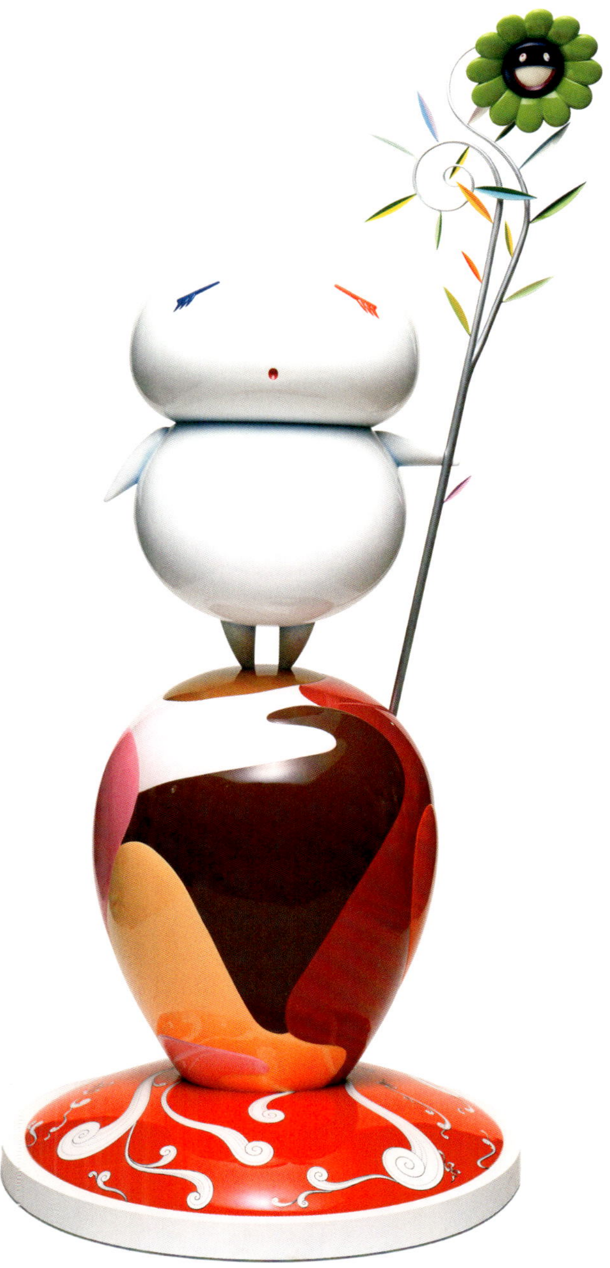

Zoucho-kun (left) and *Tamon-kun*, both 2003–05

following spread
727-727, 2006

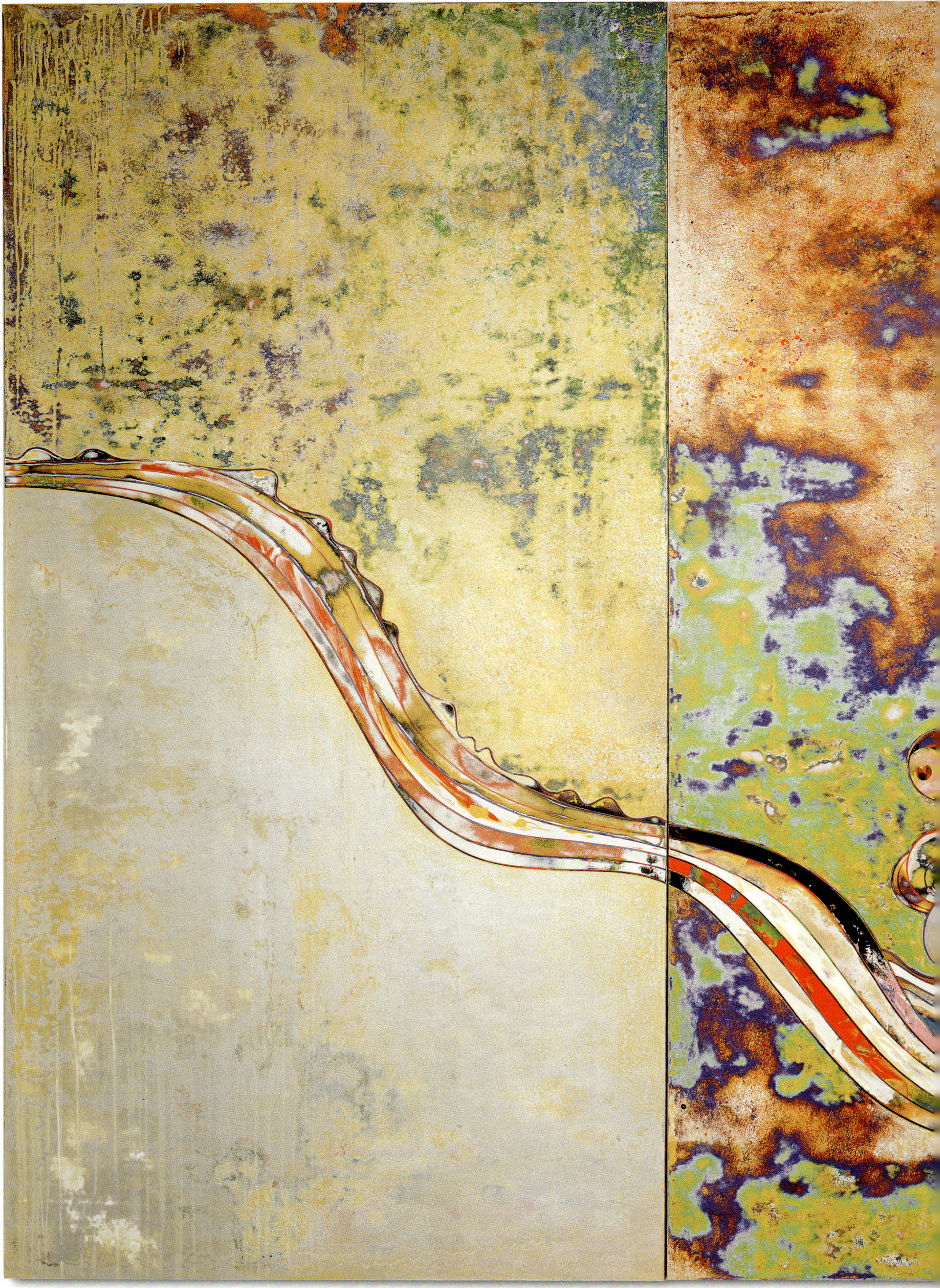

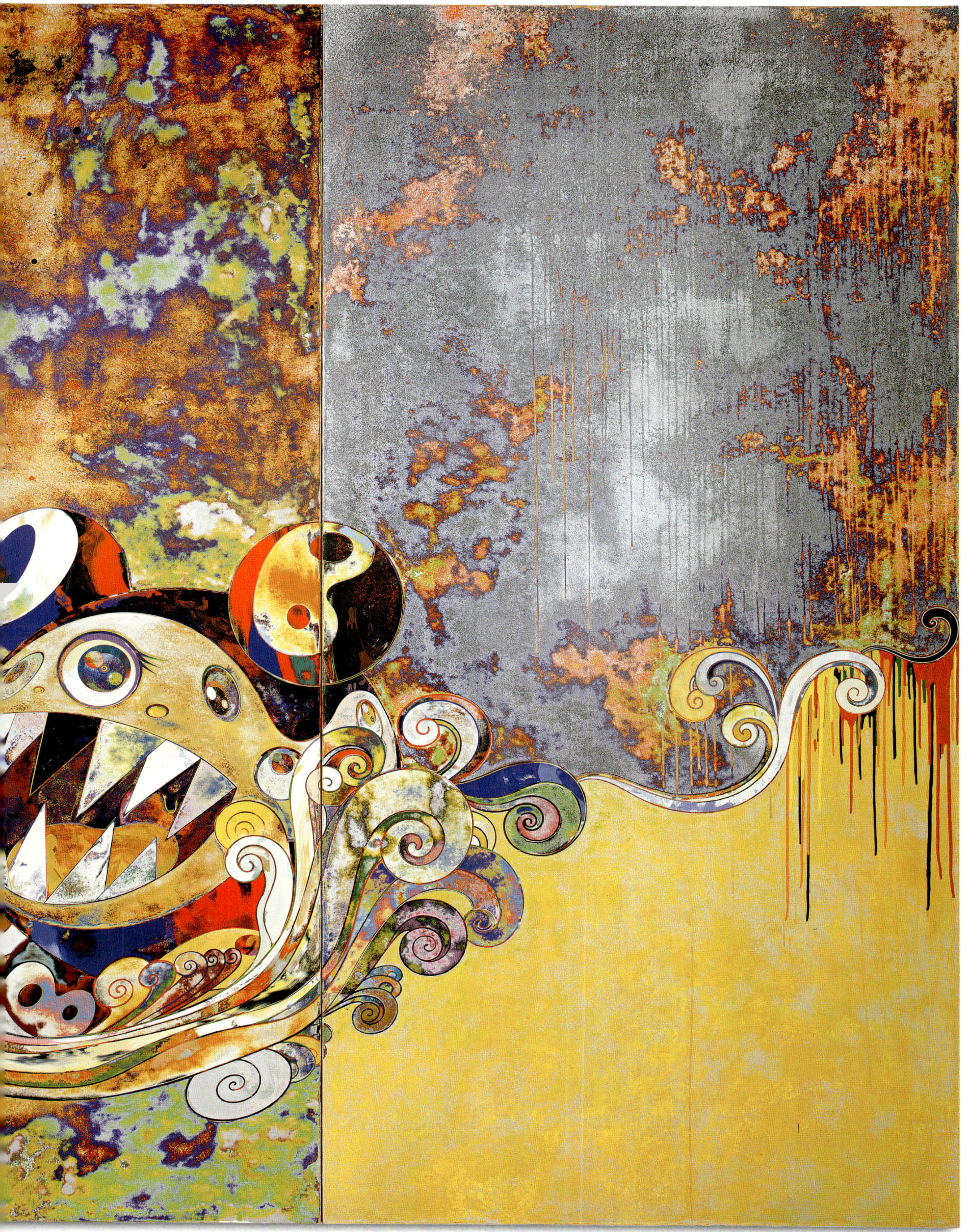

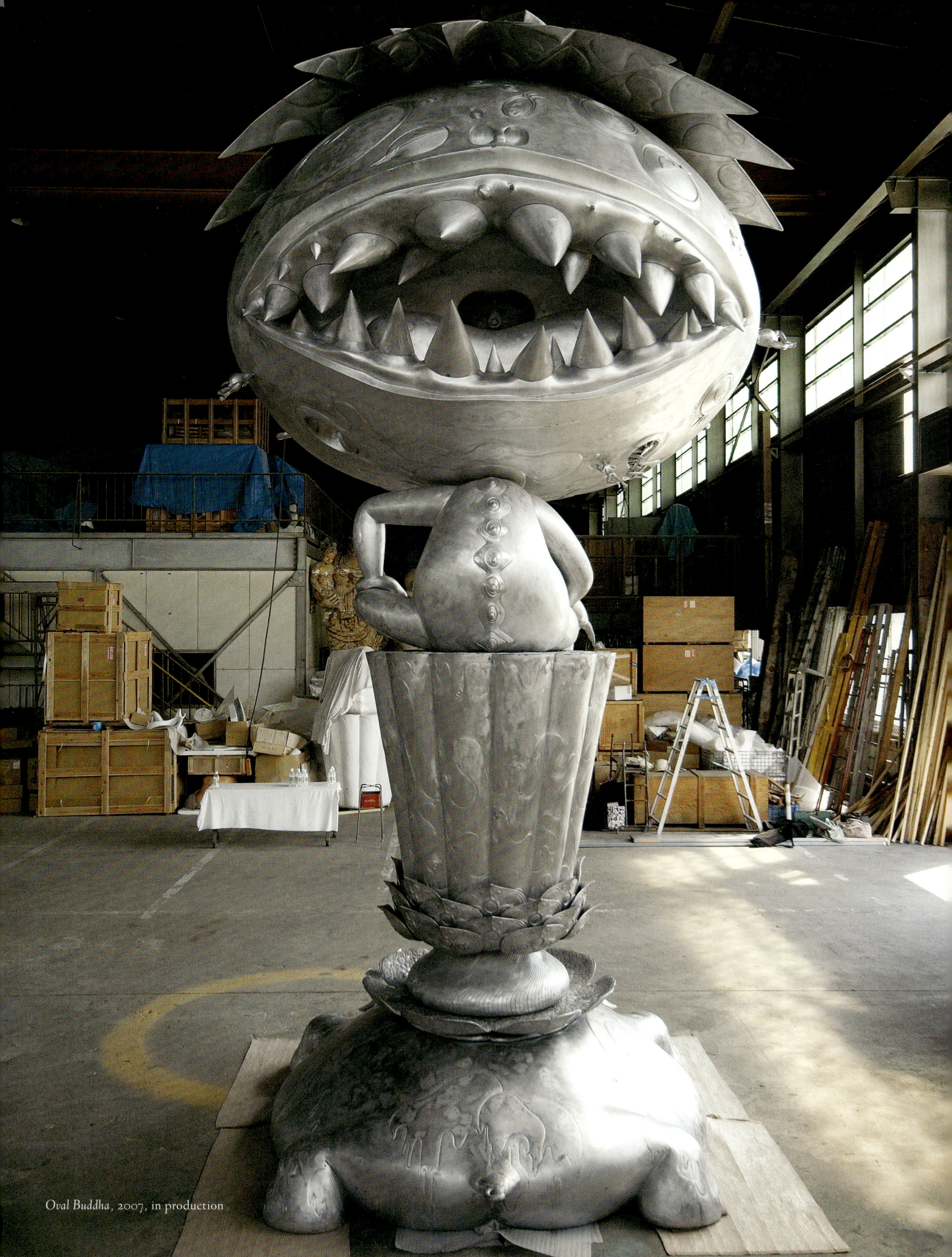

Oval Buddha, 2007, in production

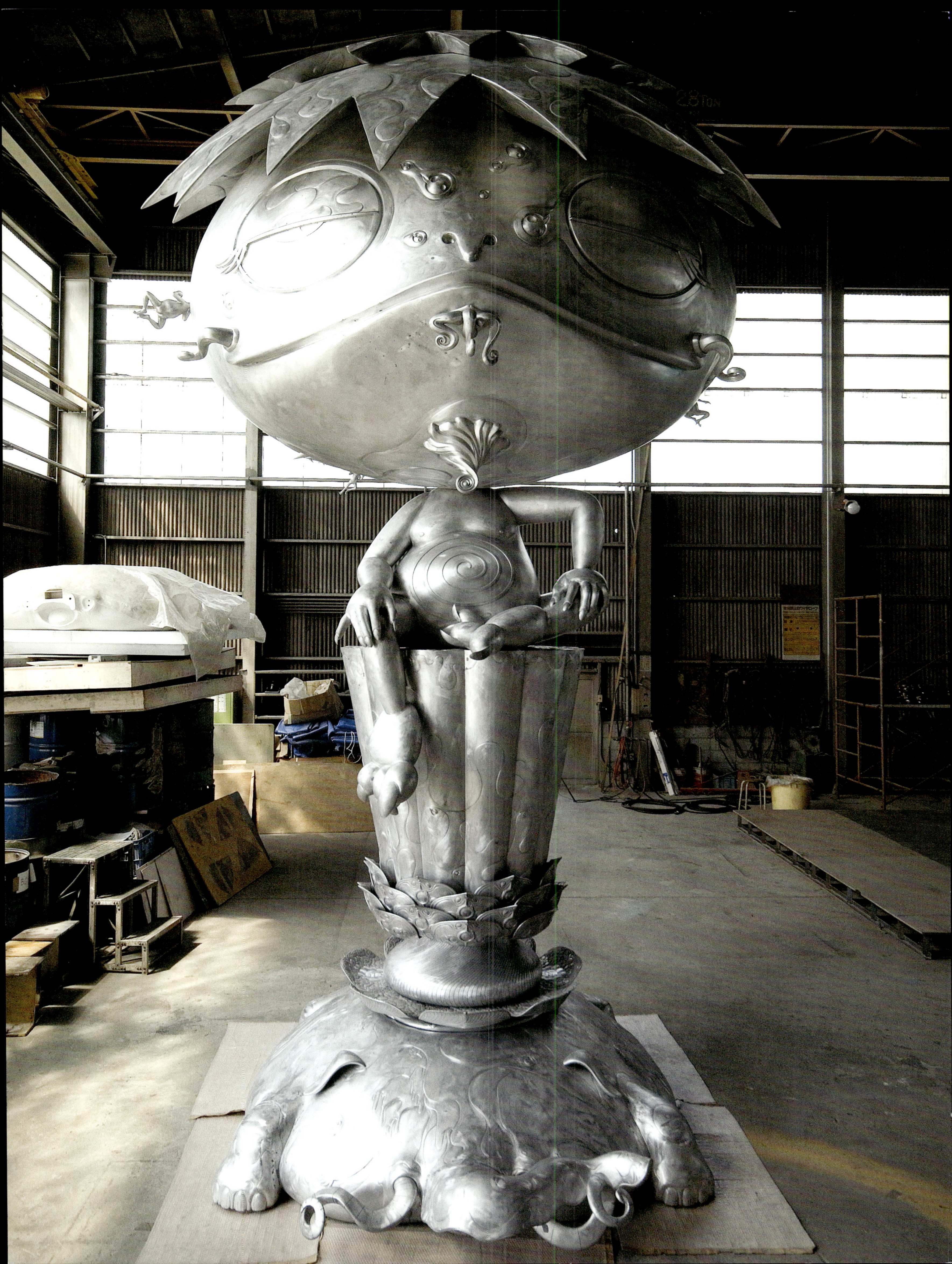

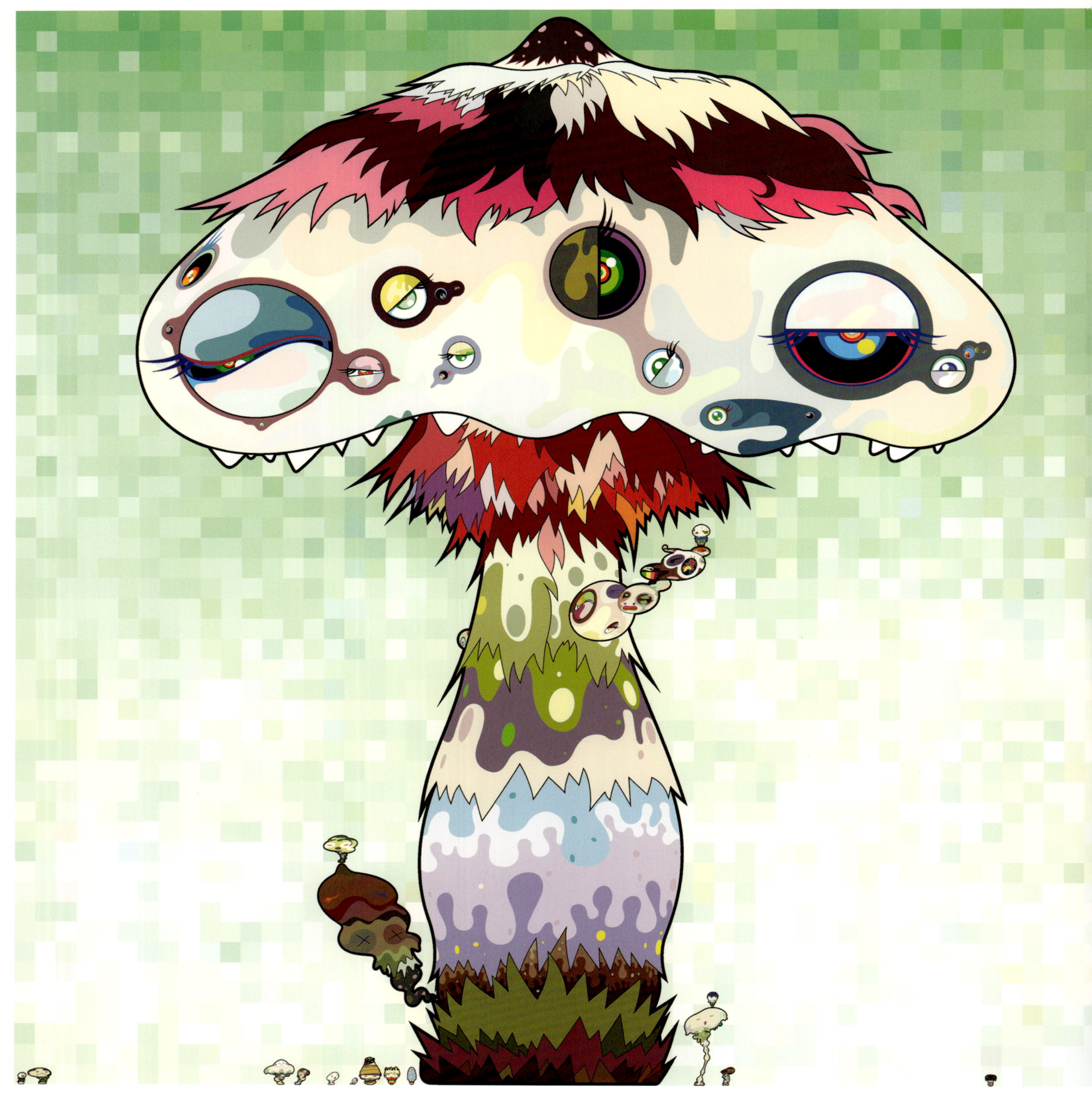

Untitled, 2007, in production

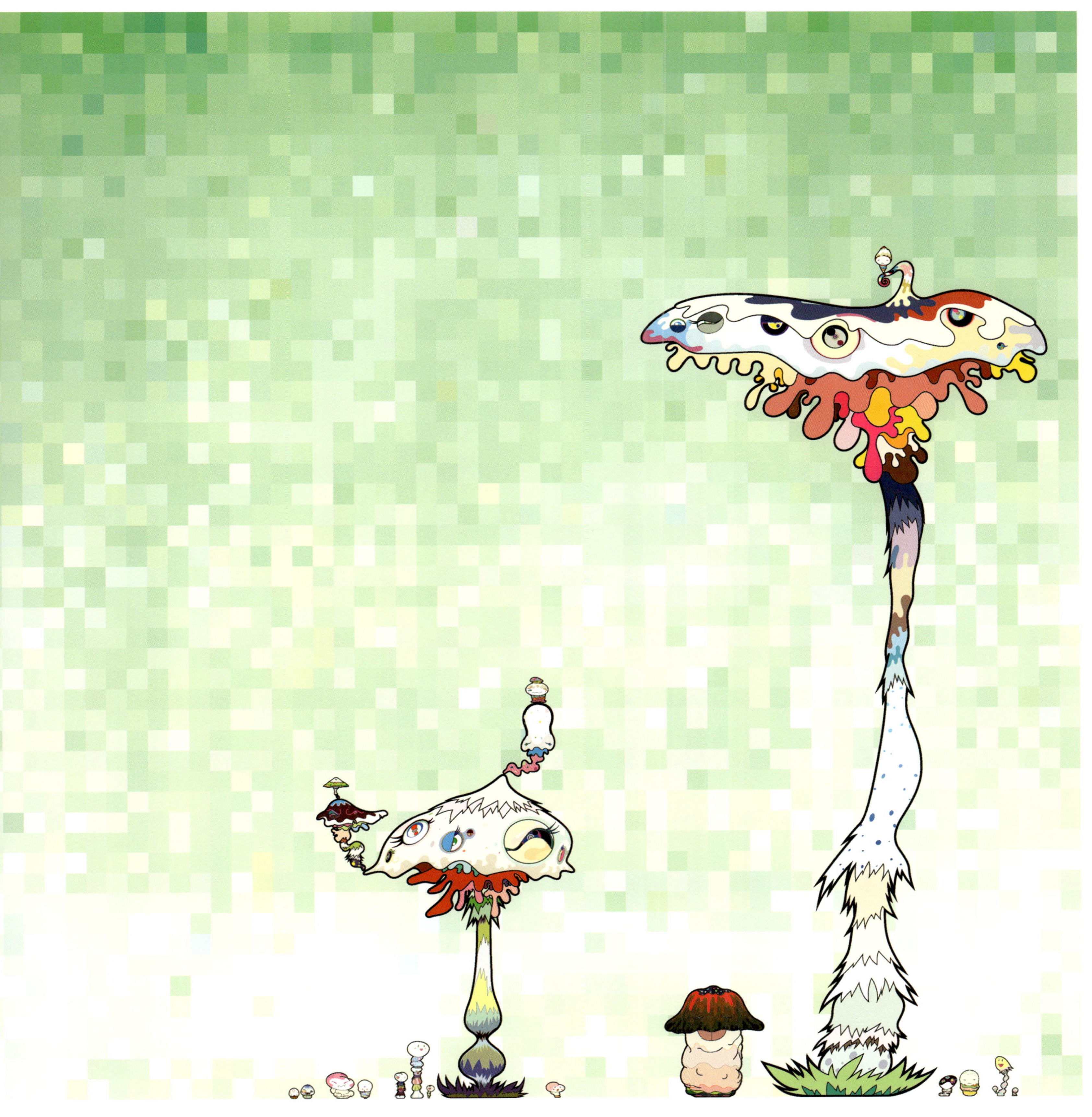

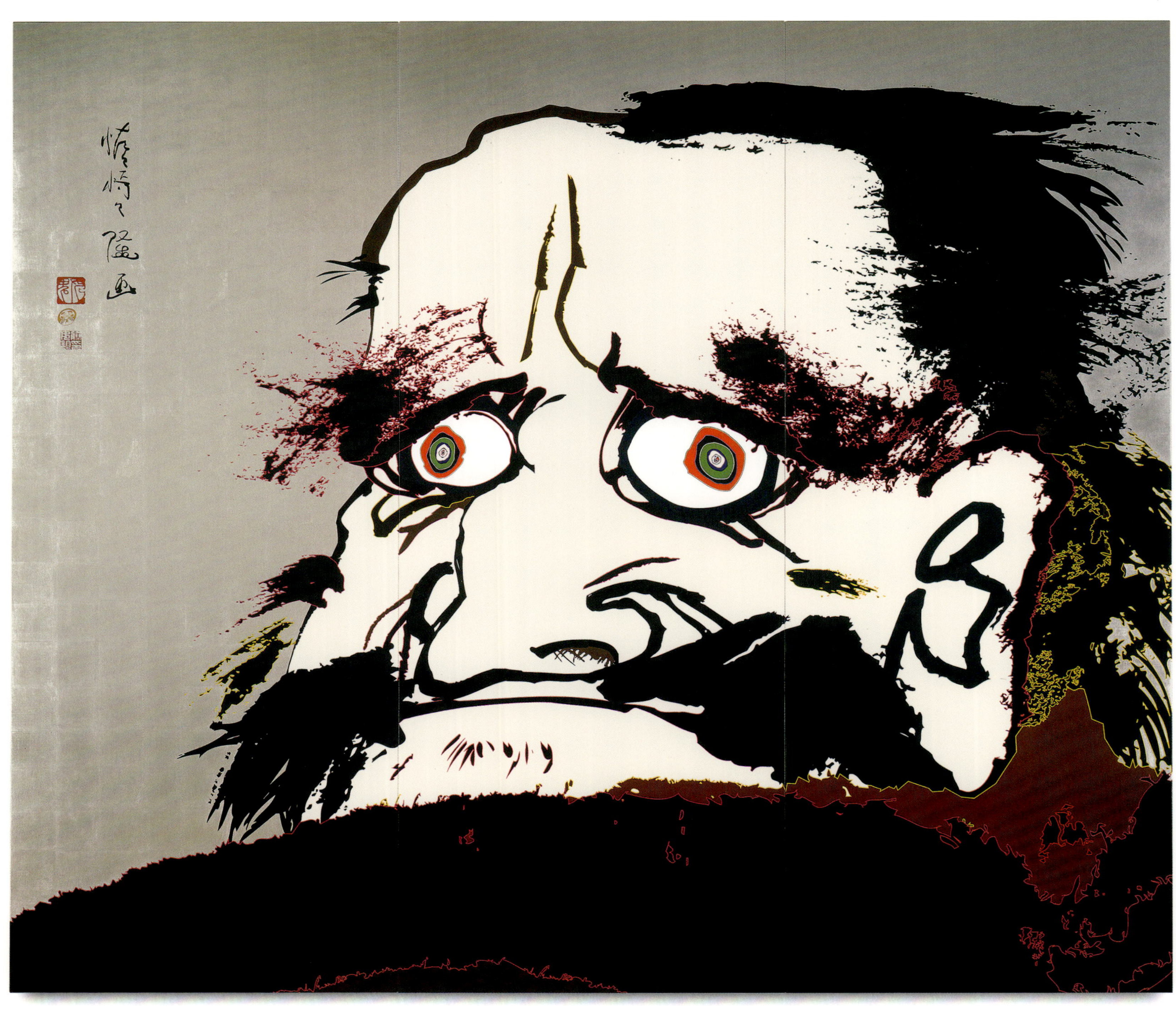

I open wide my eyes but see no scenery. I fix my gaze upon my heart., 2007

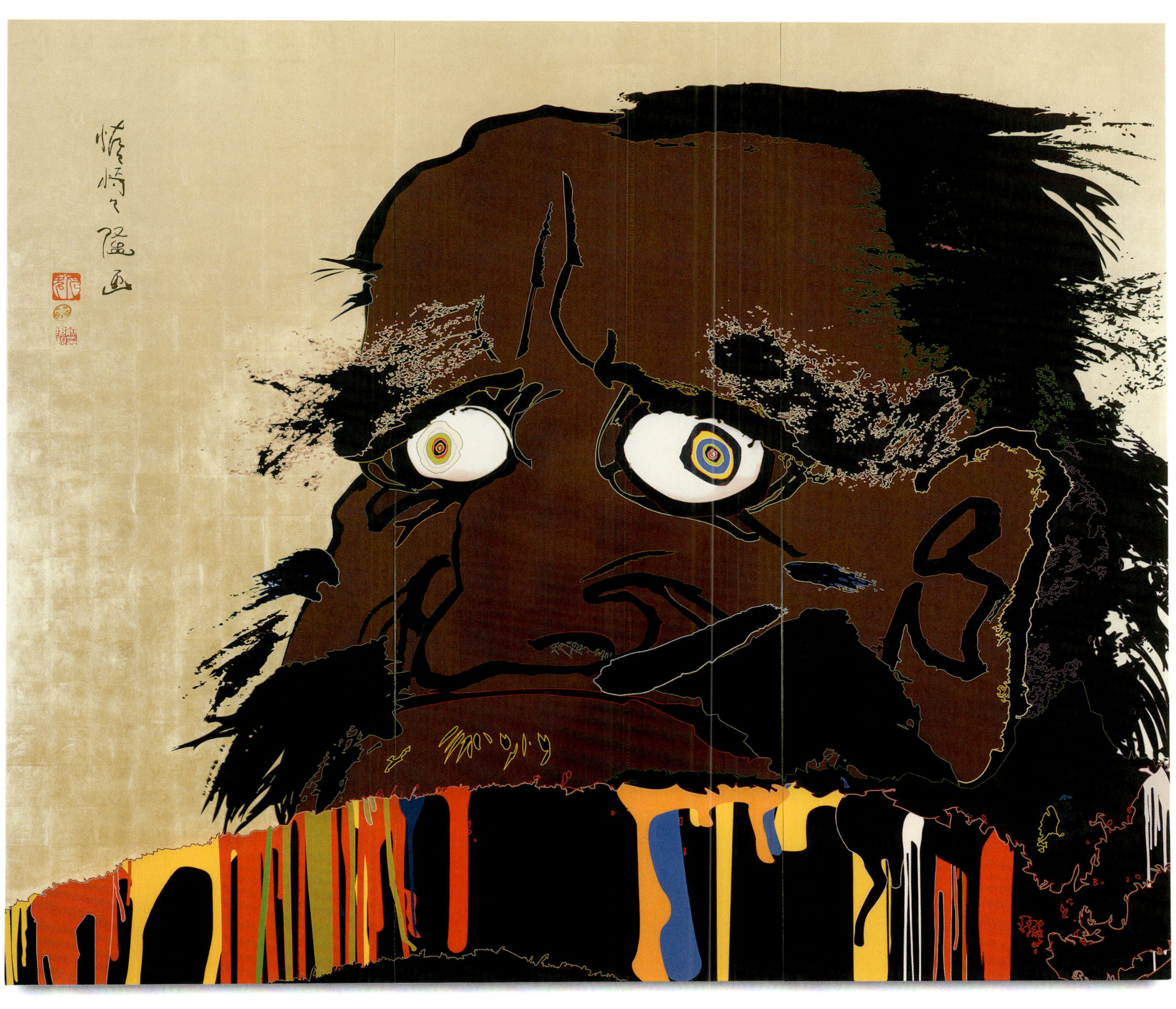

That I may time transcend, that a universe my heart may unfold., 2007

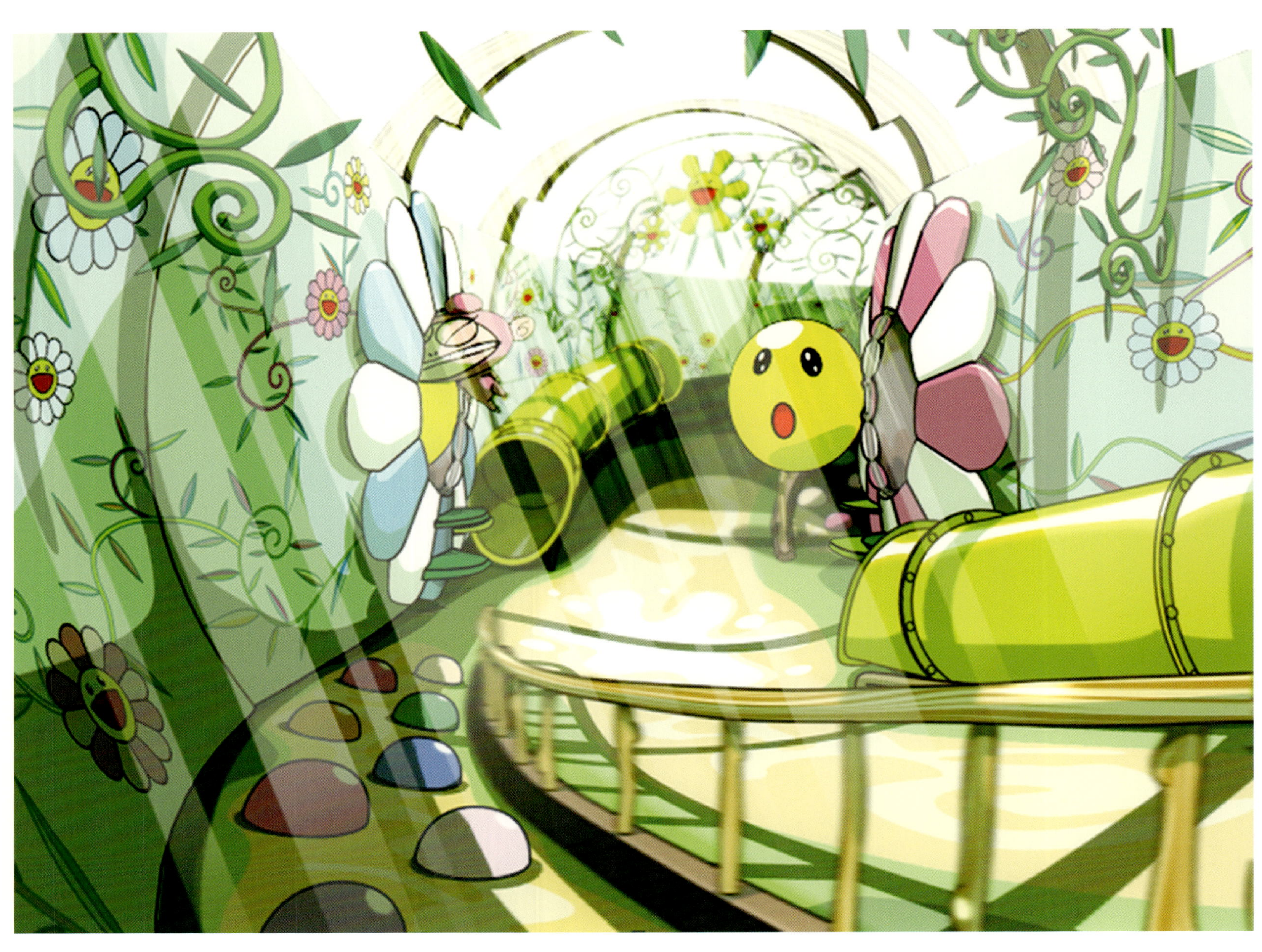

Stills from *kaikai & kiki*, 2007

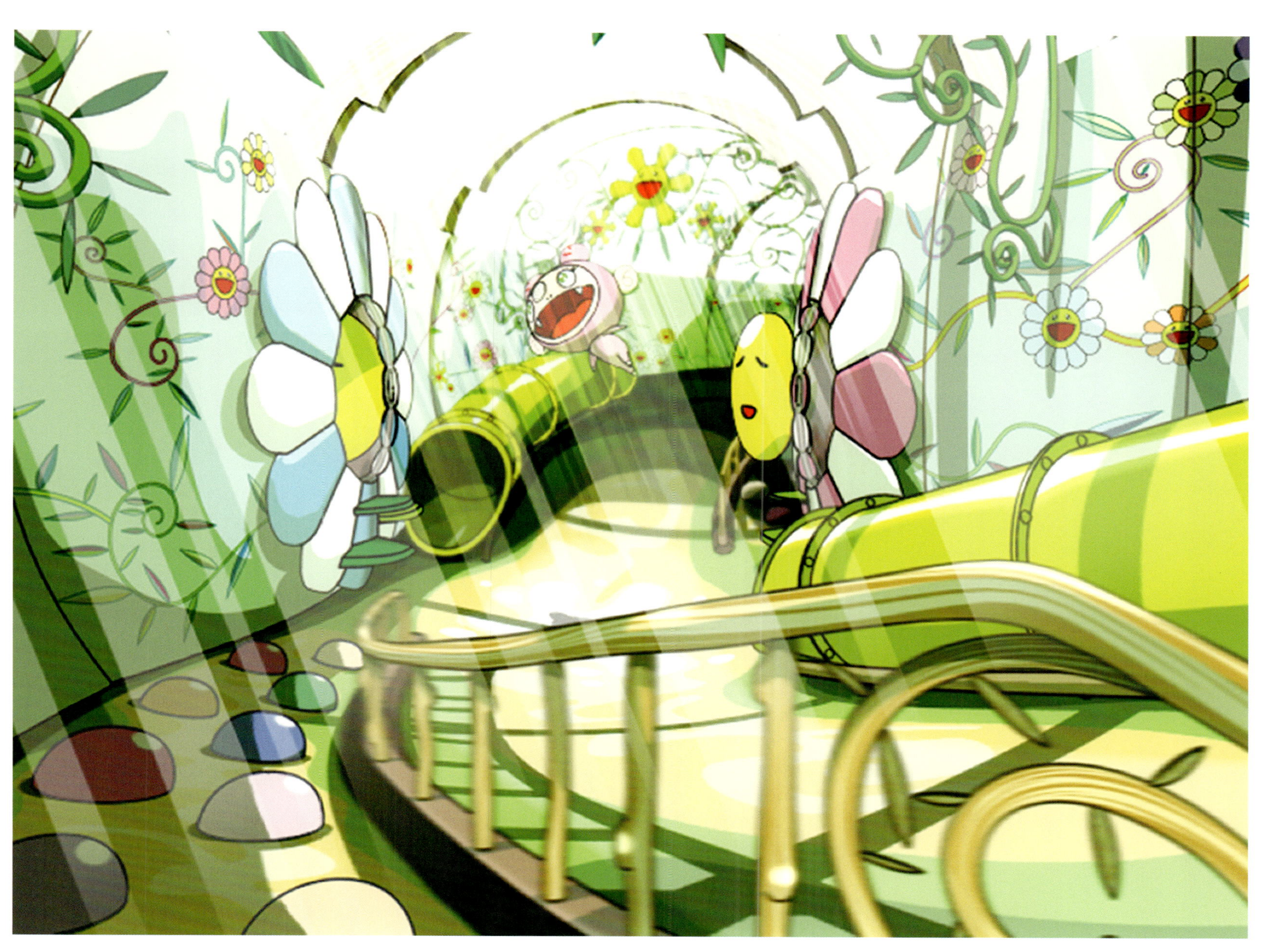

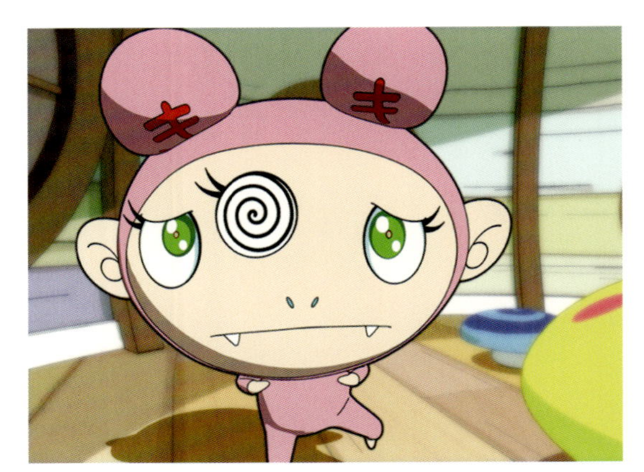
キ
キ

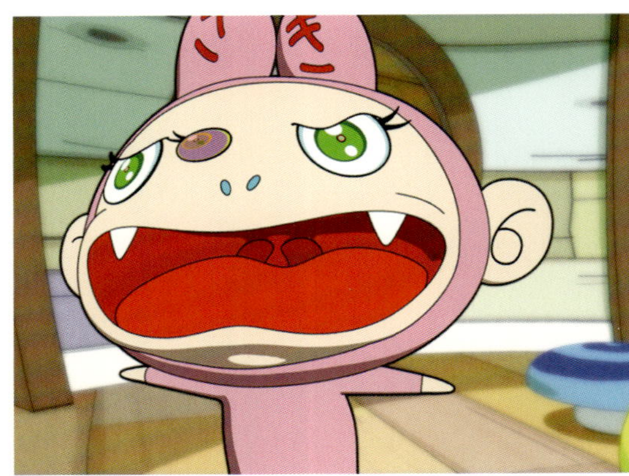

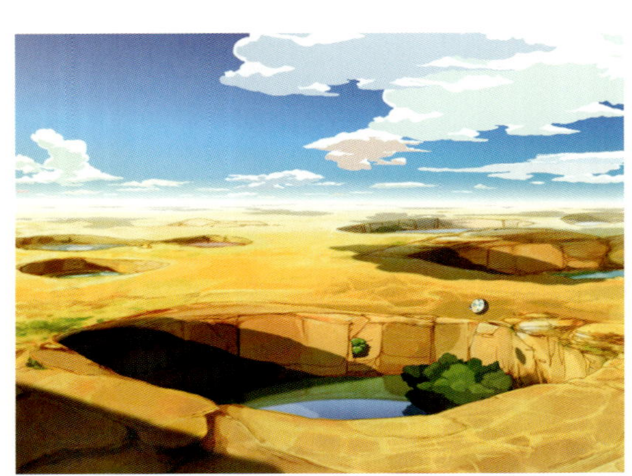

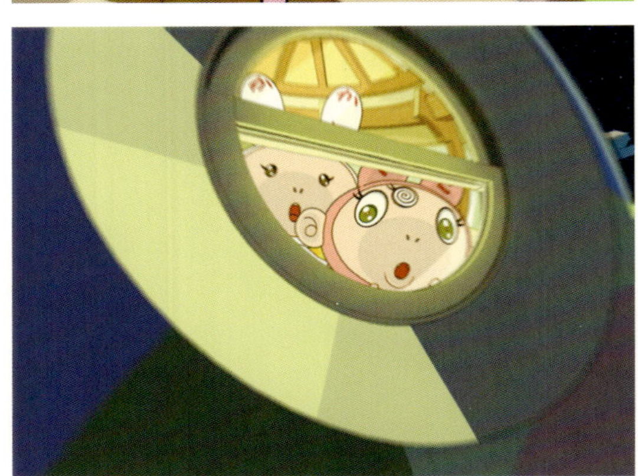

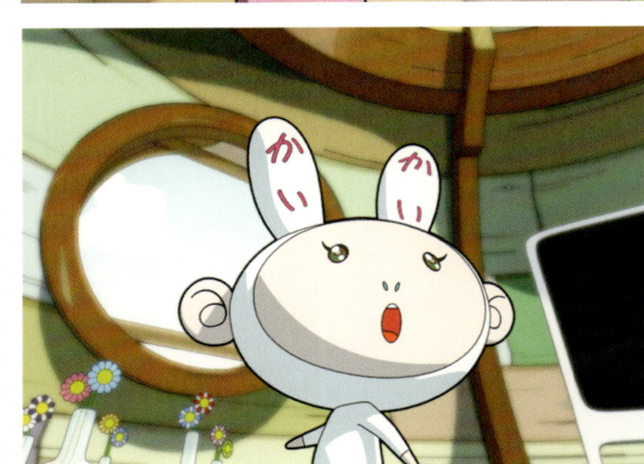
かい
かい

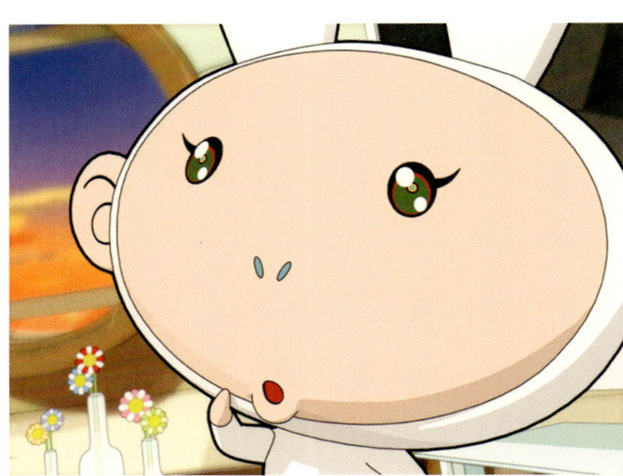

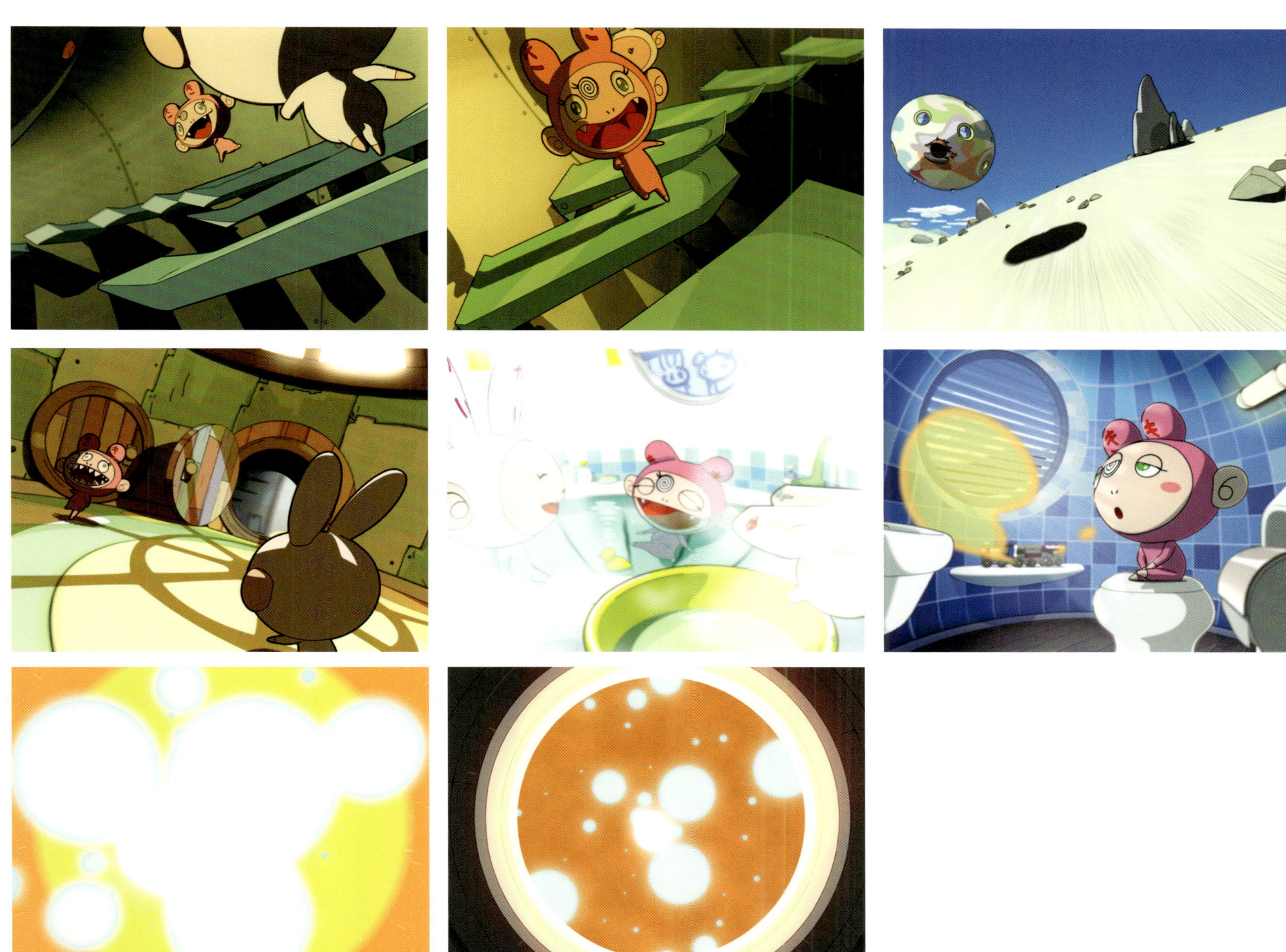

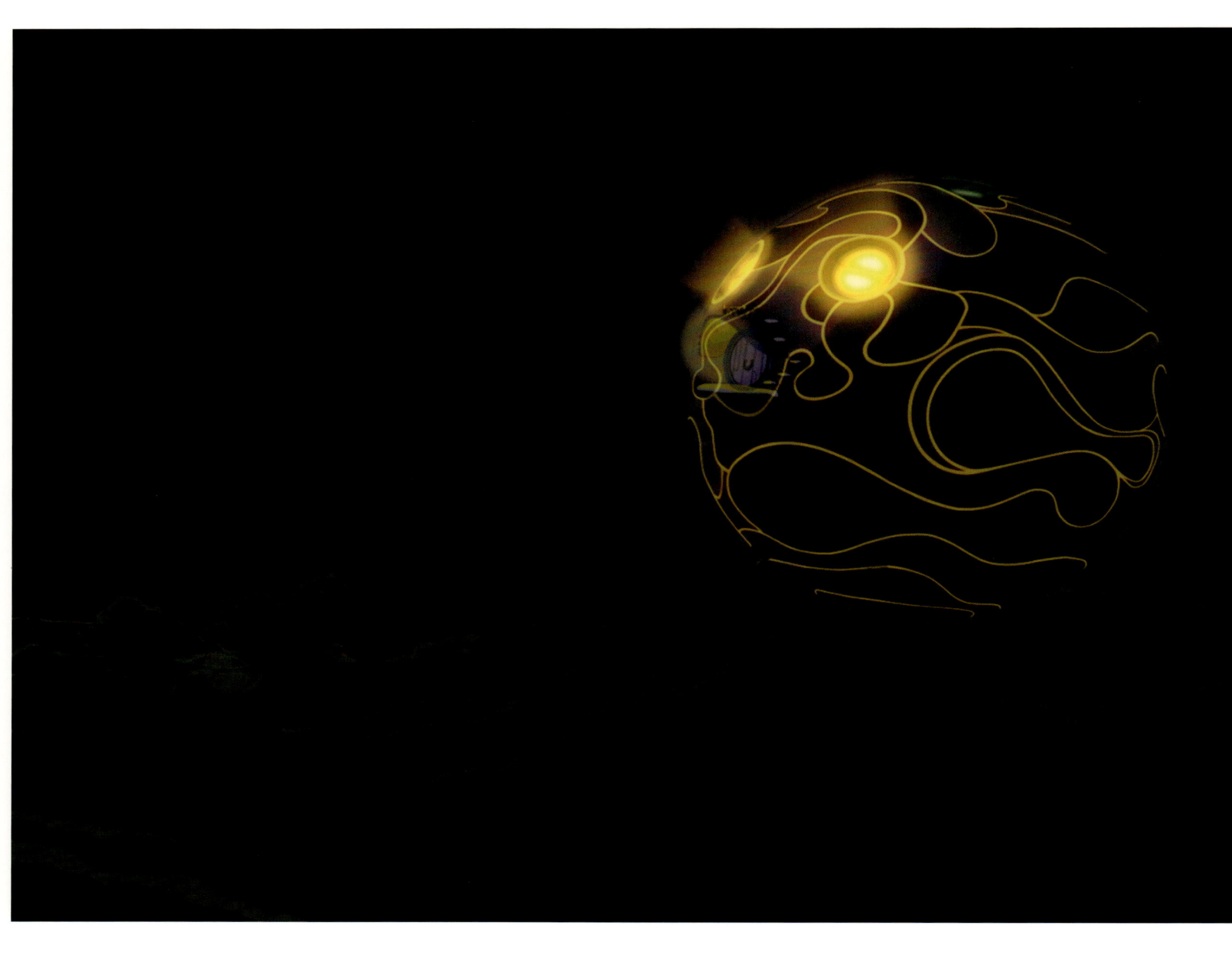

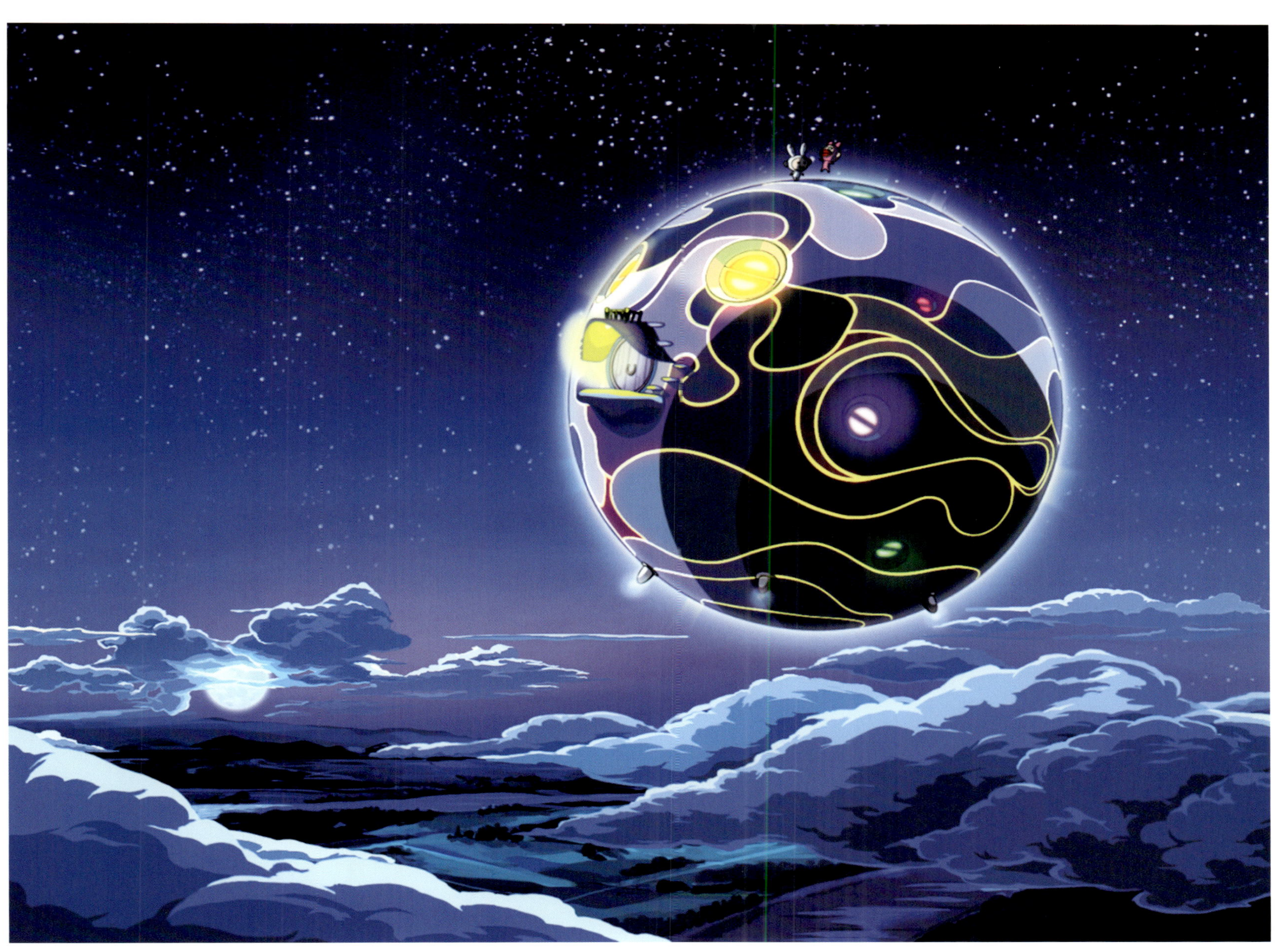

Checklist of the Exhibition

Signboard TAMIYA, 1991/2007
Plywood and sticker (branded with red-hot iron)
27 9/16 x 18 7/8 x 9/16 inches
Courtesy of the artist

Signboard TAKASHI, 1992/2007
Plywood and sticker with brand
27 9/16 x 18 7/8 x 9/16 inches
Courtesy of the artist

DOB Genesis, 1993
Acrylic and silkscreen on canvas mounted on wood
43 5/16 x 43 5/16 inches
Private collection, New York

Hiropon, 1993
Vinyl sticker on aluminum
35 7/16 x 25 9/16 inches
Private collection, Shiga, Japan

Time Bokan, 1993
Acrylic paint on wall
Dimensions variable
Courtesy of the artist

ZuZaZaZaZaZa, 1994
Acrylic and silkscreen on canvas mounted on board
59 1/16 x 66 15/16 inches
Takahashi Collection
Courtesy of Tomio Koyama Gallery, Tokyo

DOB's March, 1995
Acrylic on canvas mounted on board
27 9/16 x 39 3/8 inches
Collection of Javier and Monica Mora, Coral Gables, Florida

DOB's March, 1995
Vinyl chloride and helium
92 1/2 x 120 x 71 inches
Fluid Editions and Archives

Forest of DOB, 1995
Acrylic on canvas mounted on board
39 3/8 x 39 3/8 inches
Private collection

Mr. DOB, 1995
Vinyl chloride and helium
92 1/2 x 120 1/16 x 70 7/8 inches
Collection Martin Z. Margulies, Miami, Florida

Pschitt (blue), 1995
Acrylic on canvas
18 1/8 x 18 1/8 inches
Private collection
Courtesy of Galerie Emmanuel Perrotin, Paris and Miami

Stew (blue), 1995
Acrylic on canvas mounted on board
24 x 24 inches
Vanhaerents Art Collection, Brussels, Belgium
Courtesy of Galerie Emmanuel Perrotin, Paris and Miami

Stew (red), 1995
Acrylic on canvas mounted on board
24 x 24 inches
Vanhaerents Art Collection, Brussels, Belgium
Courtesy of Galerie Emmanuel Perrotin, Paris and Miami

Stew (yellow), 1995
Acrylic on canvas mounted on board
24 x 24 inches
Private collection, New York
Courtesy of Galerie Emmanuel Perrotin, Paris and Miami

And Then, And Then And Then And Then And Then (Blue), 1996
Acrylic on canvas mounted on board
Two panels: 118 1/8 x 118 1/8 inches overall
Collection of Queensland Art Gallery
Courtesy of Shiraishi Contemporary Art Inc., Tokyo

And Then, And Then And Then And Then And Then (Red), 1996
Acrylic on canvas mounted on board
Two panels: 118 1/8 x 118 1/8 inches overall
Collection of David Teiger
Courtesy of Blum & Poe, Los Angeles

Chaos, 1996
Vinyl chloride and helium
196 7/8 inches in diameter
Collection of Fukuoka Jisho Co., Ltd.
Courtesy of Shiraishi Contemporary Art Inc., Tokyo

DOB with Flowers, 1996–98
Acrylic on canvas mounted on board
15 15/16 x 15 15/16 inches
Collection of Matt Aberle, Los Angeles
Courtesy of Blum & Poe, Los Angeles

Miss ko², 1996
Acrylic on canvas mounted on board
39 3/8 x 39 3/8 inches
Collection of Marianne Boesky, New York

727, 1996
Acrylic on canvas mounted on board
Three panels: 118 x 180 inches overall
The Museum of Modern Art, New York
Fractional and promised gift of
David Teiger
Courtesy of Blum & Poe, Los Angeles

Hiropon, 1997
Acrylic, fiberglass, and iron, ed. 3/3
71 x 41 x 48 inches
Collections of Peter Norton and Eileen
Harris Norton, Santa Monica
Courtesy of Blum & Poe, Los Angeles

Miss ko², 1997
Oil paint, acrylic, synthetic resin,
fiberglass, and iron
100 x 46 x 36 inches
Collection of Marianne Boesky, New York

The Castle of Tin Tin, 1998
Acrylic on canvas mounted on board
Two panels: 118 1/8 x 118 1/8 inches overall
Collection of Ruth and Jake Bloom,
Marina del Rey, Calfornia
Courtesy of Blum & Poe, Los Angeles

Chaos, 1998–99
Acrylic on canvas mounted on board
15 15/16 x 15 15/16 x 1 3/4 inches
Private collection
Courtesy of Marianne Boesky Gallery,
New York

Chaos, 1998
Acrylic on canvas mounted on board
15 15/16 x 15 15/16 x 1 3/4 inches
The Ann and Mel Schaffer Family
Collection, New Jersey
Courtesy of Marianne Boesky Gallery,
New York

Chaos, 1998
Acrylic on canvas mounted on board
15 15/16 x 15 15/16 x 1 3/4 inches
Collection of Harry David, Athens
Courtesy of Marianne Boesky Gallery,
New York

Chaos, 1998
Acrylic on canvas mounted on board
15 15/16 x 15 15/16 x 1 3/4 inches
Collection of Ruth and Jake Bloom,
Marina del Rey, California
Courtesy of Blum & Poe, Los Angeles

Chaos, 1998
Acrylic on canvas mounted on board
15 15/16 x 15 15/16 x 1 3/4 inches
Collection of Ruth and Jake Bloom,
Marina del Rey, California
Courtesy of Blum & Poe, Los Angeles

Chaos, 1998
Acrylic on canvas mounted on board
15 15/16 x 15 15/16 x 1 3/4 inches
Private collection
Courtesy of Blum & Poe, Los Angeles

Chaos, 1998
Acrylic on canvas mounted on board
15 15/16 x 15 15/16 x 1 3/4 inches
Private collection
Courtesy of Blum & Poe, Los Angeles

Chaos, 1998
Acrylic on canvas mounted on board
15 15/16 x 15 15/16 x 1 3/4 inches
Private collection
Courtesy of Blum & Poe, Los Angeles

Chaos, 1999
Acrylic on canvas mounted on board
15 15/16 x 15 15/16 x 1 3/4 inches
Collection of Alan and Darryl Reichbart,
Los Angeles
Courtesy of Marianne Boesky Gallery,
New York

Cosmos, 1998
Acrylic on canvas mounted on board
Three panels: 118 1/8 x 177 3/16
inches overall
Collection of 21st Century Museum
of Contemporary Art, Kanazawa
Courtesy of Tomio Koyama Gallery, Tokyo

Cream, 1998
Acrylic on linen mounted on board
Four panels: 92 x 192 inches overall
Collections of Peter Norton and Eileen
Harris Norton, Santa Monica
Courtesy of Blum & Poe, Los Angeles

Mean of Blue, 1998
Acrylic on canvas mounted on board
15 15/16 x 15 15/16 x 1 3/4 inches
Collection of Douglas and Sherry Oliver, New York

Milk, 1998
Acrylic on linen mounted on board
Four panels: 96 x 192 inches overall
Collections of Peter Norton and Eileen Harris Norton, Santa Monica
Courtesy of Blum & Poe, Los Angeles

My Lonesome Cowboy, 1998
FRP resin, fiberglass, steel tubing, steel plate, and oil and acrylic paint; ed. 1/3
90 x 57 x 43 inches
Collections of Peter Norton and Eileen Harris Norton, Santa Monica
Courtesy of Blum & Poe, Los Angeles

PO+KU Surrealism Mr. DOB—Yellow, Pink, Blue, Purple, Green, 1998
Acrylic on canvas mounted on board
Five panels: 25 9/16 x 19 11/16 inches each
Minor Family San Francisco

DOB in the Strange Forest, 1999
FRP, resin, fiberglass, acrylic, and iron
120 x 120 x 50 inches
Collections of Peter Norton and Eileen Harris Norton, Santa Monica
Courtesy of Blum & Poe, Los Angeles

Magic Ball, 1999
Acrylic on canvas mounted on board
Seven panels: 94 1/2 x 248 x 1 15/16 inches overall
Olbricht Collection
Courtesy of Tomio Koyama Gallery, Tokyo

PO+KU Surrealism (Blue), 1999
Acrylic on canvas mounted on board
Four panels: 110 1/4 x 220 1/2 inches overall
Rubell Family Collection, Miami
Courtesy of Blum & Poe, Los Angeles

PO+KU Surrealism (Green), 1999
Acrylic on canvas mounted on board
Three panels: 110 1/4 x 161 7/16 inches overall
Collection of the Los Angeles County Museum of Art
Gift of Peter Norton and Eileen Harris Norton
Courtesy of Blum & Poe, Los Angeles

PO+KU Surrealism (Pink), 1999
Acrylic on canvas mounted on board
Three panels: 110 1/4 x 165 3/8 inches overall
Private collection
Courtesy of Blum & Poe, Los Angeles

Second Mission Project ko² (Jet Airplane Type), 1999–2007
Oil, acrylic, synthetic resin, fiberglass, and iron
21 5/8 x 76 x 73 1/4 inches
Courtesy of Blum & Poe, Los Angeles

Second Mission Project ko² (Ga-Walk Type), 1999–2007
Oil, acrylic, synthetic resin, fiberglass, and iron
88 3/8 x 69 5/8 x 51 3/4 inches
Courtesy of Blum & Poe, Los Angeles

Second Mission Project ko² (Human Type), 1999–2007
Oil, acrylic, synthetic resin, fiberglass, and iron
108 1/4 x 99 3/16 x 55 1/8 inches
Courtesy of Blum & Poe, Los Angeles

Super Nova, 1999
Acrylic on canvas mounted on board
Seven panels: 118 x 59 inches each; 118 x 413 inches overall
Collection of Vicki and Kent Logan
Fractional and Promised Gift to the San Francisco Museum of Modern Art
Courtesy of Marianne Boesky Gallery, New York

Study for Super Nova, 1999
Graphite on paper
21 13/16 x 64 1/4 inches
Collection of Vicki and Kent Logan
Fractional and Promised Gift to the San Francisco Museum of Modern Art
Courtesy of Marianne Boesky Gallery, New York

Untitled (Study for Super Nova), 1999
Mixed media, Xerox, and pen on paper
29 1/8 x 97 1/8 inches
Collection of Vicki and Kent Logan
Fractional and Promised Gift to the San Francisco Museum of Modern Art
Courtesy of Marianne Boesky Gallery, New York

Mushroom Painting Drawing, 1999
Pencil, pen, and tape on paper
8 1/2 x 20 3/4 inches
Courtesy of the artist

Study for Mushroom Painting, 1999
Computer print, tape, and marker on paper
26 x 90 1/2 inches
Collection of Martin and Rebecca Eisenberg
Courtesy of Marianne Boesky Gallery, New York

Kaikai, 2000
Oil paint, acrylic, synthetic resin, fiberglass, and iron
71 7/16 x 27 15/16 x 20 7/8 inches
Olbricht Collection
Courtesy of Galerie Emmanuel Perrotin, Paris and Miami

Kaikai with Moss, 2000
Acrylic on canvas mounted on board
23 5/8 x 23 5/8 x 1 15/16 inches
Private collection
Courtesy of Galerie Emmanuel Perrotin, Paris and Miami

Kiki, 2000
Oil paint, acrylic, synthetic resin, fiberglass, and iron
63 x 27 15/16 x 21 5/8 inches
Olbricht Collection
Courtesy of Galerie Emmanuel Perrotin, Paris and Miami

Kiki with Moss, 2000
Acrylic on canvas mounted on board
23 5/8 x 23 5/8 x 1 15/16 inches
Private collection
Courtesy of Galerie Emmanuel Perrotin, Paris and Miami

The Double Helix, Reversal, 2001
Acrylic on canvas mounted on board
Two panels: 118 1/8 x 118 1/8 inches overall
Private collection, New York
Courtesy of Tomio Koyama Gallery, Tokyo

Flower Matango (b), 2001–06
Fiberglass, resin, oil paint, lacquer, acrylic plates, and iron
Approximately 157 1/2 x 118 1/8 x 98 7/16 inches
Private collection
Courtesy of Galerie Emmanuel Perrotin, Paris and Miami

Jellyfish Eyes, 2001
Acrylic on canvas mounted on board
Five panels: 39 3/8 x 39 3/8 x 2 inches each
Courtesy of Marianne Boesky Gallery, New York

Jellyfish Eyes, 2001
Hand silk-screened wallpaper
Ten-roll set: 27 x 180 inches each
Courtesy of Marianne Boesky Gallery, New York

Melting DOB D, 2001
Acrylic on canvas mounted on board
39 3/8 x 39 3/8 inches
Collection of John A. Smith and Victoria Hughes, London
Courtesy of Tomio Koyama Gallery, Tokyo

Tan Tan Bo, 2001
Acrylic on canvas mounted on board
Three panels: 141 3/4 x 212 5/8 x 2 5/8 inches overall
Collection of John A. Smith and Victoria Hughes, London
Courtesy of Tomio Koyama Gallery, Tokyo

Time Bokan—black, 2001
Acrylic on canvas mounted on board
70 7/8 x 70 7/8 inches
Collection of Rachel and Jean-Pierre Lehmann
Courtesy of Marianne Boesky Gallery, New York

Time Bokan—blue, 2001
Acrylic on canvas mounted on board
Frame: 70 7/8 x 70 7/8 inches
Private collection, New York
Courtesy of Marianne Boesky Gallery, New York

Time Bokan—pink, 2001
Acrylic on canvas mounted on board
Frame: 70 7/8 x 70 7/8 inches
Collection of Peter Morton
Courtesy of Marianne Boesky Gallery, New York

Time Bokan—red, 2001
Acrylic on canvas mounted on board
Frame: 70 7/8 x 70 7/8 inches
Private collection, Los Angeles
Courtesy of Marianne Boesky Gallery, New York

Flower Ball (Algae Ball), 2002
Acrylic on canvas mounted on board
23 5/8 inches diameter; 1 15/16 inches in depth
Collection of Giancarlo Bonollo, Vicenza, Italy
Courtesy of Galerie Emmanuel Perrotin, Paris and Miami

Flower Ball (Kindergarten Days), 2002
Acrylic on canvas mounted on board
39 3/8 inches diameter, 1 15/16 inches depth
Private collection, New York
Courtesy of Galerie Emmanuel Perrotin, Paris and Miami

Flower Ball (3-D), 2002
Acrylic on canvas mounted on board
98 7/16 inches diameter
Private collection
Courtesy of Galerie Emmanuel Perrotin, Paris and Miami

Homage to Francis Bacon (Study of George Dyer), 2002
Acrylic on canvas mounted on board
47 1/4 x 47 1/4 x 1 15/16 inches
Private collection
Courtesy of Galerie Emmanuel Perrotin, Paris and Miami

Homage to Francis Bacon (Study of Isabel Rawsthorne), 2002
Acrylic on canvas mounted on board
47 1/4 x 47 1/4 x 1 15/16 inches
Collection of Galerie Emmanuel Perrotin, Paris and Miami

Kaikai Kiki in Peach Paradise, 2002
Acrylic on canvas mounted on board
Six panels: 63 x 137 13/16 inches overall
Collection of Florence and Philippe Segalot
Courtesy of Galerie Emmanuel Perrotin, Paris and Miami

Kaikai Kiki News, 2002
Acrylic on canvas mounted on board
47 1/4 x 47 1/4 inches
Private collection
Courtesy of Galerie Emmanuel Perrotin, Paris and Miami

Kawaii! Vacances d'été, 2002
Acrylic on canvas mounted on board
Six panels: 118 1/8 x 354 5/16 x 2 3/4 inches overall
François Pinault Collection
Courtesy of Galerie Emmanuel Perrotin, Paris and Miami

Tan Tan Bo Puking—a.k.a. Gero Tan, 2002
Acrylic on canvas mounted on board
Four panels: 141 3/4 x 283 7/16 x 2 5/8 inches overall
Collection of Amalia Dayan and Adam Lindemann
Courtesy of Galerie Emmanuel Perrotin, Paris and Miami

Cosmos, 2003
Hand silk-screened wallpaper
Twenty-sheet set: 45 1/4 x 60 1/4 inches each
Courtesy of Marianne Boesky Gallery, New York

Eye Love SUPERFLAT, 2003
Acrylic on canvas mounted on wood
70 7/8 x 70 7/8 inches
Private collection
Courtesy of Galerie Emmanuel Perrotin, Paris and Miami

Superflat Jellyfish Eyes, 2003
Vinyl floor wallpaper
Dimensions variable
Courtesy of the artist

Superflat Jellyfish Eyes 1, 2003
Silk, aluminum, and wood
Six panels: 78 3/4 x 156 5/16 x 9/16 inches overall
Private collection
Courtesy Girard Pissarro Segalot, New York, and Galerie Emmanuel Perrotin, Paris and Miami

Superflat Jellyfish Eyes 2, 2003
Silk, aluminum, and wood
Six panels: 78 3/4 x 156 5/16 x 9/16 inches overall
Collection of Linda and Harry Macklowe
Courtesy of Galerie Emmanuel Perrotin, Paris and Miami

Tongari-kun, 2003–04
Fiberglass, steel, and oil, acrylic, and urethane paint
23 x 11 1/2 feet
Collection of Richard B. Sachs, New York
Courtesy of Marianne Boesky Gallery, New York

The World of Sphere, 2003
Acrylic on canvas mounted on board
Two panels: 137 13/16 x 137 13/16 inches overall
Private collection, New York
Courtesy of Marianne Boesky Gallery, New York

Eye Love SUPERFLAT, 2004
Acrylic on canvas mounted on board
70 7/8 x 70 7/8 inches
Private collection
Courtesy of Marianne Boesky Gallery, New York

Inochi, 2004
FRP, steel, and lacquer
55 1/8 x 24 5/8 x 14 3/8 inches
François Pinault Collection
Courtesy of Blum & Poe, Los Angeles

Inochi, 2004
FRP, steel, and lacquer
55 1/8 x 24 5/8 x 14 3/8 inches
The Steven A. Cohen Collection
Courtesy of Blum & Poe, Los Angeles

Jikokkun, 2003–05
Fiberglass, steel, and oil, acrylic, and urethane paint
6 3/4 x 3 feet
Collection of the artist

Koumokkun, 2003–05
Fiberglass, steel, and oil, acrylic, and urethane paint
7 3/4 x 2 3/4 x 2 feet
Collection of the artist

Tamon-kun, 2003–05
Fiberglass, steel, and oil, acrylic, and urethane paint
9 x 3 1/2 feet
Collection of the artist

Zoucho-kun, 2003–05
Fiberglass, steel, and oil, acrylic, and urethane paint
8 1/2 x 3 3/4 feet
Collection of the artist

727-727, 2006
Acrylic on canvas mounted on board
Three panels: 118 1/8 x 177 3/16 x 2 3/4 inches overall
The Steven A. Cohen Collection
Courtesy of Blum & Poe, Los Angeles

Oval Buddha, 2007
Aluminum and platinum leaf
223 5/8 x 125 9/16 x 122 1/16 inches
Courtesy of Blum & Poe, Los Angeles

Untitled, 2007
Acrylic on canvas mounted on board
Four panels: 82 11/16 x 165 3/8 x 1 15/16 inches overall
Courtesy of Gagosian Gallery, New York

I open wide my eyes but see no scenery. I fix my gaze upon my heart., 2007
Acrylic and platinum leaf on canvas mounted on board
95 1/2 x 111 inches
Collection of Linda and Harry Macklowe
Courtesy of Gagosian Gallery, New York

That I may time transcend, that a universe my heart may unfold., 2007
Acrylic and silver gold leaf on canvas mounted on board
Three panels: 95 1/2 x 111 inches overall
The Steven A. Cohen Collection
Courtesy of Gagosian Gallery, New York

kaikai & kiki, 2007
DVD
Approximately 10 minutes
Courtesy of the artist

kaikai & kiki, 2007
Carpet
31 1/4 x 39 feet
Courtesy of the artist

kaikai & kiki, 2007
Wallpaper
25 1/4 x 10 feet
Courtesy of the artist

Selected Exhibition History and Bibliography

TAKASHI MURAKAMI
b. 1962, Tokyo;
Lives and works in Tokyo

Education

B.F.A., Tokyo National University of Fine Arts and Music, 1986

M.F.A., Tokyo National University of Fine Arts and Music, 1988

Ph.D., Tokyo National University of Fine Arts and Music, 1993

Solo Exhibitions

2007

"Tranquility of the Heart, Torment of the Flesh—Open Wide the Eye of the Heart, and Nothing Is Invisible," Gagosian Gallery, New York

"Jellyfish Eyes," Museum of Contemporary Art, Chicago

2006

"Limited/Unlimited," 34 Long, Cape Town

"The Pressure Point of Painting," Galerie Emmanuel Perrotin, Paris

Installation at Samurai, Tokyo

2005

Kaikai Kiki Exhibition, Aoi Gallery, Osaka, Japan

Takashi Murakami Print Show, Mizuho Oshiro Gallery, Kagoshima, Japan

"T1: Takashi Murakami," Fondazione Sandretto Re Rebaudengo, Turin, Italy

Installation at Roppongi Hills, Tokyo

2004

"Satoeri ko² Chan," Tomio Koyama Gallery, Tokyo

"Inochi," Blum & Poe, Los Angeles

2003

"Reversed Double Helix," Rockefeller Center, New York

"Superflat Monogram," Galerie Emmanuel Perrotin, Paris

"Superflat Monogram," Marianne Boesky Gallery, New York

2002

"Kaikai Kiki: Takashi Murakami," Fondation Cartier pour l'art contemporain, Paris; and Serpentine Gallery, London

2001
"Summon Monsters? Open the Door? Heal? Or Die?" Museum of Contemporary Art, Tokyo
"Takashi Murakami: Made in Japan," Museum of Fine Arts, Boston
"Mushroom," Marianne Boesky Gallery, New York
"Wink," Grand Central Station (organized by Creative Time), New York
"Kaikai Kiki," Galerie Emmanuel Perrotin, Paris

2000
"Second Mission Project ko[2]," P.S.1 Contemporary Art Center, Long Island City, New York
"Kaikai Kiki: SUPERFLAT," Issey Miyake Men, Tokyo
"727," Blum & Poe, Santa Monica, California

1999
"PATRON," Marunuma Art Park, Asaka, Japan
"Love & DOB," Gallery KOTO, Okayama, Japan
"The Meaning of the Nonsense of the Meaning," Center for Curatorial Studies Museum, Bard College, Annandale-on-Hudson, New York
"DOB's Adventures in Wonderland," Parco Department Store Gallery, Tokyo
"Superflat," Marianne Boesky Gallery, New York

1998
"Back Beat: Superflat," Tomio Koyama Gallery, Tokyo
"Moreover, DOB Raise His Hand," Sagacho bis, Tokyo
"Back Beat," Blum & Poe, Santa Monica, California
"Hiropon Project koko—Pity Sakurako Jet Airplane Nos. 1–6," Feature Inc., New York

1997
Gallery KOTO, Okayama, Japan
Art Gallery, State University of New York, Buffalo, New York
"The Other Side of a Flash of Light," Art Space HAP, Hiroshima, Japan
Blum & Poe, Santa Monica, California
Galerie Emmanuel Perrotin, Paris

1996
"A Very Merry Unbirthday, To You, To Me!," Ginza Komatsu, Tokyo
"727," Aoi Gallery, Osaka, Japan
"Konnichiwa, Mr. DOB," Kirin Art Plaza, Osaka, Japan
"727," Tomio Koyama Gallery, Tokyo
Gallery KOTO, Okayama, Japan
Gavin Brown's enterprise, New York
Feature Inc., New York

1995
"Mr. Doomsday Balloon," Ynglingagatan 1, Stockholm
"Crazy Z," SCAI The Bathhouse, Tokyo
Galerie Emmanuel Perrotin, Paris
"NIJI," Gallery KOTO, Okayama, Japan

1994
"Azami, Kikyō, Ominaeshi," Aoi Gallery, Osaka, Japan
"Which Is Tomorrow?—Fall in Love," SCAI The Bathhouse, Tokyo
"Fujisan," Gallery KOTO, Okayama, Japan

1993
"A Romantic Evening," Gallery Cellar, Nagoya, Japan
"A Very Merry Unbirthday!," Hiroshima City Museum of Contemporary Art, Hiroshima, Japan
Nasubi Gallery, Tokyo

1992
"Wild, Wild," Röntgen Kunst Institut, Tokyo

1991
"I Am Against Being for It," Hosomi Gallery, Tokyo
"Takashi Tamiya," Gallery Aires, Tokyo
"One Night Exhibition 8.23," Röntgen Kunst Institut, Tokyo
"Master's Thesis Show," Tokyo National University of Fine Arts and Music, Tokyo
Aoi Gallery, Osaka, Japan

1989
"Takashi Murakami: New Works," Café Tiens!, Tokyo
"Exhibition L'Espoir: Takashi Murakami," Gallery Ginza Surugadai, Tokyo

Group Exhibitions

2007

"Red Hot: Asian Art Today from the Chaney Family Collection," Museum of Fine Arts, Houston

"Land of the Samurai," Aberdeen Art Gallery, Aberdeen, Scotland

"Rockers Island: Olbricht Collection," Museum Folkwang, Essen, Germany

"Comic Abstraction: Image-Breaking, Image-Making," The Museum of Modern Art, New York

"My 2007," Colette, Paris

2006

"La collezione François Pinault: Una selezione Post-Pop," Palazzo Grassi, Venice, Italy

"Mass Production: Artists' Multiples and the Marketplace," Myers School of Art, The University of Akron, Akron, Ohio

" Japan vs. Art: Contemporary Art and Nihonga from Taikan Yokoyama and Seiho Takeuchi to Takashi Murakami," Osaka City Museum of Art, Osaka, Japan

"Radar: Selections from the Collection of Vicki and Kent Logan," Denver Art Museum, Denver

"Off the Shelf: New Forms in Contemporary Artists' Books," Vassar College, Poughkeepsie, New York

"10th Anniversary," Tomio Koyama Gallery, Tokyo

"Spank the Monkey," Baltic Centre for Contemporary Art, Gateshead, England

"Invisible Landscape," Lund City Museum, Lund, Sweden

"Surprise, Surprise," Institute of Contemporary Arts, London

"Where Are We Going?: Selections from the François Pinault Collection," Palazzo Grassi, Venice, Italy

"Exhibition of Collected Works: Secret Base," Toyota Municipal Museum of Art, Toyota, Japan

"Infinite Paintings: Contemporary Painting and Global Realism," Villa Manin Centre for Contemporary Art, Udine, Italy

"Sellout," Center for Curatorial Studies, Bard College, Annandale-on-Hudson, New York

"Dragon Veins," Contemporary Art Museum, University of South Florida, Tampa

2005

"Kaikai Kiki Exhibition," Aoi Gallery, Osaka, Japan

"Ecstasy: In and About Altered States," The Museum of Contemporary Art, Los Angeles

"'Post' and After: Contemporary Art from the Brandeis Collection," The Rose Art Museum, Brandeis University, Waltham, Massachusetts

Galerie Emmanuel Perrotin, Paris

"Japan POP," Helsinki City Art Museum, Helsinki

"Fairy Tales Forever: Homage to H. C. Andersen," ARoS Aarhus Kunstmuseum, Aarhus, Denmark

"POPulence," Blaffer Gallery, University of Houston, Houston; Museum of Contemporary Art, Cleveland; and Southeastern Center for Contemporary Art, Winston-Salem, North Carolina

"Moving Energies," Museum Folkwang, Essen, Germany

"Translation," Palais de Tokyo, Paris

"Little Boy: The Arts of Japan's Exploding Subculture," Japan Society, New York

"Colours and Trips," Künstlerhaus Palais Thurn und Taxis, Bregenz, Austria; Museum der Stadt, Ratingen, Germany

2004

"Funny Cuts: Cartoons und Comics in der zeitgenössischen Kunst," Staatsgalerie, Stuttgart, Germany

"International 04," Liverpool Biennial of Contemporary Art, Tate, Liverpool, England

"Walker without Walls," Walker Art Center, Minneapolis

"Monument to Now: The Dakis Joannou Collection," DESTE Foundation for Contemporary Art, Athens

"Modern Means: Continuity and Change in Art, 1880 to the Present," Mori Art Museum, Tokyo

"Optimo: Manifestations of Optimism in Contemporary Art," Ballroom Marfa, Marfa, Texas

"Floating Worlds," Beacon Cultural Foundation, Beacon, New York

Galerie Emmanuel Perrotin, Miami

2003

"Supernova: Art of the 1990s from the Logan Collection," San Francisco Museum of Modern Art, San Francisco

"Popular, Pop & Post-Pop: Color Screenprints 1930s to Now," Philadelphia Museum of Art, Philadelphia

"Pulp Art: Vamps, Villains and Victors from the Robert Lesser Collection,"

Brooklyn Museum of Art, Brooklyn, New York
"Splat Boom Pow! The Influence of Comics in Contemporary Art," Contemporary Arts Museum, Houston
"The Doraemon Exhibition," Sogo Museum, Yokohama, Japan; Hokkaido Asahikawa Museum of Art, Asahikawa, Japan; Matsuzakaya Museum, Nagoya, Japan; and Oita Museum, Oita, Japan
"Painting Pictures: Painting and Media in the Digital Age," Kunstmuseum, Wolfsburg, Germany
"On the Wall: Wallpaper and Tableau," Rhode Island School of Design, Providence; and The Fabric Workshop and Museum, Philadelphia
"Comic Release: Negotiating Identity for a New Generation," Regina Gouger Miller Gallery, Carnegie Mellon University, Pittsburgh
Inaugural Exhibition, Mori Art Center, Tokyo
Blum & Poe, Santa Monica, California
"Pittura/Painting: Da Rauschenberg a Murakami, 1964–2003," Museo Correr, L Venice Biennale, Venice, Italy

2002
"The Japanese Experience—Inevitable," Museum der Moderne Salzburg, Salzburg, Austria
"Drawing Now: Eight Propositions," The Museum of Modern Art, New York
"Reality Check: Painting in the Exploded Field, Selections from the Vicki and Kent Logan Collection," CCAC Wattis Institute for Contemporary Arts, San Francisco
"Chiho Aoshima, Mr., Takashi Murakami, Aya Takano," Galerie Emmanuel Perrotin, Paris
"Out of the Box: 20th-Century Print Portfolios," Philadelphia Museum of Art, Philadelphia
"The Uncanny: Experiments in Cyborg Culture," Vancouver Art Gallery, Vancouver, Canada
"POPJack: Warhol to Murakami," Museum of Contemporary Art, Denver

2001
"Casino 2001," 1st Quadrennial of Contemporary Art, Stedelijk Museum voor Actuele Kunst, Ghent, Belgium
"Jap in a Box: Mr., Tam Ochiai, Hiroshi Sugito, Yoshitomo Nara, Takashi Murakami, Masahiko Kuwahara," Stephen Friedman Gallery, London
"Form Follows Fiction," Castello di Rivoli, Museo d'Arte Contemporanea, Turin, Italy
"Murakami/Nara," Tomio Koyama Gallery, Tokyo
"Beau Monde: Toward a Redeemed Cosmopolitanism," SITE Santa Fe Fourth International Biennial, Santa Fe
"Un art populaire," Fondation Cartier pour l'art contemporain, Paris
"JAM: Tokyo—London," Barbican Art Gallery, London
"Made in Asia?," Duke University Museum of Art, Durham, North Carolina
"Public Offerings," The Museum of Contemporary Art, Los Angeles
"Painting at the Edge of the World," Walker Art Center, Minneapolis
"My Reality: Contemporary Art and the Culture of Japanese Animation," Des Moines Art Center, Des Moines; Brooklyn Museum of Art, Brooklyn, New York; Contemporary Arts Center, Cincinnati; Tampa Museum of Art, Tampa, Florida; Chicago Cultural Center, Chicago; Akron Art Museum, Akron, Ohio; Norton Museum of Art, West Palm Beach, Florida; Museum of Glass, Tacoma, Washington; and Huntsville Museum of Art, Huntsville, Alabama
"Under Pressure," Swiss Institute, New York; and Museum of Contemporary Art, Tucson
"Superflat," The Museum of Contemporary Art, Los Angeles; Walker Art Center, Minneapolis; and Henry Art Gallery, Seattle

2000
"Gendai: Contemporary Japanese Art, Between Body and Space," Centre for Contemporary Art, Ujazdowski Castle, Warsaw
"Twisted: Urban and Visionary Landscapes in Contemporary Painting," Stedelijk Van Abbemuseum, Eindhoven, The Netherlands
"The Darker Side of Playland: Childhood Imagery from the Logan Collection," San Francisco Museum of Modern Art, San Francisco
"Balls," James Cohan Gallery, New York
"00: Drawings 2000," Barbara Gladstone Gallery, New York
"Partage d'exotismes," 5e Biennale d'Art Contemporain, Lyon, France

"Yume no āto/Was vom Traum blieb...: Zeitgenössische Kunst aus Japan," Haus am Waldsee, Berlin; and Staatliche Kunsthalle, Baden-Baden, Germany

"Continental Shift: Eine Reise zwischen den Kulturen," Ludwig Forum für Internationale Kunst, Aachen, Germany

"Superflat," Parco Museum, Tokyo; and Parco Gallery, Nagoya, Japan

"One Heart, One World" United Nations, New York

"Let's Entertain: Life's Guilty Pleasures," Walker Art Center, Minneapolis; Portland Art Museum, Portland, Oregon; Centre Georges Pompidou, Paris; Kunstmuseum, Wolfsburg, Germany; Museo Rufino Tamayo, Mexico City; and Miami Art Museum, Miami

Marianne Boesky Gallery, New York

"Takashi Murakami—Miltos Manetas," NewSantandrea, Savona, Italy; and pinksummer, Genoa, Italy

"Pleasure Zone," Migros Museum für Gegenwartskunst, Zurich, Switzerland

1999

"Ground Zero Japan," Mito Art Tower, Ibaraki, Japan

"Colour Me Blind! Malerei in Zeiten von Computergame und Comic," Württembergischer Kunstverein, Stuttgart, Germany; Städtische Ausstellungshalle am Hawerkamp, Münster, Germany; and Dundee Contemporary Arts, Dundee, Scotland

Carnegie International 1999/2000, Carnegie Museum of Art, Pittsburgh

"Almost Warm and Fuzzy: Childhood and Contemporary Art," Des Moines Art Center, Des Moines; Tacoma Art Museum, Tacoma, Washington; Scottsdale Museum of Contemporary Art, Scottsdale, Arizona; P.S.1 Contemporary Art Center, Long Island City, New York; Fundacio "la Caixa," Barcelona, Spain; Crocker Art Museum, Sacramento; Art Gallery of Hamilton, Hamilton, Canada; Memphis Brooks Museum of Art, Memphis; and Cleveland Center for Contemporary Art, Cleveland

"LEGO DELUXE-LEGO EXHIBITION," Shibuya Parco, Tokyo; Sapporo Parco, Sapporo, Japan; and Nagoya Parco, Nagoya, Japan

"Painting for Joy: New Japanese Painting in the 1990s," The Japan Foundation Forum, Tokyo

"Balloon Art Festival," Shizuoka Prefectural Convention & Art Center, Shizuoka, Japan

"Pleasure Dome," Jessica Fredericks Gallery, New York

"New Modernism for a New Millennium: Works by Contemporary Asian Artists from the Logan Collection," San Francisco Museum of Modern Art, San Francisco

1998

"Tastes and Pursuits: Japanese Art in the 1990s," National Gallery of Modern Art, New Delhi, India

"Ero Pop Christmas," NADiff, Tokyo

"50 Years of Japanese Lifestyle Postwar Fashion & Design," Utsunomiya Museum of Art, Ibaraki, Japan

"Fluffy," Dunlop Art Gallery, Regina, Canada; capc Musée d'art contemporain, Bordeaux, France; P.S.1 Contemporary Art Center, New York; Louisiana Museum of Modern Art, Humlebaek, Denmark; Hayward Gallery, London; and Museum of Modern Art Kiasma, Helsinki

"The MANGA Age," Museum of Contemporary Art, Tokyo; Hiroshima City Museum of Contemporary Art, Hiroshima, Japan

"Abstract Painting, Once Removed," Contemporary Arts Museum, Houston

"Donaiyanen! Et maintenant!—La création contemporaine au Japon," Ecole nationale supérieure des beaux-arts, Paris

"Art Is Fun 9: Hand Craft and Time Craft," Hara Museum Arc, Gunma, Japan

"People, Places, Things," Marianne Boesky Gallery, New York

"Pop Surrealism," The Aldrich Contemporary Art Museum, Ridgefield, Connecticut

"Ero Pop Tokyo," George's, Los Angeles

Biennale d'art contemporain, Nouméa, New Caledonia

1997

"The 33rd 'Artists Today' Exhibition: Singularity in Plurality," Yokohama Civic Art Gallery, Yokohama, Japan

"Need for Speed," Kunstverein, Graz, Austria

"Japanese Contemporary Art Exhibition," National Museum of Contemporary Art, Seoul

"Hiropon Show '97," Shop 33, Tokyo

"Japan Today: Kunst, Fotographie, Design," MAK—Austrian Museum of Applied Arts, Vienna

"Super Body," Tomio Koyama Gallery, Tokyo
"Flying Buttress Please," Torch Gallery, Amsterdam
"Cities on the Move: Contemporary Asian Art on the Turn of the 21st Century," Weiner Secession, Vienna; capc Musée d'art contemporain, Bordeaux, France; P.S.1 Contemporary Art Center, Long Island City, New York

1996
Second Asia-Pacific Triennial of Contemporary Art, Queensland Art Gallery, Queensland, Australia
"Ironic Fantasy: Another World by Five Contemporary Artists," The Miyagi Museum of Art, Sendai, Japan
"The Time of the Pleasure of Art: Art for the Hearts of Children," Isetan Museum, Tokyo
"Tokyo Pop," The Hiratsuka Museum of Art, Kanagawa, Japan
"Sharaku Interpreted by Japan's Contemporary Artists," The Japan Foundation Forum, Tokyo
"The 39th Annual Yasui Prize Exhibition," Sezon Museum of Modern Art, Tokyo
"Romper Room," Thread Waxing Space, New York

1995
"Cutting Up," Max Protetch Gallery, New York
"Japan Today," Louisiana Museum of Modern Art, Humlebaek, Denmark; Kunsternes Hus, Oslo; Liljevalchs Konsthall, Stockholm; and Wäinö Aaltonen Museum of Art, Turku, Finland
"Transculture," 46th Venice Biennale, Venice; and Benesse House, Naoshima Contemporary Art Museum, Kanagawa, Japan
"Blind Beach," Art Space HAP, Hiroshima, Japan
"Incidental Alterations: P.S.1 Studio Artists 1994–95," The Angel Orensanz Foundation, New York

1994
"Open Air '94, Out of Bounds: Contemporary Art in the Seascape," Benesse House, Naoshima Contemporary Art Museum, Kanagawa, Japan
"The Youthful Time of Japanese Nihonga Artists from Taikan and Shunsō to DOB," Koriyama City Museum of Art, Koriyama, Japan
"Artists in Yokohama 94," Yokohama Citizens' Gallery, Yokohama, Japan
"Lest We Forget: On Nostalgia," The Gallery at Takashimaya, New York
"Shinjuku Shonen Art," Shinjuku Kabukicho, Tokyo
"VOCA '94," The Ueno Royal Museum, Tokyo

1993
"The Exhibition for Exhibitions," Kyoto Shijo Gallery, Kyoto, Japan
"Beyond Nihonga: An Aspect of Contemporary Japanese Paintings," Tokyo Metropolitan Art Museum, Tokyo
"Art Today '93, Neo-Japanology," Sezon Museum of Modern Art, Karuizawa, Japan
"oo Collaboration," Sagacho Exhibit Space, Tokyo
"The Ginbrart," Ginza, Tokyo
"Malaria Art Show, Vol. 4," Decorative, Tokyo
"Malaria Art Show, Vol. 1," February 1st Festival, Tokyo
"Artist's Shop '93,"Sai Gallery, Osaka, Japan

1992
"Nakamura and Murakami," Space Ozone, Seoul; SCAI The Bathhouse, Tokyo; Metaria Square Hotel, Osaka, Japan; and NICAF '93, Pacifico Yokohama, Yokohama, Japan
"Tama Vivant '92," Seed Hall, Shibuya Seibu, Tokyo
"Anomaly," Röntgen Kunst Institut, Tokyo
"Floating Gallery Vol. 1," Tsukishima Warehouse, Tokyo
"1st Transart Annual Painting/Crossing," Bellini Hill Gallery, Yokohama, Japan
"Artist's Shop '92," Sai Gallery, Osaka, Japan
Mars Gallery, Tokyo
NICAF Art Fair, Yokohama, Japan

1991
"Jan Hoet's Vision," Art Gallery Artium, Fukuoka, Japan
"Jan Hoet in Tsurugi," Tsurugi-cho, Ishikawa, Japan

1988
"Graduation Exhibition," Tokyo National University of Fine Arts and Music, Tokyo
Metropolitan Art Museum, Tokyo

Curated Exhibitions

2005
"Little Boy: The Arts of Japan's Exploding Subculture," Japan Society, New York

2004
"Tokyo Girls Bravo," Marianne Boesky Gallery, New York
"Chiho Aoshima, Mr., and Aya Takano," Galerie Emmanuel Perrotin at LFL Gallery, New York

2002
"Coloriage," Fondation Cartier pour l'art contemporain, Paris

2001
"Hiropon Show," Museum of Contemporary Art, Tokyo
"Superflat," The Museum of Contemporary Art, Los Angeles; Walker Art Center, Minneapolis; and Henry Art Gallery, Seattle

2000
"Superflat," Parco Gallery, Tokyo; and Parco Gallery, Nagoya, Japan
"Aya Takano: Hot Banana Fudge," NADiff, Tokyo

1999
"Hiropon 32/80," NADiff, Tokyo
"Tokyo Girls Bravo," NADiff, Tokyo; and George's, Los Angeles
"Hiropon Show," Parco Gallery, Nagoya, Japan; and Parco Gallery, Tokyo

1998
"Mr.: O-Edo Kunoichi Ninpocho," Shop 33, Tokyo
"Ero Pop Tokyo," George's, Los Angeles

1997
"Aya Takano: God Is Coming," Shop 33, Tokyo
"Tokyo Sex," NAS, Tokyo
"Hiropon Show," Shop 33, Tokyo; Manken Gallery, Kanazawa College of Arts, Kanazawa, Japan; and Iwataya Z-SIDE W<, Fukuoka, Japan

1996
"Mr. Solo Exhibition: Frone & Perrine," Shop 33, Tokyo
"Pico Pico Show," Saga-cho bis, Tokyo

Grants and Awards

2006
Heisei 17 (56th) Educational Minister Rookie of the Year, Awarded by the Agency for Cultural Affairs for the Advancement of Art
"Best Thematic Museum Show in New York City," International Association of Art Critics
11th AMD Awards, Prize of Recognition

2005
Imajiné Award, Japan Society

2004
Honorary Knighthood, Les Compagnons du Beaujolais
Tag Heuer Business Award

2003
Special Award, 46th Japan Fashion Editor Club Awards

1998
Visiting Professor, School of the Arts and Architecture, University of California, Los Angeles

Catalogues and Publications

00: *Drawings 2000 at Barbara Gladstone Gallery*. Exh. cat. New York: Barbara Gladstone Gallery, 2000. Text by Klaus Kertess.

Alonzo, Pedro, and Peter Doroshenko, eds. *Spank the Monkey*. Exh. cat. Gateshead, England: Baltic Centre for Contemporary Art; and Berlin: Die Gestalten Verlag, 2006.

Arnason, H. H., and Peter Kalb. *History of Modern Art*. 5th ed. Upper Saddle River, New Jersey: Prentice Hall, 2003.

Baqué, Dominique. *Pour un nouvel art politique: De l'art contemporain au documentaire*. Paris: Flammarion, 2004.

Beau Monde: Toward a Redeemed Cosmopolitanism—SITE Santa Fe's Fourth International Biennial. Exh. cat. Santa Fe: SITE Santa Fe, 2001. Essay by Dave Hickey.

Bloemheuvel, Marente, and Jaap Guldemond. *Twisted: Urban and Visionary Landscapes in Contemporary Painting*. Exh. cat. Eindhoven, The Netherlands: Stedelijk Van Abbemuseum, 2000.

Brehm, Margrit, ed. *The Japanese Experience—Inevitable*. Exh. cat. Ostfildern-Ruit, Germany: Hatje Cantz Verlag, 2002. Texts by Brehm and Gregor Jansen.

Carnegie International 1999/2000. Exh. cat. 2 vols. Pittsburgh: Carnegie Museum of Art, 1999.

Chiezō: Asahi gendai yōgō jiten (Asahi contemporary usage dictionary). Tokyo: Asahi Shimbun-sha, 2006.

Childhood Imagery from the Logan Collection: The Darker Side of Playland. Exh. cat. San Francisco: San Francisco Museum of Modern Art, 2000.

Coetzee, Mark. *Not Afraid: Rubell Family Collection*. London: Phaidon, 2004.

La collezione François Pinault: Una selezione Post-Pop. Exh. cat. Venice, Italy: Palazzo Grassi, 2006.

Comic Release: Negotiating Identity for a New Generation. New York: D.A.P./Distributed Art Publishers, 2002.

Dailey, Meghan, Sarah Valdez, and Jane Harris. *Curve: The Female Nude Now*. New York: Universe Publishing, 2003.

Deitch, Jeffrey, ed. *Monument to Now: The Dakis Joannou Collection*. Exh. cat. Athens: DESTE Foundation for Contemporary Art, 2004. Texts by Dan Cameron, Deitch, Alison M. Gingeras, Massimiliano Gioni, and Nancy Spector.

DOB in the Strange Forest: Takashi Murakami. Tokyo: Bijutsu Shuppansha, 1999.

Domela, Paul. *International 04*. Exh. cat. Liverpool, England: Liverpool Biennial of Contemporary Art, 2004.

Dragon Veins. Exh. cat. Tampa, Florida: Contemporary Art Museum, University of South Florida, 2006

Eccles, Tom, Anne Wehr, and Jeff Kastner. *Plop: Recent Projects of the Public Art Fund*. London: Merrell, 2004.

Fairy Tales Forever: Homage to H. C. Andersen. Exh. cat. Aarhus, Denmark: ARoS Aarhus Kunstmuseum, 2005.

Farthing, Stephen, ed. *1001 Paintings You Must See Before You Die*. New York: Universe, 2007.

Fogle, Douglas, ed. *Painting at the Edge of the World*. Exh. cat. Minneapolis: Walker Art Center, 2001. Includes texts by Fogle, Midori Matsui, and Takashi Murakami.

Funny Cuts: Cartoons und Comics in der zeitgenössischen Kunst. Exh. cat. Bielefeld, Germany: Kerber Verlag; and Stuttgart: Staatsgalerie, 2005. Texts by Kassandra Nakas, Ulrich Pfarr, and Andreas Schalhorn.

Gasparina, Jill. *Imaginaire: Mode d'emploi*. Paris: Editions Cercle d'Art, 2007.

Getlein, Mark. *Gilbert's Living with Art*. 7th ed. New York: McGraw-Hill, 2005.

Giard, Agnès. *L'imaginaire érotique au Japon*. Paris: Albin Michel, 2006.

Grenville, Bruce, ed. *The Uncanny: Experiments in Cyborg Culture*. Exh. cat. Vancouver: Vancouver Art Gallery and Arsenal Pulp Press, 2001.

Grosenick, Uta, ed. *Art Now, vol. 2: The New Directory to 136 International Contemporary Artists*. Cologne, Germany: Taschen, 2005.

Grynsztejn, Madeleine, ed. *Supernova: Art of the 1990s from the Logan Collection*. Exh. cat. San Francisco: San Francisco Museum of Modern Art; and New York: D.A.P./Distributed Art Publishers, 2003. Texts by Dan Cameron, Amada Cruz, Clara Kim, Jessica Morgan, Ralph Rugoff, and Katy Siegel.

Hoptman, Laura. *Drawing Now: Eight Propositions*. Exh. cat. New York: The Museum of Modern Art, 2002.

Ironic Fantasy: Another World by Five Contemporary Artists. Exh. cat. Miyagi, Japan: The Miyagi Museum of Art, 1996.

Japan Today: Kunst, Fotografie, Design. Exh. cat. Vienna: MAK—Austrian Museum of Applied Arts, 1997.

Kitagawa, Yujin. *Keba Keba*. Asaka, Japan: Kaikai Kiki Co., Ltd., 2003. Artwork by Takashi Murakami.

Köhn, Stephan, and Martina Schönbein, eds. *Facetten der japanischen Populär- und Medienkultur*. Wiesbaden, Germany: Harrassowitz Verlag, 2005.

Kyozon. Exh. cat. Kamloops, Canada: Kamloops Art Gallery, 2002. Essays by Kevin Ei-ichi DeForest, Monika Kin Gagnon, and Yoichi Kimura.

Lazzari, Margaret, and Dona Schlesier. *Exploring Art: A Global, Thematic Approach*. 3rd ed. Belmont, California: Thomson Wadsworth, 2007.

Lest We Forget: On Nostalgia. Exh. cat. New York: The Gallery at Takashimaya, 1994. Texts by Lynn Gumpert and Thomas W. Sokolowski.

Let's Entertain: Life's Guilty Pleasures. Exh. cat. Minneapolis: Walker Art Center, 2000.

Marcoci, Roxana, ed. *Comic Abstraction: Image Breaking, Image Making*. Exh. cat. New York: The Museum of Modern Art, 2007.

Munroe, Alexandra. "Hinomaru Illumination: Japanese Art of the 1990s." In Munroe, ed. *Japanese Art After 1945: Scream Against the Sky*, 339–50. Exh. cat. New York: Harry N. Abrams, 1994.

Murakami, Takashi. *Superflat*. Exh. cat. Tokyo: MADRA Publishing, 2000.

———, ed. *Little Boy: The Arts of Japan's Exploding Subculture*. Exh. cat. New York: Japan Society; and New Haven, Connecticut: Yale University Press, 2005.

———. *Geijutsu kigyōron* (The theory of art entrepreneurship). Tokyo: Gentosha, 2006.

My Reality: Contemporary Art and the Culture of Japanese Animation. Des Moines: Des Moines Art Center; and New York: Independent Curators International, 2001. Texts by Jeff Fleming, Takashi Murakami, and Susan Lubowsky Talbott.

Nanjō, Fumio, Dana Friis-Hansen, Akiko Miki, Yukie Kamiya, Anne Longnecker Dodds, and Yōko Miyahara. *Transculture: La Biennale di Venezia 1995*. Exh. cat. Tokyo : The Japan Foundation, 1995.

New Modernism for a New Millennium: Works by Contemporary Asian Artists from the Logan Collection. San Francisco: San Francisco Museum of Modern Art, 1999.

Nichiyō bijutsukan 1976–2006 (Sunday museum 1976–2006). Tokyo: NHK Publishing, 2007.

Nyssen, Françoise. *Takashi Murakami: Kaikai Kiki*. Arles, France: Éditions Actes Sud, 2002.

Ōshita, Kentarō. *Rikitekkusu taizen* (Liquitex creation guide). Tokyo: Bijutsu Shuppansha, 2004.

Painting Codes: I codici della pittura. Exh. cat. Montfalcone, Italy: Galleria Comunale d'Arte Contemporanea; and Cormons, Italy: Poligrafiche San Marco, 2006. Texts by Andrea Bruciati and Alessandra Galasso.

Painting Pictures: Painting and Media in the Digital Age. Exh. cat. Wolfsburg, Germany: Kunstmuseum; and Bielefeld: Kerber Verlag, 2003.

Parisot, Cecile, and Francois-Xavier Robert. *Tokyo Itinéraires*. Ed. WakuWaku. Paris: Association WakuWaku, 2006.

Phoenix, Woodrow. *Plastic Culture: How Japanese Toys Conquered the World*. Tokyo: Kodansha International, 2006.

A Portrait of Our Times: An Introduction to the Logan Collection. San Francisco: San Francisco Museum of Modern Art, 1998.

Pretty Baby. Exh. cat. Forth Worth, Texas: Modern Art Museum of Fort Worth, 2007.

Radar: Selections from the Collection of Vicki and Kent Logan. Denver: Denver Art Museum, 2006.

Reality Check: Painting in the Exploded Field—Selections from the Vicki and Kent Logan Collection. Exh. cat. San Francisco: CCAC Wattis Institute for Contemporary Art, 2002. Essay by Matthew Higgs.

Reiner, Randi and Phil Tinari. *Made in Asia?* Exh. cat. Durhan, North Carolina: Duke University Museum of Art, 2001.

Schimmel, Paul, ed. *Public Offerings*. Exh. cat. Los Angeles: The Museum of Contemporary Art; and New York: Thames and Hudson, 2001. Essays by Yilmaz Dziewior, Midori Matsui, Lane Relyea, Schimmel, Katy Siegel, Howard Singerman, and Jon Thompson.

———, ed. *Ecstasy: In and About Altered States*. Exh. cat. Los Angeles: The Museum of Contemporary Art; and Cambridge, Massachusetts: The MIT Press, 2005. Essays by Carolyn Christov-Bakargiev, Diedrich Diederichsen, Chrissie Iles, Lars Bang Larsen, Midori Matsui, and Schimmel.

Siegel, Katy, and Paul Mattick. *Art Works: Money*. New York: Thames & Hudson, 2004.

Takashi Murakami: Summon Monsters? Open the Door? Heal? Or Die? Exh. cat. Tokyo: Museum of Contemporary Art, 2001. Essays by Michael Darling, Yūsuke Minami, and Takashi Murakami.

Takashi Murakami: The Meaning of the Nonsense of the Meaning. Exh. cat. Annandale-on-Hudson, New York: Center for Curatorial Studies Museum, Bard College; and New York: Harry N. Abrams, 1999. Essays by Amada Cruz, Midori Matsui, and Dana Friis-Hansen.

Takashi Murakami: "Which Is Tomorrow?—Fall in Love." Exh. cat. Tokyo: Masami Shiraishi Contemporary Art, Inc., and SCAI The Bathhouse, 1994. Essay by Midori Matsui.

The 33rd "Artists Today" Exhibition: Singularity in Plurality. Exh. cat. Yokohama, Japan: Yokohama Civic Art Gallery, 1997.

Tillon, Fabien. *Culture Manga*. Paris: Nouveau Monde Editions, 2006.

Vitamin P: New Perspectives in Painting. London: Phaidon Press, 2002.

Washburn, Dennis. *Translating Mount Fuji: Modern Japanese Fiction and the Ethics of Identity*, cover. New York: Columbia University Press, 2006.

"Where Are We Going?" Selections from the François Pinault Collection. Exh. cat. Milan, Italy: Skira Editore; and Venice: Palazzo Grassi, 2006.

Articles and Reviews

Abbe, Mary. "Japanese Youth Culture Explodes in Walker Art Center Show." *Star Tribune*, 20 July 2001, F2.

Adam, Georgina. "Murakami to Launch Basel Fair Next Year" *Art Newspaper* (12 June 2007): 1.

Adato, Allison, Anne Driscoll, and Christian Storms. "New York City Braces for an Alien Invasion." *People* 60, no. 11 (15 September 2003): 75–76.

Aidin, Rose. "Fashion Imitating Art." *Telegraph Magazine* (November 2002): 50–53.

———. "Tokyo Rising." *Vogue UK* (November 2002): 75–78.

Albertini, Rosanna. "Superflat." *Art Press* (May 2001): 12–14.

Alleti, Vince, and Kim Levin. "Fair Game." *The Village Voice*, 21 May 1996.

Álvarez Castroviejo, Julen. "Poku: The Japanese Influence." *Lapiz*, no. 204 (June 2004): 34–49.

"Art." *House & Garden* (February 2007).

"Art and About." *Marie Claire South Africa* (November 2006): 11.

"Art Is Good Business." *Elle Taiwan* (September 2004): 214–15.

"Artist's Favorites by Takashi Murakami." *Spike Art Quarterly* (spring 2006): 10–11.

"Artists without Borders." *Brutus Japan* (September 2001). Special Takashi Murakami/Yoshitomo Nara issue.

"Artnet News: Murakami Mushroom Mania Rocks Rock Center." *Artnet Magazine* (10 September 2003), available at http://www.artnet.com/magazine/news/artnetnews2/artnetnews9-10-03.asp.

"Arty Facts." *Habitat* (November–December 2006): 122.

Asano, Masahiko. "Art to otaku no suteki na kaigō" (A beautiful meeting of art and *otaku*). *Replicant* (summer 2004): 108, 115.

———. "Otaku no teki: Murakami Takashi no meikaku naru henkō" (An enemy of *otaku*: The clear transformation of Takashi Murakami). *Bijutsu Techō* (June 2005): 104–09.

Azimi, Roxana. "Murakami, un cas sur le marché de l'art." *Le Monde*, 22–23 October 2006, 22.

Barker, Godfrey. "Smile! Your Prices Have Just Gone Up." *Art Review* (July–August 2003): 23–25.

Bates, Rob. "A Different Toon." *Smock* (July 2000).

Bayliss, Sarah. "The New Art Wallpaper: It Doesn't Just Hang There." *The New York Times*, 29 June 2003.

"Bei: Besuto tenrankai: Tēma bumon ni Murakami-san" (America: Best exhibition, Murakami-*san* wins in the themed category). *Yomiuri Shinbun Yūkan*, 13 February 2006, 15.

"Bei NY, saiyūshū tēma shō: Murakami Takashi-san kikaku no "Ritoru Bōi ni" (NY, USA: Mr. Takashi Murakami's "Little Boy" wins best themed show). *Asahi Shinbun*, 28 February 2006, 27.

Bellars, Peter. "If you can't beat' em." *Asahi Evening News*, 1 July 1994.

Bellet, Harry. "Les paradoxes de Murakami." *Le Monde*, 21 October 2006.

Bensinger, Ken. "The Gift That Might Start Giving." *The Wall Street Journal*, 22 December 2000, C3.

Bernard, Kate. "Out on the Toon." *Tatler* (February 2003).

Beyer, Charles. "Murakami's Mad World." *Gotham* (March 2001): 206–07.

Bijutsu Techō (November 2001): 9–112. Takashi Murakami special feature.

"Birds of a Feather: GEISAI #10." *Ish* (March 2006): 20–21.

Birnbaum, Molly. "The Best of Tomes." *ArtNews* (November 2006): 50.

Bizio, Silvia, and Barbara Casavecchia. " 6 chiavi per entrare nel futuro." *La Repubblica delle donne* (March 2004): 145–54.

Blum, Timothy, and Jon Kessler. "Made in Japan: Otaku: Home Alone." *Documents* (February 1993): 31–36.

Bonacossa, Ilaria. "Beyond Japanese Flatness" (interview). *Label* (winter 2005–06): 72–77.

Bonisteel, Sara. "Factory Man, New York Gets its Second Wave of Murakami as the Japanese 'Warhol' Transforms Rock Center." *New York Resident* (25 August 2003): 31.

Bors, Chris. "Report from Paris." *Artnet Magazine* (2 March 2007).

Boukobza, Julie. "Takashi Murakami." *L'Officiel de la couture et de la mode de paris* (November 2006).

Bourbon, Aude de. "Kawaii Murakami." *Chronic Art* (summer 2002): 65.

Brener, Julie. "Eye-Openers." *ArtNews* (November 2006): 122–26.

Budick, Ariella. "Meet 'Mr. Pointy': You'll Find Takashi Murakami Teasing You Somewhere between High Art and Low." *Newsday*, 22 September 2003, B6.

"Burando no-hau ikasu" (Using brand know-how). *Nihon Keizai Shinbun*, 24 March 2007.

"Calendar." *South African Home Owner* (December 2006–January 2007): 245.

Callick, Roman. "Make Way for Japan." *The American* (July–August 2007): 60–69.

Cazenave, François. "Les Mangas chez Cartier." *Air France* (June 2002): 156.

Chang, Alexandra. "Takeo Baba: Reinventing the Self." *Art Asia Pacific*, no. 39 (winter 2004): 30–32.

Charlesworth, J. J. "Takashi Murakami: Something Like a Phenomenon." *Art Review* (January 2007): 62–67.

———. "Under the Influence." *Art Review* (September 2004): 30–31.

Chen, Aric. "Paste-Testing the New Wallpaper." *The New York Times*, 13 February 2003.

Clem, Chivas. "Vuitton's Got a Brand New Bag." *Time Out New York* (1–8 May 2003): 61.

Colman, David. "Deep Inside Japan's Psyche." *The New York Times*, 8 May 2005.

Cooper, Jacqueline. "Superflat." *New Art Examiner* (September–October 2001): 58–65.

Corrigan, Susan. "Biff! Bang! Pow! Japan Goes Pop." *I-D Magazine* (May 2001): 106–10.

Cotter, Holland. "Carving a Pop Niche in Japan's Classical Tradition." *The New York Times*, 24 June 2001, 31–32.

Couturier, Elisabeth. "Murakami: Le Japonais qui cannibalise l'art moderne." *Paris Match* (19–25 October 2006): 26, 28.

Darling, Michael. "The Fire Hose Lariats of Takashi Murakami at Blum & Poe in Santa Monica." *D'art International* (fall 1998).

———. "Plumbing the Depths of Superflatness." *Art Journal* 60, no. 3 (fall 2001): 67–89.

Darren, Ressler. "Vision: Murakami." *Big Shot* (April 2005): 20–23.

Deitz, Paula. "Rice Paddy in the Sky." *The New York Times*, 7 March 2004.

Demir, Anaïd. "Kaikaï Art: Murakami Factory." *Jalouse* (November 2006).

Denny, Ned. "Cartoon Death." *New Statesman* (25 November 2002).

De Rochebouët, Béatrice. "Le sacre des stars du contemporain." *Le Figaro*, 17 November 2006.

Design Plex (December 1998): 6–17.

"Digital Contents of the Year '05: Lifetime Achievement Award," japan.internet.com, 24 January 2006.

DiPietro, Monty. "Seeing in the Rain." *ArtNews* (May 2000).

Dollar, Steve. "Japan, the Monster of Pop." *Newsday*, 8 April 2005, B4.

"Donaiyanen! et maintenant! La création contemporaine au Japon." *Ecole Nationale Superieure des Beaux Arts* (September 1998): 74–77.

"Doraemon NY jōriku" (Doraemon arrives on NY's shores). *Motto Doraemon* (spring 2005): 16.

Douaire, Pierre-Evariste, and Betty Dahmers. "Takashi Murakami: The Pressure Point of Painting." *BING* (January–April 2007): 10–17.

Drohojowska-Philp, Hunter. "Pop Go the Usual Boundaries." *Los Angeles Times*, 14 January 2001, 4, 79–80.

Dufay, Philippe. "Takashi Murakami: L'homme qui murmure à l'oreille des fleurs." *Madame Figaro*, 28 October 2006, 66–67.

Duponchelle, Valérie, and Béatrice de Rochebouët. "La Fiac 2006, de retour au coeur de Paris a misé sur l'atout lumiere du Grand Palais." *Le Figaro et vous*, 26 October 2006, 28–29.

"Exhibition to See." *Vogue Nippon* (July 2005): 51.

Falkenstein, Michelle. "Connect, Then Collect." *ArtNews* (January 2007): 102–05.

Firmin-Didob, Catherine. "Une sous-culture qui s'assume." *Télérama* (August 2002): 17–18.

"Flights of Fancy." *IDN* 10 (September 2003): 1–16.

Fox, Dan, and Mami Kataoka. "Tokyo." *Frieze*, no. 104 (January–February 2007): 146–53.

Frank, Peter. "Cultural Flatland." *Art on Paper* (March–April 2001): 22.

Frederick, Jim. "Move Over, Andy Warhol." *Time Magazine Japan* (26 May 2003): 42–44.

———. "What's Right with Japan." *Time Magazine Japan* (11 August 2003).

Friedman, Tom. "Superflat Monogram." *The New York Sun*, 1 May 2003.

Friis-Hansen, Dana. "Empire of Goods." *Flash Art* (March–April 1992).

———. Review. *The Japan Times Weekly* (7 March 1992).

Fujimori, Manami. *Bijutsu Techō* (April 1999): 133.

———. "Hontō ni yaritai no wa animēshon nandesu" (What I really want to do is animation). *OCS News*, 27 February 2004, 2–3.

Fujitsu, Ryōta. "Superflat: Battle of America." *Bijutsu Techō* (April 2001): 179–90.

Fujiwara, Erimi. "Artists without Borders Nara, Murakami." *Brutus Japan* (1 September 2001): 30–75, 122–29.

———. "'Otaku' o 'bijutsu' ni honyaku shituzuketa bōsō no 14nenkan" (14 years burning up the road translating '*otaku*' into 'art'). *Bijutsu Techō* (July 2005): 62–72.

———. "Takashi Murakami: Conceptual Art of the New Generation." *JA* (March 1992).

"Furansu ni saku Murakami Wārudo" (A world of Murakami blooming in France). *L'Officiel Japon* (January 2007): 172–74.

"Galleries." *Connaissance des Arts* (January 2001).

Galloway, Munro. "Expos/Reviews." *ArtPress*, no. 245 (April 1999): 72–73.

Gardner, Belinda Grace. "Blumenkind." *Architektur & Wohnen* (October–November 2004): 46.

Gardner, James. "Eyeball on Rock Center." *New York Post*, 17 September 2003.

Garry, Gregory. "Making a Pointy." *Flaunt* (October 2003).

"Geijutsu senshō bunka daijin shō" (Educational minister rookie of the year, advancement of art award). *Asahi Shinbun*, 16 March 2006, 37.

"GEISAI #10." *Bijutsu Techō* (November 2006): 130–37.

Génies, Bernard. "Takashi Murakami: Ivre de peinture." *Le Nouvel Observateur*, 26 October–1 November 2006.

Gilman-Sevcik, Františka and Tim. "Post-Defeat Culture." *Umělec* (Prague), no. 4 (2001).

———."Their Fantasy." *Umělec* (Prague), no. 4 (2001).

Gioni, Massimiliano. "New York Cut Up: Fragments from the Big Apple." *Flash Art*, no. 218 (May–June 2001): 97–99.

Goldberg, Itzhak. "Art et Humour." *Beaux Arts*, no. 171 (August 1998).

Gomez, Edward M. "The Fine Art of Biting into Japanese Cuteness." *The New York Times*, 18 July 1999.

Gopnik, Blake. "A Declaration of Resplendence." *The Washington Post*, 22 July 2001, G1.

———. "Twisted 'Toys': Takashi Murakami's Pop Art." *The Washington Post*, 15 July 2001, G1.

Goumarre, Laurent. "La violence du joli." *Têtu* (July–August 2002): 106–08.

Grabner, Michelle. "Painting at the Edge of the World." *Frieze*, no. 60 (June–August 2001): 116–17.

Greene, David A. "Exposure." *Spin* (March 1999): 64–65.
Griffin, Tim. "Pop Connection." *Vogue* (May 2001): 188.
———. "Left Wanting." *Artforum* (September 2003): 180–81, 246, 251.
Gropp, Rose-Maria. "Leben in der perfekten Kunst-Welt." *Frankfurter Allgemeine Zeitung*, 14 November 1998.
Gurewitsch, Matthew. "Perpetual Adolescence as a Counterweight to History." *The Wall Street Journal*, 7 April 2005, D8.
Hackworth, Nick. "Disturbing Visit to 'Toon Town." *The Evening Standard* (London), 14 November 2002.
Hageman, William. "Installment Plan." *Chicago Tribune*, 10 May 2001, sec. 5, 5.
Hall, Emily. "Flat-Sexy-Serious: High and Low Culture Collapse in the Nicest Possible Way in *Superflat*." *The Stranger* (Seattle) (8–14 November 2001): 14–15.
Halle, Howard. "Anime Kingdom." *Time Out New York*, 18–25 September 2003, 22–23.
———. "Man of the Moment." *GQ* (August 2003): 27.
Hara, Makiko. "Contemporary Japanese Art: Young Artists, Consumer Culture and Internationalization." *Parachute* (October–December 1997).
Harvey, Doug. "Superflat at Museum of Contemporary Art." *Art Issues*, no. 67 (March–April 2001): 53.
———. "P.O.'d: On MOCA's 'Public Offerings.'" *L.A. Weekly* (11–17 May 2001): 50.
Hauser, Kitty. "Superflat." *Artforum* 43, no. 2 (October 2004): 129, 286.
Heartney, Eleanor. "A Marriage of Trauma and Kitsch." *Art in America* 93, no. 9 (October 2005): 56–61.
Henry, Clare. "An Installation Full of Hot Air." *Financial Times*, 17 September 2003.
Hickey, Dave. "The Best of 1998." *Artforum* 37, no. 4 (December 1998): 94–95.
Higa, Karin, ed. "Some Thoughts on National and Cultural Identity: Art by Contemporary Japanese and Japanese American Artists." *Art Journal* (fall 1996): 6–13.
Holmberg, Ryan. "'Little Boy at Japan Society, New York." *Artforum* 44, no. 1 (September 2005): 298–99.
Howe, Jeff. "The Two Faces of Takashi Murakami." *Wired* (November 2003): 180–85.
Huckbody, Jamie. "Shooting from the Hip." *i-D Magazine* (February 2003): 80–85.
I MAGAZINE (December 1998): 14–25.
Iannaccone, Carmine. "Superflat." *Frieze*, no. 60 (June–August 2001): 114.
Ichikawa, Akiko. "Kawaii & otaku wa sekai wo sukuu?" (Cute and otaku will save the world?). *Harper's Bazaar Japan* (July 2005): 32.
"If You Do Nothing Else This Month..." *Top Billing* (Cape Town) (November 2006): 34.
"Ima sekai wo nigiwasu, Tōkyō no poppukaruchā" (Tokyo pop culture is brightening up the world). *Figaro Japon* (September 2003): 220.
"Inochi." *Bijutsu Techō* (July 2004): 11, 12.
"Interview with Takashi Murakami." *East Touch* (Hong Kong) (23 May 2006): 30–31.
Itoi, Kay. "The Wizard of DOB." *ArtNews* (March 2001): 134–37.
———. "Pop Goes the Artist." *Newsweek* (May 2001): 86–87.
———. "Japan's Year of Narakami." *Artnet Magazine* (22 October 2001), available at http://www.artnet.com/magazine/features/itoi/itoi10-22-01-asp.
———. "Japanese Generation Takes Off." *ArtNews* (summer 2002): 90.
———. "Will Murakami Move Geisai Overseas?" *The Art Newspaper* (October 2006): 51.
———. "Murakami's Guide to Success." *Artnet Magazine* (4 October 2006), available at http://www.artnet.com/magazineus/books/itoi/itoi10-4-06.asp.
Johnson, Ken. "The Innocent Yet Sinister Aspects of Japanese Animation." *The New York Times*, 24 August 2001, B30.
———. "Art in Review." *The New York Times*, 2 May 2003.
———. "O Enigma Perched on a Lotus Throne, What's on Your Mind?" *The New York Times*, 26 September 2003, B34.
Joyce, Julie. "Star Blazers: New Pop from Japan." *Art Issues*, no. 54 (September–October 1998): 23–25.
"Juxtapoz Sculpture Gallery 18: Takashi Murakami." *Juxtapoz* 6, no.1 (January–February 1999): 44–45.
Kageyama, Yuri. "Japan's Andy Warhol, Crosses Art with the Mart." *Island Life* (13 July 2003).
Kamecki, Jerzy, and Chihiro Ishida. "Flattening the Walls." *A4 Bazaar* (2006): 80–81, 94–95.
Kanai, Miki. "Torino Toraienāre no dai-ishō" (First chapter of the Torino Trienniale). *Bijutsu Techō* (1 February 2006): 154–55.

"Kachi wo tsutaeru waza wa aru ka" (Is there a way to communicate value?). *Asahi Shinbun*, 7, 14, and 21 March 2004.

Kaplan, Cheryl. "Takashi Murakami: Lite Happiness + Super Flat." *Flash Art*, no. 219 (July–September 2001): 92–97.

Kasahara, Chiaki. "Superflat: Going to America." *Kōkoku Hihyō* (March 2001): 117–24.

"Kate Moss Design." *W* (September 2003): 436–37, 453.

Kawakami, Noriko. "Torino koten wo dokusen repōto: Murakami Takashi no āto daiarī" (Exclusive coverage of his Torino solo show: Takashi Murakami's art diary). *Figaro Japon* (5 January 2006): 120–23.

Kelmachter, Hélène. "Kaikai Kiki and the Gods of Art." *Cartier*, no. 6 (2003): 82–85.

———. "Takashi Murakami: Le Pop-artiste japonais." *DADA* (December 2006): 28–29.

Kelsey, John. "Takashi Murakami at Marianne Boesky Gallery and Vanderbilt Hall." *Artext*, no. 74 (August–October 2001): 78.

Kent, Sarah. "Don't look now..." *Time Out New York* (28 June–5 July 1995).

Kimmelman, Michael. "The Hudson Valley, Inside and Out: Center for Curatorial Studies Museum." *The New York Times*, 30 July 1999.

"Kiti = Nihon no poppu-karuchā 'kawaii' no toppu aikon" (Kitty = Japan's "kawaii" pop culture's top icon). *Ichigo Shinbun*, 10 May 2005, 3.

Knight, Christopher. "Flat-Out Profound." *Los Angeles Times*, 16 January 2001.

———. "A World of Pleasures." *Los Angeles Times*, 17 July 2001, F1, 10.

Kojima, Yayoi. *Invitation* (23 September 2003): 16.

"Kokon tōsei no hyōgen wo jūsōka: Sabukaru wo junsui geijutsu ni hen'yō" (Branching out from old and new, East and West: Transforming subculture into pure art). *Kyōdō Tsūshin*, 15 January 2006.

Kondo, Kenichi. "Takashi Murakami's Lowbrow Launchpad." *Art Asia Pacific*, no. 49 (summer 2006): 35.

Konpa, Naruhiro, Katsuo Mizuguchi, Takashi Murakami, and Jeffrey Poe. "Āto ga kōkoku sareta hi" (The day art became an advertisement). *Kōkoku Hihyō* (July 2004): 125–38.

Kurabayashi, Yasushi. *Nikkei ICF* (7 July 1993): 41–44.

Kurtz, Katie. "Superflat." *Art Access* (December 2001–January 2002): 12–13.

Kusumi, Kiyoshi. "Takashi Murakami." *Bijutsu Techō* (May 1999): 125–42.

La Ferla, Ruth. "Front Row: Animating Vuitton." *The New York Times*, 8 April 2003, C16.

Larsen, Lars Bang. "Japan Today at Louisiana, Copenhagen." *Flash Art*, no. 184 (November–December 1995): 60.

Laubard, Charlotte. "Strategic Fantasy." *Technikart* (July–August 2002): 42–45.

Lefkowitz, David. "Edgy: Painting at the Edge of the World at Walker Art Center." *New Art Examiner* (September–October 2001): 66–71, 103.

Lentini, Marianna. "From the Otaku to the 'Poku Culture': The Hyperbolic Kingdom of Takashi Murakami." *Overview*, no. 6 (September 2006): 24–27.

Lieberman, Rhonda. "05.08.07: Steep Prices." Artforum.com, 8 May 2007.

Levin, Kim. "Voice Choices." *Village Voice* (May 1995).

———. "Voice Choices: Takashi Murakami." *Village Voice* (16 February 1999): 86.

Linnemeyer, Christian. "Po-ku die dekadente kunst." *Intro*, no. 63 (May 1999): 18–19.

Loyante, Benjamin. "Ici commence le pays de M. Murakami." *Connaisance des Arts* (July–August 2002): 18.

Lubow, Arthur. "The Murakami Method." *The New York Times Magazine* (3 April 2005): 48–57, 64, 76–79.

Luffy, Carol. "Japanese Art: Young Crowd, Wide Horizons." *ArtNews* (November 1994): 124–28.

Lytal, Benjamin. "A Show for Fans of Culture." *The New York Sun*, 7 April 2005, 17.

Madoff, Steven Henry. "'Pop Surrealism'—Exhibit at Aldrich Museum of Contemporary Art." *Artforum* 37, no. 2 (October 1998): 120.

Maneker, Marion. "The Giant Cartoon Landing at Rockefeller Center." *The New York Times*, 24 August 2003.

———. "Early Bids." *New York Magazine* (10 May 2004).

Marks, Peter. "A Japanese Artist Goes Global: Far-Flung Helpers Meet Demand for Takashi Murakami's Paintings." *The New York Times*, 25 July 2001, B1, 5.

Martin, Maïa de. "Délire Murakami et planète coloriage." *Art Actuel* (July–August 2002): 15–18.

Matsui, Midori. "Tokyo Pop." *Flash Art*, no. 197 (November–December 1997): 110.

———. "Takashi Murakami." *Index* 3, no. 4 (November–December 1998): 44–51.

———. "Japanese Innovators." *Flash Art*, no. 210 (January–February 2000): 90–91.

———. "Murakami Takashi ga, rekishiteki bunmyaku kara japanīzu poppuāto o hodokiakasu" (Takashi Murakami analyzes Japanese Pop art from a historical context). *Marie Claire Japan* (August 2005): 111.

Mattick, Paul. "Takashi Murakami at Marianne Boesky." *Art in America* (January 2004): 107–08.

"Maurizio and Takashi: Two Monsters Unleashed." *Whitewall* (winter 2006–07): 6, 92–107, 158–59.

McGee, Suzanne. "Cool Art, Hot Prices." *Barron's* (10 May 2004).

Meda, Maria Grazia. "Vogue Interview." *Vogue Italia* (November 2006): 46.

Menkes, Suzy. "Making a Point." *International Herald Tribune*, 16 September 2003.

Miki, Akiko. "Une brève histoire de l'art contemporain au Japon." *DADA* (December 2006): 10–11.

Milroy, Sarah. "Art Imitating Technology Imitating Life." *The Globe and Mail*, 18 March 2002.

Miura, Ryōichi. "Otaku bunka NY de sakuretsu" (A burst of *otaku* culture in NY). *Shūkan New York Seikatsu*, 26 March 2005, 1.

Miyamura, Noriko. "Kiseru x Murakami Takashi: Ongaku to āto de yumemiru mirai" (Kicell and Takashi Murakami: Dreaming of the future with music and art). *Switch* (June 2005): 94–97.

Molinari, Guido K. "Takashi Murakami." *Global Art* (March–April 1998): 106.

Mori, Teruyo. "Murakami Takashi ga kyurēshon suru nihon poppuāto ten" (An exhibition on Japanese Pop art curated by Takashi Murakami). *Spur* (July 2005): 35.

Morikawa, Ichirō. "Jichōteki na 'Nihon-zō' to teiji." (Presenting a self-deprecating image of Japan). *Mainichi Shinbun*, 23 May 2005, 6.

Muchnic, Suzanne. "Ascent of the Early Risers." *Los Angeles Times*, 1 April 2001, 4–5, 74–76.

———. "Newer Art Shows It Has Legs." *Los Angeles Times*, 19 May 2003, E1, 11.

"Murakami Journal." *BRUTUS* (1 June 2003).

"Murakami Journal: In New York."*BRUTUS* (15 September 2003): 126–43.

Murakami, Takashi. "POP + OTAKU + PO + KU." *Big* (1998).

———, with photos by Shintaro Shiratori. "Project ko² 2004 (cover)." *GQ Japan* (July 2004): 187–203.

———. In Massimiliano Gioni and Ali Subotnick, eds. "The Economy of Attention: Art and Radical Thinking in Times of Strategic Consensus." *Parkett*, no. 69 (December 2003): 165–71.

——— (as told to Katy Siegel). "On the Level." *Artforum* 43, no. 2 (October 2004): 155.

———. "Datsuryoku ni yadoru geijutsu no chikara" (The power of art that lies in letting go). *Asahi Shinbun Yūkan*, 16 May 2005, 4.

———. "Influence: Today and Tomorrow." *Art Asia Pacific Almanac* (2007): 162.

"Murakami Takashi-san ga kangaeru 21seiki no eko wa ragujuarī na bijinesu desu" (Mr. Takashi Murakami's vision of ecology in the 21st century is a luxury business). *GQ Japan* (February 2006): 44–55.

"Murakami-san ni kunshō" (An award for Mr. Murakami). *Yomitaimu* (February 2006): 3.

Myers, Terry R. "Little Boy Boom: Takashi Murakami and his Protégés Invade New York." *Modern Painters* (April 2005): 54–59.

Nakamori, Yasufumi. "Murakami Takashi no kaigai senryaku kyoten wa yappari nyūyōku ni" (Takashi Murakami makes New York his home base for overseas missions). *Bijutsu Techō* (1 September 2003): 89.

Nakamura, Eric. "The Year Otaku Broke." *Artext*, no. 73 (May–July 2001): 36–39.

———. "Superfly." *Giant Robot*, no. 21 (summer 2001): cover, 24–28.

———. "GEISAI Pride: Cultured Club." *Giant Robot*, no. 45 (January 2007): 46–49, 83.

———. "Pop Life: Transculturalist." *Giant Robot*, no. 45 (January 2007): 42–45.

Nakamura, Marie-Pierre. "Takashi Murakami." *Art Actuel* (November–December 2003): 82.

Nakamura, Ryoko Maria. "Vision of a 'Superflat' Future." *Japan Times*, 13 April 2005, 11.

"Nihon no kao" (The face of Japan). *Bungei Shunjū* (May 2004).

Nilsson, Hakan. "Japan Art Today at Louisiana." *Material* (autumn 1995).

"NY de jōretsu kangei: Murakami Takashi Ritoru Bōi" (Heated welcome for Takashi Murakami's "Little Boy" in NY). *Shūkan Shinchō*, 19 May 2005, 40.

"O-Hanashi: Ritoru Bōi no kyurētā Murakami Takashi" (Talk-corner: "Little Boy's" curator Takashi Murakami). *Asahi Shinbun*, 15 April 2005, 1.

O'Hara, Gail. "Buying Japanese: Dreamy things come in shapely packages." *Time Out New York* (4–11 October 1995).

Odagiri, Hiroshi. "Art or Not Art, That Is the Question." *Model Graphix* (25 October 1996).

Odajima, Hitoshi. "Ai wo fukkatsu saseru geijutsuka" (An artist who can bring love back to life). *Chūō Kōron* (October 2003): cover, 9–11.

Ollman, Leah. "Art That's Instantly Gratifying." *Los Angeles Times*, 28 May 2004, E28.

"100% News." *Visi* (summer 2006): 40.

"Other Side Andy Warhol." *EyesCream* (Tokyo), 1 April 2006.

Pagel, David. "Painting in Midst of Generational Conflict." *Los Angeles Times*, 1 August 1997, F28.

———. "Art Review." *Los Angeles Times*, 3 July 1998, F26.

———. "Takashi Murakami: Meet Japan's Pop Art Samurai." *Interview* (March 2001): 188–92.

Pardo, Patrick. "Flat in Japan." *NYArts* (April 2001).

Patrie, Florence. "Pulp Art: L'actualité culturelle asiatique." *Asia Pulp* (December 2006–January 2007).

Patterson, Anders. "Bubble or Squeak?" *ArtTactic* (February 2004).

Pederson, Victoria. "Reviews." *Paper* (February 1999).

Peers, Alexandra. "The Buys of Autumn." *The Wall Street Journal*, 8 November 2002.

———. "Hot Today, Cold Tomorrow?" *The Wall Street Journal*, 17 November 2003.

Perez, Magdalene. "The AI Interview: Takashi Murakami." Artinfo.com, 9 June 2006, available at http://www.artinfo.com/articles/story/17056/takashi_murakami.

Pigeut, Philippe. "Murakami Kitchissime!" *L'Œil* (December 2006): 42.

Pinchbeck, Daniel. "A Montage of Photo Exhibitions." *The Art Newspaper*, no. 89 (February 1999).

Poli, Francesco. "Takashi Murakami: Galerie Emmanuel Perrotin"; and "Let's Entertain: Takashi Murakami." *Tema Celeste* (March–April 2001): 105; 110–15.

Polsky, Richard. "Art Market Guide 2003: Takashi Murakami." *Artnet Magazine* (11 October 2003), available at http://www.artnet.com/magazine/features/polsky2/polsky10-10-03.asp.

———. "Art Market Guide 2004." *Artnet Magazine* (23 December 2004), available at http://artnet.com/magazine/features/polsky/polsky12-2-4.asp.

A Portrait of Our Times: An Introduction to the Logan Collection. Exh. cat. San Francisco: San Francisco Museum of Modern Art, 1998.

"The Power 100, #7: Takashi Murakami." *Art Review* (2003): 8.

"The Power 100, #98: Takashi Murakami." *Art Review*, no. 5 (November 2006): 135.

"Power Moves." *Art+Auction* (December 2006).

Powhida, Willam. "The Colorful World of Takashi Murakami." *The Antiquer* (March 2004): 34–35.

Prose, Francine. "Tokyo Godfather." *Black Book* (fall 2004): 184–89.

"Ragujuarī-Bijinesu no Shinkijiku wa āto ni ari!" (Luxury-business innovations are in art!). *WWD Japan*, 8 January 2007, 12–13.

Ratnam, Niru. Interview. *i-D Magazine* (February 2003): 86–88.

Raverty, Dennis. "Visions From a Sinking World: Japanese Anime at the Des Moines Art Center." *New Art Examiner* (September–October 2001): 53–57.

Ray, Amber. "Takashi Murakami Is All the Rage." *Metro* (8–10 April 2005): 10.

Richard, Frances. "Takashi Murakami at Marianne Boesky." *Artforum* 40, no. 1 (September 2001): 192–93.

Rimanelli, David. "Takashi Murakami at Bard Center for Curatorial Studies, Annandale-on-Hudson, New York." *Artforum* 38, no. 3 (November 1999): 134–35.

———. "Entries: Takashi Murakami's Louis Vuitton Show." *Artforum* 41, no. 10 (summer 2003): 41.

Rivers, Charlotte. "Takashi Murakami." *Lab* 5 (spring–summer 2003): 138–39.

Roberts, James. "Magic Mushrooms." *Frieze*, no. 70 (October 2002): 66–71.

Rockers Island: Werke der Sammlung Olbricht. Exh. cat. Essen, Germany: Museum Folkwang; and Göttingen: Steidl, 2007.

Robinson, Walter. "Murakami, Impresario." *Artnet Magazine* (26 September 2006), available at http://www.artnet.com/magazineus/reviews/robinson/robinson9-26-06.asp.

"Rohasu: Kenkō to Kankyō torendo, oshiemasu" (Lohas: Teaching health and environmental trends). *Sotokoto* (January 2007): 32–39.

Rosenblum, Robert. "Best of 2003." *Artforum* 42, no. 4 (December 2003): 120.

———. "Preview: Little Boy: The Arts |of Japan's Exploding Subculture." Artdaily.com, January 2006.

———. "Preview: Takashi Murakami at Fondation Cartier pour l'art contemporain." *Artforum* 40, no. 9 (May 2002): 80.

Rothbart, Daniel. "The Floating Art World." *NY Arts* (September–October 2003): 14–25.

Royce, Julia. "Candy Pop." *Elle U.K.* (December 2002): 59.

Rubinstein, Raphael. "In the Realm of the Superflat." *Art in America* (June 2001): cover, 110–15.

"Runaway Report." *Harper's Bazaar* (January 2003): 29.

"Saisei, shinsei 1: Kawaii sekai ni kaze" (Rebirth, new birth 1: New breeze in a cute world). *Asahi Shinbun*, 1 January 2006, 1.

Saltz, Jerry. "Imitation Warhol." *Village Voice* (31 August 1999): 65.

Sawaragi, Noi. "Takashi Murakami." *World Art* (summer 1997): 76.

———, and Fumio Nanjō. "Dangerously Cute." *Flash Art*, no. 163 (March–April 1992): 75–77.

Schimmel, Paul. "Best of 2004." *Artforum* 43, no. 4 (December 2004): 168.

Schjeldahl, Peter. "Critic's Notebook: Tokyo Pop." *The New Yorker* (9 May 2005): 14.

Scott, Andrea K. "Mushroom." *Time Out New York*, no. 290 (12–19 April 2001).

Scott, Michael. "Nuts, Bolts & Blood." *The Vancouver Sun* (7–14 February 2002): D6–7.

"Sekai wo kaeru Nihonjin" (Japanese people who are changing the world). *COURRiER Japon* (2007): 30–31.

"Sensō ni shōsha wa inai" (There are no victors in war). *Asahi Shinbun*, 27 January 2004, 27.

Shelley, Ward, and Erik Bakke. "Mob Rule: Sculpture After Hanson." *NY Arts* 4, no. 3 (1999): 10–13.

Shepherd, John. "Defining Moment: The Eye-Popping Work of Takashi Murakami Brings New Airiness to Midtown Manhattan." *House & Garden* (March 2004): 114–15.

Shin, Masa. "Vitamin Culture." *DiBi DiBi Paper* (April 1996).

"Shitte okitai Tōkyō no shin kīwādo 100/ Casa Travel" (100 new Tokyo keywords you'll want to know). *Casa BRUTUS* (May 2007): 57, 122–27.

Shū, Tomiko. "Anytime Reversed." *Studio Voice* (November 2003): 17.

Siegel, Katy. "Planet Murakami." *Art Review* (November 2003): cover, 46–53.

———. "Takashi Murakami at Marianne Boesky." *Artforum* 41, no. 10 (summer 2003): 185–86.

Smith, Roberta. "Art in Review." *The New York Times*, 5 February 1999, B35.

———. "Art in Review: Takashi Murakami." *The New York Times*, 6 April 2001, E38.

———. "From a Mushroom Cloud, a Burst of Art Reflecting Japan's Psyche." *The New York Times*, 8 April 2005, E33.

———. "Visions That Flaunt Cartoon Pedigrees." *The New York Times*, 2 March 2007.

Socha, Miles. "Artistic License." *W* (December 2002): 222.

"Spank the Monkey Street Art." *East Touch*, 21 November 2006, 98–99.

"Special Art Collection: Āto wo Kazarō" (Let's decorate art). *Vogue Japan* (May 2007): 342.

"Spring Sales Preview." *Art and Auction* (June 2003).

"State of the Arts." *Departures* (May–June 2003).

Steinberg, Marc. "Characterizing a New Seriality: Murakami Takashi's DOB Project." *Parachute*, no. 110 (April–June 2003): 90–109.

Sternberg, Claude. "Y a d'la joie!" *Femme* (June 2002): 58–59.

Stevens, Lennox. "Superfreaky! Superflat." *Entertainment Today* (23–29 March 2001): 6.

Stevens, Mark. "Toxic Cuteness." *New York Magazine* (18 April 2005): 84.

Stewart, Amy Smith. "Takashi Murakami: Superflat Monogram." *Contemporary*, no. 52 (June–July 2003): 76.

Swartley, Ariel. "For the Pop Culturati, Patterns That Say Tokyo Cool." *The New York Times*, 22 April 2001, sec. 2, 37.

"Taishū geijutsu wo sekai ni tou honyaku-sha de aritai Murakami-san" (Mr. Murakami wants to be a translator who brings popular culture to the world). *Shūkan NY Seikatsu*, 11 February 2006, 4.

"Takashi Murakami." *L'Express Styles*, 7–13 December 2006, 102.

"Takashi Murakami." *The New Yorker* (12 May 2003).

"Takashi Murakami." *The New Yorker* (29 September 2003): 25.

"Takashi Murakami and His Kaikai Kiki." *East Touch*, 21 November 2006 34–45.

"Takashi Murakami: Japan's Andy Warhol." *The Week*, 29 April 2005, 23.

"TalkArt: Takashi Murakami." *GQ South Africa* (November 2006): 32.

Tassini, Eugenio. "Murakami l'arte fatta logo." *Io Donna* (22 October 2005): 163–66.

"10 Stories about Takashi Murakami." *Luca Japan* (2003): cover, 22–61. Special issue.

Terrell, Kenneth. "Art That's Seriously Cute." *U.S. News & World Report* (29 December 2003–5 January 2004).

Thomas, Kelly Devine. "The 10 Most Expensive Living Artists." *ArtNews* (May 2004): 118–23.

Thon, Von Ute. "Angriff der Kulleraugen." *Art Das Kunstmagazine* (July 2004): 40–51.

"Tokyo Pop." *D-Mode* (November 2005): 98–101.

Tomii, Reiko. "Ritoru Bōi-ten: Murakami Takashi, isse-ichidai no yashinteki kikaku" ("Little Boy" exhibit: Takashi Murakami, ambitious project of a lifetime). *Shin-bijutsu Shinbun*, 21 April 2005, 2.

Tretlack, Philippe. "Monstres Sacres." *Elle* (30 October 2006).

Tully, Judd. "Year in Review: Beyond the Valley of the Dolls." *Art Review* (summer 2003).

Tumlir, Jan. "Takashi Murakami at Blum & Poe." *L.A. Weekly* (17–23 July 1998): 61.

———. "Tenth Reunion: Public Offerings." *Artforum* 39, no. 6 (February 2001): 120–23.

"20nin no 'Nihonjin ga katatta 'watashi no aikokushin'" (20 Japanese recount what patriotism means to them). *GQ Japan* (August 2005): 159.

Ulmer, Brigitte. "Der Star des Kunst-Pop." *Bolero* (September 2003): 44–47.

Vargel, Annieken. "Tempelridderen." *Dagbladet SØNDAG*, 3 June 2007, 30–35.

"Venetsia kara GEISAI e" (From Venice to GEISAI). *Bijutsu Techō*, 9 September 2003, 89–94.

"View: Baby Goes Bauhaus." *Vogue Living* (fall–winter 2006).

Vogel, Carol. "Inside Art: A Showcase Outdoors." *The New York Times*, 23 May 2003, E32.

———. "Inside Art: A New Friend for Mr. Pointy." *The New York Times*, 12 September 2003.

———. "The Murakami Influence." *The New York Times*, 6 April 2005, E1, 7.

———. "The Warhol of Japan Pours Ritual Tea in a Zen Moment." *The New York Times*, 7 May 2007, E1, E5.

"W Eye." *W Korea* (June 2006): 183–85.

"'Wa' no Shinsei: Tokonoma Purojekuto no Bāi" (The spirit of "Japan": The Tokonoma project). *Tokion* (April 2007): 40–41.

Walker, Hollis. "Mr. Outside Becomes Mr. Inside—For Now." *The Wall Street Journal*, 26 June 2001.

"What Inspires You? #20 Takashi Murakami." *The Face* (November 2002): 190–94.

"When Takashi Met Marc." *V*, no. 22 (March–April 2003).

Wilson, Rebecca. "Power 100: 10th, Takashi Murakami." *Art Review* (November 2004): 66.

Wilson-Goldie, Kaelen. "Satellites." *Black Book* (spring 2001): 38.

———. "Takashi Murakami." *Art & Auction* (November 2001): 121–22.

Wong, Martin. "Super Duper Flat," *Artbyte* (May–June 2001): 58–63.

"Working Proof." *Art on Paper* (July–August 2001).

Yanagihara, Hanya. "The Wonderful World of Murakami." *Departures* (September 2004): 172–77, 202–03.

Yehya, Naief. "La estetica de la abundancia de Takashi Murakami." *El Financiero* (Mexico City), 14 February 1999.

Yoshikawa, Yoshio and Yukako. *Katachi*, no. 20 (spring 1992).

The Museum of Contemporary Art, Los Angeles Board of Trustees

Photo Credits

Courtesy Blum & Poe, pp. 38, 46, 63, 71 top, 114 top, 123, 162, 168, 169 bottom, 173, 214–15, 217, photo: Joshua White, pp. frontispiece, 52, 188–89, 192–93, 196–99, 208–11, 234–35, 239, 269–71, 284–85, photo: Norihiro Ueno, pp. 170, 173, 186–87, 273–75, photo: Yoshitaka Uchida, p. 101, photo: Christopher Burke Studio, pp. 286–87; photo: © 2007 Museum of Fine Arts, Boston, p. 5; courtesy Billy Name, pp. 21 top, 132; courtesy Kaikai Kiki Co., Ltd., endsheets, pp. 31, 34, 64 top, 75, 87, 100 top, 102, 109, 114 center and bottom, 125, 131, 134–35, 147–50, 163–67, 175, 190–91, 200, 216, 218–20, 249, 254–55, 258–63, 277–81, 290–91, 294–99, photo: Mie Morimoto, pp. 21 bottom, 281, photo: Kazuo Fukunaga, pp. 49 top, 69, 185, 216–19, 232–33, photo: Mikio Kurokawa, p. 61, photo: Kikuchi Kurage, pp. 78 right, 288–89, photo: Sakae Ogura, p. 88 top, photo: Nomadic Studio, p. 97, photo: Russel Gera, p. 130, photo: Miget, p. 150 bottom, photo: Hideto Nagatsuka, p. 183, photo: Yoshitaka Uchida, pp. 212–13, photo: Norihiro Ueno, p. 223, photo: Masashi Ono, pp. 283–85; courtesy Keisuke Nemoto, p. 26 top; courtesy Marianne Boesky Gallery, pp. 29 bottom, 169 bottom, 182, 186–87, 194–95, 224–27, 230–31, 264–65, 282–83; courtesy Bob's Big Boy Restaurants International, p. 30; courtesy Galerie Emmanuel Perrotin, p. 221, photo: André Morin, pp. 33, 242–43, 248, 251, 253; photo: © The Metropolitan Museum of Art, New York, p. 39; courtesy Toyota Municipal Museum of Art, photo: Tatsuo Kayashi, p. 62; courtesy Art Resource, New York, pp. 71 bottom, 72 right; photo: Tom Powell Imaging, pp. cover, 72 left, 179–81, 277–79; photo: © Yoshizawa Memorial Museum of Art, p. 76; courtesy Gagosian Gallery, pp. 90, 292–93; photo: Adam Reich, pp. 110, 112, 127, 244–45; photo: © Minoru Hirata, p. 119 top; courtesy Keith Haring Foundation, photo: Charles Dolfi-Michels, p. 143; photo: Jason Nocito, p. 155; photo: © Alexander Troehler, Zürich, p. 156 right; photo: © Axel Heil, Fluid Archives, p. 177; photo: Andrew Kent Photography, p. 203; photo: Friedrich Rosenstiel, Cologne, pp. 204–05; courtesy 21st Century Museum of Contemporary Art, Kanazawa, pp. 206–07; photo: Jeffrey Wells Photography, Aurora, Colorado, pp. 228–29; photo: Andy Keate, London, pp. 237, 240–41; and courtesy Fondation Cartier pour l'art contemporain, Paris, p. 257.

Lenders to the Exhibition

Matt Aberle, *Los Angeles*
Ruth and Jake Bloom, *Marina del Rey, California*
Marianne Boesky, *New York*
Giancarlo Bonollo, *Vicenza, Italy*
The Steven A. Cohen Collection
Harry David, *Athens*
Amalia Dayan and Adam Lindemann
Martin and Rebecca Eisenberg
Fluid Editions and Archives
Fukuoka Jisho Co., Ltd.
Rachel and Jean-Pierre Lehmann
Vicki and Kent Logan
Los Angeles County Museum of Art
Linda and Harry Macklowe
Martin Z. Marguiles, *Miami, Florida*
Minor Family *San Francisco*
Javier and Monica Mora, *Coral Gables, Florida*
Peter Morton
Takashi Murakami/Kaikai Kiki Co., Ltd./Kaikai Kiki New York, LLC
The Museum of Modern Art, *New York*
Peter Norton and Eileen Harris Norton, *Santa Monica*
Olbricht Collection
Douglas and Sherry Oliver, *New York*
Galerie Emmanuel Perrotin, *Paris and Miami*
François Pinault Collection
Private collections
Queensland Art Gallery
Alan and Darryl Reichbart, *Los Angeles*
Rubell Family Collection, *Miami*
Richard B. Sachs, *New York*
San Francisco Museum of Modern Art
The Ann and Mel Schaffer Family Collection, *New Jersey*
Florence and Philippe Segalot
John A. Smith and Victoria Hughes, *London*
Takahashi Collection
David Teiger
21st Century Museum of Contemporary Art, *Kanazawa*
Vanhaerents Art Collection, *Brussels, Belgium*

"© Murakami" is made possible by endowment support from
the Sydney Irmas Exhibition Endowment.
The exhibition and publication are made possible by generous support
from Maria and Bill Bell. Major support is provided by
Blum & Poe, Los Angeles; Steven and Alexandra Cohen; Kathi and Gary Cypres;
Gagosian Gallery; Galerie Emmanuel Perrotin, Paris and Miami;
The Norton Family Foundation; Dallas Price-Van Breda; Janet and Tom Unterman;
Marianne Boesky; David Teiger; The MOCA Contemporaries;
The Japan Foundation; and the E. Rhodes and Leona B. Carpenter Foundation.

This exhibition is presented as part of
the Millennium on View program. The Millennium Biltmore
Hotel is MOCA's Official Hotel Sponsor.

First published in the United States of America by
The Museum of Contemporary Art, Los Angeles
250 South Grand Avenue
Los Angeles, CA 90012
and
Rizzoli International Publications, Inc.
300 Park Avenue South
New York, NY 10010

Director of Publications: Lisa Gabrielle Mark
Senior Editor: Jane Hyun
Editor: Elizabeth Hamilton
Publications Assistant: Dawson Weber
Designers: Lorraine Wild and Victoria Lam with Lauren Harden/
Green Dragon Office, Los Angeles
Decorative Initials: Kaikai Kiki Co., Ltd.
Type: Greendene by Hrant Papazian (2007) based on the font
Deepdene (F. W. Goudy, 1929–34)
Color Separations: Tony Manzella and Rusty Sena, Echelon,
Venice, California
Printer: Dr. Cantz'sche Druckerei, Ostfildern, Germany

Printed on PhoeniXmotion, Xenon, 150 g/m from paper mill
Scheufelen, Oberlenningen, Germany
PhoeniXmotion

ISBN-13: 978-1-933751-06-1 (MOCA)
ISBN-13: 978-0-8478-3003-9 (Rizzoli)

Library of Congress Cataloging-in-Publication Data
Murakami, Takashi, 1962–
© Takashi Murakami.
p. cm.
Issued in connection with an exhibition organized
by Paul Schimmel and presented
at the Museum of Contemporary Art, Los Angeles,
29 October 2007–11 February 2008.
Includes bibliographical references.
ISBN 978-1-933751-06-1
1. Murakami, Takashi, 1962—Exhibitions. I.
Schimmel, Paul. II. Museum of Contemporary Art
(Los Angeles, Calif.) III. Title.
IV. Title: Copyright Takashi Murakami.
N7359.M87A4 2008
709.2—dc22

2007024214

2007 2008 2009 2010 / 10 9 8 7 6 5 4 3 2 1
Printed and bound in Germany

cover: Takashi Murakami, *727*, 1996, detail
frontispiece: *Inochi*, 2004, detail
endsheets: stills from *kaikai & kiki*, 2007